WRITING
FROM
SOURCES

WRITING FROM SOURCES

Brenda Spatt

Herbert H. Lehman College
of the City of New York

ST. MARTIN'S PRESS   New York

Acknowledgments

"The Motor Industry" by J. D. Bernal. Reprinted from *Science and History*, Volume 3, by permission of The MIT Press, Cambridge, Massachusetts. Copyright © 1965 by The Massachusetts Institute of Technology.

"The long-range liabilities . . . ideal status symbol." Reprinted from *The Car Culture* by James Flink by permission of The MIT Press, Cambridge, Massachusetts. Copyright © 1975 by The Massachusetts Institute of Technology.

Excerpt from "Degrees: Who Needs Them?" by Blanche Blank, Autumn, 1972, *AAUP Bulletin*, a publication of the American Association of University Professors. Reprinted by permission.

Excerpt from *Birthrights* by Richard Farson, © 1974 by Richard Farson. Excerpted by permission of Macmillan Publishing Co., Inc.

Excerpt from "Game Theory" by George Stade reprinted by permission from *The Columbia Forum*. Copyright 1966 by The Trustees of Columbia University in the City of New York. All rights reserved.

Excerpt from "Science, Anti-Science, and Human Values," by John Compton, *Key Reporter*, volume 44, number 2, 1979, reprinted by permission of Phi Beta Kappa and the author.

"Survey Finds Boys Preferred as the First-born, Girls as the Second" by Jane Brody © 1974 by The New York Times Company. Reprinted by permission.

"Must Doctors Serve Where They're Told?" by Harry Schwartz © 1980 by The New York Times Company. Reprinted by permission.

Excerpt from *Criminal Violence, Criminal Justice* by Charles E. Silberman. Copyright © 1978 by Charles E. Silberman. Reprinted by permission of Random House, Inc.

Excerpt from *How Children Fail*, Revised Edition, by John Holt. Copyright © 1964, 1982 by John Holt. Reprinted by permission of Delacorte Press/Seymour Lawrence. A Merloyd Lawrence Book.

"Holdup Man Tells How to Do It" by Selwyn Raab © 1975 by The New York Times Company. Reprinted by permission.

Acknowledgements and copyrights continue at the back of the book on pages 550–551, which constitute an extension of the copyright page.

To Instructors

The design of this book was developed in freshman composition courses at several colleges in the New York City area—Borough of Manhattan Community College, Montclair State College, the State University of New York at Purchase, and Herbert H. Lehman College—over a period of eleven years. Most of the students who tested these materials had completed (or been exempted from) a first term of freshman composition. Neither advanced nor remedial, they resembled the majority of freshmen today. They were intelligent, but more often than not, they had been poorly prepared for college work, were uncomfortable expressing themselves in writing, and lacked the skills to work with the disparate sources and abstract ideas encountered in college reading. Inexperienced in analysis and synthesis, such students often feel impotent and frustrated when confronted by the necessity to write term papers, whether in English courses or in other disciplines. The object of *Writing from Sources* is to provide students with the tools to do successful academic writing and thus to raise the standard of writing in all college courses.

Writing an essay based on sources depends on a complex group of skills. In most college courses, students are less often asked to do independent thinking than they are required to work with assigned sources—textbooks, lecture notes, and outside readings. The same is true of the professional writing that will be part of their future careers; they may be asked to initiate and develop original ideas, but far more often they will need to use skills of analysis and synthesis to explain, evaluate, and integrate opinions and facts taken from other sources. In eleven years of teaching composition, I have rarely encountered a student who could—at the beginning of the term—pinpoint and paraphrase the key ideas of an essay, evaluate a group of readings, or undertake the extended synthesis necessary for presenting research. Rather, the freshman research essay typically contains "anthologies" of quotations strung together with little indication of their relationship. Few students know how to determine where the author's thought leaves off and their own interpretation begins or how to combine disparate statements culled from several authors in a single paragraph.

Traditional methods of structuring the composition course have not been effective in teaching these skills. In the typical freshman course, as it was conceived when I was in college and as it is still taught today, the research essay is customarily regarded as a separate assignment, almost as an afterthought, to be saved for the end of the term. The skills required for working with source materials rarely get integrated into the first part of the course, which is often reserved for an exploration of rhetorical modes, with a single reading (or at most a comparison of two essays) serving as the basis of the usual assignment. At the end of the term, when the research essay is suddenly introduced, students find the switch to multiple sources frightening, an unfair test of abilities that they have not been given the opportunity or the means to develop. Moreover, when the research essay is at last assigned, what is generally emphasized is library research. The locating of sources, however, is largely a mechanical process, unlikely in itself to teach students much about the skills connected with thinking or writing about what they have read. It is pointless to teach students how to compile an impressive bibliography if, when the time comes to select materials and integrate them into a coherent essay, they simply produce the familiar string of end-to-end quotations.

Writing from Sources is based on the belief that the last few weeks of the term is not the time to begin showing students how to understand, collate, and present the fruits of their research. To make the research essay the natural conclusion to the composition course, the students' work should be structured around sources throughout the term, with the synthesis of ideas and evidence the paramount objective. This text assumes that students learn best if skills are presented gradually, in lessons and assignments of progressive difficulty. Thus, comprehension and organizational skills are broken into isolated units and presented in discrete stages. In this sequential approach, each technique is first considered as an end in itself, to be explained, demonstrated, and practiced in isolation, like the skills necessary for mastering a sport. For example, quotation is thoroughly taught and applied before the student learns about paraphrase. Simple operations get practiced again and again so that they have become automatic before the student goes on to attempt more complex variations.

The text begins with a review of the writing process (Part I) emphasizing the student's most immediate and accessible source—his or her own ideas and experiences. Using oneself as the source enables the student to gain practice in imposing order over a mass of accumulated ideas without having to cope with the difficulties of understanding and assimilating information taken from written sources.

In Part II (Chapters 2 and 3) students are introduced to all the skills essential to the presentation of written source materials—basic comprehension, including annotation, outlining a source's structure, and summarizing; quotation; and paraphrase. After mastering the objective summary of a single source, students learn to incorporate quotation and paraphrase in their summaries.

In the first half of Part III students begin to combine the personal approach of Part I with the objective skills of Part II: Chapter 4 integrates source interpretation, analysis, and response in an essay composed according to the process steps detailed in Chapter 1. Chapter 5 introduces the synthesis of several sources in an essay controlled by the student's own thesis and voice. This chapter on the multiple-source essay is followed by a large number of supplementary assignments and a wide variety of materials for synthesis taken from interviews, brief written statements by students, newspapers, and oral history. Since synthesis is the single most difficult skill in academic writing, the object here is to make sure that the student selects compatible source materials and presents them understandably and accurately.

Part IV consolidates all the individual skills presented in earlier chapters as students turn to the research essay. Both the writing process and the handling of sources have by now become so familiar that students can focus on the evaluation and selection of sources gathered through research and, finally, on the documentation of these sources and on other technical matters.

Because of its scope, *Writing from Sources* is necessarily a text, an exercise book, and a reader. Twenty-two assignments and sixty-five exercises—more, obviously, than any single class could complete—offer the instructor the latitude to reinforce the text as the needs of a class or of particular students dictate. Some hundred and fifty pages of reprinted material—from authors as diverse as Francis Bacon, Simone de Beauvoir, Samuel Butler, Frances FitzGerald, Sigmund Freud, Ernest Hemingway, John Holt, Christopher Lasch, Niccolo Machiavelli, Bronislaw Malinowski, Margaret Mead, A. S. Neill, Bertrand Russell, Lewis Thomas, and E. Bright Wilson—make supplements and handouts unnecessary.

Writing from Sources is also a research-essay handbook. Chapter 10 presents MLA standards of documentation and bibliography, and Chapter 11 includes five student research essays—two on Ernest Hemingway and three on the San Francisco earthquake of 1906. The sample essays illustrate a range of quality and effort and help students to appreciate the relative merits and shortcomings of different approaches to the same topic and to recognize achievable excellence. Appendix A provides a bibliography of useful encyclopedias, indexes, and abstracts for a variety of subjects, and Appendix B lists the basic forms for notes and bibliography entries.

As I suggested at the beginning, *Writing from Sources* has benefited from the work of many students in several colleges over more than a decade. I hope that the book will now prove helpful to many new students. It is to all the students whose efforts helped shape the book that I am most deeply indebted.

Contents

PART II   MAKING YOUR SUCCESS YOUR OWN   **53**

List of Assignments, Examples, and Exercises (Including Readings)

CHAPTER 2

CHAPTER 3

CHAPTER 4

CHAPTER 6

CHAPTER 7

CHAPTER 10

CHAPTER 11

To Students

Every day, as you talk, write, and work, you use sources. Most of the knowledge and many of the ideas that you want or need to express to others originate outside yourself. You have learned from your formal schooling and, even more, from observing the world around you, from reading, from watching television and movies, and from a multitude of other experiences. Most of the time, your use of what you have learned from sources is casual, almost automatic. You do not consciously think about where you got the information; you simply go about your activities, communicating with others and making decisions on the basis of your acquired knowledge.

In college, however, using sources becomes more concentrated and deliberate. Each course bombards you with countless new facts and ideas, coming from many places and all competing for your attention. Your success depends on how well you can develop certain skills— understanding what you read and hear in your courses, distinguishing the more important from the less important, relating new facts or ideas to what you already have learned so that you can draw conclusions, and, especially, communicating your findings to others. This book is intended to help you build all of those skills, with particular emphasis on the last.

Most college writing is both informative and interpretive; that is, it contains in varying proportions both material you take from sources and ideas that are your own. Depending on the individual course and assignment, a college paper may emphasize your own conclusions supported by knowledge you have gathered or (more likely) it may emphasize the gathered knowledge, showing that you have mastered a certain body of information. In any case it will contain something of others and something of you. Therefore, if twenty students are all assigned the same topic, the resulting twenty papers will all be somewhat different.

The constant requirement to learn new material, to respond to it, and to present it to others is the essence of the academic experience. Instructors do assign papers to test your knowledge, but that is not the most important reason. The main purpose of college writing assignments is to help you consolidate what you have learned and to expand your capacity for constructive thinking and clear communication—for making sense of things and conveying that sense to others. But these are not merely academic skills; there are few careers in which success does not depend directly on them. You will listen to the opinions of your boss, your colleagues, and your customers; or read the case histories of your clients or patients; or study the marketing reports of your salespeople or the product specifications of your suppliers; or perhaps even analyze the papers of your students! Whatever your job, the decisions that you make and the actions that you take will depend on your ability to understand and evaluate what your sources are saying (no matter whether orally or in writing), to discern any important pattern or theme, and to form conclusions. As you build on other people's ideas, you certainly will be expected to remember which facts and opinions came from which source and to give appropriate credit. Chances are that you will also be expected to be capable of drafting the memo, the letter, the report, the case history which will summarize your data and present and support your conclusions.

To help you see the connection between college and professional writing, here are some typical essay topics for various college courses, each followed by a parallel writing assignment that you might have to do on the job. Notice that all of the pairs of assignments call for much the same skills: the writer must consult a variety of sources, present what he or she has learned from those sources, and interpret that knowledge in the light of experience.

Assignment	*Sources*
For a political science course, you choose a law presently being debated in Congress or the state legislature, and argue for its passage.	debates Congressional Record
As a lobbyist, consumer advocate, or public relations expert, you prepare a pamphlet to arouse public interest in your agency's program.	editorials periodical articles your own opinions
For a health sciences course, you summarize present knowledge about the appropriate circumstances for prescribing tranquillizers and suggest some safeguards for their use.	books journals
As a member of a medical research team, you draft a report summarizing present knowledge about a specific medication and suggesting likely directions for your team's research.	government reports pharmaceutical industry reports

For a psychology course, you analyze the positive and negative effects of peer group pressure.

textbooks
journals
case studies
interviews
personal experience

As a social worker attached to a halfway house for adolescents, you write a case history of three boys, determining whether they are to be sent to separate homes or kept in the same facility.

For a business management course, you decide which department or service of your college would be the likeliest candidate for elimination if the college budget were cut by 3 percent next year; you defend your choice.

ledgers
interviews
newspapers
journals

As an assistant to a management consultant, you draft a memo recommending measures to save a manufacturing company which is in severe financial trouble.

For a sociology course, you compare reactions to unemployment in 1980 with reactions in 1930.

newspapers
magazines
books
interviews

As a staff member in the social services agency of a small city, you prepare a report on the social consequences that would result from the closing of a major factory.

For a physical education course, you classify the ways in which a team can react to a losing streak and recommend some ways in which coaches can maintain team morale.

textbooks
articles
observation and
personal
experience

As a member of a special committee of physical-education teachers for your area, you help plan an action paper that will improve your district's performance in interscholastic sports.

For an anthropology course, you contrast the system of punishment used by a tribe that you have studied with the penal code used in your home or college town.

textbooks
lectures
articles
observation and
personal
experience

As assistant to the head of the local correction agency, you prepare a report comparing the success of eight minimum-security prisons around the country.

For a physics course, you write a definition of "black holes" and explain why they were discovered in the middle of the twentieth century, not earlier, not later.

books
journals

As a physicist working for a university research team, you write a grant application based on the imminence of a possible major breakthrough in your field.

For a nutrition course, you explain why adolescents prefer junk food.

textbooks
articles
interviews
observation

As a dietician attached to the cafeteria of a local high school, you write a memo that accounts for the increasing waste of food and recommends changes in the lunch menu.

For an engineering course, you describe changes and improvements in techniques of American coal mining over the last hundred years.

books
articles
observation and experience

As a mining engineer, you write a report determining whether it is cost-effective for your company to take over the derelict mine that you were sent to survey.

Because you will need to develop and use reading and writing skills throughout your academic and professional life, *Writing from Sources* will help you learn the basic procedures that are common to all kinds of academic and professional writing and will provide enough practice in these skills to enable you to write from sources confidently and successfully. Here are the basic skills:

1. *choosing a topic:* deciding what you are actually writing about; interpreting the requests of your instructor, boss, or client, and determining the scope and limits of the assignment; making the project manageable.

2. *finding sources and acquiring information:* deciding how much supporting information you are going to need (if any) and locating it; evaluating sources and determining which are most suitable and trustworthy for your purpose; taking notes on your sources and on your own reactions.

3. *deciding on a thesis:* determining the purpose and main idea of what you are writing and your probable conclusions; re-

defining the scope and objective in the light of what you have learned from your sources.

4. *organizing your material:* determining what must be included and what may be eliminated; arranging your evidence in the most efficient and convincing way, so that your reader will reach the same conclusions as you; calling attention to common patterns and ideas that will reinforce your thesis, making sure that your presentation has a beginning, middle, and end, and that the stages are in logical order.

5. *writing your essay:* breaking down the mass of information into easily absorbed units or paragraphs; constructing each paragraph so that the reader will receive a general idea which will advance your thesis, as well as providing supporting examples and details which will make the thesis convincing.

6. *giving credit to your sources:* ensuring that your reader knows who is responsible for which idea, distinguishing between the evidence of your sources and your own interpretation and evaluation; assessing the relative reliability and usefulness of each source so that the reader can appreciate your basis for judgment.

This list of skills may seem overwhelming right now. But remember: you will be learning these procedures gradually. Not many beginning college students have been adequately trained to do writing and research at the same time. In Part I, therefore, you will begin to learn about four of the six basic skills, but the essays that you will write will require no research; you will serve as your own source of ideas and information. In Part II, where you will start working with sources outside yourself, you will learn how to get the most out of what you read and how to use the skills of summary, quotation, and paraphrase to provide accurate accounts of what you have read. In Part III you will begin to apply these skills as you prepare an essay based on a single reading provided in the text and then a synthesis essay drawing on a group of sources, also provided. Finally, in Part IV, you will go to the library to locate your own sources and begin the complex process of research. From the beginning to the end of the term, you will be practicing the same basic writing skills. The gradual addition of sources and research will make the process more complex and demanding, but not essentially different.

The best way to gain confidence and facility in writing from sources is to master each skill so thoroughly that it becomes automatic, like riding a bicycle or driving a car. To help you break the task down into workable units, each procedure will first be illustrated with a variety of models and then followed by a group of exercises. You should get as much practice as you need before going on to the next step. As you go on later to write essays for other courses, you'll discover that more and more you can concentrate on *what* you are writing and forget about methods, which will have become natural.

PART I
THE WRITING PROCESS

Writing from sources depends upon two kinds of skills: selecting the materials that you are going to use and arranging those materials into an essay. In writing essays for your college courses, your materials will generally consist of other people's information and ideas, in the form of written sources like books, articles, and reports, and written transcriptions of oral sources like lectures, discussions, and interviews. But the same writing process and the same techniques of selection and arrangement must be followed when you write an essay that is based entirely on your own ideas and experiences. The best way to start gaining a working knowledge of these basic skills is for you to serve as your own source, without doing any research. For this reason, Part I asks you to work with your own ideas. Later, beginning in Part II, you will use ideas taken from books and lectures in much the same way.

This first chapter takes you very briefly through all the stages in writing a short essay and provides a grounding in the skills that are necessary for most kinds of academic assignments: narrowing your topic, gathering your ideas in notes, pinpointing your main idea, using your notes to plan an outline, and working with your notes and outline to write the sequence of paragraphs that make up an essay. Your ultimate objective is to write essays for your college courses and to use a variety of sources easily and efficiently; therefore, the emphasis here is also on the accumulation of materials. In Chapter 1, you will be asked to assemble and organize notes containing your own ideas, just as you would work with notes based on your reading, and to integrate these notes in a coherent and convincing essay.

That a good writer can write freely, without pausing to think and to plan ahead, is an illusion. Writing does not mean thinking aloud on paper. There is no way of saying "Presto!" and immediately having a five-page essay come pouring out of you. As in every act of creative design, the person in charge—you—must carefully plan and carry out each separate step, while keeping the ultimate goal somewhere in mind; otherwise, the finished product may fall apart. Nothing can be taken for granted.

In Part I, each stage of the writing process is slowed down, so that you can become thoroughly familiar with it. You will be urged to consider all your options and then to make a deliberate choice of topic, of materials, of central idea, of strategy, of paragraph sequence, and of paragraph contents. This freedom of choice gives you control over the writing process. Later, when you have practiced the skills, the stages can begin to overlap, and the entire process of writing an essay can become familiar and comfortable.

1. The Selection and Arrangement of Materials: Topics, Notes, Theses, Strategies, Outlines, and Drafts

When you receive an essay assignment, you may not know where to begin. Sometimes the subject is very broad, intended to satisfy a group of students with widely differing interests and tastes. Sometimes there is no required subject at all, with the choice left to you. But such freedom can seem frightening if you feel overwhelmed by the scope and possibilities of a wide-open subject. To make such an assignment less formidable, you must first break the subject down into its components. The aggressive image of breaking down the subject—struggle and mastery—suggests the effort of will that you must exert in the earliest stages of the writing process. You can gain the control and assurance that you need to write easily and well only if you first succeed in defining the broad subject in your own terms and make it your own.

TAKING INVENTORY

When the subject for an essay is left either broad or unspecified, your first objective is to think of a manageable topic that interests you and that suits the requirements of the assignment. As you start to work on the essay, you may find yourself having to consider and then discard a succession of topics that do not seem quite right, so you will need to provide yourself with plenty of choice. Your first step, then, is to take an inventory of all the ideas related to your broad subject that you can possibly imagine yourself writing about. At this point, don't try to anticipate which topic you will eventually choose, and don't worry about whether any of the ideas are any good. Quantity is important. Just write

3

down, as rapidly as possible, a list of everything that you can think of about your subject.

Here is such a list, a sampling of possible topics for an essay on *humor*, compiled by a student who did not know how to start writing about such a broad subject and who was searching for a starting point. The topics are in random order.

```
clowns
Charlie Chaplin
Emmet Kelly
Woody Allen
stand-up comedians
what's the difference between a clown and a comedian?
situation comedy
Archie Bunker
ethnic jokes
dirty jokes
practical jokes
does humor have an element of cruelty?
does humor have to be visual?
puns
limericks
parody
Mad Magazine
comic strips
Lucy and Schroeder
Tom and Jerry
cartoons
what makes people laugh?
```

If you look for connections between the items on the list, you will be able to follow the student's thought processes quite easily. In free association, one topic has led to the next: comic strips lead to cartoons (by way of Lucy, Schroeder, Tom, and Jerry); practical jokes lead to a question about the role of cruelty in humor. You may also have noticed that the list contains three *kinds* of topics mixed together: types of humor; examples of these types; and more abstract questions about the nature of humor. If your powers of association fail you and the flow of ideas suddenly dries up, you can extend your list by deliberately searching for new types, for different examples, for interesting questions, and for other ways of exploring the subject.

Here are some useful questions to help you generate a list of topics: What do I think about the subject? Why do I think that? What are some obvious examples? What are some unusual and strange examples? In what context or perspective do people usually think about that subject?

Does the subject break down into several types or classifications? What conditions can cause this effect or what are the effects of this condition? How can something be improved? or abused? or done differently?

Now, look at another inventory of ideas, this time dealing with the broad subject of *advertising*. Read through the sixteen topics and see if you can find any pattern to the flow of ideas as the writer moves from point to point. What are the different ways in which advertising is being viewed?

```
 1. history of advertising
 2. how advertising works
 3. how advertising benefits the consumer
 4. how an ad gets produced
 5. jobs in advertising
 6. notable advertising campaigns
 7. advertising art
 8. effects of advertising on technology: products and
    packaging
 9. original purpose of advertising
10. imagine a world without advertising
11. advertising and TV
12. false advertising
13. regulation of advertising
14. advertising as it reflects the norms of society
15. advertising and materialism
16. advertising and women
```

ASSIGNMENT 1

Assume that you have been assigned a 500- to 900-word essay (two to three typed pages). Choose *two* subjects from the list below. Write down, very quickly, all the ideas that you can think of for writing about *each* of the two subjects. (Use a separate piece of paper for each list.) Each idea can be as short as a single word or as long as a sentence; but start a new line for each new entry. You may find it convenient to number each new point in each list. Before starting your lists, get your mind working by reviewing the questions at the bottom of the previous page and at the top of this page.

adolescence	communications	death
aggression	industry	discipline and
city life	courts and law	authority
comforts of modern	courtship	doctors
life	crime	

education for small children	human rights	power
elections	inconveniences of modern life	prostitution
the environment	manners	rural life
ethics in business	manual labor	shops and supermarkets
fathers	marriage	suburban life
health	monogamy	transportation
heroes	mothers	war
housing	music	weather

ANALYZING A LIST OF TOPICS

Before you can decide on the best topic for your essay, you must examine all the possibilities on your list:

A. identify and combine topics which say the same thing in different ways;

B. identify and eliminate topics which are vague and which suggest little or nothing that is specific. There is a difference between vague and broad: a *broad* topic suggests a variety of ideas and may require a lengthy treatment to be fully developed; a *vague* topic means that you will have difficulty working out a starting point and a structure for your essay.

Here is a list of topics dealing with *cheating*, presented in five successive stages of analysis. Column A shows the list in its original random order, with repetitions of and variations on the same ideas. With Column B the writer begins to organize these raw materials by combining *one* scattered group of related topics. In Column C, the completed worksheet, you can see the entire process of analysis, with two vague and unfocused topics crossed off and related topics indicated by arrows. Column D reflects all the changes made in Column C, with similar items grouped but left in the order in which they originally appeared. Column E, the final, revised list, shows the order of topics rearranged to present a spectrum of approaches and groups minor ideas, in parentheses, after the major ideas that they support.

A. Original List

```
1. is cheating immoral?
2. cheating in marriage
```

 3. cheating is a part of life
 4. cheating your employer
 5. how to cheat on college tests
 6. the effect of cheating on society
 7. is cheating an instinct?
 8. cheating the government
 9. cheating in welfare
10. cheating on school exams
11. cheating for survival
12. cheating and its effect on children
13. cheating and TV commercials
14. does cheating indicate a criminal mind?
15. cheating the consumer through advertising
16. why cheating is prevalent in universities
17. how to avoid being cheated
18. cheating today
19. cheating to get ahead
20. cheating on income tax
21. why do people cheat?

B. Worksheet, with Aspects of the Same Idea Indicated

 1. is cheating immoral?
 2. cheating in marriage
 3. cheating is a part of life
 4. cheating your employer
 5. how to cheat on college tests
 6. the effect of cheating on society
 7. is cheating an instinct?
 8. cheating the government
 9. cheating in welfare
10. cheating on school exams
11. cheating for survival
12. cheating and its effect on children
13. cheating and TV commercials
14. does cheating indicate a criminal mind?
15. cheating the consumer through advertising
16. why cheating is prevalent in universities
17. how to avoid being cheated
18. cheating today
19. cheating to get ahead
20. cheating on income tax
21. why do people cheat?

C. Completed Worksheet

1. is cheating immoral?
2. cheating in marriage
3. cheating is a part of life
4. cheating your employer
5. how to cheat on college tests
6. ~~the effect of cheating on society~~
7. is cheating an instinct?
8. cheating the government
9. cheating in welfare
10. cheating on school exams
11. cheating for survival
12. cheating and its effect on children
13. cheating and TV commercials
14. does cheating indicate a criminal mind?
15. cheating the consumer through advertising
16. why cheating is prevalent in universities
17. how to avoid being cheated
18. ~~cheating today~~
19. cheating to get ahead
20. cheating on income tax
21. why do people cheat?

D. Condensed List with Similar Topics Grouped

1. is cheating immoral?
   is cheating an instinct?
   does cheating indicate a criminal mind?
   why do people cheat?
2. cheating in marriage
3. cheating is a part of life
   cheating for survival
   cheating to get ahead
4. cheating your employer
5. how to cheat on college tests
   cheating on school exams
   why cheating is prevalent in universities
6. cheating the government
   cheating in welfare
   cheating on income tax
7. cheating and its effect on children
8. cheating and TV commercials
   cheating the consumer through advertising
9. how to avoid being cheated

E. Final List of Topics Showing Ordered Spectrum and Major and Minor Ideas

1. cheating and its effects on children
2. cheating on school exams (how to cheat on college tests; why cheating is prevalent in universities)
3. cheating in marriage
4. cheating your employer
5. cheating the consumer through advertising (cheating and TV commercials)
6. cheating the government (cheating on welfare; cheating on income tax)
7. how to avoid being cheated
8. is cheating immoral? (is cheating an instinct? why do people cheat? does cheating indicate a criminal mind?)
9. cheating is a universal fact of life (cheating for survival; cheating to get ahead; cheating is a part of life)

Each of the first six topics suggests an examination of cheating in a different context or area of life: children, school, marriage, work, advertising, and government. The seventh topic promises to suggest some solutions to the basic problem of being cheated. Finally, the last two topics both refer to the reasons why people cheat, but they are not precisely the same. The eighth topic takes a neutral approach, neither positive nor negative, while the ninth suggests a defense or justification of cheating.

Did you notice that "cheating is a universal fact of life" did not appear on the original list of random topics? The new phrasing for this entry was invented as a convenient way of summing up the three sub-topics now placed in parentheses.

EXERCISE 1

The following list consists of random topics dealing with the subject *money.*

A. Condense this list by:
　　1. combining topics that overlap (use arrow, lines, or other symbols);
　　2. crossing out topics that are too vague.
B. Prepare a revised list of topics, using column E (above) as your model.

　　　1. is money necessary in society?
　　　2. how much money is enough?

3. why is money important?
4. money and social prestige
5. money can change personality
6. worship of the dollar
7. origins of paper money
8. money in our society
9. is money the root of all evil?
10. money and politics
11. money and elections
12. trade and barter instead of a money economy
13. a few people have most of the money in the world
14. money and the teenager
15. taxes
16. saving money
17. keeping a budget
18. gambling
19. achieving status through money
20. what constitutes greed?
21. disadvantages of having too much money
22. money and crime
23. bribery
24. money and government
25. coping with inflation: the value of money today
26. the fantasy of being rich

CHOOSING A TOPIC

Once you have pared down your original list and have a limited number of topics to choose from, you will naturally want to select the best possible topic for your essay.

Choose an Idea That Interests You

If a topic does not appeal to you, don't write about it! Don't be tempted by an apparently easy but uninteresting topic; for, if you are bored while writing your essay, your reader will probably be just as bored while reading it.

Choose a Topic That You Know Something About

No amount of interest in a topic can compensate for a complete lack of relevant knowledge or experience. For example, if you have never known or read much about families caught in the intricacies of the welfare system, you probably should not write about cheating in welfare. Of course, assignments in many of your college courses will require you to explore subjects totally new to you, and research can usually supply you with the necessary background information. But while you are still learning organizational skills, you ought to seize the advantage of working with a relatively familiar topic. Even later, when you are ready to do research, some knowledge of your subject will help you to evaluate your reading and place it in a sound perspective.

Choose a Topic About Which You Can Be Objective

Too much familiarity and too much interest in a topic can be a handicap at this stage. For example, a person whose experiences with the welfare system have resulted in very strong, inflexible opinions may be too emotionally involved with the topic to produce a well-balanced essay.

Choose a Topic That Fits the Assignment

Your instructor will generally tell you how long the essay is to be and whether or not you are to do any research. Some topics can be explored in a few pages; others require more lengthy development. Think about the topic's possibilities before you make the choice. If you decide to write about health and then plan to focus on "the incidence of infectious diseases in the Amazon region," you will need to work in the library. But if you have been asked *not* to do any outside reading, and if you are interested in "teaching children basic health care" or "the adult's right to smoke cigarettes," you may be able to base your essay on your own experience and on your understanding of the world around you.

Unfortunately, no hard and fast rules exist for choosing a successful topic. Consider the person who wants to write about cheating in the universities. Does the writer have to be a college student? a graduate? Should the writer have actually engaged in cheating, or known someone who did, in order to write a convincing essay? The answers to these questions depend on what the writer wishes the essay to be: the scope and development of the ideas; the message to be conveyed to the reader; the evidence with which the ideas are substantiated.

To sum up, all that you need to choose a reasonable topic for an essay that should not require research are the following:

1. some interest in the topic (but not to the point of obsession);
2. some ideas and opinions (but not rigid ones);
3. some knowledge you remember from your reading, from other media, from personal experience, and from the experiences of others.

EXERCISE 2

Read through the following topics, which are all starting points for an essay on *fashion*.

Write the numbers 1 through 19 down the left-hand margin of a sheet of paper.

A.   Add one broad and one narrow topic to the list (numbers 18 and 19).
B.   For each entry on the list (including your additions):
    1.   Put B next to the number of each topic that you regard as broad in scope and N next to the number of each topic that you regard as narrow.
    2.   Put R next to the number of each topic that would probably require you to do research, and NR next to the number of each topic for which your general experience would be sufficient background. (If you think that research is advisable, cite the kinds of sources that you might consult.)
    3.   For purposes of this exercise, assume that you have been assigned a short essay, averaging 500 to 750 words (or two to three type-written pages). List the numbers of the topics that you could develop in a short essay.

1. who dictates fashion? the designers or the people who wear the clothes?
2. the influence of Dior on fashions of the forties and fifties
3. how fashion is merchandized in department stores
4. the fashion industry and the economy
5. the rise of the boutique: 1960's and 1970's
6. why don't men wear bright colors?
7. men's ties: wide and narrow
8. fashion advertising
9. *Vogue* magazine over three decades
10. fashion photography
11. fashion fads
12. wearing trousers and women's liberation
13. the invention of the bra
14. women's clothes: 1880 and 1980
15. textiles: synthetics vs. natural fibers
16. hemlines up and down
17. what's the fashion capital this year?

ASSIGNMENT 2

Turn back to Assignment 1 and the two lists of topics that you compiled.

A. Revise and condense the entries for *one* of the two lists as you did in Exercise 1.
B. Then circle those topics in the revised list which do not require research and which are narrow enough to suggest a short, rather than a long, essay.
C. Choose the one topic that you want to develop into an essay of your own.

GENERATING NOTES

The selection of a topic by no means signifies that you are ready to start writing your essay. Here is one of those points in the writing process where you must slow down in order to examine your options and your intentions. If you want to make intelligent decisions about the contents and the direction of your essay, you must first find out what you think and what you know about your topic. Once you have assembled some materials to work with—in other words, once you have written down your ideas in the form of notes—you can then consider the possibilities for developing the topic and decide on a thesis or main idea. Only after you know what you want to say can you begin to plan how to best get your point across to your reader.

Finding out how much you actually know about your chosen topic and what you want to say about it involves taking another inventory, this time with a specific focus. Make a list of all the points that you might want to make about this topic. The inventory must be comprehensive. Try to think through the topic thoroughly. Ideas that occur to you belatedly during the final stages of writing can suggest an entirely new line of development and, at that point, can have a disruptive effect. It is more sensible to have all your materials at hand than to have to change your plans later in order to accommodate an afterthought. To make sure that your notes are comprehensive, use the minimum of mental censorship, just as you did when you were thinking of possible topics. Once again, as ideas pop into your head (either by free association or by a deliberate review of several possible approaches to the topic), you should jot them all down, without pausing for evaluation.

This list of ideas should not pretend to be anything else but a preliminary step. If you use a paragraph format, the notes that you generate can look like the draft of an essay. To avoid the impression that you have been producing a final product, write your notes in a column, vertical and straggly-looking and apparently disconnected, and avoid block-like "paragraphs." A page to a page-and-a-half of notes, handwritten in a column, can make an excellent beginning for a short essay. (In the interests of clarity, some of the models that you will be looking at in the next few pages run somewhat shorter than real notes would.)

Although your notes may be written in condensed form, there is no point in using a cryptic shorthand that will make no sense to you two days later. At the other extreme, it is not essential to phrase each entry as a complete sentence; however, if you naturally express your ideas in sentence form, don't fall into the trap of thinking that your notes are completed sentences from a finished essay. Your object is to jot down a number of points that you may wish to write about, not to explain each one in full detail. You are trying to discover the full range of your ideas, so your notes should be varied. Each new entry should extend or develop (rather than merely rephrase) the previous point.

Which of these two sets of notes has the greater potential for an interesting essay? Which of the two sets would you rather work from?

A. Topic: *The need for vocational training in college*
>   practical experience necessary to get a good job
>   practical experience necessary to do a good job
>   who would trust a doctor fresh out of med school?
>   book knowledge often irrelevant and unreal
>   college courses often dull and poorly taught
>   getting out into real world
>   emergency room: giving heart massage to real victim
>   helps in competition for jobs later on
>   helps to make intelligent career choice
>   actual experience makes the job real—shows you
>   disadvantages
>   too late to change career if experience comes after
>   college
>   importance of observing skilled workers actually doing the
>   job
>   someone to imitate and model yourself on
>   value of immediate criticism of your own performance
>   how to give grades for job performance?
>   earning money as soon as possible
>   helps to pay tuition
>   college is too expensive
>   is college necessary at all?

B. Topic: *The need for vocational training in our schools*

1. Every year thousands of graduates flood the marketplace, waving their college degrees, expecting careers in their majors, only to be frustrated and disappointed.

2. I believe that our society today needs more vocational education, because many students come to realize that four years of college have left them without skills that they can translate into jobs.

3. The school system should place more emphasis on vocational education as well as vocational guidance, sponsoring youths into the job market.

4. One of the reasons for the high unemployment rate in America today is the lack of vocational training in our school system.

5. The government spends too many tax dollars on less important projects, including money for the defense budget.

Although the points on List A are brief, they are perfectly comprehensible. The writer is trying to cover the topic as thoroughly as she can by including a variety of ideas. She may be raising too many issues and going off on tangents; she may not be able to develop all this material in a single short essay; but she has achieved the primary purpose of note-taking: she has plenty of ideas to choose from.

The second writer is not using the note-taking process to explore the topic thoroughly. Instead of pushing the author's ideas as far as possible, the first four entries all make essentially the same point. The writer seems to have decided to skip the inventory stage entirely and to have begun to experiment with possible opening sentences for the essay. But after the opening has been written, what material will support the assertion that vocational training is desirable?

Asking Yourself Questions

One good way to explore a topic and generate good notes is to ask yourself a few questions, writing them down and then answering them. The answers are your notes. Here, for example, are some questions that one writer asked herself about a topic which is, in itself, a question: *should everyone who wishes be able to go to college?* The writer decided to set up some choices in order to find out what her opinions really were. She wrote down the following list of questions, expressed as a series of contrasts.

Notice the deliberate attempt to look at both sides of the question.

Does a student need some preparation and a certain level of intelligence in order to do college work?

On the other hand, aren't effort and hard work enough to make a student succeed in college?

Should the serious student, who makes a real effort to compensate for his deficiencies, be given as much consideration for admission as a less serious student with proven academic ability?

Should there be a tracking system in college to allow the two types of students to attend?

Is college only important for acquiring information and knowledge?

On the other hand, what about the experience of going to college? Shouldn't we all have access to a place where everyone is striving to acquire knowledge?

For that matter, do we all have the right to demand participation in a specific kind of experience, like college?

Is college a luxury or a necessity?

Next, by examining her preliminary questions, the writer tried to work out a more basic set of questions that she could explore in her essay. Reading over her first two questions, she discovered that they were opposite sides of a single question; she was really inquiring into two kinds of qualifications which one might need to do college work. So, in effect, she "translated" her preliminary questions about specific qualities like intelligence and ambition into more general questions that could establish a broader framework for her essay. With the exception of the next-to-last question (which could not be easily re-cast into a more basic form), all the preliminary questions were thought through and expressed as broader generalizations:

Preliminary Questions	*Basic Questions*
Does a student need some preparation and a certain level of intelligence in order to do college work?	What qualifies a student to do college work?
On the other hand, aren't effort and hard work enough to make a student succeed in college?	What special abilities does college demand?

Should the serious student, who makes a real effort to compensate for his deficiencies, be given as much consideration for admission as a less serious student with proven academic ability?

Which is more important: academic ability or hard work?

Is college only important for acquiring information and knowledge?

What is the purpose of college?

On the other hand, what about the experience of going to college? Shouldn't we all have access to a place where everyone is striving to acquire knowledge?

Does one go to college to acquire knowledge or to experience an academic environment?

For that matter, do we all have the right to demand participation in a specific kind of experience, like college?

What entitles a student to a college education?

Should there be a tracking system in college to allow the two types of students to attend?

Should there be a tracking system in college to allow the two types of students to attend?

Is college a luxury or a necessity?

Does each of us have the right to attend college or are we granted the privilege of attending college?

By asking the right questions, the writer has made sure that, once her answers are written down, she will have a comprehensive set of notes and the materials for a strong essay. Setting up contrasts is not the only way to explore a topic's possibilities for development. Another successful method is to investigate causes. For example, if you are writing about a generally admired person, you might ask whether the admiration is deserved or not, and why; whether the admiration is understandable or not, and why; whether the admiration will endure (in ten months or ten years), and why. Notice how often the question "Why?" becomes the essential follow-up to a judgement, once you have made one. It is not enough to decide what you believe; it is also necessary to understand why you believe it and to make sure that your reasons are convincing.

Generating Notes and Writing from Sources

In most academic writing, you will have consulted sources by this stage of the writing process. The rest of this book deals extensively with the integration of source materials and your own ideas, but for now you should concentrate on developing notes without the distraction of outside sources. When you begin to work with sources, you will ask the same kinds of questions about your topic, and you will subject your source materials to the same kind of scrutiny as when you are writing from your own experience.

THE NEED FOR A THESIS

The early stages of the writing process are cycles of expansion and contraction. When you choose a topic, you must first spread your nets wide to gather new ideas and then filter out everything but your chosen focus. Next, as soon as you have produced a varied and loosely connected set of notes, with ideas going off in several directions at once, you must once more narrow your field of vision by establishing the boundaries of your essay. At this point, you need a firm basis for deciding which ideas in your notes shall be developed and which shall be discarded. What is it that you wish to say about your topic; that is, what single point do you want to make? The answer to this question is your thesis.

A thesis is a statement of intention and purpose, conveying what you expect the central idea of your essay to be. By committing yourself to a thesis, you are undertaking to support and validate this central idea as thoroughly and convincingly as you can. Because the thesis must be a fairly substantial generalization that stands by itself and is worth supporting, it must conform to three guidelines:

1. *The thesis should be a statement, not a question.* It is not enough to raise the question that you would like to explore; rather, the thesis represents an answer to that question.
   Unacceptable: Who should be enabled to go to college?
   Acceptable: Only students who will make the greatest effort to learn should receive the privilege of a college education.
2. *The thesis should be a complete sentence with a subject and a verb.* You cannot simply add a few details to your topic

(which is usually expressed as a phrase or a fragment). You must expand and rewrite that fragmentary topic so that your readers will understand why you want to write about it.

Unacceptable: The value of a college education.

Acceptable: Students have to understand the practical value of education if they are going to make the most of their opportunities in college.

3. *The thesis should be more than a very obvious, generally accepted fact or truth.* There can be no special skill or credit attached to convincing your readers of a point that, most likely, they already believe.

Unacceptable: College work can be difficult for poorly prepared students.

Acceptable: Since college work can be difficult for poorly prepared students, admission should depend upon an applicant's meeting certain standards of achievement.

The thesis should be broad enough and arguable enough to be worth defending. On the other hand, it should be neither so broad nor so complex that you will need a three-hundred-page book just to present the main arguments. For example, no one should undertake to prove or disprove the existence of God in the scope of a college essay, whether it is a two-page personal essay or a twenty-page research paper. Try instead to choose a thesis which you believe to be fairly controversial (i.e., some people would oppose it) and which you are sure that you can develop effectively, but don't go overboard and defend an outrageous position.

By establishing your main idea, your thesis also defines the scope and the limits that you have chosen for your essay. From now on, you should try to stay within the boundaries of your thesis and the rough notes that support it (if you add substantially to your notes, be prepared to redraft your thesis). If, for example, you have undertaken to demonstrate that "everyone suffers when individuals falsify their income tax returns," you have no business (unless you merely want to suggest a brief analogy) to write about employees who steal from giant corporations. Certainly, falsifying tax returns and stealing from corporations are both examples of people cheating large institutions; but your thesis does not promise to explore both types of cheating: it is concerned only with the falsification of income tax returns. Should you decide to expand the scope of your essay, you would rewrite your thesis to encompass the new strand of thought.

One student chose to write about "cheating in the universities" and jotted down a set of notes containing a long list of examples of students who cheated for many different reasons and in a variety of circumstances.

After reading through his notes, the student decided to try out a few theses. Would any of these make a good essay?

1. There is cheating in the universities.
2. Instances of cheating have occurred in our universities.
3. The prevalence of cheating in our university.
4. Why is cheating prevalent in our university?

In fact, none of the four is satisfactory. The first is nothing but a restatement of the topic, while an essay developing the second thesis would be restricted to the listing of a series of examples and, in effect, would be merely a transcription of the rough notes. The third and fourth theses suggest a more challenging approach, but the third is a topic or title for the essay, and the fourth is a question. Instead of simply proving that cheating prevails, why not write a thesis that attempts to answer the question raised in thesis four and that therefore explains the reasons for the prevalence of cheating? Clearly, this student has not yet explored his own reactions to the examples contained in his notes. What is his attitude toward all this cheating? Why does he think it is happening? Is it right or wrong? Finding out what he really thinks about his topic (and adding some of his ideas to the examples in his notes) could result in a far more challenging thesis:

5. Cheating is prevalent in universities today because of academic and professional pressures.
6. Academic and professional pressures make it understandable that cheating occurs in universities today.
7. Whatever the pressures experienced by students, cheating in universities today should not be condoned.

The final choice between these three satisfactory theses would depend upon the writer's point of view. The first possibility (5) is neutral, as the writer promises to discuss reasons for cheating and to suggest what they are, but refrains from any criticism. The middle thesis (6) undertakes to do the same thing, but specifies a more sympathetic approach. The last one (7) is distinctly negative, firmly expressing its intention of rejecting the practice of cheating.

EXERCISE 3

Here is a list of topics about money (taken from the list in Exercise 1), together with a set of thesis statements for each topic. Examine the theses within each group and identify the best one. Reject any thesis that is a fragment, a statement of the obvious, or a vague and undefined assertion. In some sets, you will find more than one acceptable thesis: if you were going to write a short essay, which thesis would be a practical choice?

1. Topic: How much money is enough?
    A. A person knows that he has enough money when he has some left over after his expenditure.
    B. There is no such thing as enough money.
    C. The more money we have, the more money we want to fill our needs.

2. Topic: The effects of money on the personality
    A. Having money changes the personality, because it changes how society views you and thus changes your behavior.
    B. Having money has made my personality blossom into charm.
    C. Do you know anyone whose personality has changed because of an increase in money?
    D. Money can make people arrogant and cruel.

3. Topic: The fantasy of being rich
    A. The fantasy of being rich is that one has freedom and a choice instead of being required to work under someone else's control.
    B. The fantasy of being rich can help people to progress in life until their fantasies become real.
    C. If you suddenly won a million dollars, what would you do first?
    D. She dreamed that she was Queen of Europe, smothered in jewels.

4. Topic: The disadvantages of being rich
    A. Being rich has its disadvantages.
    B. Rich people face more kidnap threats than any other class of people.
    C. The only disadvantage of being rich is that you can't take it with you.
    D. The disadvantage of being rich is that you'll never be poor.
    E. Money can't buy you love.
    F. People who become overwhelmingly rich, like Howard Hughes, become isolated because of their wealth.

5. Topic: Money and crime
    A. Crime does pay for some people.
    B. Inflation has driven some honest people with fixed incomes to shoplifting.
    C. Some people will do anything for money, even stealing and killing.
    D. Crime is often caused because people want to make a quick buck.
    E. Money leads to crime.
    F. Stealing money is the most common crime in the United States.

6. Topic: Bribery
    A. In certain public offices, bribery appears to be an accepted way of life.
    B. Many honest persons have become corrupt through bribery.
    C. Bribery was used in the Watergate scandal.
    D. Bribery is a form of temptation for many politicians.
    E. It is not wise to bribe an officer of the law.
    F. Bribery has been used for centuries, and I don't think there is any way to stop it.

7. Topic: Money and teenagers
    A. Most teenagers in New York feel that having money is more important than finishing their education.
    B. Teenagers today need more money than teenagers did twenty years ago.
    C. More teenagers are acquiring more and more money.
    D. Teenagers do not value money as they should.
    E. Teenagers today strongly believe that money is the ultimate goal of success.
    F. A teenager will best learn the value of money if he is permitted to work and is not dependent on his parents for an allowance.

Writing a Thesis from Notes

Thesis-writing, ideally, is the step *after* note-taking, not the step before. After you generate and review your notes, you have an opportunity to sift through your ideas and opinions. You cannot compose a strong thesis unless you understand your materials. Otherwise, how can you know whether you will be able to defend it?

One student who wanted to write about *private schools and public schools* knew the potential direction of her essay from the beginning: she distinctly preferred private schools. Had she immediately constructed a thesis, she might have committed herself to an overly broad and vague proposition, such as "Private schools are more desirable than public schools" or "Public schools don't work." Instead, she developed a complete set of notes, deliberately exploring the reasons for her initial preference and focusing her notes on the reasons why private schools provide a better education. Here are her notes (with details and examples omitted for the sake of clarity):

```
1. no interference from school boards; therefore innovative
   programs possible
2. parents demand value for money
```

```
3. able to choose the best school for one's child; no worry
   about zoning
4. faraway bureaucrats can't determine class sizes
5. schools need to work hard to get paying students;
   services improve
6. schools not dependent on government--political
   decisions, policy changes, budget cuts
7. able to choose between progressive and traditional
   schools and ignore local school board's policy
8. parents pay; therefore get involved in school
9. can lower-income families afford tuition? tax credits
   and scholarships?
```

To write her thesis, the student had to find a generalization which would both encompass her list of points and express the essential advantages of private schools. What do the entries have in common? Some of the points (3 and 7) stress that parents can have freedom of choice in selecting and rejecting a school. Others (1, 4, and 6) assert that, because private schools are not subject to outside control, they can have more scope for experimentation and more individualized programs. These two groups of ideas suggest that freedom of choice is the major reason for preferring a private school. However, such a thesis would not be entirely comprehensive, for there is a third group of entries (2, 5, and 8) which point out that the success of private schools results from the contract between buyer and seller: parents are concerned about their investment, and schools have to do a good job in order to compete for students. In fact (with the possible exception of the last entry), what all the notes have in common is a belief that education benefits from a free market, which encourages freedom of choice and competition. Thus, the student was able to formulate a thesis that includes, in the following order,

1. the topic of the essay;
2. the writer's own opinion;
3. her basic reasons for holding that opinion.

```
Unlike public schools, private schools provide a good
education because private enterprise encourages freedom of
choice and healthy competition.
```

EXERCISE 4

A. Write a thesis for the list of notes below. To make sure that your list is comprehensive, first try labelling each entry with a summarizing word or phrase.

Topic: *cheating for survival*

1. People feel that, if they are cheating in order to benefit themselves, they are acting correctly.
2. Cheating is natural.
3. Most people don't realize that they have cheated until it is done. Cheating is rarely premeditated.
4. People will lie and deceive others in order to get ahead.
5. Cheating is a way of life.
6. People cheat through college and work in order to get a position that is important to them.
7. Cheating will make the ladder to your chosen career a shorter one to climb.
8. Success is so important in our society that people feel it is necessary to cheat in order to be one step ahead of the next person.

B. Write a thesis for the list of notes below. To make sure that your list is comprehensive, first try labelling each entry with a summarizing word or phrase.

Topic: *discourtesy at sporting events*

1. people showing bad manners in ball parks and stadiums
2. reactions of most people to the event: intense excitement and concentration
3. spectators shocked at those lunatics who disrupt the game and call attention to themselves
4. reasons why people go to ballgames: pleasure and entertainment
5. different ways of being offensive:
   drunkenness
   trying to get on television by raising huge signs that block others' views
   heckling
   fist-fighting
6. high cost of sporting events: people want to be left alone to enjoy themselves
7. people can't concentrate on the game
8. stopping this behavior:
   ejecting hooligans from the stadium
   searching suspicious characters (for weapons or drugs or alcohol)
   not selling alcohol at these events

Writing a Thesis by Classifying Your Notes

One efficient way to define the scope and direction of your ideas is to label each entry on your list of notes with a brief identifying word or phrase. You can sometimes trace a theme or pattern within your notes if you have reduced the mass of material to a set of basic, descriptive terms.

Here is a brief set of notes for an essay analyzing the reasons why people decide to get married. The column on the right should contain a brief summary or "label" describing each reason. A single label may apply to more than one note. Try completing the column.

1. to get away from home	independence
2. to be taken care of	security
3. to avoid social disapproval	social pressure
4. for money	
5. for love	
6. to hang on to the partner	
7. for sex	
8. to have children	

What are some possible theses for an essay based on these notes?

The following five theses are worth analyzing even though only one is entirely satisfactory.

Thesis A: People get married for a variety of reasons.

This thesis, at first glance, appears to summarize the material. After all, the list does contain a variety of reasons! But the sentence only indicates that the reasons are numerous and different; it says nothing at all about the *content* of the reasons. What will the reader of the essay learn about the main motives for marriage? A good thesis should do more than echo the essay's topic.

Thesis B: People get married for pleasure, security, independence, social pressure, and principle.

This statement does no more than repeat the notes; exactly the same conclusion can be reached by glancing down the list. A good thesis integrates the writer's notes into a single summarizing idea.

Thesis C: People get married because they cannot realize their desires without marriage.

The reference to "realization of desires" moves this thesis closer to becoming a summarizing idea, for it adds an insight that one might not perceive from skimming the list. But the sentence is rather empty. What does it assert? You won't achieve your desires without marriage, so you get married because you must. But, according to the notes, what are the desires that need to be fulfilled? A good thesis presents the essay's main idea straightforwardly, not in terms of its opposite.

> Thesis D: People get married to fill emotional and social needs.

This thesis is successful because it not only provides a clear summary of the reasons for getting married, but also stands as a substantial generalization in its own right. A good thesis presents more than the sum of its notes. One wonders, however, whether marrying for money comes under the category of emotional or social needs! While it might be better to add "financial" to the statement, Thesis D is acceptable as it is.

> Thesis E: People get married for selfish reasons.

This conclusion reads so much into the list and stands so far beyond the evidence that the gap between notes and thesis is too great for credibility. The sentence does not merely summarize the list; it evaluates the reasons for getting married and comes to a negative conclusion, a conclusion that is not really implicit in the evidence as it stands. To make notes and thesis fit together, the writer would have either to omit the positive reasons from the list (and possibly add a few more self-serving ones) or to rewrite his thesis to reflect a broader spectrum of motives.

EXERCISE 5

A. Write a label describing each entry in the following list, repeating labels when you identify a repetition of the same kind of motive. Then write a shortened list of all your categories or labels.

Topic: *why do people lie?*

1. People lie because they are insecure.   self-protection

2. People lie to impress their listeners.   _____

3. People lie to protect other people.   _____

4. People lie to entertain.   _____

5. People lie to avoid punishment and embarrassment.   _____

6. People lie to inflict pain. _____

7. People lie to act out their fantasies. _____

8. People lie because they are naturally deceitful. _____

How many different categories does the list suggest to you? What possible principle of order could you use to arrange your list of labels in a sequence?

B. First, write a "label" for each reason in the list below, keeping in mind that your purpose is to look for similarities, so that related reasons can be grouped together. Try to repeat the same labels whenever you can, using a total of four to six labels.

Topic: *why do people work?*

1. to pay bills _____

2. to keep occupied _____

3. to have a feeling of responsibility _____

4. to do good deeds _____

5. to get Social Security _____

6. to protect oneself from being regarded as lazy _____

7. to satisfy one's addiction (to work) _____

8. to get out of the house _____

9. to buy luxuries _____

10. to meet new people _____

11. to get off welfare _____

12. to break the monotony of housework and child-rearing _____

13. to learn a skill _____

14. to feel emotionally well-balanced   _____

15. to have status in society   _____

16. to have a well-planned, orderly life, with a   _____
    routine

C. The list of notes for "why do people work?" lacks a thesis statement. Try writing a generalization that sums up your categories.

THE NEED FOR A STRATEGY

A strategy expresses an essay's form in the same way that blueprints express the form of a house. You may possess a great deal of information about the house that you are building: the number of rooms; the building materials; the needs, habits, and tastes of the people who are going to live there. You may be working from a list of specific ideas or requests: a fireplace; a built-in garage; a tower room. But without a plan, how can these features have any relationship to each other? In fact, how can they ever form a single, coherent structure, one that is capable of standing? In the same way, an essay cannot hold together if it is constructed from bits and pieces of notes without the binding force of a strategy.

Your essay should have a convincing effect of unity. The ideas that you choose to include in the essay should be of the same order and should be capable of blending into an integrated whole. Nothing should be included that will suggest a digressive or alien quality. In the same way, the arrangement of your materials—the application of your strategy— must support this impression of unity. Your sentences and your paragraphs should form a pattern that readers can grasp at once and then retain after they have finished reading. This pattern, this plan for arranging your ideas in some clear relationship to each other, is what most writers mean by strategy.

The relationship between ideas, between sentences, between paragraphs should remain logical and clear. There should be no gaps in the flow of information. Your readers may be surprised at the appearance of a new point; they may not have anticipated that your thoughts would take that direction; but the sense of surprise should dissolve as soon as they perceive the way in which the new idea fits into your overall plan. If the strategy has been well chosen and carried out, the meaning of the essay—its thesis—should have become completely apparent, and should even seem inevitable, by the end of the essay.

Review the list of common strategies that follows. Even if you are unfamiliar with their labels, you will recognize these strategies. You have probably used them all—singly or in combination, consciously or unconsciously—at some point in your writing and conversation. The mind thinks strategically whenever it has a purpose.

description	the depiction in detail of a person, place, object, or sensation
narration	the recounting of an event or sequence of events
exemplification	the support of a thesis with specific illustration
analysis	the division of a subject into its components to show the relations between them
process	the explanation, in order, of each step in a series of actions leading up to a result
classification	the systematic organization of subjects into categories or groups
definition	the exploration of the essential meaning of a concept or object
cause and effect	the explanation of how an event or situation has led to another event or situation
problem and solution	the description of an undesirable situation and a proposal for correcting it
argumentation	the presentation of a case designed to persuade a reader, through reason, to a point of view
comparison	the exploration of the resemblances and differences between two or more subjects
evaluation	the determination of the quality of an object, work, or situation according to particular standards

You determine your strategy by examining your materials and your thesis. You must discover for yourself the kind of essay that you want to write. In most cases, when you review your notes and thesis, you will find that they lend themselves to one or two of the common strategies and that the others would not work for *this* treatment of the topic.

The Same Topic May Lend Itself to More than One Strategy

If your notes contained a large number of reasons, you might consider *cause and effect, analysis,* or *argument*; you would have to consult your thesis before deciding on your strategy. You would choose *analysis* if you intended to stress the relationship between the reasons and to "take apart" the topic, you would choose *cause and effect* if you intended to stress the connection between reasons and consequences, and you would choose *argumentation* if you intended to support these reasons with enough evidence to prove your thesis.

You might also use more than one strategy, especially in a long essay. Thus, if the purpose of your essay were to present and solve a specific problem, you might first analyze the *cause* of the trouble and *evaluate* its deficiencies before you could start to recommend a convincing *solution*. In general, however, an essay will have a single major strategy controlling its entire length, and subordinate strategies, if any, will only be applied to short segments of the whole.

Sometimes you can anticipate your choice of possible strategies even before you have begun to generate notes about your topic. At the beginning of this chapter, there was a list of sixteen different topics for an essay on advertising. (See p. 5.) If you had chosen the first topic and recorded a mass of facts about the development of the advertising industry, which strategies could you use to plan your essay?

The most obvious choice would be *narrative*: a straightforward account of the events that took place between the appearance of the first advertisements and the current state of "Madison Avenue." You would describe what happened, and where, and when. On the other hand, if you were more interested in the way the early advertising agencies developed successful techniques for selling merchandise, then your essay would probably become an examination of that *process*. (Notice that this process essay would not resemble the process essay you might write on the topic, "how an ad gets produced," for the latter would discuss the production of a single ad.) Finally, exactly the same material might be used, in a somewhat different sequence and with a different emphasis, if you wanted to emphasize the reasons for advertising's success and you chose a *cause and effect* strategy.

Here are three possible theses that would have guided you to these three quite different strategies:

A. While advertising is as old as history, the advertising industry came of age in the twentieth century and has flourished since. (narration)

B. Successful advertising depends on a campaign that appeals to the customer's tastes. (process)

C. A principal reason for this century's boom in advertising has been America's transformation into a nation of consumers. (cause and effect)

EXERCISE 6

Look at the topics on the list below. Possible strategies for the first four have been filled in. Examine these suggestions and then decide what strategies you might use for developing the remaining topics.

Topic	*Strategy*
1. history of advertising	narrative, process, cause and effect
2. how advertising works	process, analysis
3. how advertising benefits the consumer	cause and effect, process
4. how an ad gets produced	narrative, process
5. jobs in advertising	
6. notable advertising campaigns	
7. advertising art	
8. effects of advertising on technology: products and packaging	
9. original purpose of advertising	
10. imagine a world without advertising	
11. advertising and TV	
12. false advertising	
13. regulation of advertising	
14. advertising as it reflects the norms of society	
15. advertising and materialism	
16. advertising and women	

ASSIGNMENT 3

Turn back to the topic that you decided to write about in Assignment 2.

1. Write a set of notes. (Two hand-written pages should give you a good start).
2. Examine your notes carefully; try labeling some of the entries.
3. Construct a thesis for your essay and decide on a strategy.

ORGANIZING NOTES INTO GROUPS

The strategy is a theoretical principle of organization. Now, you must put your chosen strategy into practice and apply it to your notes;

you must disentangle the jumble of ideas and redistribute them into a coherent plan for the paragraphing of your essay. By labeling your notes you have already begun to group them. Nonetheless, you should reread all your notes and consider various relations between items.

> 1. Check through the list of notes to identify and set aside any entries that are clearly irrelevant to your thesis. Group together notes that remain according to the labels you have given them.

The set of ideas that you have will be in random sequence and, in their raw form, all the points within each set will appear to have equal weight. If your notes contain nine ideas, to assume that each is equally important, that each must be presented separately and at equal length, and that your essay will therefore consist of nine paragraphs is absurd. It is equally unrealistic to bundle all nine points in a single paragraph. You might just as well conclude that all the rooms in a house should be the same size, or that a separate room should be designated for each activity, with cooking, washing dishes, and storing food each allotted a separate, enclosed space. Instead, you should analyze your notes once again, looking for similar and common themes, before you begin to consider the further organization of your essay. To make a logical allocation of paragraph space to each group of your ideas, you must first consult your strategy, just as you would consult the blueprints of your house.

> 2. Keeping your strategy in mind, decide how many different points—reasons or causes or effects or stages—you are actually intending to include in your essay. Examine the relationships between your ideas and divide your notes into a few distinct groupings or categories.

Your object for a 500-word essay would be to come up with three or four major groups, each of which would incorporate a few of the ideas on your original list.

To understand this procedure, consider the set of notes dealing with private schools, which was used (on pp. 22–23) as a model for thesis construction. The notes are here classified by label.

Topic: public schools and private schools

school's freedom of choice 1. no interference from school boards; therefore innovative programs possible

incentive 2. parents demand value for money

parents'
freedom of
choice
3. able to choose the best school for one's child; no worry about zoning

school's
freedom of
choice
4. faraway bureaucrats can't determine class sizes

incentive
5. schools need to work hard to get paying students; services improve

school's
freedom of
choice
6. schools not dependent on government--political decisions, policy changes, budget cuts

parents'
freedom of
choice
7. able to choose between progressive and traditional schools and ignore local school board's policy

incentive
8. parents pay; therefore get involved in school

parents'
freedom of
choice?
9. can lower-income families afford tuition? tax credits and scholarships?

Thesis: Unlike public schools, private schools provide a good education because private enterprise encourages freedom of choice and healthy competition.

Strategy: cause and effect

The cause-and-effect strategy is compatible with the thesis and notes. Although at first glance the writer might have considered comparison, the notes do not really explore the advantages and disadvantages of public and private schools. For a comparison essay, the writer would need a roughly equal interest in both sides of the subject. In this case, however, the writer is not so interested in describing the deficiencies of public schools as in discussing the success of private schools. A cause-and-effect strategy suits the writer's aim; in other words, it supports the essay's thesis.

Generalizing Each Group of Notes

Once you have arranged your notes into groups according to their labels, generalize each group with a sentence. In other words, explain each label with a sentence. Generalizing serves a variety of purposes. Most importantly, your generalizations test the coherence of each cluster of notes: if you cannot come up with a sentence that is supported by every note in the group, either your generalizing or your grouping is at fault. Try recasting your generalization so that it covers the entire group. Should recasting fail, cover as many ideas in the cluster as possible with your generalization and move ideas that do not fit to groups in which they do (you may have to drop some ideas altogether). Your generalizations are potential topic sentences for paragraphs in your final essay. In the following example, notice that "can lower-income families afford tuition? tax credits and scholarships?" has been crossed out; it does not adequately support the generalization "Less government intervention allows freedom of choice," nor does it fit comfortably under either of the other generalizations.

Grouped notes	*Generalizations*
able to choose the best school for one's child; no worry about zoning	
able to choose between progressive and traditional schools and ignore local board's policy	Less government intervention allows freedom of choice.
~~can lower-income families afford tuition? tax credits and scholarships?~~	
no interference from school boards; therefore innovative programs possible	
faraway bureaucrats can't determine class sizes	Less government intervention allows for greater experimentation in teaching methods and greater flexibility in classroom conditions.
schools not dependent on government—political decisions, policy changes, budget cuts	

```
parents demand value for
money

schools need to work            The profit motive will
hard to get paying              create healthy interest
students                        and competition.

parents pay; therefore
get involved in school
```

THE OUTLINE

These groupings can be rearranged as an outline for your essay. In the past, you may have had some difficulty dealing with the complexities of outlines with three or four levels and several sets of numbers and letters. Such a format can be useful for those who take a very orderly, even rigid, approach to planning and structure. But not everyone is comfortable with a multi-level outline, and it is not always necessary to use one. Certainly a middle ground lies between the formal outline and no outline at all. If you allow your strategy and notes (rather than the outline format) to control the organizing process, if you concentrate on the distribution of your notes into groups, and if you use your groups and generalizations, the outline should present few problems.

Compare the grouped notes and generalizations for the public and private schools essay with the following outline:

```
  I. Less government intervention allows freedom of
     choice.
     A. Zoning requirements can be disregarded; parents
        can choose the best school for their child's
        needs.
     B. Whatever the policy of the party in power, both
        progressive and traditional schools will be
        available.
 II. Less government intervention allows for greater
     experimentation in teaching methods and greater
     flexibility in classroom conditions.
     A. Private schools are not vulnerable to political
        decisions, policy changes, and budget cuts.
     B. Without interference from school boards,
        innovative programs can be adopted or discarded.
     C. Class sizes will not be determined by faraway
        bureaucrats.
III. The profit motive will create healthy interest and
     competition.
```

A. Parents will be more likely to become involved in their child's education since they've made an investment in the school.

B. Parents will demand value for money; schools will be forced to provide the facilities and services that they advertise.

C. Schools will work harder to gain paying students and thus improve the quality of the education they offer.

There are three important steps in the development of an outline from grouped notes:

1. *Expanding notes into sentences.* The "shorthand" entries in the list of notes have all been expanded into complete sentences. When you have reached this stage of the writing process, and especially when you are working with abstract ideas, using the sentence form helps to define each point and make it more explicit, as well as to clarify the relationship between each group of points.

2. *Planning the number of paragraphs.* This plan seems to suggest that the essay will contain three paragraphs, each one corresponding to a major group of points. However, the number of paragraphs actually depends on the complexity of each subtopic and how far the writer wants to develop it. Thus, if the writer has a good deal to say about each point in the outline, there might be as many as eight major paragraphs in the completed essay, in addition to an introduction and possibly a conclusion.

3. *Finding a principle of order.* The reasons or potential paragraphs are still in the same random order in which they appeared in the notes. When you are working with a group of ideas that are all of the same kind (e.g., all reasons or stages or solutions) and that all fit into the same strategy, it is necessary to have some basis for deciding which comes first. Thus, before beginning to write the essay, the writer needs to examine all the topics in the outline and decide on an ordering principle for the final sequence.

An ordering principle is not the same as a strategy, although both may control the sequence in which you present ideas. The following are common ordering principles:

first to last   last to first
near to far   far to near

left to right	right to left
general to particular	particular to general
universal to individual	individual to universal
negative to positive	positive to negative
least important to most important	most important to least important

Simple ordering principles arrange the contents of an essay (and the contents of a paragraph within the essay) in a spectrum. The spectrum can present a range of *time* (first to last), *space* (near to far, left to right), *extent of influence or applicability* (universal to individual, general to particular), or *value* (negative to positive, least important to most important). Any sequence, of course, is reversible.

EXERCISE 7

1. Choose a topic from the following list *or* invent a topic of your own (which fits the "why people . . ." format). Then write a list of reasons why X is true.

why people smoke	why people gamble
why people go to college	why people play tennis
why people drive cars fast	why people stay in fashion

2. Write a generalization—a thesis statement—that is broad enough to express all or most of your reasons. Avoid vague language. Remember that "a variety of reasons" is not an informative generalization.
3. Examine your list of reasons and determine which ones are similar and should be grouped together. See if you can think of a single reason broad enough to explain two or more of the original reasons on your list. Try using one-word labels which may apply to more than one reason.
4. Decide on a final sequence for your short list of reasons: least important to most important? negative to positive? social to personal?

EXERCISE 8

The following two sets of notes contain both specific examples and generalizations. Rearrange each list to establish two levels, placing the generalizations on the first level and the examples underneath. Arrange both the essay as a whole and each paragraph plan according to a principle of order or a combination of ordering principles. The notes have been narrowed so that no points will need to be discarded.

A. Thesis: *Young ladies in 1880 lived far more restricted lives than their counterparts do in 1980.*
   1. A gentleman caller could only be seen in the presence of a third person.
   2. Unacceptable behavior.
   3. Young ladies must defer to the wishes of their elders, rather than use their own judgment.
   4. A young lady's apparel.
   5. Smoking in public was unheard of for women.
   6. Relationships with young men.
   7. Trousers were never worn.
   8. A girl would expect to consult with her parents before becoming engaged.
   9. Conduct expected of young ladies.
   10. Hats and gloves were always worn out of doors.
   11. A young lady would speak to a young man only if she had been formally introduced.
   12. A young lady would never be allowed to live alone, away from her family or guardian.
   13. Young ladies were expected to conceal their feelings and present a serene and cheerful appearance.

B. Thesis: *A parole board must act in the best interests of the public and should therefore grant parole only if the prisoner seems likely to function successfully in society.*
   1. The prisoner should receive a psychiatric examination at the beginning of the prison term and before release.
   2. There should be parole with supervision for minor offenses.
   3. The board should observe whether the prisoner has cooperated with his guards.
   4. Parole should depend on rehabilitation and guidance.
   5. The board should examine the way in which the prisoner carried out his responsibilities while in jail.
   6. There should be psychiatric supervision during and after the jail term for those who commit major offenses.
   7. In certain cases, parole should always be granted.
   8. The prisoner should be placed in a halfway house, under supervision, for the first part of his parole.
   9. Second-time offenders should receive no parole and should serve the remainder of their first sentence.
   10. Parole should depend upon an examination of the prisoner's behavior.
   11. Parole should be granted to terminally ill prisoners.

12. The parole board should not attach much importance to the prisoner's assurance that he is contrite.
13. The prisoner should be given the opportunity to train for a job.
14. The parole board should observe whether the prisoner demonstrates self-control in presenting himself before the board.
15. Parole should depend on the nature and gravity of the prisoner's offense.

EXERCISE 9

For the set of notes following:

1. Write a thesis and determine the most appropriate strategy.
2. Establish categories into which the items on the list can be grouped.
3. Arrange the notes into outline format. (The notes have been planned so that no points will need to be discarded.)

Topic: *the mystique of doctors*
1. Doctors spend most of their daily lives trying to help people.
2. Patients assume that doctors have all the answers to every illness.
3. Doctors are capable of becoming tired and frustrated and making mistakes.
4. People think of doctors as very intelligent and disciplined.
5. Doctors have to do research and read new materials to be up-to-date in their specialties.
6. The portrayal of doctors on TV dramas reinforces the popular image of god-like creatures.
7. Doctors dedicate many hours to hospital work, especially when emergencies occur.
8. Our society should give doctors credit for devoting their time to their studies and to helping people.
9. Some doctors are not highly disciplined or organized and are only of average intelligence.
10. Society tends to assume that doctors are perfect.
11. There are limits to any one doctor's skill.
12. Doctors help to educate medical students.
13. People are so dependent on doctors that they refuse to consider the possibility that a doctor might be fallible.
14. Doctors have other responsibilities besides their patients.
15. People should value doctors for their time and effort spent in their profession.
16. Doctors consult with nurses and other doctors about their patients' care.

Elements of a Good Outline

The outline must be clear; it must be logical; it must say what you mean; it must map out a sequence of paragraphs. Otherwise, it will only hinder the writing of your essay. Take the trouble, then, to produce an outline that measures up to the following criteria:

1. *logical arrangement*: related ideas should be grouped together.
2. *comprehensiveness*: entries on the main levels should be broad enough to include all the ideas grouped under them.
3. *logical order*: the sequence of paragraphs and items within each paragraph should follow some logical ordering principle.
4. *unity*: the outline should contain no points irrelevant to the thesis.
5. *clarity*: the meaning of each point should be immediately evident.
6. *consistency*: all the main-level entries and all the secondary-level entries should be presented in a format that is parallel; comparable points should *all* be expressed in complete sentences or should *all* be expressed in fragmentary phrases.

Remember that an outline is a record of your intentions which, at best, will guide you through writing your essay. It is a working plan, a means to an end, not an end in itself. While you should attempt as comprehensive an outline as possible, do not expect to construct a perfectly arranged and balanced outline every time you work on an essay. Not everything in your notes will fit into your outline easily and tidily; be prepared to write down some ideas in the margin, waiting for an opportunity to incorporate them into the plan. Expect to make changes in your outline as you work; the reality of your essay is unlikely to correspond exactly to your expectations. Be as flexible as possible in your planning. Making a plan and recording it is more important than writing a perfect outline.

EXERCISE 10

Examine each of the two-level outlines below, checking

1. the distribution and sequence of points;
2. the unity of groups;
3. the clarity, consistency, and comprehensiveness of the entries.

Revise each outline so that it meets the six criteria for a good outline. Retain the same number of paragraphs: three in the first outline; five in the second.

I. Thesis: *It is everyone's fault that the welfare system is a failure.*
    A. negligent and faulty administration
        1. screening poor
        2. follow-up
        3. workers don't do their job and make mistakes; sometimes take bribes
        4. number of people on the welfare rolls is increasing
    B. clients cheat
        1. some clients try to get away with more money than they deserve.
        2. too lazy to get a job
        3. rudeness of workers.
        4. clients give workers a hard time.
    C. society's fault
        1. some people think those on welfare are lazy and look for a free ride.
        2. not encouraged to better themselves.

II. Thesis: *The practical advantages of a college degree are outweighed by the disadvantages.*
    A. advantages of a college education
        1. better jobs
        2. prestige
    B. society and a college education
        1. social status
        2. college increases one's self-esteem
    C. disadvantages of a college education
        1. college skills are seldom utilized in one's working life
        2. frustrations (e.g., lack of promotion) are encountered despite the degree.
    D. deceptions of society and college
        1. neither delivers what it promised
        2. unemployment
        3. anger and disappointment
    E. solution
        1. utilization of natural skills
        2. vocational training
        3. on-the-job training
        4. more credit given for life experience

EXERCISE 11

The six statements listed below are the main categories from an outline for an essay in favor of strict gun control. These sentences are all from the main level of the outline; subsidiary points have been omitted. All the sentences are consistent and clear; but they appear in the outline in random order. Examine all six statements and work out the most sensible sequence of ideas. Then add two subsidiary points for each main entry. Remember that the first sentence on your revised list will represent the first paragraph of the body of the completed essay, and so on.

A. Guns in the home increase the chances of fatal crimes of passion.
B. The increase in the number of crimes of violence makes it necessary to reduce the number of guns in circulation.
C. The laws controlling the possession of guns in the United States should be made uniform and consistent.
D. Possession of a gun by the average person will give little protection and may cause additional and unnecessary harm if a crime does take place.
E. Gun registration would not be an intrusion on an individual's rights: those with good reason to have a gun would be allowed to keep it.
F. Sterner rules for licensing would cause only a slight inconvenience to sportsmen.

Outlining and Paragraph Development

As you construct your outline, you should think in terms of paragraphs. If you can plan each paragraph at the outline stage, your first draft will be easy. In outlining your essay paragraph by paragraph, don't lose sight of the nature of paragraphing. Essays are divided into paragraphs for the convenience of both the reader and the writer. Ideas and information must be conveyed in limited doses, so that the reader is not overloaded. Just as a meal is divided into separate courses, so, too, a piece of writing should be divided into separate sections to regulate the flow of information and to avoid a confusion of ideas. A new paragraph serves as a signal to readers to digest the material they have absorbed and to prepare themselves for a new and different point. Paragraphs generally consist of three elements:

1. a topic sentence—a generalization that tells the reader what the paragraph is about;
2. one or more secondary generalizations explaining and clarifying the topic sentence;
3. supporting evidence, such as details, facts, and examples.

Experienced writers do not always include all three elements in every paragraph, nor do they always follow the sequence of this list, with the topic sentence first. However, until you gain writing experience and confidence, you should make sure to pinpoint a main idea in each of your paragraphs and to provide sufficient explanation and evidence to make that idea easily understandable. In most cases, this sentence will begin the paragraph. As you write your essay from your outline, your topic sentences will evolve from your primary levels.

Like an essay's thesis, a paragraph's topic sentence leads readers in the direction in which you wish to take them. It is not enough to summarize by stringing together a condensed list of the paragraph's ideas, like an inventory of contents. The topic sentence should itself contain an important idea that incorporates or relates directly to every other idea in the paragraph and has merit and interest of its own. In other words, an effective topic sentence is more than the sum of the evidence: it interprets the significance of the entire paragraph.

Writing a paragraph involves many of the same skills as writing an essay: it is the same process in miniature. In both cases, before you begin writing, make sure that you have followed the steps in this checklist:

> Have you focused on a single topic?
> Have you assembled a collection of ideas or notes?
> Have you established a topic sentence (for each paragraph) and a thesis (for the essay)?
> Have you considered possible strategies?
> Have you distinguished between main ideas and secondary evidence, details, and examples?
> Have you discarded irrelevant points?
> Have you grouped related points?
> Have you arranged the materials in a clear and logical sequence?

Your topic sentence must be consistent with the evidence contained in the body of the paragraph. If you choose to add new ideas to your paragraph after the topic sentence has been written, your outline can show you the best places to add them.

The importance of detail. As you have observed, the topic sentence has to be consistent with the evidence contained in the body of the paragraph. To ensure congruity between your topic sentence and your evidence, you should, whenever possible, assemble and carefully examine all the supporting materials for the paragraph before beginning to write the topic sentence. Should any group of entries in your outline be sparse or sketchy, then take the time to expand your notes. And, as you prepare each set of ideas for each new paragraph, make sure that your notes contain sufficient detail to make the essay convincing.

The topic sentence is supposed to tell the reader what to think about the information in the paragraph. Whether the reader actually "obeys" and accepts the topic sentence's direction depends on the effectiveness of the evidence presented in the remainder of the paragraph. One requirement is that the body of the paragraph contain some concrete points for the reader to focus on. It is very slow and difficult work to read a sequence of paragraphs that consists entirely of generalizations. A paragraph without details and examples will probably remain in the reader's mind as a vague and ephemeral impression—if it is remembered at all.

While reviewing and expanding your notes, you should also make sure that your phrasing is as concrete and clear as possible. Just as you must cite specific examples so that your reader can understand exactly what your generalizations mean, so you must express your examples in language that is exact and concise. But keep in mind that the detail, although essential, must be subordinate to the main idea of the paragraph: you do not want your descriptive examples to take over the paragraph completely.

Levels of generality. Although paragraphs are composed of a combination of generalizations (topic sentences and explanatory sentences) and supporting evidence (details, facts, and examples), do not assume that one category of ideas can, out of context, be labeled "generalizations" and a second, quite distinct category labeled "facts and examples." Consider the following statement:

> Many Indian tribes were driven from their lands and forced into reservations.

If you are writing a paragraph about the unjust way in which the Indians were deprived of their land, the statement might serve as a generalization to be supported by references to specific tribes, including facts and details about the circumstances in which those tribes were moved to new territory. If, however, you are writing a paragraph about the injustices of colonialism, the sentence about the Indians would serve as a specific example, side by side with examples referring to Africa or India or the Caribbean. If you went on to support each of your examples with still more specific evidence, you might cite some facts about the Apache or the Crow tribes. In that case, the sentence "Many Indian tribes were driven from their lands and forced into reservations" would be somewhere in the middle level of generality: it would not be the broadest generalization in your paragraph, nor would it be the most specific example. What this illustration demonstrates is that one and the same statement can serve as a topic sentence in one paragraph and as evidence for a different topic sentence in another paragraph. The context in which you are placing the sentence determines whether it generalizes or supports the paragraph.

In order to assemble your materials in a coherent paragraph, you must be able to decide which entries in your notes, for the purposes of a particular essay, will serve as generalizations or topic sentences and which ones will be incorporated into your paragraphs as supporting material. To make those decisions, you must be sensitive to the many gradations that make up a continuum between the extremes of general and specific. The following five statements will give you an idea of what is meant by continuum; they are arranged in sequence from the most general to the most specific.

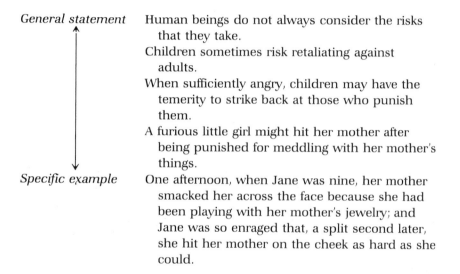

General statement Human beings do not always consider the risks that they take.

Children sometimes risk retaliating against adults.

When sufficiently angry, children may have the temerity to strike back at those who punish them.

A furious little girl might hit her mother after being punished for meddling with her mother's things.

Specific example One afternoon, when Jane was nine, her mother smacked her across the face because she had been playing with her mother's jewelry; and Jane was so enraged that, a split second later, she hit her mother on the cheek as hard as she could.

Each successive sentence is a more detailed version of the previous one. Notice that, at any level between the first and last, the sequence could go off in a different direction. Thus, the fourth level might read, "A boy could protest what he imagines was an unjust punishment by destroying his playthings as a way of striking back." In this case the specific example on the last level would have to change as well, with "Peter" or "Tommy" replacing "Jane."

When you plan a paragraph, your topic sentence can be at any level of generality. What is important is not getting all the levels into your paragraph (which is probably impractical, if not impossible) but making sure that you move between the more general levels of your topic sentences and explanatory sentences and the more specific levels of your evidence and examples. Your paragraph should be neither entirely general nor entirely illustrative; in other words, you should not stay at the same level throughout the entire paragraph. On the other hand, it is not necessary for you to make your way through every possible level of generality in order to make your paragraph convincing. For example, this series of five statements would not make a good paragraph; such a paragraph would simply make the same point on five different levels. You might start with the third level, with angry, vengeful children as the subject of your paragraph, and then cite the example of Jane (and Tommy as well, if you want additional detail) and then go on to discuss the causes of this behavior, or the best ways of dealing with it, or the effects on other siblings. The purpose of writing the paragraph is not to move through the continuum of general to specific but to develop your point as convincingly as possible. The number of middle levels that you need to include depends on the complexity of your topic and the difficulty of making it clear to your reader. If you move too gradually, your reader will be bored; if you move too abruptly, your reader will be confused.

The Completed Outline

Here is the outline for the public and private schools essay, with detailed evidence inserted after each point.

```
 I. Less government intervention allows freedom of choice.
    A. Zoning requirements can be disregarded; parents can
       choose the best school for their child's needs.
          Parents of a slow learner might be dissatisfied with the
          neighborhood public school's reputation for low reading
          scores.
          Some parents may prefer a religious education for their
          children.
    B. Whatever the current educational policy, both progressive
       and traditional schools will be available.
          In the late sixties and early seventies, many public
          schools encouraged students to learn at their own rate;
          parents who preferred a more rigorous education turned
          to private schools.
          During the present "back to basics" trend, a child who
          needs special encouragement may get individual attention
          only in a private school.
 II. Less government intervention allows for greater
     experimentation in teaching methods and greater flexibility
     in classroom conditions.
    A. Private schools are not vulnerable to political
       decisions, policy, changes, and budget cuts.
          Laws mandating balanced budgets such as California's
          Proposition 13 make it more and more difficult for
```

public schools to provide high-quality education. Educational policy can be affected by election-year promises; a newly elected official, taking over from the opposition, may make arbitrary changes.

B. Without interference from school boards, innovative programs can be adopted or discarded.

At a private school, an experimental program, like computerized instruction or ungraded classes, can be given enough time for the teachers and parents to judge its effectiveness.

The principal of a private school, who is likely to know each student and each set of parents, will be responsive to their needs and the best judge of a program's success.

C. Class sizes will not be determined by faraway bureaucrats.

It is better to have fifteen or twenty in a class than thirty or thirty-five.

III. The profit motive will create healthy interest and competition.

A. Parents will be more likely to become involved in their child's education since they've made an investment in the school.

The parents of a public school child will probably feel powerless about making and changing educational policy and so will take little interest in the day-to-day details of the child's experience.

Parents of private school children will go to meetings, visit classes, and participate in making policy.

B. Parents will demand value for money; schools will be forced to provide the facilities and services that they advertise.

A parent who pays $1000 or more on tuition will not tolerate any compromises, but will demand the latest in equipement and the best professional expertise.

C. Schools will work harder to gain paying students and thus improve the quality of the education they offer.

A neighborhood private school almost closed its doors last year when the number of students in each grade fell to fewer than ten. To maintain its enrollment and to attract new students, it re-organized its staff, hired a new headmistress, and developed a child-centered curriculum that would appeal to a majority of parents of children below the sixth grade.

ASSIGNMENT 4

Write an outline for the essay whose notes, thesis, and strategy you developed in Assignment 3.

THE ROUGH DRAFT

At this stage of the writing process, there are few guidelines to follow; you are really on your own. Every piece of writing is different from every other, and every rough draft has its own strengths and weaknesses. However, a rough draft need not be overly rough. If you have constructed an honest outline, your paragraphs should take their final form readily.

As you write your rough draft, try to maintain momentum, and put down as much as you can on paper. At this point, do not worry about polishing your writing. Checking grammar, spelling, and punctuation can wait until just before you write your final draft. Try not to get stuck over a single troublesome point. If you are taking too long to develop a difficult paragraph, make a note to spend more time on it later, and go on to the next point on your outline. But do not simply copy the sentences from your outline, one by one, putting them into paragraph form. Your generalizations may need several sentences of explanation; your examples may need a well-rounded presentation, with some background details included. Remember that your reader will probably not be familiar with your point of view and your evidence, and will need both spelled out more explicitly than you may at first think necessary.

Introductions and Conclusions

At least two paragraphs of your final essay should not be mapped out in your outline and drafted with the body of the paper: introductions and conclusions are best left until you have drafted the body of your essay. Because they present an overview of the essay, these paragraphs can only be executed properly after your ideas have been worked out.

You owe your readers an introduction as a courtesy—they should know in advance what you are writing about—and you also hope to encourage them to take an intelligent interest in what you have to say. A satisfactory introduction generally serves one or more of the following overlapping functions:

1. It describes the contents of the essay: the thesis, the scope, and the distinctive approach that makes this treatment of the topic worth reading.

2. It provides a context or background for the essay: a sense of the broader picture into which the ideas fit.
3. It suggests a reason for the reader to read the essay.

The audiences for academic and professional writing have an automatic interest in certain subjects, and, as a rule, when you address such an audience on such a subject, your introduction should be straightforward rather than seductive. You do not, however, have license to bore your readers, putting them to sleep with deadwood: "It is my intention to write an essay that describes several aspects of a problem that has long been a concern of most thoughtful people." Your readers would not only be bored, but uninformed as well, because you would not have succeeded in communicating anything to them. On the other hand, a deliberately provocative introduction can be misleading and alienating if it raises expectations that your essay does not fulfill. Do not begin by citing a startling fact or a resounding quotation if it has little to do with your thesis. Quotations and dictionary definitions provide effective openings only if they serve as keys to the contents of the essay, offering a striking insight that will prepare your readers for what follows. Generally, try to speak with your own voice and aim for a natural, rather than an impressive or unusual, tone.

Here are two examples of fairly comprehensive introductions, both taken from student essays. Which do you think is more successful? Why?

> I take my hat off to the Japanese auto industry, which in the span of just two decades has become a forty-billion-dollar-a-year auto empire. Japan is presently the world's largest exporter of cars and will soon become the world's largest auto manufacturer. Toyota, called "The Bank of Toyota" in Japan because of its tremendous cash reserves, is the world's third largest auto producer, trailing only General Motors and Ford, and Mazda has had great success with its technically advanced rotary engine and sophisticated suspension systems; Mazda is rapidly establishing an impressive name for itself as "the BMW of Japan."

> If the United States intends to break away from the monopolizing hold of the oil nations, it must try to develop an alternative energy source. Solar energy, the ultimate source of all energy and life on this planet, may provide the answer. This inexhaustible force, unappreciated for centuries, is non-polluting and free to everybody. Such a great, untapped power source could furnish this country with ten thousand times more energy than all other conventional fuels combined.

The second introduction is the more effective primarily because it makes the reader more aware of the importance of its subject and the reason for writing about it. The first introduction contains an adequate preview of the contents of the essay and the points that it will cover. A reader will assume that the essay will provide a detailed account of the reasons for the success of Toyota and Mazda. On the other hand, the essay's strategy might not be cause and effect; the writer may be about to describe the process of building such an industry or demonstrating how Toyota and Mazda solved certain problems. Because one cannot be sure exactly what the essay is going to try to do, one cannot be certain whether it will be worth reading.

The second introduction is far more straightforward and focused on its objective—an argument with a strong, clear thesis—and the reader is left in no doubt about the reasons for learning more about this subject.

If your essay is short (less than three typed pages), you will probably not need to worry about writing a separate conclusion. Your final paragraph or even final sentence can bring the essay to a satisfactory end as long as you sound a note of finality. Be careful to make your last point a major one, to express the last few sentences as generalizations, and to make the wording strong.

In a longer essay, a formal conclusion is usually included because your readers should not be expected to remember and sum up all the ideas that you have raised. The conclusion serves as a summary of the essay's contents and a restatement of its thesis (which often turns into a reassessment of the problem or issue in the light of the evidence that you have raised). You do not have to add anything new to the conclusion, but it should not sound just like the introduction. To use a cinematic analogy, the introduction represents a distance shot of unknown territory, while the conclusion is more like a review, a full camera sweep, of what has already been explored.

Here are the two conclusions that belong with the preceding introductions:

> Japan's auto success is primarily a result of the pragmatic Japanese nature. The Japanese were fortunate to possess an almost instinctive determination to build a car that uses relatively little energy and to develop an efficient means of production that allows them to charge the lowest prices. But a secondary reason for their success was an external circumstance: the world's alleged energy crisis. Without an oil shortage, America, Japan's biggest market, would still be gas-guzzling today, and America's cars would still be made in Detroit.

```
          If the United States wants to become an energy self-
     sufficient nation. with reduced unemployment, it must
     continue developing this infant energy strongly. Solar
     energy, a non-polluting, free source of power, can bring
     about a tremendous industrial expansion in the next
     decade. We may soon experience a renaissance of the sun.
```

Once again, the writer on solar energy provides a better-defined framework for his essay. While both conclusions contain a review and re-statement of the thesis, the "Japanese auto" writer offers too much new information if the body of his essay has covered the ground sketched in his introduction; he is trying too hard and too late to interest his reader, and his conclusion does not seem as straightforward or as final as the second conclusion. The "Japanese auto" writer does not make the reader certain that the essay has ended; his last sentence might easily be a transitional sentence preparing for a further discussion of Detroit's mistakes.

THE FINAL DRAFT

If you have the time, try to put your completed draft aside for at least several hours before you polish it into a final draft. When you return to your rough draft, which will have had time to "cool off," you will notice how well each paragraph leads into the next and also how smoothly the sentences within each paragraph flow. If there seem to be gaps between paragraphs and sentences, you can bridge them with transitions. Also look for the awkward phrase or word, and think about whether there is a clearer way to express that particular idea. Finally, check your grammar, punctuation, and spelling.

The actual mechanics of the final draft depend on your assignment. Instructors generally ask that the draft be typed on 8½- by 11-inch paper, double-spaced, with an inch-wide margin on each side. When you have finished, proofread: even the best typists make errors.

ASSIGNMENT 5

Using the outline that you completed in Assignment 4, write a short essay (approximately five pages or 1,500 words) by following steps seven through ten of the following guidelines. Be prepared to submit your notes, your thesis, your outline, and your rough draft along with your final draft. Your notes, outline, and rough draft should not be rewritten, but should be handed in in their original form, however messy.

A SUMMARY OF PART I: THE TEN STAGES OF WRITING A SHORT ESSAY

Step one: Choose and narrow down a topic.

Step two: Write a list of notes.

Step three: Write a thesis that gives a fair representation of the list of notes.

Step four: Choose a strategy or combination of strategies that will best carry out your thesis.

Step five: Group your notes by rearranging the points on the list. Combine repetitious points; categorize similar and related points; discard points that do not fit within the limits of the thesis; put examples and reasons next to the ideas that they illustrate.

Step six: Construct an outline, one potential paragraph at a time, starting in each case with a topic sentence that summarizes and introduces the material that you intend to present in that paragraph. Then examine the notes designated for each paragraph, making sure that there is enough concrete evidence to fully support the topic sentence.

Step seven: Write a rough draft of the body of your essay. Before writing each paragraph, check the sentence sequence for possible variations in the order of points.

Step eight: Write a brief introduction and/or conclusion; consider possible titles for your essay.

Step nine: Revise your draft, examining the entire essay for missing transitions: make sure that the sentences flow smoothly and that, wherever necessary, there is a transition from paragraph to paragraph. Also correct faulty grammar, punctuation, and spelling.

Step ten: Using 8½- by 11-inch paper and leaving adequate margins and spacing, type or neatly write the final draft. Proofread once again to catch careless errors in copying.

PART II
MAKING YOUR SOURCES YOUR OWN

So far, the essays that you have been asked to write have been taken largely from a single source—yourself. But self-sufficiency is rare in academic writing. A major purpose of a college education is for students to explore and to understand and, occasionally, to contribute to the sum of knowledge of a given discipline. Academic writers continually study the ideas of others. However good and original their own ideas may be, they are obliged to seek out the work of authorities in their field, to estimate its value and its relevance to their own work, and then to place the ideas and the words of others side by side with their own. The overall term that describes this procedure is *research*.

Except in creative writing courses, you will rarely be asked to write without a preliminary stage of careful reading and analysis. In order to make use of another person's ideas in developing your own work, you must be able to appreciate and accept (and even temporarily share) that person's point of view. Naturally, you must be willing to read extensively and be able to understand what you read. In Chapter 2, you will learn to distinguish the main ideas of an essay and to grasp the strategy and the whole plan of its development—in short, to understand the purpose, direction, and substance of the author's work. Since one useful measurement of comprehension is the ability to sum up a group of related ideas briefly, yet completely, Chapter 2 ends with some practice in mastering a source through *summary*.

In order to make use of what you have learned from your

reading and to write about your sources in essays, you must become familiar with the two basic methods of presenting sources to others—quotation and paraphrase. Your objective is fair representation. You must make it clear to your reader whether a specific idea, sentence, or sequence of sentences is the product of your work or that of another. By clearly identifying your source, you avoid the dishonest "borrowings" associated with plagiarism, which can only occur when the reader cannot determine who is responsible for what and thus gives you credit for more work than you have actually done.

Distinguishing carefully between your sources and yourself serves to protect three major interests:

it is in your own interest to receive credit for organizing and presenting an essay and for the original ideas within it;

it is in your source's interest to receive credit for certain clearly identified contributions to your essay—both ideas and words;

it is in your reader's interest to be able to to read your essay easily and painlessly and to distinguish between your work and that of your sources without any confusion.

In the interests of both your reader and yourself, your sources must be smoothly integrated into the fabric of your writing. Chapter 3 discusses quotation and paraphrase. *Quotation* makes clear that someone else is responsible for the precise phrasing, as well as the ideas contained in the quoted sentences. Through *paraphrase*, you express the ideas of others in your own words and thus demonstrate your mastery of the source and your ability to integrate these ideas into your own work. But whether you paraphrase or you quote, you must always acknowledge your source by including a clear citation of the writer's name. Although these methods of presentation are somewhat technical, calling for a high standard of accuracy, they are conventional throughout the academic world. You will use them again and again, and with practice they will become automatic.

These chapters do not assign essays for you to write. Rather, they show how to read a source, identify key facts and points, and extract them from the source in various forms. Later you will see how those facts and points can serve as material for your own writing.

2. Understanding What You Read

Before class began, I happened to walk around the room and I glanced at some of the books lying open on the desks. Not one book had a mark in it! Not one underlining! Every page was absolutely clean! These twenty-five students had all read it. They all knew that there'd be an exam at the end of the week; and yet not one of them had had the sense to make a marginal note!

Teacher of an English honors class

Why should this teacher have been so horrified? The students had fulfilled their part of the college contract by reading the text and coming to class. Why write anything down, they might argue, when the ideas are already printed on the page; all you have to do is to read the assignment and, later on, review the material by skimming through it again. Sometimes it pays to underline an important point or two; but that's only necessary for very long chapters, so that you don't have to read every word all over again. Taking notes wastes a lot of time, and, anyway, there's never much space in the margins.

ACTIVE READING

The last point is valid: narrow margins discourage frequent and legible notes. But the other comments all come from lazy readers who think that they are doing their work by letting their eyes rove over every page, line after line, chapter after chapter, until the entire assignment has been "read"—in other words, *looking*, not reading. Effective reading—reading that is active, not passive—requires concentration and the deliberate application of your mind to the material that is being absorbed. Reading is hard work. To respond to what you are learning and to participate in a mental dialogue between yourself and the author of your source is challenging. But only this kind of participation can prevent your eyes from glazing over and your thoughts from wandering off to next weekend or next summer. To become fully engaged in reading requires more than staring at the words.

As with any job, beginning and continuing the task seem much less of a strain if you have a product to show for your labors. In active reading, this product is notes: the result of contact (even friction) between your mind and the author's. As you read and reread you should be acquisitive and on the lookout for ideas that make you react. (This responsiveness resembles the topic-narrowing and note-taking stages of the basic writing process.) You should pause frequently—not to take a break but to respond to what you have read. If you have absorbed the material, you will need to take stock of what you have acquired and get used to knowing what you now know. If the reading has been difficult, these pauses provide time for you to assess the problems and figure out the questions that you should ask yourself in order to achieve full comprehension. And, as you read, your pencil should always be in your hand (assuming that you *own* the text), and a visible product should accumulate in the form of lines, checks, and comments in and around what you are reading.

Underlining

Underlining can be a sophisticated analytical skill. Its primary purpose is selection and emphasis. You are distinguishing between what is important (and presumably worth rereading) and what you can skip past on later readings. Such discrimination is never easy. In fact, it cannot really be fully achieved on a first reading, since at that point you can have little idea of what is crucial to the work's overall development.

On the other hand, underlining can also be the most primitive form of participation in reading. It can even be accomplished while the reader is half-asleep, for ideas do not have to register in the brain in order to make the pencil move across the page. Too often, underlining merely symbolizes so many minutes spent on the task: the pencil running over the page documents the fact that the eyes have run over the same lines. Many pages are underlined or colored with "hi-liter" so extensively that there is hardly anything left over: *everything* has been selected for review and retention—again, a product of passive reading.

Remember that the usefulness of underlining is selection. Some points are worth reviewing and some are not. Try underlining, and also circling and bracketing words and phrases that seem to you worth rereading and remembering, such as important generalizations and topic sentences, examples that have helped you understand a difficult point, or transitional phrases, where the argument changes. Or, in contrast, try "underlining" with an unobtrusive series of checks in the margin. Either way, deciding what to mark is the important part of the process.

Annotation

Annotation refers to the comments written in the margins surrounding a text, specifically those notes in which the reader interprets or evaluates the author's meaning, defines a word or phrase, or clarifies a point. You are annotating when you insert short explanatory "translations," summaries, or definitions in the margin; you are also annotating when you introduce something of your own: a question or counter-argument, perhaps, or a point for comparison. Annotation is different from taking notes on a separate page (a procedure which will be discussed at length in Chapter 8). Not every reading deserves to be annotated. Since the process demands a good deal of time and concentration, reserve your marginal notes for material that is especially difficult or stimulating.

Marginal notes work best if they function as an aid to memory, reminding you of ideas that you have already assimilated. Sometimes, for example, your notes will do no more than condense sentences and provide an abbreviated version of the major ideas of the text. This technique can be especially useful for review. At the other extreme, notes in the margin can remind you of where you disagreed with the author, looked at the ideas in a new way, or thought of fresh evidence. Finally, no matter what kind of marginal notes you write, try always to use your own words instead of pulling out or abbreviating a phrase from the body of the text itself. You will remember the point more easily if you have made the effort to express it yourself.

Here is an example of a passage that has been annotated. Certain difficult words have been glossed; a few ideas have been summarized; some problems and questions have been raised. Notice that annotation does not require the reader to cover the margins with comments.

THE MOTOR INDUSTRY

= untapped -- an instinct for travel?

Once the cheap car was available, the enormous latent demand hitherto unrealized for individual, family, and goods transport on the roads gave rise to a whole new industry. This should serve as an example of the lack of knowledge of the capitalist entrepreneur of where profits could be found. There is no way of assessing the real need for a new product unless a sufficient number of prototypes is available. But to supply these requires investment in plant, and the difficulty under capitalism has always been to finance such early stages. The result is that the great delay between first invention and first effective use is largely due to these purely financial considerations. *widespread? efficient? profitable?*

still true?. now marketing can make anything profitable (pet rock)

Fear of risk outweighs merit of idea and potential profit

= risk taker

= original model

The essential problem under capitalism of financing early stages of inventions depends on the expected return on investment. Even with *?*

as slow a return on capital as three percent, it will hardly pay to put up money for anything that has a reasonable chance of bringing in money only after thirty years. Even then the return would have to be at least ten times the original investment to make it worthwhile. If the development is not a certainty the prospect of finding backers in the early stages is even less. Only quick-return prospects are really worthwhile, and except in fields like antibiotics rarely involve any radically new principle. With money doled out slowly the technical difficulties tend to hold up the new developments, and hence to make them still less profitable. For the ultimate profit has to be made quickly even for patented inventions, for afterwards it goes to the cautious investors, who will put their money only on proved successes. As a result, even in the twentieth century, the average time between the essential idea and the commercial pay-off remains about a generation. Whittle had the idea of the jet engine in the early thirties. It was developed slowly for lack of funds and, despite the military need, was hardly ready by the end of the war. The situation would be different if a very large investor, which in these days could be only the State, intervened. By putting more money in at the beginning, even though most of it would be lost on failures, the development time on the remainder would be cut so short that it would pay for everything even at high rates of interest. As socialist governments get into their stride they will win the race for industrial advances unless capitalist governments change their habits or even their natures to catch up with them.

Once the profitability of motor manufacture was proved capital flowed in readily enough. A new industry grew up which was in a few years to outstrip the older engineering industries, and in large measure to absorb them. The automobile industry was, from the moment of its popular success, highly concentrated, for only the very largest concerns could meet the market demand. Alongside the new chemical and electrical combines the automobile industry took its place at the very center of monopoly capitalism. It is interesting, but not very surprising, to note that the first large-scale development of the motor-car came practically at the end of the development of the internal-combustion engine, for, with minor modifications in performance, of an essentially technical nature, it still remains what it was in 1880. What is radically new is not the car itself, however its appearance may have changed, but the mass-production methods of manufacturing it, to which we return later. The further technical development of the internal-combustion engine into the internal-combustion turbine was to come from another quarter, that of aviation.

J. D. Bernal, from *Science in History*, III

EXERCISE 12

Read the following passage carefully. Then reread it, underlining and circling key ideas and inserting annotations in the margins.

The long-range liabilities of the mass adoption of the automobile were not foreseen at the time [of its first production]. No one envisioned that the mass ownership of motorcars would ultimately entail a total per capita expenditure for cars, fuel, repairs, road building and maintenance, insurance, and loss of life and income through accidents considerably in excess of the cost of any conceivable mass-transit trolley and railroad system. Nor was it evident that the best case for the relative efficiency and economy of the motor vehicle from the perspective of either the transportation system as a whole or the individual could be made for the limited use of motor-driven trucks and buses along with rail trans-portation, not the widespread adoption of private passenger cars. That automobile exhaust would become a more dangerous and expensive pollutant than horse excreta was not foreseen. It was also overlooked that the average family did not use a horse and buggy enough, or spend enough on trolley and railroad fares, to realize a saving from switching to the automobile, the relative economy of which became apparent only when a substantial amount of driving was done.

Even had the experts recognized some of the long-range liabilities of the mass use of private passenger cars, the automobile was developed as a consumer-goods item and was diffused in response to the demands of a capitalist market economy. Americans have historically had un-bounded faith in technological progress. They have accepted as an es-sential aspect of American democracy that the marketplace and the profit motive should determine the fate of technological inventions de-fined as consumer-goods items. And they have assumed that any adverse unanticipated consequences would be corrected in time either by the market or by other technological innovations. In the early 1900s both the experts and the public concluded that the automobile promised to raise significantly the quality of life and to restructure American society through technology along lines dictated by traditional cultural values. These considerations were undoubtedly as important as the utilitarian ones in the rapid development of our automobile culture.

Individualism—defined in terms of privatism, freedom of choice, and the opportunity to extend one's control over his physical and social environment—was one of the important American core values that au-tomobility promised to preserve and enhance in a changing urban-in-dustrial society. Mobility was another. The automobile tremendously increased the individual's geographic mobility, which was closely as-sociated with social mobility in the United States. It was certain to be prized by Americans. In our traditionally mobile society the motorcar was an ideal status symbol.

James Flink, from *The Car Culture*

READING COMPREHENSION

In order to read actively and to comprehend what you read, you must ask yourself questions about your source and try to answer them.

On occasion you may wish to write your answers down, but usually answering your questions in your head is sufficient. The following questions are typical:

> What does a particular word mean?
> How should I understand a phrase?
> What is the topic sentence of the paragraph?
> What is the relationship between two points?
> What is a transitional word telling me?
> This concept is difficult: how would I express it in my own words?
> Is this point really a digression from the main idea, or does it fit in with what I've already read?
> Can the whole page be summarized briefly?
> Is there a thesis for this essay? Is it trying to make a particular point?

As this partial list suggests, you can best comprehend what you read by sweeping your mind back and forth between a specific sentence on the page and the larger context of the whole paragraph, essay, or book. You have not thoroughly mastered the meaning of the idea that you are reading about if you have not observed how it fits into the work as a whole.

Thorough comprehension takes time and careful reading. No matter how rapidly you ask and answer your questions, reaction and perception take time. In fact, it is usually on the *second* reading, when you have some sense of the overall meaning and structure of the work, that questions begin to pop into your head and your reading rate slows down.

Read "A Question of Degree" once, and then go over it more slowly a second time. During your second reading, look at the list of comprehension questions that follows the essay and attempt to answer them in your head. Some of these questions may seem very subtle to you, and you may wonder whether you would have thought of all of them. But they are model questions, intended to demonstrate what *could* be asked in order to gain an especially thorough understanding of the essay. Think of your own answer to each question.

A QUESTION OF DEGREE

Perhaps we should rethink an idea fast becoming an undisputed premise of American life: that a college degree is a necessary (and perhaps even a sufficient) precondition for success. I do not wish to quarrel with the assumptions made about the benefits of orthodox education. I want only to expose its false god: the four-year, all-purpose, degree-granting college, aimed at the so-called college-age population and by now almost universally accepted as *the* stepping-stone to "meaningful" and "better" jobs.

What is wrong with the current college/work cycle can be seen in the 2 following anomalies: we are selling college to the youth of America as a take-off pad for the material good life. College is literally advertised and packaged as a means for getting more money through "better" jobs at the same time that Harvard graduates are taking jobs as taxi drivers. This situation is a perversion of the true spirit of a university, a perversion of a humane social ethic and, at bottom, a patent fraud. To take the last point first, the economy simply is not geared to guaranteeing these presumptive "better" jobs; the colleges are not geared to training for such jobs; and the ethical propriety of the entire enterprise is very questionable. We are by definition (rather than by analysis) establishing two kinds of work: work labeled "better" because it has a degree requirement tagged to it and nondegree work, which, through this logic, becomes automatically "low level."

This process is also destroying our universities. The "practical curriculum" must become paramount; the students must become prisoners; the colleges must become servants of big business and big government. Under these conditions the university can no longer be an independent source of scientific and philosophic truth-seeking and moral criticism. 3

Finally, and most important, we are destroying the spirit of youth by making college compulsory at adolescence, when it may be least congruent with emotional and physical needs; and we are denying college as an optional and continuing experience later in life, when it might be most congruent with intellectual and recreational needs. 4

Let me propose an important step to reverse these trends and thus help restore freedom and dignity to both our colleges and our workplaces. We should outlaw employment discrimination based on college degrees. This would simply be another facet of our "equal-opportunity" policy and would add college degrees to sex, age, race, religion and ethnic group as inherently unfair bases for employment selection. 5

People would, wherever possible, demonstrate their capacities on the job. Where that proved impractical, outside tests could still serve. The medical boards, bar exams, mechanical, mathematical and verbal aptitude tests might still be used by various enterprises. The burden of proof of their legitimacy, however, would remain with the *using* agencies. So too would the costs. Where the colleges were best equipped to impart a necessary skill they would do so, but only where it would be natural to the main thrust of a university endeavor. 6

The need for this rethinking and for this type of legislation may best be illustrated by a case study. Joe V. is a typical liberal-arts graduate, fired by imaginative art and literature. He took a job with a large New York City bank, where he had the opportunity to enter the "assistant manager training program." The trainees rotated among different bank departments to gain technical know-how and experience and also received classroom instruction, including some sessions on "how to write a business letter." The program was virtually restricted to college graduates. At the end of the line, the trainees became assistant bank man- 7

agers: a position consisting largely of giving simple advice to bank customers and a modest amount of supervision of employees. Joe searched
for some connection between the job and the training program, on the
one hand, and his college-whetted appetites and skills on the other. He
found none.

In giving Joe preference for the training program, the bank had by-   8
passed a few enthusiastic aspirants already dedicated to a banking career and daily demonstrating their competence in closely related jobs.
After questioning his superiors about the system, Joe could only conclude that the "top brass" had some very diffuse and not-too-well-re-
searched or even well-thought-out conceptions about college men. The
executives admitted that a college degree did not of itself ensure the
motivation or the verbal or social skills needed. Nor were they clear about
what skills were most desirable for their increasingly diverse branches.
Yet they clung to the college prerequisite.

Business allows the colleges to act as recruiting, screening and train-   9
ing agencies for them because it saves money and time. Why colleges
allow themselves to act as servicing agents may not be as apparent. One
reason may be that colleges are increasingly becoming conventional bu-
reaucracies. It is inevitable, therefore, that they should respond to the
first and unchallenged law of bureaucracy: Expand! The more that colleges can persuade outside institutions to restrict employment in favor
of their clientele, the stronger is the college's hold and attraction. This
rationale becomes even clearer when we understand that the budgets
of public universities hang on the number of students "serviced." Seen
from this perspective, then, it is perhaps easier to understand why such
matters as "university independence," or "the propriety" of using the
public bankroll to support enterprises that are expected to make private
profits, can be dismissed. Conflict of interest is difficult to discern when
the interests involved are your own. . . .

What is equally questionable is whether a college degree, as such, is   10
proper evidence that those new skills that *are* truly needed will be delivered. A friend who works for the Manpower Training Program feels
that there is a clear divide between actual job needs and college-degree
requirements. One of her chief frustrations is the knowledge that many
persons with the ability to do paraprofessional mental-health work are
lost to jobs they could hold with pleasure and profit because the training
program also requires a two-year associate arts degree.

Obviously, society can and does manipulate job status. I hope that   11
we can manipulate it in favor of the greatest number of people. More
energy should be spent in trying to upgrade the dignity of all socially
useful work and to eliminate the use of human beings for any work that
proves to be truly destructive of the human spirit. Outlawing the use of
degrees as prerequisites for virtually every job that our media portray
as "better" should carry us a long step toward a healthier society. Among
other things, there is far more evidence that work can make college
meaningful than that college can make work meaningful.

My concern about this degree/work cycle might be far less acute, how-   12 ever, if everyone caught up in the system were having a good time. But we seem to be generating a college population that oscillates between apathy and hostility. One of the major reasons for this joylessness in our university life is that the students see themselves as prisoners of economic necessity. They have bought the media messages about better jobs, and so they do their time. But the promised land of "better" jobs is, on the one hand, not materializing; and on the other hand the student is by now socialized to find such "better" jobs distasteful even if they were to materialize.

One of the major improvements that could result from the proposed   13
legislation against degree requirements for employment would be a new stocktaking on the part of all our educational agencies. Compulsory schools, for example, would understand that the basic skills for work and family life in our society would have to be compressed into those years of schooling.

Colleges and universities, on the other hand, might be encouraged to   14
be as unrestricted, as continuous and as open as possible. They would be released from the pressures of ensuring economic survival through a practical curriculum. They might best be modeled after museums. Hours would be extensive, fees minimal, and services available to anyone ready to comply with course-by-course demands. Colleges under these circumstances would have a clearly understood focus, which might well be the traditional one of serving as a gathering place for those persons who want to search for philosophic and scientific "truths."

This proposal should help our universities rid themselves of some   15
strange and gratuitous practices. For example, the university would no longer have to organize itself into hierarchical levels: B.A., M.A., Ph.D. There would simply be courses of greater and lesser complexity in each of the disciplines. In this way graduate education might be more rationally understood and accepted for what it is—*more* education.

The new freedom might also relieve colleges of the growing practice   16
of instituting extensive "work programs," "internships" and "independent study" programs. The very names of these enterprises are tacit admissions that the campus itself is not necessary for many genuinely educational experiences. But, along with "external degree" programs, they seem to pronounce that whatever one has learned in life by whatever diverse and interesting routes cannot be recognized as increasing one's dignity, worth, usefulness or self-enjoyment until it is converted into degree credits.

The legislation I propose would offer a more rational order of prior-   17
ities. It would help recapture the genuine and variegated dignity of the workplace along with the genuine and more specialized dignity of the university. It should help restore to people of all ages and inclinations a sense of their own basic worth and offer them as many roads as possible to reach Rome.

Blanche D. Blank

Questions

Paragraph one

A. What does "false god" mean?

B. In what context can a college degree be a false god?

C. Why does Blank put "meaningful" and "better" in quotation marks?

Paragraph two

D. What is an anomaly?

E. What conclusion can be drawn from the "Harvard graduates" sentence? (Note that the obvious conclusion is not drawn at this point.)

F. What does "perversion" mean? How many perversions does Blank mention? Can you distinguish between them?

F. In the last two sentences, what are the two types of "fraud" that are described? How would you define "fraud"?

Paragraph three

H. What is the "practical curriculum"?

I. What is the danger to the universities? (Use your own words.)

J. What groups have suffered so far as a result of "compulsory" college?

Paragraph four

K. What *new* group, not mentioned before, does Blank introduce in this paragraph?

Paragraph five

L. Can you explain "'equal-opportunity' policy" in your own words?

M. What is Blank's contribution to "our 'equal-opportunity' policy"?

Paragraph six

N. What does "legitimacy" mean in this context?

Paragraphs seven and eight

O. What point(s) does the example of Joe help to prove?

Paragraph nine

P. What are the colleges' reasons for cooperating with business? (Explain in your own words.)

Q. What is the conflict of interest mentioned in the last sentence, and why is it hard to discern?

Paragraph eleven

R. Can you restate the third sentence in your own words?

S. Is Blank recommending that everyone go to work before attending college (last sentence)?

Paragraph twelve

T. Can you explain the meaning of "prisoners of economic necessity"?

Paragraph thirteen

U. What are "compulsary schools" and how would their role change if Blank's proposal were adopted?

Paragraph fourteen

V. What role does Blank envisage for the university in a healthier society? (Try not to use "museum" in your answer.)

Paragraph fifteen

W. What are the "strange and gratuitous" practices of the universities? What purpose do they serve?

Paragraph seventeen

X. What, according to Blank, would be a "rational order of priorities"? Does she see any connection at all between the work experience and the educational experience?

Consider the following answers to these questions. Do you agree or disagree with this reading of the essay?

Paragraph one

A. A false god is an idol that does not deserve to be worshipped.

B. Colleges are worshipped by students who believe that the degree will magically ensure a good career and a better life. Blank suggests that college degrees no longer have magic powers.

C. Blank uses quotation marks around "meaningful" and "better" because she doesn't believe the adjectives are applicable; she is showing disagreement, dissociating herself through the quotation marks.

Paragraph two

D. An anomaly is anything that is inconsistent with ordinary rules and standards.

E. If Harvard graduates are driving taxis, a degree does not ensure a high-level job.

F. Perversion means distortion or corruption of what is naturally good or normally done. If degrees are regarded as vocational qualifications, the university's proper purpose will be perverted, society's conception of proper qualifications for promotion and advancement will be perverted, and, by implication, young people's belief in the reliability of rewards promised by society will be perverted.

G. One kind of fraud is the deception practiced on young college students who won't get the good jobs that they expect. A second type of fraud is practiced on workers without degrees whose efforts and successes are undervalued because of the division into "better" and "worse" jobs.

Paragraph three

H. "Practical curriculum" refers to courses that will train college students for specific jobs; the term is probably being contrasted with "liberal arts."

I. The emphasis on vocational training perverts the university's traditional pursuit of knowledge for its own sake, as it makes financing and curriculum very closely connected with the economic needs of the businesses and professions for which students will be trained.

J. Blank has so far referred to three groups: students in college; workers who have never been to college; and members of universities, both staff and students, interested in a liberal arts curriculum.

Paragraph four

K. Blank introduces the needs of older people who might want to return to college after a working career.

Paragraph five

L. Equal Opportunity Policy for employment means that the only prerequisite for hiring should be the applicant's ability to perform the job.

M. Blank suggests that a college degree does not indicate suitability for employment and therefore should be classed as discriminatory, along with sex, age, etc.

Paragraph six

N. If certain professions choose to test the qualifications of aspirants, professional organizations should prove that examinations are necessary and that the best results will measure the applicant's suitability for the job. These organizations should be responsible for the arrangements and the financing; at present, colleges serve as a "free" testing service.

Paragraphs seven and eight

O. Joe V.'s experience supports Blank's argument that college training is not often needed in order to perform most kinds of work. Joe V.'s expectations were also pitched too high, as Blank has suggested, while the experience of other bank employees whose place was taken by Joe exemplifies the plight of those workers without college degrees whose experience is not sufficiently valued.

Paragraph nine

P. Colleges are competing for students in order to increase their enrollment; they therefore want to be able to assure applicants that many companies prefer to hire their graduates. Having become overorganized, with many levels of authority, the bureaucratic universities regard enrollment as an end in itself.

Q. The interests of an institution funded by the public might be said to be in conflict with the interests of a private, profit-making company; but the conflict is not apparent now that colleges choose to strengthen their connections with business.

Paragraph eleven

R. Instead of discriminating between kinds of workers and kinds of work, we should distinguish between work that benefits everyone and should therefore be considered admirable, and work that is degrading and dehumanizing and should, if possible, not be performed by people.

S. Although Blanche Blank is not insisting that working is preferable to or should have priority over a college education, she implies that most people learn more significant knowledge from the work experience than from the college experience.

Paragraph twelve

T. Young people who believe that a degree will get them better jobs have no choice but to spend a four-year term in college, whether or not they are intellectually and temperamentally suited to the experience.

Paragraph thirteen

U. Compulsory schools are grade and high schools, which students must attend up to a set age. If students were not automatically expected to go on to college, the lower schools would have to offer a more comprehensive and complete education than they do now.

Paragraph fourteen

V. Blanche Blank sees the colleges in a role quite apart from the mainstream of life. Colleges would be storehouses of tradition, to which people could go for cultural refreshment in their spare time, rather than training centers.

Paragraph fifteen

W. The universities divide the process of education into a series of clearly defined levels of attainment. Blanche Blank finds these divisions "gratuitous" or unnecessary perhaps because they are "hierarchical" and distinguish between those of greater or less achievements and status.

Paragraph seventeen

X. Blanche Blank's first priority is the self-respect of the average member of society who presently may be disappointed and frustrated at not being rewarded for his work, whether at the job or at college. Another priority is the restoration of the university to its more purely intellectual role.

EXERCISE 13

Read the following essay twice, and then answer the comprehension questions that follow. You will notice that some of the "questions" are really instructions, very much like examination questions, directing you to explain, define, or in other ways to annotate the reading. Use complete sentences and use your own words as much as you can.

BIRTHRIGHTS

There is no way to have a liberated society until we have liberated   1
our children. And right now our society is organized against them. The
ideal child is cute (entertaining to adults), well-behaved (doesn't bother
adults), and bright (capable of bringing home report cards that parents
can be proud of). Efforts of parents to produce these traits have so inhibited children that neither adults nor children can always see the
remarkable potentialities that lie beyond or outside them. Because we
have become increasingly alert to the many forms of oppression in our
society, we are now seeing, as we have not seen before, the predicament
of children: they are powerless, dominated, ignored, invisible. We are
beginning to see the necessity for children's liberation.

People are not liberated one by one. They must be liberated as a class.   2
Liberating children, giving them equality and guaranteeing their civil
rights, may seem to violate the fairly recent realizations that children
are not simply miniature adults, and that childhood is a special time of
life, with special qualities and problems. In fact, never before in history
have parents and teachers had so much "understanding" of children,
or at least of their physical and social development

[But] increased understanding and concern has not been coupled   3
with increased rights. As a consequence, children's rights have actually
diminished, for we have simply replaced ignorant domination with sophisticated domination. With increased attention to children has come
resentment. Our efforts to shape children, to reform them, to fix them,
to correct them, to discipline them, to educate them, have led to an
obsession with the physical, moral and sexual problems of children; but
they have not led to our liking them more, or realizing their potential.

By holding a limited and demeaned view of children and by segre-   4
gating them almost completely from the adult world, we may be sub-
verting their capacity for genius. It has been pointed out that we no
longer have infant and child prodigies—or at least that they are now
much rarer than before. In the past, when children were an integral part
of the community, they sometimes did show great genius. By the age
of 17 months, for example, Louis XIII played the violin. He played tennis
when he still slept in a cradle. He was an archer, and played cards and
chess, at six. Today we might worry a bit about precocity of that magnitude, but then, people took it for granted. One wonders whether we
have sacrificed genius for homogeneity and conformity. . . .

Though technically the law no longer regards them as chattels, children are still treated as the private property of their parents. The parent has both the right and the responsibility to control the life of the child. 5

It will take quite a revolution in our thinking to give some of this control back to the child. Nevertheless, the acceptance of the child's right to self-determination is fundamental. It is the right to a single standard of morals and behavior for children and adults, including behavior decisions close to home. From the earliest signs of competence, children might have, for example, the right to decide for themselves about eating, sleeping, playing, listening, reading, washing, and dressing; the freedom to choose their associates, to decide what life goals they wish to pursue. 6

Parents may argue that the right to self-determination will bring with it the risk of physical and psychological damage. No doubt some risks are involved. But under present conditions, many children are severely damaged—physically, socially, and emotionally. Compared to the existing system, the risks of harming children by accepting their right to self-determination may be greatly over-rated. Impossible as it seems, it may be that the situations we try hardest to avoid for ourselves and for our children, would be actually the most beneficial to us. One can make a good case for a calamity theory of growth—many of our most eminent people, for instance, have come from the most calamitous early childhood situations. Of course, we don't want calamities to happen to our children, but we can be a bit more relaxed about our protectiveness. 7

In any event, it's time to admit that no one knows how to grow people. 8

Since most concerns center on the problems of living with a self-determining child, our first thoughts focus on the home. While liberation cannot be truly accomplished at home—because the home is not separate from the rest of society—the situation illustrates in microcosm the dimensions of the problem as it might exist in society at large. 9

Take, for example, family mealtimes. No one should be expected to prepare a meal at a special time for children simply because they choose not to eat at the regular hour. However, most children could, with some special arrangement and training, prepare meals for themselves when necessary. Those children whose schedules demand special timetables would receive the same consideration afforded any adult member of the household in similar circumstances—but no more. 10

Loss of authority over a child in areas such as nutrition does not mean that the child cannot be influenced. In the absence of adult tyranny, adult judgment and information have to be the primary influence and are more likely to be accepted. 11

Bedtime is a case in point. Most parents know that children enjoy sleeping as much as adults do. Resistance to it comes largely from adult pressures. Because adults' sleeping habits are governed largely by the pressures to engage in productive activity during the daytime hours, we adhere to nighttime sleeping hours. Children, too, must follow daytime hours to fulfill their compulsory attendance in school. 12

If children came to these conclusions for themselves, by suffering the consequences, they would be capable in the long run of learning, as most adults have, that when we are too tired we pay for it the next day. 13

This would make the ritual of going to bed less of a vehicle through which adults and children express their mutual antagonisms. Believe it or not, bedtime is not a big issue in some homes. Children either go to bed by themselves or they are simply covered up on the spot where they drop off to sleep.

What about other physical dangers, such as children playing where   14
they might injure themselves? The first answer is that of course we cannot risk a child's death. Just as we would pull an adult out of the path of an onrushing car, we would do the same for a child. There is no double standard in an emergency situation.

In fact, children are equally concerned about safety—their own and   15
their parents'. They try, for example, to keep their parents from chain-smoking, drinking too much, getting too fat, driving dangerously, or working too hard. While they are seldom successful at this, the point is to recognize the concern and responsibility as mutual. . . .

Then there are basic changes to be made in our current living facilities.   16
Children are simply not considered important enough by those adults who design the environment. Only in places that are used exclusively by children—classrooms, playgrounds, and the like—do we find facilities built to children's scale.

Consider the daily experiences of small children—taking a shower   17
under an uncontrollable waterfall pouring down from several feet over-head, gripping the edges of a toilet seat that is far too high and too large, standing on tiptoe to reach a cabinet or a sink, trying to see in a mirror so high that it misses them completely. Then they must go out into the world to try to open doors too heavy for them, negotiate stairs too steep, reach food on tables and shelves that are too high, pass through turn-stiles that hit them directly in the face, see a film almost totally obscured by the back of the auditorium seat in front of them, get a drink out of a fountain they can't reach, make a phone call from a pay telephone placed at adult height, bang into sharp corners just the height of their heads, and risk their safety in revolving doors. Having physical reminders that there are children in the world would help to make us more alert and attentive toward them, making their lives safer and more interesting. The real advance for children will come when adults recognize them as an integral part of the community, expecting them to be around, naturally looking out for them and scaling conveniences to their size. . . .

In health, welfare, and education a child's ignorance is a strong po-   18
litical ally of adult society, and adults have learned to rely heavily on it. Because children are excluded from almost every institution in our society, they don't know what to do to gain power over their own lives. They are separated from the adult world, barred from important conversations, kept out of the rooms where decisions are made, excluded from social gatherings, dinner parties, and business meetings, and denied access to information about society and themselves. . . .

Subjecting children to such prohibitions and deceptions ultimately   19
threatens our democratic process; above all else, that process requires an independent and informed citizenry. The most potent weapon against tyranny is knowledge that is easily accessible to all. Whenever

one group decides what is and what is not desirable for another to know, whenever a "we-they" condition exists, society becomes vulnerable to totalitarian controls. The acquisition of information by the child causes adults distress for exactly the same reasons; it empowers children, and makes it less easy to control and dominate them.

Our predisposition to ignore children's concerns, deal expeditiously   20
with their questions, and deny them entry into the world of adults, is precisely the reason they tend to remain ignorant, dependent, and impotent. It's time to give up our adult privileges and made room for the autonomous child.

Individual action is vital, but it can never be sufficient. Only concerted   21
action taken on many fronts can enable children to escape their prisons. Either we do this together—or it won't be done at all.

Richard Farson

Questions

Paragraph one

A. What is the topic sentence of the first paragraph?
B. In a sentence, explain the apparent contradiction between "dominated" and "ignored" (end of first paragraph).

Paragraph two

C. Express the third sentence in your own words. Write a sentence defining "miniature adult," mentioning Farson's name somewhere in your sentence.

Paragraph three

D. How and why have children's rights diminished? What is "sophisticated domination"?

Paragraph four

E. Summarize briefly the point which the Louis XIII example is intended to prove.

Paragraph five

F. What is a chattel?
G. From your reading of the entire essay, what do you think Farson means by "control"?

Paragraph six

H. What are the two reasons for liberating children cited in this paragraph? Distinguish between the two as carefully as you can. (Note: you are not asked to distinguish between "rights.")

I. What is a synonym for "self-determination"?

Paragraph seven

J. Write a sentence defining the "calamity theory of growth."

K. What is the relationship between paragraph seven and paragraph eight? What is the function of the transition "in any event"?

Paragraph eleven

L. Express the second sentence of paragraph eleven in your own words.

Paragraph thirteen

M. State the general reason for children's liberation—not the example—that is expressed in this paragraph.

Paragraphs fourteen and fifteen

N. Summarize Farson's ideas about reciprocity.

Paragraph seventeen

O. How does Farson's description of the child's environment work both for and against his thesis? Express the last sentence of the paragraph in your own words.

Paragraphs eighteen and nineteen

P. In no more than two sentences, explain the "ignorance" argument. Which sentence in those two paragraphs would be most appropriate for quotation?

Paragraph twenty

Q. Define "autonomous child." How does the term fit into the context of Farson's whole essay?

EXERCISE 14

Read the following essay twice, and then answer the comprehension questions that follow. (You will notice that some of the "questions" are really instructions, very much like examination questions, directing you to explain, define, or in other ways to annotate the reading.) Use complete sentences and use your own words as much as you can.

FOOTBALL—THE GAME OF AGGRESSION

There are many ways in which professional football is unique among sports, and as many others in which it is the fullest expression of what is at the heart of all sports. There is no other major sport so dependent upon raw force, nor any so dependent on a complex and delicate strategy; none so wide in the range of specialized functions demanded from its players; none so dependent upon the undifferentiated athletic *sine qua non*, a quickwitted body; none so primitive; none so futuristic; none so American. 1

Football is first of all a form of play, something one engages in instinctively and only for the sake of performing the activity in question. Among forms of play, football is a game, which means that it is built on communal needs, rather than on private evasions, like mountain climbing. Among games it is a sport; it requires athletic ability, unlike croquet. And among sports, it is one whose mode is violence and whose violence is its special glory. 2

In some sports—basketball, baseball, soccer—violence is occasional (and usually illegal); in others, like hockey, it is incidental; in others still, car racing, for example, it is accidental. Definitive violence football shares alone with boxing and bullfighting, among major sports. But in bullfighting a man is pitted not against another man, but against an animal, and boxing is a competition between individuals, not teams, and that makes a great difference. If shame is the proper and usual penalty for failures in sporting competitions between individuals, guilt is the consequence of failing not only oneself and one's fans, but also one's teammates. Failure in football, moreover, seems more related to a failure of courage, seems more unmanning than in any other sport outside of bullfighting. In other sports one loses a knack, is outsmarted, or is merely inferior in ability, but in football, on top of these, a player fails because he "lacks desire," or "can't take it anymore," or "hears footsteps," as his teammates will put it. 3

Many sports, especially those in which there is a goal to be defended, seem enactments of the games animals play under the stimulus of what ethologists, students of animal behavior, call *territory*—"the drive to gain, maintain, and defend the exclusive right to a piece of property," as Robert Ardrey puts it. The most striking symptom of this drive is aggressiveness, but among social animals, such as primates, it leads to "amity for the social partner, hostility for the territorial neighbor." The territorial instinct is closely related to whatever makes animals establish 4 pecking orders: the tangible sign of one's status within the orders is the size and value of the territory one is able to command. Individuals fight over status, groups over *lebensraum*[1] and a bit more. These instincts, some ethologists have claimed, are behind patriotism and private property, and also, I would add, codes of honor, as among ancient Greeks, modern Sicilians, primitive hunters, teen-age gangs, soldiers, aristocrats, and athletes, especially football players.

The territorial basis of certain kinds of sports is closest to the surface 5
in football, whose plays are all attempts to gain and defend property through aggression. Does this not make football *par excellence* the game of instinctual satisfactions, especially among Americans, who are notorious as violent patriots and instinctive defenders of private property? . . . Even the unusual amity, if that is the word, that exists among football players has been remarked upon. . . . And what is it that corresponds in football to the various feathers, furs, fins, gorgeous colors by means of which animals puff themselves into exaggerated gestures of masculine potency? The football player's equipment, of course. His cleats raise him an inch off the ground. Knee and thigh pads thrust the force lines of his legs forward. His pants are tight against his rump and the back of his thighs, portions of the body which the requirements of the game stuff with muscle. . . . Even the tubby guard looks slim by comparison with his shoulders, extended half a foot on each side by padding. Finally, the helmet, which from the esthetic point of view most clearly expresses the genius of the sport. Not only does the helmet make the player inches taller and give his head a size proportionate to the rest of him; it makes him anonymous, inscrutable, more serviceable as a symbol. The football player in uniform strikes the eye in a succession of gestalt[2] shifts; first a hooded phantom out of the paleolithic past of the species; then a premonition of a future of spacemen.

In sum, and I am almost serious about this, football players are to 6
America what tragic actors were to ancient Athens and gladiators to Rome: models of perenially heroic, aggressive, violent humanity, but adapted to the social realities of the times and places that formed them.

George Stade

Questions

Paragraph one

A. Outline the four pairs of contrasts that Stade presents in this paragraph.

B. Express the next-to-the-last line in your own words (from "none so dependent" to "body").

---

[1]Literally, living space. The word is most often associated with the territory thought by the Nazis to be essential to Germany's political and economic security.

[2]I.e., perceptual.

Paragraph two

C. What is the difference between football and mountain climbing? (Write a complete sentence.)

Paragraph three

D. How are "occasional," "incidental," and "accidental" used in the first sentence? Try to differentiate between the three.
E. Differentiate between shame and guilt in this context.

Paragraphs one through three

F. Given the distinctions that Stade makes between football and other activities, try to summarize (in your own words) the unique quality of the game.

Paragraph four

G. Stade points out the "aggressive" as a hallmark of football; yet he also emphasizes "amity." How do the two fit together?

Paragraph five

H. How is Stade using the word "property"? Is this the usual meaning? What is the connection between property, aggression, and patriotism? (Write two or three complete sentences.)
I. Express the next-to-the-last sentence in your own words ("Not only does the helmet . . .").

Paragraph six

J. According to Stade, what is the *social function* of the football player? (Focus on the word "models.")

Entire essay

K. According to the essay, what weaknesses and strengths will the playing of football encourage? (Make two short lists.)
L. In your opinion, does Stade intend his readers (when they've finished his essay) to approve or disapprove of football? Which two sentences (not necessarily together) would you quote as support for your view?
M. Consider your answers to questions f, j, and l, and write a one-sentence thesis statement for the essay.

EXERCISE 15

Carefully read the following excerpt. Then make up a set of comprehension questions which would help a reader to understand the essay's vocabulary, structure, and meaning.

SCIENCE, TECHNOLOGY AND SOCIETY

Technology has so surrounded us with machines, techniques, and their products, that our urban society is largely an artificial world. The effects of this are many: chemical technology works massive damage in the environment; communications technology has modified our perceptions of space and time; national politics is dominated by the thirst for energy, and international politics is held hostage by a fragile nuclear arms balance. The immense growth in the scope and complexity of social institutions, with their dependence on research and development, has thrust issues of science policy into the center of political concern. Moreover, when we reflect on such issues as energy, pollution controls, the deployment of nuclear power plants, economic development, agricultural policy, medical research, and the like, we realize that decisions which affect us all are increasingly removed from the competence of ordinary people. We have reason to fear that such decisions are being made for us by some unchosen few, some priesthood of scientists, policy analysts, or management and systems engineers. In short, gains in material well-being through technology are bought at considerable political cost.

[One view] favors dismantling the entire political edifice and attempting to create small communities of a radically simpler and less technologically dependent life-style within which men and women might more fully and satisfactorily relate both to nature and to one another. . . . Such utopian experiments have some value, but they provide no general solution. They will not help developing nations or disadvantaged minorities; they will not provide political leadership; they will not aid in the search for new sources of energy or for less environmentally damaging means of large scale production.

We need, I think, to take a less apocalyptic but more difficult approach based on two principles which are in tension with one another. First, we need to affirm the fundamental reality and essential worth of the scientific and technical capacities of man—our right and responsibility to intervene in nature in order to try to improve the quality of human life, and we must recognize and accept the organized social institutions of an industrial society which go with these capacities. But, we must insist equally upon the limitations of our foresight into the environmental and social effects of using any technical tool and recognize the concentrations of special interest and power, in government and in industry, which limit our ability to control the effects of technical change even when we can anticipate them. Thus, we must be prepared to take the legal and political steps necessary to restrain abuses of technical knowledge.

There are both political and philosophical implications to the acceptance of these principles. If we seriously affirm both the possible benefits of scientific and technical knowledge and the perils in which we stand through abuse of it, we need to carry on the political process of criticism and debate against seemingly closed bureaucratic and technocratic decisions. Presidential advisory panels, Congressional and other committees, can serve in this way, but only incompletely. Ever since the advent of nuclear weapons, and in more massive fashion recently, scientifically and technically trained people, together with knowledgeable lay-people, have also organized to enter the political arena. That such groups take differing positions in the political spectrum is just the point; this is necessary in order to get before the public the fullest variety of interpretations of the facts on the SST, on nuclear power plants, on food processing, recombinant DNA research, and the like. In this way, some measure of external, knowledgeable, public criticism can be brought to bear on corporate and governmental decisions.

The philosophical point behind such action is the recognition that the scientific role in modern society has decisively shifted from a purely theoretical to a political one. As I see it, we are now able to appreciate the implications of what the propagandists for the new science told us those many centuries ago when they proclaimed, in Descartes' words, that science would make us "masters and possessors of nature." Scientific knowledge is not in fact an absolute end in itself; it is essentially technological, and therefore essentially political, that is, its costs and its benefits are necessarily of public concern. This is not to say that individual scientists are not motivated by a desire to discover the truth for its own sake, for they typically are. This is rather to say that, as an established communal activity growing out of western culture, exact natural science is best understood as part of a larger human project to objectify the natural order so as to be able to predict it, intervene in it, and control it. The application of scientific theory to the exploitation of nature is not an accident; the very forms of scientific explanation are such as to be "apt" for application. This is because the entire methodological style of natural science is one which seeks lawful relations among events. Its laws have the form: Whenever A occurs or varies in such and such a way, then B will occur or vary in such and such a way. This is a formula for action. Practical application only awaits someone's thinking that it might be profitable to try to mobilize A's in order to produce B's.

If we understand this point, we see that scientific disinterestedness is at best provisional and, in the end, impossible. Scientific inquiry serves a genuine human interest in the control of nature and, consequently, ethical and political considerations are appropriate in the planning, carrying out, and application of all research. If this philosophical thesis is taken seriously, scientists and non-scientists alike will be more likely to think realistically in the political arena on matters relating to science policy and technology assessment.

Let me put my conclusion about the confrontation between science and anti-science in the following way: There is a crucial distinction to be made between science and scientism, the view that science alone is sufficient for human understanding; and a correlative one between technology and a faith in the omnipotence of technology. Science and technology are deeply important tools with liberating social benefits as well as serious risks. Scientism and faith in technology, on the other hand, are socially destructive myths. The true targets of the humanistic critique of science are these myths which need to be exploded, both for the health of science and for the realization of our deepest human values.

John Compton, from "Science, Anti-Science and Human Values," in *Key Reporter*

DRAWING INFERENCES

When you are actively reading and annotating a text, you can sometimes begin to project your own thoughts and assumptions into what you are reading. After a while, it becomes difficult to differentiate beteen your own conjectures, inspired by what you have read, and the evidence that is actually to be found in the source. When such confusion occurs, you can easily attribute to your source ideas that are not there at all or—much more likely—ideas that you have *inferred* from your reading.

An inference means a conclusion drawn from sound evidence. It is perfectly correct to draw your own inferences from the sources that you are writing about, as long as you fulfill two conditions:

1. The inferences are clearly identified as yours, not the source's.
2. There must be a reasonable basis within the source for your inference.

When in your essay you cite a specific work as the basis of an inference, your reader should be able to go to the source, locate the evidence there, and find the evidence reasonably convincing. Thus, as you read, you should try to notice how much and what kind of authority the author is citing in support of his ideas. It is useful to distinguish between what an essay or book actually proves, what it states, what it suggests, and what it implies.

EXERCISE 16

Read "Survey Finds Boys Preferred as the First-Born, Girls as Second," and decide which of the following statements are *neither contained in nor inferred from* the contents of this article

SURVEY FINDS BOYS PREFERRED AS THE FIRST-BORN, GIRLS AS SECOND

If mothers could choose the sex of their children, a disproportionate number of boys would undoubtedly be born at first but the sex ratio at birth would ultimately even out, according to new findings of a national survey released yesterday.

The survey, which questioned 5,981 married women about their sex preferences in children, indicated that most would prefer their first-born to be a boy, followed by a girl as the second child.

Thus, in the United States at least, the survey indicates that counter to the fears of some, the ability to select the sex of offspring would not greatly distort the ultimate sex ratio of the population.

The survey findings, a part of the 1970 National Fertility Study, also indicate that at the time they were questioned, at least half of currently married women preferred to leave sex selection to nature rather than use some new technology to predetermine the sex of their children.

The National Fertility Study, first done in 1966, is based on a national random sample of married women under 45 years of age living in the United States.

If left to chance, the national sex ratio at birth is 105 boys to 100 girls, with an approximately equal chance that a family with two children would have the following combinations: boy-girl, girl-boy, boy-boy or girl-girl.

The survey findings, published in the current (May 10) issue of the journal *Science*, indicate that if sex selection were readily available and widely used, there would be a temporary "20 per cent excess of male births." This would occur mainly because most women who have not yet had children would select a boy as their first-born, giving a birth ratio of 189 boys to 100 girls.

Then, as these women select girls as their second child, the sex ratio would ultimately balance out. Among women who have already started their families, the survey showed that in subsequent births they would seek to balance the sexes of their children, which would have little, if any effect on the national sex ratio.

Thus, the authors concluded, for the total sampling of women surveyed, sex selection widely applied would yield a national sex ratio at birth of 110 boys to 100 girls. The greatest effect, they found would be an approximate doubling of the number of families who have a boy-girl combination.

The authors of the study, Dr. Charles F. Westoff, sociologist and associate director of the Office of Population Research at Princeton University, and Ronald R. Rindfuss, a research associate at the University of Wisconsin's Center for Demography and Ecology, point out certain pitfalls in their research that could alter the actual ratios.

One is the fact that men were not asked their preferences, since husbands are not in the survey sample. Other less extensive surveys have indicated that men were more likely than women to prefer sons if given a choice. Since in selecting sex of offspring, husbands might be expected to participate with wives, there may in fact result a greater proportion of male births than this study indicates.

The ultimate sex ratio may also be affected by a growth in one-child families. If such families become significantly more popular as the nation's birth rate declines, the selection of a boy as first-born may create a greater excess of males than expected.

The authors suggest that the most lasting effect of sex selection, however, would be to further endow males with the attributes characteristic of first-born children—aggressive achievers who tend to be more successful educationally and economically than later-born children, an effect that might have considerable bearing on the future of the women's movement.

Jane E. Brody, *New York Times*, 4 May 1974

1. Most American women prefer to give birth to boys.
2. Most American women prefer to give birth to boys as their first child.
3. Most married women do not have a preference for boys or for girls.
4. Most married women are eager to use the new technology to pre-determine the sex of their child.
5. Without technological intervention, more boys would be born than girls.
6. Without technological intervention, more girls would be born than boys.
7. Without technological intervention, there would be close to an even ratio of girls and boys.
8. In the long run, with or without intervention, no major change will take place in the sex ratio.
9. In the long run, with technological pre-determination of sex, men are bound to dominate the population.
10. Because women would choose girls as their second child, in the long run women would dominate the population.
11. The sex ratio of the population may be affected by pre-determination through technology.
12. Men prefer to have sons.
13. Women do want girl children.
14. Families will be happier when parents are able to control the sex of their children.
15. First-born children tend to grow more aggressive and achieve more than later children.
16. Pre-determination of sex will result in an aggressive, over-achieving population.
17. Pre-determination of sex should not be made available to would-be parents, except in special cases.

18. If pre-determination of babies' sex were readily available, husbands would encourage their wives to have more children.
19. Husbands will influence their wives to have more boys.
20. Husbands will influence wives to have a second child of the opposite sex to the first.

OUTLINING

In addition to making marginal notes and asking yourself comprehension questions, there is another way of proving to yourself that you have fully understood what you have read: outlining the author's main ideas. An outline is much more orderly and complete than marginal notes. As you learned in Chapter 1, in order to develop your own ideas you must organize your list of notes in an outline before you write an essay. This process is reversed when you are reading source material. Your outline of someone else's work becomes a preliminary stage in your understanding that person's ideas and, later on, using them in your own writing. When you outline, you are identifying the main points of a chapter or an essay, leaving them in roughly the same order as the original. In effect, you are writing a memorandum of the essay for future reference.

The wording of the entries may be taken directly from the original or (especially for main-level entries) may be expressed in your own words as inferences drawn directly from the essay. You may use both complete sentences and fragmentary phrases for your outline entries, whichever is convenient, as long as you are consistent in your choice. (That is, *all* your main-level entries may be fragments and *all* your secondary-level entries may be complete sentences; or vice versa; or everything in the outline may be written in complete sentences; or everything may be written in fragments.)

Outlining is the obvious way to record the main points of an essay whose structure is clear and straightforward. In "Must Doctors Serve Where They're Told?" for example, Harry Schwartz presents the arguments for both sides in such an orderly sequence that underlining and numbering the key phrases in the essay would probably serve as an adequate record. (Each of the main points has been italicized in the essay.) However, since Schwartz moves back and forth from positive to negative reasons, the pairing of related arguments can be shown to best advantage if you outline them.

Read "Must Doctors Serve Where They're Told?" and then carefully examine the student thesis and outline which follow. Notice that the thesis cannot do more than suggest the underlying issues, since Schwartz himself does not decisively support one side of the argument or the other.

MUST DOCTORS SERVE WHERE THEY'RE TOLD?

Should young doctors be "drafted" and forced to serve some years in areas of physician shortage? Or, less drastically, should a portion of the places in the nation's medical schools be reserved for young people who promise that in return for government financial aid they will agree to serve where the government wants them to? These and related issues have been debated in Congress for the last two years and are still unresolved. 1

Currently, it costs an estimated average of about $13,000 a year to train a medical student, but those students pay directly only about $1,000 to $6,000 in tuition. The remainder is paid by government funds, by return on endowments, by gifts and similar sources. Some lawmakers see a *compulsory service liability as a means of compensating the taxpayers for subsidizing the doctors' education.* 2

The specific proposals that have been debated in Congress have ranged from Senator Edward M. Kennedy's suggestion for a universal draft for all medical school graduates to milder schemes that would give young doctors a choice between repaying the Federal Government or serving for several years in designated areas. In New York there is already a medical training program whose students have agreed to serve two years in doctor-short areas after graduating from medical school. Those who fail to meet this "service commitment" will be required to reimburse the city and state for up to $25,000 for their free undergraduate education. 3

Some conservative economists have argued that *physician incomes, which average around $50,000, remove all excuse for government subsidy.* They would require medical students to pay the full cost, financing their way, if need be, by bank loans. Such an approach would remove the motive for any doctor draft, but many in Congress fear that this "solution" would close medical schools to children of the poor, the working class and minorities. 4

Proponents of some service requirements for young doctors usually base their arguments on the *maldistribution of doctors in this country.* In 1973, for example, California had 265 doctors per 100,000 people, more than three times as many as South Dakota's 87 per 100,000. The actual disparities are even greater, because within each state physicians tend to congregate in metropolitan areas. 5

Opponents of forced service do not deny the existence of local shortages, but they question the wisdom of *sending new physicians into shortage areas where they will have little or no help* and consultation from older, more experienced doctors. 6

Opponents also ask *whether doctors serving in isolated areas against their will are likely to give satisfactory service.* And they ask why young doctors and dentists should be singled out for coercion when government helps finance the education of most professionals and there are great inequalities in the current distribution of lawyers, accountants, architects and engineers as well. 7

But more is involved in this debate than the allocation of physicians. 8

The argument about young doctors is relevant to the broader national discussion about national economic planning and about the relative roles of government decision and market forces in directing the American economy.

On one side are those who emphasize *the obligation of government to use all its resources to reach desirable goals for all Americans.* If one assumes, as Mr. Kennedy and others do, that every American has a "right" to health care, then it seems reasonable for government to take whatever actions are needed to make sure that doctors and related personnel and facilities are available everywhere. If market forces do not produce the desired result, this school is prepared to use either government coercion or government financial persuasion. Moreover, this school of thought wants to tailor the means to the end. Thus, instead of using government money just to expand the number of doctors in general, they want to assure that doctors are available wherever needed and available, moreover, in whatever distribution of specialties Congress or its servants decide is appropriate. 9

Opponents argue that such *regulation would be contrary to all American history and tradition,* except for times of war or emergency when the military draft has been in effect. The *American emphasis, these opponents hold, is primarily upon the freedom of the individual and affords no warrant for infringing one person's freedom in order to benefit someone else.* The whole structure of publicly financed education in this country, from kindergarten to M.D. and Ph.D., it is pointed out, has developed over the decades without any related service requirement or repayment of any kind whatsoever. If doctors are drafted, it will provide a precedent for drafting other categories of Americans. 10

The issue is not peculiarly American, of course, nor is the problem of physician maldistribution confined to the United States. *In the Soviet Union and its associated Communist states,* most graduates of higher educational institutions—not only physicians—are *assigned specific work locations* for the first few years after graduation. 11

Some non-Communist countries, like Mexico, have a requirement for compulsory service for a limited time by doctors before they can go into normal practice. In Israel there is a universal service obligation for all young adults. *But in most countries of Western Europe there is no draft of young doctors.* 12

Most of the other democratic countries of the world are relatively small, both in area and population, as compared with the United States. So the advocates of a doctor draft in the United States argue that the absence of such compulsion in other countries is no conclusive argument against it here. 13

Harry Schwartz

Thesis: A decision to draft young doctors for service throughout the country will have to consider the obligations and rights of the doctors, as well as the responsibility of the government to serve the public.

I. Obligations of young doctors: public bears partial
   cost of education, entitled to compensation
   A. repayment of debt to public through service
      evidence: Kennedy plan; New York two-year term
      of service
   B. alternative: initial payment of medical school
      fees by bank loan
      evidence: extremely high incomes will allow
      ultimate repayment
      problem: possible difficulty in applying for
      initial loan.
II. Needs of the public: not enough doctors to serve the
   country
   A. ''maldistribution'' necessitates drafting: doctors
      tend to practice in certain populous states and
      cities
      evidence: California vs. South Dakota
   B. coercion would not ensure efficient service:
      inexperienced doctors would be isolated from
      guidance; unwilling doctors are inefficient.
III. Powers of the government vs. the rights of the
   individual
   A. the government is empowered to satisfy everyone's
      right to health care.
   B. public policy shouldn't encourage coercion of
      individuals to benefit others; to draft doctors
      would be an unfortunate precedent
      evidence: other professions aren't subject to a
      draft; other beneficiaries of public education
      aren't forced to repay costs.
IV. Precedents in other countries
   A. drafting doctors is routine in some countries
      evidence: Communist countries, Mexico, Israel
   B. drafting doctors is not required in many countries
      with a democratic tradition similar to ours
      evidence: Western Europe
      problem: these Western European countries are
      physically smaller than the United States and
      therefore have different requirements.

Outlining a Disorganized Essay

Occasionally, you will need to outline an essay which does not have
a clear structure, which seems to "bury" its main ideas in the surrounding
material, and which deals with two or three important points at the same

time. Such an essay is Blanche Blank's "A Question of Degree." A loose structure makes careful, point-by-point comprehension an important preliminary step in working with this essay. The ideas simply cannot be sorted out paragraph-by-paragraph. Since "A Question of Degree" is concerned with a debatable issue, and since Blank's arguments certainly merit analysis, outlining the essay becomes an interesting if complicated task.

Establishing a Thesis

Unlike Harry Schwartz in "Must Doctors Serve Where They're Told," Blank *is* attempting to convince her readers that a specific point of view is valid. An accurate thesis, then, should convey some of her distaste for the excessive value placed on college degrees. But even with the full awareness of Blank's position that comes from thorough comprehension, you may easily write an incomplete or an inadequate thesis. What is wrong with each of these potential theses?

1. According to Blanche Blank, universities need to change their outlook and curricula and return to a more traditional role.
2. Blanche Blank suggests that our present ideology about the purpose of college should be reconsidered and redefined.
3. I agree with Blanche Blank's belief that college degrees have too much importance.
4. Blanche Blank argues that employment discrimination arises from an emphasis on college degrees.
5. Blanche Blank believes that a college education isn't necessary at an early age.

A good thesis would be broad enough to cover most of Blank's argument without being so vague as to be meaningless. Consider the following criticisms of the five theses:

Thesis 1 accurately presents only one—and not the chief one—of Blank's points.

Thesis 2 is uninformative: what is "our present ideology" and what sort of redefinition is in order?

Thesis 3 is also vague: Blank may have convinced one reader, but which of her arguments did the reader find effective?

Thesis 4 is sweeping to the point of being indiscriminate: Blank does not argue that degrees are the only cause of employment discrimination, nor does she suggest that employment is the only area adversely affected by the importance attached to degrees.

Thesis 5 is simply untrue: Blank is not urging all would-be freshmen to bypass college.

The following thesis is somewhat better than the first five: it conveys something of Blank's central idea, but it omits all reference to work and the self-respect of the worker, which are ideas crucial to the essay.

> 6. In Blanche Blank's view, acquiring a college degree immediately after high school should not be considered the best way to achieve a better life.

A thoroughly acceptable thesis, however, would convey more precisely the dangers of overvaluing the college degree. Thesis 7 achieves this end:

> 7. The possession of a college degree cannot automatically lead to a better life and better earnings for a college graduate, but the universal practice of treating the degree as a prerequisite for a ''good'' job can only discourage a just and efficient system of employment.

A Outline Based on Categories

A major problem in outlining "A Question of Degree" is that Blanche Blank, like many writers, does not present her ideas one at a time, each in a separate paragraph. Because the paragraphs of this essay are crowded with ideas, you cannot simply construct an outline by pulling out a series of points and inserting them into an outline format. For example, within the following single paragraph, Blank mentions most of her main points, some more than once, and in varying order. (The numbers here are keyed to the outline on pp. 88–89.)

> What is wrong with the current college/work cycle can be seen in the following anomalies: we are selling college to the youth of America as a take-off pad for the material good life [1A]. College is literally advertised and packaged as a means for getting more money through "better" jobs at the same time that Harvard graduates are taking jobs as taxi drivers [1B]. This situation is a perversion of the true spirit of a university [3], a perversion of a humane social ethic [4A], and, at bottom, a patent fraud. To take the last point first, the economy simply is not geared to guaranteeing these presumptive "better" jobs [1B]; the colleges are not geared to training for such jobs [3]; and the ethical propriety of the entire enterprise is very questionable [1 and 2]. We are by definition (rather than by analysis) establishing two kinds of work: work labeled "better" be-

cause it has a degree requirement tagged to it and non-degree work, which, through this logic, becomes automatically "low level" [4A].

When dealing with a complex reading, you must look for organizing principles and categories of ideas when you read and reread it. Experienced readers learn to look out for points that are repeated and emphasized, so that they will find a consistent way to approach and remember what they have read. Thus, the comprehension questions that analyzed "A Question of Degree" encouraged you to stop and review the points that Blanche Blank raised. You will remember that you were asked about the different groups of people who are affected by the unfortunate worship of college degrees. The easiest way to break down the mass of assertions in Blanche Blank's essay is to use those groups as a principle of division:

A. students who are in college unwillingly;
B. college graduates who work at frustrating jobs;
C. workers who have not been to college and are undervalued;
D. true scholars who resent the decline in the quality of university life.

If you combine the first two groups (both with career expectations and both disappointed by college), you have an outline with three major entries, plus a conclusion that sums up Blanche Blank's central ideas.

> Thesis: The possession of a college degree cannot automatically lead to a better life and better earnings for a college graduate, but the universal practice of treating the degree as a prerequisite for a ''good'' job can only discourage a just and efficient system of employment.
>
> I. The frustration of students with vocational expectations
> A. Whether or not they are suited to college, students believe that they must spend four years getting a degree to get a good job.
> B. Rewarding jobs are not necessarily available, even to those with degrees.
> II. The frustration of working people without college degrees but with hopes for advancement
> A. Workers with experience and good qualifications are bypassed for promotion and denied their rightful status.
> B. Since college is considered the province of the

young, it is unlikely that an experienced older
person will seek a college education.
III. The frustration of students and teachers with
traditional views of college
    A. Instead of continuing to emphasize the traditional
pursuit of knowledge for its own sake,
universities are trying to function as a service
industry, preparing students for careers.
IV. Conclusion: deterioration of human values
    A. People are encouraged to make invidious
comparisons between less and more desirable kinds
of work.
    B. One form of educational experience is being
elevated at the expense of the others.

There are two important points to notice about this outline. First, although some people believe that an outline should be perfectly parallel—that is, all the entries should be complete sentences or all the entries should be brief phrases—consistency of presentation is not all that important (in this example, the main-level entries are all fragments and the secondary entries are all complete sentences). A more essential form of parallelism requires that all the entires be on *roughly the same level of abstraction*. Thus, the main-level entries in this outline are all very broad, while the secondary levels suggest the more specific ways in which each paragraph will be developed. In contrast, here is an excerpt from an outline in which the entries are mixed:

A. jobs aren't available
B. Joe V. disappointed
C. college students feel cheated

The example of Joe V. is used in the essay only to illustrate important ideas, not as an end in itself. Thus, entry B is *evidence* in support of entries A and C, and therefore "Joe" belongs in a more subordinate position.

A. jobs aren't available
B. college students feel cheated
   1. Joe V. disappointed

Second, all the entries in the complete Blank outline are *re-wordings* of ideas taken from the essay and are self-contained and self-explanatory. Outlines which retain the wording of the original very often fail to make sense by themselves, since phrases or sentences taken out of context usually cannot stand alone as representations of main ideas. Is this group of points easy to understand at a glance?

```
  I. Degree-granting colleges are like false gods.
 II. The college degree is regarded as a stepping-stone to
     ''meaningful,'' ''better'' jobs.
III. The ethical propriety of the entire system is in
     question.
 IV. Students see themselves as prisoners of economic
     necessity.
```

How these four points relate to each other or how they serve as arguments to support the essay's thesis is not immediately clear. On the other hand, condensing sentences into cryptic phrases is usually not much more illuminating.

```
  I. destruction of adolescents
 II. vocational schools instead of universities
III. non-degree work menial
```

Certainly, "the destruction of adolescents" is a distortion, and to appreciate Blanche Blank's argument from reading this group of entries would be impossible.

EXERCISE 17

Select one of the essays listed below, establish its thesis, and construct an outline of its main ideas. The number of entries and the number of levels, main and subordinate, in the outline will depend on the structure of the essay that you select. (For example, you may or may not need to have a subsidiary level for the presentation of evidence.)

Charles Silberman's "Poverty and Crime" on p. 227
John Holt's "Summary" from *How Children Fail* on p. 217

THE PURPOSE OF THE BRIEF SUMMARY

When you underline and annotate a text, when you ask yourself questions about its contents, when you work out an outline of its structure, you are demonstrating to yourself that you understand what you are reading. When you write a summary, you are *recording* your understanding for your own information; when you include the summary in an essay of your own, you are *reporting* your understanding to your reader.

A summary of a source is usually a condensation of ideas or information, and therefore to include every repetition and detail is neither necessary nor desirable. Rather, you are to extract only those points which you think are important—the main ideas, which in the original passage may have been interwoven with less important material. Thus, a summary of several pages can sometimes be as brief as one sentence. For the sake of clarity and coherence, you may rearrange the order of ideas.

In the kind of brief and comprehensive summary discussed here, you should add nothing new to the material that is being presented, nor (except for changes in sequence) should there be any difference in emphasis or any new interpretation or evaluation. In your role as summarizer, you should strive to remain in the background.

The brief summary is often used as part of a larger essay. For example, you have probably summarized your own ideas in the topic sentence of a paragraph or in the conclusion of an essay. When you wish to discuss another piece of writing, you generally summarize the contents briefly, in order to establish for the reader the ideas that your essay will then go on to analyze. The writer of a research essay is especially dependent upon the summary as a means of referring to source materials. Through summary, you can condense a broad range of information, and you can present and explain the relevance of a number of sources all dealing with the same subject.

Finding a Summarizing Sentence Within the Text Itself

Before you can begin to summarize a short reading—a paragraph, for example,—you must, of course, read the passage carefully and become familiar with the significance of each idea and the way it is linked to the other ideas. A successful brief summary is never merely a vague generalization, a "spin-off," loosely connected to the reading. Rather, the summary should above all be *comprehensive*, conveying as much as possible the totality of thought within the paragraph. If your reading is thorough, you may find a single comprehensive sentence in the text itself, to be taken out verbatim and used as a summary. But, as a rule, you can find your summary in the text only when the paragraph is short and contains a particularly strong and comprehensive topic sentence.

The following paragraph *can* be summarized adequately by one of its own sentences. Which one?

> Men, much as the feminists would like to build them up in order to support the myth of women as oppressed, are not all that aggressive. They are more like shy woodland creatures, fawns peeping through the thicket of masculine self-protection. A man is someone who, when his boss says something moronic, agrees. A man is someone who eats his

burnt steak in silence, rather than offend a waiter he doesn't like. A man is someone who takes you out and, when you want him to put his arms around you and kiss you, sits there carrying on a conversation. In short, all the women I know whose information about men comes from the real world and not from feminist tracts derive enormous merriment from the portrait of man as brutal enslaver. Men aggressive! they say. Ha ha, that's good. Tell us another one.

Rhoda Koenig, from "The Persons in The Office"

Don't be misled by the fifth sentence, just because it begins with "in short"; it does not summarize the paragraph. If you remove that sentence from the context of the paragraph, you will see that it provides no clues to the content. Rather, the first sentence is the summarizing topic sentence of the paragraph.

Summarizing by Combining Elements Within the Paragraph

Usually, even when there is a strong sentence to suggest the main idea of the paragraph, you will need to tinker with that sentence, expanding its meaning by adjusting the language to a more general focus. Here, for example, is a paragraph in which no one sentence is broad enough to sum up the main idea, but which contains a scattering of useful phrases:

In a discussion [with] a class of teachers, I once said that I liked some of the kids in my class much more than others and that, without saying which ones I liked best, I had told them so. After all, this is something that children know, whatever we tell them; it is futile to lie about it. Naturally, these teachers were horrified. "What a terrible thing to say!" one said. "I love all the children in my class exactly the same." Nonsense; a teacher who says this is lying, to herself or to others, and probably doesn't like any of the children very much. Not that there is anything wrong with that; plenty of adults don't like children, and there is no reason why they should. But the trouble is that they feel they should, which makes them feel guilty, which makes them feel resentful, which in turn makes them try to work off their guilt with indulgence and their resentment with subtle cruelties—cruelties of a kind that can be seen in many classrooms. Above all, it makes them put on the phony, syrupy, sickening voice and manner, and the fake smiles and forced, bright laughter that children see so much of in school, and rightly resent and hate.

John Holt, from *How Children Fail*

The object here is to combine key phrases: "a teacher who says" that she "loves all the children" "is lying to herself, or to others," and makes herself (and probably the children) "feel guilty" and "resentful." This summarizing sentence is essentially a patchwork, with the diction and phrasing drawn straight from the original; therefore it is essential either to acknowledge the borrowings (by quotation marks, as above) or, preferably, to construct an entirely new sentence, such as this one:

> Although it is only natural for teachers to prefer some students to others, many cannot accept their failure to like all equally well and express their inadequacy and dissatisfaction in ways that are harmful to the children.

Supplying a Summarizing Sentence

Finally, there are some diffuse paragraphs which offer no starting point at all for the summary and require the invention of a new generalization. How would you summarize this paragraph?

> To parents who wish to lead a quiet life, I would say: Tell your children that they are very naughty—much naughtier than most children. Point to the young people of some acquaintances as models of perfection and impress your own children with a deep sense of their own inferiority. You carry so many more guns than they do that they cannot fight you. This is called moral influence, and it will enable you to bounce them as much as you please. They think you know and they will not have yet caught you lying often enough to suspect that you are not the unworldly and scrupulously truthful person which you represent yourself to be; nor yet will they know how great a coward you are, nor how soon you will run away, if they fight you with persistency and judgment. You keep the dice and throw them both for your children and yourself. Load them then, for you can easily manage to stop your children from examining them. Tell them how singularly indulgent you are; insist on the incalculable benefit you conferred upon them, firstly in bringing them into the world at all, but more particularly in bringing them into it as your own children rather than anyone else's. Say that you have their highest interests at stake whenever you are out of temper and wish to make yourself unpleasant by way of balm to your soul. Harp much upon these highest interests. Feed them spiritually upon such brimstone and treacle as the late Bishop of Winchester's Sunday stories. You hold all the trump cards, or if you do not you can filch them; if you play them with anything like judgment you will find yourselves heads of happy, united, God-fearing families, even as did my old friend Mr. Pontifex. True, your children will probably find out all about it some day, but not until too late to be of much service to them or inconvenience to yourself.
>
> Samuel Butler, from *The Way of All Flesh*

A summary of this paragraph would recommend that parents intimidate their children and thus put them in their place. However, although such a generalization sums up the series of examples contained in the paragraph, it does not convey the fact that Butler is exaggerating outrageously. Butler's caricature of family life would not be taken very seriously by any reader familiar with the behavior of real parents and real children, and he obviously did not mean it to be taken seriously. The summary, then, would have to include not only the gist of Butler's recommendations, but also his implied point: that he does not expect anyone to follow his advice. Irony is the term used to describe the conflict between Butler's real meaning—parents are not monsters—and the meaning apparently expressed by his words. Here is a possible summarizing sentence:

> Butler ironically suggests that a parent can gain
> tranquillity and domestic happiness by tyrannizing over
> his children and making them feel morally inferior.

Notice that the summarizing sentence includes the author's name. Mentioning the author at the beginning of a summary is often an effective device.

EXERCISE 18

Read the following paragraph, and decide which of the following sentences provides the most comprehensive summary. (Only one answer is correct: state your reason for rejecting each of the other sentences.)

> Why are there laws insisting on alimony and child support? Everyone knows that men don't have an instinct to protect their young and, given half a chance, with the moon in the right phase, they will run off and disappear. Everyone assumes a mother will not let her child starve, yet it is necessary to legislate that a father must not do so. We are taught to accept the idea that men are less than decent, [that] their characters are riddled with faults. To this day I never blink if I hear that a man has gone to find his fortune in South America, having left his pregnant wife, his blind mother and taken the family car. [But] I still gasp in horror when I hear of a woman leaving her asthmatic infant for a rock group in [California] because I can't seem to avoid the assumption that men are naturally heels and women the ordained carriers of what [is moral] in our civilization.
>
> Anne Roiphe

A. Most men neglect their wives and children, and shun the responsibility of their support.

B. Since it would be impossible for society to survive properly without the protection of alimony and child support, men should be forced to provide these payments.

    C. Society falsely believes that women as mothers will never desert their offspring and that men as fathers are more likely to do so.

    D. Noting that most men only care for themselves, Anne Roiphe asks why they should be forced by law to assume the responsibility of supporting the children they've fathered.

    E. One of the reasons why the law forces men to provide alimony and child support is that society automatically assumes that women have a higher moral responsibility to their children then men do and that women wouldn't abandon that responsibility under any circumstances.

    F. Men may find many reasons for neglecting to pay alimony and child support, some of which may be valid and some not, but the laws that protect women and children should not be concerned with reasons.

    G. Anne Roiphe points out that laws insisting on alimony and child support lean heavily on men, and she inquires whether these laws are just.

EXERCISE 19

Summarize each of the following paragraphs by doing *one* of three things:

    A. underline a sentence which will serve as an adequate summary;

or

    B. change an existing sentence or combine existing phrases to create an adequate summary;

or

    C. invent a new generalization to provide an adequate summary.

1.   What usually happens is that the grandparents insist on laying down the law about the upbringing of children, or that the grandparents spoil them by seeing only the good or the bad in them. In wrong homes the children have four bosses instead of two. Even in good homes there is a strain because most of the time the grandparents keep trying to bring in their own antiquated views on childhood. Grandparents are often inclined to spoil a child by a too possessive love. This usually happens when Grandma has no real interest in life after her own family has grown. The third generation gives her a chance to begin her job anew. Under the notion that her daughter or daughter-in-law is incompetent as a mother, Grandma takes over, and the child is pulled both ways—and is apt to withdraw from *both* sides. To a child, squabbling means a loveless home, whether it be between Mother and Granny or between man and wife. And even if the squabbling is subtly hidden from the child, he is

never deceived. He *feels*, without being conscious of it, that there is no love in this house.

A. S. Neill, from *Summerhill*

2.   We must realize that becoming an educated person is a difficult, demanding enterprise. Just as anyone who spoke of intense physical training as a continuous source of pleasure and delight would be thought a fool, for we all know how much pain and frustration such training involves, so anyone who speaks of intense mental exertion as a continuous source of joy and ecstasy ought to be thought equally foolish, for such effort also involves pain and frustration. It is painful to have one's ignorance exposed and frustrating to be baffled by intellectual subtleties. Of course, there can be joy in learning as there can be joy in sport. But in both cases the joy is a result of overcoming genuine challenges and cannot be experienced without toil.

Steven M. Cahn, "If at First You Don't Succeed, Quit," *New York Times*

3.   Up to a certain point the adult bows to the official ethic of respect for the aged that has, as we have seen, asserted itself during the recent centuries. But it is the adult's interest to treat the aged [parent] as an inferior being and to convince him of his decline. He does his best to make his father aware of his deficiencies and blunders so that the old man will hand over the running of his affairs, give up advising him and submit to a passive role. Although the pressure of public opinion forces the son to help his old parents, he means to rule them as he sees fit; and so the more he considers them incapable of managing for themselves the fewer scruples he will feel.

Simone de Beauvoir, from *The Coming of Age*

4.   Stadiums are the cathedrals where fans come to worship their muscular gods, whose actions teach the gospel of corporate conformity and the survival of the fittest. Winning is the game's only goal, and linemen are the bulwark of this "holy" mission. They are the superhuman strongmen—the wall of muscle, agility and hatred—who engineer the "miracle" of touchdowns and the "grace" of victory. The names in Plimpton's record of football life hint at the energy and power of this endeavor: Bronco Nagurski, Mad Dog Curtis, Night Train Lane, Bulldog Turner, Big Daddy Lipscomb, Ox Emerson.

John Lahr, review of George Plimpton's *Mad Dukes and Bears*

5.   The death of a man or woman in a primitive group [like the Trobriand Islanders], consisting of a limited number of individuals, is an event of no mean importance. The nearest relatives and friends are disturbed to the depth of their emotional life. A small community bereft of

a member, especially if he be important, is severely mutilated. The whole event breaks the normal course of life and shakes the moral foundations of society. The strong tendency . . . to give way to fear and horror, to abandon the corpse, to run away from the village, to destroy all the belongings of the dead one—all these impulses exist, and if given way to would be extremely dangerous, disintegrating the group, destroying the material foundations of primitive culture. Death in a primitive society is, therefore, much more than the removal of a member. By setting in motion one part of the deep forces of the instinct of self-preservation, it threatens the very cohesion and solidarity of the group, and upon this depends the organization of that society, its tradition, and finally the whole culture. For if primitive man yielded always to the disintegrating impulses of his reaction to death, the continuity of tradition and the existence of material civilization would be made impossible.

Bronislaw Malinowski, from Magic, Science, and Religion

6.   . . . men are not gentle, friendly creatures wishing for love, who simply defend themselves if they are attacked, but . . . a powerful measure of desire for aggression has to be reckoned as part of their instinctual endowment. The result is that their neighbor is to them not only a possible helper or sexual object, but also a temptation to them to gratify their aggressiveness on him, to exploit his capacity for work without recompense, to use him sexually without his consent, to seize his possessions, to humiliate him, to cause him pain, to torture and to kill him. . . . This aggressive cruelty usually lies in wait for some provocation, or else it steps into the service of some other purpose, the aim of which might as well have been achieved by milder measures. In circumstances that favor it, when those forces in the mind which ordinarily inhibit it cease to operate, it also manifests itself spontaneously and reveals men as savage beasts to whom the thought of sparing their own kind is alien. Anyone who calls to mind the atrocities of the early migrations, of the invasion by the Huns or by the so-called Mongols under Jenghiz Khan and Tamerlane, of the sack of Jerusalem by the pious Crusaders, even indeed the horrors of the last world-war, will have to bow his head humbly before the truth of this view of man.

Sigmund Freud, from Civilization and Its Discontents

WRITING A BRIEF SUMMARY OF A SHORT ARTICLE

When you want to summarize an essay in a few sentences, how are you to judge which points are significant and which are not? Some essays, especially newspaper articles, have a rambling structure and short paragraphs; thus, you do not even have fully developed paragraphs in which to search for summarizing topic sentences. Are there any standard procedures to help decide which points will need to be summarized? Read "Holdup Man Tells Detectives How to Do It," and observe your own method of pinpointing the key ideas.

HOLDUP MAN TELLS DETECTIVES HOW TO DO IT

His face hidden by a shabby tan coat, the career holdup man peeked out at his audience of detectives and then proceeded to lecture to them on how easy it was to succeed at his trade in New York.

"I don't think there's much any individual police officer can do," the guest lecturer told 50 detectives yesterday at an unusual crime seminar sponsored by the Police Department. "Once I knew what the police officer on the beat was up to I wasn't much concerned about the cops."

The holdup man, who identified himself only as "Nick," is serving a prison term of 6 to 13 years. He said his most serious arrest occurred after he was shot three times by a supermarket manager—not in any encounter with the police.

When asked by a detective taking a course in robbery investigations what the best deterrent would be against gunmen like himself, Nick replied crisply: "stiffer sentences."

After being seriously wounded in his last robbery attempt, Nick said he decided it was time to retire.

I'm close to 40 and not getting any younger," he explained. "I just don't want to spend any more time in jail."

Nick also offered the detectives some tips on how robbers pick their targets and make their getaways in the city.

Except for wearing a hat, Nick said he affected no disguise. "I usually picked a store in a different neighborhood or in another borough where I was unknown."

Leads on places to hold up usually came from other criminals or from employees. There were no elaborate plannings or "casings," he said, adding:

"I liked supermarkets because there's always a lot of cash around. Uniformed guards didn't deter me because they're not armed, they usually just have sticks. It's better to pick a busy area rather than the suburbs. The chances of someone noticing you are greater in residential or suburban areas."

The detectives, sitting at desks with notepaper in front of them, were rookies as well as veterans. Besides city detectives, the audience included policemen from the Transit Authority, the Housing Authority, the Yonkers Police Department and from Seattle.

They listened carefully as Nick outlined how he or a confederate would inspect the area for signs of uniformed or plainclothes police officers.

The retired robber said he had preferred supermarkets or stores with large window advertisements or displays because these materials prevented him from being seen by passers-by on the street.

"I was always a little nervous or apprehensive before a job," he continued. "But once you're inside and aware of the reaction of the people and you know the possibilities then your confidence comes back."

Nick said he always made his escape in a car and he preferred heavily trafficked roads because it made the getaway vehicle less conspicuous than on little used side streets.

In New York, cheap handguns were selling from $15 to $70, he told the detectives. Such weapons as shotguns or automatic rifles, Nick said, could be rented for about $100 an hour.

Nick said he had been a holdup man since the age of 20 and had committed about 30 "jobs," but was uncertain of the exact number. The biggest robbery he had participated in netted a total of $8,000, and overall he got about $30,000 in his criminal activities.

Asked why he went back to robbing after his first arrest, Nick said: "I wanted whisky, women and big autos. Like most who rob I was not socially accepted. Big money elevates you above the people you think are looking down on you."

Short prison sentences, for first arrests, Nick asserted, probably do little to discourage holdup men. "I see them laying up in jail and it doesn't make any difference," he said. "They just go ahead planning the next one in a different way."

During his "on-and-off" criminal career, Nick said he had never fired any of the guns he carried.

After his one-hour appearance as a guest lecturer, Nick, his face still covered by his coat, was escorted out of the classroom back to his cell at an undisclosed prison.

Selwyn Raab, *New York Times*, 5 March 1975

Step One: Read the Entire Article More Than Once

This direction is not as simple as it sounds. Because you know that your purpose is to isolate main ideas, you may underline what you regard as the key sentences on first reading, and, from then on, look only at the "boiled-down" parts. But it would be a mistake to eliminate minor points too soon. They do have a function in the article, supporting and illuminating the central ideas. For example, the fact that Nick chose to hide his face during and after his "lecture" hardly seems worth underlining, and, in fact, would never *by itself* be regarded as a crucial point. But taken together with some of Nick's remarks, that "discardable" fact contributes to your recognition of a key point of the article: the robber's reliance on *anonymity* is his way of committing a successful crime, and Nick may at some point wish to resume his profession despite his "retirement."

Step Two: Ask Yourself the Paper's Reason for Printing the Article

What does the newspaper want its readers to learn? An inquiry into basic intention is especially important in analyzing a news article, as the journal's and journalist's purpose is frequently two-fold—to describe an event and to suggest the event's significance—and so it is easy for you to confuse the *facts* being recorded with the underlying *reasons* for recording them. Here are two one-sentence summaries of the "Nick" article that are both off the mark because they concentrate too heavily on the event:

> Nick, a convicted retired criminal, was guest speaker at a police seminar and told detectives how robbers pick their targets and make their getaways in New York.

> Nick, after committing thirty robberies, suggested to detectives some possible methods of thwarting future robberies.

Both writers seem to be overly concerned with Nick's colorful history and the peculiarity of his helping the police at all. They ignore the significance of what Nick was actually saying. The second summary—by emphasizing the phrase "thwarting future robberies"—is rather misleading and almost contradicts the point of the article; in fact, Nick is really suggesting that the police will continue to be ineffectual.

A news article can also mislead you into thinking that a headline is a summary: the headline "Holdup Man Tells Detectives How to Do It" does not cover the material in the "Nick" article, but because it is broad and vague, it "sounds" good. What, for example, is meant by the "it" of the headline—robbery or its detection? What does Nick tell the detectives? Headlines are designed to include only as much "as fits the print," and they are often written by people who do not have time to read the article.

Step Three: Look for Repetitions of and Variations on the Same Idea

There is one concrete point that Selwyn Raab and his readers and the police and Nick himself are all interested in: ways of preventing criminals from committing crimes. Not only are we told again and again about Nick's contempt for the police—the present inadequate deterrent against crime—but we are also given his flat statement that only fear of imprisonment ("stiffer sentences") will discourage a hardened criminal.

A brief summary of this article, then, would mention tough sentencing as a route to better crime prevention. But there is also a second pattern, one which was suggested above, that ought, if possible, to be incorporated into a complete summary. In Nick's opinion, his career has been a (relatively) successful one because he has managed to appear normal and blend into the crowd. The primary and secondary ideas can be joined in a summary like this one:

> Observing with contempt that the police have rarely
> been able to penetrate his "anonymous" disguise, Nick, the
> successful robber, argues that the presence of policemen
> will not deter most experienced criminals and that only
> "stiffer sentences" will prevent crime.

EXERCISE 20

Carefully read "School Fighting to End Interpreter Service for Deaf Girl, 8." Determine the article's purpose and pick out the ideas that Evans emphasizes; then write a comprehensive one-sentence summary.

SCHOOL FIGHTING TO END INTERPRETER SERVICE FOR DEAF GIRL, 8

PEEKSKILL, N.Y. — As 8-year-old Amy Rowley helped celebrate the birthday of a third-grade classmate at the Furnace Woods School in nearby Cortlandt with donut Munchkins and games, Fran Miller sat close by. Amy is deaf and Miss Miller is her personal sign-language interpreter, assigned to all her academic classes by virtue of a Federal Court of Appeals order last July after four years of legal battling.

Amy says she is doing better in school with Miss Miller's help. And her parents, who are also deaf, agree heartily. But state and local education officials say that Amy does not need an interpreter to do well academically and that they should not be required to provide one at taxpayers' expense, now about $8,000 a year.

The officials are preparing to challenge the Court of Appeals decision in the Supreme Court.

It is an emotional dispute, and one that pits the expanding rights of the handicapped against the shifting priorities of society as a whole and its ability to meet them.

"School districts have civil rights, too," said Dr. Joseph Zavarella, the principal at Furnace Woods, who argues that the Hendrick Hudson School District has provided Amy with a range of other aids—including a speech therapist, a teacher for the deaf and an FM radio transmitter—with which she has managed very well in her three years there.

"We had always said to the parents," he said, "that if we found she was failing, we might make a recommendation that a sign-language interpreter was necessary. She's been doing exceptionally well."

Nancy and Clifford Rowley were pleased with Amy's progress, but argued that she could do better with a sign-language interpreter.

In an interview the Rowleys, who are graduates of Gallaudet College, the liberal-arts college for the deaf in Washington, lip-read questions that were put to them and answered them with some help in oral interpretation from a friend.

Mrs. Rowley, who is trained as a teacher of the deaf, said tests had showed that when Amy did not have an interpreter she missed 41 percent of what was said in the classroom.

"She has the right to 100 percent of what the person is saying," Mrs. Rowley declared. "As I was growing up I actually did not know how much I was missing until I went to Gallaudet College. That is where I learned total communication."

The philosophy of total communication, Mr. Rowley, a research chemist, explained, involves mouthing words, amplification, sign language, touching and visual clues. Used in combination, the Rowleys say, the deaf can understand significantly more than they would otherwise.

The Rowleys said that the controversy had not upset Amy, but that their 11-year-old son, John, the only hearing member of the family, was affected by it and had been "left out" too much of the time.

Charles V. Eible, superintendent of the school district, said that its appeal of the Court of Appeals decision would focus on whether Amy was "getting an appropriate education" under Federal and state laws and regulations.

"Our contention is that she is, without an interpreter," he said.

Paul E. Sherman Jr., the lawyer representing the state's Education Department and the Education Commissioner, agreed, saying the local district has "done all the law requires and has gone beyond it."

He said that the main reason the state was pursuing the case was that Federal and state regulations and statutes did not require that such services be provided by local agencies. He said that if they were required, "Congress would have had to appropriate a lot more money than it has."

Sign-language interpreters for every deaf child in New York State alone would cost $100 million a year, he asserted.

Mr. Eible said that, for now, Miss Miller was being paid on a sliding scale used for substitute teachers, at a cost of about $8,000 a year, plus some medical benefits. He said he could not put an annual figure on the other services that Amy received; the time of a speech therapist, for example, is divided among several children.

The officials did not disagree with the Rowleys' contention that Amy could do better work with the help of an interpreter. The question, they said, is, What is the state's obligation?

"My son would do better if he had four teachers," Mr. Sherman remarked. "He's got a great I.Q., but is getting C's and B minuses."

Dr. Zavarella, the principal, said: "If you discount sympathy, the school district has to uphold a position with respect to the cold, hard facts. Are we capable of giving her a standard education that we promise every youngster? Can we do that without a sign-language interpreter? Our position is that we can."

Mr. Rowley said: "He misses the point. Amy is deaf and she will be deaf until the day she dies. There is no way she will be able to be equal to her classmates. He cannot compare."

The Rowleys' struggle to get an interpreter for Amy began in 1976, before she entered kindergarten, when they brought a civil complaint through the Federal Department of Health, Education and Welfare alleging that her rights were being violated. The Federal agency found in the school district's favor.

Dr. Zavarella said that Amy was given a two-week trial with an interpreter in kindergarten, and that the interpreter had concluded Amy did not need his services, partly because of her resistance and partly because her teacher was extremely sensitive to her needs.

When Amy entered first grade, the school district's committee on the handicapped concluded that she could receive an appropriate education without an interpreter. The Rowleys demanded a hearing by an independent state examiner, who upheld the committee, a decision later supported by the state's Commissioner of Education.

The Rowleys went to court, and last January Judge Vincent L. Broderick of the United States District Court for the Southern District of New York held that Amy was entitled to an interpreter when academic subjects were being taught.

He found that an "appropriate education" was one that "would require that each handicapped child be given an opportunity to achieve his full potential commensurate with the opportunity provided to other children."

The school district and the state appealed. Last July the United States Court of Appeals for the Second Circuit upheld Judge Broderick's decision 2 to 1.

Miss Miller started work late last month and Joan Conklin, Amy's home-room teacher, said Amy had begun to use Miss Miller more and more. "She's reading fine and writing fine," Mrs. Conklin said. "The only weak area is math, but she has company here."

One difference Mrs. Conklin has noticed with the interpreter present is that the other children are less likely to help Amy when she does not understand something. "They would automatically go run and help her," she said. "They have stopped."

Still, Amy is an animated participant in classroom activities. At the birthday celebration she joined the general merriment in a guessing game called "Sevenup," involving pulling donut Munchkins out of a box.

The Rowleys want their daughter to have an interpreter not just for academic subjects, but for all school activities in which verbal communication is important, music class, for example, and assemblies.

"Anything that happens within the school, that's where Amy has to learn," said Mr. Rowley. "I want her as equal to her peers."

Charlotte Evans, New York Times, 18 July 1980

WRITING A SUMMARY OF A COMPLEX ESSAY

When you are asked to summarize a reading containing a number of ideas, a reading which is abstract, disorganized, and therefore difficult to comprehend and condense, the best way to prepare for your summary is to isolate each important point and note it down in a list. Here is an essay by Bertrand Russell, followed by a preliminary list of notes, a statement of Russell's thesis, and the final summary.

THE SOCIAL RESPONSIBILITY OF SCIENTISTS

Science, ever since it first existed, has had important effects in matters that lie outside the purview of pure science. Men of science have differed as to their responsibility for such effects. Some have said that the function of the scientist in society is to supply knowledge, and that he need not concern himself with the use to which this knowledge is put. I do not think that this view is tenable, especially in our age. The scientist is also a citizen; and citizens who have any special skill have a public duty to see, as far as they can, that their skill is utilized in accordance with the public interest. Historically, the functions of the scientist in public life have generally been recognized. The Royal Society was founded by Charles II as an antidote to "fanaticism" which had plunged England into a long period of civil strife. The scientists of that time did not hesitate to speak out on public issues, such as religious toleration and the folly of prosecutions for witchcraft. But although science has, in various ways at various times, favored what may be called a humanitarian outlook, it has from the first had an intimate and sinister connection with war. Archimedes sold his skill to the Tyrant of Syracuse for use against the Romans; Leonardo secured a salary from the Duke of Milan for his skill in the art of fortification; and Galileo got employment under the Grand Duke of Tuscany because he could calculate the trajectories of projectiles. In the French Revolution the scientists who were not guillotined were set to making new explosives, but Lavoisier was not spared, because he was only discovering hydrogen which, in those days, was not a weapon of war. There have been some honorable exceptions to the subservience of scientists to warmongers. During the Crimean War the British government consulted Faraday as to the feasibility of attack by poisonous gases. Faraday replied that it was entirely feasible, but that it was inhuman and he would have nothing to do with it.

Modern democracy and modern methods of publicity have made the problem of affecting public opinion quite different from what it used to be. The knowledge that the public possesses on any important issue is derived from vast and powerful organizations: the press, radio, and, above all, television. The knowledge that governments possess is more limited. They are too busy to search out the facts for themselves, and consequently they know only what their underlings think good for them unless there is such a powerful movement in a different sense that politicians cannot ignore it. Facts which ought to guide the decisions of statesmen—for instance, as to the possible lethal qualities of fallout—do not acquire their due importance if they remain buried in scientific journals. They acquire their due importance only when they become known to so many voters that they affect the course of the elections. In general, there is an opposition to widespread publicity for such facts. This opposition springs from various sources, some sinister, some comparatively respectable. At the bottom of the moral scale there is the financial interest of the various industries connected with armaments. Then there are various effects of a somewhat thoughtless patriotism, which believes in secrecy and in what is called "toughness." But perhaps more important than either of these is the unpleasantness of the facts, which makes the general public turn aside to pleasanter topics such as divorces and murders. The consequence is that what ought to be known widely throughout the general public will not be known unless great efforts are made by disinterested persons to see that the information reaches the minds and hearts of vast numbers of people. I do not think this work can be successfully accomplished except by the help of men of science. They, alone, can speak with the authority that is necessary to combat the misleading statements of those scientists who have permitted themselves to become merchants of death. If disinterested scientists do not speak out, the others will succeed in conveying a distorted impression, not only to the public but also to the politicians.

It must be admitted that there are obstacles to individual action in our age which did not exist at earlier times. Galileo could make his own telescope. But once when I was talking with a very famous astronomer he explained that the telescope upon which his work depended owed its existence to the benefactions of enormously rich men, and, if he had not stood well with them, his astronomical discoveries would have been impossible. More frequently, a scientist only acquires access to enormously expensive equipment if he stands well with the government of his country. He knows that if he adopts a rebellious attitude he and his family are likely to perish along with the rest of civilized mankind. It is a tragic dilemma, and I do not think that one should censure a man whatever his decision; but I do think—and I think men of science should realize—that unless something rather drastic is done under the leadership or through the inspiration of some part of the scientific world, the human race, like the Gadarene swine, will rush down a steep place to destruction in blind ignorance of the fate that scientific skill has prepared for it.

It is impossible in the modern world for a man of science to say with any honesty, "My business is to provide knowledge, and what use is made of the knowledge is not my responsibility." The knowledge that a man of science provides may fall into the hands of men or institutions devoted to utterly unworthy objects. I do not suggest that a man of science, or even a large body of men of science, can altogether prevent this, but they can diminish the magnitude of the evil.

There is another direction in which men of science can attempt to provide leadership. They can suggest and urge in many ways the value of those branches of science of which the important practical uses are beneficial and not harmful. Consider what might be done if the money at present spent on armaments were spent on increasing and distributing the food supply of the world and diminishing the population pressure. In a few decades, poverty and malnutrition, which now afflict more than half the population of the globe, could be ended. But at present almost all the governments of great states consider that it is better to spend money on killing foreigners than on keeping their own subjects alive. Possibilities of a hopeful sort in whatever field can best be worked out and stated authoritatively by men of science; and, since they can do this work better than others, it is part of their duty to do it.

As the world becomes more technically unified, life in an ivory tower becomes increasingly impossible. Not only so; the man who stands out against the powerful organizations which control most of human activity is apt to find himself no longer in the ivory tower, with a wide outlook over a sunny landscape, but in the dark and subterranean dungeon upon which the ivory tower was erected. To risk such a habitation demands courage. It will not be necessary to inhabit the dungeon if there are many who are willing to risk it, for everybody knows that the modern world depends upon scientists, and, if they are insistent, they must be listened to. We have it in our power to make a good world; and, therefore, with whatever labor and risk, we must make it.

Bertrand Russell, from Fact and Fiction

First Stage: List of Notes and Determination of a Thesis

1. Should scientists try to influence the way their discoveries are used?
2. One point of view: the scientist's role is to make the discovery; what happens afterwards is not his concern.
3. Russell's point of view: scientists are like any other knowledgeable and public-spirited people; they must make sure that the products of their knowledge work for, not against, society.
4. In the past, some scientists have made public their views on controversial issues like freedom of religion; others have been servants of the war machine.
5. The power to inform and influence the public is now controlled by the news media.
6. Government officials are too busy to be well-informed; subordinates feed them only enough information to get them reelected.
7. It is in the interests of various groups, ranging from weapons makers to patriots, to limit the amount of scientific information that the public receives.
8. The public is reluctant to listen to distasteful news.
9. Since the public deserves to hear the truth, scientists, who are respected for their knowledge and who belong to no party or faction, ought to do more to provide the public with information about the potentially lethal consequences of their discoveries.

By doing so, they will correct the distortions of those scientists who have allied themselves with warmongers.

10. It is very difficult for scientists to speak out since they depend on government and business interests to finance their work.

11. While scientists cannot entirely stop others from using some of their discoveries for anti-social purposes, they can support other, more constructive kinds of research.

12. Speaking out is worth the risk of incurring the displeasure of powerful people; since the work of scientists is so vital, the risk isn't too great, especially if they act together.

Russell's Thesis: Contrary to the self-interested arguments of many scientists and other groups, scientists have a social responsibility to make sure that their work is used for, not against, the benefit of society.

Second Stage : Summary

Some scientists, as well as other groups, consider that they need not influence the way in which their discoveries are used. However, Bertrand Russell believes that scientists have a social responsibility to make sure that their work is used for, not against, the benefit of society. In modern times, it has been especially difficult for concerned scientists to speak out because many powerful groups prefer to limit and distort what the public is told, because government officials are too busy to be thoroughly informed, because scientists depend on the financial support of business and government, and because the public itself is reluctant to hear distasteful news. Nevertheless, scientists have the knowledge and the prestige to command public attention, and their work is too vital for their voices to be suppressed. If they act together, they can warn us if their work is likely to be used for an anti-social purpose and, at least, they can propose less destructive alternatives.

GUIDELINES FOR WRITING A SUMMARY

1. The summary must be comprehensive. You should review all the ideas on your list, and include in your summary all the ones that are essential to the author's development of his thesis.

2. The summary must be concise. Eliminate repetitions in your list, even if the author restates the same points. Your summary should be considerably shorter than the source. You are hoping to create an overview; therefore, you need not include every repetition or every supporting detail. Notice that the Russell summary excludes points one, four, and five on the list of notes: point one is included in the presentation of points two and three; point four is an example, one which is not essential to an understanding of the essay; and point five is not directly related to Russell's argument.

3. The summary must be coherent. It should make sense as a paragraph in its own right; it should not be taken directly from your list of notes and sound like a list of sentences that happen to be strung together in a paragraph format. In the summary of Russell's essay, a framework is established in the first two sentences, which present the two alternative views of the scientist's responsibility. The next sentence, which describes the four obstacles to scientific freedom of speech, illustrates the rearrangement of ideas that is characteristic of summary. While reviewing the list of notes, the summarizer has noticed that points six, seven, eight, and ten each refers to a different way in which scientific truth is often suppressed; she has therefore brought them together and lined them up in a parallel construction based on the repeated word "because." Finally, the last two sentences contain a restatement of Russell's thesis and point out that the obstacles to action are not as formidable as they seem.

4. The summary must be independent. You are not being asked to imitate or identify yourself with the author whom you are writing about. On the contrary, you are expected to maintain your own voice throughout the summary. Even as you are jotting down your list of notes, you should try to use your own words. In this way, you will be preparing your own presentation of the reading, instead of slavishly copying the author. While you want to make it clear that *you* are writing the summary, you should be careful not to create any misrepresentation or distortion by introducing comments or criticisms of your own. (Such distortion is most likely to occur when you strongly disagree with the material that you are summarizing.) Thus, it would not be acceptable to point out in your summary the dangers of making scientific secrets public, for that would be arguing with Russell. On the other hand, within certain limits it is acceptable to go beyond point-by-point summary, to suggest the author's implied intention, and, in a sense, to interpret the work's meaning for your reader. You might state, for example, that ours is an age which encourages inter-dependence and discourages independent action. While Russell does not say so specifically, in so many words, the assertion is certainly substantiated by the material in paragraphs eleven and twelve. Such interpretations have to be supported by evidence from the reading, and you must make it clear to your reader when you are summarizing directly from the text and when you are commenting on or inferring or explaining what is being summarized.

ASSIGNMENT 6

Summarize one of the following passages in one or a few sentences. If it seems appropriate to you, begin by making a preliminary list of points.

1.   Science begins with the observation of selected parts of nature. Although the scientist uses his mind to imagine ways in which the world might be constructed, he knows that only by looking at reality can he find out whether any of these ways correspond with reality. He rejects *authority* as an ultimate basis for truth. Though he is compelled by practical necessity to use facts and statements put forward by other workers, he reserves for himself the decision as to whether these other workers are reputable, whether their methods are good, and whether in any particular case the alleged facts are credible. He further considers it his privilege and sometimes his duty to repeat and test the work of others whenever he feels that this is desirable.

The collective judgment of scientists, in so far as there is substantial agreement, in spite of the individualistic, anti-authoritarian nature of science, is partial evidence for the validity of scientific methods. However, there are cases where universal agreement has been attained for an untruth, though this has more often been the case with sweeping generalizations than with the basic observations. Each generation of scientists has to decide for itself what it will believe, using the best available evidence and the most careful methods of interpretation. With the best luck in the world, some of these decisions will later be proved wrong, but there is no other way.

E. Bright Wilson, from *Introduction to Scientific Research*

2.   Some other characteristics of the present wave of terrorism must be mentioned: first of all, the function of the media. Terrorism aims at creating shock, and the argument of those who employ it is that the government or the society concerned will either be frightened into surrender on one or two critical matters or will be overturned and replaced by an authoritarian one which will "polarize" the issues at stake (the last motive has not, for obvious reasons, been put forward by a right-wing terrorist movement). So access to radio, press, television, is essential. If 200 people are killed in an obscure Mexican village, nobody in Mexico City will know of it, but if a bomb goes off in the Hilton Hotel, the papers will be full of it. Hence, according to one Latin American revolutionary, the change from rural guerrilla to urban terrorist in the 1960s.

On the whole, the media have not quite realized the essential role they play in terrorist tactics. As Professor Laqueur unkindly points out [in his book *Terrorism*], terrorists and newspapermen "share the assumption that those whose names make the headlines have power, that getting one's name on the front page is a major political achievement." Yet how many television producers or newspaper editors have really considered the fact that the terrorist act by itself is next to nothing, publicity is everything?

It is not only the press and television networks who play into the enemy's hands when they talk of minute terrorist organizations as if they were regular armies, or their leaders as if they had military ranks, their actions as if they had the force of law (EXECUTED! ran a recent London evening paper's headline after a terrorist murder); when the Pope recently offered himself in exchange for the hostages in the hijacked Lufthansa aeroplane, he was proclaiming the Catholic Church to be a mere branch of the media: was there nobody in the Vatican able to tell His Holiness that the real danger facing the terrorist is that of being ignored?

Hugh Thomas, "The Show of Violence," *TLS*,
18 November 1977

3.   The primary task of technology, it would seem, is to lighten the burden of work man has to carry in order to stay alive and develop his potential. It is easy enough to see that technology fulfils this purpose when we watch any particular piece of machinery at work—a computer, for instance, can do in seconds what it would take clerks or even mathematicians a very long time, if they can do it at all. It is more difficult to convince oneself of the truth of this simple proposition when one looks at whole societies. When I first began to travel the world, visiting rich and poor countries alike, I was tempted to formulate the first law of economics as follows: "The amount of real leisure a society enjoys tends to be in inverse proportion to the amount of labor-saving machinery it employs." It might be a good idea for the professors of economics to put this proposition into their examination papers and ask their pupils to discuss it. However that may be, the evidence is very strong indeed. If you go from easy-going England to, say, Germany or the United States, you find that people there live under much more strain than here. And if you move to a country like Burma, which is very near to the bottom of the league table of industrial progress, you find that people have an enormous amount of leisure really to enjoy themselves. Of course, as there is so much less labour-saving machinery to help them, they "accomplish" much less than we do; but that is a different point. The fact remains that the burden of living rests much more lightly on their shoulders than on ours.

The question of what technology actually does for us is therefore worthy of investigation. It obviously greatly reduces some kinds of work while it increases other kinds. The type of work which modern technology is most successful in reducing or even eliminating is skilful, productive work of human hands, in touch with real materials of one kind or another. In an advanced industrial society, such work has become exceedingly rare, and to make a decent living by doing such work has become virtually impossible. A great part of the modern neurosis may be due to this very fact; for the human being, defined by Thomas Aquinas as a being with brains and hands, enjoys nothing more than to be creatively, usefully, productively engaged with both his hands and his brains. Today, a person has to be wealthy to be able to enjoy this simple thing, this very great luxury: he has to be able to afford space and good tools; he has to be lucky enough to find a good teacher and plenty of free time to learn and practise. He really has to be rich enough not to need a job; for the number of jobs that would be satisfactory in these respects is very small indeed.

E. F. Schumacher, from *Small Is Beautiful*

3. Presenting Sources to Others

"I hate quotations. Tell me what you know."

Ralph Waldo Emerson (1849)

"By necessity, by proclivity, and by delight, we all quote."

Ralph Waldo Emerson (1876)

These quotations appear to be contradictory; but, in fact, they merely represent the development of one writer's understanding of his craft. Like Emerson in 1849, most writers hope to rely entirely upon what they know and to express their knowledge in their own words. But, as Emerson realized later, one rarely discovers an area of thought which has never before been explored. Someone has usually gone part of the way before; and it seems only common sense to make use of that person's discoveries. Assuming that most of your writing in college will be based directly or indirectly upon what you have read, you will need to acquire a working knowledge of the two standard methods of presenting other people's ideas to your readers: *quotation* and *paraphrase*.

BASIC QUOTATION

In academic writing, presenting the words of another writer is a basic method of supporting your own ideas. Quotation is a pivotal skill. Correct quotation tells your reader that you respect your sources, that you know how to distinguish between your own work and theirs, and that you will not make unacknowledged use of another writer's words and ideas, which is called *plagiarism*. Writers who understand when to quote understand the need to give credit to their sources both for borrowed ideas and for borrowed words. Appropriate quotation tells your readers that you know how often to quote and that you are not allowing your sources' words to dominate your writing. Quotations should not be used indiscriminately. Experienced writers hold quotation marks in reserve for those times when they think it essential to present the source's exact words.

Quoting for Support

You will often use part of another writer's work as evidence in support of one of your own points. To make sure that the evidence retains its full impact, you may decide to retain the author's original language, instead of putting the sentences in your own words. Very often, quoted material appears in an essay as an appeal to authority; the source being quoted is important enough or familiar enough with the subject (as in an eyewitness account) to make the original words worth quoting. For example, the only direct quotation in a *New York Times* article describing political and economic chaos in Bolivia presents the opinion of a government official:

> Even the Government acknowledges its shaky position. "The polity is unstable, capricious and chaotic," Adolfo Linares Arraya, Minister of Planning and Coordination, said. "The predominance of crisis situations has made the future unforeseeable."

The minister's words in themselves are not especially quotable; but his authority as representative of the government makes his words valuable evidence for the reporter's assessment of the Bolivian crisis.

Quoting Vivid Language

The wording of the source material may be so ingenious that you cannot express it in your own words, for the point would be lost. Quotation is often necessary for a sentence that is very compact or that relies on a striking image to make its point. For example, here is a paragraph from a review of a book about Vietnamese history.

> Not many nations have had such a history of scrapping: against Mongols and Chinese seeking to dominate them from the north, and to the south against weaker and more innocent peoples who stood in the way of the Vietnamese march to the rich Mekong Delta and the underpopulated land of Cambodia. Mr. Hodgkin [the author] quotes from a poem by a medieval Vietnamese hero: "By its tradition of defending the country/ the army is so powerful it can swallow the evening star."

The quotation adds authentic evidence to the reviewer's discussion and provides a memorable image for the reader.

Quoting Another Writer in Order to Comment on the Quotation

As part of your essay, you intend to analyze or comment upon a statement made by another writer. Your readers should have that writer's exact words in front of them if they are to get the full benefit of your commentary; you have to quote it in order to talk about it. Thus, when a reviewer writing about Philip Norman's biography of the Beatles wants to criticize the biographer's style, he has to supply a sample so that his readers can make up their own minds.

> Worst of all is the overwritten prologue, about John Lennon's death and its impact in Liverpool: "The ruined imperial city, its abandoned river, its tormented suburban plain, knew an anguish greater even than the recession and unemployment which have laid Merseyside waste under bombardments more deadly than Hitler's blitz." A moment's thought should have made Norman and his publishers realize that this sort of thing, dashed off in the heat of the moment, would quickly come to seem very embarrassing indeed.

Gaining Distance Through Quotation

Writers may use quotation in order to incorporate some carefully chosen evidence into their essays and, equally important, to distinguish between the writer of the essay and the writer being cited in the essay. There are a few less important reasons for using quotation marks—reasons which also involve this concept of the distance between a writer and his sources of information. For example, you may want to use quotation marks to indicate that a word or phrase is not in common or standard use. A phrase may be *obsolete*, having been dropped from current usage—the young man announced his intention of "cutting a rug" at the party that evening—or *slang*, not having yet been absorbed into standard English—she tried to "cop out" of doing her share of the work. In effect, the writer wants to both use the phrase and at the same time "cover" himself by signalling his awareness that the phrase is not quite right: he is distancing himself from his own vocabulary. It is usually better to take full responsibility for your choice of words and to avoid using slang or obsolete vocabulary, with or without quotation marks. But if the context requires such phrasing, you may use quotation marks to gain the necessary distance.

A different kind of distance can be achieved when quotation marks are used to suggest some form of irony: The actor was joined by his "constant companion." The quoted phrase is a familiar euphemism, a bland expression substituted for a more blunt term. Again, by placing it in quotation marks, the author is both calling attention to and distancing himself from the euphemism.

Quotation marks also serve as a means of dissociation for journalists who wish to avoid taking sides on an issue or making editorial comments.

> A fire that roared through a 120-year-old hotel and took at least 11 lives was the work of a "sick arsonist," the county coroner said today. Robert Jennings, the Wayne County coroner, said that he had told county officials that the building was a "fire trap."

The author of this article did not want the responsibility of attributing the fire to a "sick arsonist" or labeling the building a "fire trap"—at any rate, not until the findings of an investigation or a trial make the terminology unquestionably valid. Thus, he is careful not only to use quotation marks around certain phrases but to cite the precise source of the statement.

Direct Quotation: Separating the Quotation from Your Own Writing

The apparatus for quotation is two-fold: by *inserting quotation marks*, you distance yourself from certain words, as well as certain ideas, that appear in your writing; by *inserting a citation* containing the source's name, you give credit for both ideas and words to the original author.

Citation	*Quotation*
Somerset Maugham observed,	"To write simply is as difficult as to be good."

The simplest way to quote is to combine the citation (written by you) with the words to be quoted (exactly as they were said or written by your source). This method—called direct quotation—merely joins together or juxtaposes two quite separate statements, with punctuation (comma or colon) bridging the gap.

> St. Paul declared, "It is better to marry than to burn."

> In his first epistle to the Corinthians, St. Paul addressed lust: "It is better to marry than to burn."

In these forms of direct quotation, the quoted words are *not* fully integrated into the grammatical structure of your sentence. The comma or colon and the capital letter at the beginning of the quoted sentence, which are both separating devices, make clear that two voices are at work in the sentence. Thus, in general, you should choose this kind of direct quotation when you want to establish some distance between yourself and the quoted words. (There are many reasons for wanting to gain this distance; an obvious example would be your own disagreement with the quotation.) The colon is used less frequently than the comma, partly because it usually follows a formal introductory signal—a clause that can stand alone as a complete sentence. As such, it separates a complete idea of your own from a complementary or supporting idea in your source.

Direct and Indirect Quotation: Running Quotations into Your Sentences

You can construct a much more integrated sentence if you regard the quoted statement as the direct object of the verb:

```
St. Paul declared that "it is better to marry than to
burn."
```

In this kind of quotation, there is no signal for the reader to separate citation from quotation—no comma or colon, no capital letter; only the quotation marks indicate the presence of someone else's words. The very ordinary conjunction "that" bridges a gap which hardly exists. The effect is very smooth, and the reader's attention is not distracted from the flow of sentences. But because the complete integration of the quotation tends to blur the distinction between writer and source, one must be careful to avoid confusion. Look, for example, at the ways of quoting this first-person sentence, which was originally spoken (and not written) by a motorist: "I hate all pedestrians."

```
The motorist said, "I hate all pedestrians."

The motorist said that "I hate all pedestrians."
```

The first method, using punctuation, works well and requires no alteration in the original sentence. But in the second version, using "that," the original wording does not quite fit: the first-person "I" conflicts with the third-person "motorist"; one wonders who "I" is—the motorist or the writer! The present-tense "hate" also conflicts with the past-tense "said," and "hate" must be turned into "hated." But once the person and the tense of the original statement have been altered for the sake of clarity and consistency, only two words—"all pedestrians"—are actually being quoted:

```
The motorist said that she hated "all pedestrians."
```

If you decide not to put quotation marks around the two words taken from the original source, you are using *indirect quotation*, which is not true quotation:

```
The motorist said that she hated all pedestrians.
```

In indirect quotation, you report rather than quote what has been said.

Choosing Between the Three Kinds of Quotation

Direct quotation, without the use of "that," is probably the most appropriate method of presenting the information above. The absence of quotation marks in the indirect quotation might in some cases lead to confusion: if one were collecting evidence for a libel suit, quotation marks would be necessary to indicate that the motorist was responsible for the precise wording. *As a rule, the writer has the obligation to insert quotation marks when using the exact words of his sources, whether written or oral.* When the phrasing of a quotation is especially apt or well-known or unique, placing quotation marks around the original words is especially important.

Direct quotation:

```
Robert Ingersoll proclaimed: "I am the inferior of any man
whose rights I trample underfoot."
```

Indirect quotation:

```
Robert Ingersoll proclaimed that he was the inferior of
any man whose rights he trampled underfoot.
```

The indirect quotation conveys no clear indication of exactly who phrased this sentence. (Changing "I" to "he" and the present to the past tense does not constitute rephrasing; the basic wording of the sentence remains the same.) To imply, as this sentence could, that the wording is the writer's, not Ingersoll's, is dishonest. Thus, indirect quotation is not a method often used by academic writers. If one of the two forms of direct quotation does not seem appropriate, then the writer must invent his own phrasing to communicate the source's original statement.

As for the two kinds of direct quotation, most of the time there is no danger of inconsistency of person or tense, and you can choose between the "separated" and "integrated" versions:

```
Thomas Mann writes, "A man's dying is more the survivors'
affair than his own."

Thomas Mann wrote that "a man's dying is more the
survivors' affair than his own."
```

Both sentences do justice to this quotation. Which you choose depends upon the degree of distance that you wish to achieve.

Notice that the citation of the first sentence is in the present tense. It is generally agreed that statements which are not affected by time can be referred to in the present tense, even if the author is no longer alive. It is often useful to introduce a quotation by using the present tense. When you are devoting part of your own essay to a "discussion" with another writer, you may prefer to conduct the discussion on a common ground of time. If you use the past tense in citing statements by several writers from several different centuries, then you may have to "place" these authors in time by inserting dates as background for your readers, thus creating a cluttered impression. Instead, use the present tense (often called the *historical present*), unless your analysis of the issue in some way depends on the different historical perspective of each writer.

The Punctuation of Direct Quotations

You have already learned about punctuating the beginning of the quotation: in the first type of direct quotation, the citation is followed by a comma or a colon, while quotations preceded by "that" are introduced by no punctuation at all. There is a tendency to forget this second point and to include an unnecessary comma:

> Stendahl believed that, "to describe happiness is to diminish it."

Remember that there should be no barriers between citation and quotation, and you will not be tempted to put in that divisive comma.

There is no easy way of remembering the proper sequence of punctuation for closing a quotation. The procedure has been determined by conventional and arbitrary agreement, for the convenience of printers. Although other countries abide by other conventions, in the United States the following rules apply—and *there are no exceptions*.

1. All periods and commas are placed inside the terminal quotation marks. It does not matter whether the period belongs to *your* sentence or to the quoted sentence: it must appear before the marks. This is the most important rule, and the one most often ignored. (Don't resort to ambiguous devices like ")

> P. T. Barnum is reputed to have said that "there's a sucker born every minute."

> P. T. Barnum is reputed to have said that "there's a sucker born every minute," and Barnum's circuses undertook to entertain each and every one.

Notice that, in the second example, the comma at the end of the quotation really belongs to the framework sentence, not the quotation itself; nevertheless, it goes inside the marks.

2. All semi-colons, colons, and dashes belong after the quotation marks. They should be regarded as the punctuation for your sentence, and not for the quotation.

> George Santayana wrote that "those who cannot remember the past are condemned to repeat it"; today, we are in danger of forgetting the lessons of history.

Occasionally, when a semi-colon or a colon or (most likely) a dash appears at the end of the material to be quoted, you will decide to include the punctuation in the quotation; in that case, the punctuation should be placed inside the marks.

3. Question marks and exclamation points are sometimes placed inside the quotation marks and sometimes placed outside. If the quotation itself is a question or an exclamation, the mark or point goes inside the quotation marks; if your own sentence is an exclamation or a question, the mark or point goes outside a quotation coming at the very end of your sentence.

> It was General Sherman in 1864 who signalled: "Hold the fort! I am coming!"

> Do you agree with Dumas that "woman inspires us to great things and prevents us from achieving them"?

> Sigmund Freud's writings occasionally reveal a remarkable lack of insight: "The great question that has never been answered, and which I have not yet been able to answer despite my thirty years of research into the feminine soul, is: What does a woman want?"

> Freud was demonstrating remarkably little insight when he wrote, "What does a woman want?" citing his "thirty years of research into the feminine soul"!

To construct a sentence that ends logically in two question marks (or exclamation points) is possible: one for the quotation and one for your own sentence. In that case, one is enough—and, by convention, it should be placed *inside* the marks:

> What did Freud mean when he asked, "What does a woman want?"

These rules apply only to the quotation of complete sentences or reasonably long phrases. Whether it is a quotation or an obsolete, slang, or ironic reference, a single word or a brief phrase should be fully integrated into your sentence, without being preceded or followed by commas.

```
Winston Churchill's reference to "blood, sweat and tears"
rallied the English to prepare for war.
```

Interrupted Quotations

Sometimes it is desirable to break up a long quotation or to achieve variety in your sentence patterns by interrupting a quotation and placing the citation in the middle.

```
"I do not mind lying," wrote Samuel Butler, "but I hate
inaccuracy."
```

Notice that you have converted Butler's statement into two separate quotations, and therefore you need to use *four* sets of quotation marks: two introductory and two terminal. The citation is joined to the quotation by a comma on either side. The danger point is the beginning of the second half of the quotation: if you forget to use the marks there, then you are failing to distinguish your words from Butler's.

Double Quotations

When a quotation incorporates a second quotation, you must use two sets of quotation marks, double and single, to help your reader to distinguish between the two separate sources.

```
Goethe declared: " 'Know thyself?' If I knew myself, I'd
run away."
```

The same procedure is used even when there is no author's name to be cited.

```
A Yiddish proverb states that " 'for example' is not
proof."
```

EXERCISE 21

A. Correct the errors in the following sentences:
   1. "Beggars should be abolished, said Friedrich Nietzsche. "It annoys one to give to them, and it annoys one not to give to them".

2. Thoreau warned his readers to, "Beware of all enterprises that require new clothes."

3. The candidate said that, "He was not able to comment at this time."

4. "Is life worth living"? Samuel Butler asked? This is a question for an embryo, not for a man".

5. According to Dr. Johnson; "a man is in general better pleased when he has a good dinner upon his table than when his wife talks Greek.

6. Logan Pearsall Smith declared: "How awful to reflect that what people say of us is true"!

7. In Proust's view, "Everybody calls "clear" those ideas which have the same degree of confusion as his own".

8. Chesterton believed that "All men are ordinary men"; the extraordinary men are those who know it."

9. It's difficult for me to study at home, since there's so much noise and distraction. My sister says that "I should go to a community center to study where there are several rooms that I can use."

B. Use quotations from the group below in order to write three sentences:

> choose one quotation and write a sentence that introduces a direct quotation with separation;
> choose a second quotation and write a sentence that introduces a direct quotation with integration;
> choose a third quotation and write a sentence that interrupts a quotation with a citation in the middle.

1. Woman would be more charming if one could fall into her arms without falling into her hands. (Ambrose Bierce)

2. Imprisoned in every fat man, a thin one is wildly signaling to be let out. (Cyril Connolly)

3. I hear much of people's calling out to punish the guilty, but very few are concerned to clear the innocent. (Daniel Defoe)

4. I do not believe that civilization will be wiped out in a war fought with the atomic bomb. Perhaps two-thirds of the people of the earth might be killed, but enough men capable of thinking, and enough books, would be left to start again, and civilization would be restored. (Albert Einstein)

5. There is always a best way of doing everything, if it be to boil an egg. Manners are the happy ways of doing things. (Ralph Waldo Emerson)

6. All men's misfortunes spring from their hatred of being alone. (Jean de La Bruyère)

7. There is more felicity on the far side of baldness than young men can possibly imagine. (Logan Pearsall Smith)

8. Wars are not "acts of God." They are caused by man, by man-made institutions, by the way in which man has organized his society. What man has made, man can change. (Fred M. Vinson)

The Need for Exactitude in Quotation

Quoting is not collaborative. The author spent time and effort to work out the original wording. If you value that wording enough to want to quote it, you should respect the integrity of the sentence and leave it intact. Don't make minor changes or carelessly leave words out, but faithfully transcribe the exact words, the exact spelling, and the exact punctuation that you find in the original.

Original:

Those who corrupt the public mind are just as evil as those who steal from the public purse.

Adlai Stevenson

Inexact quotation:

Adlai Stevenson believed that "those who act against the public interest are just as evil as those who steal from the public purse."

Exact quotation:

Adlai Stevenson believed that "those who corrupt the public mind are just as evil as those who steal from the public purse."

Even if you notice an error (or what you regard as an error), you must nevertheless copy the original wording accurately. Archaic spelling should be retained, as well as regional or national spelling conventions:

One of Heywood's Proverbes tells us that "a new brome swepeth clean."

Standards of acceptable punctuation have also altered; if a comma or semi-colon looks incorrect, remember that it may be correct for the *author's* era or locality.

Dr. Johnson believed that "it is better to live rich, than to die rich."

To contemporary eyes, the comma breaking into the flow of such a short sentence seems intrusive; but it is not the reader's place to edit Dr. Johnson's eighteenth-century prose.

The need to include the precise punctuation of the original, however, applies only to the material that gets placed *inside* quotation marks. The punctuation immediately preceding or following the quoted words in the original text may be omitted and, indeed, should be omitted if the quotation will thereby fit more smoothly into your sentence.

Original:

It is better to be making the news than taking it; to be an actor than a critic.

Winston Churchill

Incorrect quotation:

Churchill observed, "It is better to be making the news than taking it;".

Correct quotation:

Churchill observed, "It is better to be making the news than taking it."

You do not have to assume the blame if there are errors of syntax, punctuation, or spelling in the material that you are quoting. A conventional device can be used to point out such errors and inform the reader that the mistake was made, not by you, but by the author whom you are quoting. The Latin word *sic* (meaning "thus") is placed in square brackets and inserted immediately after the error. The [sic] signals that the quotation was "thus" and that you, the writer, were aware of the error, which was not the result of your own carelessness in transcribing the quotation.

As you will learn in the discussion of brackets (p. 126), it is possible to deal with many errors by making the correction yourself. But, since such corrections also have to be in brackets, it is often simpler and less awkward to let the error stand and to use [sic].

In the following example, [sic] calls attention to an error in subject-verb agreement.

Richard Farson points out that "increased understanding and concern has [sic] not been coupled with increased rights."

TAILORING QUOTATIONS TO FIT YOUR WRITING

There are several devices for making corrections and changes in quotations, so that the quoted material will fit in naturally with your own sentences. Like [sic], these devices are *conventional*: you cannot improvise; you must follow generally accepted rules. Usually, these conventional rules require you to inform your reader that changes are being made; in other words, to maintain the distinction between your wording and the author's. The first way of altering quotations, however, does not require identification and depends entirely on how and where the quotation fits into your sentence. When your citation ends in "that," you make the capitalization of the first word of the quotation conform to its grammatical position in your sentence: except in the case of proper nouns and the pronoun "I," the first letter will be small, whether or not it is a capital in the original. On the other hand, when your citation ends in a comma or a colon, the first letter of the quotation will be large, whether or not it is a capital in the original.

```
The poet Frost wrote that "good fences make good
neighbors."

The poet Frost wrote, "Good fences make good neighbors."
```

As a rule, it is not necessary to indicate to your readers that you have altered a letter from small to large, or from large to small.

Using Ellipses

It is permissible to *delete* words from part of a quotation, provided that you use a symbol to indicate to the reader that there is an omission. Once aware that there is a difference between your version and the original, any reader who wants to check the omitted portion can consult the original source. Your condensed version is as accurate as the original; it is just shorter. But you must remember to insert the conventional symbol for deletion, three spaced dots, called an *ellipsis*.

> It is not true that suffering ennobles the character; happiness does that sometimes, but suffering, for the most part, makes men petty and vindictive.
>
> W. Somerset Maugham

```
Maugham believes, "It is not true that suffering ennobles
the character; . . . suffering, for the most part, makes
men petty and vindictive."
```

Notice that the semi-colon is retained, to provide terminal punctuation for the first part of the quotation. Notice also that the three dots are spaced equally. (The dots *must* be three—not two or a dozen.)

If you wish to delete the end of a quotation, and the ellipsis coincides with the end of your sentence, you must use the three dots, plus a fourth to signify the period.

```
Maugham believes, "It is not true that suffering ennobles
the character; happiness does that sometimes. . . ."
```

The first dot is placed immediately after the last letter. The sentence ends with quotation marks, as usual, with the marks placed *after* the dots, not before.

The three dots can serve as a link between two non-continuous quotations from the same paragraph, representing the deletion of an entire sentence or two, but *only* if the two sentences that you are quoting are fairly near each other in the original. Ellipses cannot cover a gap of more than a few sentences. If you do use ellipses to bridge one or more sentences, use only *one* set of quotation marks. The full quotation, with an ellipsis in the middle, is technically accurate and still continuous—a single quotation—even though it is not complete. When an ellipsis is used following a quoted complete sentence, the period of the quoted sentence is retained so that a total of four dots is used, as in the following example.

> In one sense there is no death. The life of a soul on earth lasts beyond his departure. You will always feel that life touching yours, that voice speaking to you, that spirit looking out of other eyes, talking to you in the familiar things he touched, worked with, loved as familiar friends. He lives on in your life and in the lives of all others that knew him.
>
> Angelo Patri

```
Angelo Patri observes that "in one sense there is no
death. The life of a soul on earth lasts beyond his
departure. . . . He lives on in your life and in the lives
of all others that knew him."
```

Misusing Ellipses

Ellipses should be used to make a quotation fit more smoothly into your own sentence. It is especially useful when you are working with a long passage which contains several separate points that you wish to quote. Ellipses, however, were not intended as a device to condense long, tedious quotations or to replace summary and paraphrase. If all that you want to quote is a brief extract from a lengthy passage, then simply quote that portion and ignore the surrounding material. An ellipsis is poorly used when it calls attention to itself. For a reader to wade through a sea of dots can be very distracting.

The meaning of the original quotation must always be exactly preserved, despite the deletion represented by the ellipsis.

> As long as there are sovereign nations possessing great power, war is inevitable.
>
> Albert Einstein

To simplify Einstein's words might be tempting:

```
Einstein believes that ". . . war is inevitable."
```

But it would not be accurate to suggest that Einstein believed in the inevitability of war, under all circumstances, without qualifications. To extract only a portion of this statement is to over-simplify and thus to falsify the evidence.

Another common consequence of misapplied ellipses is a mangled sentence. Deleting words from a quotation can distort and destroy its syntax and structure.

> God created woman. And boredom did indeed cease from that moment—but many other things ceased as well! Woman was God's second mistake.
>
> Friedrich Nietzsche

```
Women are certainly exciting. As Nietzsche declares, "God
created woman . . . second mistake."
```

Altering Quotations: Brackets

Brackets have a quite opposite function: ellipses signifies omission; brackets signify addition or alteration. You have already seen how to use brackets with *sic*, which is in fact a quoter's addition to and comment on the quoted material. When you wish to explain a vague word, replace a confusing phrase, suggest an antecedent, correct an error in a quotation, or adjust a quotation to fit your own writing, you insert the information *inside* the quotation, placing it in square brackets. Brackets are not the same as parentheses. Parentheses are not suitable for this purpose, for the quotation itself might already have a parenthetical statement inside it, and the reader could not be sure which parentheses contained the author's insertion and which contained yours. Instead, brackets, a relatively unusual form of punctuation, were chosen as the conventional symbol for inserted material.

The most common reason for using brackets is the clarification of an obscure word, frequently a pronoun. You may, for example, choose to quote only the last portion of a passage, and an important antecedent may be omitted:

> Man lives *by* habits, indeed, but what he lives *for* is thrills and excitement.
>
> William James

```
William James argues that "what he [man] lives for is
thrills and excitement."
```

You may also remove "he" entirely and replace it with *man*—in brackets:

```
"What [man] lives for is thrills and excitement."
```

The brackets will indicate that there has been a substitution. But, unless the presentation of both wordings seems very awkward and clumsy, it is better to quote the original as well as the clarification in brackets and thus provide your reader with all your source's words.

Brackets can also be used to complete a thought that has been obscured by the omission of an earlier sentence:

> A well-trained sensible family doctor is one of the most valuable assets in a community. . . . Few men live lives of more devoted self-sacrifice.
>
> Sir William Osler

```
Osler had great respect for his less celebrated
colleagues: "Few men live lives of more devoted self-
sacrifice [than good family doctors]."
```

Here, the quotation marks are placed *after* the brackets, even though the quoted material ends after the word "self-sacrifice." The explanatory material inside the brackets is considered part of the quotation, even though it is in the quoter's own words.

The Limitations of Brackets

Comments in brackets should be restricted to *brief* explanations; one might, for example, want to add an important date or name as essential background information. Whatever is inside the brackets should fit smoothly into the syntax of the quotation and should not be a distraction for the reader. Do not use brackets to state the obvious:

> Heinrich Heine took a cynical view of the marriage
> ceremony: "The music of a wedding procession always
> reminds me [Heine] of the music of soldiers going into
> battle."

Do not use brackets as a means of carrying on a running dialogue with
the author you are quoting:

> Sophie Tucker suggests that up to the age of eighteen "a
> girl needs good parents. [This is true for men, too.] From
> eighteen to thirty-five, she needs good looks. [Good looks
> aren't that essential anymore.] From thirty-five to fifty-
> five, she needs a good personality. [I disagree because
> personality is important at any age.] From fifty-five on,
> she needs good cash."

EXERCISE 22

1. Choose one of the quotations below. By using ellipsis, incorporate a
   portion of the quotation into a sentence of your own; remember to
   include the author's name in the citation.
2. Choose a second quotation. Incorporate a portion of the quotation
   into another sentence of your own; use the insertion of words in brackets to clarify one or more of the quoted words.

   A. Until you have become really, in actual fact, a brother to every one,
      brotherhood will not come to pass. No sort of scientific teaching,
      no kind of common interest, will ever teach men to share property
      and privileges with equal consideration for all. Every one will think
      his share too small and they will always be envying, complaining,
      and attacking one another. (Fyodor Dostoyevsky)
   B. Man, biologically considered, and whatever else he may be in the
      bargain, is simply the most formidable of all the beasts of prey, and,
      indeed, the only one that preys systematically on its own species.
      (William James)
   C. All propaganda has to be popular and has to adapt its spiritual
      level to the perception of the least intelligent of those towards
      whom it intends to direct itself. (Adolf Hitler)
   D. I not only "don't choose to run" but I don't even want to leave a
      loophole in case I am drafted, so I won't "choose." I will say "won't
      run" no matter how bad the country will need a comedian by that
      time. (Will Rogers)

E. I do not mean that there is any lack of wealthy individuals in the United States; I know of no country, indeed, where the love of money has taken stronger hold on the affections of men and where a profounder contempt is expressed for the theory of the permanent equality of property. But wealth circulates with inconceivable rapidity, and experience shows that it is rare to find two succeeding generations in the full enjoyment of it. (Alexis de Tocqueville)

CITING THE AUTHOR'S NAME

At the time of *first* reference, refer to the author by using his or her full name—without Mr. or Miss or Mrs. After that, cite the last name only. (If, however, there is a sizable gap between references to the same author, or if the names of several other authors intervene, you may wish to repeat the full name and remind your reader of the earlier citation(s).)

First reference:

```
John Stuart Mill writes, "The opinion which it is
attempted to suppress by authority may possibly be true."
```

Second reference:

```
Mill continues to point out that "all silencing of
discussion is an assumption of infallibility."
```

By citing the last name only, you are conforming to conventional usage, which discourages overly familiar and distracting references like "John says," "JSM says," "JS says," or "Mr. Mill says." You may, however, at first reference include the title of the work from which the quotation was taken:

```
In On Liberty, John Stuart Mill writes . . .
```

Avoid the habit of referring to the author twice in the same citation, once by name and once by pronoun: the repetition is tedious and unnecessary.

```
In John Stuart Mill's On Liberty, he writes . . .
```

Finally, unless you genuinely do not know the author's name, use it! There is no point in being coy, even for the sake of variety:

```
A famous man once said: "If you strike a child, take care
that you strike it in anger. . . . A blow in cold blood
neither can nor should be forgiven."
```

Your guessing game will only irritate readers who are not aware that this famous man was George Bernard Shaw.

Choosing the Introductory Verb

The citation leading up to the quotation represents an important link between your thoughts and those of your source. The introductory verb can tell your reader something about your reasons for presenting the quotation and its context in the work that you're taking it from. Will you choose "J. S. Mill says," or "J. S. Mill writes," or "J. S. Mill thinks," or "J. S. Mill feels"? Those are the most commonly chosen introductory verbs—so common that they become boring if they are used again and again. Try to get away from these stereotyped verbs, at least occasionally. (And, since the senses are not directly involved in writing, avoid "feels" entirely.) Here is a list of interesting possibilities:

insists	declares	suggests
argues	adds	proposes
concludes	explains	finds
states	agrees	continues
establishes	compares	disagrees
maintains	observes	notes

Of course, once you get away from the all-purpose category of "says" or "writes," you have to remember that verbs do not have interchangeable meanings; you must choose the verb that best suits your purpose. The citation should prepare the reader for the quotation by suggesting in advance the relationship between your own ideas (in the previous sentence) and the statement that you are about to cite. You must examine the quotation before writing the citation and define for yourself the spirit in which the author is making this point: is it being asserted forcefully? Use "argues" or "declares" or "insists." Is the statement being offered only as a possibility? Use "suggests" or "proposes" or "finds." Does the statement immediately follow a previous reference? Use "continues" or "adds." For the sake of clarity, the introductory verb can easily be expanded into a slightly longer phrase:

```
X is aware that . . .
X stresses the opposite view:
X provides one answer to the question:
X makes the same point as Y:
```

But make sure that the antecedent for the "view" or the "question" or the "point" is quite clearly expressed in the previous sentences.

Varying Your Sentence Patterns

Even if you meticulously choose a different verb for each quotation, the effect of the author's name-introductory verb-quotation combination can become repetitious and tiresome after a while. One way to achieve some variety is to place the name of the source in a less prominent position, tucked into the quotation instead of calling attention to itself. You can interrupt the quotation by *placing the citation in the middle.*

> "Knowledge is of two kinds," points out Dr. Johnson; "we know a subject ourselves, or we know where we can find information on it."

Notice that the verb and the name can be placed in reverse order when the citation follows the beginning of the quotation.

One citation is quite enough. There is no need to inform your reader twice, back to back, as does this repetitive example:

> "The only prize much cared for by the powerful is power," states Oliver Wendell Holmes. He concludes, "The prize of the general . . . is command."

Nor should you interrupt the quotation at the wrong point. The citation in the following sentence should be placed at a more logical break in syntax:

> "The only prize much cared for," states Oliver Wendell Holmes, "by the powerful is power."

Another way of avoid the monotonous "X says that . . ." pattern is by *phrasing the citation as a subordinate clause or a phrase.* Instead of

> Robert Ingersoll writes, "I am the inferior of any man whose rights I trample underfoot."

try:

> According to Robert Ingersoll, "[he was] the inferior of any man whose rights [he trampled] underfoot."

> As Ingersoll argues, an individual is "the inferior of any man whose rights [he] tramples underfoot."

> In Ingersoll's view, one is "the inferior of any man whose rights [one violates]."

In your quest for variety, however, avoid placing the citation *after* the quotation; it generally detracts from the force of the statement to have the author's name at the end, especially if the citation is pretentiously or awkwardly phrased:

> "I am the inferior of any man whose rights I trample
> underfoot," as quoted from the writings of Robert
> Ingersoll.

Two rules, then, should govern your choice of citation: don't be too fancy, but be precise!

PRESENTING AN EXTENDED QUOTATION

Occasionally, you may have reason to present an extended quotation, a single extract from the same source which runs four typewritten lines or more. For long quotations, set off the quoted passage by indenting the entire quotation on the left. Introduce an extended quotation with a colon.

1. Start each line of the quotation ten spaces from the left-hand margin; stop each line at your normal right-hand margin.
2. Triple-space before and after the quotation. Double-space *within* the quotation. (Some instructors prefer single-spacing for extended quotations.)
3. Do not use quotation marks to signify the beginning and end of the quoted passage; the indented margin (and the introductory citation) will tell your readers that you are quoting.

Here is an example of an extended quotation:

> Although he worked "hard as hell" all winter,
> Fitzgerald had difficulty finishing The Great Gatsby. In a
> letter to Maxwell Perkins, his editor at Scribner's, he
> wrote on April 10, 1924:
>
> > While I have every hope & plan of finishing my
> > novel in June . . . even [if] it take me 10 times
> > that long I cannot let it go unless it has the
> > very best I'm capable of in it or even as I feel
> > sometimes better than I'm capable of. It is only
> > in the last four months that I've realized how
> > much I've—well, almost deteriorated. . . . What
> > I'm trying to say is just that . . . at last, or

```
at last for the first time in years, I'm doing
the best I can.
```

THE QUOTATION AS PART OF YOUR PARAGRAPH

Now that you understand how to present the words of others with accuracy and appropriate acknowledgment, you must also learn to subordinate what you are quoting to the larger purpose of your paragraph or essay. Here are some suggestions for keeping quotations in their proper place.

1. *Use quotation sparingly.* If quotation seems to be your primary purpose in writing, your reader will assume that you have nothing of your own to say. Thus, unless you have a clear reason for doing so, unless you are intending to analyze a quotation, or you are sure that the wording of the quotation is essential to your argument, or you simply cannot say it in your own words, don't quote at all. In any case, do not quote repeatedly within a single paragraph.

2. *Use quotations in the body of your paragraph, not at the very beginning as a replacement for the topic sentence.* The topic sentence should establish—in your own words—what you are about to explain or prove. The quotation will normally appear later in the paragraph as supporting evidence.

3. *Let the quotation make its point; don't follow it with a word-for-word translation of its meaning.* Once you have presented a quotation, it is not necessary to provide another version of the same idea in your own words, for you would be thereby repeating the same point twice. By all means, follow up a quotation with an *explanation* of its relevance to your paragraph; but make sure that your commentary does more than echo the quotation.

In the following example, the quotation used in the development of the paragraph assumes a position that is no more or less important than any of the other supporting sentences. Notice that the inclusion of the quotation adds interest to the paragraph because of the shift in tone and the shift to a sharper, narrower focus.

```
    Some parents insist on allowing their children to
learn through experience. Once a child has actually
performed a dangerous action and realized its
consequences, he will always remember the circumstances
```

and the possible ill effects. Yvonne Realle illustrates
the adage that experience is the best teacher by
describing a boy who was slapped just as he reached for a
hot iron. The child, not realizing that he might have been
burned, had no idea why he had been slapped. The observer
noted that "if he had learned by experience, if he'd
suffered some discomfort in the process, then he'd know
enough to avoid the iron next time." In the view of
parents like Yvonne Realle, letting a child experiment
with his environment will result in a stronger lesson than
slapping or scolding the child for trying to explore his
surroundings.

EXERCISE 23

A. The first paragraph below is taken from a student essay entitled "Starting the Smoking Habit." The second passage comes from *When and
How to Stop Smoking* by Eustace Chesser. Choose one appropriate
supporting quotation from Chesser; decide where to place it in the
student paragraph; and insert the quotation correctly and smoothly
into the paragraph. Remember to lead into the quotation by mentioning the source.

Student paragraph:

Some children also smoke because they think they are
nothing in life. This act, they imagine, will give them a
more positive view of themselves, making them feel big and
tough and superior. For this purpose, they start to
imitate their parents and famous people by smoking. When
they light up cigarettes, they feel that they are being
admired and they also feel less rejected by adults. But
this feeling of acceptance is only an illusion, enabling
them briefly to break away from the reality of childhood.

Source:

The schoolboy is usually initiated by his companions. They are in fact
rebelling against their status as juveniles, for whom smoking is prohibited. To defy the ban is one way of experiencing the grown-up pleasures
which are forbidden to them.

The cigarette is a symbol of the mysterious adult world from which
they are excluded. While they are smoking they feel they are behaving
like grown-ups instead of children, and the very secrecy establishes a
bond with their smoking companions. They discover the value of to-
bacco as a social asset. This is undoubtedly one reason for its popularity.

B. The first paragraph below is taken from a student essay titled "The Compulsive Gambler." The second passage comes from *The Psychology of Gambling* by Edmund Bergler. Choose one appropriate supporting quotation from Bergler; decide where to place it in the student paragraph; and insert the quotation correctly and smoothly into the paragraph. Remember to lead into the quotation by mentioning the source.

Student paragraph:

```
     One obvious reason for gambling is to make money.
Because some gamblers are lucky when they play, they never
want to stop. Even when quite a lot of money has been
lost, they go on, assuming that they can get rich through
gambling. Once a fortune is made, they will feel really
powerful, free of all dependency and responsibilities.
Instead, in most cases, gambling becomes a daily routine
which must be performed. There is no freedom, no escape.
```

Source:

Every gambler gives the impression of a man who has signed a contract with Fate, stipulating that persistence must be rewarded. With that imaginary contract in his pocket, he is beyond the reach of all logical objection and argument.

The result of this pathologic optimism is that the true gambler never stops when he is winning, for he is convinced that he must win more and more. Inevitably, he loses. He does not consider his winnings the result of chance; to him they are a down payment on that contract he has with Fate which guarantees that he will be a permanent winner. This inability to stop while fortune is still smiling is one of the strongest arguments against the earnest assumption, common to all gamblers, that one can get rich through gambling.

ASSIGNMENT 7

1. Choose one of the following topics. Each has been narrowed down to a specific question that can be answered adequately in a single paragraph.
   A. topic: child-rearing
      question: Should children be allowed to make their own mistakes?
   B. topic: child-rearing
      question: What's the advantage of using firm discipline in child-rearing?
   C. topic: child-rearing
      question: What are some ways to bridge the gap between parents and children?

2. Ask someone you know to comment briefly on the question you have chosen, offering a suggestion or an example. Write down any part of the comment that you think might be worth quoting; transcribe the words accurately; and then show the statement to your source for confirmation of its accuracy. Make sure that you have the name properly spelled. If the first person you ask does not provide you with a suitable quotation, try someone else.

3. Answer your own question in a single paragraph of four to eight sentences, limiting the paragraph's scope to ideas which can be clearly developed in such a brief space. The paragraph as a whole should express *your* views, not those of your source. Try not to quote in the first or second sentence of your paragraph. Choose a *single* quotation from your source and integrate it into the development of your paragraph, using proper punctuation and citation and (if necessary) ellipses and brackets. If your source agrees with you, use the quotation as support. If your source disagrees, answer the objection in your own way. With your paragraph, hand in the sheet on which you originally wrote down the quotation.

QUOTING WITHOUT QUOTATION MARKS: PLAGIARISM

Quoting without quotation marks is called plagiarism. Even if you were to cite the source's name somewhere on your page, a quotation without marks would still be considered a plagiarism. *Plagiarism is the unacknowledged use of another writer's words or ideas, and the only way to acknowledge that you are using someone else's actual words is with citation and quotation marks.* Chapter 10 discusses plagiarism in detail, but what is important here is that you understand that literate people consider plagiarism to be a crime against property; that, if you plagiarize, you will never learn to write; and that plagiarists eventually get caught.

Every writer, professional or amateur, has a characteristic style or voice, which readers quickly learn to accept as the medium through which information or ideas are being conveyed. With time, the writer's voice becomes familiar and unobtrusive, so that the reader only notices that there *is* a voice when the style shifts. Then, suddenly, there is a new style and a new voice, to be first noticed, then accepted and ignored again. But when there are frequent quotations, the reader has to adjust to a series of shifts in tone and a series of strange voices. The quotation marks themselves serve as visual barriers, breaking up the paragraph into separate compartments. Removing the quotation marks does not solve the problem. Even when there is no punctuation to call attention to the shift in tone, a jarring sense of discontinuity occurs once alien voices are introduced into a characteristic style of writing.

The mixture of several distinctive voices usually suggests to an experienced reader that the work is flawed, poorly integrated, and probably plagiarized. Plagiarized essays are often identified in this way. Teachers have a well-developed awareness of style and are trained to recognize inconsistencies and awkward transitions. The revealing clue is the patched-together effect, which some teachers call a "mosaic." The next exercise should help to improve your own perception of shifting voices and should encourage you to rely on your own characteristic style as the dominant voice in everything that you write.

EXERCISE 24

The following paragraphs contain several plagiarized sentences. Examine the language and tone of each sentence, as well as the continuity of the entire paragraph. Then underline the plagiarized sentences.

The Beatles' music in the early years was just plain melodic. It had a nice beat to it. The Beatles were simple lads, writing simple songs simply to play to screaming fans on one-night stands. There was no deep, inner meaning to the lyrics. Their songs included many words like I, and me, and you. As the years went by, the Beatles' music became more poetic. Sergeant Pepper is a stupefying collage of music, words, background noises, cryptic utterances, orchestral effects, hallucenogenic bells, farmyard sounds, dream sequences, social observations, and apocalpytic vision, all masterfully blended together on a four-track tape machine over nine agonizing and expensive months. Their music was beginning to be more philosophical, with a deep, inner, more secret meaning. After it was known that they took drugs, references to drugs were seen in many songs. The "help" in Ringo's "A Little Help from My Friends" was said to have meant pot. The songs were poetic, mystical; they emerged from a self-contained world of bizarre carnival colors; they spoke in a language and a musical idiom all their own.

Before the Civil War, minstrelsy spread quickly across America. Americans all over the country enjoyed minstrelsy because it reflected something of their own point of view. For instance, Negro plantation hands, played usually by white actors in blackface, were portrayed as devil-may-care outcasts and minstrelmen played them with an air of comic triumph, irreverent wisdom, and an underlying note

> of rebellion, which had a special appeal to citizens of a
> young country. Minstrelsy was ironically the beginning of
> black involvement in the American theater. The American
> people learned to identify with certain aspects of the
> black people. The Negro became a sympathetic symbol for a
> pioneer people who required resilience as a prime trait.

PARAPHRASE

Some passages are worth quoting for the sake of their precise or elegant style or distinguished author. But many of the sources that you will want to write about in your college essays are expressed in far more ordinary language. Indeed, some sources whose *contents* warrant inclusion in your essay may be written in the jargon of an academic discipline or the bureaucratic prose of a government agency. You will not be doing your readers a favor by quoting this material. Rather, you have a positive duty *not* to quote, but to help your readers by providing them with a clear paraphrase.

Paraphrase is the point-by-point recapitulation of another person's ideas, *expressed in your own words.* By using paraphrase, you are proving to your reader that you understand the materials that you are writing about and have made them your own. Paraphrase is like summary in that both report your understanding to a reader; but, unlike a summary, a paraphrase covers a relatively short passage and reports *everything* in the passage, accurately, completely, and consecutively. When you paraphrase, you do not select, condense, interpret, or reorder the ideas; you retain everything about the original writing but the words.

Paraphrasing to Present Sources in Your Essay

Your readers depend upon your paraphrased explanations to gain a fairly detailed understanding of sources that they may never have read and, indirectly, to become convinced of the validity of your own thesis. There are two major reasons for using paraphrase in your essays, which correspond to the major reasons for using quotation.

1. Use paraphrase to present ideas or evidence whenever there is no special purpose to be gained from using a direct quotation. Many of your sources will not have a sufficiently authoritative reputation or distinctive style to justify your retaining their words. The following illustration, taken from a *New York Times* article, paraphrases a report written by an anonymous group of "municipal auditors" whose writing merits paraphrase rather than quotation:

> A city warehouse in Middle Village, Queens, stocked with such things
> as snow shovels, light bulbs, sponges, waxed paper, laundry soap and
> tinned herring, has been found to be vastly overstocked with some items
> and lacking in others. Municipal auditors, in a report issued yesterday,
> said that security was fine and that the warehouse was quicker in de-
> livering goods to city agencies than it was when the auditors made their
> last check, in August, 1976. But in one corner of the warehouse, they
> said, nearly 59,000 paper binders, the 8½-by-11 size, are gathering dust,
> enough to meet the city's needs for nearly seven years. Nearby, there is
> a 10½-year supply of cotton coveralls.
>
> Both the overstock and shortages cost the city money, the auditors
> said. They estimated that by reducing warehouse inventories, the city
> could save $1.4 million, plus $112,000 in interest. . . .

**2. Use paraphrase to give your readers a reliable and compre-
hensive account of ideas taken from a source—ideas that you intend
to explain, interpret, or disagree with in your essay.** The first illustration comes from a *Times* article on the work of the behavioral psychologist B. F. Skinner, pointing out the increasing pessimism of his
thought. As evidence, the writer of the article uses a paraphrase of material from Skinner's essay "A Matter of Consequence." Notice the limited
use of carefully selected quotations within the paraphrase.

> "Why do we not act to save our world?" [Dr. Skinner] says at the start
> of "A Matter of Consequence." The answers he offers are complex and
> bound up in the behavioral theory, which says that people do not initiate
> action on their own, but act in ways that have been successful in the
> past. But today's problems of overpopulation, pollution, energy deple-
> tion and other environmental hazards cast a pall over the future that
> promises to make it more unlike the present than perhaps at any other
> point in modern history, Dr. Skinner suggests. Therefore, solving such
> potential life-and-death problems through strategies that worked before
> is little more than a pipedream, according to Dr. Skinner.
>
> The only hope, he says, would be to get people to act on *predictions*
> of future conditions and thus alter institutions and practices. But a basic
> tenet of behavioral theory states that the environment shapes people's
> actions; and since, as Dr. Skinner notes, "the future does not exist, how
> can it affect contemporary human behavior?" The solution might be
> somehow to persuade people, through behavioral techniques, that their
> very survival might depend on their actions right now.

The next example shows how paraphrase can be used more briefly, to
present another writer's point of view as the basis for an argument. Again,
notice that the writer of this letter-to-the-editor of the *Times* has reserved
quotation to express the precise point of disagreement; the statement is

controversial, and the words of the original author are most likely to do it justice.

> In his miniature Socratic dialogue "Hong Kong's Success" (Op-Ed, Aug. 2) Stephen Beckner suggests that Hong Kong's fierce rate of economic growth is the colony's salutary and ingenious response to its peculiar geopolitical situation.
>
> As a current resident of Hong Kong, I would agree with Mr. Beckner that the unusual status of the colony has been a vital influence in defining its industrious, adaptable character. This does not, however, lead me to share Mr. Beckner's view that "by almost any standard, the city-state . . . is a fabulous success."

Paraphrasing as Preparation for Reading and Writing Essays

Paraphrase is sometimes undertaken as an end in itself. When you are reading a complex essay or chapter, writing a paraphrase of the difficult passages can help you to improve your comprehension. When you grasp an essay at first reading, when its ideas are clearly stated in a familiar vocabulary, then you can be satisfied with annotating it or writing a brief outline or summary. But when you find an essay hard to understand, the need to write down each sentence in your own words forces you to stop and review as soon as you realize that you can no longer follow the writer's sequence of thought. Thus, paraphrasing encourages you to work out ideas that at first might seem beyond your comprehension and to prove that you understand exactly what the author is saying.

Paraphrase can also be a means to an end, a preparation for writing an essay of your own. Let's assume that you are taking notes for an essay based on one or more sources. If you write down nothing but exact quotations, you will not only be doing a good deal of unnecessary transcription, but you will also be encouraging yourself to quote excessively in your essay. Instead, when you take notes, you should habitually paraphrase rather than quote, except in recording phrases or sentences which, in your opinion, merit quotation. These phrases and sentences should be inscribed accurately in your notes, with quotation marks clearly separating the paraphrase from the quotation.

Accuracy in Paraphrase

All academic writers are expected to be scrupulously correct and fluent in their presentation of material taken from their sources. While the paraphrase can only be, at best, a substitute for the original, it must be a reliable substitute. The ideas in the paraphrase should be presented in the same order as the original, and no one point should be emphasized more than another (unless the original writer chose to do so). In its adherence to the original sequence, a paraphrase resembles an outline. But when you write down the main points of a chapter or an essay in outline form—leaving them in roughly the same order—you are merely writing a list, taking down a memorandum for future reference. You are not attempting to present all the reasoning leading up to these ideas; you are only pulling out the key points, nothing more. The paraphrase, however, must suggest the scope of the original as well as the main ideas. Moreover, an outline can be very short and condensed, but a paraphrase may be as long as the original text (or even longer if there are complex ideas that need to be explained). On the whole, though, passages to be paraphrased are usually brief excerpts; you generally need to provide a full account of a single idea or piece of information rather than to present the entire context of the work in which it is found.

The paraphraser's task really resembles that of the translator. You are undertaking to master the material and to pinpoint its exact meaning; and then, as if the text were in a foreign language, you must demonstrate that you can recreate that meaning in your own voice. Like the translator, you use your own idiom, and within the scope of that idiom, you often have to rewrite the text. In a good paraphrase, the sentences and the vocabulary do not echo those of the original. Nor is it sufficient merely to substitute synonyms for key words and to leave the passage otherwise unchanged; that is plagiarism in spirit, if not in fact, for word-by-word substitution does not demonstrate that you have made the ideas your own. Do not try to imitate the phrasing of the original. The object is not rivalry; you are not expected to invent a kind of jargon that will be just as mystifying to your readers as the text that you are paraphrasing was initially mystifying to you. Strive for simplicity and clarity.

The level of abstraction within the paraphrase should resemble that of the original: neither more general nor more specific. If you do not understand a sentence, do not try to cover it up with a vague phrase that slides over the idea. Guessing in paraphrase is absolutely fatal. Instead, look up all the words; try to think of what they mean and how they are used together; consider how the sentences are formed and how they will fit into the context of your entire paraphrase; and then, to test your understanding, write it all out. Remember that a good paraphrase is a work that can make sense by itself; it is coherent and readable, without requiring reference to the original essay.

Here is a summary of the requirements for a successful paraphrase:

1. a paraphrase must be accurate;
2. a paraphrase must be complete;
3. a paraphrase must speak in the voice of the person writing the paraphrase;
4. a paraphrase must make sense by itself.

Free Paraphrase

When a paraphrase moves far away from the words and sentence structure of the original text and presents ideas in its own style and idiom, then it is said to be "free." The free paraphrase can be more interesting to write and to read than the original—provided, as always, that the substance of the source has not been altered, disguised, or substantially condensed. A free paraphrase can summarize if the original text is repetitious, and the length of a free paraphrase will probably be somewhat shorter than the original.

Here, side-by-side with the original, is a relatively free paraphrase of an excerpt from Machiavelli's *The Prince*. This passage exemplifies the kind of text, very famous and very difficult, which really benefits from a comprehensive paraphrase. *The Prince* was written in 1513, and (while the translation from the Italian used here was revised in this century) the paraphraser has to bridge a tremendous gap in time and in style in order to present Machiavelli in an idiom suitable for modern readers.

Original version

It is not, therefore, necessary for a prince to have [good faith and integrity], but it is very necessary to seem to have them. I would even be bold to say that to possess them and always to observe them is dangerous, but to appear to possess them is useful. Thus it is well to seem merciful, faithful, humane, sincere, religious, and also to be so; but you must have the mind so disposed that when it is needful to be otherwise you may be able to change to the opposite qualities. And it must be understood that a prince, and especially a new prince, cannot observe all those things which are considered good in men, being often obliged, in order to maintain the state, to act against faith, against charity, against humanity, and against religion. And therefore, he must have a mind disposed to adapt itself according to the wind, and as the variations of fortune dictate, and . . . not deviate from what is good, if possible, but be able to do evil if constrained.

A prince must take great care that nothing goes out of his mouth which is not full of the above-mentioned five qualities, and to see and hear him, he should seem to be all mercy, faith, integrity, humanity, and religion. . . . Everyone sees what you appear to

Paraphrase

It is more important for a ruler to give the impression of goodness than to be good. In fact, real goodness can be a liability, but the pretense is always very effective. It is all very well to be virtuous. but it is vital to be able to shift in the other direction whenever circumstances require it. After all, rulers, especially recently elevated ones, have a duty to perform which may absolutely require them to act against the dictates of faith and compassion and kindness. One must act as circumstances require and, while it's good to be virtuous if you can, it's better to be bad if you must.

In public, however, the ruler should appear to be entirely virtuous, and if his pretense is successful with the majority of people, then those who do see through the act will be outnumbered and impotent, especially since the ruler has the authority of government on his side. In the case of rulers, even be, few feel what you are, and those few will not dare to oppose themselves to the many, who have the majesty of the state to defend them; and in the actions of men, and especially of princes, from which there is no appeal, the end justifies the means. Let a prince therefore aim at conquering and maintaining the state, and the means will always be judged honorable and praised by every one, for the vulgar are always taken by appearances and the issue of the event; and the world consists only of the vulgar, and the few who are not vulgar are isolated when the many have a rallying point in the prince.

more than for most men, the end justifies the means. If the ruler is able to assume power and administer it successfully, his methods will always be judged proper and satisfactory; for the common people will accept the pretense of virtue and the reality of success, and the astute will find no one is listening to their warnings.

Paraphrase and Summary

To clarify the difference between paraphrase and summary, here is a paragraph which *summarizes* this same excerpt from *The Prince*:

According to Machiavelli, the ruler's only important goal is to rule. The masses will be swayed by the ruler's pretended virtue and by his success, and opposition will be ineffective. Flexibility is the wise prince's most important attribute. Although he should act virtuously if he can, and always appear to do so, it is more important for him to adapt freely to changing circumstances. "The end justifies the means."

It may be useful to review the four characteristics of the brief summary:

1. A summary is comprehensive. Notice that this one says more than "the end justifies the means." Although that may be the most important idea in the passage, it does not present the contents of the paragraph fully enough. (For one thing, the broad generalization contains no reference at all to rulers or princes and their specific circumstances—and that, after all, is Machiavelli's subject.)
2. A summary is concise. It should say exactly as much as you need—and no more. Sometimes you cannot summarize complex material in a single sentence; nor is there any reason why a summary should not take up a short paragraph. And, while this summary is four sentences long, it is still much shorter than the paraphrase.
3. A summary is coherent. As you can see, the ideas are not presented in the same sequence as that of the original passage;

nor are the language and tone at all reminiscent of the original. Rather, the summary includes only the passage's most important points, linking them together in a unified paragraph.

4. A summary is independent. What is most striking about the summary, compared with the paraphrase, is the writer's attitude toward the original text. While the paraphraser has to adapt Machiavelli's ideas and point of view, the summarizer does not. Characteristically, Machiavelli's name is cited, calling attention to the fact that the summary is of *another person's ideas.*

Both the summary and paraphrase provide the raw materials for easy reference to this passage. Which you would choose to draw upon would depend on your topic, on the way you are developing your essay, and on the length at which you wish to discuss Machiavelli. Thus, an essay citing Machiavelli as only one among many political theoreticians might easily include the brief four-sentence summary; you might then briefly comment upon Machiavelli's ideas before going on to summarize (and perhaps compare them with) another writer's theories. If, however, you were writing an essay about a contemporary politician, and if you planned to analyze the way in which your subject does or does not carry out Machiavelli's strategies, then you probably would want to familiarize your readers with *The Prince* through a fairly lengthy paraphrase. The paraphrase could then be cited at length, interspersed, perhaps, with your discussion of your present-day "prince."

Covering the Main Ideas

The minimal objective of paraphrase is to present the main ideas contained in the original reading. Without this basic coverage, a paraphrase is worthless. When an attempt at paraphrase fails to convey the substance of the source, there are three possible explanations:

1. *misreading:* The writer genuinely misunderstood what he was reading.
2. *projecting:* The writer insisted on reading his own ideas into the text.
3. *guessing:* The writer had a spark of understanding and constructed a paraphrase that roughly develops that spark, but ignores much of the original text.

Read Christopher Lasch's analysis of the changing role of the child in family life. Then examine each of the three paraphrases that follow, deciding whether it conveys Lasch's principal ideas and, if not, why it has gone astray. Then compare your reactions with the analysis that follows each paraphrase.

Original

The family by its very nature is a means of raising children, but this fact should not blind us to the important change that occurred when child-rearing ceased to be simply one of many activities and became the central concern—one is tempted to say the central obsession—of family life. This development had to wait for the recognition of the child as a distinctive kind of person, more impressionable and hence more vulnerable than adults, to be treated in a special manner befitting his peculiar requirements. Again, we take these things for granted and find it hard to imagine anything else. Earlier, children had been clothed, fed, spoken to, and educated as little adults; more specifically, as servants, the difference between childhood and servitude having been remarkably obscure throughout much of Western history. . . . It was only in the seventeenth century in certain classes that childhood came to be seen as a special category of experience. When that happened, people recognized the enormous formative influence of family life, and the family became above all an agency for building character, for consciously and deliberately forming the child from birth to adulthood.

"Divorce and the Family in America,"
Atlantic Monthly, November 1966

Paraphrase A

The average family wants to raise children with a good education, and to encourage for example, the ability to read and write well. They must be taught to practice and learn on their own. Children can be treated well without being pampered. They must be treated as adults as they get older and experience more of life. A parent must build character and the feeling of independence in a child. No longer should the children be treated as kids or servants, for that can cause conflict in a family relationship.

This paraphrase has very little in common with the original passage. True, it is about child-rearing, but the writer chooses to give advice to parents, rather than to present the contrast between early and modern attitudes towards children, as Lasch does. Since the only clear connection between Lasch and this paragraph is the reference to servants, one might safely conclude that the writer was confused by the passage, and (instead of slowing down the process and paraphrasing it sentence by sentence) guessed—mistakenly—at what it meant. Notice how assertive the tone is; the writer seems to be admonishing parents rather than echoing Lasch's detached, analytical voice.

Paraphrase B

```
      When two people get married, they usually produce a
child. They get married because they want a family.
Raising a family is now different from the way it used to
be. The child is looked upon as a human being, with
feelings and thoughts of his own. Centuries ago, children
were treated like robots, little more than hired help.
Now, children are seen as people who need a strong,
dependable family background to grow into persons of good
character. Parents are needed to get children ready to be
the adults of tomorrow.
```

This paragraph might be regarded as an example of projection. The middle sentences present Lasch's basic point, but the beginning and the end both go off on tangents, so that the paraphrase as a whole does not bear much resemblance to the original text. There is also an exaggeration: are the servants "robots"?

Paraphrase C

```
      Though the family has always been an important
institution, its child-rearing function has only in recent
centuries become its most important activity. This change
has resulted from the relatively new idea that children
have a special, unique personality. In the past, there was
little difference seen between childhood and adulthood.
But today people realize the importance of family life,
especially the family unit as a means of molding the
personalities of children from childhood to adulthood.
```

Although this paraphrase is certainly the most accurate of the three, there is still the problem of length; for, like the first two, paragraph C is hardly long enough to be a complete paraphrase. In fact, the writer seems to have succumbed to the temptation to summarize, rather than paraphrase. Lasch's main idea is undoubtedly there, but the following points are missing:

1. there is a tremendous gulf between pre–seventeenth-century and twentieth-century perceptions of childhood;
2. before the seventeenth century, it was difficult to distinguish between the status and treatment of children and that of servants;
3. child-rearing has now become of overriding ("obsessive") importance to the family;

4. children are different from adults in that they are less hardened and experienced.

The omission of point 2 is particularly damaging. The author has done a thorough job of the beginning and the end of Lasch's passage, but evidently left the middle to take care of itself. But a paraphrase cannot be considered a reliable "translation" of the original text unless all the supporting ideas are given appropriate emphasis. Here is a more comprehensive paraphrase of the passage than paraphrase C:

> Though the family has always been the institution responsible for bringing up children, only in recent times has its child-raising function become the family's overriding purpose and its reason for being. This striking shift to the child-centered family has resulted from the gradual realization that children have a special, unique personality, easy to influence and easy to hurt, and that they must be treated accordingly. Special treatment for children is the norm in our time; but hundreds of years ago, people saw little or no difference between childhood and adulthood, and, in fact, the child's role in the family resembled that of a servant. It was not until the 17th century that people began to regard childhood as a distinctive stage of growth. That recognition led them to understand what a powerful influence the family environment must have on the child and to define "family" as the chief instrument for molding the child's personality and moral attitudes.

EXERCISE 25

Each of the two readings excerpted below is followed by a group of paraphrases. Examine each paraphrase and identify those which conform to the guidelines for paraphrasing. Ask yourself whether the paraphrase contains any point that is not in the original passage and whether the key points of the original are all clearly presented in the paraphrase.

1. [One feminist assertion was that] marriage itself, in Western society, could be considered a higher form of prostitution, in which respectable women sold their sexual favors not for immediate financial rewards but for long-term economic security. . . . The difference between prostitution and respectability reduced itself to a question not of motives but of money. The virtuous woman's fee was incomparably higher, but the process itself was essentially the same; that is, the virtuous woman of the leisure class had come to be valued, like the prostitute, chiefly as a

sexual object: beautiful, expensive, and useless—in Veblen's phrase, a means of vicarious display. She was trained from girlhood to bring all her energies to the intricate art of pleasing men . . . perfecting the art of discreet flirtation, all the while withholding the ultimate prize until the time should come when she might bestow it, with the impressive sanction of state and church, on the most eligible bidder for her "hand."

Christopher Lasch, "Divorce and the Family in America"

Paraphrase A

Feminists say that marriage is an acceptable form of prostitution, a means by which "regular" women receive economic security for life. Unlike the prostitute, the virtuous woman can pick and choose whom she will play the "game" with. The game is simple. First, the woman flirts and the man responds. All the while, the woman is analyzing the man's finances as well as his emotions. If the man qualifies, a promise is made by the woman to give up her "virtue" to the man, provided that it's preceded by a ceremony involving a minister and some rings.

Paraphrase B

In Western society, decent women, like prostitutes, exchanged their bodies in a commercial transaction, not for cash, but as an investment for the future. The object of the prostitute and the unmarried woman was the same, even if the expected reward differed in kind and amount. The wife's reward was ultimately bigger, but her tactics were similar. Like the prostitute, the lady was thought of as a means of sexual enjoyment, reduced to a thing, not a person, a costly and handsome ornament, to be used to show off the wealth of the possessor. She had been taught to devote herself to the pleasure of her master, understanding how to tease and provoke, but within carefully defined limits. She did not grant her favors until she had received the legitimacy of marriage.

Paraphrase C

Matrimony in Western civilization has been little more than a superior method of using sex for hire. The honorable woman exchanges her body for a ring and a legal paper which is sanctioned by religious and by government authorities. The paper entitles the female to receive assets and properties that can be converted to cash, for the period of her marriage and not just in exchange for sexual services. Like the prostitute, all young girls are

taught from infancy the art of using their charms to
outwit unwilling males. A suitor will be stimulated to the
point where he feels that he must possess her. Then she
informs him that, if he wants her, the price is matrimony.

2. Slang is generally thought of as brusque abbreviation, but actually its
principle is circumlocutory, since it aims to bemuse the outside by adroit
verbal avoidance, paraphrasing objects rather than naming them. It is
the trickster's art: the tongue is quicker than the eye.

Peter Conrad

Paraphrase A

People tend to use slang as a shortcut to what they
really want to say. Using your own words instead of the
proper words often seems easy to one who does not
understand language. But putting words into slang is an
art and understanding slang is a talent.

Paraphrase B

Slang is usually thought of as a shortcut. Actually,
it is meant to confuse an outsider by deliberately using a
clever means of conveying the message.

Paraphrase C

To most people, slang is a shortened version of the
actual words, but, in reality, what slang does is to skirt
around the definition without touching on the meaning
precisely. It only serves to confuse someone who is not
adept in its use. Rather than calling a spade a spade,
slang finds a new and different wording, leaving those who
aren't in the know completely lost. It is the worthless
work of the word wizards.

Paraphrase D

Slang is improperly used English. Many people use
slang to confuse other people. Outsiders may be baffled at
first, but after a while they find it amusing. Given time,
these same people will try to copy this way of speaking.
Slang is used to baffle, amuse, and bewilder, perhaps for
devious reasons.

Paraphrase E

Slang is often regarded as a curt form of shorthand;
but really it is beating around the bush; the purpose of

```
slang words is to sidetrack the uninitiated by skillfully
keeping away from the real meaning, not defining the
point, but working around it. Slang is for the devious,
whose words can alter reality.
```

The Two Stages of Paraphrase

Since "translating" another writer's idiom into your own can be difficult, a paraphrase may often be written in two stages. In your first version, you will work out a word-for-word substitution, staying close to the sentence structure of the original, as if, indeed, you are writing a translation. This is the literal paraphrase. Then, once you have substituted your own words for those of the original, you work from your own literal paraphrase, turning it into a free paraphrase by reconstructing and rephrasing the sentences to make them more natural and more characteristic of your own writing style.

Writing a Literal Paraphrase

To write a paraphrase that is faithful to the original text is impossible if you are uncertain of the meaning of any of the words. You will need to use a dictionary as you paraphrase a difficult passage, especially if there is obsolete or archaic language. Try writing down a few possible synonyms for each difficult word, to make sure that you are aware of all the connotations and can choose the most precise substitute when you start writing your own version. Too often, the writer of a paraphrase forgets that there *is* a choice and quickly substitutes the first synonym to be found in the dictionary. Moreover, even when appropriate synonyms have been carefully evaluated and chosen, the first version of a paraphrase can look peculiar and sound dreadful. While the old sentence structure has been retained, the key words have been yanked out and new ones plugged in. Still, at the beginning your object is to work out the exact meaning of each sentence.

To illustrate the pitfalls of this process, here is a short excerpt from Francis Bacon's essay "Of Marriage and Single Life," written around 1600. Some of the phrasing and word combinations sound archaic and even unnatural; but, in fact, there is nothing in the passage that is inaccessible to modern understanding, if the sentences are read slowly and carefully.

> He that hath wife and children hath given hostages to fortune; for they are impediments to great enterprises, either of virtue or mischief. Certainly the best works and of greatest merit for the public have proceeded from the unmarried or childless men: which both in affection and means have endowed the public.

The passage's main idea is not too difficult to extract: unmarried men, without the burden of a family, can afford to contribute to the public good. But by now you must realize that such a brief summary is not the same as a paraphrase; Bacon's reasoning is not fully presented, and it would not be fair to pass off this sentence as the equivalent of the original. In contrast, look at these two very different *literal paraphrases* of Bacon's first sentence. (The key words have been underlined.)

> He who has a wife and children has <u>bestowed prisoners</u> to <u>riches</u>; for they are <u>defects</u> in huge <u>business organizations</u>, either for <u>morality</u> or <u>damage</u>.

> He who has a wife and children has <u>given</u> a <u>pledge</u> to <u>destiny</u>; for they are <u>hindrances</u> to large <u>endeavor</u>, either for <u>good</u> or for <u>ill</u>.

Neither sentence sounds very normal or very clear; but the second has potential, while the first is just gibberish—entirely out of keeping with the spirit and meaning of Bacon's sentence. Yet, in both cases, the inserted words *are* synonyms for the original vocabulary. In the first sentence, the words do not fit Bacon's context; in the second sentence, they do. For example, it is misleading to choose "business organization" as a synonym for "enterprises," since the passage doesn't actually concern business, but refers to any sort of undertaking requiring freedom from responsibility. "Impediment" can mean either "defect" (as in speech impediment) or "hindrance" (as in impediment to learning); but—again, given the context—it is the latter meaning that Bacon has in mind. Choosing the correct connotation or nuance is possible only if you think carefully about the synonyms and use your judgment: the process cannot be hurried.

A phrase like "hostage to fortune" offers special difficulty, since it is a powerful image expressing a highly abstract idea. No paraphraser can improve upon the original wording or even find an equivalent phrase. However, isolating the idea is important: a bargain made with life—the renunciation of future independent action in exchange for a family. Wife and children serve as a kind of bond ("hostage") to ensure one's future conformity. The aptness and singularity of Bacon's original phrase are measured by the difficulty of producing a paraphrase of three words in less than two sentences!

Writing a "Free" Version of the Literal Paraphrase

Correct though the synonyms may be, Bacon's sentence cannot be left as it is in the second paraphrase, for no reader would readily be able to understand the meaning of this stilted, artificial sentence. It is necessary to rephrase the paraphrase, making sure that the meaning of the words is retained, but making the sentence pattern sound more natural. In the first attempt at "loosening" the paraphrase, it is wise to remain as close as possible to the original sentence, leaving everything in the same sequence, but using a more modern idiom:

> Married men with children are hindered from embarking on any important undertaking, good or bad. Indeed, unmarried and childless men are the ones who have done the most for society and have dedicated their love and their money to the public good.

The second sentence (which is simpler to paraphrase than the first) has been inverted here, but the paraphrase is still a point-by-point recapitulation of Bacon. This version is quite acceptable, but not very interesting. Improvement is possible, both to clarify Bacon's meaning and to introduce a more personal voice. What exactly *are* these unmarried men dedicating to the public good? "Affection and means." And what is the modern equivalent of means? Money? Effort? Time? Energy?

> A man with a family has obligations which prevent him from devoting himself to any activity that pleases him. On the other hand, a single man or a man without children has a greater opportunity to be a philanthropist. That's why most great contributions of energy and resources to the good of society are made by single men.

The writer of this paraphrase has not supplied a synonym for "affection," assuming perhaps that the expenditure of energy and resources presupposes a certain amount of interest and concern; affection is almost too weak a motivation for the philanthropist as he is described here.

> The responsibility of a wife and children prevents a man from taking risks with his money, time, and energy. The greatest social benefactors have been men who have adopted the public as their family.

The second sentence here is the only one in all five versions that has come close to Bacon's economy of style. "Adopted the public" is not quite the same as "endowed the public" with one's "affection and means"; but nevertheless, this is a successful paraphrase because it speaks for itself. It has a life and an importance of its own, independent of Bacon's original passage; yet it makes the same point that Bacon does.

EXERCISE 26

Each of the following brief passages is followed by a *literal* paraphrase. The literal paraphrases are distortions of the originals; some inappropriate synonyms have been inserted, and no attempt has been made to understand and express the meaning of the passage as a whole. Consult the original text, and try to salvage the paraphrase.

A. Every considerable alteration in the local circumstances in which each race of animals exists causes a change in their wants, and these new wants excite them to new actions and habits. These actions require the more frequent employment of some parts before but slightly exercised, and then greater development follows as a consequence of their more frequent use.

Charles Lyell, from *Principles of Geology* (1830)

```
Each substantial change in the restricted situations in
which every kind of creature lives leads to a mutation in
their desires, and these different needs introduce them to
different performances and practices. These performances
demand that they use certain portions more often, which
earlier were hardly employed, and therefore more growth
comes as a result of their constant appliance.
```

B. The gentleman is never mean or little in his disputes, never takes unfair advantage, never mistakes personalities or sharp sayings for arguments, or insinuates evil which he dare not say out.

Joseph Hall, from *Characters of Virtues and Vices* (1608)

```
A gentleman is never abject or small in his contests,
never uses leverage or only within the confines of
impartiality; he tries not to misinterpret character or
caustic remarks or imply wickedness when he can say no
good.
```

ASSIGNMENT 8

Paraphrase the following passages, using this procedure:

1. Look up in a dictionary the meanings of all the vocabulary of which you are uncertain. Consider carefully the possible meanings of the italicized words.

2. Write a literal paraphrase of each passage by substituting appropriate synonyms within the original sentence structure. (Don't restrict yourself to changing the italicized words; use your own vocabulary throughout the passage.)
3. Revise your literal paraphrase, keeping roughly to the same length and number of sentences as the original, but using your own sentence style and phrasing throughout. (It may be helpful to put the original passage aside at this point, and work entirely from your own version.)
4. Read your "free" paraphrase aloud and make sure that it makes sense.

A. This, then, is held to be the duty of the man of wealth: To set an example of *modest, unostentatious* living, *shunning display* or extravagance; to provide moderately for all of the *legitimate wants* of those dependent upon him; and after doing so, to consider all *surplus revenues* which come to him simply as trust funds, which he is called upon to *administer*, and strictly bound as a matter of duty to administer in the manner which, in his judgment, is best calculated to produce the most beneficial results for the community—the man of wealth thus becoming the mere trustee and *agent* for his poorer brethren.

Andrew Carnegie, from *The Gospel of Wealth* (1899)

B. Children sweeten labors, but they make misfortunes more bitter; they increase the *cares* of life, but they *mitigate* the remembrance of death. The *perpetuity* by *generation* is common to beasts; but memory, and merit, and noble works are proper to men; and sure a man shall see the noblest works and foundations have proceeded from childless men, which have sought to express the images of their minds where those of their bodies have failed; the *care* of *posterity* is most in them that have no posterity.

Francis Bacon, from "Of Parents and Children" (ca. 1597)

C. The first thing that [Shakespeare had to do] with *Romeo and Juliet* was to get it licensed. No play could be produced on the London stage until it had been *certified* that no *seditious material* had crept into it that might *corrupt* the *susceptible* public. The Crown was not concerned with suppressing *indecorous* or *blasphemous material* in the theatre and it was not until the following reign [James I] that *oaths* were outlawed on the London stage. It merely wished to make sure that one of the greatest popular mediums of communication, the theatre, did not lend itself to any *propaganda* against the dignity of the government or of the Queen.

Marchette Chute, from *Shakespeare of London* (1949)

D. Since the end of World War II, investigation into the *youth subculture* has become virtually an *autonomous* branch of sociology. Disagreeing both on its scope and its relationship to adult culture, sociologists have usually agreed that the middle-class youth subculture enforces on participants *conformity to norms*, customs, modes of dress, and language fads that are different from those of adults. Although most students have viewed the youth subculture as a relatively recent development, the 19th century did spawn a variety of youth subcultures, from the intense male comradeship of college fraternities to the ebullient style of the fire company lads. The distinguishing feature of the middle-class youth subculture of the 1920s was its emphasis on physical intimacy between boys and girls. During the 1920s the greater freedom of young people toward sexuality sparked a profusion of books and articles on "our *rebellious* youth." Articles on "flaming youth" swept aside the solicitude for *exploited* minors that marked the period between 1900 and 1920. To speak of youth in the 1920s was to speak of their behavior, not their treatment. Like gang youth, middle-class young people were investigated as if they inhabited another planet, while moviemakers projected an obviously *marketable image* of Jazz Age youth. The titles tell the story: *The Perfect Flapper* (1924); *The House of Youth* (1924); *The Plastic Age* (1925); *The Mad Whirl* (1925); *Mad Hour* (1928); *Our Modern Maidens* (1929); *Our Dancing Daughters* (1929).

Joseph Kett, from *Rites of Passage* (1977)

E. In the second century of the Christian era, the empire of Rome *comprehended* the fairest part of the earth, and the most *civilized* portion of mankind. The frontiers of that extensive monarchy were guarded by ancient *renown* and *disciplined valor*. The gentle but powerful *influence* of laws and manners had gradually cemented the union of the provinces. Their peaceful inhabitants enjoyed and *abused* the advantages of wealth and luxury. The image of a free *constitution* was preserved with *decent* reverence: the Roman senate appeared to possess the *sovereign* authority, and *devolved* on the emperors all the executive powers of government.

Edward Gibbon, from *The Decline and Fall of the Roman Empire* (1776)

F. These are the times that try men's souls. The summer soldier and the sunshine patriot will, in this crisis, shrink from the service of his country: but he that stands it *now*, deserves the love and thanks of men and women. *Tyranny*, like hell, is not easily conquered: yet we have this *consolation* with us, that the harder the conflict, the more glorious the triumph. What we obtain too cheap, we *esteem* too lightly: 'tis *dearness* only that gives everything its value. Heaven knows how to set a proper price upon its goods and it would be strange, indeed, if so celestial an article as freedom should not be highly *rated*.

Thomas Paine, from *The Crisis* (1776)

G. As in war to pardon the coward is to do cruel wrong to the brave man whose life his cowardice *jeopardizes*, so in civil affairs it is *revolting* to every principle of justice to give to the lazy, the *vicious*, or even the feeble or dull-witted a reward which is really the robbery of what braver, wiser, abler men have earned. The only effective way to help any man is to help him to help himself; and the worst lesson to teach him is that he can be permanently helped at the expense of someone else.

Theodore Roosevelt, *Biological Analogies in History* (1910)

H. Except during time of panic, liberty of the press is reasonably safe from *corrupt* or *tyrannical* government. A greater present danger is from an *intolerant* majority who might try on their own or through government pressure to silence *dissent*, thereby robbing society of possible truth (if the dissenters are right), or (if they are wrong) of that clearer livelier view of truth which *emerges* when it collides with error.

John Stuart Mill, from *On Liberty* (1859)

I. I wish that the bald eagle had not been chosen as the representative of our country; he is a bird of bad moral character; like those among men who live by *sharping* and robbing, he is generally poor, and often very lousy. The turkey is a much more *respectable* bird, and *withal* a true original native of America.

Benjamin Franklin, from a letter to Sarah Bache (1784)

J. It is somewhat ironic to note that grading *systems* evolved in part because of [problems in evaluating performance]. In situations where *reward* and *recognition* often depended more on who you knew than on what you knew, and *lineage* was more important than ability, the cause of justice seemed to demand a method whereby the individual could demonstrate specific abilities on the basis of *objective criteria*. This led to the establishment of specific standards and public criteria as ways of reducing *prejudicial* treatment and, in cases where *appropriate* standards could not be specified in advance, to the normal curve system of establishing levels on the basis of group performance. The *imperfect achievement* of the goals of such systems in no way negates the importance of the underlying purposes.

Wayne Moellenberg, from "To Grade or Not to Grade— Is That the Question?" (1973)

INCORPORATING PARAPHRASE INTO YOUR ESSAY

The paraphrased ideas of other writers should never take control of your essay, but should always be subordinate to the points that *you* are making. Brevity in paraphrase is therefore often desirable, to prevent the source-material from dominating your writing and to enable the paraphrased sentence to be tucked into a paragraph in your essay. However, the presentation of the original text, whether short or long, must still be an accurate and fair representation of its ideas.

Most academic writers rely on a mixture of quotation, paraphrase, and summary to present their sources. To illustrate the way in which these three techniques of presentation can be successfully combined, here is an extract from an article by Conor Cruise O'Brien that depends on a judicious mixture of paraphrase, summary, and quotation. In "Violence—and Two Schools of Thought," O'Brien gives an account of a medical conference concerned with the origins of violence. Specifically, he undertakes to present and (at the end) comment on the ideas of two speakers at the conference.

VIOLENCE—AND TWO SCHOOLS OF THOUGHT*

Summary The opening speakers were fairly representative of the two   1
main schools of thought which almost always declare themselves when violence is discussed. The first school sees a propensity to aggression as biological but capable of being socially conditioned into patterns of acceptable behavior. The second sees it as essentially created by social conditions and therefore capable of being removed by benign social change.

Quotation The first speaker held that violence was "a bio-social phe-   2
nomenon." He rejected the notion that human beings were blank paper "on which the environment can write whatever it likes." He described how a puppy could be conditioned to **Paraphrase** choose a dog food it did not like and to reject one it did like. This was the creation of conscience in the puppy. It was done by mild punishment. If human beings were acting more aggressively and anti-socially, despite the advent of better social conditions and better housing, this might be because permissiveness, in school and home, had checked the process of social conditioning, and therefore of conscience-building. He favored the reinstatement of conscience-building, through the use of **Quotation** mild punishment and token rewards. "We cannot eliminate violence," he said, "but we can do a great deal to reduce it."

Summary The second speaker thought that violence was the result of   3
stress; in almost all the examples he cited it was stress from **Paraphrase and** overcrowding. The behavior of apes and monkeys in zoos was **Quotation** "totally different" from the way they behaved in "the completely relaxed conditions in the wild." In crowded zoos the most aggressive males became leaders and a general reign of terror set **Paraphrase** in; in the relaxed wild, on the other hand, the least aggressive

* In its original format in *The Observer*, the article's paragraphing, in accordance with usual journalistic practice, occurs with distracting frequency; the number of paragraphs has been reduced here, without any alteration of the text.

Quotation males ruled benevolently. Space was all: "if we could eliminate population pressures, violence would vanish."

Summary The student [reacting to the arguments of the two speakers] 4
Paraphrase preferred the second speaker. He [the second speaker] spoke with ebullient confidence, fast but clear, and at one point ran across the vast platform, in a lively imitation of the behavior of
Summary a charging ape. Also, his message was simple and hopeful. Speaker one, in contrast, looked sad, and his message sounded
Author's faintly sinister. Such impressions, rather than the weight of ar-
comment gument, determine the reception of papers read in such cir-cumstances.

Nonetheless, a student queried speaker two's "relaxed wild." 5
He seemed to recall a case in which a troop of chimpanzees
Paraphrase had completely wiped out another troop. The speaker was glad the student had raised that question because it proved the point. You see, where that had occurred, there had been over-crowding in the jungle, just as happens in zoos, and this was
Author's a response to overcrowding. Conditions in the wild, it seems,
comment are not always "completely relaxed." And when they attain that attributed condition—through the absence of overcrowding—this surely has to be due to the "natural controls," including the predators, whose attentions can hardly be all that relaxing, or, indeed, all that demonstrative of the validity of the prop-osition that violence is not a part of nature. Speaker two did not allude to predators. Nonetheless, they are still around, on two legs as well as on four.

The Observer, 11 February 1979

Selecting Quotations

Although we do not have the texts of the original papers to compare with O'Brien's description, this article seems to be a comprehensive ac-count of a complex discussion. The ideas are clearly presented to the reader. O'Brien provides guidelines for understanding in the summaries of the first paragraph, followed by two separate, noncommittal treatments of the two main points of view.

The ratio of quotation to paraphrase to summary works very effectively. O'Brien offers quotations for two reasons: aptness of expression and the desire to distance himself from the statement. For example, he chooses to quote the vivid image of the blank paper "on which the environment can write whatever it likes." And he also selects points for quotation that he regards as open to dispute—"totally different"; "completely relaxed"; "violence would vanish." Such strong or sweeping statements are often quoted so that the writer can dissociate himself from their implications and so that he cannot be accused of either toning down or exaggerating the meaning in his own paraphrase. In short, quote when:

1. there are no words at your disposal to reproduce the original's economy and aptness of phrasing;
2. a paraphrase would possibly alter the statement's meaning;
3. a paraphrase would not provide the necessary distance between your views and the author's.

Don't quote merely because of:

1. lack of comprehension;
2. awe for the authority of the source;
3. feelings of inadequacy;
4. laziness.

Giving Credit to Your Paraphrased Sources

There is one possible source of confusion in O'Brien's article, occurring at the point when he turns to his own commentary. In the last two paragraphs, it is not always easy to determine where his paraphrase of the speakers' ideas ends and his own opinions begin. His description (in the fourth paragraph) of the student's reactions to the two speakers appears objective. (We learn afterwards that O'Brien is scornful of the criteria that the student is using to evaluate these ideas.) But for the reader to perceive that O'Brien is describing the student's assessment, and not giving his own account of the speaker's platform maneuvers, takes a while. It would be clearer to us if the sentence began: "According to the responding student, the second speaker spoke with ebullient confidence. . . ." Similarly, in the last sentence of the same paragraph, there is no transition from the student to O'Brien as the source of commentary; yet the sentence is undoubtedly O'Brien's opinion.

This confusion of point of view is especially deceptive in the last paragraph when O'Brien moves from his paraphrased and neutral account of the dialogue between student and speaker to his own opinion: that certain predators influence behavior in civilization as well as in the wilds. It requires two readings to notice where the author is no longer paraphrasing but speaking in his own voice. Such confusions can be clarified by the insertion of citations in the appropriate places: the name of the source or an appropriate pronoun or reference label.

As you know by now, in academic writing the clear acknowledgment of the source is not merely a matter of courtesy or clarity, but an assurance of the writer's honesty. *When you paraphrase another person's ideas, you must cite his name, as you do when you quote, or else you are subject to a charge of plagiarism.* Borrowing ideas is just as much stealing as borrowing words. You leave off the quotation marks when you paraphrase, but you must not omit the citation. Of course, the insertion of the name should be smoothly integrated into your sentence, and, in writing the citation, you should follow the guidelines used for citation of quotations.

The source's name need not appear at the beginning of the sentence, but it should signal the beginning of the paraphrase:

> Not everyone enjoys working, but most people would agree
> with Jones's belief that work is an essential experience
> of life.

This sentence depends on two sources: the writer of the essay is responsible for the declaration that "not everyone enjoys working" and that most people would agree with X's views; but the belief that "work is an essential experience of life" is attributed to X. The citation is unobtrusively placed; and there are no quotation marks, so presumably X used a different wording.

The proper citation of paraphrases requires one additional precaution. When you quote, there can never be any doubt about where the borrowed material begins and where it ends: the quotation marks provide a clear demarcation of the boundaries. But when you paraphrase, though the citation may signal the *beginning* of the source material, your reader may not be sure exactly where the paraphrase *ends*. There is no easy method of indicating termination. (As you will see in Chapter 10, footnote numbers can serve as a useful signal.) Of course, it is possible to indicate the end of a paraphrase simply by starting a new paragraph. However, unity and coherence often require you to incorporate more than one person's ideas into a single paragraph.

When you are presenting several points of view in fairly rapid succession, be careful to acknowledge the change of source by citing names. You can easily signal the shift from paraphrased material to *your own* opinions by the use of the first person. Whatever you may have been told to the contrary, it is quite acceptable to use "I" in your essays, as long as you do not insert it unnecessarily or monotonously. A carefully placed "I" can leave your reader in no doubt as to whose voice he is hearing.

EXERCISE 27

A. All of the quotations in the following paragraph come from Cabell Phillips's *The 1940's: Decade of Triumph and Trouble.* Since the quoted statements are neither especially apt nor controversial, reduce the amount of quotation in the paragraph by paraphrasing. Remember to cite the source and to indicate which statements are Phillips's and which are the author's.

"The Employment Act of 1946 has never produced 'full employment' nor has it always charted a clear course through the shoals of economic upset. But without it, we almost certainly would have been in much deeper trouble than we were during many times of stress in the last 25 years." This statement confirms my point: that the Employment Act of 1946 was a law that was useful again and again in helping a staggering economy. But, if this law never produced full employment, what then was its achievement? It achieved the establishment of "an economic general staff which, like its military counterpart, was charged with detecting and averting trouble within its area of command before the trouble got out of hand. There had been nothing like it before. Such economic wisdom and policy guidance as was available to the government came from hither, yon, and everywhere—haphazard, conflicting, and often out of focus. The instrument of this new centralized function was the Council of Economic Advisers (CEA), a small and highly professional bureaucracy attached to the Office of the President. Its duty was to keep a stethoscope on the nation's economic heartbeat and to advise the President and Congress in the formulation of national economic policy, with the primary

objective of maintaining a 'full-employment economy.' "

B. All of the quotations in the following paragraph come from a single source: "Grading Students: A Failure to Communicate," by Reed G. Williams and Harry G. Miller. Since each quoted sentence appears in a different paragraph in the source essay, the student has carefully put opening and closing quotation marks around all the sentences. Restore continuity to the paragraph by:

1. examining the sentence order and altering the sequence;
2. reducing the number of quotations through paraphrase (the finished paragraph should contain only one quotation, if any).

Remember to acknowledge the authors, making clear how much of the paragraph is taken from their essay.

If grades were properly understood and read, parents,

teachers, and students could all benefit. "A notation system is

simply a shorthand means of communicating to specified audiences

judgments about a student's performance as it relates to some set

of standards." "Grading systems provide parents, students,

guidance counselors, teachers, and prospective employers with

information regarding specific knowledge, skills, and attitudes

possessed by the student." "Grades are also employed as a record-

keeping device for recording and communicating progress towards

some objective." "If grading systems are designed appropriately

they can provide teachers and administrators with information

regarding the effectiveness of their educational systems in

producing student achievement." "The student's performance must be

compared against some standard."

PRESENTING SOURCES: A SUMMARY OF PRELIMINARY WRITING SKILLS

1. *Annotation:* underlining the text and inserting marginal comments on the page. The notes can explain points that are unclear, define difficult words, emphasize key ideas, point out connections to previous or subsequent paragraphs, or suggest the reader's own reactions to what is being discussed. Annotation is the written result of the mental process of comprehension that occurs as the reader absorbs the material on the page. Since writing down marginal comments assumes the presence of a text, annotation can never serve as a substitute for or a complete reference to another person's ideas.

2. *Outlining:* constructing a systematic list of ideas that reflects the basic structure of an essay or book, with major and minor points distributed on different levels. Outlining is a reductive skill that suggests the bones of a work, but little of its flesh or outward appearance. Outlining is especially useful for covering a long sequence of material containing ideas whose relationship is easy to grasp. Densely written passages that rely on frequent and subtle distinctions and dexterous use of language are not easily condensed into an outline.

3. *Summary:* condensing a paragraph or an essay or a chapter into a relatively brief presentation of the main ideas. Unlike annotation, a summary should make sense as an independent, coherent piece of writing. Unlike paraphrase, a summary does not try to include everything. However, the summary should be complete in the sense that it provides a fair representation of the work and its parts. Summary is the all-purpose skill; it is neither crude nor overly detailed.

4. *Quotation:* including another person's exact words within your own writing. Although quotation requires the least amount of invention, it is the most technical of all these skills, demanding an understanding of conventional and complex punctuation. In your notes and in your essays, quotation should be a last resort. If the phrasing is unique, if the presentation is subtle, if the point at issue is easily misunderstood or hotly debated, the quotation may be appropriate. When in doubt, paraphrase.

5. *Paraphrasing:* recapitulating, point-by-point, using your own words. A paraphrase is a faithful and complete rendition of the original, following much the same order of ideas. Although full-length paraphrase is practical only with relatively brief

passages, it is the most reliable way to make sense out of a difficult text. Paraphrasing a sentence or two, together with a citation of the author's name, is the best method of presenting another person's ideas within your own essay.

EXERCISE 28

Consider each of the following situations, and decide which of the five skills summarized would be an appropriate method of preparation. (More than one skill may be applicable to each situation, but try to write them down in order of probable usefulness.)

1. You are about to take a closed-book exam based on materials from six different sources—about a hundred pages in all.

2. You are taking notes while listening to a TV talk-show interview with a person who is the subject of an essay that you are writing.

3. You are a social worker who has had a client transferred to her; you have a lengthy case history to absorb before the next staff meeting.

4. You are writing a term paper on a political philosopher, and have temporarily borrowed (for the weekend) one of his most important books from your teacher.

5. You are preparing to participate in a debate on foreign policy, for which you have read two books; you will be given twenty-five minutes to present your point of view.

6. You are preparing to participate in a roundtable discussion that will be debating a controversial book; the format will be conversational.

7. You have been given access to archives containing irreplacable historic letters, too fragile to be photo-copied.

8. You have taken a field trip to a museum to see a display of ancient art; two or three of the exhibits may be included on your art history

exam, but the catalogue is too expensive to buy just for a few pages of reading.

9. You are about to take an open-book exam based on a single text.

10. You are a law student looking up a crucial court decision that will be a precedent for a mock trial in which you are the prosecutor.

11. You are in the reference room of the library, checking on the historical background for the text that is the subject of your term paper; there are at least ten separate sources that you might include, but each is a brief reference.

12. You are taking notes at a one-hour lecture in your field of specialization.

13. You are interviewing an important official who has suddenly begun to talk about his political intentions.

14. You are preparing for a conference with your teacher to discuss topics for a term paper; you have narrowed down the possibilities to three books.

15. You are being given verbal instructions in the working of complex scientific apparatus which, if misused, may blow up.

PART III
WRITING FROM SOURCES

The previous two chapters have described the most basic methods of understanding another writer's ideas, and presenting them accurately and naturally, as part of your own writing. However, the units of writing with which you have been working have been extremely brief and limited: the sentence and the paragraph. Now you can combine the skills of Part II with those of Part I to develop your own ideas in a full-length essay that is based on other people's work.

When you write at length from sources, you must deal with two points of view—your own and those of your sources. As the writer you have a dual responsibility: you must do justice to yourself by developing your own ideas, and you must do justice to each source by providing a fair representation of its author's ideas. But blending the ideas of two or more people within the same essay can create competition and confusion: Who is to dominate? How much of yourself should you include? How much of your source? Moreover, in academic writing you may have to respond to a third voice—that of your teacher, who may assign a topic or otherwise set limits and goals for your essay's development.

Chapter 4 discusses four approaches to writing based on a single source. Each represents a method of reconciling competing influences on your writing and blending the voices that your reader ought to hear:

1. You can distinguish between your source and yourself by writing about the two separately, first the source and then yourself.

2. You can help your reader to understand a difficult and confusing source by presenting your own interpretation of the author's ideas.
3. You can apply a narrow, predetermined focus to your source by writing about a topic or question set by your teacher.
4. You can use your source as evidence for the development of your own ideas by writing an essay on a similar or related topic.

In the end, yours must be the dominant voice. It is you who will choose the thesis and control the essay's shape and direction; it is your understanding and judgment that will interpret and present your source materials to your reader. When you and your classmates are asked to write about the same reading, your teacher hopes to receive not an identical set of essays, but rather a series of individual interpretations with a common starting point in the same source.

The difficulties of combining your own ideas with those of your source are inevitably compounded when you begin to work with a group of sources and thus have several authors competing for representation. This is the subject of Chapter 5. It is more than ever vital that your own voice dominate your essay and that you do not end up summarizing first one source and then the next, without any perspective of your own. The method for blending a variety of sources is usually called *synthesis*. This technique is very much like the construction of the topic sentence for a paragraph; you have to look beyond the claims of any one author's assertions (as, in paragraph writing, you try to present more than one example or fact) and become aware of a broader generalization into which all of the supporting material may be subordinated. Your own generalized conclusions become the basis for your essay's thesis and organization, while the ideas of your sources serve as the evidence which supports those conclusions.

What Chapter 5 will emphasize are the standard methods of marshalling your sources: the analysis of each source in a search for common themes, the establishment of common denominators or categories that cut across the separate sources and provide the structure for your essay, the evaluation of each source's relative cogency as you decide which to emphasize, and the citation of a group of references from several different sources in support of a single point. These skills are closely related to some of the most common and useful strategies for constructing an essay: definition, classification, and comparison. The chapter ends with some specialized practice in the selection, arrangement, and presentation of sources.

4. The Single-Source Essay

Writing from a source requires that you understand another writer's ideas as thoroughly as you understand your own. The first step in carrying out any of the four strategies described in this chapter is to read carefully through the source essay, applying the skills for comprehension that you learned about in Chapter 2: annotation, outlining, and summary. Once you are able to explain to your reader what the source is all about, then you can begin to plan a rebuttal, interpretation, or analysis of the author's ideas, or you can write your own essay on the same topic.

SEPARATING SOURCE AND SELF

The simplest approach to writing about someone else's ideas is complete separation: the structure of your essay breaks into two parts, with the source's views presented first and your own reactions given equal or greater space immediately afterwards. This approach works best when you are writing about an author with whom you disagree. Instead of treating the reading as evidence in support of your point of view and blending it with your own ideas, you write an essay that first analyzes and then refutes your source's basic themes. Look, for example, at Roger Sipher's "So That Nobody Has to Go to School if They Don't Want To."

SO THAT NOBODY HAS TO GO TO SCHOOL IF THEY DON'T WANT TO

A decline in standardized test scores is but the most recent indicator that American education is in trouble.

One reason for the crisis is that present mandatory-attendance laws force many to attend school who have no wish to be there. Such children have little desire to learn and are so antagonistic to school that neither they nor more highly motivated students receive the quality education that is the birthright of every American.

The solution to this problem is simple: Abolish compulsory-attendance laws and allow only those who are committed to getting an education to attend.

This will not end public education. Contrary to conventional belief, legislators enacted compulsory-attendance laws to legalize what already existed. William Landes and Lewis Solomon, economists, found little evidence that mandatory-attendance laws increased the number of children in school. They found, too, that school systems have never effectively enforced such laws, usually because of the expense involved.

There is no contradiction between the assertion that compulsory attendance has had little effect on the number of children attending school and the argument that repeal would be a positive step toward improving education. Most parents want a high school education for their children. Unfortunately, compulsory attendance hampers the ability of public school officials to enforce legitimate educational and disciplinary policies and thereby make the education a good one.

Private schools have no such problem. They can fail or dismiss students, knowing such students can attend public school. Without compulsory attendance, public schools would be freer to oust students whose academic or personal behavior undermines the educational mission of the institution.

Has not the noble experiment of a formal education for everyone failed? While we pay homage to the homily, "You can lead a horse to water but you can't make him drink," we have pretended it is not true in education.

Ask high school teachers if recalcitrant students learn anything of value. Ask teachers if these students do any homework. Quite the contrary, these students know they will be passed from grade to grade until they are old enough to quit or until, as is more likely, they receive a high school diploma. At the point when students could legally quit, most choose to remain since they know they are likely to be allowed to graduate whether they do acceptable work or not.

Abolition of archaic attendance laws would produce enormous dividends.

First, it would alert everyone that school is a serious place where one goes to learn. Schools are neither day-care centers nor indoor street corners. Young people who resist learning should stay away; indeed, an end to compulsory schooling would require them to stay away.

Second, students opposed to learning would not be able to pollute the educational atmosphere for those who want to learn. Teachers could stop policing recalcitrant students and start educating.

Third, grades would show what they are supposed to: how well a student is learning. Parents could again read report cards and know if their children were making progress.

Fourth, public esteem for schools would increase. People would stop regarding them as way stations for adolescents and start thinking of them as institutions for educating America's youth.

Fifth, elementary schools would change because students would find out early that they had better learn something or risk flunking out later. Elementary teachers would no longer have to pass their failures on to junior high and high school.

Sixth, the cost of enforcing compulsory education would be eliminated. Despite enforcement efforts, nearly 15 percent of the school-age children in our largest cities are almost permanently absent from school.

Communities could use these savings to support institutions to deal with young people not in school. If, in the long run, these institutions prove more costly, at least we would not confuse their mission with that of schools.

Schools should be for education. At present, they are only tangentially so. They have attempted to serve an all-encompassing social function, trying to be all things to all people. In the process they have failed miserably at what they were originally formed to accomplish.

Roger Sipher, New York Times, 19 December 1977

Presenting Your Source's Point of View

Sipher opposes compulsary attendance laws. Let us suppose that you, on the other hand, can see strong advantages in imposing a very strict rule for attendance. In order for you to challenge Sipher convincingly, you will have to incorporate both his point of view and yours within a single short essay.

Since your job is to *respond* to Sipher, your first responsibility is to present his point of view to your readers. State it as fairly as you can, without pausing to argue with him or to offer your own ideas about mandatory attendance. Even though you are giving the first round to your opponent, his ideas need not dominate your essay. In fact, Sipher is more likely to dominate if you simply copy the structure of his essay, presenting and answering each of his points one by one. While at first it may seem easiest to follow Sipher's sequence of ideas (especially since his points are so clearly numbered), you will be arguing on his terms, according to his conception of the issue rather than yours. Instead, make sure that your reader understands what Sipher is actually saying before you begin your rebuttal. To do so, carry out *both* of the following steps:

1. Briefly summarize the issue and the reasons which prompted the author to write the essay. You do this by writing a brief summary, as explained in Chapter 2. Here is a summary of Sipher's article:

> Roger Sipher argues that the presence in the classroom of
> unwilling students who are indifferent to learning can

> explain why public school students as a whole are learning
> less and less. Sipher therefore recommends that public
> schools discontinue the policy of mandatory attendance.
> Instead, students would be allowed to drop out if they
> wished, and faculty would be able to expel students whose
> behavior made it difficult for serious students to do
> their work. Once unwilling students were no longer forced
> to attend, schools would once again be able to maintain
> high standards of achievement; they could devote money and
> energy to education, rather than custodial care.

You can make a summary like this one more detailed by adding paraphrased accounts of some of the author's arguments, as well as a quotation or two.

**2. Analyze and present some of the basic principles that underlie
the author's position on this specific issue.** If, throughout your debate
with the author, you remain on the surface of the topic, you run the risk
of appearing superficial in your understanding of the issue: Sipher says
mandatory attendance is bad, and you say it is good; Sipher says difficult
students don't learn anything, and you say all students learn something
useful; and so on. This point-by-point rebuttal shows that you disagree,
but it provides no context in which readers can decide who is right and
who is wrong. You have no starting point for your counter-arguments
and no choice but to sound arbitrary.

Instead, ask yourself why the author has taken this position, one which
you find so easy to reject. Where and what are the foundations of his
arguments? What larger principles do they suggest? In the case of Sipher,
what policies is he objecting to? Why? What values is he determined to
defend? Can these values or principles be applied to issues other than
attendance? You are examining Sipher's specific responses to the practical problem of attendance in order to infer some broad generalizations
about his philosophy of education. While Sipher does not state these
generalizations in this article, you would be safe in concluding that Sipher's views on attendance derive from a conflict of two principles: the
belief that education is a right that may not be denied under any circumstances, and the belief that education is a privilege to be earned.
Sipher would advocate the latter. Thus, immediately after you summarize
the article, you analyze Sipher's implicit position in a paragraph:

> Sipher's argument implies that there is no such thing as
> the right to an education. A successful education can only
> depend on the student's willing presence and active
> participation. Passive or rebellious students cannot be
> educated and should not be forced to stay in school.

> Although everyone has the right to an opportunity for
> education, its acquisition is actually the privilege of
> those who choose to work for it.

By analyzing Sipher's position, you have not only found out more about what you are actually arguing about, but you have also established a common context—eligibility for education—within which you and he differ. With a clear understanding of the differences between you, your reader will have a real basis for choosing between your opposing views. At the same time, your reader is being assured that *this* and no other is the essential point for debate; thus, you will be fighting on ground that *you* have chosen.

3. Present your reasons for disagreeing with your source. Once you have established your opponent's position, you may then plan your own counter-arguments by writing down your reactions and pinpointing the exact reasons for your disagreement. (All the statements analyzed in this section are taken from such preliminary responses; they are not excerpts from finished essays.) Your reasons for disagreeing with Sipher might fit into one of three categories:

1. you believe that his basic principle is not valid;
2. you decide that his principle, although valid, cannot be strictly applied to the practical situation under discussion;
3. you accept Sipher's principle, but you are aware of other, stronger influences which diminish its importance.

Whichever line of argument you choose, it is impossible to present your case successfully if you wholly ignore Sipher's basic principle, as Student A does:

Student A:

> Sipher's isn't a constructive solution. Without strict
> attendance laws, many students wouldn't come to school at
> all.

Non-attendance is exactly what Sipher wants: he argues that indifferent students should be permitted to stay away, since their absence would benefit everyone. Student A makes no effort to refute Sipher's point, in effect saying to his source, "You're wrong!" without explaining why.

Student B, on the other hand, tries to establish a basis for disagreement:

Student B:

> If mandatory attendance were to be abolished, how would
> children acquire the skills to survive in an educated
> society such as ours?

According to Student B, the practical uses of education have become so important that a student's very survival may one day depend on having been well educated. Implied here is the principle, in opposition to Sipher's, that receiving an education cannot be a matter of choice or a privilege to be earned. What children learn in school is so important to their future lives that they should be forced to attend classes, even against their will, for their own good. But this response is still superficial. Student B is confusing the desired object—getting an education—with one of the means of achieving that object—being present in the classroom; attendance, the means, has become an end in itself. Since students who attend, but do not participate, will not learn, mandatory attendance cannot create an educated population.

On the other hand, although attendance may not be the *only* condition for education, the student's physical presence in the classroom is certainly important. In that case, should the decision about attendance, a decision likely to affect much of their future lives, be placed in the hands of those too young to understand the consequences?

Student C:

> The absence of attendance laws would be too tempting for students and might create a generation of semi-illiterates. Consider the marginal student who, despite general indifference and occasional bad behavior, shows some promise and capacity for learning. Without a policy of mandatory attendance, he might choose the easy way out instead of trying to develop his abilities. As a society, we owe these students, at whatever cost, a chance at a good and sound education.

Notice that Student C specifies a "chance" at education. In a sense, there is no basic conflict between his views and Sipher's. Both agree in principle that society can provide the opportunity, but not the certainty, of being educated. The distinction here lies in the way in which the principle is applied. Sipher feels no need to make allowances or exceptions: there are limits to the opportunities that society is obliged to provide. Student C, however, believes that society must act in the best interests of those too young to make such decisions; for them, the principle of education as a privilege should be less rigorously applied. Students should be exposed to the conditions for (if not the fact of) education, whether they like it or not, until they become adults, capable of choice.

Student D goes even further, suggesting that society is not only obliged to expose the student to educational opportunity, but schools are responsible for making the experience as attractive as possible:

Student D:

Maybe the reason for a decrease in attendance and an unwillingness to learn is not that students do not want an education, but that the whole system of discipline and learning is ineffective. If schools concentrated on making classes more appealing, the result would be better attendance.

In Student D's analysis of the problem, the passive students are like consumers who need to be encouraged to take advantage of an excellent product that is not selling well. To encourage good attendance, the schools ought to consider using more attractive marketing methods. Implicit in this view is a transferral of blame from the student to the school. Other arguments of this sort might blame the parents, rather than the schools, for not teaching their children an understanding of their own best interests.

Finally, Student E concedes the validity of Sipher's view of education, but finds that the whole issue has become subordinate to a more important problem.

Student E:

We already have a problem with youths roaming the street, getting into serious trouble. Just multiply the current number of unruly kids by five or ten, and you will come up with the number of potential delinquents that will be hanging around the streets if we do away with the attendance laws that keep them in school. Sipher may be right when he argues that the quality of education would improve if unwilling students were permitted to drop out, but he would be wise to remember that those remaining inside school will have to deal with those on the outside sooner or later.

In this perspective, reasons of security, not education, prevail. Student E implicitly accepts and gives some social value to the image (rejected by Sipher) of school as a prison, with students sentenced to mandatory confinement.

A reasonably full response, like those of Student C and Student E, can provide the material for a series of paragraphs that argue against Sipher's position. Here, for example, is Student E's statement after it was broken down into the basic topics for a four paragraph sequence. The numbers in parentheses suggest a reordering of the topics, using the student's basic agreement with Sipher as the starting point.

danger from dropouts if Sipher's plan is adopted (3)

custodial function of school (2)

concession that Sipher is right about education (1)

interests of law and order outweigh interests of education (4)

We already have a problem with youths roaming the street, getting into serious trouble. Just multiply the current number of unruly kids by five or ten, and you will come up with the number of potential delinquents that will be hanging around the streets if we do away with the attendance laws that keep them in school. Sipher may be right when he argues that the quality of education would improve if unwilling students were allowed to drop out, but he would be wise to remember that those remaining on the inside of the school will have to deal with those on the outside sooner or later.

Student E can now develop four full-length paragraphs by explaining each section of the response and offering supporting evidence and illustrative examples.

ASSIGNMENT 9

Read "The Personal Cost of Cheating on Unemployment Insurance" and "On Cloning a Human Being" and choose, as the starting point for a summary-and-response, the essay with which you disagree most. (If you find yourself in substantial agreement with both authors, try "Birthrights," by Richard Farson, or "A Question of Degree," by Blanche Blank, both in Chapter 2.) First write a two-part summary of the essay, the first part describing the author's position and explicitly stated arguments, the second analyzing the principles underlying that position. Then present your own evaluation and rebuttal of the author's point of view. The length of your essay will depend on the number and complexity of the ideas that you find in the source and the number of counterarguments that you can muster. The minimum acceptable length for the entire assignment is two typewritten pages (approximately 500–600 words).

THE PERSONAL COST OF CHEATING ON UNEMPLOYMENT INSURANCE

The following information about unemployment-insurance abuse is a result of personal knowledge. I have misused the privilege of receiving money from the state and so have many of my friends. These abuses are widely known to both the givers and takers of the money and, in many instances, to the general public as well, yet we all go along, seeming to believe that unemployment insurance is really doing what it's meant to do: help people who have worked and are laid off for a period of time while they sincerely look for work.

Of course, there are deserving people who, perhaps after years of work, have been laid off and really do need help. Unemployment insurance should be a trust fund for them, not an unending stream of financial aid for anyone who can figure out a way of working only when he wants to and collecting the rest of the time.

It is wrong when a person who has chosen to take the risks as well as the higher pay of being a freelance worker can, when the job is finished, collect money as if he had been a full-time staff worker who was laid off.

It is wrong that a person can make $75,000 in one year and take the next year off and collect unemployment.

It is wrong when a person is offered a job in his field and can choose to refuse it, waiting for a job more to his liking sometime in the future while continuing to collect unemployment.

It is wrong when a person can collect unemployment by categorizing his job as, for example, an "animation commercial production manager," knowing that 10 such jobs exist in New York City and that they are all filled and that his abilities actually include secretarial or other skills.

It is wrong when a person works and is paid under the table and collects unemployment.

Unemployment is the standard way of life for many professional, technical and creative people in New York. Employers collude with them, writing "lack of work" on the unemployment form when the freelancer knew the duration of the job when he accepted it, or when the person quit or was fired for poor performance. Few employers have the courage to say no and go against the "everyone does it" mentality. They also contribute to abuse when they pay under the table, saving themselves money and bookkeeping expenses and allowing their workers to continue to collect unemployment money while working.

The Government plays its own part in the game, making it legal to collect as much as $125 tax free for doing nothing while the minimum wage is about $106 per week.

But most of us know all this, especially those of us who have been on that unemployment line. What we may not know is the damage to the whole person, the real price of dishonestly being on the dole. It took me a couple of years to feel and recognize the price I paid.

Physically, my energy was never lower. I felt listless much of the time.

The afternoons were the worst; people were working and I was watching the "soaps" and eating. Mentally, I was in a fog, confused and wandering, not wanting to focus on what was happening in my life. Emotionally, I felt vaguely disturbed, unworthy, generally uncomfortable, very anxious and very guilty. I was half alive, unable and unwilling to fulfill my responsibilities as an adult, to take care of myself, to give to my community. Worst of all, I was lying to myself and justifying my position.

Now, when I think back, it's so clear, but then it was so insidious.

There were so many rationalizations for taking the money: "The Government allows it." "I've worked 10 years; I've earned it." "I really am an animation commercial production manager. It's not my fault that there isn't a job in that field." "Everyone else is doing it." And finally, "I really am looking for a job," which simply was not true except for a cursory glance now and then at the want ads. None of these justifications ever made a dent in the gnawing guilt and sense of worthlessness.

Finally, I did allow myself to feel the pain of it all and stopped the downhill run in my self-esteem by accepting (in the eyes of my glorified self-image) a very simple, humble job. I discovered that in the simplicity of doing a job, any job, I began to feel self-respect for the first time in two years.

Taking money from unemployment is difficult; it hurts even when you legitimately need it and don't abuse it. But it's deadly, insidiously deadly, when you abuse it and lie to yourself about it. So to my friends who still cheat life in this way: Please stop passing the buck by blaming others and the system; check out how you really feel about it deep inside. What is the price you are paying? There is one, and it's too high.

Patricia Knack, *New York Times*, 19 February 1978

ON CLONING A HUMAN BEING

It is now theoretically possible to recreate an identical creature from any animal or plant, from the DNA contained in the nucleus of any somatic cell. A single plant root-tip cell can be teased and seduced into conceiving a perfect copy of the whole plant; a frog's intestinal epithelial cell possesses the complete instructions needed for a new, same frog. If the technology were further advanced, you could do this with a human being, and there are now startled predictions all over the place that this will in fact be done, someday, in order to provide a version of immortality for carefully selected, especially valuable people.

The cloning of humans is on most of the lists of things to worry about from Science, along with behavior control, genetic engineering, transplanted heads, computer poetry, and the unrestrained growth of plastic flowers.

Cloning is the most dismaying of prospects, mandating as it does the elimination of sex with only a metaphoric elimination of death as compensation. It is almost no comfort to know that one's cloned, identical surrogate lives on, especially when the living will very likely involve edging one's real, now aging self off to the side, sooner or later. It is hard to imagine anything like filial affection or respect for a single, unmated nucleus; harder still to think of one's new, self-generated self as anything but an absolute, desolate orphan. Not to mention the complex interpersonal relationship involved in raising one's self from infancy, teaching the language, enforcing discipline, instilling good manners, and the like. How would you feel if you became an incorrigible juvenile delinquent by proxy, at the age of fifty-five?

The public questions are obvious. Who is to be selected, and on what qualifications? How to handle the risks of misused technology, such as self-determined cloning by the rich and powerful but socially objectionable, or the cloning by governments of dumb, docile masses for the world's work? What will be the effect on all the uncloned rest of us of human sameness? After all, we've accustomed ourselves through hundreds of millennia to the continual exhilaration of uniqueness; each of us is totally different, in a fundamental sense, from all the other four billion. Selfness is an essential fact of life. The thought of human nonselfness, precise sameness, is terrifying, when you think about it.

Well, don't think about it, because it isn't a probable possibility, not even as a long shot for the distant future, in my opinion. I agree that you might clone some people who would look amazingly like their parental cell donors, but the odds are that they'd be almost as different as you or me, and certainly more different than any of today's identical twins.

The time required for the experiment is only one of the problems, but a formidable one. Suppose you wanted to clone a prominent, spectacularly successful diplomat, to look after the Middle East problems of the distant future. You'd have to catch him and persuade him, probably not very hard to do, and extirpate a cell. But then you'd have to wait for him to grow up through embryonic life and then for at least forty years more, and you'd have to be sure all observers remained patient and unmeddlesome through his unpromising, ambiguous childhood and adolescence.

Moreover, you'd have to be sure of recreating his environment, perhaps down to the last detail. "Environment" is a word which really means people, so you'd have to do a lot more cloning than just the diplomat himself.

This is a very important part of the cloning problem, largely overlooked in our excitement about the cloned individual himself. You don't have to agree all the way with B. F. Skinner to acknowledge that the environment does make a difference, and when you examine what we really mean by the word "environment" it comes down to other human beings. We use euphemisms and jargon for this, like "social forces," "cultural influences," even Skinner's "verbal community," but what is meant is the dense crowd of nearby people who talk to, listen to, smile or frown at, give to, withhold from, nudge, push, caress, or flail out at the individual. No matter what the genome says, these people have a lot to do with shaping a character. Indeed, if all you had was the genome, and no people around, you'd grow a sort of vertebrate plant, nothing more.

So, to start with, you will undoubtedly need to clone the parents. No question about this. This means the diplomat is out, even in theory, since you couldn't have gotten cells from both his parents at the time when he was himself just recognizable as an early social treasure. You'd have to limit the list of clones to people already certified as sufficiently valuable for the effort, with both parents still alive. The parents would need cloning and, for consistency, their parents as well. I suppose you'd also need the usual informed-consent forms, filled out and signed, not easy to get if I know parents, even harder for grandparents.

But this is only the beginning. It is the whole family that really influences the way a person turns out, not just the parents, according to current psychiatric thinking. Clone the family.

Then what? The way each member of the family develops has already been determined by the environment set around him, and this environment is more people, people outside the family, schoolmates, acquaintances, lovers, enemies, car-pool partners, even, in special circumstances, peculiar strangers across the aisle on the subway. Find them, and clone them.

But there is no end to the protocol. Each of the outer contacts has his own surrounding family, and his and their outer contacts. Clone them all.

To do the thing properly, with any hope of ending up with a genuine duplicate of a single person, you really have no choice. You must clone the world, no less.

We are not ready for an experiment of this size, nor, I should think, are we willing. For one thing, it would mean replacing today's world by an entirely identical world to follow immediately, and this means no new, natural, spontaneous, random, chancy children. No children at all, except for the manufactured doubles of those now on the scene. Plus all those identical adults, including all of today's politicians, all seen double. It is too much to contemplate.

Moreover, when the whole experiment is finally finished, fifty years or so from now, how could you get a responsible scientific reading on the outcome? Somewhere in there would be the original clonee, probably lost and overworked, now well into middle age, but everyone around him would be precise duplicates of today's everyone. It would be today's same world, filled to overflowing with duplicates of today's people and their same, duplicated problems, probably all resentful at having had to go through our whole thing all over, sore enough at the clone to make endless trouble for him, if they found him.

And obviously, if the whole thing were done precisely right, they would still be casting about for ways to solve the problem of universal dissatisfaction, and sooner or later they'd surely begin to look around at each other, wondering who should be cloned for his special value to society, to get us out of all this. And so it would go, in regular cycles, perhaps forever.

I once lived through a period when I wondered what Hell could be like, and I stretched my imagination to try to think of a perpetual sort of damnation. I have to confess, I never thought of anything like this.

I have an alternative suggestion, if you're looking for a way out. Set cloning aside, and don't try it. Instead, go in the other direction. Look for ways to get mutations more quickly, new variety, different songs. Fiddle around, if you must fiddle, but never with ways to keep things the same, no matter who, not even yourself. Heaven, somewhere ahead, has got to be a change.

Lewis Thomas, from *The Medusa and the Snail*

INTERPRETING WHAT YOU SUMMARIZE

Interpretation means the explanation or clarification of something that has been read, seen, or heard; the interpreter serves as go-between for the author and the reader or audience. At the United Nations, interpreters translate all the speeches into other languages so that all the delegates can understand them. A writer interprets a source by "translating" the author's ideas into terms that readers may find easier to understand and more meaningful.

In daily life, you interpret ideas and information for yourself and for others whenever you try to explain an action or event or situation. Suppose that a friend has asked you to explain the reasons for the impending bankruptcy of the drugstore on the next corner. The easiest way to do so might be to provide a full account of the reasons in chronological order, year by year, month by month: two years ago, the owner of the Best Pharmacy fell ill and was unable to supervise the store; shortly afterward, the zoning laws changed and the neighborhood became less residential; next, the chief pharmacist decided to move to the south; meanwhile, an outbreak of vandalism and petty thefts had begun; then a discount store opened a block away; only two months ago, the overworked owner had his second heart attack; and so on. Without stressing any one event, you could elaborate upon each step, providing exact dates and details to form a chronological summary of the store's gradual decline.

But if your friend only wanted a brief account of the long story, you would need to emphasize one (or more) of the reasons, probably removing it from its place in the chronological order. As soon as you make a choice and decide which piece of information to take out of its slot in the original time-sequence, you have begun to interpret the event. Of course, you must be familiar with all the stages in order to pull out one fact and confidently state that *this* was the primary reason for the pharmacy's decline. But, after weighing each fact against the others, you might finally assert that the drugstore failed because of a shift in residential patterns in that area of the city. Then (you might choose to add) this shift led to outbreaks of crime, the pharmacist's move to Florida, and the worries that brought about the owner's heart attack.

The first chronological summary was a factual list, with no attempt made to stress one idea more than the next; therefore, there was little possibility of dispute. But as soon as you condense the reasons for the drugstore's impending bankruptcy, another informed observer might refuse to accept the implications of your interpretation of events. Instead, she might claim that, in *her* view, the success of a neighborhood store always depends on the diligence of the owner and the quality of service; therefore the illness of the owner and, to a lesser extent, the departure of the pharmacist were chiefly responsible for the loss of business. Given the conflict between these two interpretations—declining residential population versus declining service—each of you might wish to expand your summary and supply some supporting evidence to reinforce your main point. The second observer might offer personal experience to back up her conclusion: after several of the substitute employees had been rude and neglectful, she and her neighbors began to shop at the discount store up the street. You, on the other hand, might cite statistics about the effect of the new zoning laws on all small businesses in the neighborhood.

The point is that both interpretations may be equally valid. Each is based on personal judgment as well as factual evidence. Each person has employed particular values and preconceptions in interpreting the actual events, which are common knowledge. (There is not always as much scope for speculation and disagreement when one is interpreting a *written* source, for the body of the material is closed and finite.) In fact, another interpretation of the same source material might emphasize a quite different idea. A stranger to the city, who has listened to both versions, might later conclude that "there are *two* main reasons why that drugstore is failing. . . ." Or, by now quite familiar with all the events (and more objective than either of the first two interpreters), he might try to encompass *all* the reasons into a single new interpretive summary: "Conditions of modern urban life do not favor the small, owner-operated business." Notice that, in order to encompass everything that has come before, this final summary is more general than the first two.

EXERCISE 29

Almost all reviews of films, plays, television programs, and books serve a dual function: they explain what the work is about and assess its value for an audience. It is important to be able to distinguish between *interpretation* (which does not explicitly pass judgment on the worth of a work) and *evaluation* (which contains the reviewer's opinion of the work and the standards which, according to the reviewer, the work should meet). Read the following review, and use different symbols to mark:

> A. passages and phrases where the author *summarizes* the plot;
> B. passages and phrases where he *interprets* (or provides additional background for) the ideas and themes of the program;
> C. passages and phrases where he *evaluates* the program.

Are there any passages that do not fall into one of the three categories above? What is their function in the review?

TV: "KAREN ANN QUINLAN" DRAMA IS SENSITIVE TO PARENTS' ORDEAL

In another "fact-based" project for television entertainment, NBC is offering, at 9 this evening, "In the Matter of Karen Ann Quinlan." The Quinlan case attracted international attention in 1975 when Karen Ann fell into a coma and was supposedly being kept alive by "extraordinary means" in a Roman Catholic hospital. Concluding from medical reports that their daughter's physical condition had deteriorated well beyond any hope of reasonable recovery, the Quinlans made the painful decision to "pull the plug" on the hospital's sophisticated machinery and put the fate of Karen Ann "in God's hands."

But, as they quickly discovered, the decision was not to be implemented so easily. Karen was 21, and Mr. Quinlan was technically no longer her legal guardian. He had to file a court petition seeking that status. The petition was discovered by a local New Jersey newspaper, and the Quinlan case vaulted into newspaper headlines and television news reports as a debate, often outrageously emotional, raged on the complicated question of maintaining life under the artificial means of modern medicine. Eventually the case reached the courts.

Hal Sitowitz's script for this television film is entirely on the side of the Quinlans. In an understandably sympathetic portrait, the parents are represented as deeply religious, compassionate and sensitive to all nuances of the case.

Complicating matters is the fact that Karen Ann, their eldest child, was adopted, and there is some irresponsible speculation that the Quinlans might have reached a different decision if one of their "natural" children had been involved.

The film firmly dismisses all such aspersions. Although the stricken figure of Karen Ann is never seen, the script contains explicit descriptions of her dreadful deterioration. Her weight has declined from 120 to 70 pounds, and her body is grotesquely contorted. Doctors agree that she has suffered irreversible brain-damage. It is continuously emphasized that "even if she comes back, she'd live like a vegetable." The parents' decision, made with extreme reluctance, simply recognizes that "she's not with us, she's not with God, she's with pipes and valves stuck into her."

Those on the side of the good-guy parents also include a young lawyer (David Huffman) and a Catholic priest (Biff McGuire). The forces of timid self-interest and blatant harassment are represented by some medical and hospital officials and seemingly most of a vulturelike press. When the reporters and cameramen descend hungrily on the hapless family, someone notes warily that "Now it all begins," a popular film line that was last used in Franco Zeffirelli's "Jesus of Nazareth," following the Resurrection.

On the whole, however, "In the Matter of Karen Ann Quinlan" is kept to a modest and carefully unsensational scale. The larger issues had been confined within—or reduced to—domestic drama. And the result is affecting, largely because of two fine performances. As Mr. Quinlan,

Brian Keith creates a character of an almost awkward but utterly convincing goodness, and Piper Laurie is brilliantly subtle and restrained in the role of Mrs. Quinlan. Using intelligent understatement, she dominates everyone and everything around her. Her performance alone makes this a production worth watching.

John J. O'Connor, New York Times, 26 September 1977

Interpreting an Essay

When you undertake to summarize a long and complex essay, one with ideas woven together, you may sometimes have to interpret and recast its contents. Your own explanation of the author's exact meaning should enable another reader to understand it more quickly and easily. In such cases, you present your interpretation of the source through a lengthy summary—through the ideas and information that you choose to explain and emphasize, through your explanations of ambiguous or contradictory ideas, through the connections that you make between apparently unrelated ideas, and through the gaps or deficiencies in the author's argument that you may choose to point out. While giving credit to the source and remaining faithful to its ideas, you will be presenting those ideas in a new and clearer light.

Since your purpose is summary as well as interpretation, you should attempt to condense the original material as much as possible, using selection and emphasis to convey to the reader what is important and what is not. Nevertheless, your version may run almost as long as the original essay. Its contents will be organized according to *your* interpretation of the source's ideas, and, because it is a summary, the readers will be hearing *your* characteristic voice, not the author's. For these reasons, the interpretive summary usually can be regarded as a separate essay in its own right.

An interpretive summary would probably be the appropriate approach in the following circumstances:

1. An essay contains a great many major ideas interwoven together.
2. An essay presents a lengthy argument whose step-by-step sequence is so complex that, if any stage is omitted, the reader of the summary will be missing something vital.
3. An essay is very disorganized and would benefit from reordering and from a recognition of the author's implicit strategy.
4. An essay is ambiguous and needs to have certain contradictions pointed out, if not resolved.

It is certainly possible for all four of these conditions to exist in a single essay, and then the summarizer will indeed be performing a service by clarifying what is obscure.

Guidelines for Writing an Interpretive Summary

After reading "The High Price of Success: You Are What You Do," study the five guidelines for writing an interpretive essay, together with the explanation of each rule as it could be applied to Heather Robertson's essay.

THE HIGH PRICE OF SUCCESS: YOU ARE WHAT YOU DO

I first watched a man cry when he was 30. They were not tears of pain or grief, but tears of anxiety. Things were not going well at work. It was a shock. For the first time I saw a man as frail, more vulnerable in many ways than myself. I began to look at men differently, my friends, men in their early thirties, men whose bravado and self-confidence I had accepted as real. I listen as they talk corporate gossip, brag of their plans and possessions, but I hear something hollow, false in their voices and as they chatter cheerfully on I see in their eyes a haunted, miserable look, the look of beasts in a zoo. I look at them—florid, fleshy from too much expense account booze, hair *Playboy* styled (seven dollars), suits ($250) which might have been cut to the same pattern from the same bolt of cloth, tense, busy, snapping their attaché cases open and shut with authority, whirring from appointment to appointment like windup automatons. They are strangers to me, although I have known them all my life. I leave their company bored by their success, depressed by their tension, contemptuous of their pretensions. It is men, not women, who are trapped.

We are the children of great expectations, the first generation of Canadians to come of age facing neither poverty nor war nor emigration. We carry a great weight of responsibility, generations of ambition and hope and sacrifice. We have inherited the earth. This pressure to realize the Canadian dream has helped women escape passivity and dependency because it offered only one measure of achievement—work. For men this obsession has been devastating.

"We are forced to *become* what we do," says a young lawyer, his black hair short, slicked down. In his white shirt and dark-blue suit he looks like something out of *Owen Marshall*. "Your occupation is your life. You can't practise law without *being* a lawyer, you have to act, think, talk and look like a lawyer. You're locked in. After a while it no longer bothers you. I don't want to be anything else. I love my life. I want to be exactly what I am." He is 32, unmarried, childless, involved in a series of casual affairs.

"Does your commitment to your work make it difficult for you to establish a lasting relationship with a woman?" I ask. He pulls back, alarmed. "You know," he says after a pause, "that's what my girl friend said when she left, that she came fourth after my work, my dog and my parents."

Women's options have increased, men's have diminished. "When I left high school," says the lawyer, "I had two choices, law or medicine, and I didn't like blood. Of course there were other choices, but they weren't presented to me."

War and unemployment no longer provide an escape from a system which manipulates men as totally and efficiently as it does women. I remember the little boys I knew in school, beating each other up, drawing skies full of fighter planes, loud-mouthed, cruel, aggressive.

"Men are trained from early childhood to be emotional amputees," says a 31-year-old businessman bitterly. He has just quit his job. "You chop off all your fingers of feeling. After a boy is three or four he doesn't go around kissing or hugging people any more and of course he doesn't cry. You learn not to be too loyal and not to take any other boy at his word. In any group of three, two will always be ganging up on the third. Every bit of leadership training teaches you to follow established authority. You learn how to exploit people, that's leadership. Women don't realize how superficial and shallow the relationships between men are. We don't see each other as people, creative individuals finding our place in the world. That's stupid rhetoric. Most men are doing jobs which have no relationship to their feeling of humanity. Christ, a peasant in Russia would have felt he was *doing* something a lot more than a man working in an office. They're both serfs. But at least a serf has a relationship with the land. In an office you don't have a relationship with anything except the company that humiliates you."

Most young men I know have already surpassed their parents' most extravagant ambitions. They flash their power and money and look around and say, "Okay, what's next?" Next, of course, is more of the same, a better job, a bigger house. It's all they know. They stifle unhappiness in liquor and handball; they take guitar lessons, ski, do dope on weekends, hustle women, trying to fill up that tiny, irrelevent compartment of their experience they've been taught to think of as their "private life," something every successful man must own, like a car. The more creative devote themselves to their work, accepting that emaciated definition of their manhood as the whole and trying to expand it by working even harder, acquiring even more power. Money becomes a substitute for the love they can neither receive nor express. They remain little boys playing games, selfish, protected, irresponsible, unable to develop the perspective that would give their world ethical structure, cynical, compulsive, prey to overwhelming fears and unconscious sexual pressures.

"Men who are anxious and unhappy work harder," says the businessman. "A woman's part in the economy is to make men anxious by depriving them emotionally. It's the mother who provides the motive force. Certainly mine did. She wanted me to make my way in the world to bring pride to her—I was an object of her success."

Power is enforced through punishment which is much more severe for boys than for girls. "It makes men nervous about power. They become preoccupied with it. Men respect their wives to the degree their wives have power over them. It makes women manipulative and crass. That's why it goes bad in bed. Once a man senses he is a victim he ceases to have sexual interest in his wife."

Anger also makes a man work harder and the most successful ones I know run on secret fury. A man usually takes out his psychic violence on his woman, laying on her all the qualities—stupidity, frigidity, vulgarity, corruption—that he most detests in himself. He flees from marriage and children, even from intimacy, as traps, proud of his independence. The woman, frozen out, often leaves. Her faithlessness justifies his cynicism and rage. He is alone. Tasted, the apple of power is ashes; he knows the loneliness and despair which is the definition of hell. How to get out? He doesn't even know the questions to ask.

Heather Robertson, *McLean's*, October 1974

Step one. *After reading the essay once, go through it again slowly, making a list of each separate idea; as you read each new sentence and paragraph, ask yourself whether the new point is individual enough and important enough to be an entry on your list.* Since "The High Price of Success" is a very digressive essay, the listing of ideas becomes an especially crucial and illuminating step. A preliminary reading suggests that Heather Robertson is chiefly concerned with the professional and personal unhappiness of Canadian men; to narrow your list, you must ruthlessly exclude (or list separately) any points, interesting in themselves, that are only loosely connected to Robertson's central theme. The numerous references to women are a good example: although the final version of your summary might contain a paragraph that contrasts men's lot with that of women, the inclusion of such a separate theme at the first stage will only confuse and complicate your list and perhaps prevent you from seeing the overall direction of the essay.

As you write the list of ideas, try to make each entry a complete sentence *in your own words.* When you retain the original author's wording, you may be including on your list phrases that sound good but do not actually stand for coherent ideas. For example, there is really very little, if anything, in the first paragraph of Robertson's essay that needs to go on your list: suggestive words like "anxiety," "windup automatons," and "bored by their success" remain meaningless unless you establish a context for them. Even the last tempting sentence—"It is men, not women who are trapped"—represents an incomplete idea: trapped by what? In fact, the list of ideas that follows begins with a reference from the *second* paragraph—the unrelenting pressures caused by the "Canadian dream."

1. The younger generation of Canadians is expected to realize their parents' hopes for prosperity and success.
2. The pressure is especially devastating for Canadian men, who have learned to live only for their work.

3. Men are not encouraged to choose between a wide range of professions; in one case, only law and medicine were acceptable.
4. The system is manipulative.
5. As children, boys are encouraged to curb their emotions and to avoid forming relationships.
6. Boys learn to strive to reach the top and become leaders; they also learn to accept the authority of those who have power over them.
7. Those men who are successful have not been satisfied by their possessions and their prestige.
8. Unable to conceive of more rewarding goals and unable to engage in satisfying relationships, some seek escape in superficial or self-destructive activities; others channel all their energies into their work to gain even greater symbols of their success.
9. Their self-absorption makes these men remain vulnerable little boys, without an understanding of the world and their place in it and without a humane system of values.
10. From childhood, boys learn to fear both punishment and those who have the power to punish.
11. Suppressing their emotions and their humanity causes these boys to grow up into cruel, exploitative men, anxious to take out their anger on those weaker than themselves.
12. These desperate men lack the knowledge and self-understanding to seek ways out of their isolation.

Step two. *Rearrange your list of points into an outline of the essay, following the author's basic strategy.*

Step three. *Using your outline of the essay, designate each main-level entry as a separate paragraph in your summary.* Stripped of irrelevancies, your list of Robertson's ideas will be short and manageable; the outlining of the source-essay and the paragraphing of your own essay are therefore almost the same process. (To review the procedure for outlining a complex essay, see Chapter 2.) The key to the process is your recognition of Robertson's strategy. This recognition comes after you have examined the original list of ideas and noticed that it includes (as the original essay does) both the reasons for the Canadian male's obsessive identification with his work and the emotional consequences of the obsession. Once you have perceived the basic *cause-effect* strategy underlying Robertson's essay, your list can be broken into two, with the items rearranged for clarity. Here is the reorganized list which serves as an outline of Robertson's essay *and* as an outline of the interpretive summary to be written about that essay:

Causes of the Obsession

1. The younger generation of Canadians has tacitly been forced to realize their parents' hopes for prosperity and success.
2. The austerity of childhood training teaches boys to curb their emotions, exalt competition, and accept the concept of an overriding authority.
3. A manipulative society no longer provides alternative options to the "acceptable" professions.

Effects of the Obsession

1. The cyclic need to gain more and more tokens of success has turned the ambitious young man into a robot; his obsessiveness has deprived him of an ethical perspective.
2. The need to suppress their anger has made many men exploitative and cruel.
3. Such men cope with their fury, disappointment, and frustration by seeking self-destructive forms of escape.

Step four. *Plan an introductory paragraph that contains a clear statement of the author's thesis and scope; if you can, include some suggestion of the essay's strategy.* Make sure that your introduction provides a fair account of Robertson's intentions. Some summarizers go beyond their legitimate function as interpreters of the original essay and wander off into digressions that the author did not include or intend. Here is the beginning of an introduction in which the summarizer's own views are attributed to Heather Robertson:

> According to Heather Robertson, men are not overly intelligent or ambitious; but they are wrapped up in themselves, full of pride. They are for the most part without drive and perseverence, easily discouraged, and they prefer to be in a secure position all the time.

This writer is manipulating Robertson's ideas in order to write an argumentative essay of her own. She even directly contradicts Robertson, who has described men as both ambitious and persevering. Later in the essay, it might be appropriate to disagree with the author, provided that it is made clear who is responsible for which point of view; but, as an introduction, the first point that the reader will encounter, such a statement can only create a false impression. Here is an introduction in which Robertson's scope, purpose, and strategy are given objectively:

> In "The Price of Success: You Are What You Do," Heather Robertson attempts to explain the reasons why so many

> Canadian men become obsessed with the achievement of
> professional success, as well as the debilitating
> physical, emotional, and moral consequences of that
> obsession. She depicts these men as stunted, trapped,
> frustrated robots, programmed to realize their goals at
> the expense of their humanity.

Step five. *As you write each paragraph, include related minor points and a few key details from the original essay, which are to be subordinated to the paragraph's central topic.* You need to convey to your reader some sense of the supporting materials that were provided in the original text. Although the actual writing of the summary's paragraphs ought to be relatively easy once the outline and strategy have been established, there are a few pitfalls to avoid. For example, you may pull a minor point out of the context of accompanying ideas, and thus inflate and distort it. One summarizer ignored Robertson's copious references to the masculine inability to show emotion and, instead, began a paragraph with the essay's *single* reference—in the first paragraph—to exactly the opposite point:

> Men are capable of showing emotion, especially when
> things are not going well.

With such a topic sentence, this paragraph must either come to a dead end, or else reverse itself!

Other errors of false emphasis are more serious since, by exaggeration, they can substantially change the meaning of the original essay. Since Robertson's references to the role of women take up more space than their thematic importance would warrant, it is easy to exaggerate their importance:

> The desire for power is instilled in males during
> childhood. Mothers activate them; they make their sons
> "objects of their own success." The son resents being
> manipulated by his mother and, in adult life, by his wife.

Notice how this author has slid from the childhood origins of the need for power (which *are* described at length in the essay) to the mother as the direct cause of this obsession. This last is an accusation that is never made by Robertson, but is taken without attribution—and misquoted—from the words of *one man*, whose opinions were quoted in the essay.

In a similar case of false emphasis (although this same "businessman" is not directly quoted), too much importance is attached to his sentiments, which are now (because the speaker is not identified) being attributed to Robertson:

> It is man's conception that women are the basic cause of
> his anxiety. He believes woman to be vicarious, sucking
> her success through his accomplishments.

The authors of these last two excerpts may have believed that the businessman whom Robertson quotes is typical of his generation. Robertson may think so, too, since she quotes only him, but she does not say so explicitly in the essay. If those interpreting Robertson's essay wish to point out how inevitable it is that such men should blame women (especially their mothers) for their ills, then they must take the responsibility for the interpretation. There are, after all, three points of view being discussed—Robertson's, the businessman's, and the interpreter's. The reader must be made aware of the exact boundary lines dividing these three points of view. The writer of a successful interpretive summary will integrate but not confuse his own opinions, those of the original author, and those of the original author's sources.

ASSIGNMENT 10

Write an interpretive summary of Christopher Lasch's "The Corruption of Sports." Before taking the first step and writing a list of ideas, consider why this essay needs and deserves to be interpreted at length.

THE CORRUPTION OF SPORTS

Among the activities through which men seek release from everyday life, games offer in many ways the purest form of escape. Like sex, drugs, and drink, they obliterate awareness of everyday reality, not by dimming that awareness but by raising it to a new intensity of concentration. Moreover, games have no side-effects, produce no hangovers or emotional complications. Games satisfy the need for free fantasy and the search for gratuitous difficulty simultaneously; they combine childlike exuberance with deliberately created complications.

By establishing conditions of equality among the players, Roger Caillois says, games attempt to substitute ideal conditions for "the normal confusion of everyday life." They re-create the freedom, the remembered perfection of childhood and mark it off from ordinary life with artificial boundaries, within which the only constraints are the rules to which the players freely submit. Games enlist skill and intelligence, the utmost concentration of purpose, on behalf of utterly useless activities, which make no contribution to the struggle of man against nature, to the wealth or comfort of the community, or to its physical survival.

In communist and fascist countries sports have been organized and promoted by the state. In capitalist countries the uselessness of games makes them offensive to social reformers, improvers of public morals, or functionalist critics of society like Veblen, who saw in the futility of upper-class sports anachronistic survivals of militarism and tests of prowess. Yet the "futility" of play, and nothing else, explains its appeal—its artificiality, the arbitrary obstacles it sets up for no other purpose than to challenge the players to surmount them, the absence of any utilitarian or uplifting object. Games quickly lose part of their charm when pressed into the service of education, character development, or social improvement.

Modern industry having reduced most jobs to a routine, games in our society take on added meaning. Men seek in play the difficulties and demands—both intellectual and physical—which they no longer find in work. The history of culture, as Huizinga showed in his classic study of play, *Homo Ludens*, appears from one perspective to consist of the gradual eradication of the elements of play from all cultural forms—from religion, from the law, from warfare, above all from productive labor. The rationalization of these activities leaves little room for the spirit of arbitrary invention or the disposition to leave things to chance. Risk, daring, and uncertainty, important components of play, have little place in industry or in activities infiltrated by industrial methods, which are intended precisely to predict and control the future and to eliminate risk. Games accordingly have assumed an importance unprecedented even in ancient Greece, where so much of social life revolved around contests. Sports, which satisfy also the starved need for physical exertion—for a renewal of the sense of the physical basis of life—have become an obsession not just of the masses but of those who set themselves up as a cultural elite.

The rise of spectator sports to their present importance coincides historically with the rise of mass production, which intensifies the needs sport satisfies while at the same time creating the technical capacity to promote and market athletic contests to a vast audience. But according to a common criticism of modern sport, these same developments have destroyed the value of athletics. Commercialized play has turned into work, subordinated the athlete's pleasure to the spectator's, and reduced the spectator himself to a state of passivity—the very antithesis of the health and vigor sport ideally promotes. The mania for winning has encouraged an exaggerated emphasis on the competitive side of sport, to the exclusion of the more modest but more satisfying experiences of cooperation and competence. The cult of victory, loudly proclaimed by such football coaches as Vince Lombardi and George Allen, has made savages of the players and rabid chauvinists of their followers. The violence and partisanship of modern sports lead some critics to insist that athletics impart militaristic values to the young, irrationally inculcate local and national pride in the spectator, and serve as one of the strongest bastions of male chauvinism.

Huizinga himself, who anticipated some of these arguments and stated them far more persuasively, argued that modern games and sports had been ruined by a "fatal shift toward over-seriousness." At the same time, he maintained that play had lost its element of ritual, had become "profane," and consequently had ceased to have any "organic connection whatever with the structure of society." The masses now crave "trivial recreation and crude sensationalism" and throw themselves into these pursuits with an intensity far beyond their intrinsic merit. Instead of playing with the freedom and intensity of children, they play with the "blend of adolescence and barbarity" that Huizinga calls puerilism, investing games with patriotic and martial fervor while treating serious pursuits as if they were games. "A far-reaching contamination of play and serious activity has taken place," according to Huizinga:

> The two spheres are getting mixed. In the activities of an outwardly serious nature hides an element of play. Recognized play, on the other hand, is no longer able to maintain its true play-character as a result of being taken too seriously and being technically over-organised. The indispensable qualities of detachment, artlessness, and gladness are thus lost.

An analysis of the criticism of modern sport, in its vulgar form as well as in Huizinga's more refined version, brings to light a number of common misconceptions about modern society. A large amount of writing on sports has accumulated in recent years, and the sociology of sport has even entrenched itself as a minor branch of social science. Much of this commentary has no higher purpose than to promote athletics or to exploit the journalistic market they have created, but some of it aspires to social criticism. Those who have formulated the now familiar indictment of organized sport include the sociologist Harry Edwards; the psychologist and former tennis player Dorcas Susan Butt, who thinks sport should promote "competence" instead of competition; disillusioned professional athletes like Dave Meggyesy and Chip Oliver; and radical critics of culture and society, notably Paul Hoch and Jack Scott.

Critics of sport, in their eagerness to uncover evidence of corruption and decline, attack intrinsic elements of athletics, elements essential to their appeal in all periods and places, on the erroneous assumption that spectatorship, violence, and competition reflect conditions peculiar to modern times. On the other hand, they overlook the distinctive contribution of contemporary society to the degradation of sport and therefore misconceive the nature of that degradation. They concentrate on issues, such as "over-seriousness," that are fundamental to an understanding of sports, indeed to the very definition of play, but that are peripheral or irrelevant to the ways they have changed in recent history.

Take the common complaint that modern sports are "spectator-oriented rather than participant-oriented." Spectators, on this view, are irrelevant to the success of the game. What a naïve theory of human motivation this implies! The attainment of certain skills unavoidably gives rise to an urge to show them off. At a higher level of mastery, the performer no longer wishes merely to display his virtuosity—for the true connoisseur can easily distinguish between the performer who plays to the crowd and the superior artist who matches himself against the full rigor of his art itself—but to ratify a supremely difficult accomplishment; to give pleasure; to forge a bond between himself and his audience, a shared appreciation of a ritual executed not only flawlessly but with much feeling and with a sense of style and proportion.

In all games, particularly in athletic contests, the central importance of display and representation serves as a reminder of the ancient connections between play, ritual, and drama. The players not only compete, they enact a familiar ceremony that reaffirms common values. Ceremony requires witnesses: enthusiastic spectators conversant with the rules of the performance and its underlying meaning. Far from destroying the value of sports, the attendance of spectators is often necessary to them. Indeed one of the virtues of contemporary sports lies in their resistance to the erosion of standards and their capacity to appeal to a knowledgeable audience. Norman Podhoretz has argued that the sports public remains more discriminating than the public for the arts and that in sports "excellence is relatively uncontroversial as a judgment of performance." The public for sports still consists largely of men who took part in sports during boyhood and thus acquired a sense of the game and a capacity to make discriminating judgments.

The same can hardly be said for the audience of an artistic performance, even though amateur musicians, dancers, actors, and painters may still comprise a small nucleus of the audience. Constant experimentation in the arts, in any case, has created so much confusion about standards that the only surviving measure of excellence, for many, is novelty and shock-value, which in a jaded time often resides in a work's sheer ugliness or banality. In sport, on the other hand, novelty and rapid shifts of fashion play only a small part in its appeal to a discriminating audience.

Yet even here, the contamination of standards has already begun. Faced with rising costs, owners seek to increase attendance at sporting events by installing exploding scoreboards, broadcasting recorded cavalry charges, giving away helmets and bats, and surrounding the spectator with cheerleaders, usherettes, and ball girls. Television has enlarged the audience for sports while lowering the quality of that audience's understanding; at least this is the assumption of sports commentators, who direct at the audience an interminable stream of tutelage in the basics of the game, and of the promoters, who reshape one game after another to conform to the tastes of an audience supposedly incapable of grasping their finer points.

The American League's adoption of the designated hitter rule, which relieves pitchers of the need to bat and diminishes the importance of managerial strategy, provides an especially blatant example of the dilution of sports by the requirements of mass promotion. Another example is the "Devil-Take-the-Hindmost Mile," a track event invented by the San Francisco *Examiner*, in which the last runner in the early stages of the race has to drop out—a rule that encourages an early scramble to avoid disqualification but lowers the general quality of the event. When the television networks discovered surfing, they insisted that events be held according to a prearranged schedule, without regard to weather conditions. A surfer complained, "Television is destroying our sport. The TV producers are turning a sport and an art form into a circus." The same practices produce the same effects on other sports, forcing baseball players, for example, to play World Series games on freezing October evenings. Substituting artificial surfaces for grass in tennis, which has slowed the pace of the game, placed a premium on reliability and patience, and reduced the element of tactical brillance and overpowering speed, commends itself to television producers because it makes tennis an all-weather game and even permits it to be played indoors, in sanctuaries of sport like Caesar's Palace in Las Vegas.

As spectators become less knowledgeable about the games they watch, they become more sensation-minded and bloodthirsty. The rise of violence in ice hockey, far beyond the point where it plays any functional part in the game, coincided with the expansion of professional hockey into cities without any traditional attachment to the sport—cities in which weather conditions, indeed, had always precluded any such tradition of local play. But the significance of such changes is not, as such critics as Jack Scott and Paul Hoch imagine, that sports ought to be organized solely for the edification of the players and that corruption sets in when sports begin to be played to spectators for a profit. It is often true that sport at this point ceases to be enjoyable and becomes a business. Recent critics go astray, however, in supposing that organized athletics ever serve the interests of the players alone or that "professionalization" inevitably corrupts all who take part in it.

In glorifying amateurism, equating spectatorship with passivity, and deploring competition, recent criticism of sport echoes the fake radicalism of the counterculture, from which so much of it derives. It shows its contempt for excellence by proposing to break down the "elitist" distinction between players and spectators. It proposes to replace competitive professional sports, which notwithstanding their shortcomings uphold standards of competence and bravery that might otherwise become extinct, with a bland regimen of cooperative diversions in which everyone can join in, regardless of age or ability—"new sports for the noncompetitive," having "no object, really," according to a typical effusion, except to bring "people together to enjoy each other." In its eagerness to strip from sport the elements that have always explained its imaginative appeal, the staged rivalry of superior ability, this "radicalism" proposes merely to complete the degradation already begun by the very society the cultural radicals profess to criticize and subvert.

What corrupts an athletic performance, as it does any other performance, is not professionalism or competition but the presence of an unappreciative, ignorant audience and the need to divert it with sensations extrinsic to the performance. It is at this point that ritual, drama, and sports all degenerate into spectacle. Huizinga's analysis of the secularization of sport helps to clarify this issue. In the degree to which athletic events lose the element of ritual and public festivity, according to Huizinga, they deteriorate into "trivial recreation and crude sensationalism." But even Huizinga misunderstands the cause of this development. It hardly lies in the "fatal shift toward over-seriousness." Huizinga himself, when he is writing about the theory of play rather than the collapse of "genuine play" in our own time, understands very well that play at its best is always serious; indeed that the essence of play lies in taking seriously activities that have no purpose, serve no utilitarian ends. He reminds us that "the majority of Greek contests were fought out in deadly earnest" and discusses, under the category of play, duels in which contestants fight to the death, water sports in which the goal is to drown your opponent, and tournaments for which the training and preparation consume the athletes' entire existence.

The degradation of sport, then, consists not in its being taken too seriously but in its subjection to some ulterior purpose, such as profit-making, patriotism, moral training, or the pursuit of health. Sport may give rise to these things in abundance, but ideally it produces them only as by-products having no essential connection with the game. When the game itself, on the other hand, comes to be regarded as incidental to the benefits it supposedly confers on participants, spectators, or pro-moters, it loses its peculiar capacity to transport both participant and spectator beyond everyday experience—to provide a glimpse of perfect order uncontaminated by commonplace calculations of advantage or even by ordinary considerations of survival.

Christopher Lasch, New York Review of Books, 28 April 1977

IDENTIFYING THE BOUNDARIES OF AN ASSIGNED TOPIC

To work out either of the first two approaches, a demonstration of your understanding of the whole source—a comprehensive sum-mary—is necessary. The third approach, however, is quite different, for it requires your focusing on *part* of the source, rather than the whole. It is usually your teacher who first assigns a reading and then presents a topic to be explored or an examination question to be answered. The purpose is to make sure that you have read and understood the assigned reading, to test your analytical skills, and to find out if you can integrate what you have read with the ideas and information that you have learned about in previous readings or in class discussion.

Since, as a rule, the object is not to test your memory, these assign-ments (even in examinations) are usually open-book, allowing you to refer to the source as often as you like. But you should have read all the material carefully in advance and outlined, underlined, annotated, or prepared the text in some other way. Whether you are expected to write at home or in the classroom, you may feel as if you are taking an informal examination; even at home there is likely to be some time pressure built into the assignment. In the discussion of this approach, assume that you are taking an open-book exam.

Reading the Question

You determine the strategy of your essay by carefully examining the focus and the wording of the question that you are being asked. You should therefore invest some time in studying the question before you begin to plan and write your essay. First of all, it is vital that you accept the fact that the scope of your essay is being defined by someone else. The person who wrote the question wants to pinpoint a single area to be explored and thus may offer you very little latitude. However restrictive it may seem, you have to stay within the boundaries of the question. If you are instructed to focus on only a small section of the text, summarizing the entire work from beginning to end is inappropriate. If you are asked to discuss an issue that is raised frequently throughout the work, paraphrasing a single paragraph or page is pointless. Further, do not include extraneous information just to demonstrate how much you know. In fact, most teachers are more impressed with aptness and conciseness than with length.

The writer of the question is really saving you the trouble of devising your own topic and strategy. As long as you pay attention to what is being asked, much of the narrowing process will have been done for you; the controlling verb of the question will usually provide you with a key. Different verbs will require different approaches. You are already familiar with the most common terms:

summarize; state; list; outline; condense; cite reasons

What is sometimes forgotten under pressure is that you are expected to carry out the instructions literally. "Summarize" means condense: the reader expects a short but complete account of the subject specified. On the other hand, "list" should result in a sequence of short entries, somewhat disconnected, but not a fully developed series of paragraphs.

Other directions may be far more broad:

describe; discuss; review; explain; show; explore; determine

Verbs like these give you a lot of rope. Since they do not demand a specific strategy, be careful to stay within the scope of the set topic, so that you do not explain or review more than the readers want to know about.

Still other verbs indicate a more exact method of development, perhaps one of the strategies that you have already worked with in Part 1:

compare and contrast; illustrate; define; show the reasons; trace the causes; trace the effects; suggest solutions; analyze

Notice that none of the verbs so far have provided an opportunity for personal comment. You have been asked to examine the text, to show off your understanding of its meaning and your awareness of its implications, but you have not been asked for your opinion. However, several verbs do request commentary:

evaluate; interpret; criticize; justify; prove; disagree

Although these verbs invite a personal response, they do not give you license to write about whatever you choose. You are still confined to the boundaries of the set subject, and you would still be wise to devote as much of your essay as possible to demonstrating your understanding of what you have read. A brilliant essay that ignores the topic rarely earns the highest grade; usually, the reader insists on being convinced that you have mastered the material. And, in fact, if you have worked hard to prepare to write the essay, to allow your impulses or your self-will to deter you from answering the set question is folly. Don't re-interpret the directions in order to write about what is easiest or what would display your abilities to best advantage or what you figured out earlier would be asked. Just answer the question on the page.

Planning and Developing the Essay

Even when you have worked out what you are expected to focus on, you are still not ready to start writing. You might be tempted to cover a few points in a page or two just to ease your tension, but since your reader also judges the way in which your essay is constructed, to begin writing without an organizational scheme is a mistake. No elaborate outline is necessary. As you would in longer essays, make a list of all the points that come into your head; reduce the list to a manageable number; and renumber the sequence. Only then are you ready to write. This process does not take very long and it can prevent unnecessary repetition, unintentional omissions, mixed-up sequences, and overemphasis. the guidelines for developing your topic can be reduced to three:

1. *Develop each point separately*. Don't try to say everything at the same time. Consult your list; say what is necessary about each item; and then move on to the next. Empty your mind of one point at a time.
2. *Develop each point adequately*. Each reason or cause or criticism deserves convincing presentation. Unless you are asked for a list, don't just blurt out one sentence and hop away to the next item. You will write a more effective essay by including some support for each of your points. Do not make brief, incomplete references to ideas which you assume that the reader will know all about. It is your responsibility to explain each one so that it makes sense by itself.
3. *Refer back to the text*. Whenever possible, demonstrate that you can cite evidence or information from the reading. If you think of two possible examples or facts, one from the source and one from your own experience or knowledge, and if you haven't enough time to include both, the safe choice will come from the source. However, you must always mark the transi-

tion between your own presentation of ideas and your reference to the source by citing its title, or the name of its author, or both. Remember never to blur the distinction between your own contribution and your source's.

Analyzing an Essay and an Essay Question

Carefully read through Margaret Mead's "A Crisis, a Challenge," and then examine the essay question that follows it.

A CRISIS, A CHALLENGE

The energy crunch being felt around the world forces us to take stock of our reckless despoiling of the earth's resources. It also provides the United States with a magnificent opportunity to initiate a transformation in our present way of life. 1

Our present way was conceived in a spirit of progress, in an attempt to improve the standard of living of all Americans, in the increasing capability of technological development to bring previously undreamed of amenities within reach of the common man. But this search has taken a form which this planet cannot support. The overdevelopment of motor transport has contributed to the near destruction of our great cities, the disintegration of the family, the isolation of the old, the young and the poor, the pollution of local air, and the poisoning of the earth's atmosphere. Our wasteful use of electricity, and our waste rather than recycling of nonrenewable resources are likewise endangering our rivers and oceans and the atmosphere which protects the planet. 2

The realization that a dramatic transformation was needed has steadily increased, but the problem was how to turn around? How to alter our dependence on motor transport? How to stop building enormous, uneconomical buildings which waste electricity night and day, all year round? How to break the deadlock between environmentalists bent upon enacting immediate measures to protect an endangered environment, and industry caught in the toils of a relentless compulsion to expand? How to turn around in our own course and not injure the young economies of the developing countries, desperate to obtain the barest necessities of food and water and light for their hungry millions? It had seemed almost impossible to turn around short of some major catastrophe which would destroy millions of lives. 3

The catastrophe has now arrived, in the energy crunch. The causes may and will be debated: How much blame to assign to government mismanagement, how much to the recent war in the Mideast, and so on. But in a more basic sense, these triggering events do not matter. They could in fact divert our attention from a much more important issue—how we are to take advantage of the crisis to move toward a way of life which will not destroy the environment and use up irreplaceable resources? 4

We can use the crisis to lead in a transformation which is needed around the world, to aim not for a shallow independence but for genuine 5 responsibility. We must not be content with half measures, following the administration's assurance that the crisis will mean only fewer Sunday drives to visit a mother-in-law, and lowered lights on Christmas trees—to be followed by an early return to normal waste and pollution.

During the inevitable disorganization of everyday life, we will be making decisions, learning new habits, initiating new research. It is vital that these activities move us forward into a new era, in which the entire nation is involved in a search for a new standard of living, a new quality of life based on conservation not waste, on protection not destruction, on human values rather than built-in obsolescence and waste. 6

As scientists who know the importance of accurate information we can press immediately for the establishment of an inquiry with subpoena power to ascertain from the industries the exact state of supplies and reserve in this country. We can press for a massive project on alternative and environmentally safe forms of energy. It should be as ambitious as the Manhattan Project or NASA, but it would have no need of secrecy. It would not aim at destroying or outdistancing other countries, but at ways of conserving our resources, in new technologies which would themselves provide new activities for those industries whose present prosperity is based on oil and motor transport and energy-expensive synthetic materials. 7

Those of us who are social scientists have a special responsibility for the relationship between measures that are to be taken and the way in which the American people and American institutions will respond. If there is to be gasoline rationing, we have to consider the importance of built-in flexibility and choice. In the United States, a rationing system will only be experienced as fair and just if it discriminates among the needs of different users, recognizes that workers have to get to work, that many people work on Sundays, that different regions of the country need different measures. Without rationing, we will set one set of users against another, one part of the country against another, encouraging such narrowly partisan measures as severance taxes through which oil-rich states will benefit at the expense of the residents of oil-less states. Rationing is a way of making the situation genuinely national, involving each American in the fate of all Americans. 8

It will be important to consider that the American people have only experienced rationing as a temporary measure in wartime. There will be danger that rationing may simply accentuate the desire to get back to normal again, with normal defined as where we were when the shortages hit us. But what we need to do is to define all measures taken, not as temporary but as *transitional*, to a saner, safer, more human lifestyle. 9

In the past, war, revolution and depressions have been the dire circumstances within which society's technologies and social institutions have been transformed. But wars are won, or lost, revolutions succeed or fail, depressions grind to an end. The situation we are in is profoundly different. An interdependent, planetary, man-made system of resource exploitation and energy use has brought us to a state where long-range planning is essential, where what we need is not a return to our present parlous state, which endangers the future of our country, our children 10 and our earth, but movement forward to a new norm, where the developed and the developing countries will be able to help each other. The developing countries have less obsolescence, fewer entrenched 19th century industrial forms to overcome; the developed countries have the scientists and the technologists to work rapidly and effectively on planetary problems.

In the past it has been only in war, in defense of one's own country 11 or one's ideals, that any people have been able to invoke total commitment. Then it has always been on behalf of one group against another. This is the first time in history that American people have been asked to defend ourselves and everything that we hold dear, *in cooperation* with all the other inhabitants of this planet, who share with us the same endangered air and oceans. This time there is no enemy. There is only a common need to reassess our present course, to change course, to devise methods by which we can survive.

Margaret Mead, Washington Post, 30 December 1973

Assume that you have been given approximately an hour to answer the following question:

> Although Margaret Mead's attitude toward the future is optimistic, she is, in fact, writing about a complex and serious problem. Considering some of her suggestions, explain why meeting the challenge of the energy crisis may be more difficult than Mead implies.

You may at first have difficulty determining the direction of your essay since the question includes *several* key words to serve as clues to your focus. The main verb that defines your task is "explain." You are being asked to account for something, to make the reader understand what may not be entirely clear. "Explain" also implies persuasion: your reader must be convinced that your explanation is valid. If you assume that the question is asking you to explain something that is confusing in Mead's essay, your task is to provide an interpretive summary of some part of her essay. If you decide that the question seeks some related point that Mead omits from her discussion, your task would be to extend her reasoning: you might have to analyze causes or consequences or apply her ideas about the energy crisis to another contemporary issue. For example, you might discuss how Mead's ideas about the energy crisis could be applied to problems of unemployment. Perhaps, however, the question is asking you to evaluate her reasoning.

In fact, the last possibility suggests the most promising approach to the essay. You are not being asked to challenge Mead's conclusions, nor to put forth counter-arguments. Rather, you must demonstrate (explain) the limitations of her argument. The question tells you—twice—that Mead may have underestimated the problem that she is attempting to solve. In effect, you are being asked to support that point of view, rather than present your own. To answer the question, you must accept the conclusion that Mead may be over-confident and then proceed to point out the deficiencies of her proposals. In a sense, writing a good essay depends upon your flexibility and your willingness to allow your views to be molded by the examiner's, at least for the duration of the exam.

The question defines the *limits* as well as the strategy of your essay. It does not permit you to dispute Mead on grounds that are entirely of your own choosing; you are firmly instructed to focus your attention on her suggestions. Given those instructions, ignoring Mead entirely and writing an essay arguing that there is no energy crisis would be foolish. What should you be evaluating in your essay and how many suggestions are "some?" Mead recommends three practical programs—the development of new sources of energy, the implementation of a scheme of rationing, and the cooperation of all nations in an attempt to conserve resources and use them wisely. These three suggestions should certainly be on the list of paragraph topics that you jot down as you plan your essay. You may either follow Mead's sequence or use your own ordering principle (most practical to least practical would be a good choice). Each of your paragraphs might begin with a summary of one suggestion, followed by your own explanation of the difficulties inherent in that plan.

Resist the temptation to devote the most space to the suggestion that would have the most immediate effect—the need to ration gas and fuel: if you write about this suggestion exclusively, you run the risk of misrepresenting Mead by making it appear as if she has only one major solution to offer. And, at the same time, you will be ignoring Mead's most significant idea, the one which serves as the principle and theme of her essay—the need for a change in our style of life. Mead predicates all her thinking on the hope—even the certainty—that people will be able to transform their expectations of what is normal and thus accept the consequences of a diminished supply of energy resources. We need to change; therefore, we will. If the greatest obstacle to the success of her proposal is the natural reluctance of human nature to accept change, then you will weaken your essay if you emphasize practical plans and neglect Mead's more abstract theme. However, you need not prove that such a transformation *cannot* take place. The question asks you only to explain the difficulties.

Introducing Your Topic

Examination essays, like all essays, require an introduction, however brief. Before beginning to explore in writing the weaknesses in Margaret Mead's argument, you should provide a short introduction that defines the author's topic and your own. Your later references to her suggestions will need a well-established context; therefore, describe Mead's overall view of the energy crisis (which might differ from someone else's) right at the outset of your essay. Although the introduction need not be longer than two or three sentences, *cite your source*—the name of the author and the name of the essay, both properly spelled—and state exactly what it is that you and your author are concerned about. To demonstrate the frustration of reading an introduction that is shrouded in mystery, following are introductions from two student essays answering the question just analyzed:

> The author's attitude is a very optimistic one, and there's nothing wrong with being optimistic. However, implementing her suggestions could turn out to be a lot more difficult than she implies. She makes strong suggestions to effect a complete transformation into a new era, such as finding an alternate and safe source of supply and setting up a rationing system.

> The big change that she recommends is to start some sort of project that is "as ambitious as the Manhattan Project or NASA." A project of this size would require a team effort from every organization in the country. It would be so big that it could quite possibly change the entire domestic policy of the country and even strengthen the morale of all citizens. People helping people may be the only way to solve major social, ecological or economic problems.

"She," of course, is Margaret Mead, and the subject under discussion is the need to save energy resources. Both students had read and understood the source essay, but both are so anxious to begin commenting on Mead's proposals that they fail to establish exactly what she wants to achieve. Here is a more informative introduction:

> In "A Crisis, A Challenge," Margaret Mead asserts that Americans will successfully adopt practical measures to reduce the excessive use of our energy resources. She recognizes that an effective program will necessitate painful changes in our long-established habits, including a less lavish standard of living, as well as beneficial changes in our national character and our individual values. Left unclear is whether the American people can be persuaded to accept these changes and whether the new attitude of responsibility and cooperation can be retained after the initial crisis is over.

Presenting Your Essay to the Reader

During in-class examinations, students often waste vital minutes by painstakingly transcribing a new copy from their rough draft. While it is crucial that your handwriting be legible, it is not at all necessary to hand in a clean copy. Teachers expect an exam essay to have sentences crossed out and words inserted. They are used to seeing arrows used to reverse sentences and numbers used to change the sequence of paragraphs. It makes no sense to write the last word of your first draft and then, without checking what you have written, immediately take a clean sheet of paper and start transcribing a copy to hand in. And, because transcription is such a mechanical task, the mind tends to wander and the pen makes errors that were not in the original draft. Use any extra time not in re-copying but in careful proofreading to locate grammatical errors and fill in gaps in continuity. As long as your corrections and changes are fairly neat and clear, your teacher will not mind reading the first draft and indeed, in most cases, will be pleased to recognize your efforts to improve your writing.

Students often choose to divide their time into three parts. For example, if you have forty minutes during which to write an essay, spend ten minutes analyzing the question and planning a strategy, twenty minutes writing the essay, and ten minutes proofreading and correcting.

EXERCISE 30

Here are four examination questions dealing with Blanche Blank's "A Question of Degree" (pp. 60–63). First analyze each question, underlining the key phrases and circling the controlling verbs. Then be prepared to discuss the strategies and boundaries implied by each question and to point out what should be included in a good answer and what should be left out.

1. How well, in your opinion, does Blanche Blank support her assertion that "discrimination based on college degrees" is as unfair a method of employment selection as discrimination according to sex, age, race, religion, or ethnic group?
2. Blanche Blank perceives a widespread and unreasonable preference for college-educated men and women in hiring for career employment. Analyze the reasons why the situation described in the essay has come about.
3. Write an essay disagreeing with Blanche Blank's belief that "we should outlaw employment discrimination based on college degrees." Explore her reasons for believing it and offer reasons for your own position.

4. Write an essay describing the most likely consequences of Blanche Blank's legislative proposal. Would the proposal produce the changes in work, education, and life that she desires?

EXERCISE 31

Read the following excerpt from Bronislaw Malinowski's *Magic, Science and Religion*. Then examine the group of questions which follows, isolating the separate focus and boundaries of each question. Be prepared to point out which parts of the reading should be referred to in order to answer each question. Finally, choose one question, and write a list of paragraph topics for an essay that will answer it. Next to each topic, note the paragraph(s) from Malinowski that you would cite in order to support your point.

These natives, and I am speaking mainly of the Melanesians who inhabit the coral atolls to the N.E. of the main island, the Trobriand Archipelago and the adjoining groups, are expert fishermen, industrious manufacturers and traders, but they rely mainly on gardening for their subsistence. With the most rudimentary implements, a pointed digging-stick and a small axe, they are able to raise crops sufficient to maintain a dense population and even yielding a surplus, which in olden days was allowed to rot unconsumed, and which at present is exported to feed plantation hands. The success in their agriculture depends—besides the excellent natural conditions with which they are favored—upon their extensive knowledge of the classes of the soil, of the various cultivated plants, of the mutual adaptation of these two factors, and, last not least, upon their knowledge of the importance of accurate and hard work. They have to select the soil and the seedlings, they have appropriately to fix the times for clearing and burning the scrub, for planting and weeding, for training the vines of the yam plants. In all this they are guided by a clear knowledge of weather and seasons, plants and pests, soil and tubers, and by a conviction that this knowledge is true and reliable, that it can be counted upon and must be scrupulously obeyed. 1

Yet mixed with all their activities there is to be found magic, a series of rites performed every year over the gardens in rigorous sequence and order. Since the leadership in garden work is in the hands of the magician, and since ritual and practical work are intimately associated, a superficial observer might be led to assume that the mystic and the rational behavior are mixed up, that their effects are not distinguished by the natives and not distinguishable in scientific analysis. Is this so really? 2

Magic is undoubtedly regarded by the natives as absolutely indispensable to the welfare of the gardens. What would happen without it no one can exactly tell, for no native garden has ever been made without 3 its ritual, in spite of some thirty years of European rule and missionary influence and well over a century's contact with white traders. But certainly various kinds of disaster, blight, unseasonable droughts, rains, bush-pigs and locusts, would destroy the unhallowed garden made without magic.

Does this mean, however, that the natives attribute all the good results 4 to magic? Certainly not. If you were to suggest to a native that he should make his garden mainly by magic and scamp his work, he would simply smile on your simplicity. He knows as well as you do that there are natural conditions and causes, and by his observations he knows also that he is able to control these natural forces by mental and physical effort. His knowledge is limited, no doubt, but as far as it goes it is sound and proof against mysticism. If the fences are broken down, if the seed is destroyed or has been dried or washed away, he will have recourse not to magic, but to work, guided by knowledge and reason. His experience has taught him also, on the other hand, that in spite of all his forethought and beyond all his efforts there are agencies and forces which one year bestow unwonted and unearned benefits of fertility, making everything run smooth and well, rain and sun appear at the right moment, noxious insects remain in abeyance, the harvest yields a superabundant crop; and another year again the same agencies bring ill luck and bad chance, pursue him from beginning till end and thwart all his most strenuous efforts and his best-founded knowledge. To control these influences and these only he employs magic.

Thus there is a clear-cut division: there is first the well-known set of 5 conditions, the natural course of growth, as well as the ordinary pests and dangers to be warded off by fencing and weeding. On the other hand there is the domain of the unaccountable and adverse influences, as well as the great unearned increment of fortunate coincidence. The first conditions are coped with by knowledge and work, the second by magic.

This line of division can also be traced in the social setting of work 6 and ritual respectively. Though the garden magician is, as a rule, also the leader in practical activities, these two functions are kept strictly apart. Every magical ceremony has its distinctive name, its appropriate time and its place in the scheme of work, and it stands out of the ordinary course of activities completely. Some of them are ceremonial and have to be attended by the whole community, all are public in that it is known when they are going to happen and anyone can attend them. They are performed on selected plots within the gardens and on a special corner of this plot. Work is always tabooed on such occasions, sometimes only while the ceremony lasts, sometimes for a day or two. In his lay character the leader and magician directs the work, fixes the dates for starting, harangues and exhorts slack or careless gardeners. But the two roles never overlap or interfere: they are always clear, and any native will inform you without hesitation whether the man acts as magician or as leader in garden work.

What has been said about gardens can be paralleled from any one of 7 the many other activities in which work and magic run side by side without ever mixing. Thus in canoe building empirical knowledge of material, of technology, and of certain principles of stability and hydrodynamics, function in company and close association with magic, each yet uncontaminated by the other.

For example, they understand perfectly well that the wider the span   8
of the outrigger the greater the stability yet the smaller the resistance against strain. They can clearly explain why they have to give this span a certain traditional width, measured in fractions of the length of the dugout. They can also explain, in rudimentary but clearly mechanical terms; how they have to behave in a sudden gale, why the outrigger must be always on the weather side, why the one type of canoe can and the other cannot beat. They have, in fact, a whole system of principles of sailing, embodied in a complex and rich terminology, traditionally handed on and obeyed as rationally and consistently as is modern science by modern sailors. How could they sail otherwise under eminently dangerous conditions in their frail primitive craft?

But even with all their systematic knowledge, methodically applied,   9
they are still at the mercy of powerful and incalculable tides, sudden gales during the monsoon season and unknown reefs. And here comes in their magic, performed over the canoe during its construction, carried out at the beginning and in the course of expeditions and resorted to in moments of real danger. If the modern seaman, entrenched in science and reason, provided with all sorts of safety appliances, sailing on steel-built steamers, if even he has a singular tendency to superstition—which does not rob him of his knowledge or reason, nor make him altogether prelogical—can we wonder that his savage colleague, under much more precarious conditions, holds fast to the safety and comfort of magic?

An interesting and crucial test is provided by fishing in the Trobriand   10
Islands and its magic. While in the villages on the inner lagoon fishing is done in an easy and absolutely reliable manner by the method of poisoning, yielding abundant results without danger and uncertainty, there are on the shores of the open sea dangerous modes of fishing and also certain types in which the yield greatly varies according to whether shoals of fish appear beforehand or not. It is most significant that in the lagoon fishing, where man can rely completely upon his knowledge and skill, magic does not exist, while in the open-sea fishing, full of danger and uncertainty, there is extensive magical ritual to secure safety and good results.

Again, in warfare the natives know that strength, courage, and agility   11
play a decisive part. Yet here also they practice magic to master the elements of chance and luck.

Nowhere is the duality of natural and supernatural causes divided by   12
a line so thin and intricate, yet, if carefully followed up, so well marked, decisive, and instructive, as in the two most fateful forces of human destiny: health and death. Health to the Melanesians is a natural state of affairs and, unless tampered with, the human body will remain in perfect order. But the natives know perfectly well that there are natural means which can affect health and even destroy the body. Poisons, wounds, burns, falls, are known to cause disablement or death in a

natural way. And this is not a matter of private opinion of this or that individual, but it is laid down in traditional lore and even in belief, for there are considered to be different ways to the nether world for those who died by sorcery and those who met "natural" death. Again, it is recognized that cold, heat, overstrain, too much sun, overeating, can all cause minor ailments, which are treated by natural remedies such as massage, steaming, warming at a fire and certain potions. Old age is known to lead to bodily decay and the explanation is given by the natives that very old people grow weak, their oesophagus closes up, and therefore they must die.

But besides these natural causes there is the enormous domain of 13 sorcery and by far the most cases of illness and death are ascribed to this. The line of distinction between sorcery and the other causes is clear in theory and in most cases of practice, but it must be realized that it is subject to what could be called the personal perspective. That is, the more closely a case has to do with the person who considers it, the less will it be "natural," the more "magical." Thus a very old man, whose pending death will be considered natural by the other members of the community, will be afraid only of sorcery and never think of his natural fate. A fairly sick person will diagnose sorcery in his own case, while all the others might speak of too much betel nut or overeating or some other indulgence.

But who of us really believes that his own bodily infirmities and the 14 approaching death is a purely natural occurrence, just an insignificant event in the infinite chain of causes? To the most rational of civilized men health, disease, the threat of death, float in a hazy emotional mist, which seems to become denser and more impenetrable as the fateful forms approach. It is indeed astonishing that "savages" can achieve such a sober, dispassionate outlook in these matters as they actually do.

Thus in his relation to nature and destiny, whether he tries to exploit 15 the first or to dodge the second, primitive man recognizes both the natural and the supernatural forces and agencies, and he tries to use them both for his benefit. Whenever he has been taught by experience that effort guided by knowledge is of some avail, he never spares the one or ignores the other. He knows that a plant cannot grow by magic alone, or a canoe sail or float without being properly constructed and managed, or a fight be won without skill and daring. He never relies on magic alone, while, on the contrary, he sometimes dispenses with it completely, as in fire-making and in a number of crafts and pursuits. But he clings to it, whenever he has to recognize the impotence of his knowledge and of his rational technique.

1. Describe some of the reasons why the Melanesians need magic. What function does it serve for them?
2. Compare and contrast the Melanesians' methods of doing their work with contemporary American work practices.
3. Does the Melanesian conception of magic derive from their dependence on nature?

4. In your opinion, is Melanesian magic a science or a religion?
5. Malinowski points out that Melanesians never confuse work and magic. Explain why the two do not overlap.
6. What is our society's equivalent magic to that of the Melanesians? Use illustrations from Malinowski to justify your answer.
7. Malinowski states that the Melanesians are astonishingly "sober" and "dispassionate" in their attitude towards sickness and death. He implies that we are not capable of such objectivity. Justify that implication, or refute it.
8. To what extent does Melanesian "magic" play a part in our reactions to and solutions to the present energy crisis? Illustrate your essay by reference to the reading.
9. How would the Melanesians explain the arrival in their society of anthropologists like Malinowski?

USING A SOURCE AS THE STARTING POINT FOR YOUR OWN ESSAY

This last approach gives you the freedom to develop your own ideas and present your own point of view in an essay that is only loosely linked to the source. You use an assigned essay to help you generate ideas and topics and to provide you with evidence or information to cite in your own essay; but the thesis, scope, and strategy of your essay are to be entirely your own.

As always, you begin by studying the assigned essay carefully, establishing its thesis and main ideas. As you read, start noting ideas of your own that might be worth developing. The essay that you are planning need not cover exactly the same material as the source essay. What you want is a spinoff from the original reading, rather than a recapitulation. If you read the essay a few times without thinking of some topics, test out some of the standard strategies for developing an essay by applying them to the source essay in ways that might not have occurred to the original author. Here, for example, are some strategies that helped to generate topics for an essay based on Blanche Blank's "A Question of Degree." You will notice that the proposed topics and the source become more and more loosely connected and that some of the final suggestions will result in essays almost entirely independent of Blanche Blank's.

Argumentation

You can argue for Blanche Blank's assertions or against them. If you disagree with her conclusions, if you believe that the role of college has not been over-emphasized, then you can follow strategy one and refute her arguments, disproving her evidence or casting doubt on her interpretation of the evidence. On the other hand, it is also possible to agree with Blanche Blank and to support and confirm her thesis by suggesting new lines of argument or citing new sources of evidence. The resulting essay would be an amalgamation of her basic ideas and yours.

You cannot always argue for or against an author's thesis; not all source essays provide clearcut assertions for you to support or refute. Several readings in this book explain and analyze a topic rather than attempt to convince the reader of a specific point of view. To understand the difference, compare "A Question of Degree" with Frances FitzGerald's "Re-Writing American History." Both Blank and FitzGerald are concerned with the ways in which the perceptions and expectations of school children may have been manipulated; but FitzGerald is trying to inform her readers and examine the evidence rather than persuade them to accept a point of view.

Process

You might describe in detail one of the processes that Blank only refers to generally. For example, you could cite your own experience to explain the ways in which teenagers are encouraged to believe that a college degree is essential, citing descriptions of high school counseling and college catalogues, and examining the expectations fostered by what young students see and read. Or, if you have sufficient knowledge, you might describe the unjust manipulation of hiring procedures or the process by which a college's Liberal Arts curriculum gradually becomes "practical."

Illustration

If you focused on a single discouraged employee, showing in what ways ambitions for better status and salary have been frustrated, or a single disillusioned college graduate, showing how career prospects have failed to measure up to training and expectations, your strategy would be an illustration proving one of Blank's themes.

Definition

Definition can sometimes result from a discussion of background. What should the work experience be like? What is the function of a university? What is an education? By attempting to define one of the components of Blank's theme in terms of the ideal, you are helping your reader to understand her arguments and evaluate her conclusions more rationally.

Cause and Effect

You can examine one or more of the reasons why college degrees have become so essential. You can also suggest a wider context for discussing Blank's views by characterizing the background—the kind of society that encourages this set of values. In either case, you will be accounting for, but not necessarily justifying, the nation's obsession with degrees. Or you can predict the consequences, good or bad, that might result if Blank's suggested legislation were passed. Or you might explore some hypothetical possibilities and thus alter the circumstances and the causes of the situation that Blank describes. What if everyone in the United States earned a college degree? What if education after the eighth grade were abolished? By taking this approach, you are radically changing the circumstances that Blank depicts, but still sharing her concerns and exploring the principles discussed in her essay.

Comparison

You can alter the reader's perspective by translating the theme of Blank's essay to another time or place. Did our present obsession with education exist a hundred years ago? Is it at this moment a problem outside the United States? Will it probably continue into the twenty-first century? Or, focusing on late twentieth-century America, you might want to contrast contemporary trends in education and employment with comparable trends in other areas of life—housing, finance, recreation, child-rearing, and communications. All of these approaches ask you to begin with a description of Blank's issue and contrast it with another set of circumstances, past or present, real or unreal. But before choosing one of these speculative topics, you must first decide whether it is practical, whether it requires research, and whether, when fully developed, it will retain some connection with the source essay. For example, there may be some value in comparing the current emphasis on higher education with monastic education in the Middle Ages. Can you write such an essay? How much research will it require? Will a discussion of monastic education help your reader better to understand Blank's ideas? Or will you immediately move away from your starting point—the value of a college degree in the 1980s—and find no opportunity to return to it? Have you a serious objective, or are you simply indulging in the comparison "because it's there"?

PLANNING THE SINGLE-SOURCE ESSAY

Consider the following development of an essay based on one of the topics suggested above. Notice that it is expressed as a question.

Topic: What is the function of a university in the 1980s?

Once the topic is established, you then follow essentially the same sequence of steps that you learned about in Part 1, beginning with the note-taking stage. Indeed, the only important difference between the two procedures is that you can use a source essay to suggest additional ideas for the notes on your list and to provide support for those ideas that you think of yourself. Try to start your list of notes before you reread the essay, to make sure that you are not overly influenced by the author's point of view and to enable you to establish some independent points. Then, review the source and add any relevant ideas to your list (remembering to indicate when an idea originated with the source and not with you).

Here is the complete list of notes for an essay defining the function of a university. The paragraph references added later, indicate which points were made by Blank and where in her essay they can be found. The thesis, which follows the notes, was written after the list was complete.

What the university ought to do
A. to increase a student's understanding of the world
   around him
        e.g. to become more observant and aware of natural
        phenomena (weather, for example) and social systems
        (like family relationships)
B. to help a student to live a more fulfilling life
        to enable him to test his powers and know more and
        become more versatile; to speak with authority on
        topics that he didn't understand before
C. to help a student to live a more productive life
        to increase his working credentials and qualify for
        more interesting and well-paying jobs (B.B., ¶ 3-9)
D. to serve society by creating a better informed, more
   rational group of citizens
        not only through college courses (like political
        science) but through the increased ability to observe
        and analyze and argue. (B.B., ¶ 3, 14)
E. to contribute to research that will help to solve
   scientific and social problems
        (not a teaching function) (B.B., ¶ 3, 14)
F. to serve as a center for debate to clarify the major
   issues of the day
        people should regard the university as a source of
        unbiassed information and counsel; notable people
        should come to lecture (B.B., ¶ 3, 14)
G. to serve as a gathering place for great teachers

```
        students should be able to regard their teachers as
        worth emulating.
  H. to allow the student to examine the opportunities for
     personal change and growth
        this includes vocational goals, e.g. career changes
        (B.B., ¶ 4)

  What the university should not do
  I. it should not divide the haves from the have-nots
        college should not be considered essential; it should
        be possible to be successful without a college degree
        (B.B., ¶ 8, 10)
  J. it should not use marketing techniques to appeal to the
     greatest number
        what the university teaches should be determined
        primarily by the faculty and to a lesser extent by
        the students; standards of achievement should not be
        determined by students who haven't learned anything
        yet
  K. it should not ignore the needs of its students and its
     community by clinging to outdated courses and programs
  L. it should not cooperate with business and government to
     the extent that it loses its autonomy (B.B., ¶ 6, 9)
  M. it should not be an employment agency and vocational
     center to the exclusion of its more important functions
     (B.B., ¶ 6, 9, 16)

  Thesis: As Blanche Blank points out, a university
  education is not a commodity to be marketed and sold; a
  university should be a resource center for those who want
  the opportunity to develop their intellectual powers and
  lead more productive, useful, and fulfilling lives.
```

Strategy

As a rule, you would consider strategies for your essay as soon as you have established your thesis. In this case, however, the choice of both topic and strategy was made at an earlier point, when you considered several possible strategies. The notes, divided into what a university should and should not do, already make it clear that the author is intending to use a definition strategy, with its emphasis on differentiation.

Outline

Having made all the preliminary decisions, you are ready to plan the structure of your essay. But before doing so, return once more to the reading and single out those portions which you will need in support of your thesis: your essay is going to be based on your own ideas and the ideas of your source, and, since writing your thesis, you have not actually checked the text of the essay. Now, you need to know whether your notes are accurate paraphrases of the source, and also how many source references you intend to make so that you can write a balanced outline. You may also need to double-check to make sure that you are giving the source credit for all paraphrased ideas.

Here, for example, is a paragraph from "A Question of Degree," together with underlinings indicating the sentences and phrases that invite paraphrases or quotation in the essay on "The Function of the University."

> Business allows the colleges to act as recruiting, screening and training agencies for them because it saves money and time. Why colleges allow themselves to act as servicing agents may not be as apparent. One reason may be that colleges are increasingly becoming conventional bureaucracies. It is inevitable, therefore, that they should respond to the first and unchallenged law of bureaucracy: Expand! The more that colleges can persuade outside institutions to restrict employment in favor of their clientele, the stronger is the college's hold and attraction. This rationale becomes even clearer when we understand that the budgets of public universities hang on the number of students "serviced." Seen from this perspective, then, it is perhaps easier to understand why such matters as "university independence," or "the propriety" of using the public bankroll to support enterprises that are expected to make private profits, can be dismissed. Conflict of interest is difficult to discern when the interests involved are your own.

You are now ready to organize your notes in groups, each of which will be developed as a separate paragraph or sequence of related paragraphs. Then, after you have set up these categories and decided on their order, incorporate in your outline some of the points from Blanche Blank's essay that you intend to use as support (or possibly to argue against). Cite the paragraph number of the relevant material with your outline entry. If the paragraph from "A Question of Degree" contains several references that you will want to place in different parts of your outline, use a sentence number or a set of symbols or a brief quotation for differentiation. Here is what one section of the completed outline would look like, incorporating notes C, M, I, and H respectively:

```
I. The university should help a student to live a more
   productive life, to increase his working credentials
   and qualify for more interesting and well paying jobs.
   (¶ 6--last sentence)
   A. But it should not be an employment agency and
      vocational center to the exclusion of its more
```

important functions. (¶ 9--"servicing agents,"
¶ 12--"joylessness in our university life," ¶ 16)

  B. It should not divide the haves from the have-nots;
success without a college degree should be possible.
(¶ 2--"two kinds of work," ¶ 17)

II. The university should allow the student to examine the
opportunities for personal growth and change; this
includes vocational goals, e.g., career changes. (¶ 4--
"an optional and continuing experience later in life")

THE TWELVE STAGES OF WRITING A SINGLE-SOURCE ESSAY

As you have seen, the procedure for planning an essay based on another text closely resembles the steps outlined in Part 1 for working without source materials. The crucial difference, of course, is that with sources you are engaged in a kind of partnership. You must strive to strike an appropriate balance between your own ideas and those of your source. It is your voice that should dominate the essay. You, after all, are writing it; you are responsible for its contents; you are controlling its effect on the reader. For this reason, all the important "positions" in the structure of your essay should be filled by you; the topic sentences, as well as the introduction, should be written in your own words and, if possible, should stress your views, not those of your author. On the other hand, your reader should not be allowed to lose sight of the source essay; it should be treated as a form of evidence and cited whenever it is relevant, but always as a context in which to work out your own purposes and assert your own thesis.

Here, again, are the stages of writing an essay, expanded to encompass writing about a source:

> *Step one:* Determine the source essay's thesis; analyze its underlying themes, if any, and its strategy; and construct a rough outline of its main ideas.
>
> *Step two:* Decide on two or three possible essay topics based on your work in step 1, and narrow down one of them. (Be prepared to submit your topics for your teacher's approval and to decide, in conference, on the most suitable one.)
>
> *Step three:* Write down a list of notes about your own ideas on the topic, being careful to distinguish in your notes between points that are yours and points that are derived from the source.
>
> *Step four:* Write a thesis of your own that gives a fair represen-

tation of your list of ideas. Mention the source in your thesis if appropriate.

Step five: Choose a strategy that will best carry out your thesis; it need not be the same strategy as that of the source essay.

Step six: Mark (by brackets or underlining) those paragraphs or sentences in the source that will be relevant to developing your topic.

Step seven: Draw up an outline for your essay. Combine repetitious points; categorize similar and related points. Decide on the best sequence for your paragraphs.

Step eight: Decide which parts of the reading should be cited as evidence or refuted; distribute references to the source among the appropriate sections in your outline. Then decide which sentences of the reading should be quoted and which should be paraphrased.

Step nine: Write the rough draft, making sure that your topic sentences express your views, introduce the material that you intend to present in that paragraph, and are written in your voice. References to the source should be incorporated smoothly, and transitions should link your paragraphs together.

Step ten: Write an introduction that contains a clear statement of your thesis, as well as a reference to the source essay and its role in the development of your ideas. You may also decide to draft a conclusion.

Step eleven: Proofread your first draft very carefully to correct errors of grammar, style, reference, and spelling.

Step twelve: Using standard-size paper and leaving adequate margins and spacing, type or neatly write the final draft. Proofread once again to catch careless errors in copying.

ASSIGNMENT 11

A. One of the three essays that follow will serve as the starting point for an essay of your own. Assume that the essay you are planning will be about four pages long, or a minimum of 1,000 words. Using steps one and two, think of at least three possible topics for such an essay, and submit the most promising (or, if your teacher suggests it, all three) for approval.

B. Plan your essay by working from notes to an outline. Be prepared to submit your thesis and outline of paragraphs (with indications of relevant references to the source) to your teacher for approval.

C. Write a rough draft after deciding which parts of the essay should be cited as evidence or refuted, distributing references to the source among appropriate sections of your outline, and determining which parts of the reading should be quoted and which should be paraphrased.

D. Write a final draft of your essay.

SUMMARY

Behind much of what we do in school lie some ideas that could be expressed roughly as follows: (1) Of the vast body of human knowledge, there are certain bits and pieces that can be called essential, that everyone should know; (2) the extent to which a person can be considered educated, qualified to live intelligently in today's world and be a useful member of society, depends on the amount of this essential knowledge that he carries about with him; (3) it is the duty of schools, therefore, to get as much of this essential knowledge as possible into the minds of children. Thus we find ourselves trying to poke certain facts, recipes, and ideas down the gullets of every child in school, whether the morsel interests him or not, even if it frightens him or sickens him, and even if there are other things that he is much more interested in learning.

These ideas are absurd and harmful nonsense. We will not begin to have true education or real learning in our schools until we sweep this nonsense out of the way. Schools should be a place where children learn what they most want to know, instead of what we think they ought to know. The child who wants to know something remembers it and uses it once he has it; the child who learns something to please or appease someone else forgets it when the need for pleasing or the danger of not appeasing is past. This is why children quickly forget all but a small part of what they learn in school. It is of no use or interest to them; they do not want, or expect, or even intend to remember it. The only difference between bad and good students in this respect is that the bad students forget right away, while the good students are careful to wait until after the exam. If for no other reason, we could well afford to throw out most of what we teach in school because the children throw out almost all of it anyway.

The notion of a curriculum, an essential body of knowledge, would be absurd even if children remembered everything we "taught" them. We don't and can't agree on what knowledge is essential. The man who has trained himself in some special field of knowledge or competence thinks, naturally, that his specialty should be in the curriculum. The classical scholars want Greek and Latin taught; the historians shout for more history; the mathematicians urge more math and the scientists more science; the modern language experts want all children taught French, or Spanish, or Russian; and so on. Everyone wants to get his specialty into the act, knowing that as the demand for his special knowledge rises, so will the price that he can charge for it. Who wins this struggle and who loses depends not on the real needs of children or even of society, but on who is most skillful in public relations, who has the best educational lobbyists, who best can capitalize on events that have nothing to do with education, like the appearance of Sputnik in the night skies.

The idea of the curriculum would not be valid even if we could agree what ought to be in it. For knowledge itself changes. Much of what a child learns in school will be found, or thought, before many years, to be untrue. I studied physics at school from a fairly up-to-date text that proclaimed that the fundamental law of physics was the law of conservation of matter—matter is not created or destroyed. I had to scratch that out before I left school. In economics at college I was taught many things that were not true of our economy then, and many more that are not true now. Not for many years after I left college did I learn that the Greeks, far from being a detached and judicious people surrounded by chaste white temples, were hot-tempered, noisy, quarrelsome, and liked to cover their temples with gold leaf and bright paint; or that most of the citizens of Imperial Rome, far from living in houses in which the rooms surrounded an atrium, or central court, lived in multi-story tenements, one of which was perhaps the largest building in the ancient world. The child who really remembered everything he heard in school would live his life believing many things that were not so.

Moreover, we cannot possibly judge what knowledge will be most needed forty, or twenty, or even ten years from now. At school, I studied Latin and French. Few of the teachers who claimed then that Latin was essential would make as strong a case for it now; and the French might better have been Spanish, or better yet, Russian. Today the schools are busy teaching Russian; but perhaps they should be teaching Chinese, or Hindi, or who-knows-what? Besides physics, I studied chemistry, then perhaps the most popular of all science courses; but I would probably have done better to study biology, or ecology, if such a course had been offered (it wasn't). We always find out, too late, that we don't have the experts we need, that in the past we studied the wrong things; but this is bound to remain so. Since we can't know what knowledge will be most needed in the future, it is senseless to try to teach it in advance. Instead, we should try to turn out people who love learning so much and learn so well that they will be able to learn whatever needs to be learned.

How can we say, in any case, that one piece of knowledge is more important than another, or indeed, what we really say, that some knowledge is essential and the rest, as far as school is concerned, worthless? A child who wants to learn something that the school can't and doesn't want to teach him will be told not to waste his time. But how can we say that what he wants to know is less important than what we want him to know? We must ask how much of the sum of human knowledge anyone can know at the end of his schooling. Perhaps a millionth. Are we then to believe that one of these millionths is so much more important than another? Or that our social and national problems will be solved if we can just figure out a way to turn children out of schools knowing two millionths of the total, instead of one? Our problems don't arise from the fact that we lack experts enough to tell us what needs to be done, but out of the fact that we do not and will not do what we know needs to be done now.

Learning is not everything, and certainly one piece of learning is as good as another. One of my brightest and boldest fifth graders was deeply interested in snakes. He knew more about snakes than anyone I've ever known. The school did not offer herpetology; snakes were not in the curriculum; but as far as I was concerned, any time he spent learning about snakes was better spent than in ways I could think of to spend it; not least of all because, in the process of learning about snakes, he learned a great deal more about many other things than I was ever able to "teach" those unfortunates in my class who were not interested in anything at all. In another fifth-grade class, studying Romans in Britain, I saw a boy trying to read a science book behind the cover of his desk. He was spotted, and made to put the book away, and listen to the teacher; with a heavy sigh he did so. What was gained here? She traded a chance for an hour's real learning about science for, at best, an hour's temporary learning about history—much more probably no learning at all, just an hour's worth of daydreaming and resentful thoughts about school.

It is not subject matter that makes some learning more valuable than others, but the spirit in which the work is done. If a child is doing the kind of learning that most children do in school, when they learn at all—swallowing words, to spit back at the teacher on demand—he is wasting his time, or rather, we are wasting it for him. This learning will not be permanent, or relevant, or useful. But a child who is learning naturally, following his curiosity where it leads him, adding to his mental model of reality whatever he needs and can find a place for, and rejecting without fear or guilt what he does not need, is growing—in knowledge, in the love of learning, and in the ability to learn. He is on his way to becoming the kind of person we need in our society, and that our "best" schools and colleges are *not* turning out, the kind of person who, in Whitney Griswold's words, seeks and finds meaning, truth, and enjoyment in everything he does. All his life he will go on learning. Every experience will make his mental model of reality more complete and more true to life, and thus make him more able to deal realistically, imaginatively, and constructively with whatever new experience life throws his way.

We cannot have real learning in school if we think it is our duty and our right to tell children what they must learn. We cannot know, at any moment, what particular bit of knowledge or understanding a child needs most, will most strengthen and best fit his model of reality. Only he can do this. He may not do it very well, but he can do it a hundred times better than we can. The most we can do is try to help, by letting him know roughly what is available and where he can look for it. Choosing what he wants to learn and what he does not is something he must do for himself.

There is one more reason, and the most important one, why we must reject the idea of school and classroom as places where, most of the time, children are doing what some adult tells them to do. The reason is that there is no way to coerce children without making them afraid, or more afraid. We must not try to fool ourselves into thinking that this is not so. The would-be progressives, who until recently had great influence over most American public school education, did not recognize this—and still do not. They thought, or at least talked and wrote as if they thought, that there were good ways and bad ways to coerce children (the bad ones mean, harsh, cruel, the good ones gentle persuasive, subtle, kindly), and that if they avoided the bad and stuck to the good they would do no harm. This was one of their greatest mistakes, and the main reason why the revolution they hoped to accomplish never took hold.

The idea of painless, non-threatening coercion is an illusion. Fear is the inseparable companion of coercion, and its inescapable consequence. If you think it your duty to make children do what you want, whether they will or not, then it follows inexorably that you must make them afraid of what will happen to them if they don't do what you want. You can do this in the old-fashioned way, openly and avowedly, with the threat of harsh words, infringement of liberty, or physical punishment. Or you can do it in the modern way, subtly, smoothly, quietly, by withholding the acceptance and approval which you and others have trained the children to depend on; or by making them feel that some retribution awaits them in the future, too vague to imagine but too implacable to escape. You can, as many skilled teachers do, learn to tap with a word, a gesture, a look, even a smile, the great reservoir of fear, shame, and guilt that today's children carry around inside them. Or you can simply let your own fears, about what will happen to you if the children don't do what you want, reach out and infect them. Thus the children will feel more and more that life is full of dangers from which only the goodwill of adults like you can protect them, and that this goodwill is perishable and must be earned anew each day.

The alternative—I can see no other—is to have schools and classrooms in which each child in his own way can satisfy his curiosity, develop his abilities and talents, pursue his interests, and from the adults and older children around him get a glimpse of the great variety and richness of life. In short, the school should be a great smörgåsbord of intellectual, artistic, creative, and athletic activities, from which each child could take whatever he wanted, and as much as he wanted, or as little. When Anna was in the sixth grade, the year after she was in my class, I mentioned this idea to her. After describing very sketchily how such a school might be run, and what the children might do, I said, "Tell me, what do you think of it? Do you think it would work? Do you think the kids would learn anything?" She said, with utmost conviction, "Oh, yes, it would be wonderful!" She was silent for a minute or two, perhaps remembering her own generally unhappy schooling. Then she said thoughtfully, "You know, kids really like to learn; we just don't like being pushed around."

No, they don't; and we should be grateful for that. So let's stop pushing them around, and give them a chance.

John Holt, from *How Children Fail*

REWRITING AMERICAN HISTORY

History textbooks for elementary and secondary schools are not like other kinds of histories. They serve a different function, and they have their own traditions, which continue independent of academic history writing. In the first place, they are essentially nationalistic histories. The first American-history text was written after the American Revolution, and because of it; and most texts are still accounts of the nation-state. In the second place, they are written not to explore but to instruct— to tell children what their elders want them to know about their country. This information is not necessarily what anyone considers the truth of things. Like time capsules, the texts contain the truths selected for posterity.

The surprise is how quickly and how thoroughly these truths for posterity have changed. And the changes have occurred not only in the past two or three decades. To read the texts published over the two hundred years of United States history is to see several complete revisions in the picture they present of the country and its place in the world. These apparently solid, authoritative tomes are in fact the most nervous of objects, constantly changing in style as well as in political content. In the nineteenth century, when the texts usually had identifiable authors, the changes could be measured in generations; in the early twentieth century, they occurred in every decade. Since the nineteen-forties, however, the practice of rewriting texts every few years has meant that children who belong to the same generation often get very different impressions of the national identity.

American-history texts gained general currency in the schools only in the eighteen-nineties. Before then, American history was not very widely taught. The public grade schools had very little history of any kind in their curricula, and the private academies that prepared students for colleges and universities concentrated on classical studies and European history. The place that American-history texts now hold as the common element in children's schooling belonged in the nineteenth century to Noah Webster's spellers and rhetoric books, and then to the McGuffey readers. The Webster and McGuffey books had snatches of American history between their catechisms and their stories, but their bent was literary, and, apart from teaching children how to read, they taught mostly manners and morals. That fact suggests that until the eighteen-nineties Americans thought of themselves as belonging to a particular culture and holding certain values; they defined themselves by that culture much more than by the fact of the nation-state. The early-nineteenth-century history texts seem to bear this proposition out, since none of them offered much information on government, on politics, or even on the shape of the country. Samuel Goodrich, who, under the name of Peter Parley, published some of the most popular of all the pre-Civil War school histories, added large quantities of pure fiction to what was an otherwise unrelieved account of earthquakes and other natural disasters. His tales about the heroism of little boys in Indian raids were there not just to make good reading but to provide moral instruction for the student.

The first school historians of the United States did not lack patriotic ardor, but they seemed to lack a means of expressing it. New England clergymen for the most part, they suffered from the circumstance that before the Revolution American history was not a proper subject for study and therefore they had little education in it. But instead of trying to compensate for this deficiency they tended to make things up. The Reverend Jedidiah Morse, a friend of Noah Webster's and the first American school geographer, wrote, for instance, "North America has no remarkably high mountains. The most considerable are . . . the Allegheny Mountains." Then, the American history they eventually wrote seemed to have very little to do with the morality they professed for it. Goodrich's more factual-minded successors concerned themselves almost entirely with violence and with events of the nature of man-bites-dog. Emma Willard, a pioneer in the education of women in the United States, wrote in the foreword to one of her histories (published in 1847) that students should study history in order to increase their virtue, and that American history was particularly appropriate in this regard, because "in comparison with these old and wily nations, the character of America is that of youthful simplicity, of maiden purity." Her text, however, describes an almost uninterrupted sequence of massacres, rebellions, Indian attacks, border skirmishes, and major wars (the wars drawn out for pages, battle by battle). In these sanguinary conflicts, the only real virtue that Americans seem to have is the negative one of not behaving quite as despicably as everyone else.

Many of the nineteenth-century text writers had decided opinions on things. For example, they did not like foreigners at all, and they had a particularly keen dislike for the Spanish. The Reverend Mr. Morse wrote of the Spanish, "Naturally weak and effeminate, they dedicate the greatest part of their lives to loitering and inactive pleasures. Luxurious without variety or elegance, and expensive with great parade and little convenience, their character is nothing more than a grave and specious insignificance." The prose style of these writers is unparalleled in the twentieth century, and, indeed, in many respects it is all downhill rhetorically from the heights of the Reverend Mr. Morse. Unfortunately, their sense of structure—their feeling for the flow of history—did not measure up to their style. They relied desperately on chronology, and some of them placed their evaluation of each President at a point in the text that corresponded to the date of the President's death, no matter how long the man had been out of office by then or what was currently going on. They told a lot of anecdotes, but these did not always advance the narrative line. One writer, for instance, reported that George Washington had introduced Lafayette to his mother at a ball after a certain battle, and that Lafayette had found the lady impressive. The story ends there. On the whole, their characterizations of historical figures, like their political analyses, tended to be thin.

The history texts of the eighteen-nineties appear at first glance to have originated in a different civilization from the one that produced the earlier texts. And that is more or less the case. The decade before the turn of the century brought, among other things, a transformation of the educational system. Since the Civil War, the number of public high schools had grown rapidly—to the point where the high schools now had more students than the private academies. While the state legislatures concerned themselves with the politics of this development (many of them started requiring courses in American history), the teachers and college professors organized national associations to set standards for the teaching profession and to bring some order to the secondary-school curriculum. This work of organization and standardization—such as was then taking place in all the professions—was accompanied by a certain change in philosophy about the nature of the scholarly enterprise. In the field of history, university professors under the influence of the German school began to explore problems of methodology and to conclude that if history was not a science (which many, such as Henry Adams, hoped it might turn out to be), then at least it was a discipline, and not just a craft practiced by men of leisure. This notion moved gradually into the schools and schoolbooks in the form of a general recognition that facts were important and certain facts more important than others.

The texts of the eighteen-nineties thus constitute a departure. In the first place, they are written in terse, declarative sentences—the so-called telegraphic style. In the second place, they are orderly to the point of compulsion. Gone are the old eccentricities of style and the old piling up of events on dates; their material is organized into themes, such as "The English Colonies" or "The Rise of Parties," the significance of each theme being stated as bluntly as possible in the chapter heading. The books give much less space to battles and much more to politics, economics, and governmental undertakings of all sorts. Institutions appear amid the welter of events—the formation of the Republic now has a significance equal to that of the Revolutionary War—and personalities are fleshed out slightly with description and pertinent anecdote. Finally, the books sound a new note of restraint. The authors clearly have their opinions, but they do not force them adjectivally upon their readers. The books have a tone of objectivity and authoritativeness. That tone is, of course, spurious—a pure formality. But seen in retrospect the assumption of this impersonal voice was as important an innovation in the history of textbooks as the discovery of perspective was in the history of painting. From the eighteen-nineties on, what the texts said about American history would appear to children to be the truth.

If the eighteen-nineties could be viewed as the Quattrocento of American-history text writing, then the period between 1910 and 1930 was surely the Renaissance of that particular form. In 1911, there appeared the first edition of David Saville Muzzey's "American History;" in 1913, the first work by the Progressive historian Willis Mason West. Subsequently, there were books by Charles and Mary Beard, by the Harvard historian Albert Bushnell Hart, and by a number of other first-rank historians, including Andrew C. McLaughlin and Wilbur Fisk Gordy. At the very end of the period, Harold Rugg began publishing his series. The new textbook authors were not simply writers for children, as the nine-teenth-century authors usually were, but professors chosen for their academic distinction and for their ability to synthesize large issues for children. Some of them were considerable prose stylists, and though their texts do not have the same flair—or sometimes even the same point of view—as their less synthetic works, the new textbook conven-tion of deadpan writing does not entirely filter out the sound of their individual voices.

Ideologically speaking, the books produced in this period were a good deal more diverse than those published in the eighteen-nineties—or, indeed, in any subsequent period until the late nineteen-sixties. Not only the authors of the books but, by and large, the new audience of sec-ondary-school teachers belonged to the Progressive political movement, and believed in political and pedagogical reform. On the right end of the spectrum were Muzzey (of whom more later) and Hart, with their aristocratic New England brand of Progressive politics. These gentlemen looked upon the Age of Enlightenment as the source of the best in the American tradition. They revered the Founding Fathers and, on their behalf, carried on the only serious attempt at ancestor worship in Amer-ican textbook history. Hart argued, typically, "One evidence that the Revolution was justified is the fact that the best and ablest men in the colonies believed that their liberty was in danger. When Benjamin Frank-lin heartily joined in the war, there must have been reason for it." For Hart and Muzzey, character was all-important, and the quality of in-dividual leaders was the central issue in politics and in history. Hart, who disapproved of Western expansionist adventures in general, wrote, "The defect of Polk's character was his lack of moral principle as to the property of our neighbor, Mexico."

On the left end of the spectrum between 1910 and 1920 was Willis Mason West. For West, the significant actors in history were not indi-viduals but economic forces, social groups, and political institutions. West specifically disapproved of the New England view of the Enlight-enment. The first of his books begins, "I have tried to correct the common delusion which looks back to Jefferson or John Winthrop for a golden age, and to show instead that democracy has as yet been tried only imperfectly among us." True to this purpose, West reports in the body of his text that the delegates to the Constitutional Convention did not believe in government by the people, that they belonged to the eight-eenth century rather than to the twentieth, and that "they represented the crest of a reactionary movement of their own day." West thought that the main value of the American Revolution lay in the fact that it opened up new opportunities to a great number of people and called forth new social energies. In writing about the late nineteenth century, West—almost alone among text writers—discussed class conflict and the "warlike" relationship between labor and capital. He was nonethe-less something of a moralist, and he was a true Progressive in that he believed in salvation by the elevation of consciousness. In the conclusion of his 1913 text, he wrote of the Progressive period, "The Nation awoke shamed . . . enmeshed in a net of intangible chains. . . . Now at the end of another twenty years, a new dawn is breaking. The moral sense of the people has grown steadily more and more alert [We have] a gallant group of leaders . . . with weapons for the strife."

These Progressive texts continued to appear throughout the twenties (textbooks being always somewhat behind the times), along with a number of conservative histories. None of the former were as politically explicit as the West book, but all carried at least some slight strain of dissent from prevailing institutions. Some of the thirties texts maintained this distance, even while introducing a very different style of political thinking. The more leftist among them reflected a hazy kind of Socialism—the ideology of the progressive-education movement, as opposed to that of the now-defunct Progressive Party. Perhaps in obedience to John Dewey's dictum that economic history is more democratic than political history, Charles Garrett Vannest and Henry Lester Smith collaborated on a text that is short on political history. Like Harold Rugg's civilization series, their "Socialized History of the United States" reports on the development of American society and tends to slight Presidents or other leaders. The approach did not result in any great narrative fluency. Of the Pilgrims, the book reports, "After a stormy voyage of over two months, they landed at Plymouth, where for the first few years they had a hard time." But books such as this were clearly not meant for the entertainment of children. They were designed to promote social reform by indoctrinating children with tolerance, coöperation, and other social-democratic virtues.

What carried over from the thirties into the forties was this tone of high moral seriousness—little more. For the period of ideological diversity—the Hundred Flowers of textbook writing—ended abruptly with the beginning of the Second World War. The warning signal was the N.A.M.-sponsored attack on the Rugg series; even before that controversy ended the publishers were dropping or revising all history texts of a similar nature and hiring new authors. Within a few years, there were no more dissenting books on the market. The political spectrum of the texts narrowed to a point somewhere in the neighborhood of Dwight D. Eisenhower and remained there for the next twenty-five years.

As might be expected, the texts of the forties give emphasis to political history, or, rather—since in many ways these texts deny the very existence of politics—to the history of government actions. The word "democracy" is not, as it was in the thirties books, a call to social action but simply the name of the American system, and the opposite of Fascism and Communism—which are not themselves very well defined. The curious thing about these books is that all of them insist upon the right to vote as the foundation stone of democracy. They do that in spite of the fact that this right exists in the Soviet Union and provides no real impediment to the rule of the Communist Party bureaucrats.

Unsurprisingly, the forties texts show a new interest in foreign affairs. In addition to a rather belated concern for Europe, they manifest a sudden rush of enthusiasm for Latin America. This enthusiasm lasts exactly as long as President Franklin D. Roosevelt's Good Neighbor Policy, leaving only one sign of its passage: the word "imperialism," which was once freely used to describe United States adventures in Asia and the Caribbean at the end of the nineteenth century, no longer applies to the United States. According to these books, imperialism is a European affair: "we" have a Monroe Doctrine and a Good Neighbor Policy. The words "we" and "our" crop up frequently in the forties texts—most prominently in the titles. Whereas the twenties books are usually called something like "An American History" or "The History of the United States" (the naming of texts never having been an occasion for much originality), those of the forties have such titles as "The Story of America" and "The Story of Our Republic," the implication of which is that the student must identify with everything that has ever happened in American history.

In the fifties, these concerns do not so much change as intensify. The morbid fear of Communism becomes an overriding passion—to the point where in some books the whole of American history appears a mere prologue to the struggle with the "Reds." Most books devote more than half of their twentieth-century history to foreign affairs and focus their attention on the question of "how the United States became a world power." American power and strength are the leitmotivs of these books. Even the War of 1812, which ended—to put the matter in its best light—in a military standoff, appears as yet another victory. Once again "we" are, according to the texts, "taking up our responsibilities" for the rest of the world. There is a fascination with patriotic symbols—the flag, Independence Hall, the Statue of Liberty. And the static, legalistic quality of the political analysis in the forties books has now hardened into a neo-Confucian mold, wherein the American political system appears eternal and unchanging. One of the major texts of the period, Henry W. Bragdon and Samuel P. McCutchen's "History of a Free People," concludes with an essay extolling the virtues of freedom not for its own sake but merely as the greatest asset in the world struggle.

For all their insistence on the wealth, strength, and virtue of the United States, the fifties texts do not have a very sunny view of the future. In the concluding sections, there are a good many grim warnings that citizens must do jury duty, pay taxes, and learn to recognize hostile propaganda. Children are also repeatedly informed that their liberties will disappear if they do not defend them properly. This, the books invariably conclude, is the most difficult and challenging period in American history. Even the sections on the wonders of science are not particularly reassuring, for where the thirties books looked forward to improvements in society and human nature, these look forward to progress only in an inhuman sphere beyond most people's control.

The texts of the fifties are notable for laying equal stress on political, social, and economic history. They give the development of American industry—a subject that was sorely neglected by their predecessors—an important place in nineteenth-century history. And while they tend to side with the Pinkertons against the labor radicals, they give nineteenth-century labor-union history as much space as they give the captains of industry. What is missing from their economic history is, first, a description of the structural changes in the American economy since the eighteen-thirties and, second, an account of how these structural changes affected American politics. But the same might be said of their political and social history: the books do not describe change or show the relationship between one kind of event and another. The nineteen-fifties texts are encyclopedias rather than history books. Their vast indexes contain references to everything under the sun, but there is no connection between one thing and another. Events stand isolated below headings of black type, like islands in some archipelago where no one has yet invented the canoe.

The texts of the sixties contain the most dramatic rewriting of history ever to take place in American schoolbooks. The political alteration began in 1965, when texts first reported the assassination of President Kennedy. From then on, problems of a new sort begin to crop up. At first, these problems are confined to the concluding sections; they come apparently from nowhere, since if one believes the rest of the books the United States, threatened though it may be from the outside, has a just and pacific society and a firm but peaceable foreign policy. Later, these problems multiply, and they spread like measles through the texts. The late-sixties editions show that foreign policy has been a problem for years, what with Suez and the Cuban missile crisis and other such challenges. Urban blight, too, has long been a problem, and black Americans have historically been discriminated against. By the early seventies, these problems are running rampant through American history; indeed, according to one book, American history is "a gnarled experience involving problems, turmoil, and conflict." Then, even while the problems are still breaking out, there is a distinct shift of emphasis from foreign policy to domestic social history. Blacks and other minority groups enter the books slowly, their way prepared by George Washington Carver. At the same time, the static, neo-Confucian style gives way to a somewhat more dynamic—or simply historical—mode of political analysis. These changes in interpretation bring with them new sets of facts or, as in the case of Reconstruction, the old set of facts used backward. To read all the editions of the sixties texts is thus a bewildering experience. What changes is nothing less than the character of the United States.

Frances FitzGerald, *The New Yorker*, 26 February 1979

POVERTY AND CRIME

Why are violent criminals drawn so heavily from the ranks of the poor? The answer lies not in the genes, but in the nature of the lives poor people lead and of the communities in which they reside. The close association of violent crime with urban lower-class life is a direct result of the opportunities that are *not* available. Psychological factors may help explain why some individuals turn to street crime and others do not. But the question posed in this chapter is not why particular individuals choose a life of crime and violence; it is why the people who make that choice are concentrated more heavily in the lower class than in the middle or working class.

Children growing up in urban slums and ghettos face a different set of choices than do youngsters growing up in middle-class neighborhoods, and they have a radically different sense of what life offers. By the time children are six or eight years old, their view of the world has been shaped by their surroundings and by their parents' as well as their own experiences. Children of the upper class and upper-middle class develop what the psychiatrist Robert Coles calls a sense of "entitlement." "Wealth does not corrupt nor does it ennoble," Coles writes. "But wealth does govern the minds of privileged children, gives them a peculiar kind of identity which they never lose, whether they grow up to be stockbrokers or communards." That identity grows out of the wide range of choices with which privileged children live—choices about toys and games, food and clothing, vacations and careers. Their identity grows out of their sense of competence as well, for they (and, to a lesser degree, ordinary middle-class children) live in a world in which their parents and, by reflection, they themselves exercise authority, in which they influence and often control their environment. They are, in a phrase, the masters of their fate; their world, as an eleven-year-old boy told Coles, is one in which "If you really work for the rewards, you'll get them." This view is confirmed in school. "Those who want something badly enough get it," the boy's fourth-grade teacher wrote on the blackboard, "provided they are willing to wait and work."

To the "children of poverty," those who want something badly enough usually do *not* get it, no matter how hard they work or how long they wait. Nothing about their own lives or the lives of their parents (or relatives or friends) suggests that "If you really work for the rewards, you'll get them." Quite the contrary: poor children grow up in a world in which people work hard and long, for painfully meager rewards. It is a world, too, in which parents and relatives are at the mercy of forces they cannot control—a world in which illness, an accident, a recession, an employer's business reverses or a foreman's whim can mean the loss of a job and a long period of unemployment, and in which a bureaucrat's arbitrary ruling can mean denial or loss of welfare benefits and, thereby, of food, clothing, fuel, or shelter.

Understandably, poor children come to see themselves as the servants, not the masters, of their fate. When I was doing research on secondary education in the late 1960s, I attended a number of high school graduations. In schools with a predominantly middle-class population, the valedictorians typically spoke of how they and their classmates would affect and change American society. In schools with a lower-class student body, the student speakers sounded a different theme. In one such school, the valedictorian read a long Edgar Guest—poem that began, "Sometimes you win, and sometimes you lose; here's luck." The poem continued in the same vein, with the refrain "Here's luck" repeated at the end of each stanza. For lower-class adolescents, this is an all too accurate assessment of the world they inhabit.

It is hard to be poor; it is harder to be poor in the United States than in most other countries, for American culture has always placed a heavy premium on "success." ("Winning is not the main thing; it is the only thing.") It is not the success ethic alone that causes problems, the sociologist Robert K. Merton observes, but the fact that the emphasis on success is coupled with an equally heavy emphasis on ambition, on maintaining lofty goals whatever one's station in life. "Americans are admonished 'not to be a quitter,'" Merton writes, "for in the dictionary of American culture, as in the lexicon of youth, 'there is no such word as "fail."'"

Crime and violence are more frequent among the poor than among members of the middle class, Merton argues, because American culture imbues everyone with the importance of ambition and success without providing everyone with the opportunity to achieve success through conventional means. And the cultural emphasis on success is greater now than it used to be: Every day of the week, in the films they see, the television programs they watch, and the public schools they attend, poor people are bombarded with messages about success—vivid images of the life style of the middle class. Television, in particular, drives home the idea that one is not a full-fledged American unless one can afford the goods and services portrayed in the commercials and in the programs themselves. To poor people, the TV screen provides a daily reminder, if any is needed, of the contrast between their own poverty and the affluence enjoyed by the rest of society.

It should not be surprising that many poor people choose the routes to success that seem open to them. To youngsters growing up in lower-class neighborhoods, crime is available as an occupational choice, much as law, medicine, or business management is for adolescents raised in Palo Alto or Scarsdale—except that lower-class youngsters often know a good deal more about the criminal occupations available to them than middle-class youngsters do about their options. In my conversations with young offenders, I was struck by the depth of their knowledge about robbery, burglary, "fencing," the sale and use of hard and soft drugs, prostitution and pimping, the "numbers" business, loan-sharking, and other crimes and rackets. In a great many cities, I was impressed, too, by their detailed knowledge of which fences, numbers operators, and other criminals were paying off which police officers, as well as by their cynicism about governmental corruption in general.

Thus the fabric and texture of life in urban slums and ghettos provide an environment in which opportunities for criminal activity are manifold, and in which the rewards for engaging in crime appear to be high—higher than the penalties for crime, and higher than the rewards for avoiding it. "It seems to me that the kind of neighborhood you come up in may make all the difference in which way you go and where you end up," John Allen suggests. In his neighborhood, most people earned their living from illegitimate activity. "Hustling was their thing: number running, bootlegging, selling narcotics, selling stolen goods, prostitution," he continues. "There's so many things that go on—it's a whole system that operates inside itself."

"Say I was to take you by it. You want some junk, then I would take you to the dude that handles drugs. You want some clothes, I could take you somewhere that handles that. You want some liquor, I could take you someplace other than a liquor store. Of course, it's all outside the law."

It is not simply a matter of opportunity; role models are important as well. "When I think about who's got the power in my neighborhood," John Allen says, "I mostly think about people who've got to the top in strictly illegal ways." As a child, his hero was a successful numbers operator: "he was about the biggest because everybody respected him, he always had plenty of money, he always dressed nice, and everybody always done what he wanted them to do. I dug the respect that he gave and that he got. . . ." "The ones you see are the ones who interest you," an ex-offender says, recalling his childhood. "If it had been doctors and lawyers who drove up and parked in front of the bars in their catylacks, I'd be a doctor today. But it wasn't; it was the men who were into things, the pimps, the hustlers and the numbers guys."

In some lower-class neighborhoods, youngsters learn to become criminals almost as a matter of course. "Education for crime must be looked upon as habituation to a way of life," the late Frank Tannenbaum wrote in 1938, in his neglected classic, *Crime and the Community*. "As such, it partakes of the nature of all education. It is a gradual adaptation to, and a gradual absorption of, certain elements in the environment." Since it would be hard to improve upon Tannenbaum's description, I shall quote from it at length.

The development of a criminal career has "elements of curiosity, wonder, knowledge, adventure," Tannenbaum wrote. "Like all true education, it has its beginnings in play, it starts in more or less random movements, and builds up toward techniques, insights, judgments, attitudes." Like all true education, it also uses whatever is available in the environment, including "such humble things as junk heaps, alley ways, abandoned houses, pushcarts, railroad tracks, coal cars." Children begin with things that can be easily picked up and carried away, and easily used or sold.

Education for crime is a social process as well—"Part of the adventure of living in a certain way in a certain environment," Tannenbaum continued. "But both the environment and the way of using it must already be there." If his career is to develop, the young criminal must have encouragement, support, and instruction from his friends and elders, particularly from what Tannenbaum calls "the intermediary," i.e., the fence. Even if he is nothing more than a junk dealer or peddler, the fence will "purchase bottles, copper wire, lead pipes, bicycles, and trinkets. He will not only pay cash which can be used to continue the play life of the growing children, for movies, candies, sweets, harmonicas, baseball bats, gloves, and other paraphernalia, but if he is a friendly and enterprising fence he will throw out suggestions, indicate where things can be found, will even supply the tools with which to rip and tear down lead pipes or other marketable materials. And the young gang will accept the suggestions and carry out the enterprise as a part of a game, each act providing a new experience, new knowledge, new ways of seeing the world, new interests."

Other factors are needed, too. There must be a cynical attitude toward the police and toward property belonging to business firms and government agencies. There must be older criminals who use adolescents as messengers or lookouts, and to whom the youngsters look for approval. And there must be a conflict between delinquent youngsters and older, more settled people who are their victims, and who call for police protection. "All these elements are part of the atmosphere, of the environment" within which education for crime proceeds.

The "slow, persistent habituation of an individual to a criminal way of life" occurs frequently and naturally in lower-class neighborhoods because so many criminal opportunities are available: numbers operations, bookmaking, and other illegal gambling enterprises; selling heroin, cocaine, marijuana, "uppers," "downers," and other drugs; loan-sharking; male and female prostitution; pimping; bootlegging and after-hours sales of alcoholic beverages; and hustling and theft in all their manifold forms.

Theft is in the very air that lower-class youngsters breathe. It is visible not just because of its frequency, but because crimes such as burglary, boosting, "clouting" (taking merchandise from a delivery truck while the driver is occupied), and stealing from parked cars are not isolated acts by isolated individuals. On the contrary, the individual act of theft is just the beginning of an elaborate process whereby "stolen merchandise is acquired, converted, redistributed and reintegrated into the legitimate property stream." This "stolen property system," as the criminologists Marilyn Walsh and Duncan Chappell call it, is an integral part of the economy of urban lower-class neighborhoods. "About 95 percent of the people around here will buy hot goods," one of William West's Toronto informants told him. "It's a bargain, they're not going to turn it down."

Reluctance to turn down a bargain is not unique to the lower class. Many middle-class people knowingly buy stolen merchandise, and some respectable merchants increase their profits by selling stolen goods unbeknownst to their customers. It is not just coincidence that a particularly good bargain is referred to colloquially as a "steal." "Everybody's looking for a bargain," the professional fence whom the criminologist Carl Klockars calls Vincent Swaggi observed. "If the price is right and a man can use the merchandise, he's gonna buy. No question about it."

Swaggi had reason to know; he was speaking from the vantage point of more than twenty-five years' experience as a fence, selling to judges, prosecutors, policemen (high officials as well as patrolmen), independent businessmen, and buyers for department stores and retailing chains, in addition to ordinary consumers. He did a booming retail business in merchandise acquired through manufacturers' close-outs and other legitimate channels; his reputation as a fence cast an aura of "bargain" over his entire inventory. "See, most people figure all of the stuff in my store is hot, which you know it ain't," Swaggi told Klockars. "But if they figure it's hot you can't keep 'em away from it. . . . People figurin' they're gonna get something for nothing. You think I'm gonna tell 'em it ain't hot? Not on your life."

For lower-class people, buying stolen merchandise is more than just a matter of picking up a bargain or accommodating the larceny that confidence men, as well as fences, tell us is in almost everyone's heart. Buying from a "peddler" at the back door may be the only way impoverished parents can afford to serve meat to their families, and patronizing a "bargain store" the only way they can afford shoes for their children's growing feet or name-brand sneakers so that teenagers do not lose face among their friends. For many poor people, too, buying stolen property is a way of buying into the American Dream, of being able to afford those consumption items—Stacy Adams shoes, Johnny Walker Black Label Scotch, a stereo or color television set, a motorcycle or ten-speed bike, a sporty-looking car—that the mass media tell them are the mark of a "successful" American. Because they lack the job titles and other devices that shore up middle-class people's sense of self, members of the lower class feel an even greater need than members of the middle class to define themselves through consumption.

Buying stolen property also provides a way of getting back at "them."* "Many people on Clay Street had had problems resulting in what they called 'getting screwed,'" Joseph T. Howell writes about the lower-class, mainly Southern white neighborhood in Washington, D.C., in which he lived for a year as a participant-observer. "For this reason, few people thought twice about 'getting back.'"

> For instance, hot merchandise was plentiful on Clay Street. At Christmas, June and Sam gave Sammy a five-speed chopper bike, listing at seventy-five dollars but for which they paid a "friend" thirty dollars. Les gave Phyllis a twenty-one-inch color TV in exchange for a new high-powered automatic rifle, both of which were hot. Les said about half of everything in their house was stolen. . . . Although few disclosed how they came upon the hot merchandise, they would usually take pride in getting an especially good deal. Having this merchandise was in no way considered dishonest.

Far from being considered dishonest, patronizing the stolen property system is a way of evening the score, of getting one's fair share in an unfair world. From a lower-class perspective, buying a name-brand item at 50 percent or more below list price is a means of correcting a social imbalance, of redressing the maldistribution of income from which they suffer. Their sense of the rightness of the enterprise is enhanced by their conviction—often right, sometimes wrong—that local merchants and local outlets of national chains sell shoddy merchandise at premium prices. Since "hot" merchandise often is stolen from "downtown" retailers as well as from factories, warehouses, trucking firms, and middle-class residences, the stolen property system (like the progressive income

---

* Frequent use of the pronoun "them" reflects both the way poor people see the rest of society and their conception of how the rest of society sees them.

tax) is a means of redistributing income from rich to poor. It may also serve to expand the overall consumer market and hence total production and employment; without the large "discounts" the stolen property system provides, Leroy Gould and his colleagues speculate, poor people might not be able to buy certain kinds of merchandise at all.

At the same time, poor people's readiness to buy stolen merchandise contributes significantly to their own poverty. Thieves do not limit their scores to middle-class targets; juveniles, addicts, and other impulsive and semiprofessional thieves tend to prey on their own communities, where apprehension is less likely. The result is a vicious circle: normally law-abiding people who have been victimized by burglary or some other form of theft feel justified in buying hot merchandise to recoup their losses as cheaply as possible; but their patronage, in turn, makes it easier for thieves and fences to dispose of their wares and encourages further theft.

Thus the stolen property system develops its own dynamic, with supply and demand feeding on one another. Because lower-class people feel aggrieved, and because they are persuaded that American society is little more than one gigantic "hustle," there is no more opprobrium attached to selling stolen merchandise than to buying it. "That's the only way to make a living up here," a deliveryman who supplemented his salary by selling merchandise he stole from his own truck told Joseph Howell. "You earn half and you steal half." The man learned his illegal trade through on-the-job training given him by a more experienced driver. "You work hard, don't you?" the older man had pointed out. "Why not take out your cut?" Why not, indeed, when the cops are known—or, what amounts to the same thing, are believed—to be taking *their* cut from the local fences, as well as from numbers runners and bankers, bootleggers, after-hours clubs, gambling joints, prostitutes, pimps, and heroin dealers.

Corruption aside, lower-class people's readiness to support the stolen property system is upheld by the benign view the rest of society takes toward fencing. Judges, prosecutors, police, and the public at large share a myopic legal tradition that focuses on individual acts of theft rather than on the stolen property system as a whole. One consequence is that judges rarely give prison sentences to fences, preferring to reserve the harsh penalty of incarceration for people they deem dangerous. Prosecutors and police administrators, in turn, are reluctant to proceed against fences. Building a strong case against a fence requires the investment of a great deal of prosecutorial and/or police time and effort, and the investment appears to be a poor allocation of resources when the end result is likely to be no more than probation or a fine for the convicted fence. From a police perspective, therefore, it often makes more sense to offer a fence protection in exchange for information. But from the perspective of people living in lower-class neighborhoods, the fact that fences go free, while burglars go to prison, serves to reinforce their cynicism about the law and law enforcement.

Charles Silberman, from *Criminal Violence, Criminal Justice*

5. The Multiple-Source Essay

Until now, your writing assignments have been either based on information that has been derived from a single source or based on ideas that you have developed yourself. You have learned to paraphrase, summarize, rearrange, and unify your evidence without sacrificing accuracy or completeness.

Now, as you begin to work with a wider range of sources, you will have to understand and organize much more diverse material. Your task is to present the ideas of your sources in all their variety, while, at the same time, maintaining your own single perspective, which encompasses all the shades of opinion. How can you describe each author's ideas to your reader without taking up a large amount of space for each one? How can you fit all your sources smoothly into your essay without allowing one to dominate? How can you convert a group of disparate ideas into an essay that is yours?

To make it easier for you to learn to deal with multiple sources, most of the examples, exercises, and writing assignments in this chapter will use materials that are brief and easy to experiment with. Most of these materials are notes taken by students during informal interviews or short, written responses to a topic or an article. In the writing assignments, you may be asked to generate your own materials by doing a series of interviews or by joining your classmates in writing down your reactions to a general question. The statements that you will work with in this chapter not only provide useful practice, but also have their equivalents in professional writing such as case notes, case studies, legal testimony, and market research.

SELECTING INFORMATION FOR A MULTIPLE-SOURCE ESSAY

In academic writing, you do not usually find the materials for an essay in a neatly assembled package. On the contrary, before beginning to organize an essay, you will often be faced with the preliminary problem of finding and selecting your materials. The first stage of a research project is traditionally the trip to the library with a topic to explore, a search for information that will later be interpreted, sifted, and synthesized into a finished piece of writing.

To demonstrate this process in miniature, assume that you have been assigned the following project, which calls for a narrow area of research rather than the range of the library's expanse of materials:

> Read an entire newspaper published on a day of your choosing during the 1930s or 1940s, and write a summary describing what life was like on that day. Your multiple sources are the assorted articles and advertisements in the day's paper.

Given the amount and variety of information contained in the average newspaper, your greatest difficulty would be to decide what and how much to include. You would hope to provide a balance of two kinds of evidence—major events that altered the fabric of most people's lives, and more ordinary happenings that could be put together and interpreted to tell a good deal about how people typically spent their days. While these events probably took place before your birth, your not having been there at the time would actually be an advantage: the outsider's distance would help you to distinguish between stories of historic importance and those that simply reflect their era.

To begin this project, you would follow these steps:

1. Read rapidly through the entire newspaper. Then read the same issue again more slowly, jotting down your impressions of important *kinds* of events or *characteristics* of daily life. Search for a pattern, a thesis that sums up what you have read.

2. Review your notes, and isolate a few main ideas that seem worth developing. Then read the issue a third time, making sure that there is really sufficient evidence for all the points that you will wish to make. Make notes of any additional information that you expect to use, and write down the page number next to each reference in your notes. Remember that you are not trying to "use up" all the available information.

3. Plan a series of paragraphs, each focusing on a somewhat different theme that is either significant in itself or typical of

the day that you are describing. Spend some time choosing a strategy for a sequence of paragraphs that not only will introduce your reader to the world that you are describing, but will also make apparent the pattern of events or thesis that you have discovered through your reading.

Drawing Conclusions from Your Information

As you write this kind of essay, you should try to help your readers form conclusions about the significance of the information that you are citing. The evidence should not be expected to speak for itself. Consider the following paragraph:

> Some popular books in the first week of 1945 were Brave Men by Ernie Pyle, Forever Amber by Kathleen Windsor, and The Time for Decision by Sumner Wells. The average price of these new, hard-cover books was about three dollars each. The price of the daily Times was three cents, and Life magazine was ten cents.

What is most interesting to the person who reads this account today is how little the reading material cost, a point that the writer properly stated explicitly somewhere in the paragraph. Three titles are cited, but nothing is said about the books. Can you tell what they were about? Why were the popular? Do they seem typical of 1945's Best Seller list? You should be careful to provide some sort of context for your evidence. Unexplained and unassimilated information is of no value to your reader, who cannot be assumed to know more than—or even as much as—you do.

In contrast, another student, writing about a day shortly after the end of World War II, built a paragraph around a casualty list in the *New York Times*. What seemed significant about the list was the fact that by the end of the war, casualties had become routine and had assumed almost a subordinate place in daily life. Notice that the paragraph begins with a topic sentence that establishes the context and draws its conclusion at the end.

> For much of the civilian population, the worst part of the war had been the separation from their loved ones, who had gone off to fight in Europe, Africa, and the Pacific. Even after the end of the war, they still had to wait for the safe arrival home of the troops. In order to inform the public, the New York Times ran a daily list of troop arrivals. However, not everyone was destined to return, and the Times also ran a list of casualties, which, on September 4, was to be found on the bottom of page 2.

Another paragraph about May 6, 1946, forms the conclusion that the post-war mid-forties were a transitional period:

> The process of switching over from a wartime to a peacetime economy was not without its pains. Then, as now, there was a high rate of unemployment. The <u>Times</u> featured a story about the million women production workers who had recently lost their jobs in war industries. Returning male and female veterans were also flooding the job market. Some working wives were waiting to see how their husbands readjusted to postwar jobs. If their ex–GI husbands could bring home enough money to support the family, they could return to their roles as housewives. If their husbands chose to continue their education or vocational training under the GI Bill, they would expect to stay on the job as long as they could.

The bulk of this paragraph appears to be a straightforward account of circumstances in support of the topic sentence containing the writer's conclusion; but she is, in fact, summarizing information taken from *sevral* articles in that day's newspaper. (Notice that, while the source of the information—the *Times*—is being cited, the identity of the reporters is not significant in this case, and no names are included.) The suggestion of a personal comment—unemployment, one gathers, is a recurring problem—adds immediacy and significance to a topic which might otherwise be remote from present concerns.

EXERCISE 32

Read the following student essay, a description of life in New York City on March 24, 1938. Analyze each paragraph and be prepared to discuss the following:

1. The writer's reasons for building a paragraph around that piece of information. (Use your own knowledge of the contents of the average newspaper today to estimate the range of choices that the writer might have had.)
2. The clarity and completeness with which the information is presented.
3. The inclusion of topic sentences that interpret the information and suggest its significance for the reader.
4. The organization of the essay: the relationship between paragraphs; the sequence of paragraphs; the unity within each paragraph.
5. The establishment of a thesis and the success of the author's attempt to characterize March 24, 1938, as typical of its era and as a contrast to her own era, decades later.

According to the New York Times, on March 24, 1938, the most important issues on people's minds were unemployment and the high increase in the cost of living. Those who were fortunate enough to have jobs were getting very low wages. To help the financial situation, measures were being taken by different city and national organizations. On page four of the Times, for example, we learn that Congress had just approved an allocation to New York State for $5,079,030, to provide extra weeks of unemployment insurance for those people who had lost their jobs and were covered by Social Security. This measure was to offer temporary help for some families. Those families that were not eligible for unemployment insurance were forced to go on relief. Another article that day states that Mayor La Guardia had proposed $9,250,000 in additional taxes to meet the increased need for welfare funds.

The high increase in the cost of living had resulted in a big rally held at Madison Square Garden on the previous day, where participants protested the high prices and the low wages. The rally was heavily attended by employees of the Fulton Fish Market, who were on strike at that time and were depending on higher salaries in order to meet the increasing cost of living. Milk, for example, had gone up from 10 to 15½ or 16 cents per quart in home deliveries and from 8 to 11½ cents per quart at grocery stores. Although nothing concrete materialized as the result of this rally, nevertheless people had made clear their feelings about the state of the economy and had brought their needs to the attention of public officials.

This prevailing financial crisis faced by so many families had brought about an awareness of the need for family planning. That week, the people of New York City started a campaign demanding that centers be opened where people could get birth control information. The city, in turn, made a decision to open such centers.

During that week, attempts were made to provide better international mail service, as well as to provide better services from the police department. The big announcement was that air mail service to and from Europe would start that summer for the first time. Another announcement was that police cars in New York City from then on would have white tops in order to make them more visible to the public.

As for advertisements, high on the list was the push-

button radio made by RCA. Diet crackers were very
prominent in advertising pages, and there were also many
cigarette advertisements, most of which featured women. A
news story reported that new car sales were increasing,
despite the state of the economy. The models most in
demand were Chevrolets, Fords, Oldsmobiles, and
Studebakers.

In the entertainment field, Sonja Henie was the top
movie star attraction. Marlene Dietrich was also very
popular for her sexy screen portrayals. The romantic movie
pair of that year was Nelson Eddy and Jeanette MacDonald.
Very popular also were Edgar Bergen and Charlie McCarthy.
Carole Lombard's Fools for Scandal was playing that week
at Radio City Music Hall with tremendous success.

The weather on that date hit a record high of 72
degrees at 3:00 PM. The same warm weather was affecting
Washington, where the cherry trees were reported to have
bloomed ahead of schedule.

We have seen that the people living in New York on
March 24, 1938, were facing similar problems to the ones
we are facing today. The unemployment situation resembled
ours, and they, too, were struggling with inflation just
as we are now. Although wages are much higher now, it is
difficult to cope with the present high cost of living. In
1938 and today, plans were being made to provide for those
people who could not earn a living. But, in the midst of
all these problems, good things happened as they do today.
The improvement of the mail service and the opening of the
1939 World's Fair were both events to be anticipated. It's
good to observe that people were rallying to speak their
minds in 1938, just as many groups today express their
beliefs openly and freely. I suppose that the most exact
parallel between 1938 and today is the weather: it is as
unpredictable now as it was then.

Generalizing from Examples

Summarizing the contents of a newspaper can cause problems for the
writer because newspaper stories describe specific incidents which often
have nothing in common except that they all happened on the same
day. Academic writing is usually not so arbitrary: a distinct, common
theme often links apparently dissimilar groups of ideas or facts, and the
writer's job is to take advantage of this common theme and to break it
down further into a few generalizations that cover several items in the
sources. This process involves the same skills as classsifying notes, or-

ganizing them into groups, and generalizing each group, all of which are discussed in Chapter 1.

Assume that you have been assigned the following exercise, which asks that you consider seven different but related situations as the sources from which two generalizations will eventually be derived:

A. In a sentence or two, write down your probable reaction if you found yourself in each of the following situations.* Write quickly; this exercise calls for an immediate, instinctive response.

1. You are walking behind someone. You see him take out a cigarette pack, pull out the last cigarette, put the cigarette in his mouth, crumple the package, and nonchalantly toss it over his shoulder onto the sidewalk. What would you do?

2. You are sitting on a train and you notice a person (same age, sex, and type as yourself) lighting up a cigarette, despite the no-smoking sign. No one in authority is around. What would you do?

3. You are pushing a shopping cart in a supermarket and you hear the thunderous crash of cans. As you round the corner, you see a two-year-old child being beaten, quite severely, by his mother, apparently for pulling out the bottom can of the pile. What would you do?

4. You see a neighborhood kid shoplifting at the local discount store. You're concerned that he'll get into serious trouble, if the store detective catches him. What would you do?

5. You're driving on a two-lane road behind another car. You notice that one of its wheels is wobbling more and more. It looks as if the lugs are coming off one by one. There's no way to pass, because cars are coming from the other direction in a steady stream. What would you do?

6. You've been waiting in line (at a supermarket or gas station) for longer than you expected and you're irritated at the delay. Suddenly, you notice that someone very much like yourself has sneaked in ahead of you in the line. There are a couple of people ahead of you in line. What would you do?

7. You've raised your son not to play with guns. Your rich uncle comes for a long-awaited visit and he brings your son a .22 rifle with lots of ammunition. What would you do?

B. Read over your responses to the seven situations and try to form a general statement (in one or two sentences) about *the circumstances in which you would take action as opposed to the circumstances in which you would choose to do nothing.* Do *not* simply list the incidents, one after the other, in two groups.

---

* Adapted from "Strategy 24" in Sidney B. Simon et al., *Values Clarification* (New York: Hart, 1972).

You can work out an answer to this exercise only by examining the group of situations in which taking action seems desirable and determining what they have in common. (It is also important to examine the "leftovers," too, and to understand why these incidents did *not* warrant your interference.) You might try looking at each situation in terms of either its *causes* or its *consequences*. For example, in each case there is someone to blame, someone who is responsible for creating the problem—except for number five, where fate (or poor auto maintenance) threatens to cause an accident. As for consequences, in some of the situations (littering, for example) there is little potential danger, either to oneself or to the public. Does this circumstance discourage action? In others, however, the possible victim is oneself or a member of one's family. Does self-interest alone drive one to act? Do adults tend to intervene in defense of children—even someone else's child—since they cannot stand up for themselves? Or, instead of calculating the consequences of *not* intervening, perhaps one should imagine the possible consequences of interference. In which situations can one expect to receive abuse for failing to mind one's own business? As always, only by examining the evidence can one discover the basis for a generalization.

The list of examples has two characteristics worth noting:

1. Each item on the list is intended to illustrate a specific and a very different situation. Thus, although it does not include every possible example, the list as a whole constitutes a *set* of public occasions for interfering with and regulating a stranger's conduct.
2. Since you probably would not choose to act in every situation, you cannot use the entire list as the basis for your generalization. Rather, you must establish a boundary line, dividing those occasions when you would intervene from those times when you would decide not to act. The exact boundary between intervention and nonintervention will differ from person to person, as will the exact composition of the smaller list of occasions justifying intervention. Thus, there is no one correct generalization.

The product of this exercise is a set of guidelines for justifiably minding other people's business. You formulate the guidelines by applying your own standards to a fairly wide sampling of possible examples.

Broad concepts offer a great deal of room for disagreement and ambiguity and are therefore susceptible to a great many interpretations. You may wish to clarify your ideas and opinions by setting up such a comprehensive set of illustrations, marking off a subgroup, and then constructing a generalization that describes what is *inside* the boundary: the common characteristics of the contents of the subgroup. Thus, in the previous exercise, one person might consider the set of seven examples and then decide to intervene only in situations 3 (the child beaten in a supermarket), 5 (the wobbly wheel), and 7 (the gift of a gun). What makes these three cases different from the others? They and they alone involve protecting some person from physical harm. This process of differentiation, followed by generalized description, is usually called *definition*, and it can serve as an essay strategy in its own right or as the basis for a *comparison, classification, argumentation*, or *evaluation* essay (see Chapter 1).

EXERCISE 33

In each of the following situations, would you give money to the person who is begging? Write yes or no.

1. A man is sitting on the sidewalk, dressed in clean-looking rags, with no visible legs and a box of pencils. There is a sign: "There but for the grace of God."
2. A woman, very untidy, but not visibly unclean, is standing quite straight on the sidewalk, entertaining the passersby by singing (very badly) at the top of her voice. It is not possible to determine whether she is drunk.
3. A man with a cane is tapping his way through a crowded subway car, politely thanking each person who drops change into his cup.
4. A fast-talking but concerned-looking young man politely makes a short speech to passengers on the subway, asking them to contribute spare change to the maintenance of a nearby school for deprived children.
5. A man with a dirty rag is wiping the windshields of cars stopping for red lights. Clearly drunk, he is arguing with some of the drivers and might prove to be a nuisance if he continues to cling to the car after the light changes.
6. A young boy is wiping the windshields of cars stopping for red lights. He is smiling politely and polishing carefully.
7. A huge old woman, looking like a rag pile, is crouching on the steps leading to a subway train, monotonously repeating, "Give me a quarter."
8. A young woman between twenty and thirty, neatly dressed in ordinary clothes (jeans and sneakers), indistinguishable from the other passengers, walks through a subway train, politely and pleasantly asking for change.
9. A spastic young woman, quite visibly handicapped and probably retarded, begs on a crowded street corner noisily and demandingly.

There is a person standing not far away who seems to be in charge of her.

10. A man dressed in a Santa Claus costume rings a bell at Christmas time; the name of a charitable organization is clearly displayed on a sign next to him.

11. A (presumably) deaf-mute young man hands out cards with sign-language instructions to passengers in the subway and then returns to retrieve the cards if the passengers do not wish to pay a token amount for them.

12. Two young musicians, clean and neatly dressed, play music professionally and pleasantly, with a sign saying, "Help us complete our studies."

Consider your motives for giving or refusing charity in each case. Under what circumstances do you give money to beggars? Without mentioning any of the specific situations described above, write—a sentence or two—your personal definition of *charity*.

ANALYZING MULTIPLE SOURCES

When you write from sources, your object is not to establish a single "right" conclusion, but, rather, to present a general statement that accommodates a variety of views. Some of these views may even conflict with your own and with each other. Because of this diversity of ideas, organizing multiple sources is more difficult than working with a series of examples, with the contents of a newspaper, or with even a highly complex single essay.

The writing process for multiple sources begins with the *analysis of ideas*: breaking a mass of information down into individual pieces and inspecting the pieces. As you scrutinize your sources, one after the other, you look for similarities and distinctions in meaning, as well as the basic principle underlying each statement. Only when you have taken apart the evidence of each source and seen how it works can you then begin to find ways of putting everything back together again in your own essay.

To illustrate the analysis of sources, assume that you have asked five people what the word "foreign" means. You want to provide a reasonably complete definition of the word by exploring all the shades of meaning or connotations that the five sources suggest. If each one of the five gives you a completely different answer, then you will not have much choice in the organization of your comprehensive definition. In that case, you would probably present each separate version of "foreign" in a separate paragraph, citing a different person as the source for each paragraph. Your biggest task then would be to decide on a sequence for the five paragraphs. But responses from multiple sources almost always overlap, as these do. Notice the common meanings in this condensed list of the five sources' responses:

John Brown: "Foreign" means unfamiliar and exotic.

Lynn Williams: "Foreign" means strange and unusual.

Bill White: "Foreign" means strange and alien (as in "foreign body").

Mary Green: "Foreign" means exciting and exotic.

Bob Friedman: "Foreign" means difficult and incomprehensible (as in "foreign language").

The common meanings are more crucial to the planning of your essay than the five sources, who have only been consulted to provide a variety of opinion. That is why the one-source-per-paragraph method should hardly ever be used (except on those rare occasions when the sources completely disagree). To write one paragraph about each person's response would be an unnecessarily repetitious and confusing way to explore the word's meaning. That essential point may become clearer to you if you imagine, briefly, that all of the connotations of "foreign" (or any other word) have come from only one source: yourself. In fact, there is not all that much difference between organizing notes taken from five separate sources and organizing notes all taken from your own thoughts. Now, it is unlikely that you would arrange the paragraphing of an essay according to the *times* when you first jotted down your ideas. You would not think: "These notes were all scribbled on May 4, so they should all go in the same paragraph." In the same way, when you organize ideas taken from multiple sources, you should reject the idea of devoting one paragraph to each page of your notes, simply because all the ideas on that page happen to have come from the same person. If you did so, each paragraph would have a topic sentence that might read, "Then I asked John Brown for his definition," as if John Brown were the topic for discussion, instead of his views on "foreign." And if John Brown and Mary Green each gets a full paragraph, there will be some repetitions because both think that one of the meanings of "foreign" is exotic." "Exotic" should dominate one of your paragraphs, not the person (or even the people) who suggested that meaning. The names of your sources should be mentioned only if you want to show where the information came from.

Analyzing Shades of Meaning

Here is a set of notes, summarizing the ideas of four different people about the meaning of the word "individualist." How would you analyze these notes?

Richard Becker: an "individualist is a person who is unique and does not "fall into the common mode of doing things"; would not follow a pattern set by society. "A youngster who is not involved in the drug scene just because his friends are." A good word; it would be insulting only if it referred to a troublemaker.

Simon Jackson: doing things on your own, by yourself. "She's such an individualist that she insisted on answering the question in her own way." Sometimes the word is good, but mostly it has a bad connotation: someone who rebels against society or authority.

Lois Asher: one who doesn't "follow the flock." The word refers to someone who is very independent. "I respect Jane because she is an individualist and her own person." Usually very complimentary.

Vera Lewis: an extremely independent person. "An individualist is a person who does not want to contribute to society." Bad meaning: usually antisocial. She first heard the word in psych. class, describing the characteristics of the individualist and "how he reacts to society."

At first glance, all the sources seem to say much the same thing: the individualist is different and "independent." It is worthwhile to examine the context in which the four sources are defining this word. First, all the responses define the individualist in terms of other people, either the "group," or the "flock," or "society." Oddly enough, it is not easy to describe the individualist as an individual, even though it is his isolation that each person is emphasizing. Whatever is "unique" about the individualist—the quality that makes him "independent"—is defined by the gap between him and everyone else. (Notice that both "unique" and "independent" are words that also suggest a larger group in the background; after all, one has to be independent *of* something!)

Having found a meaning that is common to all four sources and, just as important, having established the context for a definition, you must now look for differences. Obviously, Lois Asher thinks that to be an individualist is a good thing; Vera Lewis believes that individualism is bad; and the other two suggest that both connotations are possible. But simply describing the reactions of the four sources stops short of defining the word according to those reactions.

Richard Becker and Lois Asher, two people who suggest a favorable connotation, characterize the group from which the individual is set apart in similar and somewhat disapproving terms: "common"; "pattern set by society"; "follow the flock." Becker and Asher both seem to be suggesting a degree of conformity or sameness which the individualist is right to reject, as Becker's youngster rejects his friends' drugs. But Vera Lewis, who thinks that the word's connotation is a bad one, places the individualist in the context of a more benign society, with which the individual ought to identify himself and to which he ought to contribute.

To be antisocial is to be an undesirable person—from the point of view of Lewis and society. Simon Jackson (who is ambivalent about the word) uses the phrases "by yourself" and "on your own," which suggest the isolation and the lack of support, as well as the admirable independence, of the individualist. In Jackson's view, the individualist's self-assertion becomes threatening to all of us in society ("antisocial") only when he begins to rebel against authority. Probably for Jackson, and certainly for Vera Lewis, the ultimate authority should rest with society as a whole, not with the individualist. Even Richard Becker, who admires the individualist, draws the line at allowing him complete independence: when the individualist's reliance on his own authority leads to "troublemaking," the term becomes an insult.

EXERCISE 34

Analyze the following set of notes for a definition of the word "gossip." Then explore some ways to organize these notes by following these steps:

> A. Find the important terms or concepts that can lead to a context for defining "gossip."
> B. Write two generalizations that might serve as topic sentences for a two-paragraph essay. (Do not use "favorable" and "unfavorable" as your two topics.)

Michael Mason: pointless, trivial conversation; news gets passed; creates some kind of social tie between people; usually associated with women.

Charles Crisp: to criticize and say unpleasant things about other people; "My sister likes to gossip and pass along the latest news about everybody's private life."

Tina Thatcher: talking too much; can't trust someone to keep a secret; bad word because it means untrustworthy; "She gossips so much that I can't tell her anything."

Jill Glazer: talking about someone behind her back; harmful chatter; not to be believed, not facts; "Gossip columnists smear celebrities with their exaggerated stories."

Gerry Gadson: passing the time of day; taking an interest in other people; usually doesn't mean much; "The ladies gossiped all afternoon and exchanged some interesting stories"; the worst that you can say about gossip is that it wastes time.

Making a Chart of Common Ideas

Once you have analyzed each of your sources and discovered their similarities and differences, then you reassemble these parts into a more coherent and tidy whole. This is the first step of what is called *synthesis*. Although at first you may regard analysis and synthesis as contradictory operations, they are actually overlapping stages of a single, larger process.

To illustrate the way in which analysis and synthesis work together, let us work with a set of answers to the question: *Would you buy a lottery ticket? Why?* First, read through these summaries of all seven responses.

Mary Smith: She thinks that lottery tickets were made for people to enjoy and win. It's fun to try your luck. She looks forward to buying her ticket, because she feels that, for one dollar, you have a chance to win a lot more. It's also fun scratching off the numbers to see what you've won. Some people don't buy tickets because they think the lottery is a big rip-off; but "a dollar can't buy that much today, so why not spend it and have a good time?"

John Jones: He would buy a lottery ticket for three reasons. The first reason is that he would love to win. The odds are like a challenge, and he likes to take a chance. The second reason is just for fun. When he has two matching tickets, he really feels happy, especially when he thinks that dollars can be multiplied into hundreds or thousands. "It's like Russian Roulette." The third reason is that part of the money goes towards his education. The only problem, he says, is that they are always sold out!

Michael Green: He has never bought a lottery ticket in his life because he doesn't want to lose money. He wants to be sure of winning. Also, he says that he isn't patient enough. The buyer of a lottery ticket has to be very patient to wait for his chance to win. He thinks that people who buy tickets all the time must enjoy "living dangerously."

Anne White: Buying a lottery ticket gives her a sense of excitement. She regards herself as a gambler. "When you win two dollars or five dollars you get a thrill of victory, and when you see that you haven't, you feel the agony of defeat." She thinks that people who don't buy tickets must be very cautious and non-competitive, since the lottery brings "a sense of competition with you against millions of other people." She also knows that the money she spends on tickets goes towards education.

Margaret Brown: She feels that people who buy tickets are wasting their money. The dollars spent on the lottery could be in the bank, getting interest. Those people who buy tickets should expect to have thrown out their money, and should take their losses philosophically, instead of jumping up and down and screaming about their disappointment. Finally, even if she could afford the risk, the laws of her religion forbid her to participate in "any sort of game that is a form of gambling."

William Black: He would buy a lottery ticket, because he thinks it can be fun, but he wouldn't buy too many, because he thinks it's easy for people to get carried away and obsessed by the lottery. He enjoys the anticipation of wanting to win and maybe winning. "I think that you should participate, but in proportion to your budget; after all, one day you might just be a winner."

Elizabeth Watson: She wouldn't buy a lottery ticket because she considers them a rip-off. The odds are too much against you, 240,000 to 1. Also, it is much too expensive, "and I don't have the money to be throwing away on such foolishness." She thinks that people who indulge themselves with lottery tickets become gamblers, and she's against all kinds of gambling. Such people have no sense or self-control. Finally, "I'm a sore loser, so buying lottery tickets just isn't for me."

Since you are working with seven sources whose opinions vary widely, you must record the process of analysis by making a chart of commonly held views. To do so, you follow these two steps, which must be carried out simultaneously:

> 1. Read each statement carefully, and identify each separate reason that is being cited for and against playing the lottery by writing a number above or right next to the relevant comment. When a similar comment is made by another person, use the same number to provide a key to the final list of common reasons. *In this step, you are analyzing your sources.*

Here is what the first two sets of notes might look like once the topic numbers have been inserted:

Mary Smith: She thinks that lottery tickets were made for people to enjoy⁽¹⁾ and win⁽²⁾. It's fun to try your luck. She looks forward to buying her ticket, because she feels that, for one dollar, you have a chance to win⁽²⁾ a lot more. It's also fun scratching⁽¹⁾ off the numbers to see what you've won. Some people don't buy tickets because they think the lottery is a big⁽³⁾ rip-off; but "a dollar can't buy that much today, so why not spend it and⁽¹⁾ have a good time?"

John Jones: He would buy a lottery ticket for three reasons. The first reason is that he would love to win. The odds are like a challenge, and⁽²⁾ he likes to take a chance. The second reason is just⁽¹⁾ for fun. When he has two matching tickets, he really feels happy, especially when he thinks that dollars can be multiplied into hundreds or thousands⁽²⁾. "It's like Russian Roulette." The third reason is that part of the money goes⁽⁴⁾ towards his education. The only problem, he says, is that they are always sold out!

2. As you number each of your reasons, start to write a chart or list of reasons on a separate sheet of paper. Each reason should be assigned the number you wrote next to it in the original statement. Don't make a new entry when the same reason is repeated by a second source. Next to each entry on your chart, keep a list of the people who have mentioned that reason. *You are now beginning to synthesize your sources.*

Here's what your completed chart of reasons might look like:

Reason	*Sources*
1. People play the lottery because it's fun.	Smith; Jones
2. People play the lottery because they like the excitement of taking a chance and winning.	Smith; Jones; Green; White; Black
3. People don't play the lottery because they think it's a rip-off.	Smith; Watson
4. People play the lottery because they are contributing to education.	Jones; White
5. People don't play the lottery because they have better things to do with their money.	Green; Brown; Watson
6. People play the lottery because they like to gamble.	White; Brown; Watson
7. People who play the lottery and those who refuse to play worry about the emotional reactions of the players.	Green; White; Brown; Black; Watson

The process of synthesis starts as soon as you start to make your chart. This list of common reasons represents the reworking of seven separate sources into a single new pattern and, eventually, a single new essay.

Distinguishing Between Reasons

One of the biggest problems in making a list of topics is deciding, in cases of overlapping, whether you actually have one reason or two. Since overlapping reasons were deliberately not combined, the list above may be longer than one that you might have made.

For example, reasons one and two reflect the difference between the experiences of having fun and feeling the thrill of excitement—a difference in sensation that most people would acknowledge. You might ask yourself, "Would someone play the lottery *just for fun* without the anticipation of winning? Or would someone experience a *thrill of excitement* without any sense of fun at all?" If one sensation can exist without the other, you have sufficient reason for putting each item on your chart. Later on, the similarities, not the differences, might make you want to combine the two; but, at the beginning, it is important to keep track of just what materials you are working with.

The distinction between the thrill of excitement and the pleasure of gambling is more difficult to perceive. The former is, perhaps, more innocent than the latter and does not carry with it any of the obsessive overtones of gambling.

Resenting the lottery because it is a rip-off and resenting the lottery because the players are wasting their money appear at first glance to be similar reactions. However, references to the rip-off tend to emphasize the "injured victim" whose money is being whisked away by a public agency. In other words, reason three emphasizes self-protection from robbery; reason five emphasizes the personal virtue of thrift.

Reason seven is not really a reason at all. Many of the comments in the notes do not fit into a tidy list of reasons for playing; yet they provide a valuable insight into human motivation and behavior as expressed in lottery-playing. An exploration of the emotions that characterize the player and the non-player (always allowing for the lottery preference of the source) might be an interesting way to conclude an essay.

DECIDING ON A SEQUENCE OF TOPICS

The sequence of topics in your chart corresponds to the random order of the notes. Once the chart is completed, you have to try to decide on a more logical sequence of topics by rearranging the entries in the list. Here are two possible ways to arrange the "lottery" reasons. Which sequence do you prefer? Why?

1. fun	1. fun
2. excitement	2. rip-off
3. gambling	3. excitement and gambling
4. education	4. misuse of money
5. rip-off	5. education
6. misuse of money	6. personality of the gambler
7. personality of the gambler	

As you have learned, you can make an indirect impact on your reader by choosing a sequence that supports the point that you want to make or that, at the very least, makes the most of your ideas or your sources' ideas. In this respect, the right-hand sequence is more effective, for by contrasting the advantages and disadvantages of playing the lottery it carries out a comparison strategy. Moving back and forth between paired reasons calls attention to the relation between opposites and makes the material more interesting for the reader. But the left-hand sequence places all the "advantages" together, isolating them from the "disadvantages," and thus implies that there is no internal connection.

EXERCISE 35

Here is a set of interview notes, answering the question: *Do you think that small children learn more good things than bad things from TV?*

Martha Meade: During the day, children can watch educational shows like "Sesame Street" and game shows, which they can learn from. But police shows and other adult shows are probably too violent for children. More good things can be learned if the children go to bed early, before the violence and the "parental guidance" programs come on. But even these programs can be informative sometimes; they give you a chance to see how other people live and they also help the child to understand why people do some of the things they do.

Charles Vinson: TV doesn't really allow a child to use his mind; instead, it feeds his mind with a lot of false ideas. It makes a child passive. Also, they watch all those commercials and want me to buy everything they see. But the effect depends on the channel. For instance, PBS is educational, while the major networks display too much violence. "I would prefer to limit my child's viewing of TV, and when he is watching it, I'd like to be around to explain what's going on."

Dora Kaye: Children learn many bad things from TV because "programs showing all this violence come on, and then the children go out and try to emulate what they have seen." There are other children who are scared to walk the streets because of all the impressions they get from frightening programs. "Also, sometimes, when my children have sat in front of the TV all day long, they can hardly walk and talk anymore—they're more like vegetables."

Patricia Brewster: Definitely, more bad things come from TV, because kids watch misleading things such as commercials which are dumb and deceptive: "You spell relief r.o.l.a.i.d.s.!" Also, you see too much violence on TV, and the shows aren't very much like real life: many programs are phony. For example, crooks and cops are portrayed in ways that aren't like real-life situations.

Linda Thomas: I think that children learn more good things than bad from TV because of "Sesame Street," "Zoom," and all the other programs that are educational. After 6:00, when the violence begins to appear, children should be away from the tube. But in the day they can watch the educational shows and the stories which describe real-life situations. "Even if the kids do watch a lot of violence, it can't do that much harm, because they probably have to live around worse conditions. They can see what goes on on TV right outside their bedroom windows."

A. Read through these notes; identify distinct and separate reasons by placing numbers next to the relevant sentences; as you number each new reason, add an entry to the chart below. (The first reason is already filled in.)

Reason	*Source*
1. TV can be educational.	
2.	
3.	
4.	
5.	
6.	

B. Arrange the numbered points in a logical sequence. Be prepared to explain the reasoning behind your sequence of points.

SORTING MULTIPLE SOURCES DEALING WITH A COMPLEX TOPIC

Playing the lottery is not a subject that lends itself to lengthy or abstract discussion; therefore, charting reasons for and against playing the lottery is not difficult. The article that follows defines a social, political, and humanitarian problem and outlines two methods of dealing with it. As objective reportage, the article does not favor either "solution" or the values on which each is based. The reporter's sources, quoted in the article, simply cite aspects of the problem and the hope that the courts will deal with it.

However, fifteen students were asked to read the article and to voice their opinions, which are listed following the article. Assume as you read the article and the student opinions that you plan to address the issue and synthesize the opinions in an essay of your own.

CITY LAYOFFS HURT MINORITIES MOST

City officials reported yesterday that layoffs resulting from the fiscal crisis were having "devastating" effects on minority employment in government.

In the last 18 months, they disclosed, the city lost half of its Spanish-speaking workers, 40 percent of the black males on the payroll and almost a third of its female workers.

"You are close to wiping out the minority work force in the City of New York," said Eleanor Holmes Norton, the chairman of the Commission on Human Rights, after releasing the data in response to a request.

This dwindling employment, in turn, has put the city in "serious jeopardy" of losing various kinds of Federal aid, according to Deputy Mayor Paul Gibson, Jr.

The city's fiscal failure and the resultant layoffs have worsened the situation in such predominantly male, white agencies as the Police Department, where, after some limited gains in recent years, the ranks of women police officers have been reduced by 55 percent because of the budget crisis, according to the city's latest data.

Meanwhile, a Federal appeals court declared that Civil Service seniority was not immune from legal challenge by women police officers who were dismissed because of the city's fiscal crisis.

Scores of complaints alleging discrimination have been filed by laid-off workers, both as class members and individuals, squeezing the city between the pressures of the traditional primacy of union seniority protections and Federal equal-employment requirements.

Federal officials said yesterday they were processing the complaints, which could result in a cut-off of funds. They added that they were hoping for guidance from the United States Supreme Court this year on the clash between the seniority principle, which tends to protect male white workers, and the Federal minority employment guidelines of Federal law.

The data on dismissals, which had been quietly compiled by city officials in recent weeks, were a further indication of the price the city is paying in the campaign to balance the budget and come to grips with its huge legacy of excessive debt.

Inevitably, the requirements of the austerity drive interfere, too, with attempts to soften the layoff effects on minority-group workers and women.

For example, Commissioner Norton emphasized that the levying of budget cuts on an even percentage basis in city agencies was the best way to protect equal opportunity. But various fiscal experts intent on improving the city's management say across-the-board cutting is the worst way of economizing because it ignores the relative quality of programs.

"We had begun to make an effort," Commissioner Norton said. "But one recession takes it all out in an instant."

Since the budget crisis surfaced in the summer of 1974, the city payroll has been reduced by 40,000 jobs—two-thirds of them reported as layoffs. This was a total cut of 13 percent to the current level of about 255,000 workers, according to city records.

A maxim of the seniority system that the last hired should be the first dismissed is the chief factor preventing an even 13 percent sharing of the layoff burden without regard to race or sex, city officials say.

The austerity drive, in which the city must try to cut its spending by

$1 billion in less than three years, is forcing the conflict between what Commissioner Norton describes as "two competing and legitimate interests"—seniority and equal opportunity.

Federal and city civil rights officials were reluctant to discuss the scope of the complaints that have been filed. Werner H. Kramarsky, the state's Commissioner of Human Rights, described the issues raised as "very thorny" and extending to such questions as whether provisional, or temporary, employees should be credited with time on the job in determining relative seniority.

The available public records indicate that the state commission is handling at least 35 cases, some of them class complaints, and has sent 98 cases involving former city welfare workers to Federal officials of the Equal Employment Opportunity Commission, which already has received about 160 complaints from welfare workers alone.

The complaints are being pressed not only by women and minority group members, but also by a group of a half dozen disabled persons who contend that they were unfairly victimized in the layoff drive, according to state records.

There have been various court challenges in recent years of the seniority protections, which generally have been unsuccessful. One recent ruling threw out a racial quota program for city school principals. Federal civil rights officials emphasize that the Supreme Court is considering the issue at present and the hope is that some definitive standard will be set.

According to Deputy Mayor Gibson, minorities represented 31 percent of the payroll, but suffered 44 percent of the cuts. Males, he said, were 70 percent of the payroll and were affected by 63 percent of the cuts.

Commissioner Norton said that even before the layoffs, Federal officials had warned the city from time to time that financing for various programs would be cut off because of noncompliance with equal opportunity standards. She said that Mayor Beame had signed an executive order in 1974 committing city agencies to specific improvement programs.

Thus far there have been no Federal threats of cutoffs during the fiscal crisis, she said, apparently because the city is on record as pledging to seek a more equitable system in the event it ever resumes full-scale hiring.

But Deputy Mayor Gibson feels the situation is becoming critical. "We're losing ground," he said.

Francis X. Clines, *New York Times*, 20 February 1976

Student Opinions

Lydia Allen: The performance of a job must be the primary focus in deciding layoffs. I feel that as a whole people with more seniority in a job would perform that job best. Therefore, seniority, not minority, rights must be the deciding vote.

Grace Burrows: I believe that both sides have validity. I do feel that because minorities have been held back for so long *some* concessions should be made in their favor. Minorities were just beginning to make progress and now they will be set back once again. A person who's been on a job for a number of years shouldn't be made to suffer either.

Marion J. Buskin: I believe that an individual should be dismissed according to his ability to produce. A person with more seniority should not be allowed to keep his job if someone with less time on the job is capable of performing it better.

Robert Fuhst: I believe in seniority for job protection. If seniority doesn't prevail, then your job is based on how well you are liked and your freedom to express yourself is hampered.

John Giannini: Minorities should have a say in matters of lay-offs, especially when a large percentage of the minority is affected. Minorities and senior personnel should share lay-offs equally.

Dorothy Humphrey: I think there should be equal employment in this country. If an individual is senior in a field and satisfactorily functioning, he should remain employed. On the other hand, if a member of a minority can function even better, why not employ him instead? Production of work is what counts, not who performs it.

Rosemary McAleer: I favor seniority in employment because it is a system which does not permit discrimination. Regardless of race, color, or creed, if you have acquired more time than another employee, your job should be secure.

Marc Page: The longer a man is yoked to a job and its connected financial position, the more severe are the effects of being sundered from it. Seniority is the overriding consideration.

Megan Phillips: I feel seniority of employment is important in the job crisis because it is the only way of ensuring good and efficient services. Secondly, I feel the more mature one is in a job, the more the job becomes a part of one's welfare, as opposed to a younger person or a novice in the job, who only performs the job for the money.

Alice Reich: I think seniority in employment is an important consideration for the major reason that the benefits of seniority are hard-earned over the years. It seems unjust for a person who has given perhaps seven-eighths of his working lifetime to a job to find himself "out in the cold." Worse yet, the time of life when seniority would count is the time, very often, when other employment is unobtainable.

Robert Rivera: I feel that minority groups should be protected from job cutbacks.

The reason is that the minorities that were hired were hired to fulfill the employment clauses set up through government laws. This law deals with equal opportunity for sexes and minorities to hold jobs and offices. Since this law has been recently enforced (in the last five or six years), why should minorities then hired be affected so tremendously by unemployment?

Jesse Rogers: I feel that minority workers for the city government should be protected, because it does not seem fair that, after waiting so long to get "in," they are so easily kicked out by the unions.

Peter Rossi: I believe the federal government should compensate the minority people who were fired because of budget cuts and lack of seniority. The compensation should be the creation of new jobs and not unemployment insurance.

John Seeback: Most jobs run on the idea that the last hired are the first fired, even if the jobs held by senior workers are costing the business millions of dollars. Also, the white majority of senior workers feels superior to the minority workers on a racial basis rather than on a performance basis. Many employers also feel the minority workers are expendable: they had to hire them because of the law; now they have a good reason to fire them.

Nancy Vitale: Men and women, after putting their time and effort (not to mention their skills) into a job for a great number of years, deserve the protection of their jobs in accordance with seniority. It is unfair to dismiss a person from his longstanding position to make a position for a minority member.

When you prepare to explore a variety of opinions about a complex and perhaps controversial subject follow these steps:

1. Write a brief, objective summary of the issue under discussion (in this case, the problem described in the article). Your summary of this article would convey both the situation and the two key ideas that are stressed. Try structuring your paragraph to contrast the conflicting opinions.
2. Write a brief statement of your own point of view to suggest a possible direction for your essay.

The second step is more important than it might at first seem. Once you begin to analyze a mass of contradictory opinion, you may find yourself being wholly convinced by first one source and then another, or you may try so hard to stay neutral that you end up with no point of view of your own at all. You need to find a vantage point for yourself from which to assess the validity of the statements that you read. Of course, you can (and probably will) adjust your point of view as you become more familiar with all the arguments and evidence that your sources raise. Do not regard your initial statement of opinion as a thesis to be proven, but rather as a hypothesis to be tested, modified, or even abandoned.

3. Label your set of opinions and establish categories. For example, the group of statements following the article are all personal reactions to job layoffs and the issue of seniority protection versus equal employment opportunity. For each statement do the following:

   A. *Read each statement carefully and think about its exact significance.* First, get a rough idea of what each statement says—do a mental paraphrase, if you like. You will naturally notice which "side" the author of each statement is on. There is a tendency to want to stop there, as if the authors' positions are all that one needs to know. But your object is not only to find out which side of an issue each person is on, but also to understand *why* he has chosen that side.

   B. *Try to pick out the chief reason put forth by each person, or, even better, the principle which lies behind his argument.* Sum up the viewpoint of each person in a word or two, a phrase—inventing a distinguishing label, as if for a scientific specimen.

   C. When you have labeled most of the statements with broad concepts, the next step becomes easier. Look through all your summarizing phrases to see if there is an abstract idea, used to describe several statements, which might possibly serve as a category title. (Some change in the wording may be necessary.) Once two or three larger group titles become obvious, you should consider their relationship to each other: are they parallel? are they contrasting? Then attempt to see whether the smaller groups fit into the pattern that is beginning to form.

A Sample of the Three Steps at Work

Following is one student's exploration of the New York City layoffs article and the fifteen opinions.

Step one: summary. Here the student identifies the article to which he and his sources are responding, summarizing the issue and the nature of the conflict.

> In a February 20, 1976, article in the New York Times, Francis X. Clines reported that the budget crisis had

substantially reduced the number of minorities—blacks,
women, and Hispanics—on New York City's payroll. The
minority members laid off were the employees most recently
hired by the city to meet federal minority employment
requirements. Eleanor Holmes Norton, chairman of the
Commission on Human Rights, described the situation as a
conflict between "two competing and legitimate interests"—
the traditional principle of union seniority protection
and equal opportunity employment.

Step two: stating your own point of view (hypothesizing). Here the
student ventures an opinion that suggests the possible direction of his
essay. At this point he has not studied the group of opinions that ac-
companies the article.

Despite the legitimacy of the two competing interests,
there is a third, humane principle that goes beyond both:
in the name of fairness, the city should take the trouble
to evaluate the performance of all its employees and
dismiss those whose performance is inferior. Where a
senior employee and a minority employee share the same
performance rating but are competing for a single
position, the city should retain both employees and wait
for retirements to make room for both.

**Step three: labeling your set of opinions and establishing cate-
gories.** In this step, the student moves away from the article to examine
the opinions of others who have read the article, determining first the
position of each respondent and then the reasoning behind the position.

Lydia Allen: The performance of a job must be the primary focus in deciding lay-
offs. I feel that as a whole people with more seniority in a job would perform
that job best. Therefore, seniority, not minority, rights must be the deciding
vote.

Allen: seniority ensures performance

Grace Burrows: I believe that both sides have validity. I do feel that because
minorities have been held back for so long *some* concessions should be made
in their favor. Minorities were just beginning to make progress and now they

will be set back once again. A person who's been on a job for a number of years shouldn't be made to suffer either.

> Burrows: evades the issue——both approaches unfortunate

Marion J. Buskin: I believe that an individual should be dismissed according to his ability to produce. A person with more seniority should not be allowed to keep his job if someone with less time on the job is capable of performing it better.

> Buskin: performance should be the only criterion

Robert Fuhst: I believe in seniority for job protection. If seniority doesn't prevail, then your job is based on how well you are liked and your freedom to express yourself is hampered.

> Fuhst: seniority deserves protection (without it
>   employment becomes a popularity contest)

John Giannini: Minorities should have a say in matters of lay-offs, especially when a large percentage of the minority is affected. Minorities and senior personnel should share lay-offs equally.

> Giannini: minorities and senior personnel should share
>   burden equally

Dorothy Humphrey: I think there should be equal employment in this country. If an individual is senior in a field and satisfactorily functioning, he should remain employed. On the other hand, if a member of a minority can function even better, why not employ him instead? Production of work is what counts, not who performs it.

> Humphrey: performance should be the prevailing criterion

Rosemary McAleer: I favor seniority in employment because it is a system which does not permit discrimination. Regardless of race, color, or creed, if you have acquired more time than another employee, your job should be secure.

> McAleer: seniority protection is fundamentally the only
>   nondiscriminatory criterion

Marc Page: The longer a man is yoked to a job and its connected financial position, the more severe are the effects of being sundered from it. Seniority is the over-riding consideration.

> Page: seniority protection is the more humane policy

Megan Phillips: I feel seniority of employment is important in the job crisis because it is the only way of ensuring good and efficient services. Secondly, I feel the more mature one is in a job, the more the job becomes a part of one's welfare, as opposed to a younger person or a novice in the job, who only performs the job for the money.

> Phillips: seniority protection leads to greater
>   efficiency, i.e., performance

Alice Reich: I think seniority in employment is an important consideration for the major reason that the benefits of seniority are hard-earned over the years. It seems unjust for a person who has given perhaps seven-eighths of his working lifetime to a job to find himself "out in the cold." Worse yet, the time of life when seniority would count is the time, very often, when other employment is unobtainable.

```
     Reich:  seniority protection is the more humane policy
          (other employment often impossible for those laid off)
```

Robert Rivera: I feel that minority groups should be protected from job cutbacks. The reason is that the minorities that were hired were hired to fulfill the employment clauses set up through government laws. This law deals with equal opportunity for sexes and minorities to hold jobs and offices. Since this law has been recently enforced (in the last five or six years), why should minorities then hired be affected so tremendously by unemployment?

```
     Rivera:  the law requires that minorities be protected
```

Jesse Rogers: I feel that minority workers for the city government should be protected, because it does not seem fair that, after waiting so long to get "in," they are so easily kicked out by the unions.

```
     Rogers:  minority protection is the more humane policy in
          the light of history
```

Peter Rossi: I believe the federal government should compensate the minority people who were fired because of budget cuts and lack of seniority. The compensation should be the creation of new jobs and not unemployment insurance.

```
     Rossi:  federal government should compensate laid off
          minority employees with new jobs (implication that city
          should not lay off senior employees in order to
          accommodate minority employees in their present jobs)
```

John Seeback: Most jobs run on the idea that the last hired are the first fired, even if the jobs held by senior workers are costing the business millions of dollars. Also, the white majority of senior workers feels superior to the minority workers on a racial basis rather than on a performance basis. Many employers also feel the minority workers are expendable: they had to hire them because of the law; now they have a good reason to fire them.

```
     Seeback:  (implies that) minorities, as victims of union
          and employer prejudice, deserve protection
```

Nancy Vitale: Men and women, after putting their time and effort (not to mention their skills) into a job for a great number of years, deserve the protection of their jobs in accordance with seniority. It is unfair to dismiss a person from his longstanding position to make a position for a minority member.

```
     Vitale:  seniority protection is the more humane policy
```

From this list, the student can establish five categories that cover the range of answers. His categorical chart follows:

```
Category              Source       Note
seniority ensures     Allen
  good performance     Phillips

performance should    Buskin
  be the prevailing   Humphrey
  criterion

seniority protection  Page         (financial and emotional
  should be the                      hardship greatest for laid off
  prevailing                         senior employees)
  criterion
                      Reich
                      Vitale

                      Fuhst        (employment would be popularity
                                     contest without it)

                      McAleer      (truly nondiscriminatory
                                     policy)

minority protection   Rivera
  should be the         (legally)
  prevailing
  criterion
                      Seeback      (compensation for past and
                                     present injustices)

                      Rogers

each group should     (Burrows)
  share the burden    Giannini
                      Rossi        (federal government should hire
                                     laid off minorities; senior
                                     employees should retain city
                                     jobs)
```

EXERCISE 36

Assume that in a synthesis essay, a paragraph will be developed from each of the categories in the chart. Referring to the sources as well as the chart, write a topic sentence for each paragraph.

EVALUATING SOURCES

Although you are obliged to give each of your sources serious and objective consideration and a fair presentation, synthesis also necessitates a certain amount of evaluation and selection. No one's statement should be immediately dismissed as trivial or crazy; include them all in your chart, but do not assume that all statements are equally convincing and deserve equal representation in your essay.

The weight of a group of similar opinions can add authority to an idea. If most of your sources suggest the same reason, you will probably give that reason a proportionate prominence in your essay. However, the structure of your essay should not be governed entirely by majority rule. Your own perspective is the framework for your essay, and you must use your understanding of the topic—which is more thorough and detached than that of any of your sources—to evaluate your materials. Review the hypothesis that you formulated before you began to read and analyze the sources. Decide whether that hypothesis is still valid or whether you wish to alter it or abandon it entirely in the light of your more detailed understanding of the subject. Then, having reaffirmed your hypothesis or chosen another, sift through all the statements and decide which ones are thoughtful and well-balanced, supported by convincing reasons and examples, and which are thoughtless assertions that rely on stereotypes, catch phrases, and unsupported references. Your hypothesis, either confirmed or altered in the light of your increased understanding, becomes the thesis of your essay.

Your basic task is to present the range of opinion on a complex subject, analyzing strengths and weaknesses. You need not draw firm conclusions in your essay or provide definitive answers to the questions that have been raised. But you must have a valid thesis, an overall view of the competing arguments to present to your reader. Your evaluation of the sources will differ from someone else's, but you must assert your own point of view and assess each source in the context of your background, knowledge, and experience. You owe it to your reader to evaluate the evidence that you are presenting, partly through what you choose to emphasize and partly through your explicit comments about flawed and unconvincing statements.

WRITING THE SYNTHESIS ESSAY

Although constructing a chart of categories certainly is the most difficult part of the synthesis process, don't neglect the actual writing of the essay. Spend some time planning your sequence of ideas and considering potential strategies. Do your topic and materials lend themselves to a cause-and-effect structure, or definition, or problem and solution, or comparison? Next, before starting to write each paragraph, look back over the relevant statements in your sources. You may be fully aware of the ideas behind each point of view and the pattern connecting them all. But you may forget that your reader does not know as much as you do, and you may neglect to explain your main ideas in sufficient detail to make all the complex points clear. Remember that your reader has neither made a chart nor even read the original sources; include a certain amount of explanation in your own voice, in addition to quoting and paraphrasing specific statements.

Ideally, you should present your sources by using all three methods of reference: summary, paraphrase, and quotation. Vary the technique. Remember that, as a rule, paraphrase is a far more useful device than quoting. If you rely on quotation, you are adopting the voice of *one* source who, after all, is merely representing a single point of view. When you paraphrase someone's reaction in your own voice, you are underlining the fact that *you* are in charge, that the opinion you are citing is only one of a larger group, and that a full exploration of the topic will emerge from your presentation of all the evidence, not from any one source's opinion. That is why the first sentence of any new turn of thought (whether the topic sentence of a new paragraph or a shift of thought within a paragraph) should be presented entirely in your own voice, as a generalization, without any reference to your sources.

To summarize, each paragraph of your essay should make use of several or all of the following elements:

1. *Topic sentence:* Introduce the category or common theme, and state the idea that is the common element tying this group together.

2. *Explanation:* Support or explain the topic sentence. Later in the paragraph, if you are dealing with a complex group of statements, you may need a connecting sentence or two, showing your reader how one reason is connected to the next. For example, an explanation might be needed in the middle of the "seniority protects the worker" paragraph, as the writer moves from financial and emotional hardship for laid off senior employees to the prevention of discriminatory job conditions.

3. *Paraphrase or summary:* Present specific ideas from your sources in your own words. In these cases, you must of course *acknowledge your sources* by inserting names into your sentence.

4. *Quotation:* Quote from your sources when the content or phrasing of the original statement justifies verbatim inclusion. In some groups there may be several possible candidates for quotation; in others there may be only one; often you may find

no source worth quoting. For example, read the statements made by Page, Reich, and Vitale once again. Could you reasonably quote any of them? Although Reich and Vitale both take strong positions well worth presenting, there is no reason to quote and every reason to paraphrase. On the other hand, Page's briefer statement might be quoted, since the contrast between "yoked" and "sundered" is effective and difficult to paraphrase.

EXERCISE 37

Read the following paragraph, taken from a synthesis essay, and decide which sentences (or parts of sentences) belong to each of the five categories in the chart. Insert the proper category name in the left margin, and bracket the appropriate sentence or phrase illustrating the term. Be prepared to explain the components of the paragraph in class discussion.

Those who emphasize the upgrading of minority employment have pointed out that, since the hiring of minorities has been encouraged by governmental legislation only for the last few years, the seniority system will of necessity operate against those minorities. Thus, in the opinion of Robert Rivera, it is only fair that, during the present budget crisis, workers from minority groups be protected from cutbacks. One statement, by John Seeback, even suggests the possibility of a return to racial discrimination by white workers who have seniority and by employers, if equal opportunity laws are not enforced: "Many employers feel the minority workers are expendable: they had to hire them because of the law; now they have a good reason to fire them." In a related argument, Jesse Rogers points out that, since minorities have waited such a long time for decent job opportunities, a certain amount of preferential treatment might serve as a concrete measure of compensation. Neither Seeback nor Rogers emphasizes the abstract principle of equal opportunity implemented by law. Peter Rossi, however advocates a practical solution: the federal government should undertake "the creation of new jobs," so that, presumably, there would be enough to satisfy both groups.

Citing Sources

Throughout your essay, it is essential that you refer to your sources by name, for they are to serve as authorities for your explanations and conclusions. Although you should always cite the source's full name, whether you are quoting or not, try not to *begin* every sentence with a name, nor should you introduce every paraphrase or quotation with "says." Each sentence should do more than name a person; don't include "empty" sentences: "Mary Smith agrees with this point." If possible, each of your general points should be supported by references from several different sources, so that you will have more than one person's opinion or authority to cite.

When you have several relevant comments to include within a single paragraph, consider carefully which one should get cited first—and why. While it is not essential to name every person who has mentioned the point (especially if you have several almost identical statements), it can be useful to sum up two people's views at the same time, citing two sources for a single paraphrased statement: "Mary Smith and John Jones agree that playing the lottery can be very enjoyable. She finds a particular pleasure in scratching off the numbers to see if she has won," (Notice that the first sentence would not be possible if you *quoted* "very enjoyable." Only one source can be cited for quotation, unless both have used exactly the same wording.) If the idea under discussion was frequently mentioned in your sources, you might convey the relative weight of support by citing "five people" or "several commentators." Then, after summarizing the common response, cite one or two specific opinions, with names. (But try not to *begin* a paragraph with "several people"; remember that the topic sentence should be a generalization of your own, without reference to the supporting evidence.) Opposing views can be discussed within a single paragraph as long as the two points of view have something in common. Radically different ideas should, of course, be explained separately. Use transitions to indicate the relationship between differing opinions.

Here is an example of a paragraph that follows these guidelines. Notice that it is based on contrasting views, with a turn of thought at the word "but."

> Most people would agree that children need money to buy the things that they want: candy, small toys, games, ice cream. A regular allowance will prevent children from having to go to their parents whenever they need money for small purchases. Edward Andrews thinks that a child needs money when he goes out to buy things with his friends; otherwise, he'll feel left out. Similarly, Edna Rogers believes in giving an allowance because the child will

always have money when she needs it. But those who oppose
giving allowances argue that parents usually start such a
routine to keep children from bothering them all the time.
According to Barbara Lewis, an allowance can easily become
a means for the neglectful parent to avoid responsibility.

USES AND MISUSES OF SYNTHESIS

In synthesis, you begin with several separate sources of information—a group of statements, a collection of essays—and you proceed
to analyze each individual point of view and each conception of the topic.
In the long run, however, your object is not to present individual summaries of every source, but rather to incorporate them all in a new essay
that is designed to represent a variety of opinion. Your thorough presentation of the topic counts more than the contribution of any single
author. If the process of synthesis has been complete, coherent, and
impartial, readers of a single synthesis essay can learn just as much about
the overall topic and learn it more quickly than they would by reading
each of the source materials.

The danger is that the sources may lose much of their distinctive content. Synthesis depends not so much on distinguishing between your
materials as on recognizing their similarities. The terminology of synthesis includes such instructions as "break down" and "reduce to common denominators." "Reduction," however, has a double implication: it
suggests distillation through the elimination of impurities, but it also
leads to a loss of substance. You should not be so intent on reducing
material to a manageable form that you ignore the awkward but interesting bits of information—the impurities—which are being eliminated
from your notes. If you try to force your materials into conformity with
your synthesis chart, then you risk overlooking the individual writer's
claim to be heard as a distinct and complete voice. Synthesis is a method,
not an end in itself; uncontrolled, it can become a boa constrictor, swallowing up everything in sight.

The academic writer should be able to distinguish between material
which is appropriate for synthesis and material whose individuality
should be recognized and preserved. One-clear cut example is fiction;
another is autobiography. Assume that three writers are reminiscing
about their first jobs: one was a clerk in a drugstore, the second a telephone operator, and the third plowed his father's fields. In their recollections, the reader can find several similar themes: accepting increased
responsibility; sticking to the job; learning appropriate behavior; living
up to the boss's or customers' or father's expectations. But, just as important, the three autobiographical accounts are sharply different in their
context and circumstances, in their point of view and style. You cannot

lump them together in the same way that you might categorize statements about the lottery or opinions about TV, for they cannot be reduced
to a single common experience. In no sense are the three interchangeable; rather, they are comparable.

Synthesis and Comparison

Since synthesis cannot always do justice to the individual source
materials, a writer who is writing about several full-length essays with a
common theme may instead prefer to use comparison. In many ways,
comparison resembles synthesis. In both, there is an underlying assumption that some fruitful conclusion must result from examining the
ideas of several people, and there is also the same search for a single
vantage point from which to view these separate sources. However, there
is an important difference. While the writer of a synthesis to a large extent
constructs a new work out of the materials of the old, the writer of a
comparison leaves sources as intact as possible throughout the organizational process, so that each can retain its individuality. The components of a comparison are set out, examined, and rearranged; but they
remain individually identifiable, rather than reduced, broken down, or
chewed up.

Moreover, the functions of synthesis and comparison rarely overlap.
In academic and professional writing, you will use synthesis to assimilate
assorted facts and ideas into a coherent body of information. When you
are assigned an essay topic, and when you seek out several sources and
make use of their ideas and discoveries, you are not likely to want to
compare the information that you have recorded in your notes; rather,
you will *synthesize* that material into a complete presentation of the topic.
One of your sources may be an encyclopedia; another a massive survey
of the entire subject; a third may devote several chapters to a scrutiny
of that one small topic. In fact, these three sources are really not comparable, nor is your primary purpose to distinguish between them or to
understand how they approach the subject differently. You are only interested in the results that you can achieve by using and building on
this information. In contrast, the appropriate conditions for comparison
are rather more specific and rare: you must have two or more works of
equivalent length and complexity that deal with the same subject and
merit individual examination. Equally important, you should recognize
the differences between them; the differences will, in most cases, out-
number the similarities.

Point-to-Point and Whole-to-Whole Comparison

Point-to-point comparison is very much like synthesis. The writer selects certain points which are discussed in all the works being compared

and then describes the full range of opinion concerning each point, one at a time. Because point-to-point comparison cuts across the source essays, as synthesis does, the writer must work hard to avoid oversimplification. If you are focussing on one isolated point, trying to match it to a comparable reaction in another essay, don't forget that the works being compared are separate and whole interpretations of the topic. If not, you may end up emphasizing similarities just for the sake of making your point.

Here is a paragraph taken from a point-to-point comparison of three movie reviews:

> None of the three reviewers regards <u>Lady and the Tramp</u> as a first-rate product of the Walt Disney studio. Their chief object of criticism is the sugary sentimentality, so characteristic of Disney cartoons, which has been injected into <u>Lady</u> in excessive quantities. Both John McCarten in the <u>New Yorker</u> and the <u>Time</u> reviewer point out that, for the first time, the anthropomorphic presentation of animals does not succeed because the "human" situations are far too broadly presented. Lady and Tramp are a "painfully arch pair," says McCarten. He finds the dialogue given to the movie's human characters even more embarrassing than the clichés exchanged by the animals. Even Bosley Crowther of the <u>Times</u>, who seems less dismissive of feature cartoons, finds that <u>Lady and the Tramp</u> lacks Disney's usual "literate originality." Crowther suggests that its oppressive sentimentality is probably made more obvious by the film's use of the wide screen. McCarten also comments on the collision between the winsome characters and the magnified production: "Obviously determined to tug all heartstrings," Disney presents the birth of Lady's puppy "while all the stereophonic loudspeakers let loose with overwhelming barrages of cooings and gurglings." All the reviewers agree that the audience for this film will be restricted to dog lovers, and lapdog lovers at that.

Whole-to-whole, the other major method of organizing a comparison, creates a less fragmentary effect; the reader is more likely to gain a sense of each source's individual qualities. But unless the selections that you are writing about are fairly short and simple, this method can be far more unwieldy than point-to-point. If you discuss a series of long and complex works, and if you complete your entire analysis of one before you move on to the next, the reader may get no sense of a comparison and forget that you are relating several sources to each other. Without careful structuring, whole-to-whole comparison becomes a series of loosely related summaries, in which the reader must make all the connections and discover for himself all the parallels and contrasts.

Writers who choose whole-to-whole comparison have two ways of making sure that the structure of the comparison remains clear to the reader.

1. Although each work is discussed separately and presented as a whole, the writer should nevertheless try to present their common ideas in the same order.

Thus, whichever topic you choose as the starting point for your discussion of the first work should also be used as the starting point for your treatment of each of the others. The reader should be able to find the same general point discussed in (roughly) the same place in each of the sections of a whole-to-whole comparison.

2. The reader should be reminded that this is a comparison by frequent "cross-cutting" to works already discussed; the writer should make frequent use of the standard transitional phrases to establish such cross-references.

Initially, you have to decide which work to lead off with. The best choice is usually a relatively simple work that nonetheless touches on all the major points of comparison. Beginning with the second work, you should often refer back to what you have said about the first writer's ideas, showing the way in which they differ from those of the second. (This process can become extremely complex when you are analyzing a large number of essays, which is one reason that whole-to-whole comparison is rarely used to compare more than three works.)

Here is the second major paragraph of a whole-to-whole comparison that deals with critical reaction to the film *West Side Story*:

> Like the author of the Time review, Pauline Kael criticizes West Side Story for its lack of realism and its unconvincing portrayal of social tensions. She points out that the distinction between the ethnic groups is achieved through cosmetics and hair dye, not dialogue and actions. In her view, the characters are like Munchkins, stock figures without individual identities and recognizable motives. Natalie Wood as the heroine, Maria, is unfavorably compared to a mechanical robot and to the Princess telephone. Just as the Time reviewer accuses the film of oversentimentalizing its teenage characters at society's expense, so Kael condemns the movie's division

of its characters into stereotypical good guys and bad
guys. In fact, Kael finds it hard to account for the
popularity of <u>West Side Story</u>'s "frenzied hokum." She
concludes that many may have been overwhelmed by the
film's sheer size and technical achievements. The audience
is persuaded to believe that bigger, louder, and faster
has to be better. Her disapproval extends even to the
widely praised dancing; like the rest of the movie, the
choreography tries too hard to be impressive. In short,
Pauline Kael agrees with the <u>Time</u> review; <u>West Side Story</u>
never rises above its "hyped–up, slam–bang production."

Whether you choose point-to-point or whole-to-whole comparison depends on the nature of your materials. Whichever you choose, begin planning your comparison by establishing a chart of important ideas discussed by several of your sources. If you eventually choose to write a point-to-point essay, then your chart can become the basis for your paragraph outline. If you decide to deal with each of your essays as a whole, your chart can suggest what to emphasize and will help you to decide the order of topics within the discussion of each work. These charts can never be more than primitive guidelines; but unless you establish the primary points of similarity or difference among your sources, your essay will end up as a series of unrelated comments, not a comparison.

EXERCISE 38

Three critical reviews of the film *M*A*S*H* follow this list of questions. Read through the questions quickly, then read the reviews and return to the questions. Be prepared to discuss the answers.

1. Which of the reviews is most successful in creating a coherent image of the film? Which of the three would best enable a reader to decide whether he would like to see the film? Is there a real difference between those two questions?
2. Are all three reviewers addressing the same kind of audience? Consider the periodicals in which the reviews were first published. Do they have a similar readership? What assumption does each critic make about the probable values of the average person reading the review and watching the movie?
3. *M*A*S*H* and the reviews appeared in 1970, at the time of the Vietnam War. To what extent are the critics influenced by that circumstance? Had the movie appeared more recently, would it have been reviewed differently?

4. How does each of the critics regard the behavior of the doctors who are the main characters? To what extent are they considered competent at their jobs? Destructive? sane? heroic? How does the setting of the film—the abnormal circumstances of war—affect the three critics' conception of heroism?

5. To what extent do the three critics believe that M*A*S*H makes a valid criticism of society?

6. How does each critic describe and evaluate the humor that is characteristic of the film?

7. Denby and Kael make several allusions to other comedies, comparing M*A*S*H with previous films. What contribution to these references make to the reader's understanding of the film? Do the allusions help to make these reviews more convincing, or are they irrelevant?

8. All three critics devote a great deal of space to M*A*S*H's innovative technical effects, such as cross-cutting. Can you establish any thematic connection between each reviewer's opinion of the dialogue, editing, and camera work and his or her overall conception of the film?

9. Denby's vocabulary has been described as energetic and dynamic, which is consistent with his view of the film's liberating effect. Can you characterize the language and style of the other reviews? For example, is Greenspun's disapproval conveyed through his language? Contrast Kael's use of "surreal innocence" with Denby's "wildness of adolescence" and Greenspun's "emotional freedom" and "shocking good sense."

10. If you yourself have seen M*A*S*H, can you suggest any potential point of criticism that is not discussed by at least one of the three critics?

11. Which technique would be a more efficient and effective method of comparing the three reviews: point-to-point or whole-to-whole? Which common topics would you choose for the paragraphs of a point-to-point comparison? Which order of ideas would you use for each part of a whole-to-whole comparison?

M*A*S*H

To my knowledge Robert Altman's "M*A*S*H" is the first major American movie openly to ridicule belief in God—not phony belief; real belief. It is also one of the few (though by no means the first) American screen comedies openly to admit the cruelty of its humor. And it is at pains to blend that humor with more operating room gore than I have ever seen in any movie from any place.

All of which may promote a certain air of good feeling in the audience, an attitude of self-congratulation that they have the guts to take the gore, the inhumanity to appreciate the humor, and the sanity to admire the impiety—directed against a major who prays for himself, his Army buddies and even "our Commander in Chief."

Actually "M*A*S*H," which opened yesterday at the Baronet, accepts without question several current pieties (for example, concern for a child's life, but not a grown man's soul), but its general bent is toward emotional freedom, cool wit, and shocking good sense.

Based upon a barely passable novel of the same name (the title stands for Mobile Army Surgical Hospital, but "MASH," of course, stands for a few other things as well), "M*A*S*H" takes place mostly in Korea during the war. However, aside from the steady processing of bloody meat through the operating room, the film is not so much concerned with the war as with life inside the Army hospital unit and especially with the quality of life created by the three hot-shot young surgeons (Donald Sutherland, Elliott Gould and Tom Skerritt) who make most things happen.

But, unlike "Catch-22," with which it has already been incorrectly compared (I mean the novel, not the legendary unfinished movie), "M*A*S*H" makes no profoundly radical criticism either of war or of the Army. Although it is impudent, bold, and often very funny, it lacks the sense of order (even in the midst of disorder) that seems the special province of successful comedy. I think that "M*A*S*H," for all its local virtues, is not successful. Its humor comes mostly in bits and pieces, and even in its climax, an utterly unsporting football game between the MASH unit and an evacuation hospital, it fails to build toward either significant confrontation or recognition. At the end, the film simply runs out of steam, says good-by to its major characters, and calls final attention to itself as a movie—surely the saddest and most overworked of cop-out devices in the comic film repertory.

Robert Altman's method has been to fill the frame to a great depth with overlapping bits of action and strands of dialogue. The tracking camera serves as an agent of discovery. To a very great degree, "M*A*S*H" substitutes field of view for point of view, and although I think this substitution has a lot to do with the movie's ultimate weakness, the choice is not without its intelligent rewards.

Insane announcements over the hospital's intercom system, Japanese-accented popular American songs from Armed Forces Radio in Tokyo, bungling corpsmen, drivers, nurses—and again and again the brilliantly understood procedures of the operating room—come together to define the spirit of the film.

In one brief night scene, some MASH-men and the chief nurse meet to divide the winnings of the football game. In the distance, a jeep drives by, carrying a white-shrouded corpse. The nurse glances at it for a second, and then turns back to her happy friends—and we have a momentary view of the ironic complexities of life that "M*A*S*H" means to contain.

Among the leads, Elliott Gould suggests the right degree of coolly belligerent self-containment, but Donald Sutherland (in a very elaborate performance) supports his kind of detachment with vocal mannerisms that occasionally become annoying. Sally Kellerman plays the chief nurse, Maj. Hot Lips Houlihan—and how she earns her name is the funniest and nastiest sequence of the film. Her character changes—from comic heavy to something like romantic lead—but "M*A*S*H" really has no way of handling character change, so she mostly fades into the background.

Early in the film she is the butt of some dreadfully humiliating gags, and with her expressive, vulnerable face, she is disturbing to laugh at. It is as if she had returned from some noble-nonsense war movie of the 1940's to suggest an area of human response that the masterly sophistications of "M*A*S*H" are unaware of.

Roger Greenspun, *New York Times*, 25 January 1970

BREAKTHROUGH

*M*A*S*H*, the celebrated American comedy about three Army surgeons in the Korean War, is not a great work, but it is joyous and liberating in the way that European movies which are great works almost never manage to be. And it's the kind of movie we need in the present moment—*M*A*S*H* (an acronym for Mobile Army Surgical Hospital) may be set in Korea, but who in the audience can help thinking "Vietnam"? Sardonic antimilitary comedy suits our mood; this one may rescue us for a while from the hopelessness we feel. The film makers take for granted a certain alienation and disgust, but they don't rely on it completely for their effects, as Antonioni has in *Zabriskie Point*, his shockingly lazy vision of America as a corrupt society. Director Robert Altman and his company work with a happy, bright energy that makes you want to go along with the movie, even with the scenes that don't quite come off. They create their own world and earn the right to their attitudes. After a cautious beginning in New York and Los Angeles, Fox has now opened the movie all over the country. The Army, however, announced in late March that *M*A*S*H* would be banned on all its bases. (The ban was subsequently lifted.)

*M*A*S*H* is the breakthrough in the realm of popular culture that *The Graduate* was supposed to be and really wasn't; its great achievement is to establish an acceptable heroism. Neither solemnly forbearing in the Gregory Peck tradition, nor beautiful and ineffably sweet, as in the canting youth movies (*The Graduate*), its heroes are really something to admire. Carnal and witty, chivalrous but not soft, these men do something in the world with pride and success and have graciously retained the wildness of adolescence. Only the most unimaginative standards would find them disappointing; doubtless they aren't "mature"—that insulting, coercive notion which requires us to give up so much to succeed.

The mood of the picture is sustained by a tremendous secret excitement that passes among the three men (played by Elliott Gould, Donald Sutherland, and Tom Skerritt) and radiates from them to the audience, a tense unspoken understanding of the reality of the situation: that the war is absurd, an offense against rationality too deep for words; that the field hospital is inadequate to handle the flow of mangled bodies that pass across its operating tables; that the doctors must work with intensity, skill, and improvisatory daring to have any effect at all; and that away from their wives and civilian careers, they have been offered a second chance at recklessness and boyhood, a chance they joyously accept because it is the only way to remain sane and keep working. These doctors really know about health; they know what supports life and what kills it. The elaborate bad taste, the detailed attention to games and trivia, the constant intrigues of everyone sleeping with everyone else—all this enforced atmosphere of a disorderly summer camp or coed frat house is a kind of therapy. Several reviewers have complained that the surgeons are excessively brutal to people they don't like, but it seems natural to me that personal relations in a military emergency hospital would become exacerbated to the point where every quirk would become unbearable. The tensions are relieved either with obscenity and kidding ("If you didn't have such a good body, nurse, we'd get rid of you") or, in extreme cases, with personal vendettas.

Their wildness would be stupid and merely cruel if they weren't such good, competent surgeons. The scenes in the operating room, with blood spurting from open wounds and doctors running from body to body, are both harrowing and funny—this butcher-shop mess is war's final truth. The humor is bitter but not sick—not black comedy, but something warmer, with the outrage closer to the surface. Richard Lester tried to bring down the curtain on the traditional hypocrisy of war movies in *How I Won the War*, but his style—absurdist farce—backfired on him; his vision of war wasn't shocking and grotesque, it was just silly. Audiences were justifiably bewildered, and their resentment shifted to the movie itself. Altman sticks close to the realistic level, and his esthetic conservatism works for us: the mess in the operating room creates in us the same explosive tension and near-hopelessness that the doctors feel, and we experience the relief that they do when they get the chance to go wild.

In a movie devoted to the destruction of pretense, overelaborate or florid readings, however skillful, would be all wrong; Altman allowed his performers to improvise frequently, and they seem to be relaxed and enjoying themselves. Here, as in *Bob & Carol & Ted & Alice*, Elliott Gould is extraordinarily evocative of someone we may vaguely remember from summer camp or school; he has that air of a self-absorbed adolescent, acting out his private sense of amusement. As for Donald Sutherland, he appears to be stoned most of the time, which gives his favorite ploy of mock formality a rather muzzy and decrepit tone. These self-loving performances, probably indistinguishable from the actors' personalities, work perfectly—in the Army a man must become a "character" or he loses all individuality—whereas Tom Skerritt, who does some straight acting as a Southerner, is merely effective and likable. Almost everyone in the large cast has his own lovely moment of eccentricity or wit, and we don't see the mugging typical of supporting actors desperate to make an impression.

Since mood was more important than the details of a loosely episodic plot in which no given scene was absolutely essential, Altman could take big chances while shooting and hope for the craziness and pacing that more anxious preparation often kills; naturally, he had to throw a lot away. It would probably be impossible to do improvisation without using the sloppy sound recorded on the set; post-dubbing, the usual procedure, could never reproduce that excited intensity of actors building a scene without knowing exactly where they are going. By committing himself this way, Altman may have lost a few big laughs when dialogue overlaps (sometimes the overlap is itself funny), and there are occasional lines we simply can't hear, but he came up with the liveliest sound track on an American film in years. Many scenes begin in mid-conversation, but we catch just enough to feel the texture of relationships, the amount of living, that might be going on. It's not only the dialogue that works well. The hospital camp's loudspeaker system, for instance, becomes a major character in the movie, establishing the weirdly banal official atmosphere in which everyone must work. "The American Medical Association announced this morning that marijuana is a dangerous drug," it says, during one of the ghastly operating scenes.

Almost every minute of *M*A*S*H* is filled with detailed invention; the movie has a prodigal, throw-away quality that may remind some viewers of a vintage thirties comedy like Howard Hawks' *Bringing Up Baby*. I wouldn't be surprised if it became a college-film-society classic and was loved by generations of students.

David Denby, *Atlantic Monthly*, April 1970

BLESSED PROFANITY

"M*A*S*H" is a marvellously unstable comedy, a tough, funny, and sophisticated burlesque of military attitudes that is at the same time a tale of chivalry. It's a sick joke, but it's also generous and romantic—an erratic, episodic film, full of the pleasures of the unexpected. I think it's the closest an American movie has come to the kind of constantly surprising mixture in "Shoot the Piano Player," though "M*A*S*H" moves so fast that it's over before you have time to think of comparisons. While it's going on, you're busy listening to some of the best overlapping comic dialogue ever recorded. The picture has so much spirit that you keep laughing—and without discomfort, because all the targets *should* be laughed at. The laughter is at the horrors and absurdities of war, and, specifically, at people who flourish in the military bureaucracy. The title letters stand for Mobile Army Surgical Hospital; the heroes, played by Donald Sutherland and Elliott Gould, are combat surgeons patching up casualties a few miles from the front during the Korean war. They do their surgery in style, with humor; they're hip Galahads, saving lives while ragging the military bureaucracy. They are so quick to react to bull—and in startling, unpredictable ways—that the comedy is, at times, almost a poetic fantasy. There's a surreal innocence about the movie; though the setting makes it seem a "black" comedy, it's a cheery "black" comedy. The heroes win at everything. It's a modern kid's dream of glory: Holden Caulfield would, I think, approve of them. They're great surgeons, athletes, dashing men of the world, sexy, full of noblesse oblige, but ruthless to those with pretensions and lethal to hypocrites. They're so good at what they do that even the military brass admires them. They're winners in the war with the Army.

War comedies in the past have usually been about the little guys who foul things up and become heroes by accident (Chaplin in "Shoulder Arms," Danny Kaye in "Up in Arms"). In that comedy tradition, the sad-sack recruit is too stupid to comprehend military ritual. These heroes are too smart to put up with it. Sutherland and Gould are more like an updated version of Edmund Lowe's and Victor McLaglen's Sergeant Quirt and Captain Flagg from "What Price Glory" and "The Cockeyed World"—movies in which the heroes retain their personal style and their camaraderie in the midst of blood and muck and the general insanity of war. One knows that though what goes on at this surgical station seems utterly crazy, it's only a small distortion of actual wartime situations. The pretty little helicopters delivering the bloody casualties are a surreal image, all right, but part of the authentic surrealism of modern warfare. The jokes the surgeons make about their butchershop work are a form of plain talk. The movie isn't naïve, but it isn't nihilistic, either. The surgery room looks insane and is presented as insane, but as the insanity in which we must preserve the values of sanity and function as sane men. An incompetent doctor is treated as a foul object; competence is one of the values the movie respects—even when it is demonstrated by a nurse (Sally Kellerman) who is a pompous fool. The heroes are always on the side of decency and sanity—that's why they're contemptuous of the bureaucracy. They are heroes *because* they're competent and sane and gallant, and in this insane situation their gallantry takes the form of scabrous comedy. The Quirt and Flagg films were considered highly profane in their day, and I am happy to say that "M*A*S*H," taking full advantage of the new permissive rating system, is blessedly profane. I've rarely heard four-letter words used so exquisitely well in a movie, used with such efficacy and glee. I salute "M*A*S*H" for its contribution to the art of talking dirty.

The profanity, which is an extension of adolescent humor, is central to the idea of the movie. The silliness of adolescents—compulsively making jokes, seeing the ridiculous in everything—is what makes sanity possible here. The doctor who rejects adolescent behavior flips out. Adolescent pride in skills and games—in mixing a Martini or in devising a fishing lure or in golfing—keeps the men from becoming maniacs. Sutherland and Gould, and Tom Skerritt, as a third surgeon, and a lot of freakishly talented new-to-movies actors are relaxed and loose in their roles. Their style of acting underscores the point of the picture, which is that people who aren't hung up by pretensions, people who are loose and profane and have some empathy—people who can joke about anything—can function, and maybe even do something useful, in what may appear to be insane circumstances.

There's also a lot of slapstick in the movie, some of it a little like "Operation Mad Ball," a fifties service comedy that had some great moments but was still tied to a sanctimonious approach to life and love. What holds the disparate elements of "M*A*S*H" together in the precarious balance that is the movie's chief charm is a free-for-all, throwaway attitude. The picture looks as if the people who made it had a good time, as if they played with it and improvised and took some chances. It's elegantly made, and yet it doesn't have that overplanned rigidity of so many Hollywood movies. The cinematography, by Harold E. Stine, is very fine—full of dust and muddy olive-green tones; it has immediacy and the clarity possible in Panavision. The editing and the sound engineering are surprisingly quick-witted. When the dialogue overlaps, you hear just what you should, but it doesn't seem all worked out and set; the sound seems to bounce off things so that the words just catch your ear. The throwaway stuff isn't really thrown away; it all helps to create the free, graceful atmosphere that sustains the movie and keeps it consistently funny. The director, Robert Altman, has a great feel for low-keyed American humor. With the help of Ring Lardner, Jr.'s, script (from a novel by a combat surgeon), Altman has made a real sport of a movie which combines traditional roustabout comedy with modern attitudes. As in other good comedies, there's often a mixture of what seems perfectly straight stuff and what seems incredible fantasy, and yet when we try to say which is which we can't. "M*A*S*H" affects us on a bewildering number of levels, like the Radio Tokyo versions of American songs on the camp loudspeaker system. All this may sound more like a testimonial than a review, but I don't know when I've had such a good time at a movie. Many of the best recent American movies leave you feeling that there's nothing to do but get stoned and die, that that's your proper fate as an American. This movie heals a breach in American movies: it's hip but it isn't hopeless. A surgical hospital where the doctors' hands are lost in chests and guts is certainly an unlikely subject for a comedy, but I think "M*A*S*H" is the best American war comedy since sound came in and the sanest American movie of recent years.

Pauline Kael, *The New Yorker*, 7 February 1970

USING SEQUENCE AND ARRANGEMENT TO PRESENT MULTIPLE SOURCES

Occasionally, neither synthesis nor comparison will seem an appropriate method of presenting a group of sources to your reader. Such a problem commonly occurs when you are working with a group of first-person narratives, the testimony of those who have witnessed important events. A legal dispute might be the occasion for carefully transcribing a source's exact words, for the precise wording of each witness's evidence could be crucial to the outcome of the case. In academic writing, projects in oral history generally call for the presentation of source materials in their original form, without paraphrase or summary. Social scientists often gather the personal recollections of those whose lives have paralleled the evolution of the twentieth century. The anecdotes and reminiscences of ordinary people not only provide us with first-hand information, but also lend an immediacy to our perception of the past. For these reasons, researchers will seek out and interview those who have interesting stories to tell and then weave these stories into an oral history of a specific region, an event, or an entire era.

Transforming a group of disparate reminiscences into a coherent "history" calls for many of the skills of synthesis. These recollections of the past convey so much of their meaning through their personal, individual phrasing and style that they must be presented intact, without alteration. And yet, if they are set down in random order, they will have no form, no pattern, and no significance as a whole. They must be given shape by an objective editor, someone who understands the total effect that the stories should have upon the reader. The task of the editor, then, is 1) to analyze the meaning and implications of each separate story; 2) to form some conclusions about the significance of the group of stories, and 3) to design a sequence that will convey that significance to the reader. To carry out the third step, the editor must experiment with various arrangements, always keeping in mind the relationship between one story and the next, as well as the relationship of each to the whole. An effective arrangement is like a mosaic which forms a complete pattern, a pattern that will change if the sequence is changed.

Following, in random order, are six recollections of World War II, which can be arranged in 720 possible sequences. As you read each story, consider:

1. its topic;
2. whether its view is wide or narrow;
3. its effect on you, the reader.

Before deciding on a sequence for these reminiscences, you should first consider what overall impression or theme you would like your reader to retain after reading the entire group. The impression that you wish to make will be your unwritten thesis. Then consider which story you might want your sequence to begin with, and why; which story should come next, and next, and next; and which would make the best final impression.

1.   I can tell you a couple of stories about George S. Patton. I was a corporal in his tank corps during the war and I had the opportunity to see him in action twice. I still don't know what to make of him.

The first time we met was on an old dirt road in Germany. I was the forward observer along with my lieutenant, and we were checking out the road when we came across an old horse blocking our way. I was driving a jeep, and the road was too narrow to go around him. I slowed to a crawl and started to blow my horn, but he refused to move until we were right on top of him. Then, he ran down the road about fifty yards, stopped, and turned around to watch us. Well, I repeated this procedure several times, but the horse never left the road; he only ran down it a little further. By this time, the lieutenant and I were losing our patience, when, suddenly, we heard a roar behind us and looked back. I couldn't believe it. Here came about five jeeps and standing up in one of them was General Patton. He was some sight. With those pearl-handled revolvers and a helmet, he looked like something out of a comic book.

The old cavalryman leaped out of his jeep and lit into us. "You sons of bitches, don't you know how to handle a horse? Why the hell didn't you just get out and lead him over to the side!" With that, Patton went over to the horse and gave him a pat on the rump, and the horse trotted to the side. Then, Patton hopped back into his jeep and took off.

The next time I saw Patton, I was in a convoy heading toward the front. The tank ahead of us had somehow run over a soldier, crushing him to death and bringing the convoy to a halt. Well, again this brought Patton charging up the road to find out about the delay. When he saw the crushed body in the road, he said, "What the hell is that! Shovel that mess over to the side and burn it." With that, the body was shoveled to the side and burnt. Patton was in a rush to fight. You know, I think that Patton had more respect for horses than for men.

2. Times were tough during the war but we managed. Everything was pretty scarce then, and coupons were a big part of our life. Most of the products we used were being rationed, and ration coupons were like money. But with or without coupons, certain items were hard to come by. I remember it was difficult to get sugar and red meat, and we ate a lot of chicken. Of course, not everyone was doing badly. Inflation was pretty bad and a lot of people were cleaning up. I knew the factory I worked for was making a mint from the government. We had several contracts with the government at the time, and I remember my boss showing me the figures on the cost of production compared to the price the government was paying for the equipment. The profits were staggering. Believe me, the color of patriotism then was solid green.

3. You know what I remember? I remember Bizerte. I lost my brother there. We had joined the army in 1939 and had been together through all the fear and all the fights, but we parted company there.

Bizerte was the big city in Africa and was our last stop before the invasion of Sicily. The city wasn't occupied by the Germans and everyone was looking forward to one big bash before the invasion. Anyway, when we pulled up to the outskirts of the city, we found that it was off limits. Needless, to say, everyone was disgusted, particularly my brother. Well, my brother and about ten other guys said, "To hell with it," and decided to go anyway. I was all set to go myself, but at the last minute I was given guard duty. I told my brother I'd pull guard and meet them in town later, but later never came.

That night our company moved out. We were heading for Sicily. When my brother got back the next morning, we were gone. Well, my brother and the other men, being good soldiers, turned themselves in to the military police. However, they were not treated as good soldiers. They were charged with desertion, and later put in the stockade.

I never saw my brother after that, although we did exchange letters. In his last letter, he told me he was going to volunteer for the front and receive a full pardon. I told him to stay where he was and that he would probably be pardoned after the war anyway. Well, I guess he couldn't stand the stockade and so he volunteered. He was killed shortly before the war ended.

4. Our town was right near the German border and, as a matter of fact, everyone in town spoke German. But we were Belgians and we feared the onslaught of Hitler's army. It was strange how they arrived, too. One morning we just got up and they were there. No shots were fired and no warnings were given. We just woke up and found the German army in town.

After that, things got pretty rough. The Germans said that we were part of the Fatherland, and they wanted all the men to join the army. Most of the men, including my brothers, refused and were taken to concentration camps. But because they weren't Jews, they weren't treated too badly.

My father had a butcher store, but when the Germans took control of the food supplies and started to ration the food, my father was forced to close his store. I got a job at a drugstore, but that didn't last too long either. The man who owned the store was helping Jews escape, and it wasn't too long before he was picked up by the Gestapo. My brother later saw him in a concentration camp, where he was put to death with the Jews.

I also recall working in a small factory in town. We had a fellow employee who hated the Germans and especially Hitler. There were pictures of the "führer" everywhere, and one time he took a picture of Hitler off the wall; then he went to the bathroom and wiped his behind with the picture. Then he came out and put the picture back on the wall. It was one of the funniest incidents I can remember. Later on, though, the Gestapo found out about it and he was taken away. I never did see him again. But that's the way the war was: people just disappeared. Some came back and some didn't.

5. I was working up in the Baffin Islands during the war. That's not too far from the Arctic Circle. The army was building a post up there, and I was on the construction crew. I remember celebrating my fiftieth birthday up there, but that was no place to party. That land was the most desolate and barren area I've ever seen, and the weather was the toughest I've ever experienced. One day, when the wind was really kicking up, we lost one of the men. He went to get something in the snow, and we never saw him again.

There were a lot of draft dodgers up there, too, but the government was catching up with most of them. One I remember well was a big Swede from Minnesota. One night during dinner, he turned to me and said, "Damn, Harry, if this war can just last two more years, I'll have my house paid off." I blew my stack. I stood up and started cursing him. I had two sons overseas and I was ready to kill him, though he was twice my size. We were going out the door to settle this, when my buddy stood up. "You're twice his size, Swede, you'll have to fight me, too." Then some of the Swede's friends stood up and it looked like there was going to be a riot. Luckily, we had a strong foreman who stepped in and calmed things down. After that, though, I realized that not everyone was suffering because of the war.

6.   I don't remember too much about the war; I was only seven years old when it ended. However, I do remember a party that my mother gave for my uncle. It was the best party I ever went to. We lived in a three-family house with my aunt and my grandmother, and it always seemed like we had so much room, but this day there were people everywhere. At least, it seemed that way to me and my brothers. It was the only time in my life that my whole family was together. Even my father was there, and I hadn't seen him in a long time.

My father was an alcoholic and he didn't live with us at the time. As a matter of fact, the party was the last time and just about the only time I ever saw him sober. It was funny how everyone else was drinking, but my father didn't have anything. Why, even my mother gave me a little drink, and that was the first time I'd ever had any alcohol (at least I think it was alcohol). But my father refused everything. Actually, that's the funny thing about my father: I never saw him drink; I only saw him drunk.

Anyway, I remember my mother telling me that my uncle was a hero. He had won a bronze star and a purple heart and he'd been wounded. It was the wound that had delayed his return, but today he was being released from the hospital. I remember the moment he came through the door. He had a limp from his wound in the leg, and he was using a cane, but he looked so happy. But then my mother and my aunt started crying and pretty soon it seemed everyone was breaking out in tears. I never saw so many red eyes from people having a good time.

Determining Sequence

Here's one student's explanation for the sequence that he chose:

> I've arranged the order of these stories according to the relative effect of violence, ruthlessness, and horror that the reader might derive from each one. The sequence that I've chosen is 4-1-3-5-2-6.
>
> Story 4 is by far the most ruthless and warlike of all the stories: ruthless because of the speed with which the war pounded on an unsuspecting town overnight, and warlike in its description of the arrest and killing of the narrator's friends and relatives—for no justifiable

reason. Altogether, this story supplied the most effective picture of the horror of war.

Story 1 shows the unimportance and insignificance of human life during times of war. An animal is treated with more compassion than a human being. But this story has a narrower focus and a more humorous tone than the first; its effect is hardly as striking.

Story 3 continues at the actual scene of war. Even being held prisoner by his own side, the soldier experiences a gradual deterioration of mind and body: he would rather risk almost certain death at the front than remain in the stockade. Again, human life seems to have little value, even away from the expectable conflict between armies.

Although not as violent as the previous stories, story 5 shows the effects, good and bad, which war can have on different people. For some, it's the cause of financial gain, while for others, it means the loss of children, family, and friends. This is a mixed story and therefore a good transition from actual combat.

Story 2 is fairly mild and does not really paint much of a picture of the actual effects of war. For instance, if the first sentence were deleted, one could read the rest of the story without realizing that it had anything to do with wartime. To me, the conditions described are similar to conditions occuring all over the world during peacetime. This is a story about economic hardship—a normal condition—not about war.

Story 6 is by far the least warlike, and, actually, from the beginning, it makes little attempt to concern itself with World War II. Mostly, it's about everyday occurrences that might happen to any family in America. It's good to end the sequence with a young child, the next generation.

This writer chose to move from the most serious and intense of the stories—the one that most evokes the monstrous abnormality of war—to those that are ordinary and tranquil in their content and tone. The sequence thus traces a gradual return to the norms of peacetime. At the end, the reader should have been brought back from the state of shock and outrage prompted by the first story; thus, in a calm but concerned state of mind, he will be able to reflect on what he has read. That, at any rate, seems to be the rationale behind this student's choice of sequence.

As long as the editor applies some consistent principle to the ordering, many sequences tend to make sense. Thus, another student, working with the same six stories, might have chosen to reverse this suggested order and move towards, rather than away from, the climax or most powerful story; gradually increasing emotion is a highly effective principle of organization. As an alternative to a *spectrum*—moving from one extreme to the other, one might choose a sequence that categorizes according to content. For example, all the episodes of combat could be placed together, and the civilian scenes grouped elsewhere. Or one might gear the sequence to the perspective of the stories, beginning with the one that provides the broadest view of the subject and narrowing the focus to a minutely detailed close-up. The principle of organization might be entirely thematic. The stories could be divided, for example, into those which show human propensity for goodness and for evil. But none of these schemes would fit every set of stories. The materials must suggest the strategy; the strategy cannot be imposed on unsuitable materials.

If this collection had contained more stories, there would almost certainly have been overlapping, so that two or three stories might have described the same kind of incident, for example, prison life in the stockade *and* prison life as a POW. With more material to work with, moving gradually from one kind of story to the next is easier. Variety and contrast in your sequence make the oral history more interesting; however, your first concern should not be entertainment for its own sake, but rather the impression that the reader receives from reading the whole sequence.

SUPPLEMENTARY EXERCISES AND ASSIGNMENTS

This section contains a variety of assignments to give you practice in synthesis.

ASSIGNMENT 12

A. At the library, examine the issue of the *New York Times* that was published on the day that you were born. Most libraries keep complete microfilms of the *New York Times*. Ask your librarian how to locate and use these microfilms. (Alternatively, locate an issue of a news magazine that covers the week during which you were born.) Select the articles that seem to you to be most interesting and typical of the period, and use them as evidence in forming an account of what it was like to live on that day. This essay should not merely be a collection of facts; you are expected to suggest the overall significance of all the information that you include. Remember that your reader was almost certainly *not* born on that date, and that your job is to arouse his interest. If you like, draw some parallels with the present time, but don't strain the comparison. The essay should not run much more than 1,000 words: select carefully and refer briefly to the evidence.

B. Use a newspaper or magazine published *this week* and try to construct a partial portrait of what it is like to live in America (or in your city or town) right now. Don't rely entirely on news stories, but, instead, draw your evidence as much as possible from advertisements and features (like TV listings, classifieds, announcements of all sorts). Try, if you can, to strip yourself of personal knowledge; pretend you are a Martian if that will enable you to become detached from your familiar environment. Don't offer conclusions that the evidence does not substantiate, and don't try to say *everything* that could possibly be said.

EXERCISE 39

Make up a set of materials for a definition exercise, like the set used on pp. 239–242. Think of a representative group of examples illustrating one of the following:

A. several possible occasions for interfering in the affairs of one's family or one's friends (i.e. *private* intervention);
B. several possible occasions for complaining to authority about another person's conduct (consider the classroom and the office environments);
C. protection *or* cleanliness *or* innocence.

Remember that your list of illustrations should not be restricted to those that would satisfy your own personal definition; try to provide the broadest possible base. For that reason, if your teacher approves, it may be helpful to work on this exercise with a group of students in your class.

EXERCISE 40

A. Read the following story.

> Jack is in his third year of college and doing passing but below-average work. His mother has been insisting that he plan to enroll in law school and become an attorney, like his father. Angry at him for not receiving better grades, she has told him that under no circumstances will he get the car or the trip that he has been promised unless his average goes up one full grade. Although Jack has done slightly better work this term, he has been having trouble with his sociology course, especially with

the term paper. Twice he has asked for a conference with his teacher, but Professor Brown has told him that he isn't being paid to run a private tutoring service. So Jack has postponed writing the paper and finally puts it together hastily the night before it is due. Then, Professor Brown calls him in and tells him that the paper is disgraceful and that he has no chance of getting a passing grade or even an incomplete unless he submits a more acceptable essay by 9:00 A.M. the next day. Jack tries to explain his situation and his mother's demands, and he asks for some more time to revise the paper, but his teacher is inflexible and says, "You probably don't belong in college anyway." Since there is no way that Jack is going to be able to produce the revised essay in time, he decides to salvage the car and the trip by getting somebody to write it for him. He has heard about Victor, a recent graduate who always needs money. Victor agrees and, after some haggling about the fee, he writes an acceptable paper overnight. A few days after Professor Brown has accepted the paper and given Jack his grade, Jack gets a call from Victor, who says that, unless he gets double the original fee, he will reveal the entire transaction to Professor Brown and the Dean. Jack doesn't have the money and cannot tell his parents.

B. In your opinion, who is the worst person in the story? Write a few sentences explaining your reasons.

C. Here are some statements containing frequently expressed reasons for disliking each of the characters. Consider why each person considers his or her choice the worst person in the story. Then try to generalize about the ethical principles that lie behind each group of responses. The people who consider Jack (for example) worse than Victor are employing a particular set of values. What principles or beliefs are most important to each group? You are being asked to describe a set of *negative* opinions in terms of the underlying *positive* beliefs. Therefore, stress positive values. Try not to say, "The people who condemn Jack's mother strongly believe that she is too ambitious."

Jack's mother

Barbara Bailey: Jack's mother is trying to run his life. He is old enough to decide what he wants to do. But she is trying to make him be just like his father. She hasn't bothered to ask him whether he wants to be a lawyer. He might not even be smart enough to get through law school. She is forcing him to live up to her expectations; she is trying to live through him. Even if Jack eventually becomes successful, he will be unhappy and dissatisfied, like his mother.

Gina Britton: She is forcing her son past his natural abilities. She does not see him as a separate individual with separate needs. She should be happy that Jack is attending college and trying to get an education. But she doesn't seem to care about his feelings or his future. She is too ambitious.

Wallace Humphrey: Jack's mother should have understood that her son was trying hard to pass. If she had shown more patience and sympathy, he might have done well. She hasn't done her part as a mother, so Jack can't be a good son.

Kathy Harris: Jack's mother is threatening to punish him, not because she honestly wants him to succeed, but because she is so angry with him. In a way, she is forcing him into a desperate act. It is her demands which cause Jack eventually to become the victim of blackmail.

Mohammed Taylor: Jack's mother is very unreasonable. She expects her son to be like her husband, but they are two different people, and Jack should be treated as an individual. She is encouraging him to cheat. By bribing him, she is encouraging him to use bribery himself to get his paper written. How can he do well in his studies with a mother like her?

Summary: The people who condemn Jack's mother strongly believe __

_____

Jack

Chris Bennett: Jack is the worst person because he is not doing the work for its own sake, but for the gain he will receive from his mother. Although his teacher refused to see him, Jack shouldn't have waited to write his paper. He could have sought help from another teacher or from the tutoring center.

Dona Morrow: Jack regards college as a bargaining institution. First he bargains with his mother over his material reward; then he bargains with his teacher as to how much time he'll have for an assignment; last, he bargains with his college acquaintance over money. Jack is too greedy to enjoy life, and he doesn't want to do any work.

Josephine Navarre: Jack allows himself to be placed in this pressure chamber by trying to avoid his responsibilities, by his use of deception, by not standing up for his rights, by his unwillingness to be held accountable for his actions or lack thereof.

Bernice Richards: As a junior in college, Jack should already know how to write a paper. He sought only one source of (unwilling) help—his professor. There's no reason for Jack to get so negative about Professor Brown; he should have realized that his teacher was the inflexible type, and he should have tried to write a good paper the first time. Jack expects everyone to oblige him without making any effort. He just waits around to be bailed out by someone else.

John Suarez: School is a responsibility, just as a job is, and Jack does not live up to his responsibility. He is now in college, not high school, so we have to assume that he chose to take the course that he's failing. What will happen when he gets to law school? Who will do his work when he's defending a client? Jack is just a helpless whiner.

Summary: The people who condemn Jack strongly believe _____

_____

Professor Brown

Jack Dougherty: Professor Brown is the worst character because he could have listened to Jack's complaints and pleas for help. He isn't doing his job. He's not getting paid to tutor, but he is getting paid to teach, and helping students is part of teaching.

Andrea Notare: This story shows that some teachers don't give a damn about their students. Professor Brown is not only offensive to Jack, with no justification, but he makes impossible demands. If he'd helped Jack with his paper in the first place, maybe Jack would have received a passing grade. To expect Jack to hand in an acceptable paper in twenty-four hours is impossible and unjust.

Mary Ann Smith: Professor Brown has placed Jack in a situation which has no reasonable answer. He did not want to help Jack and yet demanded a better paper. Trapped, Jack must resort to cheating. This is ironic, since a teacher is supposed to represent learning.

Raphael Alvarez: Professor Brown appears as a person who doesn't care for his students or his profession and who teaches only for the money. His attitude is as mercenary as Victor's, but, since he's a teacher, his attitude is more hypocritical.

Summary: The people who condemn Professor Brown strongly believe

_____

Victor

Margo Drohan: Since he had already agreed on a fee, it is not right for Victor to exploit the situation and ask Jack for double the amount. He is using another person's unfortunate position for personal gain. Victor is a greedy blackmailer, and there's nothing worse than that.

Denise Generale: Victor shouldn't have agreed to help Jack with the paper. Though he is not breaking the law by writing the paper, he is helping Jack to violate the rules of the college and, unlike Jack, he has no desperate need to do so. If he's such a good writer, he should turn his talent to a legitimate business and get a decent job.

Chris Pappas: Victor has made a deal with Jack and has reneged on this arrangement in an underhanded way. He is a shake-down artist.

Harry Murphy: Victor makes his final ultimatum to Jack of his own free will; he doesn't have to do it. Unlike the other characters, he has no emotional involvement in the situation. He is intentionally mean and cruel when he asks for that money.

Tom Natoli: Victor is a criminal. He has agreed to do the work for a set fee through a verbal contract with Jack. He goes back on his word in the end, all for money (which, as everyone knows, is the root of all evil anyway), when he blackmails Jack.

Summary: The people who condemn Victor strongly believe _____
_____

ASSIGNMENT 13

All the words in the following list are in common use and have either more than one usual meaning or a meaning that can be interpreted both favorably and unfavorably. Choose one word from the list as the topic for a definition essay.

shrewd	peace	passionate
curiosity	humility	criticism
capitalism	clever	imagination
progress	ordinary	impetuous
eccentric	power	jealousy
obedience	cautious	self-interest
habit	welfare	respectable
politician	solitude	conservative
prejudice	dominance	small
ambition	culture	workman
credit	sentimental	smooth
genius	revolution	experience
duty	aggression	cheap
ladylike	glamorous	privilege
failure	passive	intrigue
poverty	failure	fashion
royalty	discipline	enthusiast
competition	self-confidence	smart
sophisticated	power	

Clarify your own definition of the word by writing down your ideas about its meaning. Then interview five or six people, or as many as you need, to get a variety of reactions. Your purpose is to become aware of several ways of using your word. You are to take careful and complete notes of each reaction that you receive. As you note reactions, consider how the meaning of the word changes and try to isolate the different circumstances and usages which cause these variations. Be alert, for example, for a discrepancy between the *ideal* meaning of the word and its *practical* application in daily life. If one person's reaction is merely an echo of something that you already have in your notes, you may summarize the second response more briefly; but keep an accurate record of who (and how many) said what. Although your notes for each source may run only a paragraph or two, plan to use a separate sheet for each person. Your notes should include not only a summary of each reaction, but, if possible, also a few quotations. If someone suggests a good definition or uses the word in an interesting way, try to record his exact words; read the quotation back to the speaker to make sure that what you have quoted is what he meant to say; and put quotation marks around the direct quotation. Make sure that the names of all your sources are accurately spelled. *Your notes should be handed in with your completed essay.*

Each person should be asked the following questions:

1. What do you think X means? Has it any other meanings that you know of?
2. How would you use this word in a sentence? (Pay special attention to the way in which the word gets used, and note down the differences. Two people might say that a word means the same thing, and yet use it differently.)
3. Is this a positive word or a negative word to use? In what situation could it possibly have a favorable or unfavorable connotation?

In listening to the answers to these questions, do not hesitate to ask, "What do you mean?" It may be necessary to make people think hard about a word that they use casually.

An analysis of your notes should result in a tentative chart of possible meanings and contexts. First, explain the most common meaning attributed to the word, according to your sources. Be sure to cite different examples of this prevalent usage. Then, in successive paragraphs, review the other connotations, favorable and unfavorable, making sure always to try to trace the relationships and common contexts among the different meanings. With your overview of all the variations of meaning, you are in an excellent position to observe and explain what the worst and the best connotations of the word have in common. There is no set length for this essay. Contents and organization are governed entirely by the kind and extent of the material in your notes.

ASSIGNMENT 14

Choose a topic from the list below or think of a question that might stimulate a wide range of responses, and submit the question for your teacher's approval. (Try to avoid political issues and very controversial subjects. You want a topic in which everyone you interview can take an interest, without becoming intensely partisan.)

Suggestions for Topics

Should wives get paid for housework?

Is jealousy a healthy sign in a relationship, or is it always destructive?

Should husbands be the decision-makers?

Should boys play with dolls?

Is "traditional" dating still desirable in the eighties?

If you could be reborn, would you change your sex?

Does it matter whether an elementary school child has a male or female teacher?

Is there a right age to get married?

What are the ingredients for a lasting marriage in the eighties?

Are there any dangers in family "togetherness"?

Should children be given the same first names as their parents?

Is it better to keep a friend by not speaking your mind or risk losing a friend by honesty?

What should a child of (pick an age) be told about death?

Is it alienating to live in a large city?

Is there anything really wrong with being a materialist?

How should "citizenship" be taught in the schools?

How should the commandment "honor thy parents" be put into practice today?

What, if anything, is wrong with the nuclear family?

Are students forced to specialize too soon in their college experience?

Should schools stay in session all year round?

Should citizens have to pay a fine for not voting?

Should movies have a rating system?

Should grade-school students be left back?

Once your topic is decided (and, if necessary, approved by your teacher), interview at least five or six people, or as many as you need to get a variety of reactions. (Some of your sources should be students in your class.) Your purpose is to learn about several ways of looking at the topic, not to argue, but to exchange views. If you wish, use the following format for conducting each interview:

Name: (first and last: check the spelling!)

Do you think . . . . ?

Why do you think so? What are some of your reasons? [later] Are there any other reasons?

Why do you think people who take the opposite view would do
so?

Do any examples come to your mind to illustrate . . . . ?

Quotation:

Take careful and complete notes of the comments that you receive. (You
will be expected to hand in all your notes, in their original form, with
your completed essay.) Keep a separate sheet for each person. If one of
your sources says something that sounds worth quoting, write down the
exact words; read them back to make sure that what you have quoted
is what the speaker meant to say; then put quotation marks around the
direct quotation. Otherwise use summary or paraphrase. Do not hesitate
to ask, "What do you mean?" or "Is this what I heard you say?" or "How
does that fit in with what you said just before?"

Make a chart of ideas from your notes and arrange the points in a
sequence of your choice. Then write an essay that presents the full range
of opinion, paraphrasing and, if desirable, quoting from representative
sources.

ASSIGNMENT 15

Read "The Art of Implying More than You Say." Then, use the twelve
statements that follow as the basis for a synthesis essay. These statements
were written by students in response to the question "Is advertising
mainly harmful or mainly beneficial to the average person?" Analyze each
statement; label each kind of reason; and organize all the labels in a chart.
Then write an essay that presents the full range of opinion, paraphrasing
and, if desirable, quoting from representative sources.

THE ART OF IMPLYING MORE THAN YOU SAY

MooMoo Milk tastes great. Keep your family healthy. Buy MooMoo Milk.
According to the above "commercial," does MooMoo Milk keep your
family healthy? If you answered yes, you're probably in the majority, but
you're wrong.

This is just one way advertisers make implied claims about their products that may not be true. The commercial doesn't say directly that
MooMoo Milk keeps your family healthy, but psycholinguistic studies
show that most people would get that impression. Recent research by
Richard Harris of Kansas State University confirms that people don't
discriminate between what is directly stated and what is implied. He
gives other examples of ways in which consumers are misled by lin-
guistic manipulation:

• The use of hedge words that weaken the statement, such as "Knock-
out capsules *may* relieve tension."

- Using comparison adjectives that give no comparison, such as "Chore gives you whiter wash." The statement is undeniably true because it could be completed with any phrase, such as, "than washing with coal dust."
- Inadequate or incomplete reporting of survey or test results.
- Using a negative question, which implies an affirmative answer: "Isn't quality the most important thing to consider in buying aspirin?" The answer might very well be no, but the assumption is yes.
- The use of expressions such as "hospital-tested" or "doctor-tested" that give little information but lend an air of scientific respectability.

Harris tested people's responses to these misleading techniques. One hundred eighty students listened to tapes of twenty mock commercials of the type frequently heard on radio and television. They heard one of two versions of each commercial containing either implied claims, or only directly asserted claims. They then were asked to decide, based on what they heard in the commercials, whether certain statements about the commercials were true, false, or impossible to judge. Half the students in both groups were given an example of an implied claim and were specifically warned not to interpret such claims as asserted ones.

The students correctly rated an average of eight out of ten of the asserted statements as true. But the students also judged seven of the implied claims as true. Even students who had been warned about implied claims rated more than half of them as true. Harris notes that the Federal Trade Commission, which regulates advertising on radio and television, has not defined a clear legal status for implied claims. What constitutes deceptive advertising is complex, and though the intent to deceive is clearly prohibited, it is difficult to substantiate.

Sherida Bush, *Psychology Today*, May 1977

Alice Dowe: I think that the average citizen gains from advertising because there are so many people who can't get out of the house to do their shopping and therefore use the phone as a means of buying things. Although sometimes we wish there weren't any commercials because we're watching a good movie, this would be a disadvantage to the people I've already mentioned and, secondly, it would be a disadvantage to the person trying to sell his or her product.

Iris Dougherty: The average citizen, on the whole, gains more advantages from advertising. Many people do not have the time to read the advertisements in the papers. They would miss out on many money-saving values, if it weren't for television advertisements. Some of these people may be old, sick and unable to move around physically. Therefore, they must rely on television and other means of advertising.

Pastor Gonzalez: The use of the communications media by manufacturers to promote sales is an intrusion and a financial detriment to all citizens. We, as citizens and consumers, are daily confronted with advertisements that claim to make one feel good, sexy, more masculine, feminine, or happier. As a matter of fact, I've had the opportunity to be involved in household-products claims substantiations. Only tests with favorable results aimed at specific consumer weaknesses were employed for the advertisements. In addition, the costs of proving and producing the advertisements are passed on to the consumer by way of higher prices on the shelf and/or reduction of active ingredients in the product.

Charles Goodman: I think that citizens benefit from advertising, because competition for your money is the goal of advertising. The company must show a better product than its competitor. The better product will get the attention of the consumers.

Chang Kee: I think that there are public disadvantages resulting from advertising. Primarily, the effect of the commercials is too persuasive. We tend to buy a certain product after seeing it on TV. Most important, advertising does harm children. They are sold sugared cereals and foods that result in tooth decay and lead to poor nutritional habits. These children have not learned to analyze advertising claims rationally, and thus they accept the claims made by the commercials.

Molly Martin: I believe advertising is an advantage to the public because of the information given out about the products. It makes it easier for us to decide personally what products will satisfy our individual needs. We all know about false advertising. But we still flock to various stores to buy that new product that we saw on TV. I'm very partial to advertising. I like reading about products and watching them on commercials. Advertising is as American as apple pie. It helps keep the economy alive and thriving and helps to keep the employment rate high. It takes thousands of people to produce and deliver products. I hope that television channels never cut out commercial advertising.

George Montespano: I strongly feel that I am at a disadvantage when I read advertisements in newspapers or watch them on television. They are mostly misleading and lack a lot of information that consumers should be aware of. A majority of us are being victimized by false advertising. Commercials make fools out of viewers by showing people who act as if they have the mentality of six-year-olds; they try to make you believe that each product is God's gift to humanity. Because commercials make things look so beautiful, people end up buying things that they don't really need and will never use—or at least use so little that it won't be worth sacrificing some vital necessity in order to get it. Sometimes, people will throw out a perfectly good article just because advertising put ideas in their heads. The whole purpose of commercials is to make money for the sponsors, not to help the consumer.

Carolyn Neilson: There are many disadvantages in advertising, but the one that I want to focus on is what's called "subliminal" advertising. This method appeals to the person's subconscious in order to persuade him to buy a certain item. For example, in liquor ads, there can often be found (under close scrutiny), a word or image associated with sex. Since sex is associated with pleasure, this message is intentionally directed to the person's subconscious mind, and the product appeals to him. He will go out and purchase the item without ever having tried it before. In this sense, advertising is not only a definite social disadvantage, but a dangerous one, because it is playing games with people's minds. Ads create a need for the product; manufacturers should instead create products to fill our genuine needs.

Allan Smith: Advertising promotes the marketing of either worthless items or falsely represented ones. This clever marketing is within the bounds of the law. For example, an electric can opener is hardly a necessity. But this item is pushed in advertising campaigns as a must for any household. And the latest model cars are advertised as if each year brings an entirely different invention. In fact, nothing is different except for a few minor exterior changes. Further, it is for these reasons that television, as the major vehicle of mass advertising, should be noncommercial. The absence of commercial television's assault on the senses would greatly change American society. For one thing, it would save us billions of dollars spent for worthless purchases.

Dean Torelli: Many people wouldn't even know that a certain product existed if it weren't for advertisements. The only thing people have to watch out for is being taken. Many ads can con people into buying a certain product. But, to the smart consumer, advertising is a very helpful way to find out what products are around, how good they are, and where to buy them.

Joann Transom: The average citizen gains from advertising, because he is made aware of the new, as well as the existing, products available in the market-place—products designed to make life easier or more comfortable. Super-market and department store ads enable people to comparison shop before actually entering a store. Advertising isn't confined to product information alone. Services to the general public are advertised, and ads concerning voter registration, the welfare program, and assistance for senior citizens inform people how and where to apply for these services.

Gary Williams: Advertising shows how competitive we are. Competition creates a tremendous amount of drive and incentive to strive for the best. When an ad achieves the goal of successfully selling a product, and when the product is fit for the public to enjoy, then you have something that everyone—the manufacturer and advertiser on down to the buyer—profits from. Ads and commercials are definitely good for business.

ASSIGNMENT 16

Read "Competency Tests in Basic Skills Cost Few Pupils Their Diplomas," and write a brief summary of its main idea. Next consider the arguments for and against the administration of minimum competency tests, as well as any other relevant circumstances that the author of the article has not touched upon. Then write a paragraph of three to five sentences in which you argue for or against testing for minimum competency in basic skills. Submit your summary and paragraph to your teacher.

The teacher will make copies of all the statements by members of your class. Label and categorize each person's response, make a chart of the labels, and write a synthesis essay presenting a well-rounded examination of the issue and its implications.

COMPETENCY TESTS IN BASIC SKILLS COST FEW PUPILS THEIR DIPLOMAS

BAKERSFIELD, Calif.—Six years ago officials of the Kern High School District, concerned about declining student achievement, installed one of the nation's first minimum-competency testing programs.

After testing 300 local workers to determine the levels of skills needed to get and hold a job, the district developed reading and mathematics tests based on the results and decreed that, beginning in 1976, no one could receive a high school diploma without passing the two tests.

The program has proved to be one of the most popular steps ever taken by the 18,000-student school district in this oil and farming community north of Los Angeles. But whether it has achieved its stated purpose of improved student performance is an open question, a question not fully answered in other districts either as the trend toward such tests has spread nationwide.

Last June's high school graduates here scored no higher on the tests than did the class of 1975. Last year Bakersfield withheld diplomas from only four out of 3,300 seniors because of the tests, in a pattern noted elsewhere as well.

"Everyone seems to feel good about the program," said James Fillbrandt, the principal of Bakersfield High School, who helped design the program. "But it doesn't seem to make much difference."

In the last four years, the movement for what educators term minimum competency programs has become the most powerful new force in American elementary and secondary education. According to Christopher Pipho of the Education Commission of the States, at least 37 states have adopted minimum competency programs, which vary widely in the level of the skills tested and the amount of remedial help required for students who fail the tests.

All the exams now test very basic skills that most students have when the enter high school. As a result of protests that its tests were too easy, New York State will institute in 1981 the first testing of skills not normally taught until high school.

Districts that have had such programs for several years report that they have improved the morale of many teachers, shaken some students out of academic lethargy and led to an infusion of millions of new state dollars into public school budgets for remedial programs.

"The competency program has made all of us sit down and think through what our goals are and what we are doing to meet them," said Susan Storms, a physical sciences teacher at Roosevelt High School in Portland, Ore., which had one of the earliest programs.

On the other hand, representatives of these districts say that virtually no students are being denied diplomas because of the tests, and they produce only mixed evidence that they have improved overall student learning. Critics frequently complain that the remedial programs to help students pass the tests have short-lived effects.

Often, teachers and other educators—many of whom opposed the adoption of minimum competency programs—have found ways to get students over the new graduation hurdles without major changes in either academic methods or student achievement.

"We have a little system going," said Dorothy Wood, a mathematics teacher at Bakersfield High School who helped develop the district's competency program. "We send students over to a 'math clinic' or a 'math lab,' where an aide gives them worksheets for each of the 15 objectives. She sits down with the kid and has him do some exercises, and then she gives him a little test and checks him off."

"We run them through the machine, and they come out knowing about the same amount as when they went in," she continued. "The question is not whether they know math, but whether they will graduate."

In virtually every state, the pressure for minimum competency has come from outside the academic community, especially from potential employers. Oregon, for example, developed one of the first statewide programs after a series of public hearings revealed a widespread belief that the high school diploma had lost its credibility.

"They said, 'A high school graduate comes to work for us, and he can't even read the safety signs in the shop,'" recalled W. R. Nance of the Oregon Department of Education.

Seventeen states, including New York, now require students to pass statewide tests in basic skills to receive a high school diploma. Others, including New Jersey and Connecticut, have instead established standards for various grade levels and give remedial help to students who fall short.

The effect of such statewide programs is just beginning to be felt, because most of the earlier minimum competency programs were started by individual school districts.

Their most conspicuous result is that they cost few students a high school diploma.

In Denver, for example, where a program has been in effect for 17 years, 1 to 3 percent of each year's senior class does not graduate because of the tests. At Westside High School in Omaha, only four out of 765 seniors failed the required tests in 1977.

Florida attracted considerable national publicity last year when a substantial percentage of juniors failed its new tests, but officials expect that when the students take the tests again this year only about 5 percent will fail.

One exception is New York City, where about 15 percent of this year's senior class had not completed the state's new reading and mathematics tests last month.

The other conspicuous feature of existing minimum competency programs is the lack of any definitive data showing that they are improving student achievement.

The most promising figures come from Florida, where 36 percent of the juniors failed the new communications test last year and 8 percent failed the math exam; the figures this year are 26 percent and 3 percent. "This is a dramatic improvement, and we are delighted," said Nan Buchanan, spokesman for the Florida Department of Education.

In Gary, Ind., which adopted reading and math tests for graduation in 1977, scores rose the first year but dropped back last year. Gordon McAndrew, the superintendent of schools, said he found comfort in the fact that the number of graduates reading below the sixth-grade level fell from 10 percent to 6 percent since the minimum competency program was established. But he added, "I wouldn't want to make any definitive judgment based on these figures."

In Berea, Ohio, a suburb of Cleveland, the number of eighth graders scoring at the level of high school proficiency has risen from 74 to 81 percent in reading and from 74 to 84 percent in math.

"The results are extremely impressive," said Dean Kelly, assistant superintendent of schools. "But I can't tell you the cause. Maybe it's just because we—parents, students and teachers—are taking school much more seriously now."

Interviews around the country suggested that minimum competency programs were popular with the public and that educators now believe that they have had some positive effects.

For example, Marzine Donaldson, a 17-year-old senior at Coral Gables High School in Florida, said, "It made us work harder."

Minimum competency programs have focused public attention on basic education, and in some cases have increased parental involvement in their children's education. "I haven't had to go to the parents," said Miss Storms, the science teacher in Portland, Ore. "Instead, they've been calling me. I think it's great."

Perhaps most important, teachers report that the programs have sharpened their professional objectives. "Whereas in the past kids who got past the 10th grade without basic skills were left to drift," said Mr. Fillbrandt in Bakersfield, "we now have remedial programs in reading and math and will soon have them in writing at the 11th grade."

Educators in Florida and elsewhere argue that the reason the tests cost few students their diplomas is that remedial programs identify weaknesses and correct them. Others, however, fear that the gains do not last very long after the competency tests.

In Bakersfield, for example, students who had passed all the math tests in 1976 and 1977 were retested last year, and only one in 10 passed them all again. The average student passed 10 of the 15 tests.

"The kids bone up and then forget," said Miss Wood. "The argument for keeping the tests is that at least they have learned it once, and perhaps it will come back when they need it."

Another frequent comment is that most students pass the tests primarily because the schools are under enormous public pressure to see that the students do so. "Schools work terribly hard to make sure nobody fails," said Robert Frahm, a Racine, Wis., journalist who recently completed a study of minimum competency programs for the Ford Foundation. "Teachers hound kids until they pass, and almost anyone can pass this kind of test if he takes it enough."

Mr. Fillbrandt said the Bakersfield program had probably benefited the more competent students who passed the tests after failing the first time around, but added that, below this level, the program had little discernible effect.

The main reason, he suggested, is that the program has not forced schools to make any major changes in teaching strategies.

"There's one huge assumption that we've been making—that teachers and students are highly susceptible to modification," he said. "But we have a highly simplistic view of change."

Edward B. Fiske, *New York Times*, 19 March 1979

ASSIGNMENT 17

Carefully read the following examples of embarrassing situations.

1. One day, I was traveling on a public bus filled with young children on their way home from school. One of the kids, a boy of about eleven years, used an indecent word. I was very embarrassed, mostly because of his age and because of the elderly people who were also riding the bus.
2. I once took a vacation trip with several acquaintances. When we boarded the bus, the husband of one of these acquaintances offered to help me with my baggage and did several other things to make me comfortable. Since he was a colleague of my husband, I accepted his help and talked to him throughout the trip. When we reached our destination, one of his children became ill. I approached the man's wife and asked if I could help in any way. She stared at me coldly and said that she could manage without my services. I walked away feeling embarrassed and rejected. She clearly thought that her husband had been too attentive.
3. When I was a child, my parents used to lie about my age in order to get me into the movies at half-price. I was dreadfully embarrassed every time they did this, since I was sure that we'd be caught.
4. As my husband and I were on the way to the supermarket, he started talking loudly. He had been drinking and he just wanted someone to yell at, so he chose me. Everyone that walked by stopped and looked at me as he kept on yelling and cursing and calling me all kinds of names. He kept this up until we got home, when we fought it out.
5. I tend to feel some embarrassment whenever anyone compliments me. Somehow, if a friend comments on my clothes or my general

appearance, I get nervous. It's almost as if I'm worried that next time I won't look as good.

6. When I was thirteen years old, I was taken to the doctor by my mother because I had an extremely high temperature. I was scared and crying, but finally relaxed a bit when I went into his office. But when the doctor asked me to lie on the couch and remove my clothing, I was so embarrassed that I ran and hid in the corner of the room. It took my mother and the nurse some time before they could get me to undress.

7. One of the situations that cause me great embarrassment is forgetting someone else's name. This usually happens in the street, when I hear my name called by someone who clearly expects me to recognize him or her. It's not so bad when it's just the name I forget; but sometimes I don't even recognize the face!

8. I sometimes get embarrassed after a conversation, if the topic under discussion has been quite foreign to me. Because I don't want to seem ignorant, I tend to nod my head in agreement or to acknowledge that I understand. Once launched into this pretense, I find it difficult to retreat. Often I get away with it, but all the while I have felt inwardly that my facade of familiarity was transparent. If I only could say, "I really don't know about that."

9. I have felt acute embarrassment in the supermarket when I have unloaded a brimming shopping cart onto the counter and, after the cashier has checked them all out, I discover that I have less money than groceries. The people behind me on line usually whisper and shuffle their feet and look irritated, and all I want is to disappear into the ground.

Now, think of a few occasions when you have felt truly embarrassed, and be prepared to write a brief paragraph describing an embarrassing situation somewhat different from those already on the list.

Once you have been given a dittoed sheet with the additional examples contributed by your classmates, analyze all of the situations in both lists, distinguishing each example from previous ones; no two instances will be alike in every respect. Your object is to analyze each situation and explain why it proved so embarrassing. Ask yourself about motives, intentions, and responsibilities. Examine the circumstances in which each incident took place; for example, consider the role of onlookers (or the "audience"). Consider also the basic human qualities that seem to be involved in the causes and the consequences of embarrassing actions. Then label and categorize each anecdote, making a chart of your categories, and prepare to write your essay.

In your essay, support each of your topic sentences by describing some of the anecdotes from your list. Make sure that you explain how each example relates to the main idea being discussed. Also make sure that each illustration is clear to your reader (who, you should assume, has not seen the original list).

Either at the beginning or the end of your essay, try to present a complete definition of embarrassment, encompassing the ideas contained in the categories that you have established.

ASSIGNMENT 18

The thirteen situations briefly described below illustrate different ways in which information can be censored or suppressed. Read through them rapidly.

1. An act of censorship that may be justifiable is one which censors the obscenities that people sometimes say on television talk shows. Is it really necessary to have to curse in order to make a joke funny?

2. The friends and relatives of an extremely sick person might wish to remove all medical encyclopedias from the household to prevent the patient from learning about his disease before the doctors are ready to inform him.

3. Preventing jurors from discussing a case that is being tried before them is usually considered justifiable because they might otherwise be influenced by the opinions of others, which might result in pre-judgment of the defendant.

4. During World War II, a commonly heard phrase was "a slip of the lip can sink a ship." Letters from sailors overseas were read to eliminate any trace of location or dates. If the enemy had no knowledge of where or when a military ship was going, the chances of the ship arriving at its destination were more certain.

5. Aware that certain stock market figures (or company reports) do not look promising, one person attempts to suppress that information so that his friend will not dispose of his holdings, and the first person can therefore sell at a profit.

6. The motion picture ratings of all movies are examples of a kind of censorship designed to protect children from listening to profane and vulgar language and from seeing explicit sex and violence.

7. A writing teacher, assigning an important essay, forbids her class to use outside readings in the preparation of the assignment.

8. When the *New York Times* obtained copies of the secret *Pentagon Papers*, an account of the U.S. involvement in Indochina, and began to publish them, the Justice Department obtained a temporary restraining order against further publication, arguing that the interests of the country would suffer "immediate and irreparable harm."

9. In Spain, actors were prevented from putting on a scene from a play called *Equus* in which there is a naked couple. Although no one in

the audience would have been forced to see the play, the government nevertheless prohibited that scene because of nudity.

10. A mother thinks it best for her young son to become a doctor, despite the boy's preference for athletics. She prevents her son from reading the sports pages at home and forbids him to play on the school teams. She believes that medicine is a more worthwhile and prestigious career than sports.

11. A cigarette company tries to persuade a magazine not to publish a new survey documenting the ill effects of smoking.

12. Some groups are lobbying to prevent the showing of X-rated films on cable television; they argue that small children might watch these movies without their parents' knowledge.

13. The commentator on a highly respected television news show has come upon information concerning the survival of a newly formed nation that is considered extremely sensitive by his network. Although the commentator feels obliged to inform his viewing audience, he is told by his superiors not to divulge any of this information at that time, or the new country will surely suffer.

Write an essay that determines appropriate limits for the public dissemination of information. Can certain facts, performances, and programs be "censored" without excessively curtailing the liberties of each citizen? In planning your essay, do not settle for dividing the examples into justifiable and unjustifiable forms of censorship. Instead, ask yourself these questions about each situation: Who will benefit? Who is being protected, and from what? Or you might ask questions about the political consequences of suppressing information: Do we invariably have a right to freedom of choice? Should we ever be deprived of the freedom to form opinions, communicate information, and watch the entertainment that we prefer? When, and why? Choose the questions that you wish to ask, and then ask them consistently as you think about and analyze each example on the list.

As you explore each one, decide whether, in your opinion, suppressing this information or imposing this censorship is justified—and why. Take notes to record your decision and your reasons in each case or to indicate your doubt if you cannot decide. As you analyze each instance, you will be engaging in three overlapping operations:

A. *interpreting* each situation;
B. starting to establish some common denominators for *categorizing* the entire group;
C. *evaluating* the various examples in order to develop your own definition of acceptable censorship and suppression of information.

Before beginning to write, make a chart of your categories. The paragraphs in your essay should form a series of generalizations characterizing acceptable and unacceptable systems of censorship. For your reader's information, briefly paraphrase—not just refer to or quote from—each situation that you discuss. (If necessary, add your own examples to those already on the list.) Use your paraphrased descriptions to support the topic sentences of your paragraphs.

ASSIGNMENT 19

Organize and complete a comparison of the three reviews of *M*A*S*H*, based on your answers to the questions in Exercise 38.

or

Write a comparison of three reviews of another film. Your first concern should be the reactions of the critics, not your own opinion of the work; you are not expected to write a review yourself, but to analyze and contrast each critic's view of the film. Try to describe the distinctive way in which each conceives of the film; each will have perceived a somewhat different film and will have a different understanding of what it signifies.

Use the *Readers' Guide to Periodical Literature* and the *Times Index* to locate possible reviews. (If you are unfamiliar with these resources, consult a librarian or Chapter 6.) For films before 1970, you can consult James Salem's *A Guide to Critical Reviews*. Don't commit yourself to a specific film until you have seen a sampling of reviews; if they are all very similar in their criticisms or all very short, choose a different subject. If you have doubts about the reviews' suitability, let your teacher see a set of copies. Be prepared to hand in a full set of the reviews with your completed essay.

EXERCISE 41

Read the following thirteen stories about the Depression. Each is a transcript of an orally transmitted reminiscence.

1. Choose the stories that you would like to include in a collection recording Depression life. Plan to work with at least ten.
2. Decide on an overall principle to govern the sequence; nothing about the order should be random or accidental. Then prepare a sheet containing: a) a statement of your principle of arrangement; b) a sentence or two for each story (in their new order), explaining the reason for its being next.
3. Write a paragraph or two summarizing what you think the reader will have learned about the Depression after reading

your set of stories. (As this summary would be placed at the end of your anthology, you can assume that the reader has already read the stories.)

1.   Aunt Bessie had worked hard for eight years putting money in the bank, a little every week. Jim, her husband, had died nearly nine years earlier, and after the money she received for the insurance was gone, she found it was necessary for her to go to work to support her family of five children.

It wasn't easy, she recalls, to work as a domestic all day and then to come home to do the same thing at night. Some nights she didn't get to bed until one o'clock in the morning. She didn't mind because at least she was working, and so many people were unemployed. She knew that by saving her money in the bank, if she ever lost her job, she would have enough saved to last her for a while. There were nearly nine hundred dollars in that bank.

On her job she heard talk of stock prices falling and some people withdrawing money from their accounts at the banks, but the day they announced the banks were closed, "I couldn't believe it. I went down to the bank and the streets were crowded; and there was a sign on the door saying 'closed by order of the Federal Government.' I fainted right there on the street. It was the greatest shock of my life; I'll never forget it. I'll remember that day as long as I live."

2.   In 1930, Mrs. James, a thirty-year-old widow who had three children to support, felt lucky to be a wage earner with the incredible salary of twenty-five cents an hour.

The hardships seemed to multiply; food was a luxury; shoes were worn far beyond normal wear; the cold-water flat was injurious to her health. But the great cooperation between families turned the hardships into a beautiful memory. Although she did not have much money, she was able to lend a dollar or two to people who had no job, while others gave her clothes which she could not afford to buy.

Her sympathetic employer asked her to accept a cut in salary, and Mrs. James often worked overtime to keep his business in operation. Workers who had cars drove each other every day, and all contributed to the cost of fuel.

According to Mrs. James, today most workers get fantastically high salaries, and everyone's standard of living has been very elevated since the Depression. Mrs. James insists that closeness between people is gone, and, in spite of the hardships of the Depression, people then felt safer and less isolated than any city-dweller can possibly feel today.

3.   Ever heard of a successful person during the Great Depression? Well, I have, and I had the opportunity of interviewing him. His name is Herman Peck, and he was rather fortunate during that unfortunate period in time. He owned and ran a tailor shop on 54th Street between 5th and 6th Avenues in New York City. Since the shop had been es-

tablished in 1907, it held on to its regular customers. Mr. Peck was able to keep right on selling made-to-order tailored suits for ladies and gentlemen, because of his customers' wealth. He catered to people like the Rockefellers, Woolworths, and many others. This is not to say that Mr. Peck was living it up, but the good days outnumbered the bad ones. It balanced out and he was able to hold onto his four employees.

Although he personally didn't suffer, he remembers having handed out pennies to pleading and outstretched hands before him. There was nothing else that he could do for them.

4.   Boy, God bless you, do you know how it was for a black family living in those days? My husband lost his job and we did not have enough savings to last us for a month. We managed to feed on the smallest amount of food until our savings completely ran out. In the morning, my husband and I drank hot water, instead of coffee or tea, sometimes without bread, until my husband left to go out to look for work or food. If he came home with food, we would have a meal; if not, we boiled onions and ate that.

On one occasion, we, as well as our neighbors, didn't have anything to eat for about two days. A few friends got together and stole some food from a market. That was the only time during the Depression that we had a good meal.

Also, we kept moving from one house to another whenever the landlord threatened that he would hurt us if we didn't pay our rent. We didn't pay the rent because we didn't have the money.

During the winter, we used to pray for snow, which enabled my husband to collect $3.00 from the city after shoveling snow all day. Don't forget that you had to be selected before you could earn that money. We prayed that we would never see another such winter during the remaining years of our lives.

5.   Although, in 1935, my grandfather had two jobs, he barely had enough to pay the rent and buy food for his family. He worked as a dishwasher and sold apples; but as long as there was food on the table, he was content. He considered himself lucky, as most of his friends were spending their afternoons standing in unbelievably long lines for food.

On Christmas morning, my mother and two aunts anxiously got up to open their presents. They usually got something extra-special, even if it wasn't very expensive. However, to their disappointment, the gifts they unwrapped were the cheapest kind of toy.

In fact, my grandfather had saved a few extra dollars to buy gifts, but he had seen a sight that made him spend his money on some other people. One day when he was coming home from work, he saw his next-door neighbor looking for food in the fly-infested garbage cans. She explained to my grandfather that her husband was sick and that her children were hungry. The next week, which was Christmas week, he had gone out and bought her children presents with most of what he'd saved. He also bought them food to put on the table at Christmas.

On Christmas morning, as grandfather was explaining to his daughters why Santa had few toys that year, their neighbor burst through the door with tears of happiness and gratitude. Realizing who Santa really was, the family all sat down to a big Christmas dinner and said a prayer of thanks.

6.   My father worked as a carpenter, while mother stayed at home taking care of our farm that consisted of six cows, four goats, and about a dozen hens. My parents ran a very small business of farm foods. The cows and goats supplied milk and the hens supplied eggs which were sold.

My father would leave for work very early in the morning and return late in the evening—a very tired and depressed man. Mother often consoled him. When he returned home from work, his dinner would be awaiting him. My little sister and I would hurry over to his side, take off his shoes, pat his forehead, and kiss him gently on the cheek. We would then receive a broad smile and a tender hug from Daddy.

After dinner, my parents would sit together outside on the porch, discussing many topics, among which would be the day's work. Daddy usually received a full day's work, but it was not every day that my mother managed to sell all of the farm produce. However, the milk always sold, because the villagers needed some for their babies, and we were the only folks in the village who sold milk and eggs. But the eggs sold more slowly, leaving us with excess eggs from day to day, which we ate for breakfast.

The Depression worsened for my family during 1933–1934. Rainfall was not as heavy as it had been in the past, and there was a drought of seven months, causing the grass to wither and die. Animals died from lack of food and water.

To sum up, I would like to say that the Depression was a time of great suffering and hardship for almost every person that I knew.

7.   In 1932, when Fred was a young man, he lost a good job at a Brooklyn garage serving as a mechanic's helper. Because the country was in the midst of a monstrous depression, Fred found himself walking the streets of midtown Manhattan every day in search of a job. One morning as he was making his usual rounds of office buildings, his eye caught a showroom displaying new Cadillacs. Fred entered the showroom and told a salesman that he wished to speak to the manager. Because the alert salesman thought that Fred might possibly be interested in purchasing a car, he promptly went into a charming sales pitch. Fred politely informed the salesman that he was not interested in buying a car, and again requested to speak to the manager. After waiting about twenty minutes, Fred was approached by a balding, middle-aged man, who immediately asked him what he wanted. Fred asked him if he'd made any car sales so far that morning. The manager uncomfortably replied that he hadn't. Fred then inquired how he ex-

pected to sell any cars with such dirty and dull-looking cars as the ones on display in his showroom. The manager was completely taken aback and stared incredulously at Fred for several seconds. On finally regaining his composure, the manager said: "Young man, you certainly have a hell of a nerve saying something like that to me. Just who do you think you are, anyway?" Fred, not once removing his jet black eyes from the manager, replied: "Sir, I don't have a lot of nerve. I need a job badly. To answer your second question, my name is Wilfred Bains." Fred promptly advised the manager that he would wash and polish all eight cars in the showroom. The man agreed.

Fred spent the entire day working on the cars. After he'd finally completed the job, he called the manager over to inspect the gleaming Cadillacs. The manager, who broke into a broad smile, was extremely pleased. He handed Fred a crisp ten-dollar bill. No smile, however, crossed Fred's face as he accepted the money. He was silently wondering how long it would take him to land a permanent job. The road ahead certainly didn't look too bright.

8. The first communion is a very important event for Catholic families. As the time drew near for my mother's first communion, she began to panic. Where would her family get the money for the clothes that she needed? She dared not ask her father, because he was always complaining about making ends meet. She thought, too, that her father's complaints were just, because he was supporting seven people on fifteen dollars a week.

My mother wanted desperately to march with her classmates in a white dress, but felt that she just could not ask her father for one. Finally, she gathered up enough courage to approach her mother about the clothes. Much to her surprise, her mother had saved up eight dollars for her to buy the white material for the big day.

The day finally arrived, and my mother had another surprise. Her father gave her a box all wrapped up and with her name on it. When she opened it, she found a pair of white shoes and a beautiful veil.

My mother says that, whenever she is experiencing money problems, this incident always comes back to her. Somehow, thinking of her first communion always makes her happy.

9. Unemployment was at its peak and factories, which a few months before had accommodated a permanent work force of hundreds, had to close their doors. Production was at a standstill. The result was vandalism, looting, and rioting, and man's most basic and animalistic force came to the surface—survival of the fittest. People stole from family, friends, neighbors, and strangers alike. Pride and morals were at their lowest, and vanity, self-esteem, and scruples had to be put aside until this crisis blew over. I remember a lady who lived in the apartment next to ours, whom we called Miss Prim, because of her prim and proper attitude. During good times, Miss Prim would have stood there and melted into the ground if her grocery bag burst in the street; she'd have done anything rather than have people see her

picking up food from the streets. Needless to say, during the Depression, things changed. I personally remember Miss Prim fighting to maintain her position in the bread lines where free soup and bread were being handed out on the street corners.

To help counteract the crisis, the government instituted work programs such as the WPA and TVA. Farmers were given subsidies to cultivate crops to be sold locally, and never have there been more backyard food gardens. Children worked for pennies and everybody did any type of work, no matter how degrading or low in salary. Mental hospitals were throbbing with business, and the police suicide prevention squad worked around the clock as many people thought it better to die than face almost certain destitution.

To this day, some say that we have not fully recovered from the after-effects of the Depression; others say it ended with World War II. It left one of the deepest scars in the history of the United States.

10. The depression is one time in my life that I'll never forget because I always wanted some type of sweet. Candy, cookies, ice cream, or cake—I'd want to eat any of them. Not understanding the Depression at that age, I thought I could get what I wanted easily.

My father was the breadwinner. He had to save every last penny because his wages weren't high enough to meet our cost of living. I would ask my father for money, but he would say that he didn't have any. My mother didn't work, so I didn't even consider asking her. I looked in drawers, corners, pants pockets, old pocketbooks, and any place where I thought there'd be money. But to no avail—I never found one red cent. My eagerness or greediness for sweets lessened because I didn't have the money to buy them. Because of the penny-pinching, I soon understood what the Depression meant and knew that I couldn't get everything I wanted.

Today, because of that penny-pinching, I try to save almost every cent, and I try to eat little or no sweets at all!

11. Before the Depression came, my father was working for General Motors at their plant in Tarrytown, New York. By the time the crash came, he had been employed there only a few years, and so did not have much seniority. My father became quite worried, for, should lay-offs occur, it would mean the end of a good salary. My father wasn't the only worker at G.M. who was worried. One day, the entire work force got together with the management and proposed that, instead of a layoff policy, the company institute a three-day work week. All the men agreed that it would be better to take a big cut in salary than to run the risk of not having any salary at all. Fortunately, the management, not only in sympathy with the position of the workers, but also realizing that the three-day work schedule would save them a considerable amount, accepted the proposal.

Before the crash, my father had been making fifty dollars a week, and in those days, that amount was considered quite good. With the reduction in his work days, his salary was cut to thirty dollars a week, a reduction of 40 percent. For the next five years, he worked for this amount, which, after taxes, came to twenty-odd dollars. My father was never bitter about this reduction, for he was grateful to still have a job when so many others were left without even that much.

12.* My dad had put all his savings into a house, and the mortgage was for fifty dollars a month at 7 percent. My dad was making only about a hundred dollars a month in 1933, so he pleaded with the landlord to cut the interest, but this bastard said no way, because, you see, he wanted that house; he wanted all the houses he could get by fore-closure, and I understand he got quite a few.

My mother tells it this way, that on paynight, the end of the month, my father would have worked himself into a frenzy of pure hate for this man who held the mortgage and wouldn't give him a break. She said that he'd be almost crazy and couldn't eat his dinner, yelled at my brother and me. And I can remember that. Then he'd put on his coat and walk half a mile to this man's house and pay him his stinking dollars, and it used to kill him. One night when he was especially bad, my mother phoned her brother Fred and he drove around and parked across the street. Dad was talking to himself as he came down the street and, as soon as the landlord opened the door, the old man started yelling at him, cursing him, like he was crazy. And I guess he was. The landlord would take the money, shut the door in my father's face, and then come back and give him a receipt.

Those nights I can remember him taking off his coat and going downstairs where he'd have a bottle of booze. He'd sit down there and curse the banks and the landlords and everybody and, you see, he was a reasonable man and this was very upsetting to us kids be-cause he was a good father. He was a very good father. About nine o'clock or so, Dad would stumble up the stairs and go into their bed-room and I could hear, because our bedroom was next door, I could hear my mother going in and saying, "Now, dear, there, there, every-thing will be all right. You'll see." She'd sit and hold his hand until he went out like a light. You know, some of the tough ones of those years, I guess, were the women. Next morning Dad would be okay, shaky but okay, and everything would be okay for another month.

You've got to think of it in his terms: one hundred bucks a month, or whatever it was. A wife, two kids, a house; that mortgage: fifty off the top; taxes, no vacations; nothing for the kids. How they did it I'll never know. Let's put up monuments all over this country to our folks. Why, the wife and I blow two hundred dollars in a weekend in Mon-treal without even trying and don't even enjoy ourselves. Just to keep our marriage from falling apart.

13.* If you want to know how your mother, if she was old enough, got

* Excerpted from Barry Broadfoot, *Ten Lost Years* (New York: Doubleday, 1973) pp. 176–77.

through the Depression, just look in the refrigerator. If it is full of junk—saucers with a few leftover sliced carrots or tomatoes, little jars with pickles that have been there a month, slices of fatty roast beef that not even a hungry dog would eat, then she was through the Depression and her family wasn't well off. Probably poor.

You never threw anything away. Keep. Save. Don't throw away. You never know when you'll need it. Make every cent count. Eat your crusts; they make your hair curly. Finish your porridge; don't you know there are starving children in China who would love to eat what you've got there?

Mother went through hell in those days, and the funny thing is that she wasn't the one who actually did the saving, the putting away, the hoarding of little bits of food. It was her mother—my grandmother. She just picked it up from her as a girl. Well, here's where the chain stops. With me. Here.

PART IV
WRITING THE
RESEARCH ESSAY

Most long essays and term papers in college courses are based on library research. Sometimes, an instructor will expect you to develop and present a topic or an issue entirely through the synthesis of sources; for other assignments, you will be asked first to formulate your own opinion and thesis and then to support that point of view by citing a few authorities. Whether your essay is to be wholly or partly substantiated by your reseach, you will still have to start your essay by finding readings and choosing sources in the library.

The research essay depends on a series of independent decisions that may present you with new problems and contradictions. On one hand, you will probably be starting out with no sources, no thesis, and only a broad topic to work with. Yet, on the other, as soon as you go to the library and start your research, you may find yourself with too many sources—shelf after shelf of books and articles from which you will have to make your own selection of readings. Locating and evaluating sources are complex skills, calling for quick comprehension and rapid decision-making. At the card catalog and indexes, you have to judge which books are worth locating; at the shelves, you have to skim a variety of materials rapidly to choose the ones that may be useful and worth reading at length; at the library table, you will have to decide which facts and information should go into your notes and which pages should be duplicated in their entirety. In Chapters 6, 7, and 8, you will be given explicit guidelines for using the library, choosing sources, and taking notes.

As you have learned, your objective in writing a multiple-source essay is to establish your own coherent structure that builds on your reading and to write an essay that blends together your ideas and those of your sources. In Chapter 9, you will find an updated, stage-by-stage description of the best ways to organize and write an essay based on complex sources. But here, again, is a contradiction. Even as you gather your materials for your essay and strive to synthesize them into a unified whole, you should also keep in mind the greatest responsibility of the researcher—accountability. From your first visit to the library, you must carefully keep track of the precise origins of each of the ideas and facts that you might use in your essay. You already know how to distinguish between your ideas and those of your sources and to make that distinction clear to your readers. Now, you also have to make clear which source is responsible for which idea and on which page of which book that information can be found—without losing the shape and coherence of your own paragraphs. To resolve this contradiction between writing a coherent essay and accounting for your sources, there is an established system of documentation that covers the familiar skills of quotation, paraphrase, and citation of authors, as well as the skills of footnoting and compiling a bibliography. The complexities of documentation are explored in Chapter 10. Finally, in Chapter 11, you will be able to examine and assess the product of all these research, writing, and documenting techniques: two sets of research essays that demonstrate—with varying sources and varying success—different ways of writing about the same topic.

6. Gathering Materials at the Library: Bibliography

Saturday, May 1
I began my first research effort at the main library
downtown. I wasn't sure just where to start, so I asked
the research librarian for the best place to find
information about the Johnstown Flood. She directed me to
the New York Times Index and the Readers' Guide to
Periodical Literature.

I checked out the Times on microfilm for June, 1889. I
found that for the first half of the month, the flood was
front-page news. I learned a lot, and I also noticed a
pattern of sensationalism. I read for two and a half hours
and I took some notes, but I wanted to hold this
information until I could compare it with some other
materials. The only problem was, where to find them?
Then I went back into the reference room and began to look
through the Readers' Guide and the subject card catalog.
In the catalog, I found The Johnstown Flood, by David
McCullough, but with only two sources of information, I
had to find more. The library was closing, so I went home
with my Times notes and the book.

Wednesday, May 5
Today I finished McCullough; I was happy to finally get a
well-rounded idea of what had really happened in Johnstown
on that dreadful day. This book was outstanding. Not only
did I learn what happened, but through its bibliography I
found other titles that I could look up. I also noticed
that most of the books, newspapers, and magazines were

dated 1889–1891. That's a long time ago; I didn't think
books that old would still be on the shelves. Instead of
going back downtown, I decided to look for some of the
more recent materials at the college library.

Thursday, May 6

After English class, I went to the reference room. In the
subject card catalog under Johnstown, I found one book:
Johnstown, from Traildust to Stardust, by Greer. The book,
however, was not on the shelf and it had not been checked
out. The reference librarian went to find the book, and in
five minutes he was back with it. I checked it out and sat
down to thumb through it. I also looked briefly at
Pennsylvania: Guide to the Keystone State, and, a few
minutes after that, Traveler's Guide to Historic Western
Pennsylvania, but they only had short paragraphs about the
region, so they weren't much help.

Friday, May 7

During lunch, I was reading the acknowledgments in
McCullough. All of a sudden, I came across the author's
special thanks to the History and Genealogy Room at the
Central Public Library. That was what I'd been hoping
for——a lead.

After work, I went down the street to the library and up
to the Genealogy Room. There I found my treasure chest. I
found Beale's Through the Johnstown Flood, O'Connor's
Johnstown: The Day the Dam Broke, and Gertrude Quinn's
Johnstown and Its Flood. I only had time to thumb through
them, and I wasn't allowed to take them out. I had to come
back on Saturday.

Saturday, May 8

I got to the library around two o'clock. I went directly
to the Genealogy Room, checked out my books for desk use,
and began to read and take notes. I can't write about any
of my problems today, because I had none.

Jesse Rogers

Jesse Rogers was a very determined and fortunate student. Nearby were
extensive library collections whose resources were readily available to
him. The books that he wanted proved to be on the shelves, not out on
loan or lost. And, equally important, Jesse Rogers went to the library
knowing that he wanted to write an essay about the Johnstown Flood.

A clearly defined topic is a great advantage when you are beginning your research. Your teacher may provide that advantage by assigning a precise topic; or you may be asked to narrow a broad subject or to develop a topic of your own choosing. If you find yourself in either of the latter two situations, you should follow essentially the same procedure for topic-narrowing that you learned about in Chapter 1.

Topic-narrowing remains a practical process, based on a realistic assessment of your circumstances. How much time do you have? What resources are available to you? How long an essay are you being asked to write? How complex a project are you ready and willing to undertake? Choosing a good topic also requires you to be reasonably familiar with the subject and with the available resources, which is why topic-narrowing continues throughout the preliminary stages of your research. But even before you start work at the library, you should invest some time in analyzing your subject and considering your options. Here are some initial approaches to topic-narrowing that have worked well for students starting their first research project.

NARROWING THE TOPIC: BIOGRAPHICAL AND HISTORICAL SUBJECTS

Biographical and historical topics have a built-in advantage: they can be defined and limited by space and time. Events and lives have clear beginnings, middles, and ends, as well as many identifiable intermediate stages. If you are not ready to undertake the full span of a biography or a complete historical event, you may wish to select a specific point in time as the focus for your essay. You can choose to examine as broad or as narrow a period as you wish. At the same time you will be reducing to a manageable size both the scope of the project and the amount of material to be read.

Assume, for example, that by choice or assignment your broad subject is Franklin Delano Roosevelt. Instead of tracing all the incidents and related events in which he participated during his sixty-three years, you might decide to describe FDR at the point when his political career was apparently ruined by polio. Your focus would be the man in 1921, and your essay might deal with any or all of the following topics—his personality, his style of life, his experiences, his idea of government—at that point in time. Everything that happened to FDR after 1921 would be irrelevant to your chosen perspective. Another student might choose a different point in time and describe the new president in 1933 against the background of the Depression. Yet another might focus on an intermediate point in FDR's presidency and construct a profile of the man as he was in 1940, when he decided to run for an unprecedented third term in office. Or the topic might be made even more specific by focusing on a single action and its causes: What, for example was FDR's attitude toward atomic research in its earliest stages? Did he anticipate using the bomb?

The writer of such a profile attempts to describe what the subject must have been like and to explore his motives and his experiences. In effect, the writer's overriding impression of character or intention serves as the *thesis*, the controlling idea of the biographical portrait. The writer undertakes to determine (on the basis of the available evidence) which facts and details about the subject relate to the thesis and which are irrelevant and to present his conclusions to the reader.

You can also view a historical event from such a specific vantage point. Your broad subject might be the Civil War, which lasted four years, or the Berlin Olympics of 1936, which lasted a few weeks, or the Johnstown Flood, which lasted a few days. If the span of time is lengthy, you might focus on an intermediate point or stage, which can serve to illuminate and characterize the entire event. The Battle of Gettysburg, for example, is a broad topic often chosen by those interested in the Civil War. Since the battle, with its complex maneuvers, lasted for three days and hardly lends itself to brief or simple narrative, you would want to narrow the focus even more. You might perhaps describe the battlefield and the disposition of the troops, as a journalist would, at a single moment in the course of the battle; in this case, your thesis might undertake to demonstrate that the disposition of the troops at this point was typical (or atypical) of tactics used throughout the battle or that this moment did (or did not) foreshadow the battle's conclusion. In fact, always assuming that sufficient material is available, you will find that narrowing your focus *too* much is difficult.

In writing about history, you may also have to consider the point of view that you wish to assume. If, for example, you set out to recount an episode from the Civil War, you might first establish your perspective: Are you writing from the Union's point of view? the Confederacy's? the point of view of the politicians of either side? the generals? the civilians? industrialists? hospital workers? slaves in the south? black freedmen in the north? If you tried to deal with *all* their reactions to your chosen episode, you would have difficulty in settling on a thesis and, in the long run, you would only end up confusing and misinforming your reader.

A similar "day in the life" approach can also be applied to events which had no specific date. When and under what circumstances were primitive guns first used in battle? What was the practical and psychological effect of gunfire on the opposing troops? What was the reaction when the first automobile drove down a village street? Or, rather than describe the effects of a new invention, you might focus on a social institution which has changed radically. What, for example, was it like to shop for food in Paris in 1810? in Chicago in 1870? in any large American city in 1945? Instead of attempting to write a complete history of the circus from

Rome to Ringling, try portraying the experience of an equestrian performer in Astley's Circus in 1770 or that of a chariot racer in Pompey's
Circus Maximus in 61 B.C.

Setting a target date enables you to focus your research. You will start
off with a practical method of judging the relevance and the usefulness
of each of your sources. As you narrow your topic and begin your reading,
watch for your emerging thesis—the single, clear impression of the person or event that you wish your reader to receive. Whether you are writing
about a sequence of events, like a battle or a flood, or a single event in
the life of a well-known person, you will still need both a thesis and a
strategy to help you to sort out your materials and to shape the direction
of your essay. A common strategy for such biographical and historical
topics is the cause and effect sequence—why a decision was made or
an event turned out one way and not another. Finally, do not allow your
historical or biographical portrait to become an exercise in creative writing. The evidence of your hypothetical witnesses must be derived from
and supported by well-documented sources, not just your imagination.
The "Napoleon might have said" or "Stalin must have thought" that you
find in some biographies and historical novels is often a theory or an
educated guess that is firmly rooted in research—and the author should
generally offer documentation and bibliography to substantiate it.

NARROWING THE TOPIC:
CONTEMPORARY ISSUES

When you write about a historical or biographical subject, you
can use the perspective of time to achieve a narrow focus by pinpointing
a date and a point of view and by deliberately excluding all other angles.
But when you work with a more abstract topic the multiplicity of possible
applications and examples may make it difficult for you to find a focus.
If the topic is contemporary, limiting your research and choosing among
the variety of conflicting sources becomes difficult. Thus, if you chose to
write about the early history of the circus, you would find an assortment
of books describing many traditional kinds of circus activity, from the
Roman arena to the turn-of-the-century Barnum and Bailey big top. But
because of the increase in the amount of information published in this
half of the twentieth century and because reviews and features are
printed—and preserved for the researcher—every time Ringling Brothers
opens in a new city, planning your reading for an essay about the role
of the circus today might be hard. Your research can be endless and the
results unmanageable unless, quite early, you decide on a single approach. If the subject that you want to write about cannot be defined
and narrowed through the persepctive of time, you will have to break it

down into its component parts and select a single aspect as the tentative focus of your essay. (You will find that many of the guides and indexes in the reference room contain not only lists of sources but also a useful breakdown of subtopics, suggesting possibilities for the direction of your essay. As an illustration, turn to the entries on advertising taken from the *Readers' Guide to Periodical Literature* later in this chapter; then turn back to Chapter 1 and review the discussion of narrowing down the broad topic of advertising (pp. 5, 30–31).

You automatically establish a narrow perspective as soon as you begin to ask questions and apply strategies. How does this topic actually work? is there a better way of doing it? What are its benefits? its dangers? which groups does it especially affect? how is it to be compared with this or that variant? Suppose that *food* is your broad subject. Your approach might be descriptive, analyzing causes and effects: you could write about some aspect of nutrition, discussing what we ought to eat and the way in which our nutritional needs are best satisfied. Or you could deal with the production and distribution of food—or, more likely, a specific kind of food—and use process descriptions as your approach. Or your approach could analyze a different set of causes: why don't we eat what we ought to? why do so many people have to diet, and why aren't diets effective? Or you could plan a persuasive essay: What would be the best way to educate the public in proper nutrition? By building your topic on a point of some controversy, you could produce an essay arguing the virtues or defects of food additives, or junk foods, or convenience cooking. Within the narrower focus of food additives, there are numerous ways to develop the topic: to what degree are they dangerous? What was the original purpose of the Food and Drug Act of 1906? Would individual rights be threatened if additives like saccharine were banned? Can the dangers of food additives be compared with the danger from alcohol? On the other hand, your starting point could be a concrete object, rather than an abstract idea: you might decide to write about the Big Mac. You could describe its contents and nutritional value; or recount its origins and first appearance on the food scene; or compare it to best-selling foods of past eras; or evaluate its relative popularity in different parts of the world. All of these topics require research.

It is desirable to have at least one narrow topic in mind before you start any intensive reading so that as you start to compile your preliminary bibliography you can begin to distinguish between sources that are potentially useful and sources that will probably be irrelevant. What you *cannot* do at this stage is formulate a definite thesis. Your thesis will probably serve as the answer to the question that you asked at the beginning of your research. Although, from the first, you may have your own theories about the answer, and although it can be helpful to consider possible theses as you read, you cannot be sure that your research will confirm your hypotheses. Your theories should remain hypothetical and your thesis tentative until your reading has given your essay content and direction.

EXERCISE 42

The following topic proposals were submitted by several students who had been assigned to write eight- to ten-page research essays. Consider the scope and focus of each proposal, and decide which ones suggest *practical* topics for an essay of this length. If the proposal is too broad, be prepared to offer suggestions for narrowing the focus.

Student A:

Much of the interest in World War II has been focused on the battlefield, but the war years were also a trying period for the public at home. I intend to write about civilian morale during the the war, emphasizing press campaigns to increase the war effort. I will also include a description of the way people coped with brown-outs, shortages, and rationing, with a section on the victory garden.

Student B:

I intend to deal with the role of women in feudal life, especially the legal rights of medieval women. I would also like to discuss the theory of chivalry and its effects on women, as well as the influence of medieval literature on society. My specific focus will be the ideal image of the medieval lady.

Student C:

My research essay will focus on the history of dance in the United States. I intend to explore the development of ballet and jazz dancing in America, with special emphasis on their earliest presentation.

Student D:

I have chosen the Lindbergh Kidnapping Case as the subject of my essay. I intend to concentrate on the kidnapping itself, rather than going into details about the lives of the Lindberghs. What interests me is the planning of the crime, including the way in which the house was designed

and the kidnapping was carried out. I also hope to include
an account of the investigation and courtroom scenes.

Student E:

My topic is going to be the importance of the banjo in
American music. I think that it will be possible to write
a history of the banjo, particularly in bluegrass music,
since the amount of information that I've found so far
doesn't seem overwhelming. If necessary, my main focus
will be the roots of banjo—playing in Appalachia.

Student F:

I would like to explore methods of travel one hundred and
fifty years ago, and compare the difficulties of traveling
then with the conveniences of traveling now. I intend to
stress the economic and social background of the average
traveler. My focus will be the Grand Tour that young men
used to take.

Student G:

I intend to explore certain kinds of revivalist religions
in America today, to describe typical experiences, and to
try to explain their interest and attraction for so many
young people.

Student H:

I intend to explain the proper methods of playing defense
in basketball, supporting my explanation with testimony
from authorities on basketball tactics. I will regard my
reader as a player coming out for my squad for the first
time, and so I'll begin with basic, fundamental skills,
such as guarding the ball and denial of the ball, and I'll
gradually move on to more difficult maneuvers. I will try
not to be too technical and I will use my own diagrams and
line illustrations.

Student I:

My essay will describe the life of a professional ballet
dancer today. I intend to begin with the way in which
dancers have to prepare themselves for their performing
career, and I will include descriptions of ballet classes.
I hope to explain the kind of emotional and physical

condition that's needed for serious work in ballet, emphasizing ways to cope with the strain of constant competition. Finally, I want to define what makes a great ballet company.

Student J:

I'd like to explore different definitions of quality in television programs. Specifically, I'd like to contrast popular and critically acclaimed TV shows of today with comparable programs ten and twenty years ago, in an effort to determine whether there really has been a decline in popular taste. It may be necessary to restrict my topic to one kind of television show—situation comedies, for example, or coverage of sports events.

Student K:

I would like to do research on several aspects of adolescent peer groups, trying to determine whether the overall effects of peer groups on adolescents are beneficial or destructive. I intend to include the following topics: the need for peer acceptance; conformity; personal and social adjustment; and peer competition. I'm not sure that I can form a conclusive argument, since most of the information available on this subject is purely descriptive; but I'll try to present an informed opinion.

EXERCISE 43

Here are fifteen different ways of approaching the broad topic of *divorce in America*. Decide which of the questions would make good starting points for an eight-to-ten page research essay. Take into consideration the practicality and the clarity of each question, the probable availability of research materials, and the likelihood of being able to answer the question in approximately nine pages. For each question that you consider practical, try to write one or two tentative theses.

1. What is the best way of dealing with the aftermath of divorce?
2. What problems does a woman encounter in picking up the pieces of her life after she has been divorced?
3. What are the primary causes of divorce today?
4. Who suffers more after divorce, husband or wife?
5. Does divorce lead to independence?

6. What has been the effect of the increased divorce rate on the American economy?
7. What can be done to protect children, who are the chief victims of divorce?
8. What are the dangers of joint custody for the child?
9. Does everyone have the right to freedom from a miserable marriage?
10. When divorce became socially acceptable, were any social benefits lost?
11. Is divorce the best answer to marital problems?
12. Are the personalities of the marriage partners significant in determining the probability of divorce?
13. Does divorce really undermine marriage, or is it strengthening the institution by encouraging only good marriages to exist?
14. Why is divorce more common in America than in many other countries?
15. What is the relationship between the increased divorce rate and women's liberation?

COMPILING A WORKING BIBLIOGRAPHY: LOCATING SOURCES

Your preliminary research in the library usually consists of three overlapping stages:

1. discovering and locating the titles of some possible sources;
2. recording basic facts about each source;
3. noting each source's potential usefulness—or lack of usefulness—to your topic.

These three steps, performed in order, usually form a continuous cycle. It is not likely that you will be able to locate *all* your sources at once, and then record all your basic information, and lastly take notes on the usefulness of all your sources. Rather, you will have to move back and forth from card catalog and reference room to stacks and back again. Even after you begin to plan and write your essay, you may find yourself back at the library, checking a new lead to a potentially useful source.

Because you may be looking at a great many titles and because, in any one session at the library, you may be at a different stage of research with several different books and articles, you should thoroughly familiarize yourself with each of the three steps.

Even before your first research essay is assigned, you should begin to familiarize yourself with your college library. Every library has a different layout, and stacks and catalogs use various kinds of numbering systems.

Find out how *your* library is organized. Most libraries provide guided tours for groups of interested students. If such a tour is not available, make your own exploratory visit. Ask yourself some of the following questions: How are the books arranged? Are the collections for the different disciplines housed in separate buildings? Do you have access to all the stacks of books? How are the guides and indexes arranged in the reference room? Is there a list of all the periodicals owned by the library? Is there a map of the reference room on the wall? What are microcards? Where are the microfilm and microcard readers, and how do you locate and sign out the cards and spools of film? Get these questions answered before you start your research; then you will not lose time by pausing in your search for a title or run the risk of losing the impetus that makes research interesting.

Since all libraries are arranged differently, there is no way that this book can tell you precisely where to find sources in your college library. However, there is a standard procedure for finding out which titles you might want to look for. Suppose that you come to the library with a broad topic in mind: you plan to write an essay about Prohibition, the period between 1920 and 1933 when the Eighteenth Amendment, prohibiting the sale and consumption of all alcoholic beverages, was in effect. What sources would be available?

The Card Catalogs

Libraries generally have three catalogs: one organized by authors, one by titles, and one by subjects. Unless you have had a specific book about Prohibition already recommended to you, your search for sources will start with the subject catalog. The way in which this catalog is organized and the way in which supplementary information is presented on each card can differ from library to library. Some libraries do not even use card catalogs, but instead place all information in a series of bound volumes, with forty or more entries per page. Moreover, a library's catalog will list only the holdings of *that* library; later on, if you need to use another library to trace certain essential sources, you may encounter new methods of cataloging. In spite of these variables, certain conventions apply to most catalogs.

Subject cards. Some cataloging systems have already broken down broad subjects into narrower topics by grouping the entries according to subtopics. For example, in one catalogue, "Prohibition" might be divided according to the following heading and subheadings:

Prohibition	three titles (cards) under the main heading
Prohibition—Great Britain	one title

Prohibition—Michigan	one title
Prohibition—Texas	one title
Prohibition—Tennessee	one title
Prohibition—United States	thirteen titles
Prohibition—U.S.—History	seven titles
Prohibition—United States	two biographies of Carrie Nation

This system enables you immediately to eliminate titles that are probably irrelevant (like Great Britain or the biographies of Carrie Nation, the temperance crusader, who died eight-and-a-half years before Prohibition became law) or titles that may be too narrow (like Michigan, Texas, or Tennessee).

Many subjects catalogs list all titles relating to a single broad topic alphabetically under the one heading. You have to judge each book's usefulness by considering its title, length, and whether it has a bibliography, and by consulting the "tracings" at the bottom of the entry card. The tracings list other subjects under which the title is listed and in this way reflect the contents of the book. On the following page are three different cards from the "Prohibition" section of a subject catalog. How would you decide which title to locate first?

The first two cards would both have clear relevance to your paper topic. The three topics listed at the bottom of the *Ardent Spirits* card are in order of their importance in the book. Thus, Kobler's main emphasis is on Prohibition and its relation to American history; you would almost certainly find some useful information there. Judging from the bottom of its card, *Repealing National Prohibition* is concerned only with Prohibition, and judging from its title, the book focuses only on the end of the period you would be concerned with; thus, its treatment is probably more detailed than the first book's. However, you might be wise to begin with *Ardent Spirits*, which would provide a better overview of the subject. If you were interested in the connection between the women's suffrage movement and the temperance movement, you might want to consult the third title. But, even though the second entry on the bottom of the card is highlighted, Prohibition is not Paulson's primary subject. (In fact, Prohibition is being highlighted only because the card is filed under that broad topic.) Moreover, the summary tells you that the book consists largely of case studies; your interest in the book would depend on what cases Paulson chooses to examine at length.

Cross-references and bibliographies. A single book may be useful for research on dozens of different topics. Placing a separate card in the catalog under every possible subject heading would result in a subject catalog overflowing with cards and an unmanageable system. Instead, most libraries use cross-referencing. A card is placed only under the subject heading that is most relevant to the book. In some libraries, either

subject heading

call number,
author

title, publica-
tion information

miscellany

PROHIBITION

HV
5089
.K67 **Kobler, John.**
Ardent spirits; the rise and fall of prohibition. New
York, Putnam ₍1973₎

386 p. illus. 22 cm. $8.95

Bibliography: p. ₍358₎–₍373₎

tracings

1. Prohibition—United States—History. 2. Temperance—History.
3. Prohibition Party. I. Title.

HV5089.K67   322.4′4′0973   73–78586
ISBN 0–399–11209–X   MARC

Library of Congress   73 ₍4₎

PROHIBITION

HV
5089
.K95 **Kyvig, David E**
Repealing national prohibition / David E. Kyvig. — Chicago
: University of Chicago Press, 1979.

xix, 274 p. : ill. ; 24 cm.

Bibliography: p. 245-266.
Includes index.
ISBN 0-226-46641-8

1. Prohibition—United States. I. Title.

HV5089.K95   322.4′4′0973   79-13516
                                                         MARC

Library of Congress   79

PROHIBITION

JF
848
.P3 **Paulson, Ross E**
Women's suffrage and prohibition: a comparative study
of equality and social control ₍by₎ Ross Evans Paulson.
Glenview, Ill., Scott, Foresman ₍1973₎

212 p. front. 23 cm.

Includes bibliographical references.

1. Woman—Suffrage—Case studies. 2. Prohibition—Case studies.
3. Equality—Case studies. 4. Social control—Case studies.   I.
Title.

JF848.P3   324′.3   72–92341
ISBN 0–673–05982–0   MARC

Library of Congress   73 ₍4₎

at the beginning or the end of the series of cards under the heading "Prohibition," you would find a card containing a list of cross-references. In other libraries, you would find a large two-volume set entitled *Library of Congress Subject Headings*, containing a standard set of cross-references found in all libraries using the Library of Congress system. Here, for example, is the listing of topics which you could look up *in addition to* Prohibition:

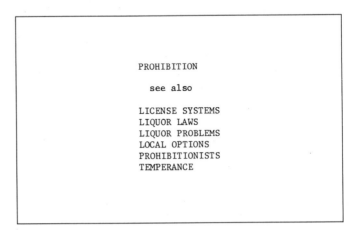

```
PROHIBITION

    see also

LICENSE SYSTEMS
LIQUOR LAWS
LIQUOR PROBLEMS
LOCAL OPTIONS
PROHIBITIONISTS
TEMPERANCE
```

The information on the catalog cards can help you indirectly to expand your list of possible titles. Look again at the sample subject cards and notice that *Ardent Spirits* contains a sixteen-page bibliography, and *Repealing National Prohibition* a twenty-page bibliography. To use these bibliographies, you would have to locate copies of *Ardent Spirits* and *Repealing National Prohibition* in the stacks. You would first copy the book's call number from the upper left-hand corner of the catalog card. There are two systems by which libraries organize their books: the Dewey Decimal system, which uses numbers followed by letters and numbers, and the Library of Congress system, which uses letters followed by numbers and combinations of letters and numbers. (At the base of each sample subject card, the Library of Congress number, used as the call number, appears on the left; the Dewey Decimal numbers are centered.) Find out which system your library uses (some use both), and, if the stacks are open to students, explore them until you find the books that you need. You may also find useful titles that you overlooked in the catalog in the vicinity of the books for which you are looking.

Once you located *Ardent Spirits* and *Repealing National Prohibition*, you would check either bibliography for more books that are relevant to your project. In this way, you could add to your own bibliography some of the titles that these authorities used in researching and developing their own work on Prohibition. Of course, you would have to find and examine these other titles before you could use them; you would check the author or title catalog, record their call numbers, and then find them in the stacks. If your library did not own these titles, you would have to decide whether any looked interesting enough to warrant a visit to another library. If you were unable to locate a vital source in any of the local libraries, you might consult your college librarian about the possibility of an inter-library loan.

Indexes

So far, your research would have been confined to books, for the subject catalog includes no periodical references. You might have found some articles cited in the bibliographies of the books that you checked; but, if you wanted to explore the sources available in periodicals and newspapers thoroughly, you would spend some time in your library's reference room, using the *Readers' Guide to Periodical Literature*, the *New York Times Index*, and one or more of the subject indexes that specifically relate to your topic.* (For an essay on Prohibition, you would look in the *Social Sciences Index*.) In the *Readers' Guide*, you can find articles taken from popular magazines with titles like "Why Repeal Will Be Coming Soon." Here's what a *Readers' Guide* entry looks like:

> After Prohibition, what? L. Rogers. New Repub 73:91–99 D 7
> '32

As you can see, the title of the article comes first, then the author's name, then the title of the periodical (often abbreviated), then the volume number, followed by a colon and the pages on which the article appears, then the month, abbreviated, the day, and the year.

In the *Times Index*, you would find topical news articles, such as "Rise in Gangland Murders Linked to Bootlegging." Here is a typical *Times Index* listing for 1933:

> 25 Buffalo speakeasies and stills raided, S 24, IV, 6:6

The title of the article is followed by the date (24 September), the section (4, indicated in Roman numerals to avoid confusion), the page (6), and the column (the sixth from the left).

Since these indexes have to cram a great deal of information into a relatively small space, they cannot afford to have too many double and triple entries, and they therefore make extensive use of cross-referencing. In the *Readers' Guide* for 1932–1933, for example, you would find four columns of articles about Prohibition, first divided into regions and then into a series of headings that include "economic aspects," "enforcement," "political aspects," "repeal," and "results." At the very beginning of the

---

* See Appendix A for a list of the most commonly used periodical indexes.

list, the reader is referred to possible headings elsewhere in the *Guide*:

> *See also*
> alcohol
> liquor problem
> liquor traffic
> liquor

It is your job to check any of the other headings which seem relevant to your topic. Occasionally, an index will not provide any "See also" lists. In a recent *Social Sciences Index*, for example, you would have to look under the broad heading of "Alcohol" to find an article about Prohibition, such as "Social Interaction in the Speakeasy of 1930." It is up to you to use your ingenuity to figure out which subjects to look up.

Summary

After you have looked in card catalogs, bibliographies, and indexes, your search would probably have led you to list and locate the following *kinds* of sources for an essay on Prohibition:

> economic and social histories for a general background of the period;
>
> congressional reports, political analyses, and legal studies of the Eighteenth Amendment;
>
> contemporary newspaper accounts, magazine articles, and memoirs describing the everyday effects of the ban on liquor;
>
> exposés of bootlegging and other criminal activities associated with Prohibition;
>
> biographies of prominent figures in the Prohibition Party;
>
> philosophy and psychology books and articles dealing with recurring forms of puritanism

At the beginning, uncertain about the precise scope and focus of your essay, you would probably find it difficult to decide which of these sources would ultimately be useful for your purpose and which would prove to be irrelevant. For one thing, you might not yet be certain exactly what you want to find out about. Would you stress the reasons for the movement towards Prohibition? the religious influence? the economic background? Prohibition as a consequence of social changes in the era after World War I? the link between Prohibition and organized crime? the effects of Prohibition on recreation and leisure time? the constitutionality of the Eighteenth Amendment? the rituals of illegal drinking? the relationship between the prohibition of alcohol in the twenties and the prohibition of marijuana decades later? the convivial scene in bars all over the nation on the day Prohibition was repealed?

Unless you know from the very beginning precisely what most interests you about your broad topic, you cannot afford to ignore or discard many of the titles that you come across. And, equally important at this stage, you cannot afford to stop the search for titles in order to examine each of the sources in detail. For the Prohibition paper you would at this stage still be trying to formulate an overall picture of Prohibition, to learn about the topic's possibilities, and to estimate the amount of material that is available and the approximate amount of time that you will need to spend on research. At the beginning, then, if you have an hour or two to spend in the library, you should spend that time at the card catalog or in the reference room, rounding out your list of possible sources and narrowing down your topic, rather than reading extensively (and taking notes) in any single work. Later on, after you have compiled a working bibliography, you will begin the "reading" part of your research, starting with the most comprehensive source. Certainly, you will want to check the stacks as soon as possible to find out if the most likely titles are available and, if they are, to check them out and take them home. But, at this point, don't spend too much time with each book. At the most, you will want to look at a book's table of contents, index, and bibliography, or flip through an article in order to gain a rough idea of its scope and relevance.

COMPLING A WORKING BIBLIOGRAPHY: RECORDING BASIC INFORMATION

A bibliography is loosely defined as a complete list of all the works that you consult in doing the research for your essay. In practice, however, there are really two kinds of bibliography, corresponding to the stages of your research. Your *preliminary* or *working bibliography* consists of all the sources that you learn about and perhaps examine as you discover what material is available and as you develop your ideas about the topic. The *final bibliography* consists of the material that you will actually use in the writing of your essay. (For a discussion of the final bibliography, see Chapter 10.)

There is a very precise format for all bibliographical entries; and, therefore, from the very beginning of your research, as you use the card catalog and the indexes, you should carefully copy down all facts that you will need later on in order to construct a complete and correct final bibliography. These notes can be written on index cards or in a separate section of your notebook. The major advantage of index cards is that, with one entry per card, the stack can be easily organized and alphabetized when you are assembling your final bibliography. But it really does not matter which method you use; what is important is that your records be accurate, readable, and reasonably consistent, so that, several weeks later, when you are working on your bibliography for submission with your essay, you will be able easily and rapidly to transform your notes into the correct format. Even though you are at the beginning of your research and cannot be sure which sources will actually become important, try not to scrawl, and do not abbreviate unless you are aware of the significance of each symbol. If your writing is illegible, you will be forced to return to the library to check your references, probably at a point when you can least spare the time. As you work from the card catalog or from one of the indexes or from a bibliography, start a fresh card or a fresh place on the page for each new item. It may help to assign a number to each new source. If you are using a notebook page, remember to leave enough space for comments about the work's potential usefulness.

Include the following facts in the notes for your bibliography:

For books:

the author's full name;
the exact title, underlined;
the name of the editor(s) (for an anthology) or the name of the translator (for a work first written in a foreign language);
the date and place of publication and the name of the publisher;
the original date of publication and the date of the new edition or reprint, if the book has been reissued;
the inclusive page numbers if you are planning to use only a single chapter or section of the book;
the call number, so that you will not need to return to the catalog if you decide to locate the book or periodical.

For articles:

the author's full name;
the title of the article, in quotation marks;
the exact title of the periodical, underlined;
the volume number and the date of the issue;
the inclusive page numbers of the article.

Later, when you locate the book or magazine article itself, remember to verify all the bibliographic information by examining the front and back of the title page of the book or the first page of the article and the title page of the periodical or newspaper. Check the spelling of the author's name; find out if the book had an editor; make sure that the place of publication was, for example, Cambridge, Massachusetts, and not Cambridge, England.

To show you what information looks like when it is placed in a conventional format, here is a final bibliography for the Prohibition essay, comprising the five works listed so far:

List of Works Consulted

Kobler, John. <u>Ardent Spirits: The Rise and Fall of
     Prohibition</u>. New York: Putman, 1973.
Kyvig, David E. <u>Repealing National Prohibition</u>. Chicago:
     Univ. of Chicago Press, 1979.
Paulson, Ross E. <u>Women's Suffrage and Prohibition: A
     Comparative Study of Equality and Social Control</u>.
     Glenview, Ill.: Scott, Foresman, 1973.
Rogers, L. "After Prohibition, What?" <u>New Republic</u>, 73 (7
     Dec. 1932), 91–99.
"25 Buffalo Speakeasies and Stills Raided," <u>New York
     Times</u>, 24 Sept. 1933, Sec. 4, p. 6.

Research is open-ended. It is impossible to judge in advance how many sources will provide adequate documentation for your topic. You need to include enough sources to support your thesis convincingly, yet not so many that they get treated superficially. Your teacher may stipulate that you consult at least five authorities, or ten, or fifteen; but that recommendation is an artificial (though realistic) one, intended to make sure that each student in the class does a reasonable and roughly equal amount of research. Certainly, without guidelines, your preliminary list of sources could conceivably reach and exceed the dozens, even the hundreds. If you wished, you could copy out whole trays of the card catalog, or whole pages of the *Readers' Guide*, or whole rows of titles on the shelves; but you would have little awareness of the contents or the relevance of your "Works Cited." An endless list of sources does not automatically demonstrate your competence in research.

What is important is not quantity, but usefulness for your purpose. Jesse Rogers did a good job in researching the Johnstown Flood, not because he located an impressively large number of sources, but because he found sufficient materials from which to construct an interesting and accurate essay. A good grade for a research essay is likely to hinge on the inclusion or omission of a few crucial sources, the works of well-known authorities, whose evidence or points of view must be considered if your essay is to be thoroughly documented. As you will learn in Chapter 7, the skill lies in distinguishing those useful sources from the irrelevant ones. Thus, it is not enough to have compiled the suggested number of source materials if the works on your list are minor or trivial or peripheral to the topic. Never settle for the first five books that come into your hands. Your research must continue until you are satisfied that you have consulted all those with a claim to be heard.

Taking Notes About the Usefulness of Each Source

In addition to the factual information that you will need for your bibliography, you should also include a few preliminary notes about the probable usefulness of each work. This third step takes place *after* you have located and briefly examined a source. These are not notes that you will later use in writing your essay, but, rather, comments that will indicate which sources may merit more thorough examination and note-taking at a later stage of your research. You simply note your initial assessment of the work's scope, general contents, strong or weak points, and apparent relevance to your topic, as well as any rough impressions about the author's reliability as a source. Often, you can write down such a comment just by examining the table of contents and leafing through the pages. (In such a case, however, the note will probably be negative since you won't be finding anything that makes you want to read further and more thoroughly.) *Don't trust to your memory.* If you neglect to note your reaction, weeks later you may find yourself wondering whether to go over to the library and check out what seems to be a likely looking title.

Keeping track of your sources by writing down preliminary comments also enables you to review the progress of your research. You can glance through your notes after each trip to the library and decide whether your topic and (perhaps) your thesis are taking shape, whether your sources are going to be numerous and thorough enough to support an essay on that topic and thesis, and whether you ought to drop a few titles from your working bibliography or go back to the card catalog and reference room to add a few new authors to your list.

Finally, your preliminary notes will be useful when it comes time to write up your final bibliography, especially if you plan to annotate it. *Annotation* means that you insert a short comment after each item in your bibliography, describing the work's scope and specific focus and suggesting its relevance and usefulness to the development of your topic. The notes are usually only a sentence or two, just enough to help your reader judge whether the source will be useful or not. In the following annotated bibliography for an essay on Charles Manson, the notes for each entry were taken, with few changes, from the earlier working bibliography.

An Annotated List of Sources Consulted

Bugliosi, Vincent. <u>Helter Skelter</u>. New York: Norton, 1974.
    A complete and excellent account of the Manson
    murders, murderers, victims, and trial.
"Case of the Hypnotic Hippie," <u>Newsweek</u>, 15 Dec. 1969, pp.

30–33. This article emphasizes the backgrounds of some Manson followers.

"Demon of Death Valley," Time, 12 Dec. 1969, pp. 24–25. There isn't a lot of material about Manson's activities here, but the article includes a discussion of the philosophy behind the murders and the atmosphere that Manson created.

"Manson's Shattered Defense," Time, 30 Nov. 1970, p. 45. The court scene is portrayed in this article, which contains a useful excerpt from Manson's testimony.

O'Neil, Paul. "Flattery, Fear, and Sex Lured His Girls," Life, 19 Dec. 1969, pp. 20–23. This is useful chiefly for an analysis of the intense power that Manson had over his followers.

Sanders, Ed. The Family. New York: Dutton, 1971. This is a very important book that presents a detailed account of the Manson case. Sanders strives to be as exact as possible.

Zaehner, R. C. Our Savage God. New York: Sheed and Ward, 1974. Purely philosophical and religious analysis of Charles Manson and his actions.

Zamora, William. Trial by Your Peers. New York: Maurice Girodias Associates, 1973. Written by one of the jurors on the Manson case in order to reveal the hidden craziness behind the trial.

EXERCISE 44

On the following pages are reproduced entries from the *Readers' Guide to Periodical Literature (1978–9)* under the comprehensive headings "Advertising" and "Television Advertising." Select one article that appears to relate directly to the topic "advertising: a powerful tool that is potentially constructive but most often abused." Locate and examine the article. Then prepare an index card containing all the information necessary for a bibliographical entry. (Although the information is the same, the form used for entries in the *Readers' Guide* is *not* the form used in the standard bibliography of a research essay; do not simply copy out the entry from the *Guide*, but make a list of the facts, indicating what each number or abbreviation signifies.) Add a few sentences describing the article's scope, focus, difficulty, and usefulness for this topic.

ADVERTISING—*Continued*

Awards, prizes, etc.

Presenting. . .the winners of Family Health's sixth annual Nutritional Advertising Awards. il Fam Health 10:28–9 F '78

Saturday review's 24th annual advertising awards. C. Tucker. il
Sat R 5:16 Jl 22 '78

Effectiveness research
See Advertising research

History
Advertising 1890 to 1930. E. Shrum. Hobbies 83: 116 + Je '78

International aspects
Gross national products. B. Solomon. il New Times 10:58–62 +
Je 26 '78

Laws and regulations
Bad aftertastes; honest advertising; study by Richard J. Semenik.
Hum Behav 7:60 S '78
See also
Advertising Corrective
Television advertising—Laws and regulations

Moral aspects
See Advertising ethics

Prize contests
In Florida: a contest winner's road to "shoppertunity" methods
of D. Haley. A. Constable. il por Time 112:13 + S 18 '78

Rates
See also
Television advertising—Rates

Testimonials
Big new celebrity boom. il Bus W p77 + My 22 '78
Johnny Miller: the selling of a loser. P. Taubman. il pors Esquire
90:50–4 + N 7 '78
Let the stellar sellar beware: P. Boone case. il por Time 111:66
My 22 '78
Rum friends. S. C. Cowley. il Newsweek 91:69 My 22 '78

Anecdotes, facetiae, satire, etc.
Endorse! Endorse! C. Neilson. Cycle 29:8 + Ap '78
ADVERTISING, Aerial
See also
Skywriting
ADVERTISING, Classified
Advertising for a man: does a nice girl like you dare to do it? V.
Tomasson. Glamour 76:58 + Je '78
I advertised for a wife. J. Gollay. por Good H 186:28 + F '78
Jobs and want ads: a look behind the words. H. E. Meyer. il
Fortune 98:88–90 + N 20 '78
ADVERTISING, Comparison
Ineffectiveness of comparative advertising. R. D. Wilson. USA
Today 107:13 Ag '78
It pays to knock your competitor. A. L. Morner. il Fortune
97:104–6 + F 13 '78
Question of taste; campaign of Taylor Wine Co. Fortune 98:33
O 23 '78
ADVERTISING, Corrective
Taking it back; corrective ads for Listerine. il Time 111:83 Ap 17
'78
ADVERTISING, Direct mail
Sales through the mails—AAP seminar looks at how it's done;
technical, scientific and medical books. J. Giusto. Pub W
214:75–7 Jl 24 '78
Survival in direct marketing. il Bus W p 148 + O 23 '78
See also
Mailing lists
ADVERTISING, Foreign
See also
Advertising—International aspects

ADVERTISING, Fraudulent

Potions, lotions & gadgets that promise a new you. il Changing
T 82:81–3 S '78

See also

Advertising, Corrective

ADVERTISING, Magazine

Deception on the beach; cigarettes. D. Seligman. Fortune
98:26+ S 11 '78

ADVERTISING, Mail. See Advertising, Direct mail

ADVERTISING, Newspaper

Get free ads in your local paper. R. Varenchik. il Mother Earth
News 55:66–7 Ja '79

See also

Books—Advertising

ADVERTISING, Outdoor

See also

Billboards

Electric signs

ADVERTISING, Personal. See Advertising, Classified

ADVERTISING, Political

Ad-versaries; use of television in Venezuelan presidential campaign. por Time 112:44+ D 18 '78

David v. Goliath; D. Garth. D. Hamill. por N Y 11:9 Ja 30 '78

Governor's race: Garth (Carey) vs. Deardourff (Duryea) New York
State. F. Ferretti. il N Y 11:95–100 S 11 '78

Jarvis goes national. por Newsweek 92:47 O 9 '78

Media mesmerists; work of D. Garth and J. Deardourff. pors
Time 112:35 O 30 '78

Selling of the comptroller; N. Regan's political commercials. S.
Marcus. N Y 12:46 Ja 15 '79

Walking pol; political gimmicks. K. Bode. New Repub 178:8–10
Je 17 '78

World according to Garth. R. S. Anson. il pors New Times 11:18–
19+ O 30 '78

ADVERTISING, Public service

Use the airways to publicize your church. C. L. Nagy. Chr Today
23:30 N 17 '78

ADVERTISING, Window. See Show windows

ADVERTISING agencies

AMF: centralizing leisure-goods ads to make the most of rub-
off sales; Benton & Bowles Inc. il Bus W p 174 My 22 '78

How Ayer engineered its Pan Am coup. il pors Bus W p88–9 S
4 '78

See also

American Association of Advertising Agencies

Black advertising agencies

Acquisitions and mergers

BBDO International buys Franklin Spier agency. M. Reuter. Pub
W-213:33–4 Ja 30 '78

Merger on Madison Avenue; Interpublic Group of Companies
acquiring SSC & B. il Time 112:91 N 20 '78

Foreign business

East-bloc linkup for Young & Rubicam; joint venture with Hun-
garian agency. Mahir Publicity Co. to open new offices in
Frankfurt and Budapest. Bus W p32 My 29 '78

Gallic invaders on Madison Avenue. il Bus W p55–6 My 8 '78

France

Galllic invaders on Madison Avenue. il Bus W p55–6 My 8 '78

Hungary

East-bloc linkup for Young & Rubicam; joint venture with Mahir
Publicity Co. to open new offices in Frankfurt and Budapest.
Bus W p32 My 29 '78

ADVERTISING art

Artist in marketplace. N. Rockwell. il Sat Eve Post 250:10–11 Ja
'78

Collectors and collecting

Corporate collectibles: the history of American business in a tin can. P. Sturm and C. Saltzman. il Forbes 121:105–8 Ap 3 '78

ADVERTISING awards. See Advertising—Awards, prizes, etc..

ADVERTISING campaigns

Not brutal—tough; Forbes' mind-reader compaign. Forbes 121:6 Mr 20 '78

ADVERTISING cards

Baseball card collecting. T. A. Brewster. il pors Americana 6:29–33 Jl '78

How to make your own photographic business cards. K. Donelson. il Peter Phot Mag 7:59–60 Ja '79

ADVERTISING characters

Around the Mall and beyond: Smokey Bear's new home at the National Zoo. E. Park. il Smithsonian 9:88–40+ N '78

ADVERTISING ethics

Advertising for trouble. il Time 111:63 Mr 20 '78

Truth or consequences. D. Finn. Sat R 5:26–7 Ja 21 '78

TELEVISION advertising

ABC visits the P.L.O; the sponsors stay home. M. J. Arlen. New Yorker 54:140 N 13 '78

Actress pickets ad industry. J. See. il por N Y 12:11 Ja 8 '79

Ad libido. D. Menaker. il Film Comment 14:20–3 N '78

Ad-monitions. Seventeen 37:30 Ja '78

Advertisements for itself; ABC program promoters H. Marks and L. Sullivan, R. M. Levine. New Times 10:77–8 Mr 20 '78

America stinks. D. K. Mano. Nat R 30:481–2, 542–3 Ap 14, 28 '78

Ban TV ads aimed at children? interviews. P. Charren; K. Broman. pors U.S. News 84:47–8 Ja 16 '78

Brainwatching. J. Mander. il New Times 12:49–51 Ja 8 '79

Capitalizing on kid-power; adaptation of address. M. Pertschuk. New Leader 61:13–15 Ja 30 '78

Confrontation with Canada over TV ads. Bus W p 142+ N 6 '78

Contrasting settings make ads memorable; study by John H. Murphy and Isabella Cunningham. D. A. Cohen. Psychol Today 12:19–20 O '78

Four arguments for the elimination of television; excerpts. J. Mander. Mother Earth News 54:144–52 N '78

How to raise hell: complaining to sponsors. R. L. Hall. il Field & S 83:124 Je '78

It's news to you, but special interests are behind the scenes. M. Massing. New Times 11:16–17 O 2 '78

Kids in commercials. S. D. Lewis. il Ebony 33:102+ Je '78

Now a few words about commercials. . .excerpt from The best thing on TV: commercials. J. Price. il Esquire 90:102–3+ O 24 '78

Sears, Roebuck: accounts closed; National Federation for Decency protest of TV sponsorship. Chr Today 22:38 Je 2 '78

Strike switches off TV ad production. il Bus W p36–7 Ja 15 '79

Telelvision: National Federation for Decency campaign against Sears, Roebuck advertising. G. Weales. Nation 227:189–90 S 2 '78

See also

Action for Children's Television (organization)

Advertising. Political

Automobile industry—Advertising

Cereal foods—Advertising

Feminine hygiene products—Advertising

Lawyers—Advertising

Phonograph record industry—Advertising

Razors—Advertising

Anecdotes, facetiae, satire, etc.

I re-write the songs. R. Rosenblatt. New Repub 178:36–7 F 11 '78

Laws and regulations

If the product is the problem, do you censor the ads? D. Dunn. il Bus W p90 Ap 3 '78

Should the FTC limit TV advertising to children? R. H. Kaspatkin. il Consumer Rep 43:432 Ag '78

Why the watchdogs are afraid to bark; ruling preventing M. Pertschuk's participation in development of curbs on television advertising aimed at children. por Bus W p33+ N 27 '78

Rates

Inflation isn't over in TV advertising rates. M. H. Zim. il Fortune 98:52–4 N 6 '78

Time purchasing

Are the TV networks selling too many ads? protest by affiliated stations. Bus W p26–7 S 18 '78

Canada

Promo that launched a thousand protests. . .D. Francis. il Macleans 92:39 Ja 1 '79

TELEVISION and business. See Business and television

TELEVISION and children

Attitude shaping kiddie TV keeps women workers in their place; study by Shirley L. O'Bryant and Charles R. Corder-Boiz il Hum Behav 7:46 D '78

Ban TV ads aimed at children? interviews, P. Charren; K. Broman. pors U.S. News 84:47–8 Ja 16 '78

Blaming the boob tube. N. E. Silberberg and M. C. Silberberg, Hum Behav 7:68–9 Ap '78

Brainwatching. J. Mander. il New Times 12:49–51 Ja 8 '79

Capitalizing on kid-power; adaptation of address. M. Pertschuk. New Leader 61:13–15 Ja 30 '78

Children and television:
Electronic fix; E. Kittrell. il Child today 7:20+ My '78
Tackling the tube with teamwork. S. L. O'Bryant and C.. R. Corder-Bolz. bibl il Child Today 7:21–4 My '78

Click! Good-by, television. P. Theroux. il Read Digest 113:29–80+ Jl '78

Cooperation between broadcasters & teachers; address. July 4, 1978. F. S. Pierce. Vital Speeches 44:658–60 Ag 15 '78

Couples; work of J. Singer and D. Singer, L. Baranski. il pors People 10:118–19+ O 9 '78

Do you have TV interference? N. Larrick. Todays Educ 67:39–40+ N '78

Have you talked to your child today? excerpt from address. B. Keeshan. il Encore 7:36 Ap 17 '78

If the product is the problem, do you censor the ads? D. Dunn. il Bus W p90 Ap 3 '78

Making the TV wasteland bear fruit; symposium, Phi Delta Kappan 59:665–75 Je '78

Seminar explores relation of books, school and TV. S. Wagner. Pub W 213:20–1+ My 8 '78

Should the FTC limit TV advertising to children? R. H. Karpatkin. Consumer Rep 43:432 Ag '78

Sugar in the morning. . .H. F. Waters and J. B. Copeland. il Newsweek 91:75 Ja 30 '78

TV up North—the kids get smarter; study by R. J.. Madigan and W. Jack Peterson. J. Horn. Psychol Today 11:106+ Mr '78

TV viewing and early school alchievement J. Perney and others. Phi Delta Kappan 59:637–8 My '78

They are doing something about TV. Changing T 32:12 Jl '78

What can parents do about unsavory TV shows? M. E. White. il por. U.S. News 84:84+ Je 19 '78

Who controls children's TV? profiles of network executives. I. Groller. il Parents Mag 53:57–60 O '78

EXERCISE 45

Below, you will find a list of six different topics for a research essay dealing with the broad subject of advertising, followed by a bibliography of twenty-eight articles, arranged in order of their publication dates. Each item in the bibliography is followed by a note giving a brief description of its contents.

Examine the bibliography carefully and then *choose a set of appropriate sources for each of the six essay topics.* You are not expected to locate and read these articles; use the notes to help you make your decisions. The bibliography is numbered to make the distribution process easier. List the numbers of the articles that you select for each topic. You will notice that many of the articles can be used for more than one topic.

Topics:

A. Does American advertising give people what they want? Is it a true reflection of our society's values?

B. What is an appropriate role for advertising in our society? What are the advertiser's responsibilities?

C. Feminists argue that the image of women created by the advertising industry has been a false and objectionable one: is that a valid claim?

D. How do advertising agencies go about manipulating the reactions of consumers? To what extent is this practice unavoidable and even acceptable?

E. How much progress did the movement to protect the consumer make during the 1970's? What was the response of the advertising agencies?

F. Are children especially vulnerable to misleading commercials? Why? How can the juvenile audience be protected?

1. "And Now a Word about Commercials," *Reader's Digest*, Oct. 1968, pp. 27–30. This is a comparatively mild criticism of TV advertising, describing several types of annoying (rather than offensive) commercials, and implying that the industry can do better.

2. "Liberating Women," *Time*, 15 June 1970, p. 93. In a slightly surprised tone, the author notes that ordinary American women are beginning to support feminist attacks against ads that show unwelcome stereotypes of women.

3. "TV Ads: Shorter Pitches at Better Prospects," *Business Week*, 23 Jan. 1971, pp. 88–89. From the ad agency's point of view, this article describes tactics that can be used to influence the buying habits

of various age groups. Specifically, it's concerned with the right time to show ads that appeal to either the old or the young.

4. Ace, Goodman. "The Uncommon Cold," *Saturday Review*, 20 Feb. 1971, p. 6. A folksy, detailed description of a deceptive ad for cough and cold medicine.

5. "The FTC Zooms in on the 'Better' Buys," *Business Week*, 20 Feb. 1971, pp. 25–26. The FTC is investigating consumer complaints dealing with false claims. The article is concerned with ways and means of regulating the advertising industry.

6. "The FTC Gets Tougher on Misleading Ads," *Business Week*, 11 Dec. 1971, p. 35. A description of the way in which one advertiser (The Sugar Association) was forced to modify an ad that presented what the FTC regarded as a false claim.

7. "Advertisers Fight Back," *America*, 8 April 1972, p. 368. This is a brief, abstract discussion of morality in advertising and pressures from consumerist organizations. It concludes that advertising is only a symptom of a more serious cultural illness.

8. "The Counter-Commercials," *Newsweek*, 5 June 1972, pp. 65–66. The article is about the growing number of public service commercials containing warnings and consumer information which, in the opinion of many commercial advertisers, threaten the structure of TV advertising. There are several examples of the need to have more balanced advertising to serve the interests of the public.

9. "Changing the Game," *Newsweek*, 17 July 1972, p. 65. Written from the point of view of ad agencies, this article stresses the threat from clients who split their business between several ad agencies.

10. Woods, Crawford. "American Pie," *New Republic*, 168 (2 June 1973), 25. This article explores the basic psychological reasons for audience gullibility; it is very hostile towards the advertising industry for daring to prey upon television viewers. There is a favorable review of a television program that provided an exposé of deceptive commercials.

11. Monahan, Anthony. "Television," *PTA Magazine*, 68 (March 1974), 8. A rather cynical review of the guidelines for children's advertising voluntarily published by the Association of National Advertisers.

12. Greenland, Leo. "Advertisers Must Stop Conning Consumers," *Harvard Business Review*, 52 (July 1974), 18–20. The consumerist point of view should be accepted by the advertising industry, which should be policing itself. Ad agencies should place more trust in the average person's common sense.

13. "The One That Cried All the Way Home," *Business Week*, July 27, 1974, p. 7. This is a review of a book that's critical of advertising,

written by a consumerist advertising man. The reviewer finds the book's criticisms of the ad industry too strong, especially in the light of inflation, which is creating problems for all ad men.

14. Krugman, Herbert E. "What Makes Advertising Effective?" *Harvard Business Review*, 53 (March–April 1975), 96–104. This is a scientific examination of methods of making an effective ad. Written from the agency's point of view, the article is full of advertising jargon and statistics, and seems rather repetitive.

15. Field, Roger. "The Great Paper Towel Deception," *Science Digest*, 77 (May 1975), 86–88. This offers a single illustration, in great detail, of the false claims and trickery presented in the commercial for Bounty towels.

16. "More Truth in Advertising," *Time*, 2 June 1975, p. 6. This is a basic protest against advertising hype, especially ads that are based on testimonials by celebrities.

17. "Recession Rip-offs," *McCall's*, 102 (July 1975), 34–35. Two or three illustrations of deceptive ads, specifically those offering employment or soliciting investment.

18. Bever, T. G., et al. "Young Viewers' Troubling Response to TV Ads," *Harvard Business Review*, 53 (Nov.–Dec. 1975), 109–120. This is a long essay, mostly about children's fantasies, written in academic language which isn't too easy to understand. There's a good section on what's needed to make a valid economic judgment before purchasing.

19. "The FTC's Ad Rules Anger Industry," *Business Week*, 1 Nov. 1976, p. 30. This article seems very objective. It presents the ad industry's point of view and also the consumer's. The topic is the new guidelines for food and drug advertisement.

20. "An Art Director Who Has a Way with Words Also Has a Book Coming from Abrams," *Publishers Weekly*, 17 Jan. 1977, pp. 55–56. A detailed profile of George Lois and how he develops ad campaigns.

21. "Really Socking It to Women," *Time*, 7 Feb. 1977, pp. 57–59. According to ad agencies, ads and commercials that abuse women stimulate sales. The article cites examples and tries to explore the reasons for this trend.

22. "Buy the Product, Not the Package," *Changing Times*, 31 (April 1977), 21–23. This is a discussion of impulse buying, describing deceptive and manipulative packaging and the consumer's gullibility. It contains advice on how to prevent being fooled by false advertising.

23. Seldin, Joseph J. "A Long Way to Go, Baby," *The Nation*, 16 April 1977, pp. 464–66. This article discusses sterotyped images of women presented in ads and commecials, using guidelines from NOW as a frame of reference. The author suggests that such ads are

unavoidable since they are merely reflecting generally accepted social values. The author is president of an ad agency.

24. Rosenblatt, Roger. "Those Little Eyes So Helpless and Appealing," *New Republic*, 27 April 1977, p. 33. The emphasis here is on the use of adolescent sexuality in ads, linked to the interest in child prostitution. The author suggests that such trends may be a kind of revenge on women and on the young.

25. Bush, S. "The Art of Implying More than You Say," *Psychology Today*, 10 (May 1977), 36. This describes the way in which the wording of an ad can protect an advertiser from false claims. Such ads feature "implied claims." The article stresses public gullibility.

26. "Battle over Comparative Ads," *Dun's Review*, 60 (Nov. 1977), 60–62. This discusses whether the use of a rival's product in an ad will help to raise sales. Possible dangers are cited (e.g., lawsuits). The article is written from the advertiser's point of view.

27. "Advertising for Trouble," *Time*, 20 March 1978, p. 15. A brief article built around two racist ads which are also sexist in their depiction of women.

28. Hurst, Lynda. "Modifying Media Imagery," *Atlas World Press Review*, April 1978, pp. 36–37. The author describes an increasing reaction against TV commecials that contain degrading depictions of women. The article is useful for its description of the stereotypes of women contained in many ads.

ASSIGNMENT 20

I. Choose a broad topic for a research essay.
   A. If you have *a person or an event* in mind, but do not have sufficiently detailed knowledge to decide on a focus and target date, wait until you have done some preliminary reading. Start with an encyclopedia article or an entry in a biographical dictionary; then use the card catalog and any bibliographies that you find along the way. Decide whether your topic is recent enough to have been featured in available newspapers and periodicals, and consult the appropriate indices.
   B. If you want to write about a *contemporary issue*, examine some of the entries dealing with that topic in recent volumes of the *Readers' Guide* or the *New York Times Index*; then formulate a few questions which you might undertake to answer.

II. Compile a preliminary bibliography for an essay of eight to ten pages, consulting the relevant card catalogues and indexes. At this point, you need not examine all the sources, take notes, or plan the organization of your essay. Your purpose is to assess the *amount* and, as much as possible, the *quality* of the material that is available. Whether or not your teacher asks you to hand in your preliminary bibliography, make sure that the publication information that you record is accurate and legible. Distinguish between the sources that your library has available and the sources that may be difficult to obtain.

III. Submit a topic proposal to your teacher, describing the probable scope and focus of your essay. (If you are considering more than one topic, suggest a few possibilities.) Be prepared to alter the specifics of your proposal as you learn more about the number and availability of your sources.

7. Gathering Materials at the Library: Evaluating Sources

While compiling a preliminary bibliography, a student has located a promising group of sources. She intends to focus her essay on high school dropouts: specifically, she wants to discuss the age at which adolescents should be allowed to leave school. At the library, the student has consulted indexes and bibliographies, and has collected references to several books and articles, all of which, according to their titles, seem to be relevant. Some of these authors will have a better claim to being cited as authorities than others. Since all the names are unfamiliar to her, which should she read first? How can she hope to weigh one source of evidence against another and decide whose ideas will receive prominence in her essay?

First of all, the student can try to find out something about each author's credentials for writing about high school students. Is the writer a teacher? an administrator? an educator? or a journalist, presenting second-hand information? Are the source's qualifications consistent with the subject? Someone who specializes in the kindergarten years may not be the best person to offer opinions about sixteen-year-olds. On the other hand, one might not think that an economist would be an authority to consult about high school dropouts; yet, if he has made a study of the job market and the career prospects of workers without high school certificates, then an economist's evidence and recommendations would be well worth including in a research essay. Would a social psychologist be a useful source? An answer would depend on the nature of the work: a study of abnormal social patterns in adolescents might be rather remote from the everyday problem of determining the minimum age for leaving high school, but a study of juvenile delinquency might suggest connections between teenage crime and teenage dropouts. Consider the article in Chapter 4 about strict attendance policies in grade school. What *were* Roger Sipher's qualifications for making such tough recommendations?

Consider also "A Question of Degree" in Chapter 2. Who *is* Blanche Blank, and why should we believe her claim that we have grossly inflated the value of a college degree? When she wrote "A Question of Degree," was she the employee of a company that denied her promotion because she lacked a B.A.? a college graduate seeking a more interesting job? a housewife, anxious to return to college? or a college teacher who specialized in education (as, in fact, she is)? What difference would this information make to your understanding of her essay?

On the other hand, you may be asked to write about a writer or a group of writers (in an anthology, perhaps) whose names are all familiar to you and whose importance and credentials cannot be in doubt. Why, then, would you need to find out more about these authors? Would they have been chosen for inclusion in an anthology if their authority were questionable? Once again, how can knowledge of the source help in the writing of your research essay?

APPROACHES TO SOURCE EVALUATION

You should not try to examine information or ideas in isolation, in a vacuum. The mind, the personality, and the experience of an author (as well as the times in which he lived) are generally well worth knowing something about, if only to provide a context for understanding his meaning. There may be some significant connection between the author's background—education, previous writings, professional interests, political leanings, life experience—and the ideas in the book or article that you are planning to write about. Finding out about an author's credentials and background not only helps you to decide whether the source is trustworthy, but also enables you to make allowances for an individual approach to the subject and (in some cases) for bias.

In this sense, "bias" is not a bad word, nor is it quite the same thing as "prejudice." Bias means special interest or personal angle: the line of thought that this person would be expected to pursue, which might affect his opinion about the subject that interests you. Few knowledgeable people are entirely detached or objective, whether about their pet interests and "hobbyhorses" or about the area of learning which has been their life's work. To some extent, the awareness of bias can weaken your belief in the author's credibility. It is the person who is both knowledgeable and without bias whose opinions tend to carry the most weight. Nevertheless, it is a mistake to discount a good idea automatically just because you believe that the writer's ideas may reflect his special interests. Once you have identified a possible bias, then you can either disregard it as harmless or adjust your judgement to allow for its influence.

Learning the facts about an author's background does not necessarily permit you to make assumptions about his probable point of view. Jumping to conclusions can be dangerous. For example, according to their biographies, two of the authors whose writings are included in this book, E. Bright Wilson and J. D. Bernal, were engaged during World War II in the development of new weapons. Yet, on the basis of that information, it would be foolish to try to trace a cause-and-effect connection between these activities and the ideas presented in their essays. What is important is not their common experience of arms research, but the use that they made of this experience in the development of their ideas about scientific responsibility; and in this respect the two scientists differ quite sharply. In general, the purpose of enquiring about the author's life and work is to understand more about the wider context of the work that you are creading so that the relatively small area on which you are focusing—a single essay, a chapter in a book, even a brief quotation—will open up, expand, and become that much more revealing and interesting.

Authors

Where do you go to find out about a writer's background? Possibly to the book itself. The preface may contain biographical information, and the "blurb" on the paper cover will probably describe the author (but frequently in such laudatory terms that much of the information may have to be discounted). Periodicals may provide a thumbnail biography of an article's author at the bottom of its first page, or at the end of the article, or in a group of authors' biographies at the beginning or end of an issue. What you should look for are details about the author's education, professional experience, and published works. These are facts, not susceptible to cosmetic improvement, and they can tell you quite a bit about the writer's probable approach to the subject of your research. Look out for vague descriptions: "a freelance writer who frequently writes about this topic" can describe a self-styled authority or an ignorant amateur. You can also consult one of the many biographical dictionaries, encyclopedias, and indexes. Some of them, however, are not very informative. *Who's Who*, for example, will give you some basic facts about positions held and works published; but you may need to know a good deal about the academic world to interpret this information, and you may not find out very much about the author's characteristic beliefs, associations, or enthusiasms.

As an illustration of this evaluating process, let us look more closely at the author of "A Crisis, a Challenge," one of the readings in Chapter 4. Margaret Mead is a very famous name, yet you may have often read and heard that name without really knowing what she is famous for. Thus, to find out something about her achievements and her credentials for solving the energy crisis, you stop in the library and check one of the biographical reference works. (If you know where these books are shelved, this can take less than ten minutes.) In the index to *Current Biography*, you find a listing for Margaret Mead's obituary in the 1978 volume; to supplement that brief paragraph, you can also look up the complete article on Mead in an earlier volume. Here is the obituary, followed by a few excerpts from the much longer 1951 article (which ends with references to twelve other sources of information about Margaret Mead).

> **MEAD, MARGARET** Dec. 16, 1901–Nov. 15, 1978. One of world's foremost anthropologists; pioneered in research methods that helped to turn social anthropology into a major science; curator emeritus (from 1969) of American Museum of Natural History, with which she had been associated since 1926; taught at Fordham, Columbia, and other universities; made many expeditions, to Samoa, New Guinea, Bali, and other parts of South Pacific; author of hundreds of articles and more than a score of books, including all-time best-seller *Coming of Age in Samoa* (1928); commented on American institutions in such books as *And Keep Your Powder Dry* (1942) and *Male and Female* (1949); promoted environmentalism, women's rights, racial harmony, and other causes; died in New York City. See *Current Biography* (May) 1951.
> *Obituary*
> NY Times A p1 + N 16 '78

> Before leaving [on her second field trip to the West Pacific], Miss Mead completed her now well-known book *Coming of Age in Samoa* (1928). The work was praised in the New York *Times* as "sympathetic throughout . . . but never sentimental" and as "a remarkable contribution to our knowledge of humanity," it went into five printings within two years and has been twice reissued. . . .
> . . . [Mead] published *And Keep Your Powder Dry* (1942), subtitled *An Anthropologist Looks at America* and described in the *Library Journal* as "American character outlined against the background of the seven other cultures" the author had studied.
> Dr. Mead during World War II "wrote OWI pamphlets and interpreted GI's to the British" (*Saturday Review of Literature*) and also served (1942–5) as executive secretary of the committee on food habits, the National Research Council. She was a visiting lecturer at Teacher's College (1945–51) and has further served as consultant on mental health, as a member of the committee on research of the mental health division of the National Advisory Mental Health Council of the United States Public Health Service and as a member of the interim governing board of the International Mental Health Congress. . . .

What do you learn from this information? Margaret Mead was a scientist, thoroughly familiar with the rigorous methods, the complexities, and the delays of scientific research; therefore, she is unlikely to be wishfully optimistic about breakthroughs in the search for new sources of energy. Moreover, Margaret Mead was a *social* scientist, specifically, an anthropologist; she was accustomed to studying the whole of a community or society, assessing its customs, its stability, its morale, its probable responses to challenges and emergencies; therefore, her training would make her both comprehensive and objective in her description of America's response to the energy crisis. Nor did Margaret Mead restrict her writing to anthropological studies of remote tribes; this article is by no means her first comment on the American scene, and so her analysis and predictions gain the credibility that comes with repeated observation. The environment was one of Margaret Mead's special concerns; thus, one can understand and place in context the fervor with which she pleads her case. And, finally, the popularity of her best-selling scientific work suggests that her readers would be more likely to accept her analysis of the crisis and even her stringent solutions—rationing, a less luxurious style of life—than they would the ideas of an author who was less well-known and whose background had been exclusively academic.

On the other hand, the fact that Mead was a popularizer—one who takes dry and difficult ideas and makes them understandable to a wide public—helps to explain why "A Crisis, a Challenge" may seem facile, with many of its assertions unsupported. (Notice that it was written for the *Washington Post*, not for a scholarly journal.) There is clearly a difference between the writings of Margaret Mead, the anthropologist, and those of Margaret Mead, the social commentator. Provided that one realizes that "A Crisis, a Challenge" belongs in the latter category, the article has a place in a research essay as an example of one scientist's contribution to the debate on an issue of popular concern.

Although finding out about your sources may enhance your understanding of what you read, it should never be allowed to dominate the research process. Certainly, if your preliminary bibliography contains twenty books, and you merely want to choose a few for an essay in which no single source will be emphasized, don't waste your time looking up each author at length in the reference room. If, however, you are building a paper around a subject for which there are clearly going to be only one or two highly important sources, and if you feel uneasy about your ignorance of their qualifications and characteristic opinions, invest some time in reading a few articles *about* these authors and their writings. Try book reviews, especially reviews of the books that you intend to cite, or articles cited in *Biographical Index*. In the end, you may have to fall back upon your research instincts, which can become remarkably acute if you spend some time comparing the content and style of the sources that you come across.

EXERCISE 46

Read the twelve statements published by the *New York Times* on 1 May 1979 under the heading "Going to Work in 2001." The remarks were excerpted from a series of long papers delivered at a symposium, "Working in the 21st Century."

A. Consider the professional background of each of the commentators, and decide whether, in each case, you can reasonably conclude that the statement reflects some special interest on the part of the author. (Although your primary focus should be the statement's content— the predictions and suggestions—enlarge your understanding of the writers' various points of view and purposes by also becoming aware of the characteristic style of the economist, the journalist, and so on.) Choose three authors whose interests seem very different, and, in a short paragraph for each, describe the writer's point of view or "bias"; explain your reasoning.

B. Choose one of the four topics listed below. Imagine that you are planning an essay on that topic, and pick out a group of statements (at least five and no more than seven) that would be appropriate for citation in your essay. (The hypothetical essay can be either descriptive or argumentative.)

1. 2001: A return to old-fashioned morality
2. 2001: Changes in politics and the class system
3. 2001: The need for greater productivity
4. 2001: A day in the life of a typical worker

> A.   Our Government tells us that their predictions indicate, and if they bear any fruit at all, that by the year 2050, if the current inflationary trends persist, we will be living in the situation in which a loaf of bread is going to cost $37.50, a medium-sized car, $281,000, and a modest home in an average neighborhood, nearly $3.5 million. Since per-capita consumer debt in our country is already right now at 20 percent of annual income, then perhaps the real question, in terms of the 21st century, will be how to break the bonds of economic and human bondage.
>
> As for myself, I can only suggest that the most effective counterbalance to the corporate state's pyramiding of America will be a dynamic and progressive democratic socialist movement, indifferent to previous ideologies or theories; rather, I think, it will be a socialism spawned from economic, political and social necessity through a very pragmatic approach, championing the common goal, as opposed to narrow, parochial self-interest—and that includes my own institution as well. The counterbalance, as I view it, will be a people-oriented socialism, clashing with the corporate state socialism which I think currently exists.
>
> William W. Winpisinger, President, International
> Association of Machinists and Aerospace Workers

> B.   The big political divisions of the future are likely to be between those who advocate a higher and higher material standard of living, on the

one hand, and those who feel that such a rise in material acquisition is growing less important and that the quality of human experience is far more important. In this line-up, old-fashioned New Deal liberals and old-fashioned materialistic conservatives are likely to find themselves on the same side. Indeed, just such divisions are beginning to shape up in our politics today. By contrast, those who believe in pluralism both in terms of rights of self-expression and in terms of life-style are likely to be drawn together in a new coalition, supported by those groups striving to be recognized by the mainstream and consumerist types.

We are rapidly losing the economic determinism of our politics. In the future, redistribution of the opportunities to partake of quality-of-life experiences, to join together in new common cause to enhance the living of life instead of simply redistributing wealth is likely to be the focus of the American scene.

Louis Harris, pollster

C. A noticeable effect on working life of high energy cost will be a re-duction in the mobility of people. Transportation will become much more expensive and will be subject to fuel-supply interruptions. Most forecasts call for this problem resulting in an increase in mass transit into the center city. However, I don't think this route will be followed, even though it would increase energy efficiency. It seems to me more likely, given our present trends, our life-style preferences, and a still substantial but reduced mobility, that we will see the development of both smaller cities and satellite complexes around larger cities. These smaller cities and satellite complexes will contain all the elements of living—commercial, industrial and residential areas—in close prox-imity.

The trend, I think, will be to eliminate commuting, rather than in-crease its efficiency through mass transit. People will tend to live much closer to their work.

William E. Bonnet, Vice President for Environmental
Assessment, The Sun Company

D. Numerically, the "family" of today will remain strong compared with other living arrangements, but "household" will have to be regarded as the consumer buying unit. Single households, childless couples, groups of adults living together, single-parent groups—all of these remain real-ities of the households of the late 1970's and early 1980's. Within the family, informal and trial marriages, marriage-contracts, role reversal, children's rights—love remains.

If forced to name a few long shots, I would mention the following:

• An unexpected rise in birth rate, perhaps near the turn of the cen-tury, as perceptions about women's roles change again, possibly trig-gered by underemployment in the work force. (This is pure speculation.)

• Child-rearing as a profession.

  • Technology permitting the choice of sex of one's offspring and perhaps some genetic attributes as well.
  • A drop in the rate of formation of single-person households as the
economic advantages of multiple-wage-earner households become apparent.

Theodore J. Gordon, President of the Futures Group
and former Chief Engineer of the Saturn Program,
McDonnell-Douglas Astronautics

E.   As the American economy becomes more labor-intensive as a result
of the shift towards service, clerical and knowledge work, the *attitudes*
of workers become central factors in national productivity. In the industrial sector, uncooperative, recalcitrant and obstreperous workers
can be automated out of the process of production—and productivity
will rise as a result.
      But in a mature, post-industrial economy (such as America's), the
success or failure of the national enterprise rests on the willingness of
individual workers to take responsibility for the quality and quantity of
their work, to take initiative in those increasingly frequent situations
that cannot be routinely handled, to show a real interest in the welfare
of customers, suppliers and fellow-workers. Because of increasing bal-
ance-of-payments deficits and the declining dollar, American managers
may no longer be able to afford to play golf on company time, and
American workers may no longer be able to afford to goof-off or sabotage
cars on the assembly line. The nation can only afford such behavior if
it doesn't want oil, bauxite, coffee, French wines and Japanese radios.

James O'Toole, Associate Professor of Management,
Southern California Graduate School of Business

F.   The most conspicuous failing of self-conscious living Tom Wolfe accurately needled as the "Me Decade." It will outlast the decade.
      And people will continue to use it to dismiss the massive healthy
movement going on behind its smokescreen.
      That's fine.
      Whether or not individuals are Freudian, societies undoubtably are.
Denial precedes acceptance.
      And close attention to self, by its very limitations, precedes close at-
tention to others—responsibility in fact, though a bit different from the
familiar dutiful kind.

Stewart Brand, Editor (and founder) of *The Whole
Earth Catalog* and *CoEvolution Quarterly*

G.   We have a very low investment rate in this country, say 17 percent of
gross national product. But as I've looked at energy and its requirements,
as I've looked at the requirements for containing air and water pollution
which require another 1 percent of gross national product investment
by 1985, as I've looked at the fragmentary data on what we require to

get a rational transport system, one where the trains don't fall off the tracks and the bridges don't threaten to cave in, as I look at problems of water generation, conserving ground water, perhaps transferring water, soil conservation—I look at productivity and the requirements are indeed where I think we ought to add another half percent at least to gross national product. It's palpable to me that we're a society where, if we face these supply problems, you ought to have an investment rate of 20-21-22 percent of G.N.P. Which is no astonishing figure because that's what European countries generally have and the Japanese have 35. I drive this home because this is one very practical operational meaning of this approach from the supply side. But, once we break loose from the fixations of the past we're going to be looking at the people in the slums of the Northern, Midwestern cities not as a sad social problem but as real live bodies that we need for the working force and there will be plenty of jobs.

W. W. Rostow, Professor of Economics,
University of Texas, Austin

H.   I suspect that America's ongoing quest for growth in a global society will be described by the relationship between the future public-policy environment and the entrepreneurial function in our country, and more specifically whether or not the American value system will remain supportive to the entrepreneurial spirit and sanction the appropriate rewards.

We can be sanguine about America's quest for growth, provided our society remains supportive to structural evolution which accommodates the increasing mix of services in our economic profile, and allows the dynamics of comparative advantages to permit our economy to evolve toward higher levels of productivity. And we can also be sanguine to the extent that our neighbors in the global community manage their own economies in complementary fashion. If the net result is the unshackling of the entrepreneurial function over the global marketplace, our prospects can be very bright indeed.

George J. Voijta, Executive Vice President, Citibank N.A.

I.   I see collective bargaining continuing through the remainder of this century and on into the next. The subject matter of bargaining is not likely to change much—wages, hours and working conditions. New problems will inevitably arise involving health, pensions as well as job security in face of environmental and energy considerations.

But there is a professionalism that has developed on both sides of the bargaining table that enhances the capability of industry and labor to cope with these problems. It is likely to increase.

Theodore W. Kheel, labor mediator

J.   Starting within the office itself, the daily personal-interaction pattern will change first. Most of the printed-paper routines that consume so much time (and space) will be gone. Mail-sorting, opening, stamping, physical transportation or searching will decrease significantly but not disappear. During the transition to a (relatively) paperless office, some of these functions will occur at a central location for conversion to electronic form and transmission throughout the business.

There will be fewer reasons to move around the immediate office and the building and thus the social structure of the office will change.

Will we see in office workers the boredom and reactions in health and attendance we now see in highly automated factories? Will we be wishing our letter or file was produced in midweek? What novel excuses will be invented to meet the new person on the fifth floor?

Walter A. Hahn, Congressional Research Service, Washington

K.   My own hope (and I cannot pretend that it is much more than wishful thinking) is that the traditions of this country, with its dedication to the principles of individual dignity and social justice, and the basic good sense of our people will keep us from riding a totalitarian treadmill into the 21st century. I prefer to believe and to expect that the magnitude of the nation's present and prospective problems will cause us to seek democratic solutions based on re-establishment of a foundation of trust in the adaptability of our institutions and the integrity of our leaders, public and private. The erosion of that trust is our single most troublesome roadblock; none of our institutions will be susceptible of enduring repair until the virtue of their performance begins to match the piety of their protestations.

A. H. Raskin, labor specialist

L.   There is no shortage of useful, productive work that needs to be done in this country. The nation's housing stock is dilapidated. Unrepaired railbeds are a barrier to adequate transportation. New energy systems are needed. We can train toward these needs, target our resources towards them, use them to build the momentum for a new productive upsurge. If we combine this reconversion from military to useful civilian production with a new policy that curbs the power of multinational corporations, we can revitalize the manufacturing sector and create the new, good jobs we need.

The same national planning we bring to the goods-producing sector must be brought to the provision of services. We must analyze what the nation needs, look at approaching trends and try to anticipate changes in the way we live.

William Lucy, Secretary-Treasurer, American Federation
of State, County and Municipal Employees

Dates of Publication

One indication of a work's usefulness for your purpose is its date. If the essay on high school dropouts is intended to be a survey of past and

present policy, you would deliberately want to choose some representative works published at various intervals over the last few decades. However, if you are addressing yourself only to present-day conditions, drawing heavily on material published in the forties or fifties would be
pointless (unless you wanted to include some predictions that might or
might not have come true). An article that takes for granted school attendance laws that no longer exist or social conditions (like the draft)
that have changed would be of little value in preparing an essay about
contemporary dropouts. However, you may find older sources with theoretical content that is not dated, such as discussions of the role of
education in the formation of personality.

In judging the usefulness of a source, you may need to know the difference between primary and secondary sources. A *primary source* is a
work which is itself the subject of your essay or (if you are writing a
historical research essay) a work written during the period that you are
focusing on which gives you direct or "primary" knowledge of the period. The term is frequently used to describe an original document—
like the Constitution, for example—or memoirs and diaries of historical
interest, or a work of literature which, over the years, has been the subject
of much written commentary. Any commentary written both *after* and
about the primary source can, in turn, be called the *secondary source.*
Thus, a history textbook is a secondary source.

While you generally study a primary source for its own sake, the secondary source is important—in many cases, it only exists—because of
its primary source. If you are asked to write an essay about *Huckleberry
Finn* and your instructor tells you not to use any secondary sources, you
are to read *only* Mark Twain's novel and not consult anyone else's commentary. Carl Sandburg's biography of Abraham Lincoln is a secondary
source if you are interested in Lincoln, but a primary source if you are
studying Sandburg. And if you read the *Times* in order to acquire information about life in America on a certain date, you are using the newspaper as a primary source, since it is your direct object of study; but
when you look up a *Times* review of a book or a movie you want to write
about, then you are locating a secondary source in order to acquire more
information about your primary subject.

In the sciences and social sciences, the most recent sources usually
supersede earlier ones. However, that rule does not apply to secondary
sources written about historical and biographical subjects. For example,
Forster's biography of Charles Dickens, written in the nineteenth century,
is still considered a valuable and interesting work, in part because Forster
knew Dickens and could provide much firsthand information. However,
research is always unearthing new facts about people's lives. Thus, in
many ways, Forster's work has been superseded by new biographies
which feature the latest information. In fact, for a biographical or historical essay, you would do well to consult both "contemporary" works

(written at the time of the event or during the subject's lifetime) and the most recent studies. But the works in the middle—written only a few years after your target date and without the perspective of distance—often lack authenticity or objectivity.

If you are in doubt about using a source, check to see whether the author has included footnotes and a bibliography; well-documented works tend to be the most reliable. But the absence of documentation is not the only reason for distrusting a source. You can also suspect that a book should not be taken seriously just by glancing through it. If the source is written in a superficial or frivolous or overly dramatic style, then you would be wise to suspect its claim to authority.

Finally, try dividing the available sources into three groups: those you know that you will want to use; those you reject on sight; and those you are doubtful about. Be aware of the reasons for your doubts and indicate those reasons in the notes for your bibliography. Then, at some point in your research, you can check the qualifications of those sources with your instructor or with reference works; or, at the end, you can simply annotate your bibliography so that your reader is made aware of your judgments and your reasons for proceeding with caution.

SELECTING SOURCES THAT WORK WELL TOGETHER

In Chapter 5, when you learned how to write about a group of sources, the process was simplified to make your work easier: the sources were all of the same kind, homogeneous, and therefore relatively easy to synthesize. The statements in each group all came from students who had roughly the same skills and experience, and whose opinions were therefore comparable. But in real research at the library, the sources that you find may have nothing at all in common but their subject.

Periodicals provide a clear-cut example, for they are published for a variety of specific audiences with well-defined interests and reading habits and (in some cases) social and political views. Since the readership varies so greatly, articles on the same subject in two different periodicals are likely to be very different in their point of view and presentation. An article on dropouts in one of the well-known women's magazines is likely to be reassuring and helpful, filled with concrete advice to parents. It will not have the same purpose nor cite the same kinds of evidence nor be expressed in the same kind of vocabulary as an article of comparable length published the same year in *Psychology Today*, which, in turn, will probably not resemble a scholarly essay on dropouts in the *Journal of the American Psychological Association* or the *American Journal of Sociology*. An equivalent article in *Newsweek* or *Time* will be shorter and snappier, filled with vivid, concrete illustrations. Consider these characteristic differences when you are establishing research priorities and deciding which articles to consult and to include in your essay.

Books are potentially even more difficult to synthesize since they vary so greatly in length, purpose, and presentation. Suppose that in researching your paper on high school dropouts you have found three very different books, all published recently. One contains 285 pages exclusively about dropouts; chapter after chapter is filled with statistical studies and case histories presented in dense detail and in an abstract language which requires concentration to absorb. The second book is a comprehensive study of the high school curriculum and its present levels of achievement; there is one thirty-page chapter about dropouts and student morale in general. Finally, the third source is an educational handbook, directed at future teachers, with a page and a half devoted to the importance of making students stay in school; the issue is presented broadly and rhetorically, as if part of a stirring speech.

Can these three sources be integrated into the same essay? All three are certainly relevant to the topic, and each may be interesting and useful in itself. But the difference in depth among them is so radical that it is hard to see how the three can be used together in a single essay. And, indeed, the one thing that you should not do is to plunk down excerpts from these three sources side by side, in adjoining sentences. If they are to be integrated at all, you must first recognize and then communicate to your reader that the three sources are not equivalent.

This does not mean that all of your sources should cover the same range of ideas, should be roughly the same length, and should employ much the same vocabulary and depth of evidence. Working with materials of the same order of difficulty may be convenient, but developing a balanced bibliography that offers a variety of approaches to the topic is more important. You must remain sensitive to the *kinds* of sources that you are using and recognize the nature of your materials. This awareness begins when you begin your research. As you glance through an article or a chapter in a book, ask yourself whether the content is primarily theoretical or practical. How often does the author offer evidence to support his conclusions? What kind of evidence? Or does the book's thesis depend on a series of broad propositions, linked together into an argument? What is the scope of the book? Is the focus narrow, with the entire work centered around one person's experience? Or does it sum up the work of others and present a comprehensive picture of the research that has been done in the field? Finally, be alert to the kind of language and rhetoric that the author is using, and make mental (or even written) notes about its difficulty.

Your awareness of the differences between your sources will help you to determine your research priorities. You would not begin your research by taking notes from the 285-page book on dropouts; not everything in it would relate to your eventual thesis. Instead, you would begin with the single comprehensive chapter from the second source, which would give you an overview of the subject and help you to narrow your own thesis and establish your own approach to the topic. Once you have a working list of the specific points that interest you, it might not be necessary for you to work through all 285 pages of the first source. And don't forget the third work, the handbook, which might suggest a broad perspective that could give you a better understanding of your topic, as well as provide you with an excellent quotation or two.

INTEGRATING YOUR SELECTED SOURCES

Once you have become familiar with all three sources and have become aware of their differences and their relative usefulness, how do you integrate them into your essay? Unless the framework is large enough to incorporate them all smoothly, you may simply decide to exclude the one that does not mesh easily with the others. You do not want to distract your reader by moving back and forth abruptly from extremely broad statements of policy to minute citations of case studies or statistical evidence, especially if the different segments are expressed in a completely different vocabulary and style. Even if you attempt the difficult task of paraphrasing all three and thus provide a common denominator of your own style, you will still need to insert transitions between the sources to prepare your reader for the shift from one approach to the next. Thus, in an essay of only six or seven pages, you would be wise to restrict your sources to those which blend well together because they are of the same order of difficulty. The writers you cite do not have to agree with each other; rather, their scope and methods should be roughly similar.

For a short essay you would have to decide in the early stages of your research which kind of source will best suit the development of your thesis. How complex will your essay be? How sophisticated is your argument? Does it require support from complex case studies? If you intended to prove that dropouts came from a clearly specified kind of family environment, you would probably need to cite scholarly sources, like the 285-page dropout book. On the other hand, you might want to argue that the dropout rate could be linked to a general decline in standards of education, drawing to some extent on your own high school experience. This thesis would be "popular" in its approach to the subject and would require less rigorous sources. Remember that a popularization is a simplification of a difficult subject; popular essays could not exist without the evidence to be found in longer and more complex works. In a sense, a college research essay has to be popular since it is valuable as evidence of the student's understanding of the subject, rather than as a contribution to scholarly knowledge.

In determining whether or not to use the popular approach, remember to consider the level of the course that you are taking. An introductory course is intended to help you grasp the broad concepts that are basic to the discipline; thus, your instructor does not expect you to go out of your depth in hunting scholarly sources for your essay. On the other hand, in an advanced course, you are preparing to do your own research, and so you have to demonstrate your understanding of the work of others as well as the methods that are commonly used in that field. In an advanced course, the popular approach can be superficial.

In a longer essay of ten pages or more, you should have much less trouble blending ill-assorted sources. With fairly leisurely development, you can position each source in the place where it is most appropriate and where it will have the most convincing effect. Thus, for the dropout essay the fine quotations that you might have gleaned from the brief handbook could be placed in the introduction or conclusion of your essay; the theories relating curriculum to student morale could be included in your preliminary presentation of your argument; and you would cite the detailed evidence of the longest source in support of your own ideas or as part of your survey of the work already done in this field. In short, these very different sources could be used together successfully, provided that you did not give your reader the impression that they were interchangeable in their usefulness.

In your search for a well-balanced bibliography, make sure that you include only what you yourself really understand. The point here is that you are an amateur who cannot yet be expected to compete with the professionals on their own terms. If you retain the amateur's approach— keen interest, fresh point of view, respect for authority and for experience—you can choose sources that help you learn. But if you find yourself consulting and citing sources whose writing makes no sense to you, no matter how eminent and qualified these authorities may be, your essay will be a failure; for you will be pretending a mastery of the subject that you do not actually have. Write only about what you understand.

EXERCISE 47

Examine the following preliminary bibliography of articles for a research essay on the broad topic of *divorce*. The bibliography is followed by two excerpts from the *New York Times Index*, one from 1973 and one from 1980, each containing a selection of articles.

A. Make up two *narrow* topics, one focused on divorce in recent years, the other suggesting a retrospective approach and including the last few decades.
B. Carefully read the bibliography and the selections from the *Times Index*, and consider the probable contents of each article, as suggested by the title; the kind of periodical it appears in; the length; and the date of publication. What can you conclude about each article?
C. Determine your research priorities for each of your two topics by choosing a list of the five articles that you believe ought to be located and consulted first. Record your two lists.

Ackerman, N. W. "Divorce and Alienation in Modern Society," *Mental Hygiene*, 53 (20 Oct. 1966), 118–26.

"Bazaar's After-divorce Survival Guide: Symposium," *Harper's Bazaar*, 109 (July 1976), 26–31.

Cadden, V. "The Myth of the Civilized Divorce," *Redbook*, 140 (Feb. 1973), 89.

Cantor, D. F. "The Right of Divorce," *The Atlantic Monthly*," 218 (Nov. 1966), 67–71.

Cerling, C. E. "When Love Fails: Consultation on Divorce and Remarriage," *Christianity Today*, 19 Nov. 1976, pp. 54–55.

Davis, K. "Statistical Perspective on Marriage and Divorce," *Annals of the American Academy*, 272 (Nov. 1950), 9–21.

DeWolf, R. "No-fault divorce," *The Nation*, 216 (23 April 1973), 527–29.

"Divorce, New York Style," *Newsweek*, 21 March 1966, pp. 31–32.

"Divorce Rates Climbing, Increase Is World Wide," *Science Newsletter*, 55 (21 May 1949), 326.

"Divorced Execs; Study by Eugene Jennings," *Human Behavior*, (7 Dec. 1978), 49–50.

Gold, Herbert. "Divorce as a Moral Act," *Atlantic Monthly*, 200 (Nov. 1967), 115–18.

Goode, W. J. "Social Engineering and the Divorce Problem," *Annals of the American Academy*, 272 (Nov. 1950), 86–94.

Hacker, A. "Divorce à la Mode," *New York Review of Books*, 26 (3 May 1979), 23–27.

Hanks, G. F. "What Every Divorced Woman Should Know About Taxes," *Essence*, 9 (March 1979), 66–76.

"High Cost of Divorce in Money and Emotions," *Business Week*, 10 Oct. 1975, pp. 83–86.

Horner, L. "I Have Two Mothers and Two Fathers," *Good Housekeeping*, 132 (Feb. 1951), 52.

Hughes, E. J. "The Catholics of New York," *Newsweek*, 21 March 1966, p. 23.

Hunt, M. M. "The Formerly Married," *Newsweek*, 21 Oct. 1966, pp. 105–06.

———. "Help Wanted: Divorce Counselor," *New York Times Magazine*, 1 Jan. 1967, pp. 14–21

James, T. F. "Divorce, an Emotional Disease," *Cosmopolitan*, 146 (March 1959), 36–43.

Kirkpatrick, J. D. "Child of Divorce," *Parents' Magazine*, 21 (Sept. 1946), 194.

———. "Do Working Wives Risk Divorce?" *McCall's*, Sept. 1976, p. 42.

Lobsenz, N. M. "No-fault Divorce—Is It Working?" *Reader's Digest* 112 (March 1978), 113–16.

Monahan, T. P. "How Stable Are Re-Marriages? Records in Iowa and Missouri," *American Journal of Sociology*, 58 (Nov. 1952), 280–88.

"Money Side of Divorce," *Changing Times*, 27 (Sept. 1973), 29–32.

Murdock, G. P. "Family Stability in Non-European Cultures," *Annals of the American Academy*, 272 (Nov. 1950), 95–201.

Newsman, S. C. "Needs and Future Prospects for Integrating Marriage and Divorce Data with Other Vital Statistics," *American Public Health*, 39 (Sept. 1949), 1141–44.

"Nobody Tells You: By a Divorcee," *Woman's Home Companion*, 78 (Jan. 1951), 4.

O'Sullivan, S. "Single Life in a Double Bed," *Harper's*, 251 (Nov. 1975), 45–48.

Pierce, P. "Divorce and the Negro Woman," *Ebony*, July 1967, 84–86.

Seldin-Schwartz. "Diary of a Middle-aged Divorcé," *MS.*, 4 (April 1976), 84–87.

Thompson, D. "Don't Divorce Your Child," *Ladies Home Journal*, 64 (Jan. 1947), 6.

Traile, M. "More Orphans in America than in Bomb-Riddled Europe?" *American Home*, 36 (Jan. 1946), 28–29.

Wiegner, K. K. "High Costs of Leaving," *Forbes*, 123 (19 Feb. 1979), 44–49.

Younger, J. T. "Love Is Not Enough: Divorce and Feminism," *New Republic*, 19 June 1976, pp. 8–9.

New York Times Index, 1973, "Divorce, Separations and Annulments"

United States. See also subhead NYS

Conn Superior Ct Judge E W Ryan awards Mrs A Malash divorce because husband had not spoken to her for yrs and would not even acknowledge her presence in room; dismisses Malash countersuit charging cruelty, Ja 6,59:3

Ariz Sup Ct agrees to dispose of 194 old divorce decrees that have never been filed and therefore are not officially valid; decrees were discovered in business papers of V L Hash,

Phoenix lawyer who died in '66 without having filed them with county clerk; his niece says it was common practice in Maricopa County not to file decrees, dating from' 24-55, until atty was paid, Ja 7,66:1

Intermarriage and divorce cited as factors in erosion of Jewish families in US, F 9,40:1

Article on increasing number of women who, with psychological encouragement of women's liberation movement, leave home and marriage because of discontent and lack of personal fulfillment; 2 women describe their reasons for leaving their husbands and children and results of their estrangements; illus, F 16,44:3

Vermont man G J Chicoine imprisoned over 5 yrs for nonpayment of $2550 in support to estranged wife; sentenced because Superior Ct Judge Larrow felt he was hiding $90,000; never received jury trial; Vermont Legal Aid files petition for writ of habeas corpus, F 18,53:1

Article on Sun Valley (Idaho), where wealthy women go to ski while they fulfill state's 6-wk residency requirement to get valid divorce, Mr 18,66:1

L Friedman rev of const questions posed by current alimony laws; illus, Mr 25,IV,6:4

C R Davenport, Agr Dept official, indicated on charges of hiring private detective to place electronic listening device on telephone of his estranged wife, Ap 10,37:1

Nevada Sen approves, 13 to 7, bill providing for 'no-fault' divorce, Ap 18,45:2

NJ Judge S J Ruggiero calls for elimination of adversary proceedings in state's divorce procedure in essay published by NJ Law Journal; contends that 'adversary proceedings in divorce cases are detrimental to parties and against public interest'; says problem is that lawyers have task of seeking revenge for their clients; says he has not formulated program of reforms, but that '71 divorce reform law, which instituted 'no fault' concept in dissolving marriages, is step in right direction, Je 10,81:1

39 of the 420 married Amer POWs recently returned from Vietnam either have gotten or are getting divorces, according to Pentagon rept, Je 12,2:4

A Martin comment describing hurt he feels at wife's decision to seek divorce; drawing; deplores lack of communication which led to situation; defends traditional values of marriage and family, Je 25,33:2

J Clinthorne, research associate for Community Council of Greater NY, has computed additional cost that divorce brings to moderate-income family; family that could get by on $10,000 after taxes before divorce will need $12,000 after divorce; housing expenses go up 63% with need to maintain 2nd apartment; food costs go up about 7%; wife will also need separate medical coverage; other added expenses are cost of 2 telephones, duplication in spending on newspapers, magazines, etc, and double contributions and spending for charity, church and gifts; expenses increase as children grow older; study was designed to give families contemplating divorce an idea of what it will cost; table showing breakdown of annual budget of divorce family, Jl 5,43:5

New York Times Index, 1980, "Divorce, Separations and Annulments"

Ethelyn (Morgan) Daniel, who, 5 years ago, was focus of widely publicized matrimonial trial in which Justice Bentley Kassal ruled that her husband, Charles Morgan, help her through medical school after divorce, receives MD degree from Albert Einstein College of Medicine of Yeshiva University; invites Kassal to graduation; case recalled in light of divorce reform pending in NYS Legislature; Daniel and Kassal illus (M), Je 6,II,4:4

NYS Court of Appeals rules that a woman living with a man to whom she is not married may be entitled to a share of his assets if she can prove they had an 'express' oral agreement; opinion (Morone vs Morone), was authored by Associate Judge Bernard S Meyer, who refers repeatedly to rights of 'a couple;' lawyers for Frances Morone describe ruling as 'a monumental, landmark decision' (M), Je 7,1:3

Article on 'equitable distribution' divorce bill passed by NYS Legislature and major impact it could have on property awards, negotiated as well as contested. Dr Doris Jonas Freed, legal scholar, comments (M), Je 10,II,19:1

NJ Supreme Court, in separate divorce cases decided this week, rules that former wife's earning capacity must be considered before amount of alimony or child support payments be increased and that physical separation of a couple and payment of support money are not incontrovertible evidence that a marriage is dead, for purposes of equitable distribution of property; says in absence of qualifying separation agreement, any property acquired before actual filing of divorce complaint has to be included in determining property settlement (M), Je 15,26:2

Geraldine Greene comment on effect of divorce on grandparents, who are sometimes caught in middle of marital disputes and who often must shoulder unexpected child-rearing responsibilities; drawing (M), S 28,XXII,22:3

Marvin Mitchelson, Hollywood divorce lawyer, demands community property payments for Mrs Desmond Ryan in divorce proceedings, Los Angeles, over 5 years, even in event of husband's death (S), S 29,II,8:6

Los Angeles court rules Stanley Benton-Rudich and former husband David P Rudich must share custody of couple's Rolls-Royce (S), O 2,II,2:3

Dr Sheila Schwartz, author of The Solid Gold Circle, novel about divorce, discusses plight of middle-aged women who face divorce after years of being dependent on successful husbands; por (S), O 5,XXII,11:1

Suffolk County (NY) school professionals from 4 districts are trained in handling emotional problems of children whose parents are divorced or separated; psychotherapist Maida Berenblatt comments on course she designed; illus (M), O 19,XXI,4:5

US Supreme Court to hear California case on whether military retirement pay may be divided between spouses as part of divorce settlements; case is important to military families because pension is often couples' largest asset (S), O 21,14:3

Editorial on expected US Supreme Court decision on rights of military couples in divorce cases; holds military pensions should be shared in divorces, like other assets acquired during marriage, N 7,26:1

Shelby Moorman Howatt article expresses sadness and bewilderment at friends' divorce after 20 years of marriage; drawing (M), N 9,XI,34:3

National Center for Health Statistics reports 1.17 million divorces in '79, 3.5% over '78 (S), N 16,63:3

Michael Norman article on extended family relationships created by divorce, remarriage and child custody arrangements; illus; describes delicate modus vivendi worked out by spouses and former spouses concerned with rearing children of their former marriages; focuses on families living in Menlo Park (Calif), Lincoln (Neb) and Opelika (Alaska) (L), N 23,VI,p28

NJ state Judge Conrad W Krafte rules that person who contributes financially and emotionally to spouse's professional education is entitled to share of 'present value' of that education after divorce; finds degree is 'property' or physical asset subject to equitable settlement under NJ divorce law; orders Dr Robert Lynn to pay former wife Bonnie $61,377 over 5 years as 20% share of medical license he earned in '75; notes wife supported Lynn throughout schooling (S), D 7,60:3

EXERCISE 48

Each of the passages below has been extracted from a longer article (or, in one case, a book) on the general subject of alcoholism. These excerpts all deal specifically with the causes of alcoholism, and some are especially concerned with teen-age alcoholics.

Carefully examine the distinctive way in which each passage presents its information:

    A. the amount and kind of evidence that is cited;

    B. the expectations of the reader's knowledge and understanding;

    C. the relative emphasis on generalizations and abstract thinking;

    D. the characteristic tone and vocabulary.

Take into consideration what you may already know about these publications and the audience for each. Then decide whether there would be any difficulty in using these sources together in a single research essay on teen-age alcoholism.

Write a thesis for such an essay, and then decide which three sources you would definitely use in writing your essay. Be prepared to justify your choice.

  A. **ALCOHOLISM.** Alcoholism is a chronic illness, psychic or somatic or psychosomatic, which manifests itself as a disorder of behavior. It is characterized by the repeated drinking of alcoholic beverages, to an extent that exceeds customary dietary use or compliance with the social customs of the community and that interferes with the drinker's health, or his social or economic functioning. Many special categories of alcoholics have been identified, including "alcohol addicts," who cannot control their drinking, and "alcoholics with complications." The latter are those whose excessive drinking has led to recognizable physical or mental sequels.

    Causation.—There are two leading schools of etiological theory. Alcoholism is believed by one school to be a manifestation of neurosis, due to inadequate or arrested development of personality and rooted in early childhood. A constitutional predisposition to psychic deviation is often assumed. The deviation is thought to take the form of alcoholism rather than some other disturbance when environmental conditions favor recourse to intoxication as a defense against the unconscious stresses connected with personal and social life responsibilities. The incidence of alcoholism in a population, therefore, depends on how frequently the combination of constitutional predisposition, inadequate rearing and permissive circumstances occurs.

    The second school attributes alcoholism to a biochemical defect, either of the endocrines or of metabolism or of some other kind, which provokes an uncontrollable craving specifically for alcohol. The inci-

dence of alcoholism in different populations is thought to be related to
the frequency of the causative defect, most often assumed to be genet-
ically determined.

Still others regard alcohol itself as the addiction-causing substance
but must rely on one of the preceding explanations to account for the
different frequencies of alcoholism in various ethnic, cultural and geographic populations, and for the immunity of the vast majority of drinkers.

from *Encyclopedia Americana*

B.   Many theories regarding the causes of alcoholism have been proposed, yet none has gained widespread acceptance. Alcoholism has
been related to physiological, psychological, and sociological factors.
Among physiological causes that have been proposed are nutritional
deficiencies, metabolic defects such as abnormal enzyme levels, disturbed glandular functions, abnormal levels of various body chemicals,
and allergic reactions. Proposed psychological causes have included oral
cravings, repressed homosexual traits, pleasure fixation, unconscious
urges to destroy oneself or to dominate others, feelings of inferiority or
insecurity, and many others. Sociological factors are cited on the basis
of the relationship between cultural patterns and incidence of alcoholism. For example, drinking is almost universal among Orthodox Jews
and native Italians, but the incidence of alcoholism is quite low. In these
groups, alcoholic beverages have established roles in religious and social
traditions.

At least some research evidence has been presented to support each
of the possible causes of alcoholism, but no single theory of causation
has been adequately proven. In fact, there probably is no single cause
of all alcoholism. More likely, alcoholism is the result of many complex
factors acting together.

The concept of alcoholism as a disease is widely accepted today and
is well within the medical definition of disease. The alcoholic is regarded
as a sick person rather than as a weak or sinful person. Although there
have been attempts to describe "the" alcoholic personality type, alcoholics can be found among all personality types.

Kenneth L. Jones, from *Drugs and Alcohol*

C.   Moderate drinking behavior, too, is influenced by what people expect
from alcohol. The person who knows that a drink relaxes and loosens
him up can expect the same of others, and the expectation makes socializing easier. To be sure, physiology can play a role even in some of
the fantasies that alcohol encourages—e.g., power. In *The Drinking Man*,
David C. McClelland, a psychological researcher at Harvard, contends
that men often drink in order to feel stronger, and that the illusion of
power is at least partly the result of physical causes. With distilled spirits
in particular, he says, not only is alcohol absorbed quickly, but the burning sensation in the throat triggers adrenalin. "These diffuse sensations

of increased strength are readily absorbed into fantasies of increased power," says McClelland.

But nobody has been able to improve greatly upon the analysis offered by Selden Bacon, the retired director of the Rutgers alcohol center, in a lecture at Yale in 1944. Individuals in modern society, said Bacon, are relatively self-contained, specialized in their interests, and competitive. Yet they'd like to enjoy "unsuspicious, relatively effortless joint activity." In a social gathering, alcohol diminishes suspicion and eases competitive tensions, eventually dissolving "the barriers usually present between strangers in our society."

Experts are just beginning to understand that there are a lot of different routes to alcoholism. Executive alcoholism, for example, usually seems to begin in mid-career. Ralph E. Tarter, research psychologist at the Carrier Clinic in New Jersey, thinks the reason is that the executive is "goal oriented and driving; he's working on something, is mentally balanced, and not bored. But he acquires what amount to bad habits that carry him away eventually. The executive is the typical conditioned drinker . . . the lunch, the club car, the cocktail party. He starts out using alcohol as a strategy or a tool for personal gain, like the man who says a drink makes him more fluent or convincing, or as a response to pressure. If it works, it becomes learned behavior—a bad habit."

A relatively new concern for the people who deal with alcoholism is the increasing drinking by children. More kids in their teens are indeed drinking, and some are acquiring the habit even earlier in life; alcohol seems to have currently replaced marijuana, amphetamines, and barbiturates as the drug of choice among the young. Tarter finds that some teenagers coming into the Carrier Clinic "arrive here after only a year or two of drinking, and already are having blackouts and withdrawal symptoms." Don Cahalan, one of the authors of the A.D.P. book, says that "there are a hell of a lot of people aged fourteen to twenty-one who will be moving into our statistics soon. The youthful drinking means to me that in five years we are going to have more alcohol-related crimes and more alcoholics."

Yet generalized dire predictions of trends in youthful drug abuse have more often been wrong than right. Five years ago, there was much fretful anticipation that a generation of drug-saturated kids would grow up to be either junkies or marginally functional heavy marijuana smokers. It hasn't happened. Moreover, to become an alcoholic in the broad definition of the word is a long process. "It generally takes eight or nine years of hard work to become an alcoholic," says Mark Keller.

What's most important is the social context of the drinking. Youths are starting to drink earlier because they are doing just about everything earlier, including dating and sleeping with each other. As Keller observes, "Drinking is a rite of passage, and all of those rites are taking place at earlier ages."

How they will eventually handle alcohol depends to a great extent upon what they learn about the culturally accepted drinking style. Children will tend to drink according to the examples their parents and peers set. Some cultures have historically had low rates of problem drinkers—most notably, Jews, Chinese, and Italians. It's not that all of these groups have great numbers of abstainers, or are light drinkers; the Italians, in fact, are among the world's heaviest drinkers. But children are exposed from their earliest years to a temperate drinking practice—the Italians drink much of their wine with meals, for example, and Jews accord it a special place in family religious celebrations. Alcohol does not acquire the "forbidden fruit" image that tempts the young drinker to assert his or her independence through excess.

> from "Changing Habits in American Drinking,"
> *Fortune*, October 1976

D.   So numerous are problem drinkers becoming among the young that Alcoholics Anonymous has begun opening local groups exclusively for them all over the nation.

Sober at age 11. At one meeting of an AA "youth" organization in California's San Fernando Valley, "The Los Angeles Times" reported, one member was honored for his first year of sobriety. He was 11 years of age.

At the same meeting, a 10-year-old boy reported he had been sober for a month.

What is causing this youthful binge?

A 30-year-old alcoholic, a member of an AA group in Washington, D.C., who started drinking when he was 17 years of age, offered this explanation:

"Kids are getting scared of drugs. They feel safer with a bottle. They don't see alcohol as addictive, and it's more socially acceptable. For one thing, it is legal.

"Besides, parents encourage their kids to drink, rather than to do drugs. I went to a wedding of a teen-age couple not long ago, and the parents served beer at the reception. They said it was better to have kids drunk on beer than off somewhere lighting up joints."

Another factor: the growing popularity, especially among the young, of "pop" wine. Sales of this generally inexpensive and sweet wine have soared from 3 million gallons in 1968 to 33 million in 1971, the latest available figures.

Many young people are mixing alcohol with other drugs, such as marijuana, barbiturates and amphetamines, to get a "double high."

One man's experience. A 22-year-old member of Alcoholics Anonymous in Washington, D.C., who started drinking at 14 explains:

"I drank to get drunk as fast as possible. I was putting down beer, wine, whisky, even rubbing alcohol. Then I started taking pills—mostly amphetamines and acid—to speed up the process. Man, I had blackouts that lasted from three to 18 hours."

Students of alcoholism point out that this young man's experience is rare. They say the large majority of young people experience no serious problem because of drinking. They note that, for untold generations, youngsters have been taking that first drink as a rite of passage.

from "Rising Toll of Alcoholism," *U.S. News and World Report,* 29 October 1973

E.   With the establishment of the NIAAA in 1970 has come a spate of research on drinking role-models and their effects on young people. Because the average eighteen-year-old has spent 15,000 hours in front of a television set—4,000 more than he has in the classroom—television and other media are often blamed as alcohol's greatest promoters. Alcohol is touted as the drug of choice in radio and television commercials and on sitcoms and cartoons, in which drunken behavior is considered funny.

In many high schools, alcohol education is provided in the health curriculum, but more is taught about the repeal of prohibition than about alcohol's potentially addictive and destructive properties. "Any money that's spent on prevention goes for assembly programs in which an alcoholic gets up and does his drunkalogue for the kids," says an alcoholism counselor in Dallas. "They all feel sorry for him, but they don't believe anything like that is going to happen to them."

To counter drinking role-models, NIAAA is planning to triple the amount of money it spends on education for young people. Several states are increasing local funding for pilot education programs, and even the liquor industry is attempting to help solve the problem. Public-service messages developed by the Distilled Spirits Council of the United States received nearly $4 million worth of broadcast time during National Football League games in 1978. The United States Brewer's Association has budgeted $2.6 million for alcohol education for youths in an attempt to curtail movements to ban advertising of its products in the broadcast media.

"Jeanne," Anna asks, "what do you think you could do that would improve your situation?"

Jeanne draws hard on her cigarette and exhales a cloud of blue smoke. "I don't know," she says. "My mother says she'll see me again if I go through a detoxification program. She thinks drinking is screwing up my life. I guess everybody here has heard that before."

Mark, his right leg twitching madly, interjects. "Well, not all of us are here because we have drinking problems."

"Yeah," adds Don, "a lot of us are here because of our families."

"Yes," Anna says, "but we're all familiar with the problem. There isn't anybody here who hasn't had a problem either with their own drinking or their family's, is there?"

Carol, a tall, slender seventeen-year-old with a round face, liquid brown eyes and short, flaxen hair, raises her hand tentatively. Next to her sits Jill, her best friend, who is tapping Carol's thigh, encouraging her to tell the group about her boyfriend and how his drinking is affecting her.

"This is my first time," Carol says shyly. "Jill got me to come. I don't have any trouble with my own drinking or anything like that, and my parents just drink socially. But this guy I've been going out with for three years, Rob, he's just been drinking more and more."

Jill glances at her friend. "It's like I'm about three months ahead of Carol," she says. "Our boyfriends are best friends, too, and I had to break up with mine a few months ago after going through the same thing."

"What happens to your boyfriend when he drinks?" Anna asks.

"I hate him when he drinks," Carol says, less nervous now. "He either gets real childish or real aggressive. He always drinks with his friends, and I just get pushed aside. He has to have this big macho image in front of them. And last night I told him I was going to this meeting, or maybe to an Alateen meeting, and he got real mad. He kept saying that he didn't have a problem."

"The weirdest part," Jill adds, "is that you start going out with this one person and you end up with this other person. When we first started going out, we didn't do that much drinking, but then we both started to go downhill and I straightened out and he didn't."

At the bottom of the hill for Jill was thirty-four ounces of vodka, which she drank in forty-five minutes in the woods that surround her high school. She remembers getting tangled in a thorn bush, then nothing until she woke up from a three-day coma in a hospital. She had attended three Alateen meetings before her accident to try to cope with her mother's alcoholism ("My whole family on my mother's side is alcoholic") and has missed few meetings since. "My mother stopped drinking last year. It was right after my accident, and at about the same time it started getting bad with my boyfriend, so I just stayed.

"When I'd talk to my boyfriend about his drinking," she continues, "he'd just sit there with this serious face and let me go through the whole thing, everything I learned at Alateen about the psychology and why you need it. Then at the end he'd just laugh. So I found myself going back to my former habit just to keep up with him, to keep him. But it's not worth it. You look at your family and the way your friends are drinking and you're thinking, you know, I could end up like that."

"Are you dating anybody now?" Anna asks.

"Yeah," Jill says glumly, "but he's a big drinker, too. You know, they say people from alcoholic families are attracted to alcoholic people. It seems everybody I date ends up having a problem."

"Maybe you're looking for a father figure," says Peter, a high-school junior with dark, curly hair.

"That's not so farfetched," Carol says to her friend. "You used to say you never had a relationship with your father."

"Well," says Jill, "it's been better since he stopped. When I was younger, I didn't really know what was going on. All I knew is that I could never bring kids over to the house because they might see my father strung out."

from "Teenage Alcoholics," Michael Segell,
Rolling Stone, 31 May 1979

EVALUATING SEVEN SOURCES:
AN EXAMPLE

Assume that you are gathering information for an essay about Ernest Hemingway's life in Paris in 1924 and 1925. From your introductory reading, you have already become familiar with some of the basic facts. You know that Hemingway and his wife, Hadley, traveled to Paris with their infant son, Bumby; that the Hemingways had very little money; that they associated with many of the literary expatriates who lived in Paris at the time; that they took occasional trips to Spain for the bull-running and to Austria for the skiing; and that Hemingway was working on *The Sun Also Rises.* Now, through research, you are intending to fill in the details that will enable you to construct a portrait of Hemingway and his Paris experiences. You have collected a preliminary bibliography of nine books (a list which could, in fact, easily have been expanded to fifteen or twenty, but which has been cut down to a manageable size for the purpose of this hypothetical discussion). Here is the annotated preliminary bibliography; the comments are based on a rapid examination of each book.

Baker, Carlos. *Hemingway: A Life Story.* New York: Scribner's, 1969. 563 pages of biography, with one hundred pages of footnotes. Everything seems to be here, presented in great detail.

Donaldson, Scott. *Hemingway: By Force of Will.* New York: Viking, 1977. The material isn't organized chronologically; instead, the chapters are thematic, with titles like "Money," "Sex," "War," etc. Episodes from Hemingway's life are presented within each chapter. The introduction calls this "a mosaic of [Hemingway's] mind and personality." Lots of footnotes.

Fenton, Charles. *The Apprenticeship of Ernest Hemingway: The Early Years.* New York: Viking, 1954. A well-documented book, but with a very narrow focus. It covers 1916–1923, and, although Hemingway's experiences are described, the author's chief purpose is to relate them to the development of his writing. Might not be useful, even if I were working on an earlier period.

Gurko, Leo. *Ernest Hemingway and the Pursuit of Heroism.* New York: Crowell, 1968. This is part of a series called "Twentieth Century American Writers": a brief introduction to the man and his work. After fifty pages of straight biography, Gurko discusses Hemingway's writing, novel by novel. There's an index and a short bibliography, but no notes. The biographical part is clear and easy to read, but it sounds too much like a summary.

Hemmingway, Ernest. *A Moveable Feast.* New York: Scribner's, 1964. This is Hemingway's own version of his life in Paris. It sounds authentic, but there's also a very strongly nostalgic tone, so I'm not sure how trustworthy it is.

Hemingway, Leicester. *My Brother, Ernest Hemingway.* Cleveland: World, 1962. It doesn't sound as if the family was very close. For 1924–1925, he's using information from Ernest's letters (as well as commonly known facts). The book reads like a third-hand report, very remote; but L. H. sounds honest, not as if he were making up things that he doesn't know about.

Hemingway, Mary Walsh. *How it Was.* New York: Knopf, 1976. This is Hemingway's fourth wife, and she didn't meet him until 1944, so hardly any of her information is of any use. Sounds unreliable—she has long extracts of dialogue, but doesn't seem to have carried a tape recorder everywhere.

Hotchner, A. E. *Papa Hemingway.* New York: Random House, 1955. This is called a "personal memoir." Hotchner met Hemingway in 1948, and evidently hero-worshipped him. Hemingway rambled on about his past, and Hotchner tape recorded much of it. The book is their dialogue (mostly Hemingway's monologue). No index or bibliography. Hotchner's adoring tone is annoying, and the material resembles that of *A Moveable Feast*, which is better written.

Sokoloff, Alice Hunt. *Hadley, the First Mrs. Hemingway.* New York: Dodd, Mead, 1973. This is the Paris experience from Hadley's point of view, most of it taken from her recollections and from the standard biographies. (Baker is acknowledged.) It's a very slight book—102 pages— but there's an index and footnotes, citing letters and interviews which some of the other biographers might not have been able to use.

Examining the Sources

From these annotations, it seems clear that two of the sources should have been eliminated immediately. Fenton's purpose is critical rather than biographical, and, even more important, neither he nor Mary Hemingway is concerned with the period between 1924 and 1925. The notes on the other seven sources seem to be the outgrowth of two separate processes. In the first place, the student is observing basic facts about each biography—the length of the book, the amount of documentation, the potential bias of the writer (if it is easily recognized), and the way in which the material has been organized. But there are also several comments on tone, impressions of the way in which the information is being presented: "sounds like . . ." or "reads like . . ." How were these impressions formed? How did a rapid examination of random passages lead to an assessment of the relative value of each source?

Let's begin with the biography which, according to the annotations, seems to be the most thorough and complete. Here is Carlos Baker's account of Ernest and Hadley Hemingway immediately after their arrival in Paris:

> The first problem in Paris was to find an apartment. Ezra's *pavillon* in the rue Notre Dame des Champs was too cold and damp for the baby, but there was another available flat on the second floor of a building farther up the hill. It was a pleasant street sloping down from the corner of the Avenue de l'Observatoire and the Boulevard du Montparnasse, an easy stroll from the Luxembourg Gardens, where Hadley could air the baby, a stone's throw from an unspoiled café called La Closerie des Lilas, and much closer to Gertrude Stein's than the former walk-up apartment in the rue du Cardinal Lemoine. The whole neighborhood was a good deal prettier and more polite than that of the Montagne Ste.-Geneviève, though not much quieter. The Hemingways' windows at Number 113 looked down upon a sawmill and lumberyard. It was owned and operated by Pierre Chautard, who lived with his wife and a small dog on the ground floor. The whine of the circular saw, the chuff of the donkey-engine that drove it, the hollow boom of newly sawn planks being laid in piles, and the clatter of the ancient camions that carried the lumber away made such a medley that Ernest was often driven to the haven of the Closerie des Lilas to do his writing.
>
> In the apartment itself, a dark tunnel of a hall led to a kitchen with a stone sink and a two-ring gas burner for cooking. There was a dining room, mostly filled by a large table, and a small bedroom where Ernest sometimes worked. The master bedroom held a stove and double bed, with a small dressing room large enough for the baby's crib. Hadley quickly rehired the *femme de ménage*, Madame Henri Rohrbach, who had worked for her off and on before. Marie was a sturdy peasant from Mur-de-Bretagne. She and her husband, who was called Ton-Ton, lived at 10 bis, Avenue des Gobelins. Her own nickname was Marie Cocotte, from her method of calling the chickens at home on the farm in Brittany. She took at once to the child and often bore him away in a carriage lent by the Straters to see Ton-Ton, who was a retired soldier with time on his hands. Madame Chautard, the wife of the owner of the sawmill, was a plump and childless woman with brassy hair and a voice so harsh that it made the baby cry. She seemed to be envious of Hadley's motherhood. Watching the child drink his daily ration of orange juice she could only say scornfully, *"Il sera un poivrot comme sa mère."** Of the baby's many nicknames—Gallito, Matt, and Joe—the one that stuck was Bumby, which Hadley invented to signify his warm, plump, teddy-bearish, arm-filling solidity which both parents admired and enjoyed.

What makes Baker's description so effective is the impressive amount of detail. One cannot help believing a biographer who offers so much specific information about everyone and everything with even the remotest connection to his subject. One expects to be told what Hemingway ate for dinner and, indeed, in reporting the novelist's skiing trip to

---

* "He'll become a lush like his mother."

Schruns, Baker tells us that the cook prepared "great roasts of beef, with potatoes browned in gravy, jugged hare with wine sauce, venison chops, a special omelette soufflé, and homemade plum pudding." Of course, when every possible lead is followed so thoroughly, you are sometimes told more than you want to know, and the profusion of detail can interfere with your immediate comprehension of events. There's a house-that-Jack-built effect in the sentences about the Hemingways' nursemaid who was a "sturdy peasant from Mur-de-Bretagne," who had a husband named Ton-ton, who lived in the Avenue des Gobelins, whose nickname was the result of . . . and so on. Nevertheless, Baker tells a good story and his description of the apartment is effective: notice the evocation of the sounds that Hemingway must have heard from his windows.

Next, in sharp contrast to all this detail, we have a comparable passage from the biography by Leo Gurko (which the bibliography described as "a summary"). Gurko is dealing with the same material as Baker, in less than one-tenth the space, and naturally offers much less detail:

> Paris in the 1920s was everyone's catalyst. It was the experimental and fermenting center of every art. It was highly sophisticated, yet broke up naturally into small intimate *quartiers*. Its cafés were hotbeds of intellectual and social energy, pent up during the war and now released. Young people from all over the world flocked to Paris, drawn not only by the city's intrinsic attractions but by the devaluation of the franc.
>
> The young Hemingways settled on the Left Bank, and since they were short of money, rented modest rooms in an ancient walk-up. They moved several times, taking flats that were usually on the top floor, five or six flights up, commanding good views of the roofs of Paris. This was somehow in tune with a passion to absorb the city. Hemingway did much of his writing in cafés, where he would sit for hours over a beer or *Pernod* with paper spread before him. He took long walks through the streets and gardens, lingered over the Cézannes in the Luxembourg Museum, and let the great city permeate his senses.

Now, the camera eye is no longer trying for a close-up. Gurko is *outside* the scene, describing what he, the observer, has seen over the distance of time. Baker, in contrast, is trying as much as possible to draw the reader into the scene and to share the Hemingways' own perception of Paris; wherever possible, Baker is inconspicuous. But Gurko does not hesitate to tell his reader what to think—about Paris, about its expatriate population, and about the Hemingways. Notice in this short passage how Gurko moves from verifiable facts to his own hypotheses:

> . . . The Hemingways put themselves on short rations, ate, drank, and entertained as little as possible, pounced eagerly on the small checks that arrived in the mail as payment for accepted stories, and were intensely conscious of being poor. The sensation was not altogether unpleasant. Their extreme youth, the excitement of living abroad, the sense

of making a fresh start, even the unexpected joy of parenthood, gave their poverty a romantic flavor.

Gurko's book does not document his sources; the reader is asked to accept Gurko's assertion that being poor in Paris was "not altogether unpleasant" for Hemingway, because of its romantic connotations. Other biographers however, do not agree with this statement. Remember that Gurko's hypothesis is one man's opinion and is not to be confused with evidence or presented as such in a research essay. Acceptance of this opinion depends on Gurko's credentials as an authority on Hemingway and on what established authorities have to say.

Here's a final excerpt from Gurko's biography, as a starting point for a second group of comparisons. Notice his tendency to generalize and summarize and, especially, to speak for Hemingway. Then contrast Gurko's approach with that of Alice Sokoloff:

> He was becoming increasingly devoted to imaginative writing, to the point where his newspaper assignments and the need to grind out journalistic pieces were growing more and more irksome. Another threat to his work was the "arty" atmosphere of Paris. The cafés of the city, he soon recognized, were filled with aesthetes of one kind or another who wanted to be artists, talked incessantly and even knowledgeably about art, but never really produced anything. There were a hundred of these clever loafers and dilettantes for every real writer. Hemingway developed a contempt and even fear of them, perhaps because there was in him, as in most genuine artists, a feeling of uncertainty about his own talent. He drove himself to hard work and avoided the café crowd as much as he could.
>
> Leo Gurko

> It was a worldly crowd, full of intellectual and artistic ferment, some of it real, some of it bogus, some of them obsessed with their own egos, a few of them deeply and sincerely interested in Ernest's talent. The Hemingways' finances were as restricted as ever, but these people "could offer them all the amenities, could take them anywhere for gorgeous meals," could produce any kind of entertainment and diversion. Although Ernest accepted it all, Hadley thought that he resented it and always kept "a very stiff upper front to satisfy himself." He did not want "simply to sink back and take all this," but the success and admiration was heady stuff and he could not help but enjoy it.[1] Hadley used to be wryly amused when Ernest and Gertrude Stein would talk about worldly success and how it did not mean anything to them.[2] The fact that this was true for a part of him, and that he despised anything false or pretentious, was a source of inner conflict which sometimes expressed itself in malice.

[1] John Dos Passos, *The Best Times* (New York: New American Library, 1966), p. 143.

[2] Interview with Hadley Richardson Hemingway Mowrer, January 18, 1972.

Alice Sokoloff

Sokoloff's conclusions differ from Gurko's: she points to a conflict in Hemingway's reaction to his Paris acquaintances, and offers footnotes to support her suggestion. In another sense, Sokoloff's commentary is limited: because the subject of her biography is Hadley Hemingway, she is describing events as much as possible from Hadley's point of view. Even when writing about Ernest's actions or reactions, Sokoloff uses Hadley as an intermediary observer. Thus, this version of the Hemingways' experience is colored by Hadley's subjectivity. On the other hand, Sokoloff's presentation makes it fairly easy to figure out where Hadley's version leaves off and the biographer's account begins, and the story is told coherently.

Leicester Hemingway's account of his brother's life is far more confusing; most of his information comes from letters, and he makes little attempt to sort out the contents into a structure that is accessible to the average reader:

> Things were going very well for Ernest, with his home life as well as with his writing. Bumby was beginning to talk and Ernest was learning that a child could be more fun than fret. With wife and son he took off for Schruns in the Vorarlberg when good skiing weather set in. For months they were deep in the snow up there, working and enjoying the sports, before returning to Paris in mid-March.
>
> Ernest wrote the family that when they camped in the mountains, up above 2,000 meters, there had been lots of ptarmigan and foxes, too. The deer and chamois were lower down.
>
> He said Bumby weighed twenty-nine pounds, played in a sand pile with shovel and pail, and was always jolly. His own writing was going very well. *In Our Time* was out of print and bringing high prices, he said, while his stories were being translated into Russian and German. . . .
>
> Hadley added other details, thanking the family for the Christmas box which had been delayed more than two months in customs, but had arrived without damage to the fruit cake—Mother's one culinary triumph besides meat loaf. She wrote that Bumby had a wonderful nurse who had taken care of him while she and Ernest spent days at a stretch in mountain huts to be near good snow.

Ernest's writing is mixed up with Bumby's pail and shovel and fruitcakes for Christmas. This is certainly raw material, with no interpretation at all by the biographer for the reader to discount or accept; but the material is stitched together so crudely that one has to spend time sorting out important details from trivia. Certainly, this biography would be a poor choice for the student who was beginning research on this topic; but the details might provide interesting background once the events of 1924–1925 were made more familiar by other biographies.

Finally, here are four descriptions of Hemingway as a baby sitter, odd-job man, and scavenger, all dealing with similar experiences:

Ernest was working fairly hard. He awoke early in the spring mornings, "boiled the rubber nipples and the bottles, made the formula, finished the bottling, gave Mr. Bumby a bottle," and wrote for a time at the dining-room table before Hadley got up. Chautard had not begun his sawing at that hour, the street was quiet, and Ernest's only companions were Mr. Bumby and Mr. Feather Puss, a large cat given them by Kitty Cannell and named with one of Hadley's nicknames. But Ernest was truly domestic only in the early mornings. He took the freedom of Paris as his personal prerogative, roving as widely as he chose. There was a gymnasium in the rue Pontoise where he often went to earn ten francs a round by sparring with professional heavyweights. The job called for a nice blend of skill and forbearance, since hirelings must be polite while fighting back just enough to engage, without enraging, the emotions of the fighters. Ernest had befriended a waiter at the Closerie des Lilas and sometimes helped him weed a small vegetable garden near the Porte d'Orléans. The waiter knew that he was a writer and warned him that the boxing might jar his brains. But Ernest was glad enough to earn the extra money. He had already begun to save up to buy pesetas for another trip to Spain in July.

Carlos Baker

When there were the three of us instead of just the two, it was the cold and the weather that finally drove us out of Paris in the winter time. Alone there was no problem when you got used to it. I could always go to a café to write and could work all morning over a *café crème* while the waiters cleaned and swept out the café and it gradually grew warmer. My wife could go to work at the piano in a cold place and with enough sweaters keep warm playing and come home to nurse Bumby. It was wrong to take a baby to a café in the winter though; even a baby that never cried and watched everything that happened and was never bored. There were no baby-sitters then and Bumby would stay happy in his tall cage bed with his big, loving cat named F. Puss. There were people who said that it was dangerous to leave a cat with a baby. The most ignorant and prejudiced said that a cat would suck a baby's breath and kill him. Others said that a cat would lie on a baby and the cat's weight would smother him. F. Puss lay beside Bumby in the tall cage bed and watched the door with his big yellow eyes, and would let no one come near him when we were out and Marie, the *femme de ménage*, had to be away. There was no need for baby-sitters. F. Puss was the baby-sitter.

Ernest Hemingway

. . . As he grew older (and *A Moveable Feast* was the last book he finished), Hemingway laid increasing stress on the poverty he suffered in Paris. Without question, Ernest and Hadley Hemingway lived on a relatively scant income during those years, but they were never so badly off as the writer, in retrospect, liked to believe.

In any case, poverty is vitually apotheosized in *A Moveable Feast*. As the title hints, a gnawing hunger for food and drink symbolizes Hemingway's indigence. According to the legend constructed in this book, Hemingway worked all day in his unheated garret, too poor to buy firewood or afford lunch. At least he does not tell here the unlikely yarn that appears in A. E. Hotchner's biography: the one about Hemingway catching pigeons in the Luxembourg Gardens in order to satisfy a rumbling stomach. But poverty, and its symbolic hunger, are nonetheless celebrated. "You got very hungry when you did not eat enough in Paris," Hemingway writes, because of the good things on display in the *pâtisseries* and at the outdoor restaurants. Mostly he and Hadley survived on leeks (*poireaux*), but at least so frugal a diet enabled one to savor, truly, the joys of eating well when an unexpected windfall made it possible for them to dine out.

Scott Donaldson

Ernest wanted me to see the neighborhood where he had first lived; we started on Rue Notre-Dame-des-Champs, where he had lived over a sawmill, and slowly worked our way past familiar restaurants, bars and stores, to the Jardin du Luxembourg and its museum, where, Ernest said, he fell in love with certain paintings that taught him how to write. "Am also fond of the Jardin," Ernest said, "because it kept us from starvation. On days when the dinner pot was absolutely devoid of content, I would put Bumby, then about a year old, into the baby carriage and wheel him over here to the Jardin. There was always a *gendarme* on duty, but I knew that around four o'clock he would go to a bar across from the park to have a glass of wine. That's when I would appear with Mr. Bumby—and a pocketful of corn for the pigeons. I would sit on a bench, in my guise of buggy-pushing pigeon-lover, casing the flock for clarity of eye and plumpness. The Luxembourg was well known for the classiness of its pigeons. Once my selection was made, it was a simple matter to entice my victim with the corn, snatch him, wring his neck, and flip his carcass under Mr. Bumby's blanket. We got a little tired of pigeon that winter, but they filled many a void. What a kid that Bumby was—played it straight—and never once put the finger on me."

A. E. Hotchner

Characteristically, Baker describes exactly how the father tended his son, pausing to explain the full name and the origins of their cat. Hemingway himself, years after the event, describes much the same relationship, but with a completely different emphasis and set of details. The two passages are not in conflict; but they are not at all the same kind of writing and, in fact, they provide an excellent illustration of the difficulties of combining two sources written in two different modes for two different kinds of audience. The Hemingway who reminisced for A. E. Hotchner offers a somewhat different version of the same experience, a version criticized in Donaldson's extract, which is an attempt to distinguish between nostalgia and truth. Unlike Gurko's, his presentation is detailed; unlike Baker, he takes an outsider's stance; and the combination, backed up by documentation, is quite convincing.

In what order, then, would you consult these seven books for full-scale research? You might begin with Gurko's brief account, to establish the sequence of events, and then fill in the details by reading Baker's longer version. Donaldson gets pushed down the list to third or fourth, primarily because his biography is not chronological; gathering the scattered references to 1924 will be easier once the overall chronology has been made clear by Gurko and Baker. Now, you can draw on the details to be found in the works by "interested" parties: wife, brother, friend, and the author himself. And, at intervals, you should stop reading and note-taking to compare these various versions of one life and determine which of the sources was in a position to know the truth—the man himself, thirty years later? his correspondence at the time? records left by his wife (whom, in fact, he divorced in 1929)? his biographers, whose information is presented second-hand? a combination of all the sources?

EXERCISE 49

Choose one of the passages listed below (all of which can be found in the earlier chapters of this book) and:

A. Find out some information about the author's background and write a paragraph describing his qualifications for writing about this subject.
B. Think about the suggested research topics that accompany the references, and state whether and why the passage would be a suitable source to consult if you were writing an essay on that topic.
C. For each passage, write down one more research essay topic for which the passage would be a suitable source.

1. Bertrand Russell: "The Social Responsibility of Scientists" (Chapter 2, p. 104)
   a) The arms race
   b) The power of the media
2. A. S. Neill, excerpt from *Summerhill*, (Chapter 2, p. 95)
   a) The case for grandparents
   b) The need for freedom in childhood
   c) The case against family life
3. Simone de Beauvoir, excerpt from *The Coming of Age* (Chapter 2, p. 96)
   a) The conflict between the generations
   b) The plight of the aged

4. Andrew Carnegie, excerpt from *The Gospel of Wealth* (Chapter 3, p. 154)
   a) American tycoons at the turn of the century
   b) In support of private charity
5. Lewis Thomas, excerpt from *The Medusa and the Snail* (Chapter 4, p. 178)
   a) The dangers of scientific experiment
   b) The practicability of cloning
6. Bronislaw Malinowski, excerpt from *Magic, Science, and Religon* (Chapter 2, p. 96, Chapter 4, p. 205)
   a) Primitive customs in American society
   b) Modern ways of dealing with death

EXERCISE 50

In the middle of the night of November 29, 1942, a Boston nightclub called the Cocoanut Grove burned down, resulting in the deaths of at least three hundred people. Read the following three accounts of this disaster, and be prepared to discuss the differences in content, organization, tone, purpose, and point of view. What is the thesis of each article? Consider how you would use the three articles in a single research essay dealing with the Cocoanut Grove disaster. Are these three versions interchangeable?

300 KILLED BY FIRE SMOKE AND PANIC IN BOSTON RESORT— DEAD CLOG EXITS—Terror Piles Up Victims as Flames Suddenly Engulf Nightclub—Service Men to Rescue—Many of Them Perish—Girls of Chorus Leap to Safety—150 Are Injured

BOSTON, Sunday, Nov. 29—More than 300 persons had perished early this morning in flames, smoke and panic in the Cocoanut Grove Night Club in the midtown theatre district.

The estimate of the dead came at 2 A.M. from William Arthur Reilly, Fire Commissioner, as firemen and riggers searched the ruins for additional bodies. It was a disaster unprecedented in this city.

The chief loss of life resulted from the screaming, clawing crowds that were wedged in the entrance of the club. Smoke took a terrific toll of life and scores were burned to death.

At the Boston City Hospital officials said there were so many bodies lined up in corridors that they would attempt no identifications before daybreak.

Commissioner Reilly stated that an eyewitness inside the club said the fire started when an artificial palm near the main entrance was set afire.

Martial law was clamped on the entire fire area at 1:35 A.M. Sailors, Coast Guardsmen, shore patrolmen and naval officers dared death time and again trying to get at bodies that were heaped six feet high by one of the entrances.

Firemen said that many bodies were believed to have fallen into the basement after the main floor collapsed.

A chorus boy, Marshall Cook, aged 19, of South Boston, led three co-workers, eight chorus girls and other floor show performers totaling thirty-five to an adjoining roof from the second-floor dressing rooms and from there they dropped to the ground from a ladder.

Scores of ambulances from nearby cities, the Charlestown Navy Yard and the Chelsea Naval Hospital poured into the area, but the need for ambulances became so great that even railway express trucks were pressed into service to carry away victims. At one time victims, many of them dead, lay two deep in an adjoining garage.

Many of the victims were soldiers, sailors, marines and Coast Guardsmen, some of them junior officers, visiting Boston for a weekend of merrymaking. In the throng were persons who had attended the Holy Cross-Boston College football game.

Scores of dead were piled up in the lobbies of the various hospitals as the doctors and nurses gave all their attention to the 150 injured.

A "flash" fire, believed to have started in the basement, spread like lightning through the dance floor area, and the panic was on. All available nurses and priests were being called into the disaster area.

Among the dead were a marine and one who appeared to be a fireman. Casualties were arriving at hospitals so rapidly that they were being placed in the corridors wherever a suitable place could be found.

It appeared probable that the greatest loss of life was in the newly opened lounge of the night club in Broadway. Here, one policeman said, burned and suffocated persons were heaped to the top of the doors, wedged in death.

The night club was a one-and-a-half story building with a stucco exterior. The blaze was said to have broken out in the basement kitchen at 10:17 P.M. just as the floor show performers were preparing for their next performance. Performers on the second floor were met by terrific smoke and flame as they started downstairs. Their stories were the only ones available, as those who had escaped the dance floor and tables were too hysterical to talk.

A temporary morgue and hospital were set up in the garage of the Film Exchange Transfer Company at the rear of the club in Shawmut Street. At least fourteen persons, suffocated and lying in grotesque positions, were lying on the garage floor at one time, while scores of injuries were cared for by garage workers and others.

The city's Civilian Defense Workers were called to the scene to maintain order and to give first aid to those suffering from burns and smoke inhalation. Every hospital in the area soon was loaded with the victims.

At least thirty-five performers and their friends were rescued by the quick actions of Marshall Cook, a South Boston boy. He was met by a blast of flame as he started down stairs, went back to the dressing room and organized those caught there.

He then smashed his way through a window, carrying away the casing.

Through this opening he led a group to an adjoining room, where a small ladder was found. The ladder was not long enough to reach the street, but Cook and several other male performers held the top end over the roof's edge and guided the women over the side. They had to jump about 6 feet to reach the ground.

At the City Hospital bodies were piled on the floors, many so burned that there was no attempt to identify them immediately. Many service men were among the victims, many of whom were partly identified through their uniforms.

Buck Jones, the film star, was believed to be one of the victims.

Among the first at the scene was the Rev. Joseph A. Marcus of Cranwell School, Lenox, who administered the last rites for at least fifty persons. In the meantime, thirty or forty ambulances rushed to the fire, these coming from Lynn, Newton, and Brookline. Despite the hindrances caused by automobiles parked in the streets, some of the dead and injured were taken from nearby buildings, where they had been left covered only by newspapers.

Abraham Levy, a cashier at the Cocoanut Grove, said there were about 400 in the place, including many sailors.

Sailors saved many lives, pulling people through the doors and out of danger. A fireman said that he saw at least thirty bodies lying on the floor, and that he believed some of them were firemen.

Among the spectacular escapes were those of two of the eight chorus girls, who leaped from the second floor and were caught by two of the male dancers. They were Lottie Christie of Park Drive, Boston, and Claudia Boyle. They jumped into the arms of Andrew Louzan and Robert Gilbert. Louzan and Gilbert had climbed out of a window of their dressing room to an adjoining roof and then descended by ladder.

New York Times, 30 November 1942

CATASTROPHE: BOSTON'S WORST

Holy Cross had just beaten Boston College: downtown Boston was full of men & women eager to celebrate or console. Many of them wound up at Cocoanut Grove: they stood crowded around the dimly lighted downstairs bar, filled the tables around the dance floor upstairs. With them mingled the usual Saturday night crowd: soldiers & sailors, a wedding party, a few boys being sent off to Army camps.

At 10 o'clock Bridegroom John O'Neil, who had planned to take his bride to their new apartment at the stroke of the hour, lingered on a little longer. The floor show was about to start. Through the big revolving door, couples moved in & out.

At the downstairs bar, a 16-year-old busboy stood on a bench to replace a light bulb that a pranksh customer had removed. He lit a match. It touched one of the artificial palm trees that gave the Cocoanut Grove its atmosphere; a few flames shot up. A girl named Joyce Spector sauntered toward the checkroom because she was worried about her new fur coat.

Panic's Start. Before Joyce Spector reached the cloakroom, the Cocoanut Grove was a screaming shambles. The fire quickly ate away the palm tree, raced along silk draperies, was sucked upstairs through the stairway, leaped along ceiling and wall. The silk hangings, turned to balloons of flame, fell on table and floor.

Men & women fought their way toward the revolving door; the push of bodies jammed it. Near by was another door; it was locked tight. There were other exits, but few Cocoanut Grove patrons knew about them. The lights went out. There was nothing to see now except flame, smoke and weird moving torches that were men & women with clothing and hair afire.

The 800 Cocoanut Grove patrons pushed and shoved, fell and were trampled. Joyce Spector was knocked under a table, crawled on hands & knees, somehow was pushed through an open doorway into the street. A chorus boy herded a dozen people downstairs into a refrigerator. A few men & women crawled out windows; a few escaped by knocking out a glass brick wall. But most of them, including Bridegroom John O'Neil, were trapped.

Panic's Sequel. Firemen broke down the revolving door, found it blocked by bodies of the dead, six deep. They tried to pull a man out through a side window; his legs were held tight by the mass of struggling people behind him. In an hour the fire was out and firemen began untangling the piles of bodies. One hard bitten fireman went into hysterics when he picked up a body and a foot came off in his hand. They found a girl dead in a telephone booth, a bartender still standing behind his bar.

At hospitals and improvised morgues which were turned into charnel houses for the night, 484 dead were counted; it was the most disastrous U.S. fire since 571 people were killed in Chicago's Iroquois Theater holocaust in 1903. One Boston newspaper ran a two-word banner line: BUSBOY BLAMED. But the busboy had not put up the Cocoanut Grove's tinderbox decorations, nor was he responsible for the fact that Boston's laws do not require nightclubs to have fireproof fixtures, sprinkler systems or exit markers.

Time, 7 December 1942

[COMMENTARY]

On the last Sunday morning of November, 1942, most inhabitants of greater Boston learned from their newspapers that at about the time they had gone to bed the night before the most terrible fire in the history of their city had occurred. The decorations of a crowded night club had got ignited, the crowd had stampeded, the exits had jammed, and in a few minutes hundreds of people had died of burns or suffocation. Two weeks later the list of dead had reached almost exactly five hundred, and the war news was only beginning to come back to Boston front pages. While the Allied invasion of North Africa stalled, while news was released that several transports engaged in it had been sunk, while the Russians and the Germans fought monstrously west of Stalingrad and

Moscow, while the Americans bombed Naples and the RAF obliterated Turin and conducted the war's most widespread raids over western Europe, while the Japs tried again in the Solomons and mowed down their attackers in New Guinea, while a grave conflict of civilian opinion over the use of Admiral Darlan developed in America and Great Britain, while the anniversary of Pearl Harbor passed almost unnoticed—while all this was going on the Boston papers reported it in stickfuls in order to devote hundreds of columns to the fire at the Cocoanut Grove. And the papers did right, for the community has experienced an angry horror surpassing anything that it can remember. For weeks few Bostonians were able to feel strongly about anything but their civic disaster.

There is irony in such preoccupation with a minute carnage. In the same fortnight thousands of men were killed in battle. Every day, doubtless, more than five hundred were burned to death, seared by powder or gasoline from bombed dumps, in buildings fired from the sky, or in blazing airplanes and sinking ships. If these are thought of as combatants meeting death in the line of duty, far more than five hundred civilians were killed by military action in Germany, Italy, France, Great Britain, Russia, China, Australia, and the islands of the Pacific. Meanwhile in two-thirds of the world civilians died of torture and disease and starvation, in prison camps and wire stockades and the rubble of their homes—they simply came to their last breath and died, by the thousand. At a moment when violent death is commonplace, when it is inevitable for hundreds of thousands, there is something grotesque in being shocked by a mere five hundred deaths which are distinguished from the day's routine only by the fact that they were not inevitable. When hundreds of towns are bombed repeatedly, when cities the size of Boston are overrun by invading armies, when many hundreds of Boston's own citizens will surely be killed in battle in the next few weeks, why should a solitary fire, a truly inconsiderable slaughter, so oppress the spirit?

That oppression provides perspective on our era. We have been so conditioned to horror that horror must explode in our own backyard before we can genuinely feel it. At the start of the decade our nerves responded to Hitler's murdering the German Jews with the outrage properly felt in the presence of cruelty and pain. Seven years later our nerves had been so overloaded that they felt no such outrage at the beginning of a systematic effort to exterminate an entire nation, such as Poland. By progressive steps we had come to strike a truce with the intolerable, precisely as the body develops immunity to poisons and bacteria. Since then three years of war have made the intolerable our daily bread, and every one of us has comfortably adapted to things which fifteen years ago would have driven him insane. The extinction of a nation now seems merely an integral part of the job in hand. But the needless death of five hundred people in our home town strikes through the immunity and horrifies us.

The fire at the Cocoanut Grove was a single, limited disaster, but it exhausted Boston's capacity to deal with an emergency. Hospital facilities were strained to the limit and somewhat beyond it. If a second emergency had had to be dealt with at the same time its victims would have had to wait some hours for transportation and a good many hours for treatment. If there had been three such fires at once, two-thirds of the victims would have got no treatment whatever in time to do them any good. Boston is an inflammable city and it has now had instruction in what to expect if a dozen hostile planes should come over and succeed in dropping incendiary bombs. The civilian defense agencies which were called on justified themselves and vindicated their training. The Nurses' Aid in particular did a memorable job; within a few hours there was a trained person at the bed of every victim, many other Aids worked to exhaustion helping hospital staffs do their jobs, and in fact more were available than could be put to use. Nevertheless it was clearly demonstrated that the civilian agencies are nowhere near large enough to take care of bombings if bombings should come. There were simply not enough ambulances; Railway Express Company trucks had to be called on to take the injured to hospitals and the dead to morgues. The dead had to be stacked like cord wood in garages because the morgues could take no more; the dying had to be laid in rows in the corridors of hospitals because the emergency wards were full. The drainage of doctors into the military service had left Boston just about enough to care for as many victims as this single fire supplied. Six months from now there will be too few to handle an equal emergency; there are far too few now for one twice as serious. One plane-load of incendiaries would start more fires than the fire department and its civilian assistants could put out. There would be more injured than there are even the most casually trained first-aiders to care for. Hundreds would be abandoned to the ignorant assistance of untrained persons, in streets so blocked by rubble and so jammed with military vehicles that trained crews could not reach them even when trained crews should be free. Boston has learned that it is not prepared to take care of itself. One doubts if any community in the United States is.

Deeper implications of the disaster have no direct connection with the war. An outraged city has been confronting certain matters which it ordinarily disregards. As a place of entertainment the Cocoanut Grove was garish but innocuous and on the whole useful. It had been called "the poor man's Ritz"; for years people had been going there to have a good time and had got what they were looking for. With the naïve shock customary in such cases, the city has now discovered that these people were not receiving the minimum protection in their pleasures to which they were entitled and which they supposed they were receiving.

The name of the night club suggests the kind of decorations that cluttered it; the public supposed that the law required them to be fireproof; actually they burned like so much celluloid. The laws relating to them were ambiguous and full of loopholes; such as they were, they were not enforced. The public supposed that an adequate number of exits was required and that periodic inspections were made; they were not. There were too few exits for the customary crowds, one was concealed, another could not be opened, and panic-stricken people piled up before the rest and died there by the score. The public supposed that laws forbidding overcrowding were applied to night clubs and were enforced; on the night of the fire the place was packed so full that movement was almost impossible, and it had been just as crowded at least once a week throughout the years of its existence. The public supposed that laws requiring safe practice in electric wiring and machinery were enforced; the official investigations have shown that the wiring was installed by unlicensed electricians, that a number of people had suspected it was faulty, and that in fact officials had notified the club that it was violating the law and had threatened to take action—but had not carried out the threat. Above all, the public supposed that an adequate building code taking into account the realities of modern architecture and modern metropolitan life established certain basic measures of protection. It has now learned that the Boston building code is a patched makeshift based on the conditions of 1907, and that though a revision which would modernize it was made in 1937, various reasons have held up the adoption of that revision for five years.

These facts have been established by five official investigations, one of them made by the Commonwealth of Massachusetts in an obvious expectation that the municipal authorities of Boston would find convincing reasons to deal gently with themselves. They have turned up other suggestive facts. The Cocoanut Grove was once owned by a local racketeer, who was murdered in the routine of business. The present owners were so expertly concealed behind a façade of legal figureheads that for twenty-four hours after the fire the authorities were not sure that they knew who even one of them was and two weeks later were not sure that they knew them all. An intimation that financial responsibility was avoided by a technically contrived bankruptcy has not yet been followed up as I write this, and other financial details are still lost in a maze of subterfuges. It is supposed that some of the club's employees had their wagescale established by terrorism. Investigators have encountered, but so far have not published, the customary free-list and lists of those entitled to discounts. Presumably such lists contemplated the usual returns in publicity and business favors; presumably also they found a use in the amenities of regulation. Names and business practices of the underworld have kept cropping up in all the investigations, and it is whispered that the reason why the national government has been conducting one of them is the presence at the club of a large amount of liquor on which the latest increase in revenue taxes ought to have been paid but somehow had not been.

In short, Boston has been reminded, hardly for the first time, that laxity in municipal responsibility can be made to pay a profit and that there can be a remunerative partnership between the amusement business and the underworld. A great many Bostonians, now writing passionate letters to their newspapers and urging on their legislators innumerable measures of reform, have gone farther than that. They conclude that one of the reasons why the modernized building code has not been adopted is the fact that there are ways of making money from the looser provisions of the old code. They suppose that one reason why gaps and loopholes in safety regulations are maintained is that they are profitable. They suppose that one reason why laws and regulations can be disregarded with impunity is that some of those charged with the duty of enforcing them make a living from not enforcing them. They suppose that some proprietors of night clubs find that buying immunity is cheaper than obeying safety regulations and that they are able to find enforcement agents who will sell it. They suppose that civic irresponsibility in Boston can be related to the fact that a lot of people make money from it.

But the responsibility cannot be shouldered off on a few small grafters and a few underworld characters who have established business relations with them, and it would be civic fatuousness to seek expiation for the murder of five hundred citizens in the passage of some more laws. The trouble is not lack of laws but public acquiescence; the damaging alliance is not with the underworld but with a communal reverence of what is probably good for business. Five hundred deaths in a single hour seem intolerable, but the city has never dissented at all to a working alliance between its financial interests and its political governors—a partnership which daily endangers not five hundred but many thousand citizens. Through Boston, as through every other metropolis, run many chains of interests which might suffer loss if regulations for the protection of the public's health and life were rigorously enforced. They are sound and enlightened regulations, but if they should be enforced then retail sales, bank clearings, and investment balances might possibly fall off. The corner grocery and the downtown department store, the banks and the business houses, the labor unions and the suburban housewife are all consenting partners in a closely calculated disregard of public safety.

Since the system is closely calculated it usually works, it kills only a few at a time, mostly it kills gradually over a period of years. Sometimes however it runs into another mathematical certainty and then it has to be paid for in blocks of five hundred lives. At such times the community experiences just such an access of guilt as Boston is feeling now, uncomfortably realizing that the community itself is the perpetrator of wanton murder. For the responsibility is the public's all along and the certain safeguard—a small amount of alertness, civic courage, and willingness to lose some money—is always in the public's hands. That means not the mayor's hands, but yours and mine.

It is an interesting thing to hold up to the light at a moment when millions of Americans are fighting to preserve, among other things, the civic responsibility of a self-governing people. It suggests that civilians who are not engaged in the war effort, and who feel intolerably abased because they are not, could find serviceable ways to employ their energies. They can get to work chipping rust and rot from the mechanisms of local government. The rust and rot are increasing because people who can profit from their increase count on our looking toward the war, not toward them. Your town may have a police force of no more than four and its amusement business may be confined to half a dozen juke joints, but some percentage of both may have formed a partnership against your interests under cover of the war. Certainly the town has a sewage system, a garbage dump, fire traps, a rudimentary public health code, ordinances designed to protect life, and a number of Joe Doakes who can make money by juggling the relationship among them. Meanwhile the ordinary hazards of peace are multiplied by the conditions of war, carelessness and preoccupation increase, and the inevitable war pestilence is gathering to spring. The end-products do not look pleasant when they are seen clearly, especially when a community realizes that it has killed five hundred people who did not need to die.

Bernard DeVoto, *Harper's*, February 1943

8. Gathering Materials at the Library: Taking Notes

The availability of copying machines provides a tempting alternative to taking notes. However, note-taking is by no means an obsolete skill. Some sources, like newspaper articles, are difficult to copy clearly; others contain only one or two useful sentences and are not worth the expense of copying.

Moreover, when you have found a group of sources worth copying, what do you do with the stack of xeroxed pages? In effect, you have merely moved the raw materials from the library to your desk. How do you turn them into an essay? In order to take inventory and start working on your *essay* (as distinguished from your *research*), you must separate the important points from the irrelevancies which surround them. Of course, you could work out your strategy of organization by cutting up each page and sorting your vital passages into separate piles; but unless you identify each source clearly on each bit of cut-up paper, you may easily lose track of its origin.

It therefore makes sense to take notes as part of the research process, to express as much of the information as you can in your own words, and, at the same time, to make copies of the most important passages, so that you will have the originals to refer to if your notes let you down. There is no substitute for good notes.

TAKING GOOD NOTES

The following guidelines should help your note-taking:

1. *Try to complete your survey of the library's resources and work out a preliminary bibliography before you start to make copies*

or take notes. Not only will you get a good idea of what materials are available and the probable extent of your research, but your survey can also enable you to make sure that your preferred topic is a practical one. If you start taking notes before you are certain of your precise focus, you may waste a good deal of time. You may discover, for example, that there is very little documented information about the gunfight at the O.K. Corral, and thus decide to shift your focus to Wyatt Earp. Or the amount of technical material about Lindbergh's flight in the *Spirit of St. Louis* might overwhelm you, with the result that you switch to Lindbergh's opposition to America's entry into World War II.

2. *Use paraphrase and summary rather than quotation.* If you write down sentence after sentence, word for word from your source, you might as well save time and use a copying machine. Remember that the longer you keep the language of the original author, the more difficult it will be to make the transition to your own writing style. If your first draft reads like an anthology of quotations, then you will find it hard to make your essay coherent and intelligible. The cannibalized sources will still be in control. Take the trouble *now* to master each new idea by putting it in your own words.

3. *Make sure that your notes make sense.* Remember that you won't remember everything and that you will have seen a vast number of similar pages by the time you begin to organize your essay. Spell everything out, just as you will have to spell everything out for your reader. Plan to include a certain number of facts to serve as your supporting evidence. It is not enough to say that "X's father lost his job." What was his job? Why did he lose it? What did he do instead? Later on, you may find that these details are irrelevant and will not fit into the shape of your essay; but if you do need supporting evidence, you will find it more convenient to look in your notes than to go back to the library.

4. *Differentiate your own ideas from those that you are paraphrasing.* Taking notes is often an intellectually stimulating experience, probably because it requires so much concentration and because your reading rate is slowed down. You are therefore likely to have plenty of comments about the source that you are paraphrasing. As you develop your own ideas and include them in your notes, be careful to differentiate them from contributions of your sources. Later on, you will want to know exactly which ideas were yours and which were your source's. Square brackets ([ ]) for your own ideas are a good way of making this distinction.

5. *Keep a running record of page references.* In your essay, you will have to cite a page number for each reference, and these must be correct pages, not approximate guesses. It is therefore not enough to write "pp. 285–91" at the top of the note card or sheet. Three weeks later, or three hours later, how will you remember on which of the six pages you found the point that you want to cite in your essay? If you are writing a lengthy set of notes that paraphrase your source, make a slash and insert a new page number to indicate exactly where you turned the page. This is especially important for quotations. Of course, it is vital that you immediately put quotation marks around quotations. Later on, you will never remember who said what (although you may be surprised at the improvement in your prose style).

6. *Keep a master list of your sources, assigning a code number or symbol to each one.* Having a code to identify each source that you intend to use in your essay is an advantage. As you take notes, you can use an abbreviation or code number to identify each new source; when you begin a new card or sheet, you won't have to repeat all the basic information.

Using Note Cards—One Fact per Card

The traditional method of taking notes is to write a single fact or piece of information on one three- by five-inch index card. Cards each containing a single note are easily sorted into stacks; they can also be left at home when you go back to the library. On the other hand, index cards can stray from the pile and become lost. A stack of cards should be kept under control with a sturdy rubber band.

In fact, only certain topics lend themselves to note cards, topics which require the collection of small, fragmentary bits of information, like facts or brief descriptions, which fit easily on to an index card. (Eight- by ten-inch cards or sheets of paper may be more suitable for an abstract topic that depends on complex sources, with each one discussed at length.) Whether you write on small cards or long sheets, make sure that you *write on one side only*, and be careful to label each separate unit of information with its exact source and page number, using abbreviations, symbols, or numbers.

One student, taking notes for an essay describing the 1871 fire that devastated Chicago, used the one-fact-per-card method. At the top of the following page is a typical note card.

The empty space that is left on this card may seem wasteful, but the

**One fact
per card**

25

Estimate of 1,000 dead

NY Times, 10/15/1871
p. 1

**Notes grouped
by topic**

10

<u>fire-fighting</u>

all engines and hose carts in city came (<u>NYT</u>, 10/8, p. 5)

water station on fire, with no water to put out
small fires (*Hall*, p. 228)

all engines out there; fire too big to stop (<u>NYT</u>, 10/8
p. 5)

fire department "demoralized"; bad fire previous
night; men were drinking afterwards; fire
marshal "habitually drunk" (<u>NYT</u>, 10/23, p. 2)

**Below, notes
grouped
by source**

<u>Source H</u>

NY Times, 10/15/1871, p. 1

1. city normal again
2. still martial rule; Gen. Sheridan in charge
3. citizens working at night to watch for new outbreak of fire
4. newspapers moved to other locations
5. estimate 1,000 dead
6. earlier reports of looting and loss of life not exaggerated
7. waterworks won't open till next day
8. two-thirds of city still using candlelight
9. suffering mostly among "humbler classes"
10. businessmen are "buoyant"
11. bread is 8¢
12. saloons are closed at 9:00 P.M. for one week

method enables the writer, later on, to label and place all the cards that refer to *casualties* in a single pile. If the card contained information relating to two different categories, the same card would have to be placed in two separate piles, which would defeat the purpose of the organizational system. Notice that, to keep track of all the notes, the writer has assigned a number to the card.

Notes Grouped by Topic

A second student used a more sophisticated system that combines note-taking and preliminary organization. Early in the note-taking process, the student put down a piece of information on a card that was to be devoted to notes about *fire-fighting* only. Thereafter, every time the student came across a new point about fire-fighting—no matter what the source—it was added to the card. Such organization requires a list, either written or mental, of note topics, which may also be identified by number. (See the second card on the previous page.)

Because the notes are grouped according to topic, this student will find organizing an outline easier than will the first student. But preliminary synthesis during the note-taking stage is practical only with relatively short items. An author's open-ended theorizing can destroy this tidy system by forcing the note-taker to devote card after card to a single idea from a single source. (Notice that none of the sources on the "fire-fighting" card seems to be offering any lengthy opinions about the fire.) For this reason, when you organize notes by topic, you may prefer to use long sheets of paper, in order to be prepared for any kind of material and not to be cramped for space.

Notes Grouped by Source

Instead of putting one point on each card or one topic on each card, a third student chose to use one source per sheet. This system "uses up" one source at a time and calls for a long sheet of notes in which the information is presented in the order of its appearance in the source. (See the example at the bottom of the previous page.)

Notice that to simplify the essay's organization, this student numbered each item on the sheet and also gave each sheet a code letter. When the time comes to synthesize these notes into paragraph topics, the student can establish a category dealing with, say, *food supplies*, find the relevant references to that topic, and place the code numbers under that heading. While drafting the outline, the writer would find H-11 under the heading *food supplies* and have immediate access to information about the price of bread after the fire. (For further explanation of this process, see Chapter 9, p. 405.)

TAKING NOTES FROM ABSTRACT SOURCES

As the sample notes suggest, research on the Chicago fire mostly uncovered factual details about circumstances and incidents which occurred during and after the catastrophe. The research notes are therefore brief, factual summaries. Taking notes becomes quite a different proposition when the source consists of generalizations and evidence used to develop complex ideas; for the note-taker must constantly struggle to understand and paraphrase abstract thinking. To illustrate the difficulties, here is a brief extract from *Victorian Cities*, by Asa Briggs. Assume that the book is being consulted for an essay on "The City One Hundred Years Ago."

> The industrial city was bound to be a place of problems. Economic individualism and common civic purpose were difficult to reconcile. The priority of industrial discipline in shaping all human relations was bound to make other aspects of life seem secondary. A high rate of industrial investment might mean not only a low rate of consumption and a paucity of social investment but a total indifference to social costs. Overcrowding was one problem: displacement was another. There were parts of Liverpool with a density of 1,200 persons to the acre in 1884: rebuilding might entail the kind of difficulties which were set out in a verse in *The Builder* of 1851:
>
> > Who builds? Who builds? Alas, ye poor!
> > If London day by day "improves,"
> > Where shall ye find a friendly door,
> > When every day a home removes?

The paragraph may seem hard to understand on first reading because Briggs is developing his image of the industrial city through a series of abstract words combined into phrases—"economic individualism," "common civic purpose," "industrial discipline," and "low rate of consumption."

These difficult abstractions, typical of the social sciences, are tossed into the paragraph as if everyone understood them. Fortunately, the essential point is repeated in several different ways and supported by some straightforward facts about the density of population in Liverpool. The passage ends with quite a different kind of evidence: the verse-quotation which suggests that, earlier in the century, people were already aware of the dangers of unlimited expansion.

Note A

> Briggs, p. 491
>
> If capital is being used for industrial expansion and personal profit, the same money can't be used for social services. [This was before the welfare state.] Because production was paramount, no one worried that living conditions were impossibly crowded or that people were evicted or moved to allow for industrial expansion. Example: Liverpool -- 1,200 per acre in 1884. Fear of improvement ("If London day by day 'improves'") [sounds like urban renewal and the inner city cycle today -- renovating slum brownstones becomes fashionable]

The researcher here has made a point of avoiding the original phrasing, and thus avoided the danger of quoting the author's words without acknowledgment. The researcher's brief comments in square brackets, clearly distinguished from the notes on Briggs, suggest possible points for development in the research essay.

If one does not expect to refer to Briggs in any detail, it would be sufficient to make a note that summarizes his basic point more briefly:

Note B

> Briggs, p. 491
>
> Danger of industrialization: profit becomes more important than social values. Expansion results in a highly dense population and the need for relocating existing neighborhoods.

In taking good notes everything depends on achieving an adequate understanding of the author's meaning. The following example, however, suggests that the researcher did not bother to puzzle out the complexities of the paragraph and, instead, tried a few wild guesses:

Note C

> Briggs, p. 491
>
> A city of crowded business brings chaos. People couldn't find a job. Your rights meant nothing. Industries didn't respect people's real needs. The cities were overcrowded because industrial investments were poor.

With the possible exception of the first sentence, none of these points can be correctly attributed to Briggs, whose meaning has been entirely distorted. On the other hand, the attempt to play it safe by copying out the phrases verbatim is not successful either:

Note D

> Briggs, p. 491
>
> Problems of the industrial city:
> 1. "economic individualism"
> 2. "common civic purpose" difficult to reconcile
> 3. "industrial discipline" takes priority over "all human relations"
> 4. "high rate of social investment" and "total indifference to social costs"
> 5. "over-crowding"
> 6. "displacement"

Although this information is beautifully laid out in outline form, with quotation marks carefully inserted, there is no evidence at all that the researcher has understood a word of Briggs's paragraph. Moreover, using an outline format makes it hard to recognize the relationships among these concepts. When the time comes to include a reference to Briggs in the research essay, this student will not have the faintest idea how the phrases fit together.

EXERCISE 51

In 1937, the German airship *Hindenburg* caught fire near Lakehurst, New Jersey, killing thirty-six people. Two of the many eyewitness accounts were by Leonhard Adelt and Margaret Mather, both passengers on the ship. Read these two passages and then evaluate the following sets of notes prepared by students writing about the Hindenburg disaster. Consider the following criteria:

1. Does one get a good sense of the experience from reading the notes?
2. Which sets of notes are reliable? complete?
3. Do any of the notes omit anything important?
4. Which notes quote excessively?
5. Does the note-taker recognize that the two sources often confirm each other's testimony, and indicate when they agree?
6. Would the notes make sense to someone who had not read the original?
7. Which sets of notes would you prefer to work from if you were writing an essay on the Hindenburg?

With my wife I was leaning out of a window on the promenade deck. Suddenly there occurred a remarkable stillness. The motors were silent, and it seemed as though the whole world was holding its breath. One heard no command, no call, no cry. The people we saw seemed suddenly stiffened.

I could not account for this. Then I heard a light, dull detonation from above, no louder than the sound of a beer bottle being opened. I turned my gaze toward the bow and noticed a delicate rose glow, as though the sun were about to rise. I understood immediately that the airship was aflame. There was but one chance for safety—to jump out. The distance from the ground at that moment may have been 120 feet. For a moment I thought of getting bed linen from the corridor in order to soften our leap, but in the same instant, the airship crashed to the ground with terrific force. Its impact threw us from the window to the stair corridor. The tables and chairs of the reading room crashed about and jammed us in like a barricade.

"Through the window!" I shouted to my fellow passengers, and dragged my wife with me to our observation window.

Reality ceased with one stroke, as though fate in its cruelty was yet compassionate enough to withdraw from its victims the consciousness of their horror. I do not know, and my wife does not know, how we leaped from the airship. The distance from the ground may have been 12 or 15 feet. I distinctly felt my feet touch the soft sand and grass. We collapsed to our knees, and the impenetrable darkness of black oil clouds, shot through with flames, enveloped us. We had to let go of each other's hands in order to make our way through the confusion of hot metal pieces and wires. We bent the hot metal apart with our bare hands without feeling pain.

We freed ourselves and ran through a sea of fire. It was like a dream. Our bodies had no weight. They floated like stars through space.

Leonhard Adelt

I was leaning out of an open window in the dining saloon with many others including the young aviator, who was taking photographs. He told me that he had taken eighty during the trip. When there were mysterious sounds from the engines I glanced at him for reassurance.

At that moment we heard the dull muffled sound of an explosion. I saw a look of incredulous consternation on his face. Almost instantly the ship lurched and I was hurled a distance of fifteen or twenty feet against an end wall.

I was pinned against a projecting bench by several Germans who were thrown after me. I couldn't breathe and thought I should die suffocated, but they all jumped up.

Then the flames blew in long tongues of flame, bright red and very beautiful.

My companions were leaping up and down amid the flames. The lurching of the ship threw them repeatedly against the furniture and the railing, where they cut their hands and faces against the metal trimmings. They were streaming with blood. I saw a number of men leap from the windows, but I sat just where I had fallen, holding the lapels of my coat across my face, feeling the flames light on my back, my hat, my hair, trying to beat them out, watching the horrified faces of my companions as they leaped up and down.

Just then a man—I think the man who had exclaimed "Mein Gott" as we left the earth—detached himself from the leaping forms, and threw himself against a railing (arms and legs spread wide) with a loud terrible cry of "Es ist das Ende."

I thought so too but I continued to protect my eyes. I was thinking that it was like a scene from a medieval picture of hell. I was waiting for the crash of landing.

Suddenly I heard a loud cry: "Come out, lady!" I looked and we were on the ground.

Margaret G. Mather

Student A:

    All of a sudden there was complete silence and not a
    sound from the motors of the airship. Everybody in the
    airship "stiffened." Leonhard Adelt suddenly "heard a dull
    detonation from above, no louder than a beer bottle
    being opened." L.A. knew that the "airship was aflame."
    The only way to save one's life was to jump. This meant
    the jump was for 120 feet. All of a sudden, "the airship

crashed to the ground with terrific" speed. The force was
so high that Margaret Mather "was hurled a distance of
fifteen to twenty feet against an end wall."

Student B:

"The motors were silent, and it seemed as though the
whole world was holding its breath." "At that moment we
heard the dull and muffled sound of an explosion." "Almost
suddenly the ship lurched and I was hurled a distance of
15 or 20 feet against an end wall." This is the beginning
described by two passengers that were on the Hindenburg of
1937. After a long voyage over the Atlantic and being so
close to their destiny, this was too much of a shock for
them to handle. All the passengers had to escape death.
Some were fortunate, others weren't. "I was pinned against
a projecting bench by several Germans who were thrown
after me. I couldn't breathe, and thought I should die,
suffocated, but they all jumped up." Everyone ran for
their life.

Student C:

We heard the dull muffled sound of an explosion. I saw
a look of incredulous consternation on his face. . . . The
ship lurched and I was hurled a distance of 15 or 20 feet
. . . then the flames blew in, long tongues of flame,
bright red and <u>very beautiful</u>. My companions were leaping
up and down amid the flames.––they were streaming with
blood.
I sat just where I had fallen, holding the lapels of
my coat over my face, feeling the flames light on my
back.––threw himself against a railing with a loud
terrible cry of "Es ist das Ende."
––like a scene from a medieval picture of hell. I was
waiting for the crash of the landing.

Student D:

Adelt: "The motors were silent"
Mather: "Dull muffled sound of an explosion"
Adelt: "I turned my gaze towards the bow and noticed a
rose glow . . ."
Mather: "The ship lurched and I was hurled a distance of
fifteen or twenty feet against an end wall."
Adelt: "its impact threw us from the window to the stair
corridor."

Mather: "Then the flames blew in"
Mather: "I saw a number of men leap from the windows."
Adelt: "We leaped from the airship."

Student E:

before crash:
Adelt: "The motors were silent" "I heard a light, dull
detonation from above, . . ." "I turned my gaze towards the
bow and noticed a delicate rose glow"
Mather: "Mysterious sounds from the engine" "dull muffled
sound of an explosion" "then the flames blew in, long
tongues of flame, bright red and very beautiful"
after crash:
Adelt: "Through the window!" I shouted to my fellow
passengers, . . ." ". . . how we leaped from the airship.
The distance from the ground may have been 12 or 15 feet,"
. . . "impenetrable darkness of black oil clouds, shot
through with flames" . . . "a sea of fire."
Mather: ". . . where they cut their hands and faces against
the metal trimmings. They were streaming with blood."

Student F:

"I turned my gaze towards the bow and noticed a
delicate rose glow, as though the sun were about to rise."
The blimp catches on fire; the only means of escape is
jumping to the ground. Distance from the ground
approximately 12 or 15 feet when couple jumped out of
"airship." People "beat the hot metal apart with our bare
hands without feeling pain." How mind works when in life
and death situation. No pain. People had to run through
fire one at a time.
Mather: "mysterious sounds from the engine." She was
leaning out of dining saloon, heard sounds of explosion.
People thrown 15 or 20 feet after hearing explosion.
Flames came into room after people thrown. "lurching of
ship threw them repeatedly across furniture and the
railings."

Student G:

There was an inexplicable silence followed by a
"light, dull detonation from above, no louder than the
sound of a beer bottle being opened." Then it was observed
that the airship was on fire looking like "the sun were
about to rise." There was the realization that the only

chance for survival was to abandon the ship. By the time
the decision to jump and the action itself was
implemented, the ship had crashed (from 120 feet). Upon
impact, everything in the ship (chairs, tables, people)
was tossed about. Reality became suspended "as though fate
in its cruelty was yet compassionate enough to withdraw
its victims the consciousness of their horror."

EXERCISE 52

Reread the three articles dealing with the Cocoanut Grove Fire of 1942
at the end of the previous chapter. Head one group of cards or one sheet
of paper "The Causes of the Fire," and take a set of notes on that topic.
Head another group of cards or sheet of paper "The Fire's Intensity and
Speed," and take a second set of notes on the second topic. Each set of
notes should make use of all three sources.

EXERCISE 53

Assume that you are planning an essay about King Henry VIII and that
you have come across the following source, published in 1971, in the
library. After doing a preliminary evaluation of the passage, considering
its length and date of publication, take a set of notes for an essay about
"Henry VIII's predilection for marriage."

>   If the English royal household was more restrained than its French
> counterpart, the explanation has much to do with the fact that Henry
> Tudor was far more inhibited than his Valois cousin. The possession of
> six wives obscures the issue, and even contemporaries could not help
> confusing matrimony with lust: "Who," wrote Richard Hilles to Henry
> Bullinger, "judging of the King by his fruits, would ever believe him to
> be so chaste a character" as to leave Anne of Cleves a maiden after having
> been married to her for a month? Yet Henry was neither ribald nor bawdy
> nor particularly lusty. In fact the King was exceedingly touchy about his
> sex life, answering the Imperial Ambassador's argument that perhaps
> God had ordained the succession to remain in the female line by shout-
> ing three times over: "Am I not a man like others?" The question for
> Henry was rhetorical, but later generations have had their doubts. Is the
> sovereign who goes through wives "as some men go through socks" like
> other men? A single matrimonial catastrophe might be accepted as bad
> luck, but four marriages which end in disaster must have a common
> explanation. The psychologist J. C. Flugel may have been correct in say-
> ing that unconsciously the King was driven forward and at the same
> time repelled by his craving for sexual rivals, for incest and for chastity
> in his wives, thereby making his marriage-couch a nightmare of recrim-

inations, fears and frustrations. All these "desires," says Flugel, "are closely interconnected" and are "derived from the primitive Oedipus complex." Or possibly it can be argued that the King knew or feared himself to be deficient in bed; certainly one of the rumoured charges directed against George Boleyn, the Queen's brother, was that he and his sister had gossiped about Henry's clumsiness as a lover and his lack of potency and staying-power. Or again the explanation may be more brutally prosaic. As that excellent ecclesiastic of the Church of England, Bishop Stubbs, put it: the portraits of the monarch's many wives are, "if not a justification, at least a colorable occasion for understanding the readiness with which he put them away." In truth, the question must be left unanswered. All that can be said is that the King did seem to have had a habit of involving himself in canonical incest by persistently marrying within the prohibited degree; but whether by accident or un-conscious design neither Henry nor, probably, his spiritual confessor could say.

Whatever the psychological speculations, there is evidence that Henry may not have been like most other men in that he was a rather prudish individual, uncomfortable with smut and easily embarrassed by sex. In 1538 he was negotiating for a new wife and informed the French Am-bassador that "I will trust no one but myself; marriage touches a man too closely." He wanted Francis, he said, to send to Calais an assortment of eligible French damsels so he could "see them and enjoy their society before settling on one." With wry Gallic humor, Castillon deliberately misunderstood, and asked the King whether he "would perhaps like to try them all, one after the other, and keep for yourself the one who seems the sweetest. It was not thus, Sire, that the Knights of the Round Table treated their ladies in old times in this country." Bluff King Hal is said to have blushed crimson and dropped the subject.

Lacey Baldwin Smith, from Henry VIII: The Mask of Royalty

EXERCISE 54

Assume that you are planning an essay about King Henry VIII and that you have come across the following source, published in 1754, in the library. After doing a preliminary evaluation of the passage, considering its length and the biography's date of publication, take a set of notes for an essay about "Henry VIII's popularity with his subjects."

It is difficult to give a just summary of this prince's qualities: he was so different from himself in different parts of his reign, that, as is well remarked by Lord Herbert, his history is his best character and descrip-tion. The absolute uncontrolled authority which he maintained at home, and the regard which he acquired among foreign nations, are circum-stances which entitle him, in some degree, to the appellation of a *great* prince; while his tyranny and barbarity exclude him from the character of a *good* one. He possessed, indeed, great vigour of mind, which qualified him for exercising dominion over men; courage, intrepidity, vigilance, inflexibility: and though these qualities lay not always under the guidance of a regular and solid judgment, they were accompanied with good parts and an extensive capacity; and every one dreaded a contest with a man who was known never to yield or to forgive, and who, in every controversy, was determined either to ruin himself or his antagonist. A catalogue of his vices would comprehend many of the worst qualities incident to human nature: violence, cruelty, profusion, rapacity, injustice, obstinacy, arrogance, bigotry, presumption, caprice: but neither was he subject to all these vices in the most extreme degree, nor was he at intervals altogether destitute of virtues: he was sincere, open, gallant, liberal, and capable at least of a temporary friendship and attachment. . . .

It may seem a little extraordinary, that notwithstanding his cruelty, his extortion, his violence, his arbitrary administration, this prince not only acquired the regard of his subjects, but never was the object of their hatred: he seems even, in some degree, to have possessed, to the last, their love and affection. His exterior qualities were advantageous, and fit to captivate the multitude: his magnificence and personal bravery rendered him illustrious in vulgar eyes: and it may be said with truth that the English in that age were so thoroughly subdued, that, like eastern slaves, they were inclined to admire those acts of violence and tyranny which were exercised over themselves, and at their own expense.

David Hume, from The History of England, Volume III

EXERCISE 55

Read the following excerpt from an essay (printed in the August 3, 1975, issue of *The Observer*, a British newspaper) about the career and personality of George Washington. Then take *four separate sets of notes* from this passage, using four separate cards or sheets, as if you were preparing an essay on *each* of the following topics:

1. The personality of George Washington
2. The presidency, as molded by George Washington
3. The consolidation of power in new and developing nations
4. The economic objectives of the founding fathers

It was the threat to property that at least helped to make Washington a revolutionary. It was another threat to property that made him President. By 1787, with no strong central government, the new States seemed to be disintegrating. In Massachusetts, an uprising led by Daniel Shays, a dissatisfied farmer, set the alarm bells ringing hundreds of miles south in Virginia. "Thirteen colonies pulling against each other will soon bring ruin to the whole," wrote Washington from Mount Vernon. "We are," he warned, "fast verging to anarchy and confusion." So once again

Washington rode to Philadelphia, to preside over the revision of the Articles of Confederation in Liberty Hall, the meeting that produced an entirely new Constitution. Historians have since noted that the men who drew up this Constitution were overwhelmingly members of the professional and propertied classes: 29 were university graduates, many were lawyers, at least 14 were land speculators, at least 24 were lending money at interest, at least 11 had mercantile and manufacturing connections, at least 15 owned slaves, and perhaps 40 owned public securities.

In Liberty Hall the propertied classes set out to produce a new form of government that would be strong enough to protect property rights, and yet not so strong that it could become another tyranny. The man who chaired the Constitutional Convention was Washington—mostly in dead silence, large and brooding and impressive—and it was Washington who was the propertied classes' natural choice as first President: he was, as Hamilton said, "indispensable."

But although the American Revolution can be, and sometimes is, seen as a capitalist racket, with Washington its leading racketeer—the landowner who fought the war to facilitate a land-grab in the west, and became President to secure the war's gains for the future stockholders of General Motors—it is undeniable that he did not want the Presidency. He was not healthy; he was tired; he loved Mount Vernon; above all, he once again felt inadequate.

As President, it is true, he did maintain a system that kept the new country safe for property; but he did much more than that. He gave the new nation stability. He did not, as some feared, become a king. He stamped the office with his own profound respect for constitutionalism. Most important of all, he solved the problem of the succession. As Professor Martin Lipset of Harvard has pointed out, with a sideways look at the liberation movements of the twentieth century, especially in Africa, nothing is harder about independence than the transfer of authority after independence has been achieved. Having repudiated the old authority, how do you legitimize the new? Washington solved this problem by sheer strength of character: he *was* authority personified—and although his second term was stormier than his first, his critics mostly preferred to criticise him behind his back. When he stepped down, refusing to run for a third term, the Presidency, as an office, was an established fact. Luckily, unlike the Kennedys, he was sterile; Martha had four children before she married him, but no children by him. The first President went back to Mount Vernon and died two years later, with his name attached to the new capital city (the name "Washingtonople" was fortunately rejected), but not to a new political dynasty.

Michael Davie, "Washington—The Truth Behind the Legend"

9. Presenting the Results of Your Research: Organizing and Writing the Essay

The research essay should be planned and written in exactly the same way that you would work on any other essay. Whether you are working with your own ideas, or your observations about other people, or your comments about another writer's essay, or statements made by a group of people, the process is always the same. In each and every case, you are starting out with written notes—facts, ideas, suggestions, comments, opinions—that serve as the raw materials for your synthesis. From these notes, you establish a sequence of separate generalizations to be used as topic sentences; and, in doing so, you work out the basic structure of your essay. What distinguishes the organization of the research essay from that of the essays that you have previously written is nothing more than the unusually large quantity of notes. The term "notes" in this context refers to any of the products of your research, such as your own summaries and paraphrases, quotations, Xeroxed copies of pages and articles, class lecture notes, and stories clipped from newspapers.

TAKING INVENTORY

At this stage, you search for ideas worth developing by reviewing all the major points that you have learned and thought about in the course of your research. From these ideas, you can now select the core of your essay. You select the main ideas of your research essay by carefully reading through all your notes. As you read, you look for and write down any points that seem especially important to understanding and explaining your topic. In other words, you take a *new* set of notes from your old set and thus reduce the accumulated mass of information to a manageable size. You must take inventory and produce a working version of your notes, a relatively brief list of generalizations that can be rearranged, tried out in different versions, and eventually converted into an outline of topic sentences. This new set of notes is *not* supposed to be a summary of your research, nor should you attempt at this point to summarize any single source.

Your new notes will be a random list of vaguely related items. At this early stage of organization, there is no special reason to place the names of the sources next to your new list of ideas; not every statement in your new list will get included in your essay, and you are not yet at the point where you need to decide which source should be used to support which topic sentence.

This inventory of your research is not only an essential stage in the organization of your essay, but it is also the point at which the content of the essay really becomes the product of your own thinking. Until this stage, most of what you have written down has been extracted directly from the sources; your own individual reactions and opinions have probably been restricted to the occasional comment in square brackets. Now, when you sift this information and evaluate it, you are deciding what you are going to write about. Each point that you jot down, however brief and however fragmentary, should be expressed in your own words; it should be *your* version of the idea. Even if it is a point that has appeared in ten different articles (and has been noted on ten different index cards), you are now, in some sense, making it your own. By choosing this idea and not another, and by blending your own combination of the ideas that you have been working with, you are preparing to stamp your essay with your own personality.

DEVELOPING A THESIS AND SELECTING A STRATEGY

Once your list of general ideas has been completed, once you have read through all of your research notes and decided which points are worth writing about, it is time to take inventory again. Evaluate your list. If your new notes take up more than a couple of pages, try to reduce the number of ideas, avoiding duplication and combining similar statements. Some points will be in the mainstream of your research, discussed by a sizable number of your sources. Others, however, will seem more peripheral; you may find it difficult to cite a variety of evidence in their support, and you may wish to exclude them from your master outline. Eliminate what seems to be minor or remote from the topic or inconsistent with most of your research notes.

Next, consider what remains on your list. How do these ideas relate to the topic with which you began your research? How do they help to establish a thesis? Are you working with a collection of reasons? consequences? problems? dangers? Try to find some common bond. Then try to conceive of an overall strategy for your essay—cause-and-effect? problem-and-solution? explanation of a procedure? evaluation of reasons for an argument? If you are developing a historical or biographical topic, see if your information naturally divides into units that might correspond to the separate parts of your essay. Did the event fall into distinct narrative stages? What aspects of the scene would an observer have noticed? Which of your subject's activities best reveals his personality? In other words, decide what is to be included and what is to be discarded. Finally, when your list of topics is relatively firm, remember to arrange them in a logical sequence, carrying out your strategy and developing your thesis in a clear direction.

CROSS-REFERENCING

When you have developed a list of major topics that will roughly correspond to the paragraphs of your essay, then and only then are you ready to link up that tentative outline with the materials of your research. Remember to leave plenty of space between the items on your outline, and also remember to assign a number or a letter to each point. Now, once again, slowly reread all your research notes, this time keeping your master-list of topics right in front of you. Every time you come across something in your notes which might be cited in support of a topic on your outline, immediately:

1. place the number or letter of the point in your outline next to the reference in your notes;
2. place the source's name (and the number of the note-card, if you have used that system) under the item on your outline.

To illustrate cross-referencing, here is another excerpt from the notes for an essay on the Chicago Fire, followed by three paragraph topics taken from an outline for that essay.

Notes:

Source G

<u>Times</u>, October 11, "The Ruined City," p. 1

1. the fire has stopped and there has been some "blessed rain"
2. 20–30 people have died in their homes
3. plundering everywhere—like a scene of war
   VII a. a thief suffocated while trying to steal jewelry from a store

       b. people who were caught pilfering had to be released
         because the jail burned down

VI   4. water for drinking from the lake

     5. people dying of exposure

V   6. little food; people searching the ruins

V   7. difficulties of transporting supplies

VII   8. meeting of citizens at church to help protect what was
        left, to help homeless, and to provide water if
        further fires broke out

Outline:

V. Feeding the homeless

    Source G, 6, 7

VI. Providing basic services

    Source G, 4

VII. Protecting life and property

    Source G, 3, 8

This cross-referencing system is essential if you are going to make full use of your notes and if you are going to avoid time-consuming searches for references later on when you are writing the essay. At the end of this procedure, your outline will have a list of the relevant sources following each main point, and your research notes will have code numbers in most of the margins. Notice that a few of the items on the sheet of notes for Source G have no cross-references next to them. Some will be placed under the headings of other topics in this outline, and they have not here been given their reference numbers. Items 2 and 5 in the notes, for example, would probably come under the heading of Casualties. On the other hand, not all the notes will necessarily get used in the essay; some items will simply not fit into the topics chosen for the outline and will be discarded.

In the next stage, as you prepare to write a paragraph or two about each topic on your outline, you will need only to consult those sources which you have already selected, and, without hesitation, you will be able to move to the exact point in your notes that you need to cite. The more notes that you have collected, the more important it is that you take pains to be thorough during the preliminary organization. Don't start to write your essay, don't start to sort your note-cards until you have completed both your basic outline and your cross-referencing.

EXERCISE 56

Read the following set of notes for an essay on the Chicago Fire, and:

A. write an outline of topics for an essay to be called "Coping with Disaster: The Aftermath of the Chicago Fire";
B. cross-reference the notes with your outline.

As you consider the scope and depth of the information in these notes, remember that you can return to any of the sources, if you wish, and add details or examples to develop a topic which does not have enough supporting information.

Source A

The Story of Chicago, Jennie Hall, Chicago, Rand McNally, 1911, pp. 220–39

1. Sunday, October 8, 1871
2. factors: flimsy wooden buildings (222), hot and dry summer (220)
3. theories: a match was dropped or a lantern was knocked over (Mrs. O'Leary's cow)
4. began at 9:00 west side of the river on DeKoven and Jefferson St. slums—little shacks burned quickly (222)
5. watchman in the court house turned in an alarm to the wrong box (222)
6. all engines and hose carts in the city came (222)
7. everything along the river burned (222-3)
8. flames 100 feet high (223)
9. people panicked trying to get to safety—running wildly (223)
10. Business district: money, mail, possessions all burned (225)
11. Tribune Bldg. supposed to be fire proof—it burned too (226)
12. gas tanks exploded spreading fire rapidly (226)
13. Water Station—Chicago Ave. Pump Station on fire—no water to put out small fires (228)
14. same people went to "The Sands"—small strip of beach (230)
15. Tuesday—fire still burning—17,000 buildings burned (232)
16. General Sheridan sent for tents, rations for people (234)
17. Relief committee distributed provisions and money (234)
18. lumber merchants volunteered not to raise prices (239)

Source B

<u>Chicago, A Chronological and Documentary History</u>, Howard S. Furer, NY, Oceana Publications, pp. 82-4 (original documents and ordinances)

1. October 8, 1871: proclamation by Mayor R. B. Mason
   a. a "terrible calamity"
   b. objective: "preservation of order and the relief of suffering"
   c. special police hired to protect what's left and keep order
   d. men of fire and health departments act as special police
   e. "It is believed the fire has spent its force and all will soon be well"
2. October 10, 1871: ordinance (83)
   a. price of bread was fixed at 8¢ a loaf (10 oz. size) for ten days
   b. anyone selling bread higher will be liable for a penalty of $10. for every sale
   c. request for caution in using fire and request to avoid kerosene lights; water supply still too limited
   d. request for citizens to serve as special policemen; blocks should organize their own guards
   e. avoid using streets in burnt districts until walls are leveled
   f. saloons to close at 8 PM
3. Building Construction Ordinance (1872) (84)
   a. not rebuild wooden buildings if damaged more than 50%
   b. the roof, the outsides and the dividing walls be fireproof
   c. permit must be obtained for building
   d. building permits required to carry on various types of businesses

Source C

<u>The Great Chicago Fire</u>, Robert Cromie, McGraw Hill, 1956

1. in November, two weeks inquiry into causes of fire and conduct of services; no blame fixed (277)
2. popular theory: O'Learys' cow—cow definitely kicked over lamp
   unclear whether Mrs. O'Leary did or didn't bring the lamp to the barn (278)
   newspaper reports very contemptuous of the O'Learys— "stupid"—"no intelligence" [sounds like a scapegoat]
   suggestion that the O'Learys were having revenge for

being removed from welfare (in fact, they were never
on welfare) (279)

3. popular theory: anarchists (280)

4. popular theory: fire extinguisher salesman, in revenge
   for poor sales, to show off his product (280)

5. popular theory: punishment from heaven--"divine
   retribution for the burning of Atlanta by Sherman's
   army" (278)

Source D

NY Times, October 8, 1871, "The Fire Fiend," p. 5

1. fire starts 11 A.M.--starts in planing mill; wind
   blowing fresh

2. children wrapped in blankets and thrown out second-
   story windows to safety

3. another fire a short distance away; all the engines tied
   up there; engines called for city-wide; engines arrive,
   but fire is too big to be stopped

4. spreads with "incredible rapidity"--houses made of wood
   in that area

5. half the population of the city is gathered at scene

6. tugs drawing away boats down the river

7. 1:30 A.M.: one may see to read half a mile from the site
   of the fire

Source E

Times, October 9, "Fires in Chicago," p. 1

1. estimate losses at $250,000 to $300,000--half-insured

2. fires affected factories, two mills, and lower-class
   dwellings primarily

3. "The flames are raging with increased fury in every
   direction and God's mercy can only save the city from
   utter destruction. A fearful panic prevails all through
   the streets where people are rushing to and fro and
   weeping and wailing."

4. sparks flew across the east side of the river and set a
   wooden building on fire that was directly adjoining the
   Chicago Gas house; if gas house burns, there will be no
   light for the city

5. entire city may burn

6. constant ringing of the alarm bell

Source F

<u>Times</u>, October 10, "A City in Ruins," p. 1

1. a violent SW prairie wind fills the air "with fiery messengers of destruction before which the cheaper tenements . . . melted away like wax."
2. 12,000 buildings have burned (rumor); all public buildings, banks, hotels.
3. 100,000 people homeless
4. hundreds of horses, cows, and domestic animals killed
5. streets lined with household goods
6. waterworks intact, but water shut off in certain parts of the city

Source G

<u>Times</u>, October 11, "The Ruined City," p. 1

1. the fire has stopped and there has been some "blessed rain"
2. 20-30 people have died in their homes
3. plundering everywhere--like a scene of war
   a. a thief suffocated while trying to steal jewelry from a store
   b. people who were caught pilfering had to be released because the jail burned down
4. water for drinking from the lake
5. people dying of exposure
6. little food; people searching the ruins
7. difficulties of transporting supplies
8. meeting of citizens at church to help protect what was left, to help homeless, and to provide water if further fires broke out
9. speculation of cause: Late on evening of 8th, a boy (O'Leary) went to the stable on DeKoven Street with a kerosene lantern to milk his cow. The lantern was kicked over by the cow
10. fire mostly affected run-down and obsolete buildings (acc. to reporter, a blessing in disguise)

Source H

<u>Times</u>, October 15, "The Chicago Fire," p. 1

1. city normal again
2. still martial rule; General Sheridan in charge
3. citizens working at night to watch for any new outbreak of fire
4. newspapers moved to other locations

```
 5. estimate 1,000 dead
 6. earlier reports of looting and loss of life were not
    exaggerated
 7. waterworks won't open until next day
 8. two-thirds of the city still using candlelight
 9. suffering mostly among the "humbler classes"
10. businessmen are "buoyant"
11. bread is 8¢
12. saloons are closed at 9:00 for one week [conflict with
    Source B/2f]
```

Source I

Times, November 23, 1871, "Chicago," p. 2

```
1. cause of fire: combination of circumstances
  a. moderate to high winds from a point between N to S and
     W fire kept changing direction
  b. wooden buildings—from one to six blocks in width
     mansard roofs encouraged fire
  c. drought for previous three months; city highly
     flammable
  d. fire intensified into an invincible force—great
     momentum "a heat so terrible that no human agency
     could resist it"
  e. fire department demoralized: bad fire previous night:
     some men had been drinking afterwards; fire marshal
     habitually drunk
  f. "judgment of god"
```

ASSIGNMENT 21

Below are two sets of subjects for a research essay, with a list of readings for each set. You are to work on one of these subjects. First, read through all of the relevant passages. (In a full-scale research project, these readings would form a substantial part, but not all, of your sources.) Then, develop a tentative list of main ideas, based on these sources, that ought to be discussed in an essay dealing with your subject. Include also your own ideas on the subject. Each point in your list should suggest the focus of a paragraph or group of paragraphs in the essay. As you work on your list consider possible theses for the essay and, later on, the strategy that will best fit your thesis and materials. After you have a substantial list of topics and a tentative thesis to pursue, reread the passages, cross-referencing the topics on your list with the relevant paragraphs from the essays. While you do not have to "use up" everything in all of the readings, you should include all relevant points. Your outline should be capable of being developed into an eight- or ten-page essay.

Set A:

What is the best environment for learning?

or

Who should decide what and how children learn?

Readings for Set A:

Blanche Blank, "A Question of Degree" (p. 60)

Steven Cahn, from "If at First You Don't Succeed, Quit" (p. 96)

Edward B. Fiske, "Competency Tests in Basic Skills Cost Few Students Their Diplomas" (p. 294)

Richard Farson, "Birthrights" (p. 69)

Frances FitzGerald, "Rewriting American History" (p. 221)

John Holt, from *How Children Fail* (p. 217)

Roger Sipher, "So That Nobody Has to Go to School if They Don't Want To" (p. 169)

Lewis Thomas, "On Cloning a Human Being" (p. 178)

Set B:

Why are decisions about the use of scientific knowledge so difficult to make?

or

Who should be responsible for the way in which scientific discoveries are applied?

Readings for Set B:

J. D. Bernal, from *Science in History* (p. 411)

Jeremy Bernstein, from *Experiencing Science* (p. 412)

John Compton, from "Science, Technology and Society" (p. 77)

William Lowrance, from *Of Acceptable Risk* (p. 415)

Margaret Mead, "A Crisis, a Challenge" (p. 199)

J. Ravetz, from *Scientific Knowledge and Its Social Problems* (p. 417)

Bertrand Russell, "The Social Responsibilities of Scientists" (p. 104)

Lewis Thomas, "On Cloning a Human Being" (p. 178)

E. Bright Wilson, from *An Introduction to Scientific Research* (p. 109 and p. 419)

from SCIENCE IN HISTORY

One basic distinction between science as such and the generalized techniques from which it arose and to which it is still attached is that it is essentially a literate profession. It is something recorded and transmitted in books and papers, as distinct from the handing on by practical example of the traditional crafts. As such, it was from the very start an occupation limited to the upper classes or to a minority of gifted individuals who managed to win acceptance into them in return for loyal service. This limitation has had several effects on the character of science. It has retarded it by keeping out of science the great majority of the naturally gifted people of all classes who might have contributed to it. At the same time it has ensured that those thinking and even experimenting about science, at least until the time of the Industrial Revolution, should have had very little acquaintance with practical arts and so, in matters of natural science, have not known what they were talking about. Nor could they understand, because they did not themselves feel, the practical needs of common life and, therefore, they had no stimulus to satisfy them by the use of science.

This identification of science with the governing and exploiting classes has, from the earliest times of class division, which arose five thousand years ago with the first cities, engendered a deep suspicion of science, and book-learning generally, in the minds of peasants and, to a lesser degree, of the working classes. However well intentioned were the efforts of the philanthropic philosophers, the people could not but feel that in practice they would result in changes that would bring them no good, and were likely to enslave them more completely or, alternatively, throw them out of work. The first scientists were regarded as magicians capable of unlimited mischief, and this attitude persisted into late classical times when popular feeling, often allied with religion, was sullenly and sometimes violently against the philosophers who were identified, with some justice, with the interests of the upper classes of the hated Roman Empire. In the Middle Ages science existed only on sufferance, and even after its rebirth the same popular reaction was to be seen in the machine wreckers of the Industrial Revolution. Today we can still see it in the reactions to the latest triumph of science, the atom bomb. The combined effect of the contempt and ignorance of the learned, and of the suspicion and resentment of the lower orders, has been, through the whole course of civilization, a major hindrance to the free advance of science.

J. D. Bernal

from EXPERIENCING SCIENCE

A great deal has been written about how the decision to make the Super was reached. Rabi, as a member of the General Advisory Committee, participated in the decision. I asked him what his recollections were of what had happened, and he said, "The Atomic Energy Commission was asked to give the president advice on whether or not to initiate a crash program to make a hydrogen bomb, and it asked the Advisory Committee." At that time—October of 1949—the members of the Advisory Committee, in addition to Rabi and Oppenheimer, were James Conant; Lee DuBridge; Enrico Fermi;* Hartley Rowe, an engineer

---

* The "Super" was the hydrogen bomb. I. I. Rabi won the 1944 Nobel Prize for physics and was chairman of the General Advisory Committee to the Atomic Energy Commission from 1952 until 1956. J. Robert Oppenheimer was director of the atomic energy research project at Los Alamos, N.M., from 1942 to 1945 and preceeded Rabi as chairman of the General Advisory Committee. Conant, a chemist, was president of Harvard from 1933 until 1953 and was chairman of the National Defense Research Committee during World War II. DuBridge was a University of Rochester physicist. Fermi won the 1938 Nobel Prize for physics and headed atomic bomb research at the University of Chicago during World War II.

who had worked on materials procurement for the Manhattan Project; Cyril Smith, a metallurgist who had been in charge of the metallurgy division at Los Alamos during the war; Oliver E. Buckley, president of Bell Laboratories and an expert on guided missiles; and Glenn Seaborg, of Berkeley, a noted chemist who shared the Nobel Prize for chemistry with E. M. McMillan in 1951, for their discoveries of the transuranium elements. "It was a real crisis time, and the whole problem was so entangled that it is difficult for me to remember all the ins and outs of our debate. In fact, the debate was recorded but the tapes were deliberately destroyed soon afterward. It is a great pity that we cannot hear the voices of Fermi and Oppenheimer and the rest in that very fateful discussion," Rabi went on. "The problem that came up was this: All through the period at Los Alamos, and before, there had been a proposal for a bomb called the Super, on which work was being done. The general idea was to cause a fusion reaction involving hydrogen." Hydrogen nuclei (protons) are "fused" by confining them in close proximity at exceedingly high temperatures. When the fusion takes place, the resultant nucleus— deuterium, for example—is less massive than the sum of the masses of its constituents. This mass loss is converted into energy according to Einstein's formula $E = mc^2$, m in this case standing for the mass loss. "It was an interesting idea, except that whatever specific theoretical proposal was made didn't seem to produce a self-propagating chain reaction," Rabi went on. Such a reaction was necessary to generate enough energy to cause a large-scale explosion. "Beautiful and clever calculations were made about it, and even more brilliant calculations to show that it wouldn't work. It began to be more and more evident that if there were such a device it would have to be enormous. A ship would be needed to hold it. And then there was the question of how it would be set off. Would the fusion process spread—"propagate"— throughout the nuclear fuel or simply confine itself to a small part of it? Would it cool off after you got it ignited? Since it would be at a very, very high temperature, would the device radiate away that heat and cool off before it could explode? Nevertheless, after the Russian explosion, certain people thought that we did need some counterthrust. And Lawrence, Alvarez, and Teller felt that the only thing to do was to go full tilt for this Super. In fact, during the Los Alamos period some people felt that it should have higher priority than the ordinary fission bomb. "We shouldn't dillydally with the fission bomb but go for the Super"—so said some very eminent physicists. Not very sensible, but very eminent. I wonder what they think about that now. Anyway, after the Russian explosion they wanted to go ahead with a specific Super model. This model is what came up before the committee. There were two objections to it. In the first place, it was a very chancy thing, because, basically, we didn't know how to make it. And then, just about this time, it was shown that it wouldn't work, it wouldn't propagate—at least, not that particular model. But the general kind of thing they were talking about would have been absolutely devastating if it had worked, because it was so big. Well, the Super people pressed the Atomic Energy Commission to give this program first priority. They wanted to try various configurations of this general type. There was no way we had of refuting these models in general. A man could come in with some configuration and be strongly in favor of it, and it might take three months or more of calculations, by some very brilliant people, to find out if it had a chance. There were no experiments, and the constants weren't known, or anything of that sort. It was like dealing with some of the perpetual-motion people. You show them why something doesn't work, and they say, 'Fine. Thank you,' and the next day they're back with a modification.

"In any event, there was strong agreement within the committee that we should not go ahead. We all agreed that if it could be made to work it would be a terrible thing. It would be awful for humanity altogether. It might give this country a temporary advantage, but then the others would catch up—and it would just louse up life. Fermi and I said that we should use this as an excuse to call a world conference for the nations to agree, for the time being, not to do further research on this."

Rabi and Fermi wrote, in an addendum to the full committee's report to the AEC, "The fact that no limits exist to the destructiveness of this weapon makes its very existence and the knowledge of its construction a danger to humanity as a whole. It is necessarily an evil thing considered in any light. For these reasons we believe it important for the president of the United States to tell the American public and the world that we think it is wrong on fundamental ethical principles to initiate the development of such a weapon."

"Fermi and I felt that if the conference should be a failure and we couldn't get agreement to stop this research and had to go ahead, we could then do so in good conscience," Rabi said. "Some of the others, notably Conant, felt that no matter what happened it shouldn't be made. It would just louse up the world. So the committee unanimously agreed not to go ahead with it with this high priority, especially since we were doing very well in the development of the fission bomb. One member was absent—Glenn Seaborg—and I don't know how he would have voted if he had been there for the discussions. Well, the committee's report to the AEC caused a lot of flak—a lot of consternation—in some circles, and especially with the Berkeley group and Teller. I think we persuaded some members of the commission, but one, Lewis Strauss, got into an absolute dither. The Berkeley people and Strauss went around and talked to newspapermen all over, and to the House and the Senate, and whatnot. Furthermore, it was just about then that Klaus Fuchs was arrested in London for espionage on behalf of the Soviet Union." Fuchs had been at Los Alamos from December of 1944 to June of 1946, working on, among other things, the primitive Super program. He was in a unique position to have complete knowledge of American efforts up to that point to make a Super. "All of this got to President Truman and built up such a head of steam that he was practically forced to declare that he was going to give the Super top priority. Now, around this very time, some experiments that were suggested by Teller and Ulam"—this was Stanislaw Ulam, a brilliant Polish-born American mathematician, who was at Los Alamos during and after the war—"gave rise to a new idea for making a thermonuclear reaction. It bore no relation to the original Super, and in a fairly short time it was shown to be a practical thing, which could be calculated. And the General Advisory Committee backed it—with reluctance, because of all the problems it would create. But it was not the horrendous first thing. It was a terrible thing, but not the original Super. It came not long after Truman's original decision, so the two devices got mixed up in people's minds. Now, I never forgave Truman for buckling under pressure. He simply did not understand what it was about. As a matter of fact, after he stopped being president he still didn't believe that the Russians had had a bomb in 1949. He said so. So for him to have alerted the world that we were going to make a hydrogen bomb at a time when we didn't even know how to make one was one of the worst things he could have done. It shows the dangers in this kind of thing. He didn't have his own scientific people to consult and give him an impartial picture."

Jeremy Bernstein

from OF ACCEPTABLE RISK

In many ways we are better off than we used to be. In a sense we now have the luxury to worry about subtle hazards which at one time, even if detected, would have been given only low priority beside the much greater hazards of the day. Whereas once the outright poison, lead arsenate, was at issue, we have come through several generations of much less toxic agents and now worry about what may be marginal effects of our current pesticides. We have largely gotten lead out of our food; the worst we have to contend with now is an occasional trace dissolving into food from a lead-soldered can seam. But the canning art itself has improved so much that cases of food poisoning, once common, are now so rare as to make the front pages of newspapers. As we worry about the disinfectant hexachlorophene in soap, we should also remember the harsh carbolic acid it has replaced and the surgical operations it has made safer; and, incidentally, we should be grateful for the retirement of that backyard hazard, the lye pot. Surely no case needs to be made for the public health and pharmaceutical revolutions—the conquering in this country of malaria and typhoid and smallpox and polio and tuberculosis and the nutritional deficiency diseases. By comparison with the rickets and pellagra of ages not long past, our anxieties over supplemental vitamins and weight-reducing artificial sweeteners seem trivial. There are signs that our great rivers, lakes, and urban atmospheres are clearing, even if distressingly slowly. The move toward making our workplaces less hazardous is gaining momentum. Consumers have found collective strength, and *caveat emptor* no longer strictly governs the market. In the United States infant mortality in the first year of life is now down from thirteen percent in 1900 to about two percent—a fivefold decrease in seventy-five years.

We don't mean to be overly sanguine; most certainly there are problems, many of them urgently demanding resolution. That is why we have written this book. But in the safety issue, historical perspective is particularly enlightening, leaving us viewing our contemporary condition, as the biologist René Dubos expresses it, as "despairing optimists."

Notice the many different, but interdependent, reasons for the progress sketched above. In part, scientific advance was responsible, bringing forward empirical evidence about the subtle risks of Paris green, lead chromate, and the early food preservatives. Technology provided less harsh antiseptics, devised more efficacious and less risky pesticides and pharmaceuticals, and—together with extraordinary medical and public health innovations—established a rational basis for health protection.

At the same time and partly because of scientific advance, people's values and expectations changed. Discomforting discoveries were forced by the extraordinary growth in our social and physical scale. We have been startled into profound realizations, no less profound for having become commonplace; that the balance of nature is much more precarious than we had presumed; that nature's complex web is easily rent by our clumsy passage; that "there is no longer any 'away' into which to throw things"; that it is crucial that we stop fouling our earthly nest; and that what we do today will affect not only ourselves, and not only our children, but our descendants for many generations to come.

Much of the change has been closely coupled to the mechanisms of government. The 1906 Pure Food and Drugs Act was passed to combat the atrocities of food and drug adulteration and fraud; subsequent replacements and amendments have greatly extended government regulation of the safety of food and food additives, pharmaceuticals, cosmetics, radiation, and medical devices. The 1947 Federal Insecticide, Fungicide, and Rodenticide Act brought those agricultural and public health chemicals under government scrutiny. So also with the Coal Mine Health and Safety Act (1969), the Clean Air Amendments (1970), the Occupational Health and Safety Act (1970), the Consumer Product Safety Act (1970), and many others. A bureaucracy, for which even the usual journalistic "vast" is inadequate, has grown to include a Food and Drug Administration, an Environmental Protection Agency, an Occupational Safety and Health Administration, a Consumer Product Safety Commission, and an assortment of other agencies charged with regulating the products we buy and the surroundings in which we live and work. Legislative and administrative developments have evolved apace with social values as reflected in court determinations of the rights of workers, the liabilities of manufacturers, and the assignment of responsibilities for preserving the environment. Most evaluations of the efficacy and efficiency of these changes are mixed. To be sure, some of these developments have succeeded in protecting individuals from threats against which they would otherwise be defenseless. But others have simply compounded the problems, strewn red tape, and advanced the bureaucratization of society.

We would be remiss not to add the following note. Although we have indeed conquered many of the classical scourges and are in many ways better off than ever before, we currently find ourselves confronted by some new hazards that can fairly be said to appear "monstrous." They are problems which we don't yet know very much about: the radiation, steam explosion, theft, sabotage, and waste disposal hazards of the rapidly growing civilian nuclear power program; the poorly understood effects of attempts to modify the world's weather; the effects of freons and other manmade agents on the protective sunlight-filtering ozone shield of the upper atmosphere. Other such problems are being recognized. Their apparent monstrousness lies principally in their physical and temporal scale. The potential consequences are unprecedentedly widespread and terrible, indifferent to political boundaries. Some of these consequences may prove to be reversible only with great difficulty, with decades or even centuries having to pass before the mishap can be undone. We are now adopting many innovations for widespread use faster than we can even hope to learn about their consequences, thus tragically outsmarting ourselves. Further, the "scale of decisionmaking" involved here transcends that of all previous decisional situations except the uniquely bizarre ones of modern warfare; the decision of one small group can influence the well-being of an entire nation for many years to come, and what one nation decides can affect the fate of millions, or even billions, of unconsulted people around the world.

William Lowrance

from SCIENTIFIC KNOWLEDGE AND ITS SOCIAL PROBLEMS

Science has traditionally been portrayed as an activity whose morality could be nothing but the best. The search for truth is innocent and ennobling; and the eventual benefits to mankind through the advance of knowledge and power, further secure the moral status of science. The very idea of a scientist being a thief, a swindler, or a man who offers his opinions for sale, is near to being a contradiction in terms.

The contrast between the working ethics of science, and that of politics, or business, is so strong as to induce a belief that scientists must be born, or at least made, as superior beings. This picture of the perfect morality of science had its strong basis in reality, both in the practice and in the self-consciousness of science in the academic period. For then, the favourable social conditions, and the effective arrangements for the protection of property, were sufficient to ensure that the working ethics of science would serve to resolve all the social problems encountered in its experience.

In the longer perspective of history, the moral innocence of academic science appears as a temporary feature, a happy accident of circumstances. For the problem of responsibility for powerful knowledge had been recognized by the practitioners of fields ancestral to science, in all the previous centuries. Such knowledge, including magic, alchemy, and parts of astrology, was to be restricted to those who could use it wisely; and hence it was transmitted in an oral or cryptic tradition to initiates in a brotherhood. Of the pioneers of the scientific revolution, Bacon and Descartes, although disbelieving in magical powers, retained this moral sense. Even in his Utopian "New Atlantis," Bacon had the sages of "Solomon's House" deciding which secrets they would reveal to the State, and which not; and Descartes stated a "scientist's oath" of classic simplicity: I would not engage on projects which can be useful to some only by being harmful to others. But Galileo, whose general style of work was so much more like that of a "scientist" than any other natural philosopher of his time, was totally lacking in such a sensitivity. He considered himself as having the right to proclaim philosophical truth as he saw it, and was utterly unconcerned with the possible social effects of his unsettling doctrines. It is probable that he was sure that God's truths, which he was announcing, could not be harmful; but in practice he was demanding the influence over men's minds resulting from his pronouncements, while denying responsibility for the consequences of his actions. His moral position was made even more complex by the fact that while fighting heroically for the truth of natural philosophy as he saw it, he was not at all averse to making money privately through the sale of inventions to the highest bidder.

With the rise to dominance of the "mechanical philosophy," or more correctly with the dehumanization and disenchantment of Nature for the educated common sense of European civilization, the expected powers of scientific knowledge were reduced, and hence also the responsibilities of men of science. The association of natural science with "progress," first with that of the intellect in the eighteenth century, and then with industry in the nineteenth, removed any fears concerning the applications of science from the traditions of self-awareness within science. Hence it was as moral innocents that a group of distinguished physicists urged the American government to produce an atomic bomb. Although such a device clearly had its dangers, ordinary human morality dictated that there should be no risk of Hitler having sole possession of such a bomb. But, some six years later, what had been conceived as a deterrent weapon in the struggle against Fascism, was used on the civilian population of a nation near to surrender; and not once, but twice. Were the scientists who initiated the Manhattan Project morally responsible for the victims of Hiroshima and of Nagasaki? This is not an easy question to answer; but whatever the judgement, it is clearly not one which can be reached by an argument within the traditional working ethics of science.

Thus, first with the Bomb, and more recently through involvement in runaway technology, the world of science has been faced with genuinely moral problems. They concern the responsibility of an individual for the immediate and remote effects of his actions. Such problems are difficult, if not insoluble. The inherited working ethics of science offer no guidance; and the traditional claim of benefit for humanity has, in its realization, produced this darker side. Whatever else will happen to the ideology of science, it can never again claim innocence.

A few decades is a moment in the life of a civilization, and does not even cover the working life of a scientist. The sudden transformation of the social activity of science, rendering its traditional ethics obsolete and its ideology hollow, has caught many a scientist in a personal tragedy. That of Einstein is the most famous; the incidental relation $E = mc^2$, arising from his profound studies in the philosophy of nature, became the magic formula for the sorcery of the atomic bomb, for whose creation he was at least partly responsible. There are doubtless many other such cases: the President of the University of Pennsylvania, formerly a distinguished physicist, found himself in an unpleasant situation when, after repeated denials, he was forced to admit that germ-warfare research was being conducted secretly on his campus. Calling for his resignation, the student newspaper explained that, as an elderly man, he found himself involved in problems whose existence he could not have conceived when, as an old-fashioned scientist, he took office some years previously.

For many generations, up to but not including the present, the study of nature has been among the most serene of occupations. To be sure, the work is arduous and even hazardous; but many an eminent scientist turned with relief from the turbulence and faction of politics, commerce, and even institutional religion, to the innocent contemplation of the unchanging and impersonal laws of nature. In less than a generation's time, that haven has been lost. Science is in flux. Many who entered it as a refuge from the intellectual and moral squalor of ordinary society find, in their advancing years, that they are involved in administering just another bureaucratic establishment. They are enmeshed in the demands of society and the State; they must accomplish the administrative and social tasks of getting high-quality craftsmen's work out of a set of manpower-unit employees; and in participating in the leadership of their field, they must cope with the insoluble practical and moral problems which emerge when corruption sets in.

For the industrialization of science has produced another set of moral problems, internal to science but still incapable of solution through a working ethic that was conceived in terms of the search for truth, and organized around the protection of well-defined intellectual property. As the ideal of truth has become obsolete, and the location of intellectual property has shifted, this ethic has lost its relevance. The very naturalness of such conditions as shoddy science and entrepreneurial science ensures that they are connected to good work by a multiplicity of continuous gradations. A scientific entrepreneur may produce a piece of genuinely good work, but then use it for further inflating the stock of his establishment; has he violated the ethics of science? A piece of work may be condemned as shoddy, but may then be defended as the best work a particular man could do in a difficult field; the assessment of quality of scientific results is subtle enough, and who can be sure of the intentions of another? And if a man does not wish to belong to a community of colleagues of the traditional sort, and does not need it for the building of his personal career in science, how can the informal penalties of disapproval be applied against him? Thus there is no escape from moral problems in science, even in the purest of pure science, except perhaps in those enclaves which have not yet been affected by industrialization and its social consequences.

J. Ravetz

from AN INTRODUCTION TO SCIENTIFIC RESEARCH

There is much criticism of scientists today for their alleged indifference to the uses to which their discoveries may be put. Scientists are blamed by many, for example, for contributing to the horrors of modern war. The fact is that the same people who now condemn scientists as soulless and amoral for their wartime work would have been the first to cry "Treason!" if any had refused to assist their country during the war.

Nevertheless, the scientist has to consider moral factors before undertaking a new problem. This is particularly true in applied research, whose effects are more easily predictable. Since few applied scientists are independent agents, serious personal dilemmas can arise when a scientist believes that the work he is doing for an industrial firm has either no social usefulness or actually harmful consequences. Frequently the difficulty arises from the fact that work done by him is exaggerated or applied in directions never intended. Often this is done by the advertising departments of his employer's firm. It is the right and duty of scientists to protest against these misuses of their work, and most of them will do so, even at the risk of losing their jobs. In this they are supported by the great majority of their colleagues, who in fact look down upon those who permit their names or their work to be improperly exploited. If the other components of the business world had as high a level of ethical responsibility as is generally maintained by scientists, there would hardly be grounds for criticism.

It is practically impossible for the pure scientist to predict the moral consequences of his choice of a problem, however much he may wish to do so. The wisest man living cannot foresee all the future effects of a new basic discovery and correctly balance the good uses against the bad. It is hard for nonscientists to believe this but very important that they should be repeatedly shown the evidence which supports it. Even after the fact, who would be bold enough to say that the study of radioactivity should never have been begun? Even aside from the atom bomb, it is impossible to untangle its influence on today's life, but it certainly had a strong effect on theories of atomic structure, chemistry, genetics, electronics, astrophysics, and geology. In fact, like so many other fundamental discoveries, it is mixed into every branch of science today and therefore into every branch of technology. It is impossible to imagine modern life existing without a knowledge of radioactivity, so much so that one is tempted to say that its discovery was, or would have been, forced upon man by the march of events.

Finally, the primary aim of pure science is not the laying of foundations for future inventions but the pushing back of the wall of ignorance and superstition which surrounds the human race. When an eclipse of the sun is no longer a dreaded manifestation of the gods' displeasure but an eagerly anticipated chance to test refinements of the laws of motion of the heavenly bodies, it would seem that undeniable progress has been made. Let those who decry science come out into the open and say that they prefer ignorance to understanding, darkness to light.

But scientists are, and correctly so, under tremendous moral pressure to work incessantly for the proper utilization of their work by society. This must include strenuous efforts to educate the public, not only on the facts of science, a discouragingly vast job in view of the ignorance in this field of even most college graduates, but also on the basic aims of science, its effects, and the climate necessary for its advancement. In this enterprise most scientists are inhibited by their well-grounded fear of dealing in any way with the press. Almost every scientist has at some time yielded, as a matter of duty, to requests for interviews with newspaper reporters. In spite of the most solemn promises, his reward is all too frequently a distorted and sensational article which serves no public purpose and damages his reputation. After such experiences, many scientists shun the press as the plague.

Nevertheless the public should receive information about scientific advances, and some way should be worked out to give it to them. Reporters frequently promise to show their write-ups to the scientist for correction, but they do not always live up to these promises. This check also provides little protection from the headline writers, who reporters claim are out of their reach. A perfectly sound article on an anthropological expedition is of little help if headed by: "Harvard Savant Discovers Savage Love Nest." Perhaps the best procedure is to work through an experienced press officer who understands the scientist's viewpoint and who also is in a position to apply some pressure on the newsmen.

E. Bright Wilson

INTEGRATING YOUR SOURCES INTO PARAGRAPHS

Writing the text of a research essay is rather like putting a mosaic together. Each paragraph has its basic design, established by its topic sentence. Carrying out the design might require you to present a group of reasons or examples to illustrate the main idea, or to provide an extended explanation to develop that idea in greater detail, or to compare two elements introduced in the topic sentence. These are the same paragraphing patterns that you use in all of your writing. What makes the research essay different is the origin of the materials, assembled from many sources, *not* the way in which they are organized or presented.

Imagine that the notes which you have taken from several different sources are boxes of tiles, each box containing a different color. You may find it easier to avoid mixing the colors and to work only with red tiles or only with blue, or to devote one corner of the mosaic to a red motif and another to a blue. In the same way, you may find it both convenient and natural to work with only one source at a time and to avoid the decisions and the adjustments that must be made when you are combining different styles and approaches. But, of course, it is the design and only the design that dictates which colors should be used in working out the pattern; and it is the topic sentence which dictates which evidence should be included in the paragraph. Therefore, whichever topic you have decided to discuss in a given paragraph, you must work with *all* the relevant information that you have gathered about that topic, whether it comes from one source or from many. Of course, there may be an abundance of materials; you may find it impossible to fit every available detail or comment into the paragraph without overloading its structure through excessive repetition. These rejected pieces may not fit into another part of the essay; instead, they will go back into their boxes as a back-up or reserve fund of information.

At the same time, the criteria for judging the quality of a paragraph remain the same—clarity, coherence, and unity. Don't attempt to call attention to the variety of your sources at the expense of your design. You must strive to integrate your materials so that no one reading your essay will be distracted by their different origins; your reader should not be made aware of any breaks or disharmony between the various points. On the other hand, your materials should not be so completely assimilated that you fail to provide appropriate acknowledgement of your sources. As you will learn in the next chapter, the apparatus of footnoting will act as a running record of your research. Your reader observes the little numbers, consults the notes, and becomes aware of the diverse origins of these smoothly integrated pieces of information.

Here, then, are the basic rules for paragraph construction, adjusted to fit the requirements of the research essay:

1. Each paragraph should possess a single main idea, usually expressed in the topic sentence. That topic or design controls the distribution and arrangement of all the information in the paragraph. Everything that is included should develop and support that single idea, without any striking digressions.
2. The body of the paragraph will probably contain a combination of information taken from a variety of sources. The number of different sources that you will include in any one paragraph depends partly on the number of authors in your notes who have touched on that point and partly on the contribution each can make to the development of your topic.

PROVIDING A CLEAR ACCOUNT OF YOUR EVIDENCE

Worth noting again is that if your research has been thorough, you may find yourself with more information than you can easily integrate into your paragraph and run the risk of overcrowding it. You may have collected four or five examples from several different sources to illustrate the topic sentence of your paragraph, and each of these instances in its original text may have filled several sentences or several paragraphs or several pages. Interesting as they all may be, for you to give each a comparable amount of space is impractical. You must select the example or examples on which you will focus and either disregard or briefly refer to the others. But if you go to the other extreme and your account of an example is too brief and cursory, your reader will not understand its significance and your reasons for including it. Your object is to supply just enough information about that example to make your reader appreciate its interest and its relevance to your topic.

In the following complete paragraph the writer is eager to assert her main idea, but her examples are presented as afterthoughts:

> Advertising uses women amorally. This condition should be publicized, and the sooner the better for every member of the reading public. For the past half century, the giant and not-so-giant corporations have succeeded in portraying an image of women that ranges from downright stupidity (Parker Pen: "You might as well give her a gorgeous pen to keep her checkbook unbalanced with") to the object of sadistic sex (Vogue's "The Story of Ohhh . . ." which included shots of a man ramming his hand into a woman's breast). Women today are being awakened to these debasing and degrading tactics.

The parentheses here are being used to wedge the examples into an already overloaded sentence. This writer is counting on having an exceptionally patient reader, who will pause long enough to identify and interpret the significance of these parenthetical illustrations.

In contrast, here is a paragraph from an essay about the novelist F. Scott Fitzgerald, in which four different explanations of an incident are presented, each at suitable length. The writer is describing an affair between Fitzgerald's wife, Zelda, and Edouard Jozan, a young Frenchman. (Notes have been deleted.)

> There is a lack of agreement about the details of the affair as well as its significance for the Fitzgeralds' marriage. According to one of Fitzgerald's biographers, Jozan and Zelda afterwards regarded it as "nothing more than a summer flirtation." But Ernest Hemingway, in his memoirs, wrote much later that Scott had told him "a truly sad story" about the affair, which he repeated many times in the course of their friendship. Gerald and Sara Murphy, who were present that summer and remembered the incident very well, told of being awakened by Scott in the middle of a September night in order to help him revive Zelda from an overdose of sleeping pills. The Murphys were sure that this incident was related to her affair with Jozan. Nancy Milford, Zelda's biographer, believes that the affair affected Zelda more than Scott, who, at that time,

> was very engrossed in his work. Indeed, Milford's account
> of the affair is the only one which suggests that Zelda
> was so deeply in love with Jozan that she asked Scott for
> a divorce. According to an interview with Jozan, the
> members of this triangle never engaged in a three-way
> confrontation; Jozan told Milford that the Fitzgeralds
> were "the victims of their own unsettled and a little
> unhealthy imagination."

This paragraph gives a brief but adequate account of what is known about the events of that summer of 1924. The writer does not try to rush through the four accounts of the affair, nor does he reduce each one to a phrase or a label, as if he expected the reader to have prior knowledge of these people and their activities. Placed in the context of the whole essay, the paragraph probably provides enough information for the reader to judge whose interpretation of the affair is closest to the truth.

DOING JUSTICE TO YOUR SOURCES

Perhaps the greatest disservice that you can do your sources is to distort them so that your reader is left with a false impression of the opinions held by a writer or a group of writers whom you have cited in your essay. One way of shading an argument to suit your own ends is to misrepresent the strength of the opposition. Let us assume that you are working with a bibliography of ten articles. Three clearly support your point of view, but four of the others are openly opposed, and the rest avoid taking sides, emphasizing related but less controversial topics. If your essay cites only the three favorable articles and the neutral ones, and if you avoid any reference to the views of the opposition, you have not provided a satisfactory argument. Such ostrich-like tactics will not convince your reader that your opinions are right; on the contrary, your unwillingness to take on the opposition can only suggest that your point of view must have some basic flaw. If you omit the troublesome sources from your bibliography and pretend that they do not exist, then your reader, who is likely to be familiar with some of the arguments on both sides, will wonder at your inability to locate and cite sources that fairly represent the opposition's views. Thus, a one-sided presentation will either make you appear to be wholly biased or will damage your credibility as a thorough researcher. If the sources are available in the library, and if their views are pertinent, then they should be represented and, if you wish, refuted in your essay.

Sometimes, distortions can occur accidentally, because you have presented only a *partial* account of a source's views. In the course of an article or a book, an author may examine and then reject or accept a variety of views before making it clear which are his own conclusions. Or he may have mixed opinions about the issue and see merit in more than one point of view. If you choose to quote or paraphrase material from only one section of such a work, then you must find a way to inform your reader that these statements are not entirely representative of the writer's overall views.

When ideas get distorted, it is not usually the source who has been guilty of ambiguity; more often, the cause has been the researcher's poor comprehension or careless note-taking or hasty reading. Remember to check through the entire section of the article or sequence of your notes *before* you attribute an opinion to your source, to make sure that you are not taking the statement out of context or ignoring a more comprehensive statement in the next paragraph or on the next page, which may be more typical of the writer's thinking. Remember that a common argumentative strategy is to set up a point with which one basically disagrees in order to shoot it down shortly thereafter. Don't confuse a statement made for the sake of argument with a writer's real beliefs. A thorough reading of the entire source will usually leave you with the correct impression, which you must communicate to your reader.

Occasionally, a writer may be tempted to distort a source deliberately because he is so anxious to uphold his point of view that he will seize upon and cite any bit of material which looks like corroborative evidence. Very often, however, the words of the source have to be twisted to fit the argument, and the true intentions are warped to suit the preconceived ideas of the writer. This is one of the worst kinds of intellectual dishonesty—and one of the easiest for a suspicious reader to detect: one has only to look up the source oneself. If you cannot muster sufficient arguments and if your sources' evidence does not clearly and directly support your side, then you should seriously consider switching sides or switching topics.

Here is a fairly clear instance of such distortion. In an essay on the need for prison reform, Garry Wills is focusing on the general deficiencies of our society's punitive system, not the death penalty (or lack thereof). But the student who is citing Wills in his research essay on the left is writing specifically in support of capital punishment. To make Wills's arguments fit into the scheme of this essay, the student has to make some suspiciously selective references. Here are two paragraphs from the research essay, side by side with the source:

Although the death penalty may sound very harsh and inhumane, is this not fair and just punishment for one who was able to administer death to another human being? A murderer's victim always receives the death penalty. Therefore, the death penalty for the murderer evens the score, or, as stated in the Bible, "an eye for an	*Revenge:* The oldest of our culture's views on punishment is the *lex talionis,* an eye for an eye. Take a life, lose your life. It is a very basic cry—people must "pay" for their crimes, yield exact and measured recompense. No one should "get away with" any crime, like a shoplifter taking something unpaid for. The desire to make an offender suffer equivalent pain (if not compensatory *excess* of pain) is very deep in human nature, and rises quickly to the surface. What is

eye, and a tooth for a tooth." According to Garry Wills, "take a life, lose your life." Throughout the ages, society has demanded that man be allowed to right his wrongs. Revenge is our culture's oldest way of making sure that no one "gets away with" any crime. As Wills points out, according to this line of reasoning, the taking of the murderer's life can be seen as his payment to society for his misdeed.

Another argument in defense of capital punishment is its effect as a deterrent against future murderous acts. It seems likely that, if a would-be killer knows the price he'll have to pay, he will stop and think twice before committing murder. Garry Wills points out that long ago, before prisons came into existence, minor criminals were punished by shaming them through public humiliation, like branding or the stocks. Law-abiding citizens were encouraged to ridicule and mock them, and, for violent crimes, there was public execution. These methods were excellent deterrents for all those who viewed the punishments. Today, instead, as Wills reminds us, we have very high and thick prison walls, which keep prisoners out of the public eye and off the streets. Has justice been truly served by this form of punishment?

lynching but an impatience with even the slightest delay in exacting this revenge? It serves our social myth to say that this impatience, if denied immediate gratification, is replaced by something entirely different—by an impersonal dedication to justice. Only lynchers want revenge, not those who wait for a verdict. That is not very likely. Look at the disappointed outcry if the verdict does not yield even delayed satisfaction of the grudge.

The importance of revenge is seen in the fact that the demand for a death penalty is often greatest in cases where no other motive can be observed—with the psychotic or deranged killer or rapist or child-abuser; with those who have committed crimes of passion, where deterrence of the similarly afflicted is not possible. Such cries for redress have little to do with social utility—especially when it is an outsider or outcast who is being punished (an Indian on the frontier, a black in the old South). One cannot pretend to be instilling respectability in a people denied that respectability from the outset.

. . . the man who "pays his debt" gives society something useful because he offers his body as an object lesson to others, who might commit the same crime if they did not see his grisly example set before them.

This was, of course, the reason for public execution and penance in the days before prisons were invented. People were locked in the stocks to be ridiculed. They were deprived of an ear or branded, to give all citizens a mnemonic lesson on the wages of crime. But our crooks are hidden away, not brandished in public. Certain parts of society are very aware of the prisons, but not in ways that scare them off—the ghettos commune with their prison-extensions, so as to make prison walls seem inevitable. Others are deterred—but mainly those who need no such harsh deterrence. The middle class citizen is frightened of prison just as he is scared to death of the ghetto. But his type also fears any loss of respectability—fines, bankruptcy, scandal, lost jobs and opportunities. All those things hedge his actions, deter him, even apart from jail—which is a comparatively distant threat.

In both paragraphs the writer is citing only the preliminary part of Wills's argument and thus makes him appear to be a supporter of capital punishment. Wills is being misrepresented because (unlike the writer) he had the sense to examine the views of the opposing side and give them a fair hearing before presenting his own arguments. The ideas that the student cites are not Wills's, but Wills's rendition of commonly accepted assumptions about punishment. It is not entirely clear whether the writer of the research essay has merely been careless, failing to read past the first few sentences of each section, or whether he deliberately twisted the essay to his own advantage. These excerpts do not make Wills's views on the death penalty entirely clear, but they certainly cannot be converted into a defense of executions, public or private.

INTEGRATING YOUR SOURCES: AN EXAMPLE

To illustrate the need for careful analysis of sources when you write your paragraphs, the following example works with a group of passages, all direct quotations, which have been gathered for a research essay on college athletics. The paragraph developed from these sources must support the writer's thesis: colleges should, in the interests of both players and academe, outlaw the high-pressure tactics used by coaches when they recruit high school players for college teams. Of the following statements, the first three come from college coaches describing recruiting methods that they have observed and carried out; the last four are taken from books that discuss corruption in athletics. Notice that all seven sources address much the same point, which is to be the focus of the paragraph—the prevalence of recruiting high school stars as an alternative to developing the students that the admissions office happens to deliver.

> I think in the long run, every coach must recognize this basic principle, or face the alumni firing squad. Recruiting is the crux of building a championship football team.
>
> Steve Sloan, Texas Tech

> Athletics is creating a monster. Recruiting is getting to be cancerous.
>
> Dale Brown, Louisiana State University

> You don't out-coach people, you out-recruit them.
>
> Paul "Bear" Bryant, University of Alabama

> It is an athletic maxim that a man with no special coaching skills can

win games if he recruits well and that a tactician without talented players is a man soon without a job.

Kenneth Denlinger

There is recruiting in varying degrees in every intercollegiate sport, from crew to girls' basketball and from the Houston golf dynasty that began in the mid-50's to Southern California importing sprinters and jumpers from Jamaica.

J. Robert Evans

The fundamental causes of the defects in American college athletics are too much commercialism and a negligent attitude towards the educational opportunity for which the college exists.

Carnegie Foundation, 1929

[*Collier's* magazine, in 1905, reported that] Walter Eckersall, All-American quarterback, enrolled at Chicago three credits short of the entrance requirement and his teammate, Leo Detray, entered the school before he even graduated high school. In addition the University of Minnesota paid two players outright to play in a single game (Nebraska: 1902). A quarterback and an end also from Minnesota admitted shaving points during the 1903 Beloit game.

Joseph Durso

Which of these ideas and observations might contribute something to the development of a paragraph describing the prevalence of commercialism in the recruitment of athletes? In other words, which statements deserve to be represented in this paragraph by paraphrase or perhaps by direct quotation?

I think in the long run, every coach must recognize this basic principle, or face the alumni firing squad. Recruiting is the crux of building a championship football team.

This very broad generalization initially seems quotable, largely because it sums up the topic so well; but, in fact, because it does no more than sum up the paragraph topic, it does not advance your argument any further and need not be included if your topic sentence says the same thing. (In general, you should write your own topic sentences rather than letting your sources write them for you.) The phrase "alumni firing squad" might be useful to cite in a later paragraph, in a discussion of the specific influence of alumni.

Athletics is creating a monster. Recruiting is getting to be cancerous.

Coach Brown's choice of images—"cancerous" and "monster"—is certainly vivid; but the sentence as a whole is no more than a generalized opinion about recruiting, not an explanation of *why* the situation is so monstrous. To be lured into quoting this in full for the sake of two words would be a mistake.

> You don't out-coach people, you out-recruit them.

This is the first statement that has advanced a specific idea: the coach may have a *choice* between building a winnning team through recruiting and building a winning team through good coaching; but recruiting, not coaching, wins games. Coach Bryant, then, is not just wringing his hands for rhetorical effect, as the first two coaches seem to be. His seven-word sentence is succinct, if not elaborately developed, and would make a good introduction to or summation of a point which deserves full discussion.

The remaining four statements suggest a wider range of approach and style. The last two, dealing with recruiting practices in 1903 and 1929, might be more appropriate for citation in another paragraph of the essay, one which discusses the early background of college sports.

> Walter Eckersall, All-American quarterback, enrolled at Chicago three credits short of the entrance requirement and his teammate, Leo Detray, entered the school before he even graduated high school. In addition, the University of Minnesota paid two players outright to play in a single game (Nebraska: 1902). A quarterback and an end also from Minnesota admitted shaving points during the 1903 Beloit game.

This passage is as much concerned with corruption as recruiting and indicates that commercialism is nothing new in college athletics. Although the information is interesting, there would be no point in quoting these examples in their original phrasing. The passage is little more than a list of facts, presented in a straightforward but rather dull fashion; the language is not worth preserving verbatim.

> The fundamental causes of the defects in American college athletics are too much commercialism and a negligent attitude towards the educational opportunity for which the college exists.

In contrast, this extract from the 1929 Carnegie Foundation study is phrased in abstract language that is characteristic of foundation reports and academic writing in general. This style can be found in most of the textbooks that you read (including this one) and in many of the sources that you use in college. The foundation presents its point clearly enough and raises an important idea: an athlete recruited to win games (and earn himself fame and fortune) is likely to ignore the primary reason for going to college—to acquire an education. Nevertheless, there is no compelling reason to *quote* this statement. Remember that you include quotations in your essay to enhance your presentation; the quotation marks automatically prepare the reader for a treat, something special, worth singling out. But the prose here is too colorless and abstract to give the reader anything to focus on; a paraphrase that elaborates the idea of the student's motivation is preferable.

> There is recruiting in varying degrees in every intercollegiate sport, from crew to girls' basketball and from the Houston golf dynasty that began in the mid-50's to Southern California importing sprinters and jumpers from Jamaica.

This statement presents a quite different level of information; it is full of detailed references, specifically, a list of sports, including some not known for their cutthroat recruiting practices. But the presence of details does not of itself justify quotation. Will these references be at all meaningful to the reader who is not familiar with the "Houston golf dynasty" or the Jamaican track stars? To know that recruitment is not limited to "cash" sports, such as football, is interesting, but the specifics date quickly: in a few years, they may no longer be a useful frame of reference for most readers.

> It is an athletic maxim that a man with no special coaching skills can win games if he recruits well and that a tactician without talented players is a man soon without a job.

Largely because of parallel construction, the last comment sounds both sharp and solid. In much the same way as Coach Bryant's seven words, but at greater length, Kenneth Denlinger sums up the contrast between coaching and recruiting, and suggests which one has the edge. Because the statement gives the reader something substantial to think about and because it is well phrased, Denlinger is probably worth quoting.

   Should the writer include both the statements, by Bryant and by Denlinger, which say essentially the same thing? While Bryant's firsthand comment is commendably terse and certainly authoritative, Denlinger's is more complete and self-explanatory. A solution might be to include both, at different points in the paragraph, with Bryant cited at the end to sum up the idea that has been developed. Of course, the other five sources need not be excluded from the paragraph. Rather, if you wish, all five may be referred to, by paraphrase or brief reference, with their authors' names cited.

   Here is *one* way of integrating this set of statements into a paragraph:

> In college athletics, what is the best way for a
> school to win games? Should a strong team be gradually

```
built up by training ordinary students from scratch, or
should the process be shortened and success be assured by
actively recruiting players who already know how to win?
The first method may be more consistent with the
traditional amateurism of college athletics, but as early
as 1929, the Carnegie Foundation complained that the focus
of college sports had shifted from education to the
material advantages of winning. Even earlier, in 1903,
there were several instances of players without academic
qualifications who were "hired" to guarantee victory. And
in recent years excellence of recruiting has become the
most important skill for a coach to possess. Kenneth
Denlinger has observed, "It is an athletic maxim that a
man with no special coaching skills can win games if he
recruits well and that a tactician without talented
players is a man soon without a job." It follows, then,
that a coach who wants to keep his job is likely to
concentrate on spotting and collecting talent for his
team. Coaches from LSU, Alabama, and Texas Tech all
testify that good recruiting has first priority throughout
college athletics. According to Bear Bryant of Alabama:
"You don't out-coach people, you out-recruit them."
```

SELECTING QUOTATIONS

Now that you are working with a great variety of sources, it may be all the more difficult to limit the number of quotations in your essay and to choose quotable material. If you are doubtful about when and what to quote, review the guidelines for quotation in Chapter 3 and Chapter 5. As a rule, the more eminent and authoritative the source, the more reason to consider quoting it; but make sure that eminence does not bring with it a complexity of style that makes it unreadable. Never quote something just because it sounds impressive, and avoid bland generalizations which do not have much substance. Most important, the style of the quotation—the level of difficulty, the choice of vocabulary, and the degree of abstraction—should be compatible with your own style. Don't force your reader to make a mental jump from your own characteristic voice and wording to a far more abstract or flowery or colloquial style. Of course, the need for a consistent voice does not mean that your essay should lack all variety; nor are you expected to exclude significant but difficult quotations by authors whose style is so distinctive that it cannot be paraphrased.

When the time comes to decide whether and what to quote, stop and observe your own reactions. After an interval, reread your rough draft fairly rapidly. If you find any quotation difficult to understand on the first try, if you find that you are moving from one "language" to another as your eyes move from your own text to the quotation, then either attempt to paraphrase the point, or leave it out entirely. If your mind becomes distracted or confused or blank, your reader's will be, too. In the long run, the writers that you will want to quote will be the ones whom you understand and enjoy.

Quoting Primary Sources in Biographical and Historical Essays

When you are working on a biographical or historical research essay, you will probably encounter special problems deciding whether or not to quote. You may be trying to recreate an unusual personality or event and thus wondering whether the quoted material is uniquely characteristic or descriptive of your subject, necessitating quotation rather than paraphrase. Primary sources often have a special claim to be quoted. You would be more likely to include one of Hemingway's descriptions of Paris in 1925, without alteration, than a comparable sentence by one of his biographers. A person who witnessed the Johnstown Flood has a better claim to have his original account transcribed verbatim than does the reporter describing the same event from the newsroom.

Sometimes you must quote your source at length to convince your reader of a point which he might possibly be reluctant to accept. In the following example, George Washington's own phrases present us with some unpalatable facts. Notice how the author's topic sentence places Washington's attitude towards slavery in the context of his age, and thus mitigates the effect of the quotations:

> The most charitable description of Washington's attitude to slavery is to say that he accepted the Virginia labor practices of his time. It is painful to read, in his account books, his careful notes of the cash value of a slave who died. When, before the Revolution, he sent a recalcitrant slave to be sold in the West Indies, he wrote to the captain of the ship to say that "Tom" should be kept handcuffed until the ship sailed, adding that "he is exceedingly healthy and strong, and good at the hoe . . . which gives me reason to hope he may, with your good management, sell well, if kept clean and trimmed up a little when offered for sale." But his attitude changed: by 1797, two years before his death, he had resolved "never again to become the master of another slave by purchase." In the same year he wrote, "I wish from my soul that the Legislature of this State could see the policy of a gradual abolition of slavery."

If you are quoting in order to remain faithful to your subject's characteristic turn of phrase, it is essential that you make the exact source of the quotation quite clear to your reader. Here, for example, is an excerpt from a student essay describing Charles Dickens on holiday in France in 1853:

> On first beholding Boulogne, Dickens was enraptured. He immediately wrote home to a friend expressing his delight in the beauty of the French countryside and of the town. "He raved about the rustic qualities of the people. . . ." He raved about the "fresh sea air" and about the "beauty and repose of his surroundings."

The first "He raved" tells us at once that the biographer, not Dickens, is being quoted, and the reader cannot be sure which of the two is responsible for "fresh sea air" and "beauty and repose," since the biographer may, in fact, be quoting from Dickens's letters. (Single quotation marks inside the double quotation marks might have been used to make this distinction.)

The placement of the quotation marks in the next excerpt makes it easier for us to believe that the words are Dickens's own. The novelist is describing the house that he has rented, the Château des Moulineux:

> Dickens rattled off a list of phrases in his attempt to describe this idyllic place. It was to become his "best doll's house," "our French watering place," and "this abode of bliss." More than anything else it would become a "happy, happy place."

On the other hand, such a group of separately quoted phrases can create an awkward, disconnected effect, and the strategy should not be used too often. As always, there should be a good reason for placing words within quotation marks.

Descriptions are often more difficult to paraphrase than ideas and therefore tend to be presented in a sequence of quoted phrases. If you read that the walls of the room were painted sea-green and the furniture was made out of horsehair and covered with light-brown velvet, you may find it next to impossible to summon up appropriate synonyms to paraphrase these standard descriptive terms. "Crin de cheval" covered with fuzzy beige fabric? Mediterranean colors decorating the walls? The result is hardly worth the effort, and the new descriptions will probably be a distortion of the original. On the other hand, the original sentences that contain such bits of objective description are frequently not worth careful preservation in quotation marks. If the man's eyes were dark blue, don't alter the phrase to "piercing blue" or "deep azure" or "ocean pools." If you place "dark blue" in a sentence that is otherwise your own, it will be permissible to avoid the quotation marks entirely.

EXERCISE 57

The following paragraphs are excerpted from a biographical essay describing the novelist Herman Melville in his last years. The author of this essay has scrupulously placed in quotation marks all the words and phrases that he found in his sources. Consider the purpose of the essay, which was to create a full and accurate portrait of Melville's style of life, and then examine these excerpts. Decide which quoted phrases can and should be eliminated through paraphrase, and which phrases should remain in quotation marks. Your object is to achieve a less distracting presentation, without any loss of accuracy.

On the second floor there was a "narrow iron-trimmed porch, furnished with Windsor and folding canvas chairs." It was on the second floor, facing "bleak north," where Melville's study-bedroom was located. "It was a carpetless room, gloomy and monastic in appearance." The room and its "small black iron bed, covered with dark cretonne," were dominated by a "great mahogany desk." The desk, with its writing surface of "pebbled green paper" had four shelves of books. The desk and its bookcase were "topped by strange plaster heads." On the side of this study-bedroom was pasted a motto, "Keep true to the dreams of thy youth." Adjoining Melville's room in this house located near the University Club of New York was the "sunny and comfortable" room of Melville's wife, Elizabeth. Here, sitting in a big armchair, Herman Melville could relieve the "dark privacy" of his own cell.

It was a household in which ill health and depression afflicted the principal occupants. Elizabeth (Bessie) Melville, the oldest of the Melville daughters, suffered from a crippling arthritis, and although the "family always discussed [her] ailments in physical terms . . . they would appear to have been in part psychosomatic." Herman Melville's wife, Elizabeth, suffered from a "hay fever which incapacitated her . . . in the summer" and a depression that was a result of her life with her husband. Yet, like her bright sunny room in contrast to her husband's room of gloom, "she did not encase herself in a funereal or ascetic environment." "Her life with a genius husband brought her much that she was emotionally unequal to; yet her loyalty and devotion to him were unswerving."

or

Bring to class passages from a descriptive biography or narrative that you have found difficult to paraphrase. Underline the phrases for which there appear to be no synonyms.

EXERCISE 58

The unfinished student paragraphs below are followed by brief excerpts from sources.

1. Decide which of the excerpts contains the most appropriate sentence for quotation. (It is not necessary to quote a passage in its entirety.) For the purposes of this exercise, assume that all the sources are qualified authorities.
2. Paraphrase the other excerpts.
3. Complete the paragraph by using both paraphrase and quotation, citing two *or* three sources. Maintain a consistent tone and (except for the quotation) a single voice. Do not digress too far from the topic sentence.

A. Student Paragraph:

    Love and marriage have taken on a new appearance.
    Books, magazines, movies and television have impressed
    upon people that, through love and marriage, a complete
    state of euphoria could be achieved. Love was forever and
    could conquer all. . . .

Sources

Our society expects us all to get married. With only rare exceptions we all do just that.

Mervyn Cadwallader

Doesn't popular psychology, brandishing the banner of Freud with more enthusiasm than knowledge, tell us, in effect, that any male who stays single is selfish or homosexual or mother-dominated and generally neurotic? And any unmarried female frustrated (or worse, not frustrated) and neurotic? A "normal" person, we are told, must love and thereupon marry.

Ernest van den Haag

[For all of us,] love has, in a word, become a value—perhaps the supreme one—something undubitably worth while in itself and something capable by its own magic of making other things valuable either as means or as adornments.

Joseph Wood Krutch

B. Student Paragraph

As human beings, we constantly have images, fantasies, and aspirations about love and romance, and we spend our lives trying to act them out. But not all of our fantasies can be put into action. We store them away and, as each situation arises, we reach into our unconscious and pull out an appropriate image to act out. . . .

Sources

[When we say that] we love someone we mean that the image of that person in our mind is highly charged with constructive, affectionate, and generous feelings. . . . What the person is actually like, or how he appears to other people and how they feel about him, does not come into the picture except indirectly. . . . If we are particularly anxious at the moment to fall in love, we help it along by picking out the lovable things to emphasize in our image, denying or neglecting the undesirable qualities.

Eric Berne

In our society, people commonly marry in a romantic haze, usually ignorant of the traits, needs and aims of their spouses. They marry an image, not a person. The image is partly a construction of their needs and fantasies—much like the interpretations made of a psychologist's ambiguous inkblots.

Sidney M. Jourand

As a matter of fact most fantasies consist of anticipations. They are for the most part preparatory acts, or even psychic exercises for dealing with certain future realities.

C. G. Jung

[Psychotherapists] show that fantasies go in typical cycles. The stammerer fancies himself a great orator . . . the poor man fancies himself a millionaire. . . . All seek compensation through fantasy.

Violet Staub de Laszlo

C. Student Paragraph

It can be very difficult to decide the extent to which a nation is responsible for its destructive acts during wartime. Authorities don't seem to be able to make clear distinctions between peacetime behavior and the necessities of war. . . .

Sources

[War crimes] involve [conventional] violations of the law or customs of war, such as murder, ill treatment, or deportation of the civilian population of occupied territory, murder or ill treatment of prisoners of war or persons on the seas, killing of hostages, plunder of public or private property, wanton destruction of cities, towns, or villages, or devastation not justified by military necessity; [or] crimes against humanity, which concern murder, extermination, enslavement, deportation, and other inhumane acts committed against any civilian population, either before or during a war, or persecutions on political, racial, or religious grounds in execution of or in connection with any other war crime.

Encyclopaedia Britannica

The right of belligerents to adopt means of injuring the enemy is not unlimited. . . . [for example, an occupying army must respect] family honor and rights, the lives of persons, and private property, as well as religious convictions and practices.

The Fourth Hague Convention (treaty signed in 1907)

The soldier who kills a man in obedience to authority is not guilty of murder.

Gratian (12th century)

War consists largely of acts that would be criminal if performed in time of peace—killing, wounding, kidnapping, destroying or carrying off other people's property. Such conduct is not regarded as criminal if it takes place in the course of war, because the state of war lays a blanket of immunity over its warriors.

Telford Taylor

ASSIGNMENT 22

Write an essay of at least seven pages based on the outline developed in Assignment 21.

10. Presenting the Results of Your Research: Acknowledging Your Sources

When you engage in research, you are continually coming into contact with the ideas and the words of other writers; consequently, the opportunities to plagiarize—by accident or by intention—increase tremendously. You must therefore understand exactly what constitutes plagiarism. *Plagiarism is defined as the unacknowledged use of another person's work, in the form of original ideas, strategies, and research, as well as another person's writing, in the form of sentences, phrases, and innovative terminology.* Plagiarism is the equivalent of theft; but the stolen goods are intellectual rather than material. And, like other acts of theft, plagiarism is against the law; the copyright law, which governs publications, requires that authorship be acknowledged and (if the "borrowed" material is of sufficient length) that payment be offered to the writer.

Plagiarism also violates the moral law which dictates that each person be allowed to take pride in, as well as profit from, the fruits of his labor. Put yourself in the victim's place. Think about the best idea that you ever had, or the paragraph that you worked hardest on in your last paper. Now, imagine yourself reading exactly the same idea or exactly the same sentences in someone else's essay, with no mention of your name, with no quotation marks. Would you accept the theft of your property without protest?

The plagiarist is not only guilty of robbery; he is also guilty of misrepresentation or cheating. The person who bends or breaks the rules concerning authorship, who does not do his own work, will be rightly distrusted by his classmates, by his teachers, and by his future employers, who may equate a history of plagiarism with dishonesty, incompetence, or the desire to avoid work. One's future rarely depends on getting a better grade on a single assignment; on the other hand, one's reputation may be damaged if one resorts to plagiarism in order to get that grade.

But plagiarism is dangerous for a more immediate and practical reason.

As you observed in Exercise 24, an experienced teacher can usually detect plagiarized work quite easily. If you are not skilled enough to write your own essay, you are unlikely to do a good enough job of adapting someone else's work to your needs. Plagiarism is inherently a self-destructive act; it represents a confession of failure, an inability to do—even to attempt to do—the job. Remember that anyone can learn to write well enough to make plagiarism an unnecessary risk.

DECIDING WHEN ACKNOWLEDGMENT IS NECESSARY

Fortunately, there are guidelines to help you determine what can and what cannot safely be used without acknowledgment, and these guidelines mostly favor complete documentation.

Documenting Information

A conservative rule of thumb is that you must cite a source for all facts and evidence in your essay that you did not know, think, or believe before you started your research. Knowing when to acknowledge the source of your knowledge or information largely depends on common sense. For example, it is not necessary to document the fact that there are fifty states in the United States or that Shakespeare wrote *Hamlet* since these are points of common knowledge. On the other hand, you may be presenting obscure information, like facts about electric railroads, which you have known since you were a child, but which may be unfamiliar to your readers. Technically, you are not obliged to document that information; but your audience will trust you more and will be better informed if you do so. In general, if the facts are not unusual, if they can be found in a number of standard sources, and if they do not vary from source to source, from year to year, then they can be considered common knowledge and need not be documented.

Documenting Ideas Taken from Your Source

Your object is both to acknowledge the source and to provide your reader with the fullest possible background. Let us assume that one or more of the ideas that you are writing about was firmly in your mind—the product of your own intellect—long before you started to work on your topic. Nevertheless, if you come across a version of that idea during your research, you should cite the source, even though the idea was as much your own as the author's. Of course, in your acknowledgement, you might state that so-and-so is confirming *your* theories and thus indicate that you had thought of the point independently. (For examples of such acknowledgments see the "basketball" essay on p. 453.)

Documenting the Source of Your Own Ideas

Perhaps, in the course of working on your essay, you develop a new idea of your own, stimulated by one of your readings. You should make a point of citing the source of inspiration and describing how and why it affected you. (For example: "My idea for shared assignments is an extension of McKeachie's discussion of peer tutoring.") The reader should be made aware of your debt as well as your independent effort.

Most important, you will not receive greater glory by plagiarizing. On the contrary, most teachers believe that, if a student is energetic enough to understand and digest the ideas of others, to apply them to his topic, and to place them in his own words, then he deserves to receive the highest grade for his mastery of all the basic skills of academic writing. There are, however, occasions when your teacher asks you not to use secondary sources and thus makes it impossible for you to acknowledge your debt. In such cases, you would be wise to undertake no background reading at all, so that the temptation to borrow or steal will not arise.

Plagiarism: Stealing Ideas

If you present another person's ideas as your own, you are plagiarizing *even if you use your own words*. Here is an illustration: The paragraph on the left, by Leo Gurko, is taken from a book, *Ernest Hemingway and the Pursuit of Heroism*; the paragraph on the right comes from a student essay on Hemingway. Gurko is listed in the bibliography and is cited as the source of several quotations elsewhere in the essay. But the student does not mention Gurko anywhere in *this* paragraph.

The Hemingways put themselves on short rations, ate, drank, and entertained as little as possible, pounced eagerly on the small checks that arrived in the mail as payment for accepted stories, and were intensely conscious of being poor. The sensation was not altogether unpleasant. Their extreme youth, the excitement of living abroad, the sense of making a fresh start, even the unexpected joy of parenthood, gave their poverty a romantic flavor.

Leo Gurko

Despite all the economies that they had to make and all the pleasures that they had to do without, the Hemingways rather enjoyed the experience of being poor. They knew that this was a more romantic kind of life, unlike anything they'd known before, and the feeling that everything in Paris was fresh and new, even their new baby, made them sharply aware of the glamorous aspects of being poor.

The language of the student paragraph does not require quotation marks, but unless he acknowledges Gurko in a note, the student will be guilty of plagiarism. These impressions of the Hemingways, these insights into their consciousness, would not have been possible without Gurko's biography—and Gurko deserves the credit for having done the research and for having formulated the interpretations. After reading extensively about Hemingway, the student may have absorbed these biographical details so thoroughly that he feels as if he had always known them. But the knowledge is still second-hand, and the source must be acknowledged.

Plagiarism: Stealing Words

When you quote a source, remember that the quoted material will require *two* kinds of documentation: *the acknowledgment of the source of the information or ideas* (through a footnote and possibly through the citation of the author's name in your text) and *the acknowledgment of the source of the exact wording* (through quotation marks). It is not enough to supply a footnote and then indiscriminately to mix up your own language and that of your sources. The footnote number tells your reader nothing whatever about who is responsible for the choice of words. Here is an excerpt from a student essay about Henrik Ibsen, together with the relevant passage from its source:

When writing [Ibsen] was sometimes under the influence of hallucinations, and was unable to distinguish between reality and the creatures of his imagination. While working on *A Doll's House* he was nervous and retiring and lived in a world alone, which gradually become peopled with his own imaginary characters. Once he suddenly remarked to his wife: "Now I have seen Nora. She came right up to me and put her hand on my shoulder." "How was she dressed?" asked his wife. "She had a simple blue cotton dress," he replied without hesitation. . . . So intimate had Ibsen become with Nora while at work on *A Doll's House* that when John Paulsen asked him why she was called Nora, Ibsen replied in a matter-of-fact tone: "She was really called Leonora, you know, but everyone called her Nora since she was the spoilt child of the family."

P. F. D. Tennant,
Ibsen's Dramatic Technique

While Ibsen was still writing A Doll's House, his involvement with the characters led to his experiencing hallucinations that at times completely incapacitated his ability to distinguish between reality and the creations of his imagination. He was nervous, distant, and lived in a secluded world. Gradually this world became populated with his creations. One day he had the following exchange with his wife:

Ibsen: Now I have seen Nora. she came right up to me and put her hand on my shoulder.
Wife: How was she dressed?
Ibsen: (without hesitation) She had a simple blue dress.

Ibsen's involvement with his characters was so deep that when John Paulsen asked Ibsen why the heroine was named Nora, Ibsen replied in a very nonchalant tone of voice that originally she was called Leonora, but that everyone called her Nora, the way one would address the favorite child in the family.[5]

The footnote at the end of this passage may refer the reader to Tennant's book, but there is no indication at all of the debt that the student owes to Tennant's phrasing and vocabulary. Phrases like "distinguish between reality and the creatures of his imagination" must be placed in quotation marks, and so should the exchange between Ibsen and his wife. Arranging these sentences as dialogue is not a solution.

In fact, the problem here is too complex to be solved by the insertion of a few quotation marks. The student, who probably intended a paraphrase, has substituted some of his own words for Tennant's; however, because he keeps the original sentence structure and many of the original words, he has only succeeded in obscuring some of his source's ideas. At times, the phrasing distorts the original idea: the student's assertion that Ibsen's hallucinations "incapacitated his ability to distinguish between reality and the creatures of his imagination" is very different from "[Ibsen] was sometimes under the influence of hallucinations and was unable to distinguish between reality and the creatures of his imagination." Many of the substitutions change Tennant's meaning: "distant" does not mean "retiring"; "a secluded world" is not "a world alone"; "nonchalant" is a very different quality from "matter of fact." Prose like this is neither quotation nor successful paraphrase; it is doubly bad, for it both plagiarizes the source and misinterprets it.

EXERCISE 59

Here are two excerpts from two books about the Great Depression of the 1930s. Each excerpt is followed by a passage from a student essay that makes use of the ideas and the words of the source, without any acknowledgment at all. Compare the original with the plagiarized passage; insert the appropriate quotation marks; underline the paraphrases.

A. *Source:*

Without income or housing to hold them together, many families disintegrated. A father without a job, who washed dishes, made beds, sat around and failed to provide food, lost status in his family. If minor tensions already existed, the father's position could become intolerable. A few fathers committed suicide, but many more unemployed fathers and older children started drifting around the country, presumably looking for work, but perhaps really seeking escape through activity. The drift of a million or more of these "migrants of despair" was aimless, but generally towards warm areas, where each city tried to keep the wayfarers moving to someplace else. Although in many cities they could get a meal, they could not stay.

In the larger cities the major burden of relief fell first on private donors, and then on voluntary organizations, such as the Red Cross, Salvation

Army, Community Chest, and, as these exhausted their resources, on small local and state appropriations. . . . In small cities, conditions were often worse than in the major centers. A survey of 59 cities of upstate New York in the winter of 1930–1 revealed that most of them had no relief programs. "By the fall of 1931," says Professor Irving Bernstein, "muncipal relief—private and public—was bankrupt in virtually every city in the United States," and it is estimated that unemployment rose 50 per cent in the next 18 months.

T. C. Cochran, The Democratic Experience

Student Essay:

Many families were savagely struck by the loss of their livelihood, and without income or housing to hold them together, many families disintegrated. Many fathers copped out by committing suicide, and others drifted aimlessly around the countryside, seeking employment or escape from the harsh realism of the era.

The social agencies which were established to give relief to the poor and destitute were hit hard by the unusually heavy burden they had to bear. The Red Cross, the Salvation Army and Community Chest exhausted their resources. Furthermore, scores of cities had no relief programs, and by the fall of 1931, municipal relief—public and private—was bankrupt in virtually every city in the United States.

B. Source:

Before the end of 1929 the entire economy began to snowball downhill. Consumer buying declined sharply and the public, leery of banks, cached currency in safe-deposit boxes and mattresses. Every kind of business suffered, and had to discharge employees; they, unable to find other jobs, defaulted installment payments and exhausted savings to live. To some extent the misery was relieved by the charity of employed relatives, or by returning to a parental farm; but America, unlike Britain, then had neither social security nor unemployment insurance. This tailspin of the economy went on until mid-1932 when around 12 million people, about 25 per cent of the normal labor force, were unemployed. In the cities there were soup kitchens and breadlines. Factory payrolls dropped to less than half those of early 1929. Shanty towns, where the jobless gathered to pick over a dump, grew up; bankrupt mills and garment lofts were reopened by unscrupulous promoters who paid a dollar a day to men and half that to girls. Small towns in the farm belt were almost deserted by their inhabitants. Some farmers resisted eviction and foreclosure by force of arms.

Samuel Eliot Morison, The Oxford History
of the American People

Student Essay:

> The signs of the depression were made visible by the sharp decline of consumer buying and the downward plunge in the economy before the end of 1929. Matters became worse when the public, leery of banks, withdrew their deposits to their mattresses. Suffering businesses had to discharge their employees. As the working class found it difficult to secure alternative employment, they defaulted on installment payments and exhausted savings to live. The difficulty was made more pronounced by the absence of social security and unemployment insurance. People were attracted to pick over dump areas and shantytowns. Farmers fought against eviction and foreclosure with force of arms.

ENDNOTES

So far, the only methods of documentation that you have been taught to use have been the system of quotation marks—to acknowledge words—and the system of citing the source's name in the text—to acknowledge authorship. The latter method only works efficiently when you are using one or two sources, for you will only have to interrupt your essay once or twice to supply the necessary publication information.

When you work with excerpts from a variety of sources, the standard method of documenting them is with endnotes or footnotes. In the past, footnotes (so called because of their placement at the bottom of the page) were used in all types of writing; now, they appear mostly in dissertations and printed material. Endnotes (or, simply, notes) for college research papers appear at the end of the essay and are numbered to correspond to "superior" numbers in the text. Notes do three important things for your reader: they show where you have found your information; they enable readers to go to your sources to get more information; and they allow you to add explanatory comments of your own.

Providing Proof of Research

As you know, you have an obligation to provide complete information about your sources. When you cite the author's name and the work's publishing history, you are, in effect, providing proof of its existence and thereby establishing your credibility. By citing the work and the date and the page, you are assuring your reader that your research was honest, that you have not made up fictitious sources and quotations.

The entire apparatus of documentation originally evolved as an aid to scholarship, not as a means of torturing unfortunate students. By providing an efficient method of displaying one's sources, the inventors of this system made it both convenient and obligatory for scholars to make their research visible and accessible to their readers. Just as important, notes, like quotations and citations, help to distinguish your ideas from those of your sources. A reader skimming over a well-documented essay can have no doubt about who was responsible for what.

Providing Follow-up References for Your Readers

Those who read about your research are often doing so to acquire knowledge. Since they may very well want to know more about your subject, you should give them the option of going back to the library and locating the basic materials that you have used. Certainly, the essay's bibliography can serve this purpose, but not even the most thoroughly annotated bibliography is going to send readers to the right book and the right page that will contain more information about a specific topic discussed in the paper. What is needed, then, is a direct link between an interesting sentence or paragraph in the paper and the source in the library that will satisfy the readers' interest.

The notation system demands very little effort from readers. The note number appears directly in the text; it is keyed to a note at the end of the essay that cites a relevant book or article. In the note readers are given background information about the source—the publisher, the periodical, the date, and even the right page number—so that no time will be wasted in skimming through the source at the library.

Providing Additional Explanation

A note can also serve as a depository for pieces of information other than source citations, information that you do not want cluttering up your text. As you write, there is inevitably going to be material that does not quite fit into the text of your essay. You may be faced with the choice of either excluding an interesting bit of information or fitting it in by wrenching apart the organization of your paragraph. Do neither; instead, put it in a note. For this purpose, you may use extra pieces of information taken from the source that you are already citing *or* your own ideas, which do not actually require documentation. You are obliged to maintain a fairly tight focus and structure for the text of your essay; but there are no firm rules about style in notes. In this sense, notes serve as the file cabinets of the research essay.

SEPARATING TEXT AND DOCUMENTATION

Notes limit the number of distracting interruptions in your text. You do not have to stop the flow of your paragraph to insert full documentation, the dry facts about publishers and page numbers; instead, you use the smallest possible symbol, a number indicating that there is some information placed elsewhere. The reader's eye takes note of the number, but if he does not care to follow up the signal, he just continues reading, with the minimum of interruption.

Notice, for example, how fragmented and distracting the paragraph about recruiting college athletes would become if you stopped every time you wanted to insert full documentation about your sources. Remember, six sources are being cited in this passage, and, even if you lumped the three coaches together, full documentation would interrupt the paragraph's flow:

> . . . But, as early as 1929, the Carnegie Foundation complained that the focus of college sports had shifted from education to the material advantages of winning. (See Kenneth Denlinger, in <u>Athletes for Sale</u>, published in New York by Thomas Y. Crowell in 1975, p. 22.) Even earlier, in 1903, there were several instances of players without academic qualifications who were "hired" to guarantee victory. (Examples can be found in Joseph Durso's <u>The Sports Factory</u>, published in New York by the Times Book Company, in 1975. On page 6, Durso quotes from a <u>Collier's</u> magazine series of 1905.) And in recent years, excellence of recruiting has become the most important skill for a coach to possess. Kenneth Denlinger has observed: "It is an athletic maxim that a man with no special coaching skills can win games if he recruits well and that a tactician without talented players is a man soon without a job." (See Denlinger's <u>Athletes for Sale</u> in the reference a few sentences back in this paragraph, p. 3.) . . .

If you substitute numbers for those intrusive parentheses and, in effect, direct your reader to look elsewhere, you give your reader the option of either checking and following up your sources or settling for the names cited in your text.

In this revised, properly documented version of the "recruiting" paragraph, you can see notes being used for all three purposes. They cite sources and specific pages and provide some additional background, such as the names of the two coaches not quoted in the text.

In college athletics, what is the best way for a school to win games? Should a strong team be gradually built up by training ordinary students from scratch, or should the process be shortened and success be assured by actively recruiting players who already know how to win? The first method may be more consistent with the traditional amateurism of college athletics, but as early as 1929, the Carnegie Foundation complained that the focus of college sports had shifted from education to the material advantages of winning.[1] Even earlier, in 1903, there were several instances of players without academic qualifications who were "hired" to guarantee victory.[2] And in recent years, excellence of recruiting has become the most important skill for a coach to possess. Kenneth Denlinger has observed, "It is an athletic maxim that a man with no special coaching skills can win games if he recruits well and that a tactician without talented players is a man soon without a job."[3] It follows, then, that a coach who wants to keep his job is likely to concentrate on spotting and collecting talent for his team. Coaches from LSU, Alabama, and Texas Tech all testify that good recruiting has first priority throughout college athletics. According to Bear Bryant of Alabama: "You don't out-coach people, you out-recruit them."[4]

[1] The Carnegie Foundation study is cited in Kenneth Denlinger, Athletes for Sale (New York: Crowell, 1975), p. 22. According to this study, a chief reason for the trend towards athletic, not educational, success was Cecil Rhodes's insistence that candidates for Rhodes scholarships have "fondness for and success in manly outdoor sports."

[2] A series in Collier's magazine in 1905 entitled "Buying Football Victories" refers to two football players who were permitted to enter college before they'd graduated from high school and to two other players who were given sums of money to play in a single game. Cited in Joseph Durso, The Sports Factory (New York: Times Books, 1975), p. 6.

[3] Denlinger, p. 3.

[4] Dale Brown of LSU is cited in Barry McDermott, "Who Is Kidding Whom?" Sports Illustrated, 17 January 1976, p. 17; Steve Sloan of Texas Tech is cited in Steve Sloan, A Whole New Ball Game (Nashville, Tenn.: Broadman, 1975), p. 106; and the quotation from Paul "Bear" Bryant cited in

```
this paragraph comes from D. Keith Mano, "Say 'Cheese,'
Mom and Pop," Sports Illustrated, 15 March 1976, p. 41.
```

Numbering and Placement of Notes

As you can see from the example, note numbers are raised slightly above the line (you move the typewriter roller up one-half turn) and inserted into the text immediately after the punctuation following the reference, without any surrounding symbols such as parentheses or dashes. In other words, the note number is placed at the *end* of the relevant material, whether that material is quoted, paraphrased, summarized, or briefly mentioned. By convention, the reader assumes that the number signals the end of the material from that source; anything after the number comes from the writer's own thoughts or from a new source that will be documented later.

Notes are numbered consecutively: if you have twenty-six notes in your essay, the number of the last one should be 26. A note may contain more than one piece of information, but it remains a single note with a single number. *Under no circumstances* should you have two note numbers placed together, like this:[7, 8]. On the other hand, each note should contain at least one distinct piece of information. Never write a note which says only, "See footnote 3." The reader should be told enough to make it unnecessary to consult footnote 3 unless he wishes to. When you are revising your first draft and checking your documentation, read through your essay once, just to make sure that each reference to a source is covered by a note and that each note number has been placed to the right of the punctuation mark following the end of the reference. (Note: when a reference ends before a dash, the number precedes the punctuation.)

THE BASIC FORM OF THE NOTE

In this book, as in most writing courses and in many fields of study, documentation follows a standard format. (Some fields in the social and natural sciences may use different forms; ask your instructor and then consult the alternate methods described in Appendix B, pp. 542–549.) Like bibliography entries, notes follow two basic forms, one for books and one for articles.

For books, follow this sequence:

1. *author's full name, first name first, followed by a comma.* (If the author is anonymous, skip this step and start with the title.)

2. *the title of the book, underlined, followed by a comma.* You may wish to cite only part of a complete work: a chapter or an essay, a poem or an introduction. In that case, the section that you are citing should have quotation marks around it and be followed by the word "in" and the underlined title of the whole work. Usually, you need not include the name of the chapter in your note if the entire work is by a single author. But if you are using a collection of pieces by various authors—an anthology or a casebook, for example—then your note should contain the title of the specific section that you cite in your essay.

3. *the place of publication (followed by a colon), the name of the publisher (followed by a comma), and the date—in that order, inside parentheses, with a comma following the closing of the parentheses.* In footnotes, punctuation is not to be improvised: if a colon is supposed to appear between place and publisher, then you cannot substitute a semi-colon or a comma. When you look at a book's title page, you may find more than one city cited as the place of publication; use only the first one listed.

4. *the page number of the idea or the quotation that you are acknowledging.* The note ends with a period.

Citation of a book

[1] Steve Sloan, <u>A Whole New Ball Game</u> (Nashville, Tenn: Broadman, 1975), p. 105.

Citation of part of a book

[2] George P. Elliott, "Against Pornography," in <u>Perspectives on Pornography</u>, ed. Douglas A. Hughes (New York: St. Martin's, 1970), p. 83.

For articles, follow this sequence:

1. *author's full name, first name first, followed by a comma.* (If the article is anonymous, skip this step and start with the title.)

2. *the title of the article, in quotation marks, followed by a comma (placed inside the final quotation marks).*

3. *the title of the periodical or newspaper, underlined, followed by a comma.*

4. *for periodicals published four times a year or less, the volume (and issue) number, followed by date of issue (month and year, or year alone) in parentheses. For monthly and weekly periodicals and for daily newspapers, the complete date, without*

parentheses, directly follows the underlined title. The date is followed by a comma.

5. *the page number of the idea or the quotation that you are citing.* (For a periodical published quarterly or less frequently and numbered by volume, the page number is placed at the end of the note without any preliminary p. or pp.) The note ends with a period.

Citation of an article from a magazine that appears once, twice, or four times a year

³ Sheila Tobias and Carol Weissbrod, "Anxiety and Mathematics: An Update," Harvard Educational Review, 50, No. 1 (Feb. 1980), 65–66.

Citation of an article from a monthly or weekly magazine

⁴ Bruno Bettelheim, "Freud and the Soul," The New Yorker, 1 March 1982, p. 52.

Citation of a newspaper article

⁵ Walter Sullivan, "U.S. Science Reassessing Its Status," New York Times, 2 Jan. 1979, p. 82.

There are also rules for the placement and spacing of the items in the note. The first line of each note is indented 5 spaces, as a paragraph is, with the number slightly raised, as the corresponding number is raised in the text of your essay. Endnotes are double-spaced throughout. The second and all other lines within each note should return to the same margins that you set for the text of your essay; don't squeeze the notes together in the middle of the page. (This is the reverse of the format for the bibliographical entry, in which the first line is at the margin and the remainder is indented.) The second and all subsequent notes should look exactly the same as the first, beginning with an indentation and a raised number.

Notes

Indent 5 spaces; raise number ½ space; skip 1 space; return to margin for next line. Indent new note 5 spaces.

¹ Helen Block Lewis, Psychic War in Men and Women (New York: New York University Press, 1976), p. 43.

² Norman N. Holland, The Dynamics of Literary Response (New York: Oxford University Press, 1968), p. 75.

If you are noting sources with a complex publishing history, you will need to use more elaborate variations of the five basic forms. For example, you may wish to cite a source that comes in several volumes or that has been through several editions or that is part of a series. For additional models, see Appendix B, which you should consult frequently as you work on the documentation for your research essay.

Because these forms are arbitrary, they are difficult to remember. Most people, even experienced researchers, tend to forget the correct note forms when they are not working with them every day; and so they keep a handbook or style manual available to recheck forms that they have used dozens of times. Sloppy notes can even affect grades—which is a pity, since you need only look up the appropriate forms each time you work on a research essay.

Finally, you cannot write a proper note if you do not have all the information about the source. Whether you take notes or provide yourself with pages from a copying machine, remember always to write down the information that you will need for your notes. Look at the front of the book or periodical and write down the publishing history. And, as you work on the first draft of your essay, include the author's name and the relevant page number in parentheses after every reference to one of your sources, to serve as a guide when you write your notes.

Second References

The basic type of note that is illustrated above is known as the *long form* because it includes a good deal of information and thus takes up a fair amount of space. If you are using the same source more than once in your essay, there is no point in writing out the long form each time. Of course, you must have a separate note, with a new number, each time that you cite that source, but now you can use the *short form*.

The most convenient, all-purpose short form consists of the author's name and a page number:

> [3] Denlinger, p. 3.

You may have noticed this note among those for the "recruiting" model on p. 447. In this case, the short form can be used because there is already a long-form note for Denlinger on record in a previous note. Use the short form as soon as you are entitled to do so; there is no point in making your reader plough through all the publication information again and again.

If your notes include two sources by authors with the same last names, add first names to avoid confusion. If you cite more than one work by the same author, add the title. If there is no author, use the title alone. If the title is long, use a shortened title made up of a few key words.

> [5] Henry Adams, p. 25.
> [6] Beowulf, p. 12.
> [7] Baldwin, Beale Street, p. 85.

EXERCISE 60

A. Correct the errors of form in the following notes.

1 Martin Tolchin, "South Bronx: A Jungle Stalked by Fear: "New
          York Times" January 15, 1973, 1

  2 Richard Severo. "The Horrors of Heroin" in Reader's Digest,
          1/70, page 2.

          3 "Anonymous," "Lambert Houses" <u>Architectural Record</u>,
      Jan. 74, 32.

          4 Constance J. Foster, "You don't need to Punish" in
      Parent's Magazine, (Volume 7), Oct 1947, p. 17.

          5 Ratcliff, T. S. <u>The Child and Reality</u>, (Science
      House, New York, 1970) pgs. 57-8.

          6 Richard Severo. "The Horrors of Heroin," <u>RD</u>, p. 3.

B. Using the following information (which is in random order), write out
   five notes in proper format.

   1. John Holt's book How Children Fail, published by Pitman Publish-
      ing Co. in New York, 1964, an item on page 170
   2. Thomas Szasz, from The Right to Health, which is one essay in a
      collection called Moral Problems in Medicine, edited by Samuel
      Groutz, published by Prentice-Hall, Englewood Cliffs, New Jersey
      in 1976, page 470.
   3. It's Called Repentance by Leonard Orland in the New York Times
      of 11/2/77 on page 35.
   4. A chapter called The Nature of Battle, taken from The Face of Battle
      by John Keegan, published by the Viking Press of New York City
      in 1976. The chapter spans pp. 17 to 31.
   5. An article in the New York Review, volume XXIV, 4/28/77 by Chris-
      topher Lasch, called The Corruption of Sports. Page nos. 24-6.

Noting a Complex Sequence of Sources

   To illustrate the proper insertion of note numbers, here is an excerpt
from a research essay on defensive tactics in basketball, followed by the
pertinent endnotes. (These paragraphs are taken from the middle of the
essay; the writer has already provided long forms for his sources in the
earlier notes, so only short forms are needed here.) Try reading through
the text twice, once straight through and then, the second time, pausing
at each number to glance at the right note.

Defensive rebounding is another very simple tactic; but it takes many games and hours of practice to be performed correctly. Rebounding occurs when a shot is missed. The team that gains possession afterwards has secured the rebound and is now on offense. Since seven out of every ten junior high school shots are missed,[18] there are many advantages for the team that gains the most rebounds. We emphasize to our team that, if the rebound is obtained, we can control the tempo of the game.[19] We also stress that, if our opponents are going to score, they should be forced to earn their basket. If an offensive player rebounds a ball, he is in a good position to score. No defensive team wants to allow the opponents two or three shots at the basket because, sooner or later, they'll score.[20]

There are certain steps to master before you become a good rebounder. Mental preparation is what enables our team and other small teams to out-rebound taller ball clubs. You must be aggressive[21] and conditioned to believe that every shot attempted will be missed.[22] When the shot is in the air, one or all the defensive players should yell "Shot!"[23] Each defensive player should take an opponent and block him off wherever he (the offensive player) is standing.[24] When the ball hits the rim or backboard, the defensive player should jump into the ball.[25] (See figure 3.) "The key to successful rebounding is to play the man, and not the ball," points out Nat Holman.[26] A common error in defensive playing is that, once the shot is in the air, the players don't "box out" their opponents.[27] They go straight to the basket. The offensive rebounder will follow, and then it's just a question of who is taller or who is the better jumper. My fellow coaches and I stress the "position defense" that's recommended by Pete Newell and Red Auerbach.[28] We want our defensive players to box out their man as far away from the basket as possible, leaving plenty of room for a bad bounce. We take pride in our defense, and our tall men are aware that the six-foot area around the basket is our area, not theirs.

[18] Dobbs, p. 27.
[19] Goodrich, p. 21.
[20] Pinholster, p. 231.
[21] Hawkins, p. 127.
[22] Goodrich, p. 23.

[23] Pinholster, p. 216.

[24] Ray Meyer deviates from the other coaches, saying, "The defensive player should take two steps back and let the offensive rebounder come to him." I disagree. The defensive player should go and meet the offensive player and thus cut off any momentum that the latter might obtain. Meyer, p. 58.

[25] Hawkins, p. 125. Also, Pete Newell, p. 89; Goodrich, pp. 21–22; Meyer, p. 38; Pinholster, p. 27.

[26] Holman, p. 149.

[27] Meyer, p. 58.

[28] Newell, p. 71, and Auerbach, p. 178. The defensive man should always be positioned correctly, usually between the ball and the man he's guarding. If your man has the ball, you should be positioned between the basket and the ball handler. Once the shot is attempted, you should be in a good position to box out your opponent immediately.

Notice that the writer has combined his personal knowledge of the game (he has coached a team) with evidence that he has gathered in his research. Thus, he must make a special effort to document only what he has acquired from other sources and to let the reader know that the knowledge of tactics is his own. Occasionally, he makes a point that he has learned from experience and which also has been corroborated by one of the coaches whom he is citing. Thus, in the sentence ending in note 19, the writer uses the first person to assert his mastery of the point; were it not for the note number, we would not be aware that support for this statement was being offered.

In fact, throughout the paragraphs the tone is personally authoritative, and the sources are relegated to a subordinate position in the notes. There is nothing wrong with this exclusion of sources from the text. Indeed, it may be because names are not cluttering the text that the paragraphs seem well integrated, with brisk pacing and reasonably smooth continuity. But because the reader has encountered so few citations in the text, the quotation and the names Holman and Newell in the second paragraph seem rather intrusive (Auerbach, on the other hand, is well enough known to be worth citing). Having kept references out of the text for so long, the writer might have done better to maintain his independence throughout the essay.

Finally, for an essay that cites so very few sources *directly*, there seems to be a rather large number of notes. But all of them are justified since a different authority is being cited in virtually every sentence. This kind of documentation occurs only when a writer has achieved a certain amount of independence from his sources and is not merely organizing each paragraph around a single authority. Instead, he is using whatever information is available to support his own decided views on the topic.

Signaling the Transitions Between Sources

The student who wrote the "basketball" research essay had enough confidence to write about his subject without citing many sources in his text. However, since most students go to considerable trouble to find and select the right materials to support their ideas, they tend to paraphrase and quote from their sources and thus keep them before the reader's eye. After all, the reader may not appreciate the range of research unless the writer cites the names of the sources at appropriate intervals in the text. Of course, citation should be as unobtrusive as possible, without unnecessary repetition, so that the reader is not distracted by the constant appearance of certain names. In general, the citation of the author's name serves as the standard signal to your reader that you are starting to use source material; the note number signals the point of termination for the material covered by a single note.

These starting and stopping signals become especially important when you are finishing with one source and moving on to the next, all within the same paragraph. If a name is not cited, the reader will not be aware that a new source has been introduced until he reaches the second footnote number. Here is a brief passage from an essay which illustrates this kind of confusion:

> 1946 marked the beginning of the post-war era. This meant the demobilization of the military, creating a higher unemployment rate because of the large number of returning soldiers. This also meant a slow-down in industry, so that lay-offs also added to the rising rate of unemployment. As Cabell Phillips put it: "Motivation [for the Employment Act of 1946] came naturally from the searing experience of the Great Depression, and fresh impetus was provided by the dread prospect of a massive new wave of unemployment following demobilization."[2]
>
> [2] Cabell Phillips, The 1940's: Decade of Triumph and Trouble (New York: Macmillan, 1974), pp. 292-93.

Here, it is the placement of the citation that creates the problem. The way in which the name is introduced into the paragraph firmly suggests that Cabell Phillips is responsible for the quotation and only the quotation. (The fact that the quotation is nothing more than a repetition of the first three sentences, and therefore has no business being included in the essay, has also probably occurred to you.) Anyone reading the essay will assume that note 2 covers only the material that starts with the name and ends with the number; the coverage is not expected to go back any further than the beginning of the sentence. Thus, in this passage, the first three sentences are not documented. Although it is highly probable that the writer derived all his information from Phillips, *The 1940's* is not being acknowledged as the source. "Probably" is not an adequate substitute for clear documentation. Either Phillips's name should be included somewhere at the beginning of the paragraph (the second sentence would be a good place), or the note should explain exactly how much material note 2 is covering. (See "umbrella notes," pp. 462.)

Signaling the *end* of a source reference in your text presents fewer problems. As you have learned, the appearance of the note number denotes the end of that source's contribution, and, as a rule, the numbers are placed at the ends of sentences. But occasionally you may need to insert a number in mid-sentence if that single sentence contains references to two different sources. For example, you might want to place a number in mid-sentence to indicate exactly where the source's opinion leaves off and your own begins:

> These instances of hiring athletes to play in college games, cited by Joseph Durso,[2] suggest that recruiting tactics in 1903 were not as subtle as they are today.

If the note number were put at the end of the sentence, the reader would assume that Durso was responsible for the comparison between 1903 and the present; but he is not. It is only the examples which must be documented, not the conclusion drawn from these examples. In this case, the *absence* of a note number at the end of the sentence signals to the reader that this conclusion is the writer's own.

Here is a passage in which the techniques of documentation have been used to their fullest extent and the transitions between sources are clearly indicated. This example is taken from Jessie Bernard's "The Paradox of the Happy Marriage," an examination of the woman's role in American marriage. At this point, Bernard has just established that more wives than husbands acknowledge that their marriages are unhappy:

> These findings on the wife's marriage are especially poignant because marriage in our society is more important for women's happiness than for men's. "For almost all measures, the relation between marriage, happiness and overall well-being was stronger for women than for men," one study reports.[11] In fact, the strength of the relationship between marital and overall happiness was so strong for women that the author wondered if "most women are equating their marital happiness with their overall happiness."[12] Another study based on a more intensive examination of the data on marriage from the same sample notes that "on

each of the marriage adjustment measures . . . the association with over-all happiness is considerably stronger for women than it is for men."[13] Karen Renne also found the same strong relationship between feelings of general well-being and marital happiness: those who were happy tended not to report marital dissatisfaction; those who were not, did. "In all probability the respondent's view of his marriage influences his general feeling of well-being or morale";[14] this relationship was stronger among wives than among husbands.[15] A strong association between re-ports of general happiness and reports of marital happiness was also found a generation ago.[16]

[11] Norman M. Bradburn, *The Structure of Psychological Well-Being* (Chicago: Aldine, 1969), p. 150.
[12] Bradburn, p. 159.
[13] Susan R. Orden and Norman M. Bradburn, "Dimensions of Mar-riage Happiness," *American Journal of Sociology* 73 (May 1968), 731.
[14] Renne, p. 64.
[15] Among white couples, 71 percent of the wives and 52 percent of the husbands who were "not too happy" expressed marital dissat-isfaction; 22 percent of the wives and 18 percent of the husbands who were "pretty happy" expressed marital dissatisfaction; and 4 percent of the wives and 2 percent of the husbands who were "very happy" ex-pressed marital dissatisfaction. Renne, p. 63.
[16] Gordon Watson, "Happiness among Adult Students," *Journal of Educational Psychology* 21 (1930).

This paragraph contains six notes to document the contents of seven sentences. Four different works are cited, and, where the same work is cited in two consecutive notes (11 and 12; 14 and 15), the reference is to a different page. Note 14 (which uses the short form) covers a sentence and a half, from the name "Karen Renne" to the number itself. Note 15 is used for the presentation of additional evidence to support the point made in the text; these statistics would certainly have disturbed the con-tinuity of the paragraph had they not been relegated to a note. Finally, there is no page reference in note 16, since Bernard is referring the reader to the entire article, not a single part of it.

Bernard quotes frequently, but she never juxtaposes quotations from two different sources, and she is careful to use her own voice to provide continuity between the quoted extracts. Notice, too, that one is never in doubt as to the source of information. Although Bernard does not always cite the name of the author, we are told in each case that there is a source—"one study reports"; "the author wondered"; "another study based on a more intensive examination of the data on marriage from the same sample"; "Karen Renne also found." These phrases not only ac-knowledge the source but also provide vital transitions between these loosely related points.

Using Notes to Acknowledge Multiple Sources

Bernard's documentation is made complex by the complex nature of her subject. In contrast, here are two extracts from an essay which describes Charles Dickens's experiences while on holiday in France. The text is straightforward description, but the details recounted here have been built up through complex research; therefore the writer must use numerous notes to document her numerous sources:

> Dickens's regular work habits involved writing at his desk from about nine in the morning to two in the afternoon;[45] this left a good deal of time for other pursuits. Some of his leisure each day was regularly delegated to letter-writing, some to walking and riding in the open air.[46] Besides this regular routine, on some days he would devote time to reading manuscripts which Wills, his sub-editor on <u>Household Words</u>, would send to him for revision and comment.[47]

> [45] Butt and Tillotson, p. 19; Pope-Hennessy, p. 248.
> [46] Pope-Hennessy, p. 305, quoting Nathaniel Sharswell Dodge.
> [47] Forster, p. 65; Johnson, 702.

> As for the practicalities of life, Dickens attempted to instill into his children such good habits as neatness and punctuality,[65] and gave a "worried attention to their education."[66] Dickens provided well for the children that summer: the house at Bolougne and the surrounding gardens were delightful playgrounds, complete with a pond full of goldfish.[67]

> [65] Johnson, 751-52.
> [66] Dupee, p. 155.
> [67] Pope-Hennessy, p. 310.

In both passages, three notes are needed for three or fewer sentences, because a different biographer is the source for each piece of information. Thus, for example, to combine notes 65 and 66, and to cite both Johnson and Dupee in a single note, would confuse, rather than simplify, the acknowledgments. Obviously, it is Johnson who describes Dickens's concern for neatness and punctuality, and it is Dupee who is responsible for the phrase "worried attention to their education." Without the separation into two notes, the reader could not be sure who said what.

More important, the writer of this essay is not only leaving her sources tidily labeled, but (in note 45) she is also providing her reader with a choice of references. She has come across the same information in more than one biography, has noted the duplication of material in her notes, and has decided to demonstrate the thoroughness of her research by citing all the references in a row. This kind of multiple note uses the same format as an ordinary note. (In this case, all the citations are second references, calling for the short form, which cuts down on the paperwork.) The list of citations should be linked together with a semi-colon.

Sometimes, your sources for a single point will not all be equally good: one of them may be more thorough or more convincing than the others and thus should be given an unequivocal first position, with a terminal period at the end. Immediately afterwards, you would write "Also" and follow that with as many other sources for that same point as you have found. Here is what the note would look like:

> [21] Johnson, 757. Also, Forster, p. 126; Pope–Hennessy, p. 310.

But remember that you cannot string along a series of source citations unless they are being used to support exactly the same point in your text.

EXERCISE 61

The following paragraph has been properly noted. There are, however, relatively few names cited in the text, so that the reader has to rely on the placement of the note numbers to determine which points are supported by research and which points are the writer's own ideas. Read through the paragraph; underline all the material which has been taken from documented sources; put brackets around all the material which seems to be the writer's own.

> The development of certain habits starts innocuously enough with the desire to achieve adult status[1] and social acceptance.[2] It's usually at adolescence that one takes one's first drink or cigarette or gambles for the first time.[3] This is done as a gesture, a statement which says the person is adult enough to handle a cigarette or a drink, or mature enough to gamble a sum of money. There's an aura of glamor associated with smoking and drinking, which has been promoted by the entertainment media. Aside from the familiar advertisements which attempt to sell cigarettes and alcohol,[4] an entire generation was influenced by the romantic films of the forties. These films generally stressed the kind of sophistication and independence exemplified by actresses like Lana Turner, who flaunted convention with the eternal cigarette in her hand. Or they created an image of intimacy like that implied by the shared cigarette of Bette Davis and Paul Henreid. Similarly, war films and west-

erns demonstrated the "manliness" of asking for a drink or lighting a cigarette as an alternative to demonstrating fear; in Eustace Chesser's view, this ritual was shown to be the only acceptable way for a man to handle anxiety.[6] It was appropriate, for example, to offer a dying man a cigarette. A mystique thus arose around the handling of the cigarette or the type of drink preferred and the way it was ordered. The person trying to achieve adult status would emulate the film personality he was trying to identify with.[7] Films also glamorized gambling to a lesser extent: the cool "gentleman" player would lose at poker in the saloon, proceed to buy the boys a drink with his last silver dollar, and thereby win the respect and admiration of all.

EXERCISE 62

The following paragraph, taken from a research essay about the Depression, is based on source materials which can be found in Exercise 59. Compare the paragraph with its sources, and then decide where the footnote numbers should be placed. Insert the numbers, making sure that the source material is distinguished from the writer's own contributions to the paragraph.

> Poverty and anxiety threatened many families during the Great Depression. Historians have described the large floating population who had left home and were on the road, seeking a job or a meal. T. C. Cochran describes this drift of a million or more of these "migrants of despair" as "aimless," for most cities did not welcome the vagabonds or allow them to remain. According to Samuel Eliot Morison, a large number of the people living in small rural towns abandoned their homes, while some city dwellers, unemployed, returned to the countryside. For some fathers who remained at home, unable to support their families, the sense of guilt and failure was so great that suicide occasionally seemed the only escape. However, in a sense, the depression may have increased family solidarity. Morison does point out that those who were down-and-out could return home or seek help from relatives who were better off. In times of crisis, the extended family can provide a refuge.

Avoiding Excessive Notes

There is no special advantage or merit in accumulating a large number of notes. An abundance of notes does not in itself indicate sound research, and excessive notation results only in clutter. A great many numbers scattered throughout a few sentences may be justified only by the alternate use of a group of sources or (less likely) by an essay full of provocative, confusing, or contradictory material which necessitates commentary in explanatory notes. The following paragraph illustrates the wastefulness of excessive notes:

> In his letters, Dickens indicated that he was enjoying the relaxing atmosphere at the Château de Molineaux: "I warrant the pure air, regular hours, and perfect repose of this place to bring you around triumphantly";[41] and "if you have anything to do, this is the place to do it in. And if you have nothing to do, this is also the place to do it to perfection."[42] Dickens's experience confirmed his testimonial: within two days of his arrival, he was well again[43] and devoting his time to the completion of his work as if he'd never been ill at all.[44]

> [41] Hutton, p. 15.
> [42] Hutton, p. 14.
> [43] Hutton, p. 16.
> [44] Hutton, p. 16.

Although it is true that the writer is citing three different pages from Hutton, these pages are consecutive. Why stretch the documentation to four notes on four separate lines? Perhaps the writer was nervous about leaving the quotations undocumented, and did not want to wait until the end of the paragraph. But, at the very least, the number of notes could be halved, with 41 (Hutton, pp. 14–15) appearing at the end of the quotation, and 42 (Hutton, p. 16) placed at the end of the paragraph.

Here is another example of documentation which, this time, is not only excessive, but also confusing:

> In contrast to London, this setting was an idyllic one: the house stood in the center of a large garden complete with woods, waterfall, roses,[35] and "no end of flowers."[36] For a fee, the Dickenses fed on the produce of the estate and obtained their milk fresh from the landlord's cow.[37] What an asset to one's peace of mind to have such a master of cooperation for a landlord as they had[38] in the portly, jolly M. Beaucort![39]

> [35] Forster, p. 145.
> [36] Forster, p. 146.
> [37] Forster, p. 146.
> [38] Pope–Hennessy, p. 310; Johnson, p. 758; Forster, p. 147.
> [39] Forster, p. 147.

Clearly, the entire passage is taken from three pages in Forster's biography, and a single note would serve to document the entire paragraph. What information is contained in the sentence leading up to note 38 that could justify the sudden expanded acknowledgment of three sources? The note does not say. And what's the function of 39? Is it only Forster who's aware that M. Beaucourt is portly and jolly? To avoid tiring or irritating the reader, the writer here would have been well-advised to ignore the corroborative evidence in Pope-Hennessy and Johnson and employ a single reference to Forster, or else explain why the corroboration is important. This writer was undoubtedly proud of the 150 notes which document the twelve-page essay; but she seems more anxious to show off her hours in the library than to provide a readable text for her audience.

Using Umbrella Notes

Occasionally the logical sequence of your ideas requires you to use the same source for several sentences or even for several paragraphs at a stretch. Instead of repeating "Hutton, p. 41" over and over again, use a single note to cover the entire sequence as an umbrella might cover more than one person. An "umbrella" note simply means that you are leaving the reader in no doubt as to how much material the note is covering.

> [12] The information in this paragraph is derived from Laurence Hutton, ed., <u>Dickens–Collins Letters</u> (New York: Harper, 1892), p. 41.

If you are writing the kind of essay that encourages the citation of names in the text, an umbrella note is not usually necessary; your reader can figure out the coverage by assuming that the name and number signify the beginning and ending points. But biographical and historical essays do not generally afford the sources much visibility in the text, and an umbrella note is often useful.

Of course, such a blanket statement about coverage can be extended too far. You cannot use an umbrella note to cover more than one of your paragraphs, and if you use two sources in a paragraph, in your note you must make clear which source covers which material—cite your sources in the order in which you refer to them in your paragraph. Umbrella notes must also be used with caution when you are quoting. Because the umbrella is providing the reference for a long stretch of material, the citation usually includes several pages; but how will the reader know on which page the quotation appears? You can, of course, add this information to the note itself:

> [41] The information in this paragraph is derived from Hutton, pp. 14–16. The two quotations from Dickens's letters are from pages 15 and 14 respectively.

If you end up using too many umbrella notes, or if you expect a single note to guide your reader through the intricacies of a long paragraph, you will have abused the device. Your essay will have turned into a series of summaries, with each paragraph covering a single source; that is not what a research essay is supposed to be.

EXERCISE 63

Each of the following passages is accompanied by the relevant notes. After careful examination, improve the documentation by eliminating unnecessary notes, placing the numbers properly, and introducing umbrella notes where they seem appropriate. If necessary, rearrange the sequence of information in the text.

The United States first became interested in the atomic bomb in October of 1939.[1] This was when a letter, signed by Albert Einstein, was personally delivered to the White House by Alexander Sachs.[2] Sachs, a New York financier, was a friend and an economic adviser of President Roosevelt.[3] This letter was written by Einstein at the urging of fellow refugee physicists: Leo Szilard, Eugene Wigner, and Edward Teller.[4] Like Einstein, these men had all fled Europe and Hitler's new order.[5] They had no doubt that Germany would bend every effort to develop a superweapon like the atom bomb.[6] They drafted the letter setting forth the dangers created by uranium fission.[7] They then enlisted the aid of Sachs to reach the President.[8]

The President was impressed by the Einstein letter detailing the likelihood that Germany would want to develop an atomic bomb that would certainly lead to world conquest.[9] He decided immediately to create a committee that would give governmental financial assistance to American universities engaged in uranium research.[10] Since the first splitting of a uranium atom in Germany in 1939, it had been thought that a bomb with incredible destructive force might be built if enough fissionable material could be produced.[11] This material had to be either U–235, a rare isotope of uranium, or plutonium, a newly discovered element, knowledge of which was limited to American and British scientists.[12] Both would be extremely difficult, if not impossible, to produce.[13]

[1] Stephane Groueff, <u>Manhattan Project</u> (Boston: Little, Brown, 1967), p. 10.

[2] Groueff, p. 10; Robert Jungk, Brighter than a Thousand Suns (New York: Harcourt, Brace, 1956) p. 84.

[3] Groueff, p. 10; Jungk, p. 84.

[4] Groueff, p. 10; Jungk, p. 85.

[5] Groueff, p. 10; Jungk, p. 85.

[6] Groueff, p. 10.

[7] Groueff, p. 11; Jungk, p. 85.

[8] Groueff, p. 11; Jungk, p. 86; "Atomic Bomb Loosed on Hiroshima," New York Times, August 7, 1945, p. 4.

[9] Groueff, p. 12.

[10] Groueff, p. 12.

[11] Groueff, p. 4.

[12] Groueff, p. 4; The World Book Encyclopedia (Chicago: Field Enterprises, 1965), p. 830.

[13] Groueff, p. 5.

George Bernard Shaw was very conscious of his physical appearance. In his preoccupation with his weight, he was constantly dieting.[26] Each morning, he weighed himself and made sure that he had not gained even an ounce.[27] His meals were tailored towards this dieting, and everything that he ate was weighed.[28] The meals never included meat, for he was a strict vegetarian.[29] Although Shaw was certainly very conscious of his health,[30] it was really his extreme vanity that kept him on this daily regimen.[31] He was generally thought to be uncommonly vain.[32] He was always turning to admire himself when he passed mirrors.[33] Although his eyesight was not good, he refused to wear glasses, and so he frequently didn't acknowledge the people he passed by, simply because he couldn't tell who they were.[34] And Shaw always loved to have his picture taken.[35]

[26] Minney, p. 171.

[27] Minney, p. 171.

[28] Minney, p. 171.

[29] Ervine, p. 309.

[30] Stephen Winsten, Jesting Apostle: The Private Life of Bernard Shaw (New York: Dutton, 1957), p. 113.

[31] Minney, p. 171.

[32] Minney, p. 171.

[33] Minney, p. 169.

[34] Minney, p. 172.

[35] Minney, p. 172.

Using Explanatory Notes

Sometimes the reader of a research essay feels confused and distracted, not by excessive notes and citations, but by excessive information. Writers who have done a thorough job of research sometimes have more material than they know what to do with; thus, they may be tempted to use up every single point on every last note-card and to cram all the available information into their essays. The result is that the paragraphs tend to bulge at the seams with random bits of information, and readers will find it hard to retain any sense of continuity. To illustrate this point, here is a contrast between two paragraphs dealing with the same topic: one streamlined, the other bulging. Again, the subject is Dickens; this time, we are given an explanation of the reasons for the French holiday:

In 1853, three of Dickens's closest friends had died,[8] and the writer himself, having become even more popular and busy since the publication of <u>David Copperfield</u>,[9] began to complain of "hypochondriacal whisperings" and also of "too many invitations to too many parties."[10] In May of that year, a kidney ailment that had plagued Dickens since his youth grew worse,[11] and, against the advice of his wife, he decided to take a holiday in Boulogne.[12]

[8] The friends were Mr. Watson, Count d'Orsay, and Mrs. Macready. Forster, p. 124.
[9] André Maurois, <u>Dickens</u> (New York: Frederic Ungar, 1934), p. 70.
[10] Forster, p. 125.
[11] Charles Dickens, <u>Letters</u>, ed. G. Hogarth (New York: Walter Black, n.d.), p. 350. Also, Johnson, p. 757.
[12] Tillotson, Dickens's doctor, was the only one who encouraged him to set off for Boulogne, Tillotson himself had been there the previous October. Johnson, p. 757.

Dickens needed a holiday because he felt tired and overworked. Throughout his life, Dickens had taken on new projects, like writing books, acting in plays, or managing them, or both,[21] and "conducting" his own magazine with dynamic energy.[22] Dickens had hired the prospective domestic staff for Urania Cottage, the house of his friend, Miss Coutts; he'd chosen the house for himself and he'd become involved with her moving in many other ways.[23] He preferred the title "conductor" to editor when applied to himself and his magazine <u>Household Words</u>. In fact, just before he left his home for France in June, 1853, Dickens

> was still pouring his customary energy into everything he
> did; he was doing daily work for Miss Coutts,[25] managing
> the magazine, which had been created in 1859 and was
> issued weekly,[26] dictating A Child's History of England to
> his sister-in-law Georgina,[27] and attending the "feasts
> and festivals" that made up part of his social life.[28] But
> at this age, he found it hard to undertake all these
> ventures with his customary energy. Edgar Johnson comments
> that, at this period, just before the summer of 1853,
> Dickens felt tired.[29] Perhaps the recurrence of his
> childhood kidney problem was a blessing in disguise: it
> enabled him to escape from London to Boulogne.

One does not need notes to observe that the paragraph contains too much information unrelated to its topic. If the writer wishes to mention Dickens's friend Miss Coutts, or Dickens's job as editor of *Household Words*, she should discuss these matters at greater length elsewhere. The writer should have kept her mind on the holiday at Boulogne instead of running down every possible lead, relevant or irrelevant. Whether the extraneous material should be distributed in other paragraphs of the essay, placed in the notes, or simply omitted is a hard decision to make without examining the entire essay and its structure. But the first, much shorter, paragraph suggests that some related but less important detail can be put into the notes, where, if wanted, it is always available. The reader of the first paragraph has been given a choice: he can absorb the essential information through the paragraph alone, or he can examine the topic in depth, through reading the paragraph and notes. But the reader of the second passage must assimilate a mass of unconnected detail about Dickens's career; getting to Boulogne simply takes too long.

EXERCISE 64

Read each of the following paragraphs, paying special attention to unity and coherence. Place in the notes any information that you find loosely related to the paragraph's focus. Draw a line through any material that you find wholly unrelated to the topic. Put brackets around the material to be moved, and use arrows to indicate the appropriate note for each piece of information that you are removing from the paragraph.

> Since Dickens tried to pack so much activity into each
> day of his holiday, one wonders when he had time for his
> nine children--Charles, born in 1837; Kate, 1839; Francis,
> 1844; Sydney, 1847; Mary, 1838; Walter, 1841; Alfred,
> 1845; Henry, 1849; and Edward, 1852.[52] Since July 3, the

children had been with their parents, and on that day,
their father wrote to his friend Lemon that the children
had arrived "all manner of toad-like colors" from their
trip across the channel.[53] In this description and in
other references to them in letters to his wife, we can
see evidence of Dickens's feeling for the children: very
often he refers to them as "the darlings," sends them his
love,[54] and refers to them by nicknames that perhaps only
another father might appreciate: "Keeryleemoo" (either
Walter or Francis); "the jolly post boy" (Henry);[55]
"Lucifer Box" (Kate);[56] and "Plornishghenter" (Edward).[57]
Many of the boys had been named for great literary men of
the time, which suggests their father's hopes for their
future: Edward Bulwer-Lytton, Henry Fielding, Sydney
Smith, and Alfred Tennyson.[58]

[52] Johnson, Genealogical Chart 5.
[53] Johnson, p. 759.
[54] Dexter, pp. 159-60.
[55] Dexter, p. 167.
[56] This name is not mentioned in the letters, but it
can be found in Johnson, p. 751.
[57] Dexter, p. 175.
[58] Pope-Hennessy, p. 373.

Another good friend to Charles Dickens was his sister-
in-law. Georgina had lived with the family ever since the
parents had returned from an American tour in June, 1842.
She had grown attached to the children while the couple
was away.[82] She now functioned as an occasional secretary
to Dickens, specifically when he was writing A Child's
History of England, which Pope-Hennessy terms a "rather
deplorable production." Dickens treated the history of his
country in a very unorthodox manner.[83] Dickens must
have felt close to Kate since he chose to dictate the
History to her; with all his other work, Dickens always
worked alone, writing and correcting it by himself.[84]
Perhaps a different woman would have questioned the
relationship of her younger sister to her brother; yet
Kate Dickens accepted this friendship for what it was.
Georgina used to take over the running of the household
whenever Kate was indisposed. Kate was regularly too
pregnant to go anywhere. She had ten children and four
miscarriages in a period of fifteen years.[85] Kate probably
found another woman to be quite a help around the house.[86]

Pope–Hennessy suggests that Kate and her sister shared Charles Dickens between them.[87]

[82] Pope–Hennessy, pp. 179–80.
[83] Pope–Hennessy, p. 311.
[84] Butt and Tillotson, pp. 20–21.
[85] Pope–Hennessy, p. 391.
[86] Pope–Hennessy, p. 179.
[87] Pope–Hennessy, p. 287.

THE FINAL BIBLIOGRAPHY

The bibliography is always listed on a separate sheet at the end of your research essay. Which works you include in your final bibliography may depend on the wording and intention of your assignment. There is an important difference between a list of works that you have *consulted or examined* and a list of works that you have *cited or actually used in the writing of your essay*. Your instructor may restrict your bibliography to "Works Cited," or you may be asked to submit a list of "Works Consulted." Remember that one purpose of a "Works Consulted" bibliography is to help your readers to find appropriate background information, not to overwhelm them with the magnitude of your efforts. An indiscriminate collection of thirty-five titles can appear to be pointless self-advertisement if, in your essay, you actually cite only five sources.

On the whole, a sensible final bibliography of "Works Consulted" for an undergraduate essay consists of all the sources that you examined (in other words, actually held in your hand and looked at) which proved to have a clear bearing on your topic, whether you actually used them in your essay or not. If, for example, you consulted a book *in the hope* that it contained some relevant information, and if you then discovered that it provided no pertinent material, what would be the point of citing such an irrelevant title in your final bibliography? You might, of course, choose to include certain sources for negative reasons: to prevent your readers from repeating your mistake and attempting to consult works with misleading titles in the belief that they might be useful. Finally, if you have been unable to locate a source and have thus never yourself examined it, you may not ordinarily include it in your final bibliography, however tempting the title may be.

THE CORRECT FORMAT FOR YOUR FINAL BIBLIOGRAPHY

Here are the guidelines for bibliographical entries:

1. Notice that each bibliographical entry is indented in reverse of a note: the author's last name appears at the margin; the second line of each entry (if there is one) starts five spaces in. This format enables the reader's eye to move quickly down the list of names at the left-hand margin.
2. Each entry is double-spaced, with double spacing between the entries.
3. The bibliography is in alphabetical order, according to the last name of the author. If there are two authors, only the first has the last name placed first: "Woodward, Robert, and Carl Bernstein." If an author has more than one work included on your list, do not repeat the name each time: alphabetize or arrange chronologically by publication date the works by that author, place the name at the margin preceding the first work, and, for the second (and subsequent) title(s), replace the name with a row of ten hyphens followed by a period and two spaces.

```
Freud, Sigmund. Civilization and Its Discontents. London:
     Hogarth, 1930.
----------. Moses and Monotheism. New York: Knopf, 1939.
May, Rollo. Love and Will. London: Souvenir, 1970.
```

If the work that you are citing is unsigned, alphabetize it according to the first letter of the title, and place the title at the margin.

4. A bibliographical entry for a book is read as a list of three items—author, title, and publication information—with periods between each piece of information. All the information must always be presented in exactly the same order that you see in the model bibliography above. Place of publication must precede publisher and date; a colon must separate place and publisher; a comma must separate publisher and date. For a periodical reference in a bibliography, the items included are author and article title, each followed by a period; periodical title, followed by a comma; volume and/or number, followed by date in parentheses and a comma; and the pages spanned by the article, followed by a period.

```
Tobias, Sheila, and Carol Weissbrod. "Anxiety and
     Mathematics: An Update." Harvard Educational Review,
     50, No. 1 (Feb. 1980), 61-67.
```

(See Appendix B for models illustrating more complex kinds of bibliographical entries.)
5. Each entry terminates with a period.

The Annotated Bibliography

Annotating your bibliography is an excellent way to demonstrate the quality of your research. But, to be of use, your comments, though brief, must be informative. The following phrases do not tell the reader very much: "an interesting piece"; "a good article"; "well-done": "another source of well-documented information." What is well done? Why is it interesting? What is good about it? How much and what kind of information does it contain? Although it need not be detailed, a good annotated bibliography will answer some of these questions.

Examine the following bibliography carefully, noting the way it presents the basic facts about author, title, and publication, as well as a fair range of evaluative information. If the annotations were omitted, these entries would still be perfectly correct, for they conform to the standard rules for bibliographical format. Without the annotation, one would simply have to change the heading to "Works Consulted" or an equivalent title.

ANTON CHEKHOV IN 1912: AN ANNOTATED BIBLIOGRAPHY

Bruford, W. H. <u>Chekhov and His Russia</u>. London: Paul, Trench, Trubner, 1948. Excellent material about Russia and the social background which helped to influence Chekhov's writings.

Edwards, Christine. <u>The Stanislavsky Heritage</u>. New York: New York University Press, 1965. Edwards seems to be very well acquainted with her subject. The book is interesting and valuable in understanding the impact of the Moscow Art Theatre on Chekhov's craft.

Gillés, Daniel. <u>Chekhov: Observer Without Illusion</u>. Translated by Charles Lam Markmann. New York: Funk and Wagnalls, 1968. A very lively biography, written with enthusiasm for his subject.

Gorky, Maxim. "Anton Chekhov: Fragments of Recollections." <u>Reminiscences of Tolstoy, Chekhov and Andreev</u>. London: Hogarth, 1948. Not useful for biographical facts, but supplies very descriptive details about Chekhov's personality and outlook upon life.

Hingley, Ronald. <u>Chekhov: A Biographical and Critical Study</u>. London: George Allen & Unwin, 1950. A very good biography. A unique feature of this book is the appendix, which has a chronological listing of all English translations of Chekhov's short stories.

Macdonald, Alexander. "A. Chekhov: The Physician and the Major Writer." <u>Journal of the American Medical Association</u>, 229 (1974), 1203–04. A two–page appreciation of Chekhov's career as a doctor. This is interesting reading with apt quotations from Chekhov, especially the references to Chekhov fighting the cholera epidemic.

Magarshack, David. <u>Chekhov: A Life</u>. 2nd ed. 1953; rpt. Westport, Conn.: Greenwood Press, 1970. A valuable biography by an author who is also an accomplished translator of Russian literature.

Muchnic, Helen. <u>An Introduction to Russian Literature</u>. New York: E. P. Dutton, 1947. A small paperback, without enough material to be of any assistance for research.

11. The Research Essay

An effective research essay depends on the integration of the many variables that have been explored throughout this book as overlapping stages in the writing process. However, a research essay must also conform to a few basic mechanical rules:

1. Type your essay. Use a dark ribbon and double-space throughout.
2. Use 8½- by 11-inch paper, and type on only one side of the page.
3. Leave one-inch margins on all sides.
4. Number each page after the first.
5. Proofread your essay and insert any corrections neatly, in ink.

Check with your instructor for any other special rules that may apply to the assignment.

TWO SAMPLE RESEARCH ESSAYS

Following are two student research papers on the same subject, as well as the instructor's comments on each. The papers were written in response to this assignment:

> Write a research essay, five to ten typewritten pages in length, in which you explore a few years of Ernest Hemingway's early career as a writer. As you state your thesis, try to relate the events of this period to Hemingway's artistic development.

Both students concentrate on roughly the same period, but each addresses the subject from a somewhat different perspective. The bibliographies also differ. Compare the essays, noting the strengths and weaknesses of each.

Sharon Boyd
Intro. to Amer. Lit.
April 4, 1983

The Making of a Novelist: Ernest Hemingway, 1925-1926

Before becoming the spokesman of the "lost generation," Ernest Hemingway had to find--or possibly create--himself. Between the publication of his first stories and poems in 1923 and his first great critical success with the novel The Sun Also Rises, Hemingway crowded his life with people, places, and physical activity. With Western Europe as his arena, Hemingway struggled--with poverty, real or imagined artistic impotence, his wife, other writers, and even Spanish fighting bulls. All of these struggles, people, and places played a role in molding, in a few short years, the complex and controversial "Papa" Hemingway.

Ernest Hemingway began writing The Sun Also Rises, his first novel, on his twenty-sixth birthday, July 21, 1925, in Valencia.[1] Dedicated to his work,[2] he would begin writing in bed each morning.[3] During August Hemingway continued his work in Madrid, often writing in the coolness of a cafe, until the summer heat became so unbearable that he and his wife Hadley were forced to move on to Hendaye.[4] Hemingway increased his feverish pace, working more intensely than ever before.[5] In a little, inexpensive beachfront hotel,[6] he would often write into the early morning hours, going to sleep, then awakening with fresh phrases that he was eager to write down.[7]

   The couple returned that fall to their Paris apartment at 113 rue Notre Dame des Champs, where, only two months after beginning, Hemingway completed the novel.[8] The writer's determination to conclude the book left him drained.[9] However, the intensity of the effort was typical of Hemingway—he seemed to have an insatiable appetite for whatever interested him at that moment.[10] And, in order to meet the demands of his work, Hemingway required isolation whenever he wrote.[11]

   In Paris, "the town best organized for a writer to write in,"[12] Hemingway's apartment seemed like the least likely refuge for a writer. Besides the noise of the sawmill below and the lack of warmth,[13] he had to contend with the distractions of his baby boy, Bumby.[14] In order to allow her husband more peace, Hadley would sometimes borrow a baby carriage and take the child through the streets of the city,[15] leaving the writer to grapple with his work and the cold in the small room in which he wrote.[16]

   Many times Hemingway would escape the chill and the clatter of morning by taking a short walk to the Closerie des Lilas cafe.[17] Equipped with two pencils, pencil sharpener ("a pocket knife was too wasteful"), blue notebooks, and his good-luck charms—a rabbit's foot and a horse chestnut—carefully tucked away in his right pocket,[18] Hemingway would have little problem writing as he occasionally sipped on a café crème while the waiters busied themselves with their cleaning.[19] The writer liked the unspoiled ambiance of the place and ridiculed the pretentious attention seekers who frequented such cafes as the Dôme and the Rotonde.[20] He wrote that such spots "anticipated the columnist as the daily substitute of immortality." It was Hemingway's contention that the Closerie was a good cafe because the people there were genuine and nobody was on display.[21]

Hemingway's affinity for the unaffected also led him to the Negre de Toulouse restaurant, where he and Hadley became very friendly with the entire staff.[22] Amidst the napkins of red and white checks, the purple mimeographed menus and the diluted Cahors wine,[23] the couple would have their afternoon meal.[24] They would frequently meet friends at the restaurant, and, though not as often, in each other's apartments.[25]

While entertaining at home, the writer might proudly point out an important Miró painting that he had bought for Hadley's thirty-fourth birthday (although he couldn't really afford it).[26] Both had been very excited over the acquisition and scoffed at criticism for indulging in such luxuries when money for bare essentials was at a minimum.[27]

In mid-December of that year (1925), despite their financial difficulties, the Hemingways were able to flee from their cold apartment and live in Austria at surprisingly little cost.[28] Always susceptible to accidents and illnesses,[29] Hemingway developed a severe cold that forced him to bed upon his arrival at Schruns,[30] a village located in the Austrian Vorarlberg. Because his father was prone to attacks of angina,[31] and, having suffered the same ailment himself, Hemingway feared that a reccurence of such an attack would prove fatal.[32]

His short stay in bed, however, allowed him the pleasure of reading, writing letters, eating well,[33] and, in general, happily bemoaning a confinement that made him the center of attention.[34] Nestled in the comfort of his featherbed, Hemingway would discuss the art of fiction with F. Scott Fitzgerald,[35] a good friend of his ("I had no more loyal friend than Scott when he was sober").[36] They would talk of various topics for writing, with war being at the top of Hemingway's list (followed by, but not necessarily in order of impor- tance, "love, money, avarice, murder and impotence")[37]

Indeed, even at this early stage of his career, Hemingway seemed to have developed a basic philosophy of writing. His ability to perceive situations clearly and to capture the exact essence of the subject (which was invariably of a common nature)[38] might have stemmed from a disciplined belief that each sentence had to be "true" and that a story had to be written "as straight as you can."[39] In order to maintain this "truth," Hemingway would not stop writing until he was sure of what was to occur next.[40] In addition, he had taught himself to ignore his work from the moment he stopped until the time he resumed writing. Hemingway feared that too much attention to his work might leave him artistically "impotent," but as he absorbed what was going on around him, his mind would subconsciously busy itself with ideas.[41]

Another maxim in Hemingway's arsenal of beliefs was his aversion to being confronted by talk of his work. Apparently, it was part of the writer's creed that any praise paid directly to the artist was an "open dis- grace."[42] However, Hemingway had no reservations about reading some chapters of the still unpublished The Sun Also Rises to his friends, the Gerald Murphys, and glowing in their complimentary comments.[43] Sometimes, however, the moody Hemingway would ignore the opinions of friends and his wife.[44]

An example of stubborn behavior occurred in November of 1925: tired of being compared with the well-established Sherwood Anderson, Hemingway began a satire of Anderson's Dark Laughter called The Torrents of Spring and finished it within a week. Not meaning to hurt the elder writer's feelings,[45] Hemingway considered the parody a harmless prank. He thought that writers were fair game for each other, as long as they remained sincere in their criticism.[46] However, others doubted Hemingway's motives, believing that it was all a clever ploy to break a contract with his publisher. In fact, the contract was canceled and resulted in the beginning of Hemingway's long association with Max Perkins of Scribner's.[47]

Thus, the product of Hemingway's struggle to rewrite The Sun Also Rises at Schruns during the winter of 1925 and 1926 would ultimately end up in the hands of a new publisher;[48] and, despite the distractions of his illness and the Murphys,[49] he was able to concentrate on finishing the book as he pounded away at his "noisy old Corona."[50]

Still, life in the Vorarlberg was hardly all work and no play. Hemingway's recreational activities included billiards,[51] bowling, poker,[52] and, of course, skiing. With characteristic enthusiasm, and despite a "trick knee and a bad eye,"[53] Hemingway immersed himself in the sport, because he wanted to be the best.[54] Skiing also seemed to bring out his disgust for limp-limbed phonies: "the spiral fracture had not become common then and no one could afford a broken leg." Hemingway attributed this prevention of injuries to leg muscles that were strengthened by the absence of ski lifts.[55]

Mealtime was an event in itself at Schruns.[56] The Hemingways and their friends would season mountains of food with much laughter.[57] The eager eaters might help themselves to hare, venison,[58] or trout.[59] These delicacies would be washed down by various wines and beers.[60] Although Hemingway would occasionally get "slightly tight," he appeared to have a good hold on his liquor. Indeed, he admired the villagers for their own drinking abilities and seemed to fit in well with them—— drinking and singing songs of the mountains.[61]

Hemingway's zest for life extended to women also. His wandering heart seemed only to be exceeded by an even more appreciative eye.[62] Hadley was aware of her husband's flirtations and of his facility with women.[63] Yet, she had no idea that something was going on between Hemingway and Pauline Pfeiffer, a fashion editor for Vogue magazine.[64] She was also unaware that Hemingway delayed his return to Schruns from a business trip in New York, in February 1926, so that he might spend some more time with this "new and strange girl."[65]

When a remorseful Ernest Hemingway finally rejoined his family in Austria, he was able to continue where he had left off——skiing, socializing, playing with Bumby, and completing the rewrite of his novel.[66] This aura of serenity, however, was dealt a strong, if not fatal, blow when the Hemingways returned to Paris and joined Pauline around Easter of 1926.[67] After a drive in the country with an unusually hostile Miss Pfeiffer, Hadley's suspicions were aroused and she questioned her husband about Pauline. Hemingway was enraged that she should bring such information out into the open and stormed out of their apartment, leaving a tearful wife behind.[68]

Still, the writer thought that he and Hadley would be able to continue the charade of being happily married.[69] Hemingway's behavior certainly appeared to support John Dos Passos's contention that Ernest was "hard on his women."[70] That summer, when Miss Pfeiffer joined the Hemingways at Juan-les-Pins, it was difficult for Hadley to keep up the cruel pretense of domestic tranquility.[71] In fact, she thought it most unlike her husband to subject her to such humiliation.[72] Ironically, it was here, amongst the crumbling of the Hemingway family, that friends began calling the writer "Papa."[73]

In early July, the "ménage à trois" journeyed to the festival of Pamplona and the same deceptive conditions persisted. When Miss Pfeiffer had to return to Paris, the Hemingways traveled on to San Sebastián and Madrid, where they were followed by Pauline's missives. In Valencia, a full year after Hemingway began his novel, the writer finally admitted that his marriage was in ruins.[74] Friends were shocked to learn of the break-up and even Hemingway appeared to be stunned by the reality of the separation.[75]

Strangely, there didn't seem to be any traces of bitterness between the estranged couple. Hadley reconciled herself to the fact that her husband was always susceptible to affection.[76] Hemingway, after proofreading the final manuscript of The Sun Also Rises, sent it to Max Perkins on August 27, 1926, with the following dedication: "This book is for Hadley and for John Hadley Nicanor."[77]

Notes

[1] Carlos Baker, ed., Hemingway and His Critics: An International Anthology (New York: Scribner's, 1969), p. 30. This was the only specific date available—other books were vague or seemingly incorrect. Baker, p. 152, mentions that he began working in Valencia; on p. 173 Baker documents the sending of the finished manuscript to Max Perkins as August 27, 1926. I chose this date as the ending of the period under examination because not only had Hemingway given final approval to the novel, but also had signaled the end of an era in his own private life with the farewell dedication of the book to his wife and son.

[2] Carlos Baker, Ernest Hemingway: A Life Story (New York: Scribner's, 1969), p. 152. Also, Alice Hunt Sokoloff, Hadley: The First Mrs. Hemingway (New York: Dodd, Mead, 1973), p. 85.

[3] Baker, ed., p. 31. Also, Baker, p. 152.

[4] Baker, ed., p. 31. It was not unusual for Hemingway to seek the shelter of a cafe, as later references will bear out in the text.

[5] Baker, p. 153. Also, Sokoloff, p. 82.

[6] Baker, ed., p. 31.

[7] Baker, p. 153–54.

[8] Baker, p. 155.

[9] Baker, p. 155. Also, Sokoloff, p. 82.

[10] John Dos Passos, The Best Times (New York: NAL, 1964), p. 185. Also, Ernest Hemingway, A Moveable Feast (New York: Scribner's, 1964), p. 12. In the words of

Notes 2

Hemingway, "I always worked until I had something done."

[11] Baker, p. 170. Also, Hemingway, p. 186.

[12] Hemingway, p. 182.

[13] Baker, p. 123. Also, Sokoloff, p. 69.

[14] Sokoloff, p. 70. The couple constantly were making up nicknames for everyone. Hemingway's was "Tatie," "Tiny," or "Wax Puppy," and Hadley was known as "Hash," "Cat," or "Feather-Kitty." Two-year-old "Bumby's" real name was John Hadley Nicanor.

[15] Sokoloff, p. 70.

[16] Sokoloff, p. 70. Also, Baker, p. 123. Sokoloff calls it "a little boxlike room," while Baker refers to it as a "small bedroom."

[17] Sokoloff, p. 69. Also, Hemingway, p. 92. Sokoloff states that the cafe was located "just down the street on the Boulevard du Montparnasse." Hemingway writes that this was his "home cafe--the [other] swell places were far away."

[18] Hemingway, p. 91.

[19] Hemingway, p. 197.

[20] Hemingway, p. 81. Also, Sokoloff, p. 69.

[21] Hemingway, p. 81. Information in the two previous sentences comes from the page cited.

[22] Sokoloff, p. 73.

[23] Hemingway, pp. 99, 101.

[24] Hemingway, p. 99. Also, Sokoloff, p. 73. Typical offerings of the menu were not provided in the cited sources.

[25] Sokoloff, p. 73.

[26] Baker, p. 73. Actually, Hemingway rolled dice with Evan Shipman for the rights to pay the 5,000 francs

for the painting entitled "The Farm." Hadley was born November 9, 1891, making her almost eight years older than her husband.

[27] Baker, p. 158. Also, Sokoloff, p. 83, and Hemingway, p. 198.

[28] Dos Passos, p. 158. Also, Hemingway, p. 198. Hemingway lists the actual price as "about two dollars a day."

[29] Dos Passos, p. 142: "I've never known a man who did so much damage to his own carcass . . . when it wasn't an accident it was a sore throat."

[30] Sokoloff, p. 83.

[31] Sokoloff, p. 70.

[32] Sokoloff, p. 84.

[33] Baker, p. 161. Hemingway's reading list included Thomas Mann's Buddenbrooks, Turgenev's Fathers and Children, Maugham's Of Human Bondage, Conrad's Within the Tides, and Tolstoi's War and Peace. On page 162, Baker notes that Hemingway would take Captain Marryat's Peter Simple to bed with him.

[34] Sokoloff, p. 84.

[35] Baker, p. 161.

[36] Hemingway, p. 184.

[37] Baker, p. 161. In Baker's words, war "offered maximum material combined with maximum action."

[38] Dos Passos, p. 143. Also, Harold Loeb, The Way It Was (New York: Criterion, 1959), p. 218.

[39] Hemingway, pp. 12, 183.

[40] Hemingway, p. 12.

[41] Hemingway, p. 13. Information in the last three sentences comes from the page cited.

[42] Hemingway, pp. 127, 150.

[43] Baker, p. 166. Also, Hemingway, p. 209. In Baker's words, Hemingway "wagged his tail with pleasure." The apparent contradiction between the last two sentences of this paper may be attributed to a change in Hemingway's viewpoint over the years. Indeed, what seems to be the same incident (reading aloud to the Murphys), in Hemingway's words, "is about as low as a writer can get and much more dangerous than glacier skiing."

[44] Sokoloff, p. 83.

[45] Dos Passos, p. 158.

[46] Baker, p. 170. Information in the preceding comes from the page cited.

[47] Baker, p. 160. In the words of Mike Strater, it was a "cold-blooded contract-breaker." Since both writers were published by Horace Liveright, it would be unwise for the publisher to risk the wrath of the firmly entrenched Anderson for the sake of the relatively unknown Hemingway. The contract (in Baker's words) "stated very clearly [that] Liveright's option on his first three books would lapse if they rejected Book Number Two." So Hemingway became a free man.

[48] Hemingway, p. 202. He called it his "most difficult job of rewriting."

[49] Baker, pp. 161, 166.

[50] Baker, p. 167.

[51] Baker, pp. 161–62.

[52] Hemingway, p. 201.

[53] Loeb, p. 194. These infirmities were results of war wounds suffered in Italy in the service of the Red Cross.

[54] Dos Passos, p. 158.

[55] Hemingway, p. 199. The quotation and the information in the following sentence come from the page cited.

[56] Hemingway, p. 201.

[57] Dos Passos, p. 159.

[58] Hemingway, p. 201, writes, "We were always hungry"; and he appears to take particular delight in describing the fare: "jugged hare with a rich red wine sauce, and sometimes venison in chestnut sauce."

[59] Dos Passos, p. 159.

[60] Dos Passos, p. 159. Also, Hemingway, p. 201, and Loeb, p. 230. Loeb writes that besides the usual red and white wines, there were "thirty kinds of beer."

[61] Loeb, pp. 283, 231. Also, Hemingway, p. 202.

[62] Hemingway, p. 102. He seemed to pay special attention to their hair and the way in which they were "built."

[63] Sokoloff, p. 84. In Hadley's own words, women "had a habit of falling in love with Ernest."

[64] Baker, p. 159. Ironically, Miss Pfeiffer's first perception of Hemingway was that of a "rough, unshaven loafer" (in the words of Baker).

[65] Hemingway, p. 210. Also, Baker, p. 165.

[66] Sokoloff, p. 85.

[67] Baker, p. 168.

[68] Baker, p. 168. Also, Sokoloff, p. 86. The information in the previous two sentences comes from the pages cited—with one exception. Sokoloff makes no mention of any crying.

[69] Sokoloff, p. 87.

[70] Dos Passos, p. 143. These were the author's own words.

Notes 6

[71] Baker, p. 171. In Baker's words, "there were three of everything: breakfast trays, bicycles, bathing suits drying on the line."

[72] Sokoloff, pp. 88–89.

[73] Baker, p. 171.

[74] Baker, p. 172.

[75] Baker, p. 172–73. Hemingway took Gerald Murphy's offer to use his studio at 69 rue Froidevaux.

[76] Sokoloff, p. 90.

[77] Baker, p. 173.

Annotated Bibliography

Baker, Carlos. Ernest Hemingway: A Life Story. New York:
    Scribner's, 1969. A thorough biography with
    detailed notes and sources. Interesting reading and
    an invaluable guide.

Baker, Carlos, ed. Hemingway and His Critics: An
    International Anthology. New York: Hill and Wang,
    1961. Although the book is a critical study in
    general, George Plimpton's interview with Hemingway
    does provide useful biographical information.

Dos Passos, John. The Best Times. New York: NAL, 1966.
    The author may have forgotten many facts in these
    memoirs, but his perceptions are still clear.

Hemingway, Ernest. A Moveable Feast. New York:
    Scribner's, 1964. Fragmentary and posthumous
    portrait of Paris in the twenties. Although it
    lacks much factual information, the author's style
    makes the book come alive.

Loeb, Harold. The Way It Was. New York: Criterion, 1959.
    Reminiscences of one of Hemingway's closest
    acquaintances evoke inevitable comparisons between
    Loeb and Robert Cohn in The Sun Also Rises. The
    author has an irritating habit of providing dates
    without giving the year. Abrupt ending is a
    disappointment to serious researchers.

Sokoloff, Alice Hunt. Hadley: The First Mrs. Hemingway.
    New York: Dodd, Mead, 1973. Brief account of the
    young couple from a wife's point of view. Anyone
    expecting to find any juicy revelations will be
    disappointed.

Remarks:

This was an extremely enjoyable essay—very pleasant to read. Your focus and approach are exactly what I wanted, and I especially commend your ability to synthesize facts into a coherent paragraph. You also do well with a limited base of research. There are some points of dating and authenticity that could be made clearer; it is sometimes hard to tell just how composite your portrait is and just how reliable your sources are. The footnoting is good. The two greatest weaknesses, on the whole, are the structure and the completeness of the essay. You paragraph too often. Although the breaks are not disastrous in a narrative essay like this one, the habit could be very distracting and fragmenting if you indulge it in a straight critical essay. More important, you don't offer enough background, especially in the second half. You could have expanded the whole marriage-Pauline section so that a reader might have clearly understood all the relationships. Although the last pages suffered the most, there were several other points at which I could have benefited from more elaboration in text or in notes. All in all, two more pages would have made a world of difference.

Ben Goetz
Intro. to Amer. Lit.
April 4, 1983

Ernest Hemingway: The Early Years

The world discovered Ernest Hemingway with the
publication of The Sun Also Rises. The author was only
twenty-seven years old. Although in many respects
Hemingway remained an emotional adolescent for life, he
was, by 1926, as old as the century, which, in the wake
of World War I, considered itself very old. Wounded
during the war, Hemingway spent the next several years
packing his life with experience, working and playing
and exulting and suffering with a manic intensity. These
few years also saw the emergence of a major novelist,
and because Hemingway is a "writer who deliberately
projects his own personality and life as central to his
work,"[1] the events of these years are worth recounting.

F. Scott Fitzgerald had discovered Hemingway
somewhat earlier. In the early autumn of 1924, from the
Villa Marie at St. Raphael, on the French Riviera,
Fitzgerald wrote to his editor at Scribner's, Maxwell
Perkins. Part of Fitzgerald's letter concerned "a young
man named Ernest Hemingway, who lives in Paris (an
American) . . . and has a brilliant future. . . . I'd look
him up right away. He's the real thing."[2]

The publication of The Sun Also Rises established

Hemingway as "the real thing" not only for his literary peers but for the public at large. He had begun writing the novel in July 1925,[3] on holiday in Madrid with his wife, Hadley. The Hemingways had just arrived in Madrid after a disappointing trip to the fiesta of San Fermin at Pamplona,[4] where a year earlier they had thrived on the intensity of the celebration:

> The fiesta began with fireworks and continued through a noisy week of drinking and dancing, with religious processions and special Masses in the Churches, and bullfights every afternoon. Each morning at dawn Ernest roused Hadley to watch the bulls come galloping down a mile and a half of cobblestoned streets to the pens in the Plaza de Toros. Ahead of the bulls ran all the young bucks of Pamplona, flirting with death. . . . Between times came the riau-riau dancing. . . . The celebration reached its daily climax each afternoon at the bullfights.[5]

Upon seeing his first bullfight, Hemingway immediately became an aficionado, enthusiastically wanting to learn all about the art of bullfighting. He treated bullfighting not as a visceral experience, but as a literary or artistic one.[6]

In that summer of 1925, Hemingway anxiously anticipated his return to Pamplona, gathering money from his friends for train fare, hotel reservations, and tickets to the bullfights. The Hemingways planned to stay at the Hotel Quintana, owned by Juanita Quintana, a

bullfighting fan and friend of many matadors. Before
going to Pamplona the Hemingways planned to fish for
trout in the Spanish town of Burguete, where they would
rendezvous with their friends Bill Smith, Don Stewart,
and Harold Loeb. The whole trip, however, became a
travesty of the Hemingways' past trips to Spain. Fishing
in Baguete was ruined by loggers who, working in the
forests, had littered the streams with refuse, and the
Hemingways' traveling companions were not as congenial
as they had once been. Don Stewart, who had been with
the Hemingways at Pamplona in 1924, recalled that all
had changed: "The atmosphere [in 1924] had been much
like that of a college reunion, pervaded by a kind of
boyish innocence and a sense of relief." In 1925 the
Hemingways also discovered that they were no longer the
only Americans in Pamplona; high society, driving in
from Biarritz, had appeared.[7]

The party broke up, and the Hemingways proceeded to
Madrid, staying at the Pension Aguilar in the Calle San
Jerónimo. After a side-trip to Valencia, the Hemingways
returned for a few days to their pension in Madrid,
where Hemingway worked on The Sun Also Rises. They then
proceeded to the beach resort of San Sebastián and from
there across the border to Hendaye, where they were
surrounded by purple mountains and white beach. Hadley
entrained for Paris on August 12; Hemingway left Hendaye
to join her on August 19, and by then the first draft of
his novel covered two hundred and fifty notebook pages.[8]

Carlos Baker describes the twenty-six-year-old
Ernest Hemingway:

4

[He was] six feet tall and usually weighed 210
pounds . . . He wore a size eleven shoe. His
eyes were brown, his complexion ruddy, and
there were dimples in both his cheeks . . . His
hair at first was brownish black and straight
. . . His gait was rolling and purposeful. He
had a habit of standing poised on the balls of
his feet, and there was often a noticeable
side-to-side motion of his head when he talked
or listened. Acute listeners could detect a
slight speech impediment in which ls and rs
tended to take on the semblance of the w
sound.[9]

Sometimes the young Hemingway was deliberately old and
hard, affecting a swagger or an incipient scorn; at
other times he was naive, sensitive as a boy.[10]

By August of 1925 Ernest and Hadley Hemingway had
lived in Paris for almost four years.[11] Their address,
113 rue Notre-Dame-des-Champs, was near the corner of
the Avenue de l'Observatoire and the Boulevard du
Montparnasse, and the Hemingways' windows overlooked a
sawmill and lumberyard. The apartment was composed of a
dark hall which led to a kitchen equipped with a stone
sink and two-ring gas burner. There were also a dining
room, a small bedroom, a master bedroom with a stove and
double bed, and a dressing room, where their infant son
Bumby slept.[12] To keep the apartment "warm and cheerful," he and Hadley burned boulets, lumps of coal dust
shaped like eggs, in their wood fire.[13]

Hemingway had taken possession of the apartment

after he had resigned, in January 1924, from his job as an overseas correspondent for the Toronto Star. Aside from his journalistic writing, Hemingway had had a volume of his short stories and poems published by Robert McAlmon. McAlmon, an American, was a short story writer and poet who had married an heiress and become founder and editor of Contact Editions.[14]

Soon after Hemingway's return to Paris following World War I, he had accepted a job as assistant editor of the Transatlantic Review, a literary journal founded by Ford Madox Ford.[15] The review published works by many of the future lions of the literary world, but it was short-lived, publishing its last issue in December 1924.[16]

During that time Hemingway had begun to experiment with storytelling. Silas Huddleston, a contemporary in Paris, writes of the young Hemingway's aspirations:

> I happened to be the president of an association to which he [Hemingway] belonged, and at its meetings he would chat with me about his ideals and his ambitions. He was seeking a simple, realistic style. He wanted to set down life as he saw it. Conversation in novels was too highfalutin. He intended to make it as he supposed it to be.[17]

Hemingway would also discuss his work with Gertrude Stein, whom he met in March, 1922.[18] Hemingway later wrote about a visit Miss Stein paid him and his wife at their home. After entering their home, Gertrude Stein

made herself comfortable and proceeded to read all of
Hemingway's short stories; the only one she did not like
was "Up in Michigan." Stein felt that Hemingway's sexual
descriptions in this story made the piece unaccrochable; it couldn't be published because of its language
and therefore was silly. Hemingway responded, "But what
if it is not dirty but it is only that you are trying to
use words that people would actually use? That are the
only words that can make the story come true and that
you must use them? You have to use them." Stein
reiterated her feelings about the unaccrochable.
Hemingway "did not argue about this nor try to explain
again what [he] was trying to do about conversation."[19]

Conversations with Gertrude Stein were again on
Hemingway's mind in the Autumn of 1925. Continuing The
Sun Also Rises in Chartres in late September, Hemingway
played with the notion of calling his book The Lost
Generation. The title had come from a story Stein told
him. She had gone to a garage to have her car repaired
and had complimented the owner on the efficiency of his
workers. The owner replied that these were young workers
who learned fast; it was those in the age group 22 to 30
who could not be taught. They were a lost generation. By
the end of his trip to Chartres, Hemingway had decided
against calling his novel The Lost Generation; instead
he chose The Sun Also Rises.[20]

In October 1925 a collection of Hemingway's early
stories, In Our Time, was published.[21] Reviews were
generally good, but Hemingway was galled that one of his
short stories was favorably compared to the work of the
American writer Sherwood Anderson. Hemingway decided to
avoid any future comparisons between himself and

Anderson, and set out to write a parody of Anderson's work; this lampoon, called The Torrents of Spring, was written in an unserious, offhanded way.[22] Gertrude Stein reacted to the book by telling a hurt Sherwood Anderson that "Hemingway's character is such that he had to kill off his rivals."[23] Hemingway's friend, John Dos Passos, thought the book amusing but not good enough to follow on the heels of In Our Time. Hadley very much objected to The Torrents of Spring, hating what Hemingway had done to Anderson but seeing that her husband was determined to publish it, regardless of her or Anderson's feelings.[24]

Pauline Pfeiffer was the one person who thoroughly enjoyed The Torrents of Spring[25] "Small boned and lively as a partridge,"[26] Pauline had met the Hemingways briefly at the beginning of 1925. She was at first unimpressed with Ernest Hemingway, thinking him "rather coarse in both manner and appearance." Pauline, who was an editor for Vogue in Paris, had by the winter of 1925 overcome her initial dislike of Hemingway, and had become one of Hadley's closest friends.[27]

Later that winter, on December 12, 1925, Ernest and Hadley Hemingway went on a skiing vacation in Shruns, Austria, an idyllic resort in the Vorarlberg mountains:

> After going through Switzerland you came to the Austrian frontier at Feldkirch. The train went through Liechtenstein and stopped at Bludenz where there was a small branch line that ran along a pebbly trout river through a

valley of farms and forests to Shruns, which was a sunny market town of sawmills, stores, inns and a good, year round hotel called the Taube where we lived.[28]

The Hemingways loved Shruns; they skied, drank beer and wine, and ate hare and venison. They walked trails, past farmhouses where women spun wool into yarn.[29] Hemingway, however, needed the rest, having developed a case of laryngitis from reading The Torrents of Spring to Gerald and Sara Murphy, new friends he and Hadley had made. Hemingway spent most of his first week at Shruns in bed, reading and writing. He planned to begin revising and typing The Sun Also Rises as soon as he was cured of his infection.[30]

Pauline Pfeiffer was getting ready to join the Hemingways at Shruns; she was in Paris buying skis and making preparations to spend the Christmas and New Year's holiday with them. When Pauline arrived at Shruns a thaw had set in and there was no skiing, but she was not dismayed. "Just to be near Ernest was enough. She was now, and she knew it . . . in love with him, and the problem was to keep Hadley from guessing as much."[31] Pauline was still in Shruns when Hemingway, in a New Year's Day letter to Scott Fitzgerald, wrote that he was thinking about making a trip to New York. Hemingway had sent the manuscript of The Torrents of Spring to Horace Liveright, the American publisher of In Our Time. Liveright had rejected The Torrents of Spring, feeling it was not lighthearted enough and unusually cruel to Sherwood Anderson.[32] Hemingway later wrote that "It was necessary that I leave Shruns to go to New York to rearrange publishers."[33] Thus, Hemingway left Hadley and their son in Shruns, and journeyed to Paris in preparation of his voyage to New York. He reached Paris in January, 1925, and spent considerable time with Pauline, who had journeyed there with him. Hemingway was now inexorably in love with two women.[34]

The seven days that Hemingway had planned to spend in New York were extended to nineteen. When Hemingway returned to Paris he dined with Zelda and Scott Fitzgerald, who were preparing to leave for Nice; he agreed to consider joining them on the Riviera in April.[35]

Hemingway did not immediately leave Paris for Shruns; he spent some more time with Pauline at her apartment on the rue Picot.[36] Hemingway recalls, "When I got back to Paris I should have caught the first train from the Gare de l'Est that would take me down to Austria. But the girl I was in love with was in Paris then, and I did not take the first train, or the second or the third."[37]

In March, 1926, John Dos Passos and Gerald and Sara Murphy visited the Hemingways in Shruns; at the time Hemingway enjoyed their company and read them passages from The Sun Also Rises.[38] Later, however, Hemingway was to bitterly describe the visit as "the year the rich showed up." John Dos Passos, according to Hemingway, was the pilot fish who led the rich Murphys to Hemingway.

> The rich came led by the pilot fish. A year
> before they would never come. There was no
> certainty then. The work was as good and the

happiness greater but no novel had been
written, so they could not be sure. . . . But
this year they were sure and they had the word
from the pilot fish who turned up too. . . .
The pilot fish was our friend of course.[39]

At this time writer Kay Boyle was living in a villa
in Grasse, in the south of France. She was visited by
her sister Jean, who worked for Paris Vogue and brought
with her as a guest a co-worker, Pauline Pfeiffer. One
week prior to their arrival, a daily letter had been
delivered to Boyle, for Pauline, from Ernest Hemingway.
Boyle's sister later explained to her that Hadley
Hemingway and Pauline were best friends, and that
Hemingway wrote to Pauline asking her to buy perfume
made in Grasse, and lingerie available in Cannes, as
gifts for Hadley. Boyle recounts: "In a few months
everything would be different. . . . Hadley would have
been put aside, and in her place Pauline Pfeiffer would
be Mrs. Hemingway; for the letters he had written her to
Grasse had nothing to do with a particular kind of
perfume, or a particular kind of lingerie."[40]

The Hemingways were back in Paris by Easter of
1926; in those few months before the final break, their
marriage deteriorated. Hemingway and Hadley quarreled
over Pauline, and, because of a persistent cough of
Bumby's, had to rearrange their plans to go to Spain in
the summer. Hemingway went alone to Madrid in the second
week of May.[41]

The trip to Spain began unsatisfactorily; Madrid
was unseasonably cold, the bullfight on Saturday, May
15, was canceled owing to a lack of superior bulls, and

on Sunday a heavy blanket of snow canceled the fights for that day. During his stay in Madrid, Hemingway did manage to complete three short stories and write to Sherwood Anderson to explain that The Torrents of Spring was not meant as a "personal attack."[42]

While Hemingway was in Spain, Hadley went with Bumby to Cap d'Antibes, where she first stayed in Gerald and Sara Murphy's guest house. Antibes was a wonderful place to relax,[43] but soon after Hadley arrived Bumby was quarantined with whooping cough: "The Fitzgeralds had recently moved from the Villa Paquita at Juan-les-Pins to the much larger villa St. Louis. . . . Their lease on the smaller house had not expired and they offered it to Hadley, who . . . moved to keep the quarantine."[44]

Hemingway arrived at the Villa Paquita after three weeks in Spain, and he and Hadley appeared to be on good terms. Hemingway showed Scott Fitzgerald a copy of The Sun Also Rises; Fitzgerald suggested several cuts in the opening chapter, and Hemingway agreed to the change. On May 28, 1926, while he was still on the Riviera, Hemingway's The Torrents of Spring was published, and the majority of reviewers found it to be an amusing parody.[45]

Soon after Hemingway arrived at Cap d'Antibes, he and Hadley were joined by Pauline Pfeiffer.[46] In July 1926 the Hemingways, Pauline, and the Murphys went again to the fiesta at Pamplona, lodging at the Quintana Hotel, where the Hemingways had stayed the year before. Hemingway was remembered from his past visits to Pamplona; he and his entourage were the center of attention, drinking sherry and eating roasted almonds, "surrounded by Spaniards who shot wine into Ernest's mouth from their wineskins." Hemingway and Gerald appeared briefly in the bullring; Gerald executed a passable veronica, and Hemingway dived over a bull's horns, lying face down on its back until it collapsed.[47]

There was some strain in the relationship between Ernest and Gerald Murphy, for there was some feeling on Hemingway's part that Gerald wasn't tough enough. Hemingway was also slightly competitive with Murphy. Murphy's daughter Honoria was called "daughter" by her father; Gerald occasionally would address other women by this appellation. When Murphy called Pauline Pfeiffer "daughter" he noticed that Hemingway started to address her the same way, and didn't like it when Gerald did it. "As a result of these undercurrents, Gerald never was as close to Hemingway as he was to Zelda and Scott Fitzgerald."[48]

The undercurrents in the Hemingway marriage could no longer be kept beneath the surface; on hearing that they were separating, Gerald Murphy invited Hemingway to use his studio in Paris, on the rue Froidevaus, and Hemingway accepted.[49] The marriage of Ernest and Hadley Hemingway ended simultaneously with the beginning of Hemingway's reputation as an author of importance. He would never again be the person who had lived in Paris "when we were very poor and very happy."[50] His associations with little magazines like the Transatlantic Review and Contact also ended with the publication of The Sun Also Rises.[51] The early Paris years became the foundation on which the legend was built.

Notes

[1] Cleanth Brooks, et al., "Ernest Hemingway," in
<u>American Literature: The Makers and the Making</u>, II (New
York: St. Martin's, 1973), p. 2250.

[2] F. Scott Fitzgerald, <u>Letters</u> (New York:
Scribner's, 1963), p. 167.

[3] Carlos H. Baker, <u>Ernest Hemingway: A Life Story</u>
(University Park, Pa.: Pennsylvania State University
Press, 1969), p. 155.

[4] Baker, p. 147.

[5] Baker, p. 112.

[6] Robert McAlmon, <u>Being Geniuses Together, 1920–
1930</u>, rev. and enl. Kay Boyle (New York: Doubleday,
1968), p. 180.

[7] Baker, pp. 147–50.

[8] Baker, pp. 151–54.

[9] Baker, p. ix.

[10] McAlmon, p. 175.

[11] Nicholas Joost, <u>Ernest Hemingway and the Little
Magazines: The Paris Years</u> (Barre, Mass.: Barre
Publishers, 1968), p. 1.

[12] Baker, pp. 122–23.

[13] Ernest Hemingway, <u>A Moveable Feast</u> (New York:
Scribner's, 1964), p. 11.

[14] Baker, pp. 106–22. Hemingway quit the <u>Star</u> after
a dispute with its city editor, Harry Hindmarsh.

[15] James R. Mellow, <u>Charmed Circle: Gertrude Stein
and Company</u> (New York: Praeger, 1974), pp. 266, 242.

[16] Mellow, p. 270. Also Baker, pp. 82, 125.
Hemingway raged over Ford's "megalomaniacal blundering"

that led to the demise of the Transatlantic Review.

[17] Silas Huddleston, Bohemian, Literary and Social Life in Paris (London: Harrap, 1928), p. 144.

[18] Mellow, p. 262. Also Baker, p. 82. When the Hemingways left for Paris in 1921, they had a letter of introduction from Sherwood Anderson to Gertrude Stein, who, with her companion, Alice B. Toklas, lived on the rue de Fleurus. According to Mellow, "she collected Picasso and other modern painters, looked like an Erdmutter, and talked like an angel."

[19] Hemingway, p. 15.

[20] Baker, pp. 155-58.

[21] Mellow, p. 262.

[22] Baker, p. 158.

[23] Mellow, p. 278.

[24] Baker, p. 159. Hemingway first met Dos Passos, a Chicagoan, on the front in Italy during World War I (Baker, p. 42).

[25] Baker, p. 159.

[26] McAlmon, p. 201.

[27] Baker, p. 142. Hemingway met Pauline and her sister Virginia at Harold Loeb's.

[28] Hemingway, p. 198.

[29] Hemingway, p. 202.

[30] Baker, p. 161. The Murphys were a wealthy American couple who had lived in France (both in Paris and at Cap d'Antibes) since 1916. Gerald Murphy was an accomplished painter.

[31] Baker, p. 162.

[32] Baker, pp. 162-63.

[33] Hemingway, p. 210.

[34] Baker, p. 164.

[35] Baker, p. 165.

[36] Baker, p. 165.

[37] Hemingway, p. 210.

[38] Baker, p. 166.

[39] Hemingway, pp. 207–09.

[40] McAlmon, pp. 201–05.

[41] Baker, pp. 168–69. "April and May were dark and wet. . . . When Hadley remarked one day that she had reason to think he was in love with Pauline, his face flushed and he drew himself up. Hadley, said he, should not have mentioned the matter. By bringing it out in the open, she had broken the chain that might have held them together. His implication, as Hadley caught it, was the fault was hers for having spoken."

[42] Baker, pp. 169–70.

[43] Calvin Tomkins, <u>Living Well Is the Best Revenge</u> (New York: Viking, 1971), pp. 96–97. "In the early twenties, Antibes was still a provincial town. The telephone service shut down for two hours at noon and ceased altogether at seven P.M. . . . The long, quiet days centered on the beach, the garden, and the port, where from 1925 on the Murphys kept a boat."

[44] Baker, p. 170.

[45] Baker, p. 170. "Ernest resolved almost at once to lop off the first fifteen pages of manuscript. The whole biography of Brett Ashley and Mike Campbell, and the autobiography of the narrator, Jake Barnes." This trimming was characteristic of Hemingway's esthetic theory.

[46] Baker, p. 171.

Notes 4

[47] Tomkins, p. 98.
[48] Tomkins, p. 100.
[49] Baker, p. 171.
[50] Hemingway, p. 211.
[51] Joost, epilog.

Annotated Bibliography

Baker, Carlos H. Ernest Hemingway: A Life Story.
        University Park, Pa.: Pennsylvania State Univ.
        Press, 1969. An imcomparable aid for anyone
        wanting to know about every part of Ernest
        Hemingway's life. This is what is called a
        definitive biography. The index is very helpful
        for anyone tracking down a certain period of
        Hemingway's life, as the material is listed
        chronologically.
Brooks, Cleanth, R. W. B. Lewis, and Robert Penn Warren.
        American Literature: The Makers and the Making.
        Vol. II. New York: St. Martin's, 1973. An
        anthology with useful critical and historical
        introductions to each author represented.
Fitzgerald, F. Scott. Letters. New York: Scribner's,
        1963. A small selection of letters to Ernest
        Hemingway; not exceedingly useful for direct
        information on Hemingway, but uniquely
        informative about an era Fitzgerald and Hemingway
        shared.
Hemingway, Ernest. A Moveable Feast. New York:
        Scribner's, 1964. Paris, thirty years later,
        through rose-colored glasses. Interesting,
        nostalgic, and, of course, with the kind of
        atmosphere that Hemingway is so adept at
        creating, but it should not be considered the
        final word when writing about Hemingway in the
        twenties.

Bibliography 2

Huddleston, Silas. Bohemian, Literary and Social Life in
    Paris. London: Harrap, 1928. Interesting
    description of Paris in the twenties, enhanced
    considerably by the fact that it was written when
    it happened, and thus is a good primary source.
Joost, Nicholas. Ernest Hemingway and the Little
    Magazines: The Paris Years. Barre, Mass.: Barre
    Publishers, 1968. Comprehensive, though rather
    dry, account of Hemingway's contribution to the
    literary journals in the early twenties. Some
    good background information on Hemingway. At
    times the author palpably idolizes his subject.
McAlmon, Robert. Being Geniuses Together, 1920-1930.
    Revised and with supplementary chapters by Kay
    Boyle. New York: Doubleday, 1968. McAlmon was in
    the thick of Parisian life during this era, and
    writes with understandable authority about it.
    Boyle writes with acuity about the people she
    knew. Definitely worth reading if you want to
    know about the era and those who peopled it.
Mellow, James R. Charmed Circle: Gertrude Stein and
    Company. New York: Praeger, 1974. Exuberant book
    about Gertrude Stein and the company she kept.
    Nuggets of information about Hemingway and
    everyone else who passed through her salon.
Tomkins, Calvin. Living Well Is the Best Revenge. New
    York: Viking, 1971. Slim volume about a singular
    couple, Gerald and Sara Murphy. While they
    weren't part of "the lost generation," they knew
    and were friendly with most of them. Some
    insights into Hemingway. Quick, enjoyable
    reading.

Remarks:

These are the weaknesses of your essay, some of which are more serious than others:

1. The narrow base of research. If, in fact, Baker is the only available full biography, then you cannot be strongly criticized for emphasizing a single source and for failing to alternate sources and cross-reference key points. But the essay ends up being rather thin and Baker-ridden.

2. The structure of the essay really has the wrong focus. At the beginning, the focus seemed promising enough; but you end up trying to cover much too much time. The essay becomes a narrative of the Hemingway's travels during a period of many months, instead of a profile of Hemingway at a given point. Aside from the confusion about dating (and you really should have kept your reader better informed about the passing of time) and the omission of references to Sun *for pages and time (so that one forgot what the focus was supposed to be), the major casualty here was the sense of personality. Increasingly as the paper advanced, your paragraphs became a mass of little details or an anecdote detached from any special point. Instead of having strong topic sentences, revealing of H's personality, you gradually moved into your point, so that only by the end of the paragraph did I become aware of the focus. That's a backwards technique. Ideally, you should have abandoned the blow-by-blow-through-time approach. One paragraph about* Torrents; *one paragraph about their propensity for travel; one paragraph about bullfighting; two or three* CONNECTED *paragraphs about the deterioration of their marriage—you might as well have condensed time, since you can't tell the chonological story as well as Baker. (That's precisely why I ask you to focus on just a few years; you don't have the scope or space to do a proper narrative.)*

3. Your judgment about what to put in the notes and what to put in the text was a bit uncertain. I definitely got the feeling that there were too many minor details in the text, but that may have been a result of the absence of topic sentences to establish the reason for including the details. Your tendency to quote at length was a more serious error; quote only when you absolutely cannot help it (or perhaps when it is your subject that you are quoting). The style of many of your long quotations was most undistinguished; you could easily have paraphrased as successfully.

EXERCISE 65

A. Following are three research essays about the San Francisco earth-quake of 1906. The essays vary in quality as well as length. Read each essay and check it against this list, taking notes as you progress.

1. Does the essay have a single focus which is clearly established and maintained throughout?
2. Does the writer have a thesis or a consistent point of view about the events being described?
3. Does the narration have a beginning, middle, and end?
4. Does the essay begin with an informative introduction?
5. Does the essay end on a conclusive note?
6. Does each paragraph have a clear topic sentence?
7. Does each paragraph contain one and only one topic?
8. Are the paragraphs long enough to be convincing? Does each point get supported by facts and information?
9. Does the writer build up a complete and well-balanced picture of the event?
10. Does the development of the essay depend entirely upon the dry listing of facts and events, or does the writer offer explanations and relevant commentary?
11. Does the writer use transitions to signal the relationship between separate points?
12. Does the reader get a sense of the relative importance of the sources being used?
13. How many pages of source material were actually used in re-searching the essay?
14. Does the writer use one source for long stretches at a time, or are multiple sources cited to support individual points?
15. Is there the right number of notes? too many? too few?
16. Is it clear how much material is covered by each note? Are um-brella notes used when appropriate?
17. Do notes provide important explanatory information? Do notes contain unnecessary or excessive information? Is there material in the essay which might be better placed in the notes?
18. Are the quotations well-chosen? Are there enough? too many?
19. Is paraphrase properly used? Is the style of the paraphrase con-sistent with the style of the writer of the essay?
20. Does the writer use enough citations? Does the text of the essay make it clear when the writer is using a specific eyewitness source, and who that person is?
21. Is the essay convincing? Did you believe what you read?

B. Give each essay a grade. Then write a general comment of three to four sentences which justifies and explains your grade.

James Gould
History 102
Section 8
May 19, 1983

The Aftermath of the San Francisco Earthquake

San Francisco has long been plagued by earth tremors. "Severe quakes had been felt in 1864, 1898, and 1900, but it was not until 5:13 A.M. of April 18, 1906, that the rocky masses of the San Andreas Fault, the greatest fracture anywhere on the earth's crust, heaved violently and doomed San Francisco as it then existed."[1] The quake was followed by a fire that destroyed the center of the town and burned on until April 21, when the ashes were wetted down by rain.[2]

The water mains broke, the gas works blew up, and the chief of the fire department perished when the chimney of his home fell on him as he slept in bed. By mid-morning the fire department resorted to dynamiting the downtown business district to stop the flaming fury which was being blown rapidly by a west wind, obliterating everything in its path.

In a few short hours most of San Francisco was in ruins.[3] "Four square miles, making up 512 blocks in the centre [sic] of town, were gone, along with 28,000 buildings and a total property value of about $500,000,000."[4] Approximately 700 people had died and approximately 250,000 people were left homeless.[5] The homeless took refuge in the Presidio, Richmond District, and Golden Gate Park. Tents were set up, then outdoor kitchens, and a makeshift operating room, where several babies were born.[6] The city was far from beaten. Henry Miller, a millionaire cattle rancher, gave out free beef to the homeless for seven days, and a merchant, Raphael Weill, imported trainloads of clothes and personally walked through the tent cities to see that everyone was clothed.[7]

On every side there was death and suffering. Hundreds were injured, either burned, crushed, or struck by falling pieces from the buildings.[8] San Franciscans insist on telling one, "It wasn't an earthquake that destroyed us, it was the fire." Starting in the business section down near Montgomery Street and the district south of Market Street, the giant flames swept towards Russian Hill, Chinatown, North Beach, and Telegraph Hill.[9]

Famed author Jack London looked down California Street and saw "two mighty walls of fire advancing from the east and south."[10] Several houses were saved on Telegraph Hill by the Italians pouring wine on the flames, and A. P. Giannini saved all the cash in the Bank of Italy (now the richest bank in the world, the Bank of America) by hauling it off in a vegetable cart to his home on the Peninsula.[11]

Under a special message from President Roosevelt, the city was placed under martial law. Hundreds of troops patrolled the streets and drove the crowds back, while hundreds more were set at work assisting the fire and police departments. The strictest orders were issued, and in true military spirit, the soldiers obeyed. During the afternoon three thieves were shot on sight while working in the ruins. The curious were driven back at the breasts of the horses that the cavalrymen rode and the crowds were forced from the level district to the hilly section in the north.[12]

The lore of the earthquake and the fire has become overlaid with much sentiment, but in recent years seismologists and structural engineers have been reminding San Franciscans that this could happen again. There have been charges that the new office towers could not withstand another earthquake like the one in 1906 and that the next great rumbling of the San Andreas Fault may take a vastly greater toll.[13]

Within a remarkably short time San Francisco began the struggle to rehabilitate itself. Owing to the courage and energy of the people, within a year following the catastrophe the city was taking on a somewhat normal appearance. The new structures were planned along more costly and substantial lines. With the aid of San Francisco banks and the money received from insurance companies, the city arose to a beautiful San Francisco once again.[14]

A poem written by Laurence W. Harris reflects the feelings of those who lived through the disaster:

> From the ferry to Van Ness you're a God
> forsaken mess
> But the damndest finest ruins nothing more and
> nothing less.[51]

Notes

[1] Kenneth Lamott, "San Francisco," <u>New Encyclopaedia Britannica</u>: <u>Macropaedia</u>, 1980 ed.

[2] Lamott, p. 219.

[3] Barnaby Conrad, <u>San Francisco: A Profile with Pictures</u> (New York: The Viking Press, 1959), p. 30.

[4] Lamott, p. 219.

[5] Lamott, p. 219.

[6] Conrad, p. 30.

[7] Conrad, p. 31.

[8] Conrad, p. 32.

[9] Conrad, p. 29.

[10] Conrad, p. 33.

[11] Conrad, p. 33.

[12] Conrad, p. 32.

[13] Conrad, p. 32.

[14] Lamott, p. 219.

[15] Conrad, p. 35.

A List of Sources

Conrad, Barnaby. <u>San Francisco: A Profile with Pictures</u>.
    New York: Viking, 1959.
Lamott, Kenneth. "San Francisco." <u>Encyclopaedia
    Britannica: Macropaedia</u>. 1980 ed.

Noel Vitale
History 102
Section 8
May 19, 1983

The San Francisco Earthquake

The crack in the earth beneath California, later entitled the San Andreas fault, yawned a warning of its existence and its powerful strength in 1857 when it pulled the earth apart for forty miles. The break in the earth's crust spread open twenty feet wide before the earth sealed shut again. This same fault caused the area around San Francisco to rumble during 1865, and it shook the city again in 1890 and 1898. Andrew Lawson, in 1893, was the first to actually locate the existence of the cause of these earth tremors, and he named this potential hazard after San Andreas Lake. At the time of his discovery, he voiced his prediction that the area beneath and around San Francisco ". . . was marked by tilting and movements that may yet be active."[1] But the attitude of the San Franciscans was that there was "nothing to worry about, because there's nothing that can be done about it. Besides, a good shake is not half so bad as a twister or a hurricane bearing down on you."[2]

Unaware of any impending disaster in San Francisco, other history-making events around the world on April 17, 1906, received public attention. In Russia, the Czar had crushed a revolution. In London, a group called the Suffragettes were picketing 10 Downing Street. The world was mourning three disasters--a mine tragedy in the Calais mine in France, an earthquake in Formosa,[3] and the eruption of Mt. Vesuvius in Italy.[4] In the United States, some people believed that cars would eventually replace horses, and Geronimo, 76 years old, took his eighth wife.[5] In San Francisco, on the evening of April 17, music lovers went to hear Enrico Caruso singing the leading role of the opera Carmen.[6] On that same day, in Los Angeles, the city had collected $10,000 for the victims of the Vesuvius disaster. Little did anyone know that on April 18, there would be victims of an earthquake in San Francisco who would need this aid even more.[7]

Officer Leonard Ingham of the San Francisco Police Department had not been sleeping well for two months previous to April 1906. In his dreams, he saw the Palace Hotel[8] burning and the people of San Francisco being driven into the sea by a fire which scorched the land. His recurrent, terrifying, dream, in which he saw his hometown consumed by flames, motivated him to make a personal survey of the fire potential of the city. Officer Ingham found that every area, from the "squalor" of Chinatown to the "expensive residential quarter between Powell and Van Ness Avenue," contained a high proportion of wooden buildings. On Monday, April 16, Leonard Ingham had an exceptionally vivid, realistic, dream of the impending San Francisco disaster. The following day, he acted upon his foreboding dream in two ways. First, he made an appointment with Police Chief Dinan to report his findings and the fears that he had for the city's welfare. Second, he purchased a $2,000 fire insurance policy on his house.[9] Officer Ingham did not have a nightmare on the night of April 17. He slept well until 5:00 A.M., when a noise in the street woke him up. The sound was the clatter of milk bottles on a cart. At that time, "the milkman was having trouble pacifying his excited horse."[10]

The fear of the destruction of San Francisco by fire, which Leonard Ingham felt, was not isolated. Dennis Sullivan, Chief of the San Francisco Fire Department, was also distressed over the dangerous, potential fire hazards of the area. Furthermore, his fears were founded on solid evidence. The Fire Chief had read the October, 1905, report by the National Board of Fire Underwriters:

> San Francisco has violated all underwriting
> traditions and precedents by not burning up;
> that it has not done so is largely due to the
> vigilance of the fire department, which cannot
> be relied upon indefinitely to stave off the
> inevitable.[11]

This same report also claimed that the San Francisco water system was inadequate and that the hydrant system was insufficient for distributing water in the event of a fire.[12] Chief Sullivan had fought for years for money to build a better water-supply system for the city. He suggested that an auxiliary salt-water system should be built, and he urged that the existing cisterns beneath the streets should be utilized better. His pleas and suggestions fell on deaf ears because the Fire Department had always been successful in combating fires with their existing facilities.[13] From these recorded facts, it seems obvious that both Dennis Sullivan and Leonard Ingham greatly feared the disastrous fire that they felt would eventually endanger the city. Neither one of them realized how close at hand the catastrophe actually was.

On April 18, 1906, the San Andreas fault once again pulled the earth apart. The initial explosive impact, along the Humboldt County coastline, that the tear in the earth surface made on the land went briefly unobserved before the "rip" began traveling south on its quick, ominous, devastating, 200-mile journey toward San Francisco.[14] Part of the path which the "rip" traveled would find it racing south at two miles a second beneath the ocean. The tremor was noticed by the crew members who were aboard two vessels at that time. These men weren't even aware of what they had experienced. The movement of the ocean floor along the San Andreas fault below the schooner John Campbell caused the ship to rise into the air, then splash back into the sea.[15] Those on board ran to the railing to see what the ship had rammed. They saw nothing. Captain Svenson made the following entry in the Campbell's log: "Sudden motion, unexplained. The shock felt as if the vessel [had been] struck. . . ."[16] The steamer Argo was similarily shaken at sea by the moving San Andreas fault. While forty fathoms above the open ocean floor, the crew members felt as if the ship had been hit by a "depth charge at point blank range."[17] The earthquake emerged from the sea within seconds at Point Arena, California, ninety miles north of the Argo's destination. From there, the quake

continued traveling south, moving and changing the
earth's surface as it tore toward unsuspecting San
Francisco.[18]

On the morning of April 18, Bailey Millard woke up
early. He was an artist and he wanted to capture the
tranquility of an awakening San Francisco on canvas. He
had a panoramic view of the city below from the terrace
of his villa and he intended to ". . . capture the rise
of the sun as it embraced the Bay and shoreline,
sheening all it touched with gold." As he worked on <u>When
Altruria Awoke</u>, he listened to the bells of old St.
Mary's calmly announce the hour; it was five o'clock in
the morning.[19]

Only twelve minutes later, Bailey Millard's paints
spilled, his easel was destroyed, and his canvas was
torn.[20] The earthquake had struck San Francisco.[21]

As he heard the bells of old St. Mary's tolling
frantically, Bailey Millard now looked from his villa at
a completely different city. San Francisco was "rocking
and rolling" below him. He saw waves of earth, two to
three feet high, going over the land, and he saw
chimneys, spires, cornices, brick walls, and wooden
buildings deteriorating.[22] Then, he experienced peace
for ten seconds when the tremors temporarily halted. The
second phase of the quake followed.[23] "In seconds,"
Thomas reports, "the earthquake changed the shape of the
city."[24]

Two other people saw the earthquake--Jesse Cook, who
was a policeman on duty, and John Barrett, who was the
city-desk news editor of the <u>Examiner</u>.[25] Jesse Cook saw
it coming up Washington Street as he stopped to talk

with Al Levy. Sergeant Cook recalled hearing a sound
which was "deep and terrible" before actually seeing
anything. He recalled that "the whole street was
undulating. It was as if the waves of the ocean were
coming toward me, and billowing as they came."[26] Jesse
Cook was sent flying by the shock waves, and he saw
people and animals crushed by falling bricks.[27] John
Barrett was only a few blocks from Washington Street
when the earthquake struck. He found himself pinned to
the ground by an invisible vacuum which pushed him down
flat on his face: "It was as though the earth was
slipping quietly away from under our feet." As he looked
around at the crumbling city, he noted that the buildings seemed to be "dancing."[28] One writer, during
the peak of the earthquake, gave a brief description of
what it felt like: the movement of the earth, during the
quake, reminded him of a "terrier shaking a rat."[29]

Elsewhere in the trembling city, Officer Leonard
Ingham saw smoke and flame, and he realized that "his
nightmare had come true." He reported to work after
sending his wife away from San Francisco.[30] Fire Chief
Sullivan and his wife were not as fortunate. Both were
injured when the smokestacks from the California Hotel
fell through the roof of the firehouse of Engine
Company #2. The Fire Chief received head and chest
injuries and he never regained consciousness.[31] Enrico
Caruso gave the most unusual performance of his life on
that day when he appeared on the balcony of his Palace
Hotel suite. Though terrified, he sang to the people
below and he tried to show the world that he hadn't been
afraid at all, but he never came to San Francisco
again.[32] Arnold Genthe, a world-famous photographer,

said that he had gone to sleep with "the music of Carmen . . . still ringing in my ears." He awoke to find his Chinese porcelains smashed, his cameras ruined and his photographs destroyed.[33] He walked downtown where he got a small 3A Kodak camera and took pictures of people.[34] His photographs are purposefully out of focus, and he utilized light from behind his subjects.[35] Genthe's photographs are, to this day, "things of terrible and breathtaking beauty."[36]

Following the earthquake, there was a terrible silence. Though everyone went into the street after the quake, those few who were able to speak only whispered.[37] Samuel Dickson, seventeen years old in April 1906, describes the aftereffect of the shock with extreme clarity:

> It was cold; the fog was almost a drizzle. People whispered to each other. I don't know why, but they all spoke in low voices as though they were afraid that any loud noise might suddenly start the earth careening again.[38]

However, one person, Brigadier General Frederick Funston, reacted quite differently. Upon looking around him, he saw smoke from the beginning fires and he saw the "stunned" people. He soon realized that, once the shock of the disaster faded, panic would set in unless the citizens were handled firmly. He promptly appointed himself the military governor of San Francisco and surrounded himself with 2,000 men who were willing to take orders.[39] The behavior of the people of San Francisco during this time of crisis is still regarded by fellow San Franciscans with pride. The rumors of brutality existing during this period are unfounded. Though death and destruction were everywhere, the mood of the city was one of tenderness. Judge Isadore L. "Ike" Harris, said it all when he exemplified the period as one in which there was ". . . a brotherhood of man such as I wish could come without tragedy."[40]

According to historians Gordon Thomas and Max Morgan Witts, "The policeman's recurring nightmare had predicted the fire with uncanny accuracy—the course it would travel, beginning south of the Slot, sweeping up Market Street to engulf the Palace Hotel."[41] At 2:30, the water jets in the Palace, which distributed the water contained in the hotel's private water supply, stopped spraying water. The reservoirs that had contained 130,000 gallons of water were empty. The fire continued to advance toward the Grand Hotel.[42] The Palace Hotel eventually did catch fire, but people continued to cheer the red, white, and blue, which still flew from its roof. When the hotel was destroyed, the American flag was the last part of it to burn.[43]

Following the earthquake more than 50 fires broke out.[44] The fire department fought the flames with anything that they could. "Many of the men dropped, literally, from exhaustion before the last flame died."[45]

Dickson observed Italian-American families' formation of a most unusual fire fighting brigade on Telegraph Hill. When the fire tried to climb the Hill, there was no water to put it out. Entire families fought the flames as ". . . into the street they rolled their precious barrels of red wine. And with buckets and with sacks soaked in red wine, the brigade fought flame with wine." They were extremely successful in saving their homes and the "fragrance of red wine blessed the hill for many months after the smell of smoke and fire had blown away."[46]

The Boston Evening Transcript claimed, "The breaking of the mains handicapped [the firefighters], of course, but it is doubtful if they could have coped with the conflagration even if they had [had] plenty of water."[47] The firemen fought the blaze not only without water, but also without the experienced leadership of their chief.[48] The other factors which led to the destruction of the city included the lack of communication, and the limited extent of the firefighting force—585 firemen and 50 pieces of firefighting equipment.[49] For days and weeks following the fire, the people of San Francisco looked for answers to the question "What if . . .?"[50]

The memory of the 1906 earthquake remains with San Franciscans. The city held a "Festival of Progress" on the 50th anniversary of the quake. The San Francisco area was shaken up again in 1957 by an earthquake, but it wasn't comparable to the one in 1906.[51] There are landmarks, also, in San Francisco, which serve as reminders of the 1906 disaster. "Portals of the Past" stand in Golden Gate Park.[52] There is a plaque, honoring Fire Chief Sullivan, on the facade of the new Engine House #2 on Bush Street.[53] Anyone can see in the floor of the main post office building cracks that have been there since the morning of April 18, 1906. There are other buildings in San Francisco that survived the earthquake and are still standing--the Fairmont and St. Francis hotels, the old mint, the Ferry Building and the Merchants' Exchange.[54]

Notes

[1] Gordon Thomas and Max Morgan Witts, <u>The San Francisco Earthquake</u> (New York: Stein and Day, 1971), p. 28.

[2] William Bronson, <u>The Earth Shook, The Sky Burned</u> (Garden City, N.Y.: Doubleday, 1959), p. 19.

[3] Thomas and Witts, p. 35.

[4] Thomas and Witts, p. 20.

[5] Thomas and Witts, p. 35.

[6] Thomas and Witts, p. 21; also, Samuel Dickson, <u>Tales of San Francisco</u> (Stanford, Calif.: Stanford University Press, 1957), p. 205.

[7] Bronson, p. 17.

[8] Thomas and Witts, pp. 21–22, describe how the Palace Hotel was built to withstand earthquakes and fire: "It was said in San Francisco, that if the Palace ever burned down, the city itself would also be gutted." The hotel's foundation was sturdy. There was an abundant supply of water stored at the hotel site and an intricate, effective system of delivering the water, when needed, within the hotel to combat fires.

[9] Thomas and Witts, pp. 22–23.

[10] Thomas and Witts, p. 56. In this same book, on page 14, there is the hypothesis that animals sense an impending quake first. This can be born out in the case of the San Francisco earthquake on page 54 which cites examples of restless horses and barking dogs.

[11] Thomas and Witts, p. 24; also, Bronson, p. 19.

[12] Bronson, p. 21; also mentioned in Thomas and Witts, p. 25.

[13] Bronson, p. 21.

[14] Thomas and Witts, pp. 66–68. These pages contain a detailed description of the path of destruction which ripped through California on April 18th.

[15] What the crew actually experienced was a "kickback from the rip" because the actual break in the ocean floor was located miles ahead of the vessel. The schooner Campbell was 150 miles from San Francisco when these shock waves were registering around the world.

[16] Thomas and Witts, p. 65. All the above information, and the explanation in the preceeding footnote, was derived from this source.

[17] Thomas and Witts, p. 66. The Argo is also mentioned in Bronson, p. 31.

[18] You can check Thomas and Witts, p. 68, for an account of the destruction at the Agnews State Insane Asylum, in San Jose, where more than 100 people died. This same information is given in Bronson, p. 29, where it is also recorded that in Santa Rosa, "every brick building in town was down." It should be noted that the entire area affected by this earthquake was 20 to 40 miles wide and 200 miles long, according to Bronson, p. 29.

[19] Thomas and Witts, pp. 59–60.

[20] Thomas and Witts, p. 70.

[21] The earthquake struck at 5:12 A.M. according to Thomas and Witts, p. 61. "Exact clocks showed the onset of the quake to be a few seconds after 5:12 A.M." This same page, as well as Bronson, p. 24, verify that the Ferry Building clock was fast. However, Thomas and Witts

claim it stopped at 5:14, and Bronson says it stopped at 5:15.

[22] Thomas and Witts, p. 70.

[23] Thomas and Witts, p. 71. This time sequence is also verified by Bronson, p. 35, in Jesse Cook's account of the quake. The entire earthquake lasted more than 60 seconds. Part one was 40 seconds long, during which the intensity of the tremor mounted. Then it stopped for 10 seconds. Next, the earth shook for 25 seconds more during which time the tremor's intensity diminished.

[24] Thomas and Witts, p. 63.

[25] Thomas and Witts, p. 69.

[26] Bronson, p. 24.

[27] These facts are combined from Thomas and Witts, p. 69, and Bronson, pp. 33–35.

[28] Thomas and Witts, p. 69. On p. 71 of the same book, Bailey Millard also claimed that the skyline was dancing.

[29] Bronson, pp. 25.

[30] Thomas and Witts, pp. 76–77.

[31] Bronson, pp. 29 and 36. Unfortunately, Fire Chief Sullivan never had the opportunity to explain all the details that he had in mind for an improved San Francisco water system, or any alternative plans which he might have had for fighting a major fire. He died three days later. p. 40.

[32] Thomas and Witts, p. 75.

[33] Samuel Dickson, Tales of San Francisco (Palo Alto: Stanford Univ. Press, 1957), p. 626. On page 627, it is noted that his Chinatown pictures were safe.

[34] Bronson, p. 41, and Dickson, p. 627.

[35] Thomas and Witts, p. 142.

[36] Dickson, p. 626.

[37] Bronson, p. 25.

[38] Dickson, p. 223.

[39] Thomas and Witts, p. 77. Further information about Funston's actions is given by Thomas and Witts, on pages 102 and 103. It is stated here that Funston "took charge of the city." He did not have any authority to assume this position. However, he could not have maintained it without the approval of the mayor.

[40] Dickson, 223–27; also, Bronson, p. 189. Dickson gives a fantastic account of life following the quake. He acknowledges, that ". . . social barriers were broken down, discarded, and everybody was friendly with everybody else."

[41] Thomas and Witts, p. 126.

[42] Thomas and Witts, p. 124.

[43] Thomas and Witts, pp. 26–27.

[44] Bronson, p. 34.

[45] Bronson, p. 65.

[46] Dickson, p. 577.

[47] Bronson, p. 67.

[48] Bronson, p. 65, also p. 67.

[49] Bronson, p. 67. It should be mentioned here that dynamite also played a role in fighting the fire. Its use is mentioned in all three books but I chose not to go into detail about it.

[50] Bronson, pp. 148–50. These pages contain several theories about the causes of the fire.

[51] Bronson, pp. 188–89.

[52] Bronson, p. 187.

[53] Bronson, p. 91.

[54] Bronson, p. 185.

Annotated Bibliography

Bronson, William. The Earth Shook, The Sky burned.
    Garden City, N.Y.: Doubleday, 1959. This book
    provides a very clear account of the earthquake; it
    is detailed and easy to read.
Dickson, Samuel. Tales of San Francisco. Palo Alto,
    Calif.: Stanford Univ. Press, 1957. Only one part
    of this very long book is devoted to the
    earthquake. The author retells stories about the
    disaster, which makes them seem like fiction. This
    is useful for background, but not as a primary
    source of information.
Thomas, Gordon, and Max Morgan Witts. The San Francisco
    Earthquake. New York: Stein and Day, 1971. This is
    the most thorough and up-to-date of the sources.

Ann Wallbridge
History 102
Section 8
May 19, 1983

A City in Ruins: The San Francisco Earthquake

"I'm going to heaven in a chariot of fire! Don't you hear the rumble of the chariot wheels? It's coming low to get me!" cried a patient at the State Insane Asylum at Agnews.[1] The brick building collapsed, killing eighty-seven patients and eleven nurses, and pinning many others alive under the debris.[2]

It was 5:13 A.M. on April 18, 1906, when the earthquake that destroyed this building and thousands of others struck San Francisco.[3] The earthquake was caused by a sudden refracturing along the San Andreas fault and registered 8.3 on the Richter scale.[4] Although it lasted only seventy-five seconds, the damage done and the number of lives claimed as a result were staggering.[5] The "most destructive incident in terms of human life" was the collapse of the Valencia Hotel in the Mission District, which crushed the life out of the hotel's eighty occupants.[6]

John Barrett, an editor of the San Francisco Examiner said: "It was as though the earth was slipping quietly away from under our feet. There was a sickening sway, and we were all flat on our faces."[7] People ran into the street panic-stricken as chimneys fell and buildings cracked.[8] In general, those who remained indoors escaped with their lives, though scores were hit by articles thrown to the ground by the shock.[9]

Fire sprang up everywhere. Fire Chief Dennis T. Sullivan had created an extensive firefighting plan in the event that San Francisco was threatened by a massive blaze.[10] However, when the earthquake hit, the cupola of the California Hotel crashed through the roof of Sullivan's house, leaving him fatally injured.[11] It was said that if he had not been injured, he would have devised a plan and saved the city. However, it is more likely that he would have been as ineffectual as Assistant Fire Chief John Dougherty, who took his place while San Francisco burned:[12] the water supply was cut off and, when fires started in various sections, there was nothing to do but let the buildings burn.[13] In a futile attempt to check the flames, dynamite and even artillery were used.[14] The wooden-frame buildings which had been built because they endured the strain of an earthquake better than brick buildings were speedily being devoured by the spreading blaze.[15] Sections of the city were being destroyed. South and north of Market Street, dozens of fires were raging out of control.[16] Chinatown was burned to the ground.[17]

The last message to leave San Francisco was sent by the Chief Operator at the Postal Telegraph office at 2:20 P.M.:

> The city practically ruined by fire. It's
> within half a block of us in the same block.
> The Call Building is burned out entirely, the
> Examiner Building just fell in a heap. Fire
> all around us in every direction. . . . They

are blowing standing buildings that are in the
path of the flames up with dynamite. It's
awful. There is no communication anywhere and
entire phone system is busted. I want to get
out of here or be blown up.[18]

At this moment, the Postal wire went dead.[19]

As thousands of people left the city, transportation was at a premium. The rate for a two-horse carriage
rose from $2.00 an hour, to $5.00, then $30.00--
"anything fightened people would pay."[20]

Disorder grew and looting began. Thieves robbed
abandoned buildings and wholesale liquor houses, and
even removed valuables from dead bodies lying in the
street.[21] Frederick Fulston, Commanding General of the
Department of California, called out all the Army troops
available for rescue work and for police action,[22]
despite the fact that nobody but the President of the
United States can order regular troops into any city.[23]
San Francisco's Mayor, Eugene Schmitz, quickly drafted a
proclamation:

> The Federal Troops, the members of the
> Regular Police Force and all Special Police
> Officers have been authorized by me to Kill
> any and all persons found engaged in Looting
> or in the Commission of Any Other Crime.[24]

The city was under martial law.[25] Thieves came to
loot, families came looking for relatives, and visitors
arrived to watch the "spectacle of San Francisco
burning." The Army "had all it could handle without
tourists," so Fulston closed the city completely.[27]

4

People were desperate for food and water. "Extortion was running wild over the city."[28] A New York Times correspondent was obliged to pay twenty-five cents for a small glass of mineral water.[29] "A loaf of bread, normally five cents, was now a dollar; a dozen eggs, five dollars."[30]

To remedy the situation, one soldier walked into a profiteering bakery, announced that the price of bread was back to five cents, and "stood guard as the people made their purchases."[31]

At seven o'clock Saturday morning, April 21, the fire was over.[32] Approximately 520 blocks of San Francisco had been burned, and 28,188 buildings destroyed.[33] Hundreds of thousands had left the city.[34] "The banking district, the wholesale district, factories, every retail store of any consequence, had gone up in smoke."[35] Casualties were estimated at seven hundred.

In spite of the vast problems, there was much hope. Almost immediately, plans were made to rebuild the city.[36]

Notes

[1] John Castillo Kennedy, The Great Earthquake and Fire (New York: Morrow, 1963), p. 13.

[2] Kennedy, p. 14.

[3] Jay Robert Nash, Darkest Hours (Chicago: Nelson-Hall, 1976), p. 490.

[4] Stephen Taber, "Local Effects of the San Francisco Earthquake," Journal of Geology, 14 (May 1906), 305.

[5] Nash, p. 491.

[6] Nash, p. 494.

[7] Nash, p. 492.

[8] New York Times, 19 April 1906, p. 1.

[9] Times, April 19, p. 1.

[10] Nash, pp. 491–92.

[11] Kennedy, pp. 16–17.

[12] Kennedy, p. 25.

[13] Times, p. 1.

[14] "San Francisco and Its Catastrophe," Scientific American, 28 April 1906, p. 347.

[15] Times, p. 1.

[16] Kennedy, p. 27.

[17] Nash, p. 505.

[18] Kennedy, p. 71.

[19] Kennedy, p. 71.

[20] Kennedy, p. 30.

[21] Kennedy, p. 30.

[22] Kennedy, p. 33.

[23] Kennedy, p. 35.

[24] Kennedy, p. 65.

[25] Times, p. 2.

Notes 2

26 Times, p. 1.
27 Kennedy, p. 76.
28 Kennedy, p. 77.
29 Times, April 20, 1906, p. 1.
30 Kennedy, p. 77.
31 Kennedy, pp. 77-78.
32 Kennedy, p. 188.
33 Kennedy, p. 191.
34 Kennedy, p. 191.
35 Kennedy, p. 191.
36 Charles F. Richter, "Earthquakes," Encyclopaedia
Britannica: Macropaedia, 1980 ed.

Bibliography

Kennedy, John Castillo. The Great Earthquake and the
     Fire. New York: Morrow, 1963.
Nash, Jay Robert. Darkest Hours. Chicago: Nelson-Hall,
     1976.
New York Times, 19 April 1906, p. 1.
Richter, Charles F. "Earthquakes." Encyclopaedia
     Britannica: Macropaedia, 1980 ed.
"San Francisco and Its Catastrophe." Scientific
     American, 28 April 1906, p. 347.

Appendix A. Some Useful Reference Sources

Here are some points to remember when you use the reference works listed on the following pages:

1. You can find sources for your essay by looking in the *subject card catalog,* by looking in the *bibliographies of standard works* on your subject, by looking at the brief bibliographies at the end of *encyclopedia articles,* by looking under the broad subject headings in *general-interest bibliographies* and *periodical indexes,* and by looking in the *indexes and abstract collections* that deal with the specific subject in which you are doing research.

2. Some reference sources are entirely bibliography: they consist of long lists of articles and (sometimes) books, each followed by the essential publication information. These indexes are usually arranged by topic. You may have to check several broad headings before you find the articles that you need. If, for example, you are doing research on educational television, you would look up "education," "television," and the names of some of the programs that you intend to write about. Most indexes are cross-referenced.

3. Some reference sources are called "abstracts" because they contain abstracts or paragraph summaries of many (but not all) of the articles published each year in that discipline. Abstracts often have two sections: the first contains a series of summaries of articles, chosen for their special interest or excellence and arranged by subject; the second contains a list of all the articles published in that field in that year. (Occasionally, you will find a modified form of abstract, in which several articles are each given a one-sentence summary.) First

you look up the specific subject that you are interested in and glance at the summaries. Then you get the publication information about the articles relevant to your research by looking up their *authors* in the second section of the reference work. Although abstracts give you a convenient preview, you will find that many of the articles are highly technical and may therefore be difficult to read and write about.

4. Some of the periodical articles that you want to consult may be available only on microfilm, microfiche, or microcards. Ask the reference librarian to help you to use the system and its apparatus. With the proper explanations, even the most unmechanical people can become adept at using these tools of the modern library.

5. If you can't find a specific reference work or if you are not sure which one to use, check with a librarian. As long as you can tell librarians the broad or (preferably) the narrow subject of your research, they will be willing and able to help you.

GENERAL ENCYCLOPEDIAS

Collier's Encyclopedia. 24 vols. with annual supplements. New York: Crowell-Collier, 1981. Easier to read and understand than the old *Britannica* or *Americana.*

Encyclopedia Americana. 30 vols. with annual supplements. New York: Americana Corporation, 1978. Use the index volume to locate your subject within the longer encyclopedia.

Encyclopaedia Britannica. 14th ed. 24 vols. with annual supplements and periodic revisions (through 1973). Chicago: Encyclopaedia Britannica, 1929. Dated and more sophisticated than the 15th edition, but retained by many libraries for the excellence of its articles.

New Columbia Encyclopedia. 4th ed. 1 vol. New York: Columbia University Press, 1975. A single-volume encyclopedia, especially good as a starting point.

New Encyclopaedia Britannica. 15th ed. 30 vols. with annual supplements and periodic revisions. Chicago: Encyclopaedia Britannica, 1974. Use the "Micropaedia" to find your subject in the 19-volume "Macropaedia." A disappointing successor to earlier editions; the "Micropaedia"/"Macropaedia" arrangement is annoyingly inconvenient.

SPECIALIZED ENCYCLOPEDIAS

Encyclopedia of World Art. 15 vols. New York: McGraw-Hill, 1959–68.

McGraw-Hill Encyclopedia of Science and Technology. 15 vols. Rev. ed. New York: McGraw-Hill, 1966. Current articles appear in supplementary yearbooks.

McGraw-Hill Encyclopedia of World Drama. 4 vols. New York: McGraw-Hill, 1972.

New Grove Dictionary of Music and Musicians. 20 vols. Ed. Stanley Sadie. Washington, D.C.: Grove's Dictionaries of Music, 1980.

Sills, D. L., ed. *International Encyclopedia of the Social Sciences.* 17 vols. New York: Macmillan, 1968. Includes articles on anthropology, economics, history, law, political science, psychology, and sociology. Volume 17 is an index.

GENERAL INDEXES

Book Review Digest. New York: H. W. Wilson, 1905–present. *Book Review Digest* includes excerpts from reviews as well as lists of references.

Book Review Index. Detroit: Gale Research Co., 1965–present. *Book Review Index* lists reviews of books on literature, art, business, economics, religion, and current affairs.

Editorials on File. New York: Facts on File, 1970–present. Selected editorials on subjects of contemporary interest, with each editorial proceeded by a summary of the issue being discussed.

Facts on File. New York: Facts on File, 1941–present. Summaries of issues and events, with selected bibliographies.

New York Times Index. New York: New York Times, 1851–present.

Popular Periodical Index. Camden, N.J.: Popular Periodical Index, 1971–present. Includes magazines such as *New York, Playboy, Rolling Stone,* and *TV Guide.*

Readers' Guide to Periodical Literature. New York: H. W. Wilson, 1905–present. Includes listings of articles in many general-interest magazines, especially news magazines and women's magazines.

Vertical File Index. New York: H. W. Wilson, 1932/1935–present. Lists pamphlets on all subjects.

BIOGRAPHICAL SOURCES

Annual Obituary. New York: St. Martin's, 1981–present. Annual collection of profiles of prominent individuals who died during the year (1980–   ), arranged by month of death date.

Biographical Index. New York: H. W. Wilson, 1947–present. Organized like *The Readers' Guide,* listing articles about contemporary celebrities.

Current Biography. New York: H. W. Wilson, 1940–present. Consists of full-scale articles (like encyclopedia entries) about prominent people. Use the index to find the right year for the person that you are researching.

Dictionary of American Biography. 16 vols. New York: Scribner's, 1974. Articles contain basic information about notable figures in American history. (Do not use this source for contemporary figures.)

New York Times Obituary Index 1858–1968. New York: New York Times, 1970.

SEMI-SPECIALIZED INDEXES AND ABSTRACTS

Humanities

Humanities Index. New York: H. W. Wilson, 1974–present. Annual volumes include reviews of books and performances as well as a listing of articles on issues and new developments in all the humanities.

Art Index. New York: H. W. Wilson, 1929–present.

MLA International Bibliography of Books and Articles in the Modern Languages and Literature. New York: Modern Language Association, 1921–present.

Music Index. Detroit: Information Service, 1949–present. Includes reviews listed under composer and title.

The Philosopher's Index. Bowling Green, Ohio: Bowling Green State University, 1967 to present. Articles on philosophy and its relation to art, religion, the humanities in general, and history.

Salem, James. *A Guide to Critical Reviews.* 5 vols. New York: Scarecrow, 1966. Theater reviews, listed by playwright, with title index.

Physical and Biological Sciences

Applied Science and Technology Index. New York: H. W. Wilson, 1958–present. Includes references to a large number of scientific and technological periodicals.

Biological and Agricultural Index. New York: H. W. Wilson, 1964–present.

Chemical Abstracts. Easton, Pa.: American Chemical Society, 1907–present.

Engineering Index. New York: Engineering Index, 1920–present.

Lasworth, Earl. *Reference Sources in Science and Technology.* Metuchen, N.J.: Scarecrow Press, 1972.

Science Abstracts. London: Institute of Electrical Engineers, 1898–present. Summaries of articles about physics.

Social Sciences

Guide to U.S. Government Serials and Periodicals. McLean, Virginia: Documents Index, 1964–present. A cumulative index directs the user to the correct volume.

Public Affairs Information Service Bulletin. New York: P.A.I.S., 1915–present. Includes pamphlets and government documents and reports as well as periodical articles. Covers an unusually large number of periodicals. Emphasizes factual and statistical information.

Social Sciences Index. New York: H. W. Wilson, 1974–present.

White, Carl M., et al. *Sources of Information in the Social Sciences.* 3d ed. Chicago, American Library Association, 1973.

SPECIALIZED INDEXES AND ABSTRACTS

Business

Accountants' Index. New York: American Institute of Certified Public Accountants, 1944–present. Lists articles about accounting, data processing, financial management, and taxation.

Business Periodicals Index. New York: H. W. Wilson, 1958–present. Lists articles from over a hundred periodicals dealing with new developments and methods in business management.

Personnel Literature. Washington, D.C.: U.S. Civil Service Commission, 1969–present. Lists articles about administration, supervision, management relations, and productivity.

Education

Education Index. New York: H. W. Wilson, 1929–present.

Current Index to Journals in Education. Phoenix, Arizona: Oryx Press, 1969–present.

History

America: History and Life. Santa Barbara, Calif.: American Bibliographical Center, Clio Press, 1964–present. Includes references to 2,000 publications dealing with past, recent, and present history. Part A consists of abstracts; Part B consists of one-sentence summaries of articles, grouped under topic headings.

Historical Abstracts. Santa Barbara, Calif.: American Bibliographical Center, Clio Press, 1955–present. Part A deals with modern history from 1450 to 1940; Part B deals with mid-twentieth-century history. The index is in the Winter issue.

Law

Index to Legal Periodicals. New York: H. W. Wilson, 1952–present. In addition to a listing of articles by subject and author, there is a table of cases and a group of book reviews.

Library Science

Library and Information Service Abstracts. London: The Library Association, 1970–present. Materials about information dissemination and retrieval, as well as library services.

Nursing and Health

Index Medicus. Bethesda, Md.: National Library of Medicine, 1961–present. Lists articles of medical interest and includes a bibliography of medical book reviews.

International Nursing Index. New York: American Journal of Nursing, 1966–present.

Nursing and Allied Health Index. Glendale, Calif.: Nursing and Allied Health Corp., 1956–present. Articles listed include health education and social services as they relate to health care.

Political Science

Barone, Michael, ed. *Almanac of American Politics.* Boston: Gambit, 1972–present. Lists sources for information about local and national public affairs.

International Political Science Abstracts. Paris: International Political Science Assn., 1951–present. Summaries of articles on political science and international relations.

Sage Public Administration Abstracts. Beverly Hills, Calif.: Sage Publications, 1979–present. Summaries of books, articles, government publications, speeches, and research studies.

Psychology

Psychological Abstracts. Washington, D.C.: American Psychology Assn., 1927–present. Use the three-year cumulative subject and author indexes; for example, 1978–80 are indexed together.

Social Work

Human Resources Abstracts. Beverly Hills, Calif.: Sage Publications, 1965–present. Summarizes developments in areas such as poverty, manpower, and distribution of human resources.

Journal of Human Services Abstracts. Rockville, Md.: Project Share, 1976–present. Summarizes articles concerning the provision of public services as they relate to public administration, education, psychology, environmental studies, family studies, nutrition, and health services.

Sage Family Studies Abstracts. Beverly Hills, Cal.: Sage Publications, 1979–present.

Social Work Research and Abstracts. Albany, New York: National Association of Social Workers, 1965–present. Selected research articles as well as abstracts of other articles in the field of social welfare.

Sociology

Sociological Abstracts. New York: Sociological Abstracts, Inc., 1953–present. Includes articles on mass communications, ecology, and women's studies.

INDEXES TO STATISTICAL COMPILATIONS

American Statistics Index: A Comprehensive Guide and Index to the Statistical Publications of the U.S. Government. Washington, D.C.: Congressional Information Service, 1973–present.

Statistical Yearbook. New York: United Nations Department of Economic and Social Affairs, 1949–present. International statistics.

Appendix B. Some Basic Forms for Notes and Bibliography Entries

Book by a Single Author

Note:

> [1] Laurence R. Veysey, <u>The Emergence of the American University</u> (Chicago: Univ. of Chicago Press, 1965), p. 125.

Bibliography entry:

Veysey, Laurence R. <u>The Emergence of the American University</u>. Chicago: Univ. of Chicago Press, 1965.

Note:

> [2] Jerry G. Gaff, <u>Towards Faculty Renewal</u> (San Francisco: Jossey–Bass, 1975), p. 42.

Bibliography entry:

Gaff, Jerry G. <u>Towards Faculty Renewal</u>. San Francisco: Jossey–Bass, 1975.

Book by Two Authors

Note:

> [3] Neil Postman and Charles Weingartner, <u>Teaching as a Subversive Activity</u> (New York: Dell, 1969), p. 103.

Bibliography entry:

Postman, Neil, and Charles Weingartner. <u>Teaching as a Subversive Activity</u>. New York: Dell, 1969.

Book by Several Authors

Note:

    [4] David Riesman, et al., <u>The Lonely Crowd</u> (New Haven: Yale Univ. Press, 1950), pp. 93-94.

Bibliography entry:

Riesman, David, Nathan Glazer, and Reuel Denney. <u>The Lonely Crowd</u>. New Haven: Yale Univ. Press, 1950.

Essay from a Collection Written by Different Authors

Note:

    [5] R. K. Webb, "The Victorian Reading Public," in <u>From Dickens to Hardy</u>, ed. Boris Ford (Baltimore: Penguin, 1958), p. 214.

Bibliography entry:

Webb, R. K. "The Victorian Reading Public." In <u>From Dickens to Hardy</u>. Ed. Boris Ford. Baltimore: Penguin, 1958, pp. 205-26.

Book Published in Several Volumes

Note:

    [6] Alexis de Tocqueville, <u>Democracy in America</u>, ed. Phillips Bradley (New York: Knopf, 1945), II, 145.

Bibliography entry:

Tocqueville, Alexis de. <u>Democracy in America</u>. Ed. Phillips Bradley. 2 vols. New York: Knopf, 1945.

Book Published in a Reprinted Edition

Note:

    [7] George Orwell, <u>Animal Farm</u> (1946; rpt. New York: Signet, 1959), p. 64.

Bibliography entry:

Orwell, George. <u>Animal Farm</u>. 1946; rpt. New York: Signet, 1959.

Book That Is One Volume in a Series

Note:

⁸ The London Stage 1729–1747, ed. Arthur H. Scouten, Part 3 of The London Stage 1600–1800 (Carbondale, Ill.: Southern Illinois Univ. Press, 1961), p. lxv.

Bibliography entry:

Scouten, Arthur H., ed. The London Stage 1729–1747. Part 3 of The London Stage 1600–1800. Carbondale, Ill.: Southern Illinois Univ. Press, 1961.

Note:

⁹ Jerry G. Gaff, Institutional Renewal through the Improvement of Teaching, New Directions for Higher Education, No. 24 (San Francisco: Jossey–Bass, 1978), p. 47.

Bibliography entry:

Gaff, Jerry G. Institutional Renewal through the Improvement of Teaching. New Directions for Higher Education, No. 24. San Francisco: Jossey–Bass, 1978.

Article in an Encyclopedia

Note:

¹⁰ "American Architecture," Columbia Encyclopedia, 3d ed. (1963).

Bibliography entry:

"American Architecture." Columbia Encyclopedia. 3rd ed. (1963).

Publication of a Corporation, Foundation, or Government Agency

Note:

¹¹ Gerry, An Outdoor Sports Company, How to Camp and Leave No Trace (Denver, 1972), p. 3.

Bibliography entry:

Gerry, An Outdoor Sports Company. How to Camp and Leave No Trace. Denver, 1972.

Note:
    [12] Marsha Manott, <u>Parents and Pot</u> (Washington, D.C.:
National Institute on Drug Abuse, 1979), p. 37.

Bibliography entry:

Manott, Marsha. <u>Parents and Pot</u>. Washington, D.C.:
    National Institute on Drug Abuse, 1979.

Article in a Periodical Numbered by Volume

Note:
    [13] J. H. Plumb, "Commercialization of Childhood,"
<u>Horizon</u>, 18 (Autumn 1976), 17.

Bibliography entry:

Plumb, J. H. "Commercialization of Childhood." <u>Horizon</u>, 18
    (Autumn 1976), 16–29.

Article in a Monthly Periodical

Note:
    [14] David Loye, "TV's Impact on Adults," <u>Psychology
Today</u>, April 1978, p. 88.

Bibliography entry:

Loye, David. "TV's Impact on Adults." <u>Psychology Today</u>,
    April 1978, pp. 87, 88, 90, 93–94.

Article in a Weekly Periodical

Note:
    [15] Karl E. Meyer, "Television's Trying Times,"
<u>Saturday Review</u>, 16 Sept. 1978, pp. 19–20.

Bibliography entry:

Meyer, Karl E. "Television's Trying Times." <u>Saturday
    Review</u>, 16 Sept. 1978, pp. 19–23.

Article in a Newspaper

Note:
    [16] Constance Rosenbloom, "The Plight of the Working
Mother," <u>Daily News</u>, 14 May 1979, p. 41.

Bibliography entry:

Rosenbloom, Constance. "The Plight of the Working Mother."
    Daily News, 14 May 1979, p. 41.

Note:

   [17] Hugh Price, "Leave School Gates in Place," New
York Times, 26 March 1982, Sec. A, p. 16.

Bibliography entry:

Price, Hugh. "Leave School Gates in Place." New York
    Times, 26 March 1982, Sec. A, p. 16.

Article Without an Author

Note:

   [18] "How to Get Quality Back into the Schools," U.S.
News and World Report, 12 Sept. 1977, p. 32.

Bibliography entry:

"How to Get Quality Back into the Schools," U.S. News and
    World Report, 12 Sept. 1977, pp. 31–34.

Lecture

Note:

   [19] Louis Auchincloss, Erica Jong, and Gloria Steinem,
"The 18th Century Woman," Symposium at the Metropolitan
Museum of Art, New York, 29 April 1982.

Bibliography entry:

Auchincloss, Louis, Erica Jong, and Gloria Steinem. "The
    18th Century Woman." Symposium at the Metropolitan
    Museum of Art, New York. 29 April 1982.

Film

Note:

   [20] Stanley Kubrick, dir., Dr. Strangelove, Columbia
Pictures, 1963.

Bibliography Entry:

Kubrick, Stanley, dir. <u>Dr. Srangelove</u>. Columbia Pictures,
    1963.

Television Program

Note:

   21 <u>Serge Pavlovitch Diaghilev 1872-1929: A Portrait</u>,
prod. Peter Adam (BBC), Hearst/ABC, 12 July 1982.

Bibliography entry:

<u>Serge Pavlovitch Diaghilev 1872-1929: A Portrait</u>. Prod.
    Peter Adam (BBC), Hearst/ABC, 12 July 1982.

Short Forms

   22 Veysey, p. 81.
   23 Gaff, <u>Institutional Renewal</u>, p. 7.
   24 Gaff, <u>Faculty Renewal</u>, pp. 81-82.
   25 "Quality in the Schools," p. 42.
   26 Tocqueville, II, 155.

SOME OTHER METHODS OF DOCUMENTATION

Notes Combined with Page Numbers in the Text

If you are using very few source-references in your essay, it is both
acceptable and desirable to provide only one note, at the first reference;
thereafter, instead of writing a long list of notes to the same source, cite
the page number of that source in the body of your essay.

For example, if your essay is exclusively about Sigmund Freud's *Civilization and Its Discontents*, document your first reference to the work
with a complete note, citing the edition that you are using.

   1 Sigmund Freud, <u>Civilization and Its Discontents</u>
(Garden City, N.Y.: Doubleday, 1958), p. 72. All further
citations refer to this edition.

This single note explains to your reader that you are intending to use
the same edition whenever you cite this source. All subsequent references
to this book will be followed by the page reference, in parentheses, usually
at the end of your sentence.

```
Freud has asserted that "the greatest obstacle to
civilization [is] the constitutional tendency in men to
aggression against one another . . ." (p. 101).
```

This method is usually used in essays on literary topics when you are focusing on a single author, without citing secondary sources. The technique will also work with a small group of sources, provided that you use them one at a time: two pages on Hemingway, the next two pages on Fitzgerald, and so on. It is only when you keep moving back and forth from one author to another that you must use the standard method of documentation to keep a more firm and complete record of what you are citing and where it comes from.

Bibliography Combined with Author and Year in the Text

Newer techniques of documentation which require no notes at all are now being used in the sciences and some of the social sciences. Instead of a series of numbers in your text keyed to a list of separate notes, your documentation is linked directly to your bibliography. In the method used by economics, sociology, and other social sciences, after you refer to a source, you insert (in parentheses) the author's last name and the work's publication date in the place where you would have inserted the superscript for a note.

```
America's colleges began to make room for the individual
sciences in 1711 when William and Mary established a
professorship of natural philosophy and mathmatics
(Rudolph, 1977).
```

The reader then uses Rudolph's name to turn to the bibliography and find complete publication information about this book.

If you cite the author's name in your own sentence, it is not necessary to repeat it in parentheses. But when you are quoting or paraphrasing a precise point from your source, most teachers require that you add the page number to the date.

```
Toffler (1971, pp. 30-31) measures that growth [of
knowledge] in terms of published books, observing that by
the mid-1960s, the world output of books in a single day
matched Europe's production of books in a whole year prior
to 1500.
```

Your bibliography remains essentially the same as the one you would use for a traditionally documented research essay. However, since the identification of sources greatly depends on the dates that you cite, you must be careful to clarify the dating, especially when a single author has published two works in the same year. Here, for example, is an excerpt from a bibliography which carefully distinguishes between three sources published in 1972:

> Carnegie Commission on Higher Education. The Campus and the City: Maximizing Assets and Reducing Liabilities New York: McGraw-Hill, 1972a.
> Carnegie Commission on Higher Education. The Fourth Revolution: Instructional Technology in Higher Education. New York: McGraw-Hill, 1972b.
> Carnegie Commission on Higher Education. The More Effective Use of Resources: An Imperative for Higher Education. New York: McGraw-Hill, 1972c.

And here is how one of these sources would be documented in the text:

> In its report on The More Effective Use of Resources, the Carnegie Commission on Higher Education (1972c, p. 105) recommended that "colleges and universities develop a 'self-renewal' fund of 1 to 3 percent each year taken from existing allocations."

Numbered Bibliography

In this method, used primarily in the abstract sciences, you number each entry in your bibliography. Then, the citation in your essay consists of the number of the work that you are referring to, placed in parentheses. Remember to include the page number if you quote from your source.

> The following theorem is a strengthening of Theorem 2 of Joel, Shier, and Stein (2).
>
> The following would be a consequence of the conjecture of Mcmullen and Shepher (3, p. 133):

You may arrange your bibliography in alphabetical order or in the order in which you cite the sources in your essay. Consult your teacher or a style sheet that contains the specific rules for your discipline.

Remember: The decision to choose traditional footnoting or one of the methods using the bibliography is not really yours to make. Ask your teacher which method is appropriate for your course and your paper topic.

ACKNOWLEDGMENTS (*continued from p. iv*)

"School Fighting to End Interpreter Service for Deaf Girl" by Charlotte Evans ©
1980 by The New York Times Company. Reprinted by permission.

"The Social Responsibility of Scientists" by Bertrand Russell from *Fact and Fiction*.
Reprinted by permission of George Allen & Unwin.

Excerpt from *Small Is Beautiful: Economics As If People Mattered* by E. F. Schumacher. Copyright 1973 by E. F. Schumacher. Reprinted by permission of Harper
& Row, Publishers, Inc.

"Violence—and Two Schools of Thought" by Connor Cruise O'Brien reprinted
by permission of The Observer News Service.

"So That Nobody Has to Go to School if They Don't Want To" by Roger Sipher
© 1977 by The New York Times Company. Reprinted by permission.

"The Personal Cost of Cheating on Unemployment Insurance" by Patricia Knack
© 1978 by The New York Times Company. Reprinted by permission.

"On Cloning a Human Being" from *The Medusa and the Snail* by Lewis Thomas.
Copyright © 1974, 1979 by Lewis Thomas. Reprinted by permission of Viking
Penguin Inc. This selection appeared originally in *The New England Journal of
Medicine*.

"TV: 'Karen Ann Quinlan' Drama Is Sensitive to Parents' Ordeal" by John J. O'Connor © 1977 by The New York Times Company. Reprinted by permission.

"The High Price of Success: You Are What You Do" by Heather Robertson, copyright 1974 by Heather Robertson, Canada. Reprinted by permission.

"Divorce and the Family in America" by Christopher Lasch, *Atlantic Monthly*,
November 1966. Reprinted by permission of the author.

"A Crisis, A Challenge" by Margaret Mead reprinted by permission of the Institute
for Intercultural Studies. This article originally appeared in the *Washington Post*.

Excerpts from *Magic, Science and Religion* by Bronislaw Malinowski from *Science,
Religion and Reality*, ed. James Needham, 1925, published by SPCK. Reprinted by
permission of The Society for Promoting Christian Knowledge.

Excerpt from *America Revised* by Frances FitzGerald © 1979 by Frances Fitz-
Gerald. First appeared in *The New Yorker*. By permission of Little, Brown and
Company in association with the Atlantic Monthly Press.

"City Layoffs Hurt Minorities Most" by Francis X. Clines © 1976 by The New York
Times Company. Reprinted by permission.

Movie review of *M*A*S*H* by Roger Greenspun © 1970 by The New York Times
Company. Reprinted by permission.

"Breakthrough" by David Denby. Copyright © 1970 by The Atlantic Monthly Company, Boston, Mass. 02116. Reprinted with permission.

Excerpt from *Deeper into Movies* by Pauline Kael © 1970 by Pauline Kael. First
appeared in *The New Yorker* January 24, 1970. By permission of Little, Brown and
Company in association with the Atlantic Monthly Press.

"The Art of Implying More than You Say" by Sherida Bush reprinted from *Psychology Today* magazine. Copyright © 1977 Ziff-Davis Publishing Company. Reprinted by permission.

"Competency Tests in Basic Skills Cost Few Pupils Their Diplomas" by E. Fiske © 1979 by The New York Times Company. Reprinted by permission.

Excerpts from *Ten Lost Years* by Barry Broadfoot. Copyright © 1973 by Barry Broadfoot. Reprinted by permission of Doubleday & Company, Inc.

Excerpts from *Readers' Guide to Periodical Literature*, Copyright © 1978, 1979 by The H. W. Wilson Company. Material reproduced by permission of the publisher.

Excerpts from *Times Index*, 1973 and 1980, © 1973 and 1980 by The New York Times Company. Reprinted by permission.

"Changing Habits in American Drinking" by Burke, © 1976 by Time Inc. All rights reserved. Repinted by permission of *Fortune* Magazine.

"Rising Toll of Alcoholism: New Steps to Combat It" from *U.S. News & World Report*, October 29, 1973. Copyright 1973 by the publisher and reprinted with their permission.

Excerpt from "Teenage Alcoholics" by Michael Segell, *Rolling Stone*, #292, May 31, 1979, by Straight Arrow Publishers, Inc., © 1979. All rights reserved. Reprinted by permission.

Excerpts from Carlos Baker, *Hemingway: A Life Story*. Copyright © 1968, 1969 by Carlos Baker; copyright © 1969 by Mary Hemingway (New York: Charles Scribner's Sons, 1969). Reprinted with the permission of Charles Scribner's Sons.

"300 Killed by Fire" © 1942 by The New York Times Company. Reprinted by permission.

"Boston's Worst" copyright 1942 Time Inc. All rights reserved. Reprinted by permission from *Time*.

"The Easy Chair" by Bernard DeVoto. Reprinted from *Harper's*, February 1943, by permission of Mrs. Bernard DeVoto, owner of copyright.

Excerpt from *Henry VIII: The Mask of Royalty* by Lacey Baldwin Smith. Reprinted by permission of Jonathan Cape Ltd.

"Washington—the Truth Behind the Legend" by Michael Davie. Reprinted by permission of The Observer News Service.

Excerpts from *Experiencing Science* by Jeremy Bernstein. Copyright © 1978 by Jeremy Bernstein. By permission of Basic Books, Inc., Publishers, New York. This material first appeared in *The New Yorker*.

Excerpts from *Of Acceptable Risk* by William W. Lowrance. Copyright © 1976 by William Kaufmann, Inc., Los Altos, CA 94022. All rights reserved. Reprinted by permission.

Excerpt from *Scientific Knowledge and its Social Problems* by Jerome R. Ravetz, © Oxford University Press 1971. Reprinted by permission of Oxford University Press.

Excerpt from *Introduction to Scientific Research* by E. Bright Wilson. Reprinted by permission of McGraw-Hill Book Company.

Excerpts from review of Tom Wicker's *A Time to Die* by Garry Wills. Reprinted by permission of the author and the author's agents, Scott Meredith Literary Agency, Inc., 845 Third Avenue, New York, New York 10022.

Index